D1230149

THE MISCELLANEOUS WORKS OF
JOHN BUNYAN

General Editor: Roger Sharrock

VOLUME VIII

INSTRUCTION FOR THE IGNORANT

LIGHT FOR THEM THAT SIT IN DARKNESS

SAVED BY GRACE

COME, & WELCOME, TO JESUS CHRIST

INSTRUCTION
FOR THE
IGNORANT:

Being a Salve to cure that great want of Knowledg which ſo much reigns both in young and old.

Prepared, and preſented to them in a plain and eaſie Dialogue, fitted to the Capacity of the weakeſt.

809

By JOHN BUNYAN.

Hoſ. 4. 6. *My People periſh for lack of Knowledg.*

LONDON,
Printed for *Francis Smith* at the Elephant and Caſtle in *Cornhil*, near the Royal-Exchange, 1675.

Title-page of the Bodleian copy of *Instruction for the Ignorant* (1675)

JOHN BUNYAN

Instruction for the Ignorant

Light for Them that Sit in Darkness

Saved by Grace

Come, & Welcome, to Jesus Christ

EDITED BY

RICHARD L. GREAVES

OXFORD

AT THE CLARENDON PRESS

1979

Oxford University Press, Walton Street, Oxford OX2 6DP

OXFORD LONDON GLASGOW
NEW YORK TORONTO MELBOURNE WELLINGTON
KUALA LUMPUR SINGAPORE JAKARTA HONG KONG TOKYO
DELHI BOMBAY CALCUTTA MADRAS KARACHI
NAIROBI DAR ES SALAAM CAPE TOWN

British Library Cataloguing in Publication Data

Bunyan, John
The miscellaneous works of John Bunyan.
Vol. 8 : Instruction for the ignorant; [and], Light for them that sit in darkness; [and], Saved by grace; [and], Come, & welcome to Jesus Christ. – (Oxford English texts).
1. Theology, Protestant – History
2. Dissenters, Religious – History
I. Series II. Greaves, Richard Lee
III. Sharrock, Roger
823'4 BR75 77–30369
ISBN 0–19–812736–7

Printed in Great Britain
at the University Press, Oxford
by Eric Buckley
Printer to the University

TO

ROBERT B. HANNEN

AND

E. P. Y. SIMPSON

GENERAL EDITOR'S PREFACE

SINCE the middle of the nineteenth century, there has been no complete edition of Bunyan's works. The author who is known to the world for *The Pilgrim's Progress* was a prolific preacher and writer. As his first editor and friend, Charles Doe, the comb-maker of Southwark, said: 'Here are Sixty Pieces of his Labours and he was Sixty Years of Age.' Apart from his spiritual autobiography, *Grace Abounding to the Chief of Sinners*, and the three allegorical fictions, *The Pilgrim's Progress*, *The Life and Death of Mr Badman* and *The Holy War*, these include sermons, theological treatises, biblical commentaries, and controversial works directed against the Quakers, the Latitudinarians (in the person of Edward Fowler), and the strict-communion Baptists; all these works are cast in the form of the popular sermon, with analysis of the text, abundant quotation from Scripture, a frequent employment of numbered heads and a meeting of objections by a series of questions and answers, and 'uses' or applications of the doctrine extracted from the text (these last usually conclude the work).

The purpose of this edition is to present all that Bunyan wrote in a text based on the earliest available editions, but incorporating those additions and revisions in later editions published during the author's lifetime which may reasonably be judged to have been made by Bunyan or to have received his approval. In fact, the method is that observed in the Oxford editions of *Grace Abounding* and *The Pilgrim's Progress*. As in those editions, colloquial forms and irregular grammar (such as plural subjects with singular verbs) have been retained. The punctuation, capitalization, and italicization are those of the originals, though here the editors have corrected obvious printers' errors and inconsistencies, and anything in the accidentals which might be merely confusing to the reader. A short textual introduction with title-page transcriptions precedes each work; it includes information on the printers, a list of seventeenth-century editions, and a mention of later reprints that are of any importance.

The reader of Bunyan's *Miscellaneous Works* is more likely to be a social or ecclesiastical historian, a theologian or a psychologist, than a literary student. The introductions to the various works thus aim to give an adequate account of the background of Nonconformist life in the period, as well as of Bunyan's own life and career as minister of the Bedford separatist church and visitor to its associated churches in the eastern counties and in London. Explanatory notes have been kept to a minimum. However, a good measure of individual freedom has been left to editors in respect of the introductions and notes; it seemed, for instance, that *The Doctrine of the Law and Grace-Unfolded*, Bunyan's chief theological treatise, required a fairly full consideration of his particular version of the theology of the two covenants, a dialectical system which may be said to provide the basic structure informing every work in these volumes, and indeed underlying the drama of salvation and damnation in *The Pilgrim's Progress* and the other allegories.

The first attempt at a complete edition was that of Charles Doe in the Folio of 1692. This was announced in an advertisement in *Mercurius Reformatus* for 11 June 1690:

> Mr. *John Bunyan*, author of *The Pilgrim's Progress*, and many other excellent Books, that have found great acceptance, hath left behind him Ten Manuscripts prepared by himself for the Press before his Death: His Widow is desired to print them (with some other of his Works, which have been already printed but are at present not to be had), which will make together a book for 10s. in sheets, in Fol. All persons who desire so great and good a work should be performed with speed, are desired to send in 5s. for their first payment to Dorman Newman, at the King's Arms in the *Poultrey*, London: Who is empower'd to give receipts for the same.

A year later, Doe issued a pamphlet, *The Struggler* (1691), telling of his efforts to bring out a collected edition of his friend's works. But when the Folio finally appeared, it contained only ten works apart from the previously unpublished ones obtained from Bunyan's widow and her son John. These were, in the order in which they appeared: *Saved by Grace*, *Christian Behaviour*, *I Will Pray with the Spirit*, *The Strait Gate*, *Gospel-Truths Opened*, *A Vindication of Some Gospel-Truths Opened*, *Light for Them that Sit in Darkness*, *Instruction for the Ignorant*, *The Holy City: Or*, *The New Jerusalem*, *The Resurrection of the Dead*. It seems likely that Doe ran into trouble over copyrights, and was therefore not able to bring out the second volume that he had planned. It is noteworthy that none of Bunyan's best-selling books are represented in the Folio; it is difficult to imagine Nathaniel Ponder, another publisher in the Poultry, surrendering his control over that valuable property *The Pilgrim's Progress*; and it is significant that the Folio was finally published by William Marshall, and not by Dorman Newman, who had issued both editions of *The Holy War*. The Folio was published by subscription, and the many copies extant suggest that the subscription-list was a long one.

A second edition of the Folio was issued in 1736–7, and this included the second volume with those writings which Doe had been unable to assemble. The edition was edited by Ebenezer Chandler and Samuel Wilson (the son of Bunyan's friend John Wilson) and published by E. Gardner and John Marshall (the son of William Marshall). Three books were still not included, but these are found in the third edition of the collected works which appeared in two volumes in 1767, and was thus the first truly complete edition. There is a preface by George Whitefield. Another collected edition in six volumes by Alexander Hogg appeared in 1780.

In 1853 the complete works were re-edited by the devoted Bunyan scholar, George Offor. In the twentieth century this has continued to be the only collected edition available to the scholar. It contains an amount of painstaking if amateurish bibliographical information, and a verbose and often melodramatic evangelical commentary; as John Brown (Bunyan's biographer and minister of Bunyan Meeting, Bedford, 1854–1903) said: 'His notes . . . are occasionally a little superfluous, sometimes indeed raising a smile by their very simplicity.' Offer's edition was revised and reissued in three volumes (Edinburgh and London, 1860–2). There was also an edition in four volumes by Henry Stebbing (1859).

The great disaster of Bunyan studies was the fire which destroyed a great part of the Offor Collection when it was to be auctioned at Sotheby's in 1865 (Tuesday, 29 June). Many of the surviving volumes came into the possession of Sir Leicester Harmsworth, and at the sale of the Harmsworth Collection at Sotheby's in February 1947 passed into various public libraries. Some remained in the family or were bought back by it, and at the death of Richard Offor, George Offor's grandson and former Librarian of the University of Leeds, were presented to Elstow Moot Hall in Bunyan's birthplace. Several of the copies consulted by the present editors are badly charred books from the Offor Collection.

Coleridge once drew a distinction between the Bunyan of genius and the Bunyan of the conventicle. If we accept this, the bulk of the works in this new edition represent the Bunyan of the conventicle; but Coleridge's romantic premisses, which we have in part inherited, draw a far sharper line between genius and the man rooted in his historical accidents than accuracy will admit. There is much strong, plain, effective exhortation in the awakening sermons; many of the poems in *A Book for Boys and Girls* are real poems; more important, the *Miscellaneous Works* bring us up against the raw material, the subsoil, on which the spirit of English Puritanism which we breathe in *The Pilgrim's Progress* and experience in its historical succession is founded.

ROGER SHARROCK

CONTENTS

ILLUSTRATIONS

REFERENCES AND ABBREVIATIONS

[*The place of publication, unless otherwise stated, is London*]

BUNYAN'S WORKS

The Works of That Eminent Servant of Christ, Mr. John Bunyan, ed. Charles Doe (1692)	*1692 Folio*
The Works of John Bunyan, ed. George Offor (3 vols., Glasgow, Edinburgh, London, 1861)	Offor
The Miscellaneous Works of John Bunyan, general editor Roger Sharrock (Oxford, 1976–)	Oxford Bunyan
Grace Abounding to the Chief of Sinners, ed. Roger Sharrock (Oxford, 1962)	*G.A.*
The Pilgrim's Progress from This World to That Which Is to Come, ed. J. B. Wharey, rev. Roger Sharrock (Oxford, 1960)	*P.P.*

OTHER WORKS

John Brown, *John Bunyan: His Life, Times and Work*, rev. ed. Frank Mott Harrison (1928)	Brown
Calamy Revised, ed. A. G. Matthews (Oxford, 1934)	*C.R.*
The Church Book of Bunyan Meeting, 1650–1821, facsimile edition with intro. by G. B. Harrison (1928)	*Church Book*
Dictionary of National Biography	*D.N.B.*
Documentary Annals of the Reformed Church of England, ed. Edward Cardwell (Ridgewood, New Jersey, 1966; reprint of the 1844 Oxford edn.)	*Documentary Annals*
Joyce Godber, *History of Bedfordshire, 1066–1888* (Bedford, 1969)	Godber
Richard L. Greaves, *John Bunyan* (Abingdon, 1969)	Greaves
Oxford English Dictionary	*O.E.D.*
David Ogg, *England in the Reign of Charles II*, 2nd edn. (Oxford, 1956)	Ogg
H. R. Plomer, *A Dictionary of the Printers and Booksellers . . . from 1668 to 1725* (Oxford, 1922)	Plomer

Roger Sharrock, *John Bunyan* (1968)	Sharrock
William York Tindall, *John Bunyan, Mechanick Preacher* (New York, 1934)	Tindall
Transactions of the Congregational Historical Society	*Trans. Cong. Hist. Soc.*

INTRODUCTION

(i) *Bunyan in the Period of Renewed Persecution* (1675–1677)

IN the later 1670s Bunyan's fame spread to London. After his final release from prison in 1676, 'he preached the Gospel publickly at *Bedford*, and about the Countries [i.e. counties], and at *London*, with very great success, being mightily followed every where'. The works in this volume are the by-products of this constant preaching.

> When Mr. *Bunyan* preached in *London*, if there were but one days notice given, there would be more people come together to hear him preach, than the Meeting-house would hold: I have been to hear him preach . . . [to] about twelve hundred at a Morning-Lecture by seven a clock, on a working day, in the dark Winter time.
>
> I also computed about three thousand that came to hear him one Lords day at London, at a Townsend Meeting-house . . .[1]

The latter place would be Mead's church in Stepney, built in 1674. Among other likely places in London where Bunyan preached are Plaisterers' Hall and Girdlers' Hall (where George Griffith preached) and Pinners' Hall (where Anthony Palmer and George Fownes, and later Richard Wavel preached, and where Bunyan's presence in 1682 is reliably attested).[2] Contacts with other Nonconformist ministers were naturally increased in these years. Bunyan associated with Stephen More, across the Thames at Winchester Yard, Southwark, where the cobbler Samuel How used to preach.[3] He also knew John Gammon of Boar's Head Yard, the author of *Christ, a Christian's Life*. Both Gammon and More were supporters of open communion. It was in Gammon's church near Whitechapel that

[1] *1692 Folio*, pp. 873–4.

[2] *The Greatness of the Soul* (1683) is described on the title-page as 'First preached in Pinners Hall'. Cf. Brown, pp. 366–7.

[3] Tindall, p. 87, and see William Agutter's sketch of his life prefixed to his edition of How's *The Sufficiency of the Spirit's Teaching* (1835), xii–xiii.

Bunyan preached his last sermon on 29 August 1688; and he died at the home of the grocer John Strudwick, a member of George Cockayne's church in Leadenhall Street.

The years in which these works were published were years of difficulty for the Bedford church and its associated churches after a short period of freedom. The story leads up to Bunyan's arrest and second imprisonment for some months in 1676 for illegal preaching. These are also the years preceding the publication of the First Part of *The Pilgrim's Progress* in 1678.[1] At Parliament's insistence the Declaration of Indulgence was cancelled on 8 March 1673, which prompted public rejoicing in the streets of London. The preceding month the Commons resolved to bring in a Bill to provide relief for Protestant Dissenters, but as finally passed in March it was amended so as to become the first Test Act. Nonconformists were legally barred from civil and military offices and places of trust under the Crown.[2] Their over-all strategy began to change. 'Nonconformists were beginning to realize by 1675 that they could wield considerable influence of an indirect kind in corporations', and they sided with the Country in its struggle with the Court party.[3] Bunyan himself later became involved in the contest for control of the corporations.[4] The Presbyterians also opted to work for some form of comprehension with the Anglicans. Rejecting '*Disloyal or Rebellious Principles*' and opposing 'the Congregational way', one of their spokesmen (possibly John Humfrey[5]) stated their case in 1675:

It hath pleased His Majesty by several Gratious Overatures to commend an union of his Protestant Subjects to the consideration of Parliament. A Design full of all Princely Wisdom, Honesty, and Goodness . . . [We desire] a further latitude in the present constituted order, that such may be received; and this we call *Comprehension* or *Accomodation*.[6]

[1] Sharrock, pp. 48–9.

[2] *The Statutes of the Realm* (1810–28), v. 782–5; Ogg, pp. 365–8.

[3] R. Tudor Jones, *Congregationalism in England, 1662–1962* (1962), p. 95.

[4] 'A Continuation of Mr. Bunyan's Life', in *G.A.*, p. 170.

[5] Roger Thomas, in *The English Presbyterians: From Elizabethan Puritanism to Modern Unitarianism* (1968), p. 95.

[6] *The Peaceable Design; Being a Modest Account of the Non-Conformist's Meetings* (1675), pp. A4^r, 2, 53, 57; cf. pp. 58, 63–4.

But since this accommodation included use of the Book of Common Prayer, and a system of parish rather than gathered churches, Bunyan would have adamantly rejected it.

The outlook of the Anglican establishment is reflected in *A Seasonable Discourse against Comprehension*, published in 1676 in response to *The Peaceable Design*. It warned Charles II that to grant the proposed accommodation 'will expose your Majesty to the restless importunity of every Sect or Opinion, and of every single Person also, who shall presume to dissent from the Church of *England*'. The old cry linking toleration to chaos and civil war was raised: 'Different Opinions and Practices in matters of Religion (especially when cherished and indulg'd) do naturally improve into contentious *Disputes*; and these Disputes, if not restrain'd, break out into Civil Wars.' If the Presbyterians were accommodated in the Church of England, the anonymous author warned, it would be tantamount to pulling down the walls of the church, leaving it defenceless.[1] This repressive Anglican view towards even the Presbyterians is indicative of the prevailing mood in the country during the years in which Bunyan again found himself in legal difficulties.

The licences issued in connection with the Declaration of Indulgence were finally revoked at the beginning of 1675,[2] though by then the Anglicans had suffered considerable losses. In 1676 the Archbishop of Canterbury bemoaned the fact that 'many left the Church upon the late Indulgence, who before did frequent it'.[3] As one of those responsible for the Anglican defections, Bunyan was an early target of the authorities, particularly of Dr. William Foster. Foster was the brother-in-law of Francis Wingate, the Justice of the Peace before whom Bunyan appeared after his arrest in November 1660, and who may have suggested the use of the Elizabethan conventicle act against Bunyan.[4] He was made commissary in the Archdeaconry of Bedford in 1674, and in this capacity issued a warrant for Bunyan's arrest on 4 March 1675, for teaching at a conventicle. The warrant specified that Bunyan 'hath divers times

[1] *A Seasonable Discourse against Comprehension* (1676), pp. 9, 10, 17.

[2] Thomas Richards, *The Religious Census of 1676*, Supplement to *The Transactions of the Honourable Society of Cymmrodorion* (session 1925–6; pub. 1927), p. 2.

[3] Lambeth MS. 639, fol. 168b, cited in Richards, pp. 2–3.

[4] Godber, p. 234; Oxford Bunyan, ii. xxxix–xl.

within one Month last past in contempt of his Majestie's good Lawes preached or teached at a Conventicle meeting'.[1] The Conventicle Act of 1670 (22 Car. II c. 1) had been used against Nehemiah Coxe and other members of the Bedford church in May 1670. Although a first offence for the preacher carried a maximum fine of £20, which could be doubled for the second offence, Foster chose on that occasion to imprison Coxe for making remarks critical of the Church of England. The Act allowed fines for offenders of 5*s.* for the first offence and 10*s.* for the second, but the zealous Foster imposed fines as high as 40*s.*, £3, and £5. In Bunyan's case in 1675, it is not known if the warrant was served, or if he went into hiding (probably in another county) for a period of time. If he did appear before Foster, he may well have followed his own example in 1660 or Coxe's in 1670 and spoken his mind, which could have resulted in brief imprisonment as well as a fine. When Foster and his deputy registrar, William Johnson, sent a report on 10 April 1675, giving information about the previous visitation of the Archdeaconry to the Bishop of Lincoln, they stated that 'John Bunnion, tinckar' had been presented by the churchwardens for refusal to attend church and receive the sacrament, and was therefore excommunicated.[2]

Was Bunyan imprisoned, or fined, or in hiding? His preface to *Instruction for the Ignorant*, published by Francis Smith in 1675, provides a hint. Although he prepared this catechism 'for publick and common benefit', 'I could do no less (being driven from you in presence, not affection) but first present you with this little Book . . .' This would indicate that he was either in the county gaol or away from Bedford, probably with Cockayne, Palmer, Griffith, or Owen, or other London Dissenting ministers. Another clue is offered by Charles Doe, who wrote: 'And after he was released again, they took him again, and put him in Prison the third time, but that proved but for about half a year.'[3] The context indicates that Bunyan was imprisoned twice before his release in 1672, but this is not so. Could Doe have meant to indicate that the second release came after a short imprisonment in 1675? If not, Bunyan

[1] A facsimile of the warrant is in Brown, facing p. 266.

[2] Joyce Godber, 'The Imprisonments of John Bunyan', *Trans. Cong. Hist. Soc.* xvi (Apr. 1949), 28.

[3] *1692 Folio*, p. 873.

avoided the warrant, and, given the preface to *Instruction to the Ignorant*, was probably in London by the spring of 1675.

The Church of England kept up its pressure on Nonconformity in 1675 and 1676, despite continuing attempts toward accommodation. In 1675 the fear of Catholicism prompted Tillotson, Stillingfleet, and others to hold conferences with moderate Dissenters like Richard Baxter and Thomas Manton.[1] Herbert Croft, Bishop of Hereford, called for some accommodation in *The Naked Truth*, published in 1675. In November of the same year the Duke of Buckingham proposed a Bill for the relief of Dissenters on the grounds of national benefit. Most of the Anglican bishops, however, were opposed to such comprehension. They were led by the inveterate opponent of Nonconformity, Archbishop Sheldon. Early in 1676 he sent a letter to the Bishop of London, for circulation among his diocesans in the Province. Three queries were to be made: the number of persons or families in each parish; the number of Catholic Recusants; the number of Protestant Dissenters.

> Amongst other specious pretences [he wrote] the consideration of the number of dissenters hath been an argument much insisted upon, as if their party were either too formidable to be suppressed, or that the combination of the several factions being infinite, it were but lost labour to re-enforce the censure and execution of the laws provided against them.

Sheldon believed such assertions were 'groundless and untrue', and indicated that 'the just number of dissenters' was to be made known so that their 'practicable' suppression could be undertaken.[2] The results were favourable, and helped to introduce the Test Act of 1678.[3] Bishop Sherlock commented approvingly of the Census: 'The nonconformists of all sorts (including papists as well as others) were computed to be in proportion to the members of the Church of England, in the year 1676, as one to twenty; a number in proportion too small to have any natural strength to hurt the constitution.'[4]

[1] *D.N.B.*, s.v. [2] *Documentary Annals*, ii. 340–2.

[3] *Statutes of the Realm* v. 894–6; J. P. Kenyon, *The Stuart Constitution, 1603–1688; Documents and Commentary* (Cambridge, 1969), pp. 448–51; Ogg, pp. 516–17.

[4] *Documentary Annals*, ii. 341 n.

In Bedfordshire 99 of the 131 parish incumbents reported the presence of Nonconformists. Other records, including those of assizes, for the period 1660 to 1689, reveal the presence of Nonconformists in fourteen other parishes. 'The percentage of Nonconformity [in Bedfordshire] is 8%',[1] a figure that probably errs on the low side. The attempt of Sheldon and his subordinates to enforce Anglican worship prompted Bunyan to make an implicit comparison of them with the false apostles who urged the early church to retain the practice of circumcision. 'SUPPOSE Men should attempt to burthen the Church of God with unnecessary Ceremonies, and impose them, even as the false Apostles urged Circumcision of old . . .'[2] This statement was made in Bunyan's discourse, *Saved by Grace*, which was probably completed in mid or late 1676, after the census was taken, but before Bunyan was again put in gaol. The discourse, which in subject-matter reiterates much that was said in *The Doctrine of the Law and Grace Unfolded*,[3] contains a general reference to the renewed pressures of the Anglican-Tory forces on Nonconformists in 1675–6: 'How do they shuck at the Cross? and how unwilling are they to lose that little they have for God, though all they have was given them to glorifie him withal?'[4]

It was in these times that Bunyan endured his last imprisonment. He had been excommunicated in 1675 for refusing to attend services and receive the sacrament at St. Cuthbert's church, and for refusing to appear in the Archdeacon's court to answer these charges. The court then initiated action against Bunyan by procuring a *significavit* which the Bishop of Lincoln sent to Chancery. There a writ *de excommunicato capiendo* was issued, empowering the sheriff of Bedfordshire to gaol Bunyan as a prisoner of the Crown. Legally, however, the bishop retained the right to absolve the prisoner and thus obtain his release. Bunyan was imprisoned once again, probably in December 1676.

A cautionary bond, dated 21 June 1677, was offered to Bishop Thomas Barlow of Lincoln to procure Bunyan's release. It outlines the entire case:

Whereas John Bunnyon of the parish of St. Cuthbert in the Towne[,]

[1] Godber, p. 239.
[2] Below, p. 221.
[3] Oxford Bunyan, ii, *passim*, on the covenant of grace.
[4] Below, p. 209.

County and Archdeaconry of Bedd' within the Diocese of Lincoln hath been presented at the Visitacion of the said Archdeacon of Bedf' by the Churchwardens of the said parish for refuseing to come to his said parish Church to heare divine servise and to receive the Sacrament of the Lord's Supper according to the lawes established in that behalfe, And whereas the said Archdeacon or his Officiall lawfully appoynted hath lawfully summoned the said J. B. to appeare before them or either of them at the Archdeacon's Court in Bedf' aforesaid the next Court day next following such his said Summons . . . to answer the said presentment, which Summons being lawfully executed upon the said J.B., And the said J.B. wilfully neglecting or Refuseing to appeare before the said Archdeacon or his Officiall at the said Court was by the said Archdeacon or his Officiall decreed Excommunicate and was soe publiquely denounced in the said parish Church of St. Cuthbert and for his obstinate and willfull perseverance under the said Sentence of Excommunication beyond the space of Forty days hath been Certifyed to the Bishopp of the said Diocese, and a Significavit for a writt de Excommunicato capiendo thereupon decreed and transmitted into the Chancery and the said writt thereupon Issued forth and executed and the said J. B. taken into Custody by the Sheriffe of the said County of Bedf' where he shall Remayne a prisoner. And whereas Request has been made for the said J. B.'s absolucion and releasement upon sufficient Caucion tendered in this behalf by the above named and bounded Th. K. and R. B., if therefore the said J. B. shall after lawfull Summons given by the said Reverend father Th., Lord Bishop of Lincoln or the said Archdeacon of Bedf' or his Officiall appeare and performe and obey the King's Majestie's Ecclesiastical Lawes and the Mandates of the Church . . . That then this obligacion to be voyd or els etc.[1]

The two sureties were Thomas Kelsey and Robert Blaney. Kelsey was later present at the induction of John Wilson as minister of the Hitchin church in April 1678. Blaney had been clerk to the Haberdashers' Company from 1654 to 1662, and was, according to an informer, a former confidant of Oliver Cromwell. Kelsey and Blaney lived in the parish of St. Giles, Cripplegate, where Cockayne's congregation was located. Because membership lists for this church do not begin until *c.* 1696, it is not known if they were members.[2]

[1] Reprinted in Godber, *Trans. Cong. Hist. Soc.* xvi. 30–1.

[2] C. Bernard Cockett, 'George Cockayn', *Trans. Cong. Hist. Soc.* xii (April 1935), 231.

It is likely, however, that Cockayne persuaded Owen to intervene with Bishop Barlow, his former tutor at Queen's College, Oxford, on Bunyan's behalf,[1] and obtained the two sureties from his church because they were not within the jurisdiction of the Bishop of Lincoln.[2] The activities of Cockayne and Owen in 1677 thus point to London as the place of Bunyan's hiding in 1675 (if he was not in Bedford gaol). Cockayne and his people would have been well acquainted with his trouble with Foster in 1675, and would have been anxious to secure his release in 1677. But whatever happened in 1675, Bunyan's London connections served him in good stead two years later.

Before leaving Bunyan's last imprisonment, it should be noted that it provided him with a good opportunity to write *Come, & Welcome, to Jesus Christ*, and to make any final revisions of the first part of *The Pilgrim's Progress*, which was entered in the Stationers' Register on 22 December 1677, and licensed the following February.

The 1670s were consequently busy years for Bunyan. The early years of the decade were involved with organizing Nonconformity in Bedfordshire and contiguous areas and with procuring release from twelve years' imprisonment. They were also the years of doctrinal controversy with Edward Fowler, Thomas Paul, William Kiffin, and Henry Danvers; the controversies are reflected in his writings of 1675–8. The 1670s are also a decade in which his travels increased in the areas south and east of Bedford. Trouble with the authorities in 1675 and 1676 involved at least one further period in prison. Yet Bunyan emerged in 1677, not broken but triumphant, despite the likelihood of what another minister referred to as 'those fiery trials we have just cause to suspect are approaching'.[3]

[1] W. G. Thorpe argues that the friend who urged Owen to intervene on Bunyan's behalf was Ichabod Chauncy, second son of Harvard President Charles Chauncy. Ichabod practised medicine at Bristol, where he was also known for defending Protestant Dissenters. *Proceedings of the Society of Antiquaries*, 2nd series, xii (1887–9), 10–17.

[2] Godber, *Trans. Cong. Hist. Soc.* xvi. 28–30.

[3] *Letters of John Pinney, 1679–1699*, ed. Geoffrey F. Nuttall (1939), p. 8. Pinney, ejected from his living at Broadwindsor in 1662, was licensed as a Nonconformist in 1672, and presumably spent the decade 1672–82 at Bettiscombe, preaching and living as a gentleman farmer (pp. ix–xi; see *C.R.*, s.v.). Pinney received a letter from Isaac Clifford, written probably *c.* 1666 from the Dorchester gaol, commenting on his imprisonment: 'The fear of a prison is more than the harm. We have great cause to praise God, who hath made a prison very comfortable' (p. 1).

(ii) *Discipline in the Church, 1671–1678*

On a less dramatic level the 1670s were also years in which Bunyan faced a continuing involvement in the disciplinary problems of the Bedford church. On 21 March 1671 letters had to be sent to neighbouring churches explaining the excommunication of Robert Nelson and Richard Deane. These men had ceased attending Bedford church, the former having been 'profanely bishopt' in the Church of England.[1] Sister Witt was accused of railing on 16 September 1673, and excommunicated on 18 October. The same October meeting also concerned itself with the fact that some members were having difficulties paying their debts. On 10 April 1674 Elizabeth Bisbie had to be admonished for 'immodest lieing in a chamber' with a young man; Sister Landy, for card playing and failure to receive communion; and Elizabeth Maxey for disobeying her parents.[2] Elizabeth Bisbie was again admonished for immodesty on 7 May, and excommunicated on 29 May 1674. Elizabeth Burtwood fell prey to the same problem, and was rebuked at the same May meeting of immodestly keeping company with young men at the Elstow fair.[3]

The entries for 1675 are sparse, and include no disciplinary problems. The renewal of persecution may have had a sobering effect, or the entries may simply be incomplete. In April 1676 Sister Cooper of Weston (Westoning, south of Ampthill?[4]) was admonished in a meeting at Gamlingay for going to hear 'the nationall ministers and through Gods mercy receaved instruction', which led to her public repentance at the next monthly meeting. The meeting on 23 May, however, was again faced with the problem of a young lady's demeanour towards young men. The offender, Sarah Caine, was admonished for her behaviour and for slighting the church. In January 1677 Oliver Thodye had to face the church to acknowledge that he had broken the Sabbath and brawled with his neighbours. Approximately a year later a meeting at Gamlingay

[1] *Church Book*, pp. 44–5.

[2] Ibid., p. 54.

[3] Ibid., p. 55.

[4] William Dell, an early friend of Bunyan, owned land in the Westoning hamlet of Samshill, where Bunyan was arrested in November 1660. Eric C. Walker, *William Dell: Master Puritan* (Cambridge 1970), p. 177.

withdrew communion from William Gardiner of that town for unseemly and scandalous conduct towards a woman.[1]

The joy of Bunyan's release in June 1677 must have been somewhat tempered by the problems arising later that year with Edward Dent, who had been given the responsibility in 1672 to teach at Edworth. Communion was withdrawn from Dent.

> The matter of fact charged opon [upon] him was for being negligent and unfaithfull as to the management of his sister's imployment which [he] was intrusted with, and all soe for contracting many debts which he neither was able to pay nether did he so honestlye and christianly take care to pay his creditors in due time as he oft [ought] though he had bine often exhorted to it, and admonished before by his brethren.

Dent repented and was received back into communion on 17 March 1678 at Gamlingay.[2]

Dent's restoration was virtually coupled with the withdrawal of communion in March 1678 from another man whose name appeared on the 1672 application. William Man's house at Stagsden was licensed as the place in which John Fenne would teach. Yet at Cotton End Man was disciplined for 'carrying himselfe immodestly towards a woman as lived in Sheford, kiseing of hir, and atempting uncleanenese with hir . . .'. In May a full meeting of the church at Cotton End learned that Man had committed fornication with several women. He was thereupon 'cast out of the Church, and deliver[ed] . . . up to Satan, for the destruction of the flesh, and that his sperit may be saved in the day of the Lord Jesus'.[3] In July 1678 Mary Fosket, following an earlier admonition, was publicly rebuked for passing on gossip about an untrue scandal involving an old church stalwart, Thomas Honylove, who had been fined for attending the 1670 conventicle at John Fenne's house at which Nehemiah Coxe preached.[4] At the November meeting William Man was permitted to speak regarding his sexual offences, and the church agreed to take the matter into consideration again. And, finally, on 12 March 1679 John Stanton was admonished for beating his wife.[5]

[1] *Church Book*, pp. 59–60. [2] Ibid., p. 66. [3] Ibid.

[4] Ibid., p. 67; *A True and Impartial Narrative of Some Illegal and Arbitrary Proceedings . . . in or near the Town of Bedford* (1670), p. 6.

[5] *Church Book*, pp. 67, 68.

These disciplinary cases cover a period of eight years, from 21 March 1671 to 12 March 1679. Absence from church and sometimes worshipping in the Church of England were frequent problems, involving four or perhaps five accused members in these years. Some allusion to the problem of non-attendance, as well as to that of perfunctory attendance, appears in Bunyan's 1676 discourse, *Saved by Grace*, where he complains:

THEY sin in their most exact and spiritual performance of Duties; they pray not, they hear not, they read not, they give not Alms, they come not to the Lord's Table, or other holy Appointments of *God*, but in, and with much coldness, deadness, wandrings of heart, ignorance, mis-apprehensions, *&c.* They forget *God*, while they pray unto him; they forget Christ, while they are at his Table; they forget his Word, even while they are reading of it.[1]

Serious financial difficulties over debts also involved an unspecified number of members at Bedford during these eight years, but only the major case of Edward Dent is specifically indicated. The other offences dealt with concerned only a single offender each: railing, card playing, disobedience to parents, sabbath breaking, brawling, gossiping, and wife-beating. The serious disciplinary issues confronting Bunyan and his colleagues in these years were thus sexual and those of non-attendance and debts.

A sampling of disciplinary problems in other churches will provide a background for the Bedford experience. Discipline, of course, was taken seriously by the Nonconformists. Baxter even regarded the exercise of discipline (but in a parish context) as the principal issue between Anglicans and Nonconformists: 'The utter neglect of Discipline by the over-hot Prelates had caused all our Perplexities and Confusions; and in this point is the chiefest part of our Difference with them indeed, and not about Ceremonies.'[2] Such Puritan discipline is encountered in the House Beautiful, where Christian sojourned on his pilgrimage through life.

A general survey of Baptist record books in the seventeenth century reveals that the major problems were drinking, sexual laxity (more often involving women members of the church than

[1] Below, p. 209.

[2] Cited in Roger Thomas, *The Beginnings of Nonconformity* (1964), p. 34.

men), witchcraft, business transactions, marrying someone of a different religious persuasion, non-attendance, frequenting Anglican services, and doctrinal matters.[1]

The Baptist Henry Denne, Bunyan's defender in 1659 against Thomas Smith, Professor of Arabic at Cambridge, was responsible for helping to found a Baptist church at Warboys, Hunts. The church records have a gap between 1663 and 1682, but a number of disciplinary problems occurred in 1662. Three of these involved sexual conduct (fornication and adultery); two involved non-attendance; four involved telling lies; and an unspecified number involved eating blood, contrary to Acts xv. There were also charges of improperly treating a wife, marriage to someone outside the church, frequenting an alehouse, forgery, evil conduct, cursing, drunkenness, hypocrisy, and adherence to the Quakers. Most of those accused at Warboys in 1663 were involved with multiple offences.[2] The number and variety of charges indicate a more serious discipline problem here than at Bedford.

Denne also helped to found the Baptist church at Fenstanton, Hunts. Denne's eldest son, John Denne of Caxton, was an elder here, and opposed Bunyan's position on open membership and communion.[3] On 29 August 1676 this church, noting 'the remisiveness that hath been too long in the church concerning the due punishing [of] offenders, whereby our hands have been weakened, have now resolved to look more strictly thereinto...'.[4] The church at this point included eighty-four names on its roll, but thirty-eight of these had died and four had been excommunicated. In this small congregation there were a number of discipline cases in 1677, reflecting the recent decision to punish offenders. Three people were accused of non-attendance; two, of refusal to reform as the church directed; and one, of schism (for opposing his wife's excommunication!). Another case involved marital discord, which allegedly hindered the couple's fellowship in the church. The records

[1] T. Dowley, 'Baptists and Discipline in the 17th Century', *Baptist Quarterly*, xxiv (Oct. 1971), 161–4.

[2] *Records of the Churches of Christ, Gathered at Fenstanton, Warboys, and Hexham, 1644–1720*, ed. Edward B. Underhill (1854), pp. 277–9. Cf. Horace A. Hyde, *The Warboys Baptists* (Newcastle upon Tyne, [1963]).

[3] Greaves, pp. 21–2, 137–44.

[4] *Records of . . . Fenstanton*, pp. 254–5.

also indicate the readmission of a woman formerly separated from the church for marrying out of it.[1] These offences are generally less serious than those at Warboys. The absence of sexual and financial charges provides a contrast with Bedford's experience.

The Baptist church at Amersham, Bucks., was separately constituted by John Griffiths of Dunning's Alley, London, in December 1675. It continued to maintain ties with Griffiths, even when he was in Newgate prison. It was also in contact with another leading Baptist, Benjamin Keach, whom Bunyan reputedly visited in London.[2] There were few disciplinary problems at Amersham in the early years of its existence. In January 1677 one of the men was reproved 'Abought his Calling vpone such to pray as doth not own Beleuers Baptisme...'. In May 1678 the church called into account one of its members who was retiring as a constable for not giving a pregnant woman lodging on a rainy day for fear he would receive no compensation. The same man had to be dealt with on several occasions for not attending church.[3]

Discipline occupies a major portion of the church records of the Seventh Day General Baptist church in London (known as the Mill Yard church, because it began meeting at Mill Yard, Goodman's Fields, in 1692). In May 1675 a man was admonished for failure to keep the sabbath, marrying outside the church, and breaking his covenant with the church. In June one woman was accused of showing importunity for church communion. In June and July another woman was excluded from communion for showing disrespect towards her husband and for telling lies. Also in July a married couple was accused of unbecoming conduct. In October the church raised the issue of a woman's heterodox views on the Jews and their worship. The entries in the church book for 1676 include a number of disciplinary cases, as do all four entries for 1677. The only entry for 1678 deals with a quarrel between two women in which one was accused of being a busybody.[4] In contrast

[1] Ibid., pp. 255–64.

[2] Tindall, p. 125; Sharrock, p. 102.

[3] *The Church Book of Ford or Cuddington and Amersham in the County of Bucks.*, ed. W. T. Whitley (1912), pp. 201, 204–8, 211–12, 214–15.

[4] *Mill-Yard Minutes, being the Church Book of the Seventh Day General Baptist Congregation, 1673–1840, with Registers and Records*, photocopy in Dr. Williams's Library, fols. 5–21.

with Bedford, which was strict by modern standards, the Mill Yard church was repressive and legalistic.

The exercise of discipline by Bunyan and his colleagues at Bedford was, for the times, moderate. This was in keeping with the later testimony of John Wilson and Ebenezer Chandler, Bunyan's successor at Bedford, that Bunyan was 'useful' as a pastor 'by the Accuracy of his Knowledge in Church-discipline, and readiness to put that in practice in the Church (as occasion offered) which he saw was agreeable to the Word of God, whether Admonition, or Excommunication, or making up Differences, or filling up Vacancies, or paring off Excrescencies'.[1]

(iii) *Catechetical Literature*

Bunyan's catechism, *Instruction for the Ignorant*, was completed in 1675 either in the Bedford county gaol or, more likely, in London. It can best be appreciated in the general context of seventeenth-century Protestant catechisms.

The multiplicity of catechisms that poured from the presses in this century reflect the struggle to capture the minds of young people. When Bunyan wrote his catechism he in effect enlisted to defend his cause in this 'catechetical war', which was but one aspect of the broader 'holy war' he so dramatically allegorized. Leadership for the Anglicans in this struggle came from no less persons than the Archbishops of Canterbury. William Laud, for example, had earlier ordered the clergy to catechize, and forbade them to preach on controversial subjects.[2] Gilbert Sheldon's position is clearly stated in a letter to his suffragans, dated 6 February 1672.

> The king's most excellent majesty being truly sensible, that the growing increase of the prevailing sects and disorders amongst us, proceeds chiefly from the general neglect of instructing the younger sort of persons (or their erroneous instruction) in the grounds and principle[s] of true religion, is therefore pleased to command me, that in his name I require your lordship (and by you the rest of my brethren the bishops of this province) that . . . you will . . . reinforce

[1] *1692 Folio*, sig. A2^{r}.

[2] Christopher Hill, *The Century of Revolution, 1603–1714* (Edinburgh, 1961), p. 90.

doctrinal controversy over justification between Bunyan and Fowler is reflected in the latter's preface to John Worthington's catechism. Fowler made the usual charges that ineffectual catechizing in the home was responsible for the problems of the Church of England. Then, almost certainly with Bunyan in mind,[1] he wrote: 'The *Christian Religion* is no *Speculative* but a purely *Practical* Science, and . . . *the* design and business thereof is (though those that would not have it so will not see it) to make men *inwardly* and *really* Righteous, to purify our souls . . ., and endue us with a God-like and divine nature.'[2]

Nonconformist arguments for the importance of catechizing give less significance to the social aspects of the ideological contest, and stress more narrowly religious concerns. Writing to his former church at Fordham, Essex, John Owen remarked that, next to preaching, catechizing was his most important work. (One notes the order of priorities, as contrasted with the Anglican view.) Owen had two catechisms printed for its members 'meerly because the least part of the Parish are able to read it in writing, my intention in them being, principally, to hold out those necessary truths, wherein you have been in my Preaching more fully intrusted . . .'.[3] Joseph Alleine, a noted preacher at Taunton, Somerset, stressed the importance of family catechism in the light of 'how jejune, and liveless, and insipid the more publick exercises of religion somewhere are . . .'.[4] Owen Stockton, the diarist who preached alternately at Colchester and Ipswich,[5] similarly stressed, in *A Treatise of Family Instruction* (1672), the duty of each parent and master to provide children and servants with instruction in Scripture to promote

[1] At the end of Worthington's catechism the publisher Richard Royston lists five of his other publications, including a work by Fowler or his curate, *A Manifest Discovery of the Gross Ignorance . . . of One John Bunyan*. Sherlock's catechism is also one of the five.

[2] Fowler's preface to Worthington, *'ΥΠ-ΤΎΠΩΣΙΣ 'ΥΌΓΙΑΙΝΌΝΤΩΝ ΛΌΌΩΝ*, *A Form of Sound of Words: Or, a Scripture-Catechism* (1673), sig. A7^v^. Worthington (1618–71) was rector of Ingoldsby, Lancs., in 1666, and shortly thereafter became a lecturer at Hackney. *D.N.B.*, s.v.

[3] Owen, *The Principles of the Doctrine of Christ: Vnfolded in Two Short Catechisms* (1645), sigs. A2^v^–A3^r^. This work was reissued in 1684.

[4] Alleine, *A Most Familiar Explanation of the Assemblies Shorter Catechism* (1672), sig. A2^r^. For Alleine see *D.N.B.*, s.v.

[5] *D.N.B.*, s.v.

their salvation and edification. His *Scriptural Catechism* (1672), using only Bible verses to answer catechetical questions, was designed to be used as an aid in this endeavour.

The purposes for which Bunyan intended his catechism are akin to those expressed by Owen, Alleine, and Stockton. Like Owen, he hoped the contents of his brief work would remind those to whom he had preached 'of first things'. Like Stockton, he also looked upon the catechism as a means, 'if God will', for the conversion of unbelievers. It was 'wholsom Medicine' for sinners to 'read, ponder, and receive', and 'a Salve to cure that great want of Knowledg which so much reigns both in young and old'.[1]

In its form, there is little that sets Bunyan's catechism apart from others. He uses the obvious question and answer format. Scriptural citations are placed in the text, though marginal placement is also common among other catechetical authors. Bunyan includes a moderate number of citations, certainly more than some authors, who use few or none.[2] Edward Wetenhall, for example, opposed trends 'to stuff up the Margins of such Catechisms with numerous Citations of Scripture, most of them very impertinent'.[3] In length Bunyan's catechism is also moderate. It holds a position between a number of shorter works (often running only between ten and twenty-five pages) and a group running into hundreds of pages (up to Towerson's approximately 1,100 pages). Bunyan's is about equal in size to the catechisms by George Fox, Thomas Grantham (the British Library copy of which includes a John Bunyan signature), Richard Sherlock, John Owen, John Worthington, and Edward Wetenhall.

In terms of organization, Bunyan's catechism is equal to or better than nearly all others examined. It is clearly arranged in six parts. At this point, however, the uniqueness of Bunyan's work becomes

[1] Below, p. 7 and title-page of *Instruction*.

[2] See, e.g., Alleine, op. cit.; Lowth, op. cit.; Owen, the shorter catechism in op. cit.; Thomas Grantham, *St. Paul's Catechism* (1687); anon., *The Catechism of the Church of England Briefly Paraphrased and Explained* (1688); Francis Peck, *The Kernell of Christianity* (1644); G[eorge] F[ox], *A Catechisme for Children* (1657). For Grantham see *D.N.B.*, s.v.

[3] Wetenhall, *The Catechism of the Church of England, with Marginal Notes* (1678), sig. A3ᵛ. Wetenhall (1636–1713) became curate of St. Werburgh's, Dublin, *c.* 1672, and thereafter chantor of Christ Church, Dublin. He served as Bishop of Cork and Ross from 1679 to 1699, and as Bishop of Kilmore and Ardagh from 1699 on. *D.N.B.*, s.v.

apparent. The parts are these: an opening section of doctrinal questions and answers; a section on confession of sin; a section on faith; a section on prayer; a section on self-denial; and a brief sermon conclusion. This differs strikingly from traditional catechisms, with their sections on baptismal vows, expositions of the Apostles' Creed, the Ten Commandments, the Lord's Prayer, and the sacraments, and normally concluding with various prayers.[1] Many other catechisms, of course, do not follow this pattern, in either structure or contents. Generally, Puritan and sectarian catechisms display more flexible organization and less formality in content.

The Puritan William Perkins prepared a rather short, straightforward catechism, published originally in 1591, and reissued in 1677, two years after Bunyan's catechism. Perkins organized his catechism around six themes: the nature of God, the nature of man, how to escape damnation, how to receive the benefits of Christ's work, how to obtain faith (through preaching, prayer, and the sacraments), and the state of man after death. The catechism is concluded with a brief paraphrase of the Ten Commandments, a short exposition of the sacraments, and a brief but vivid description of hell. The virtues of clarity and simplicity made this a popular catechism.[2] An even briefer catechism by Thomas Wolfall was also organized around six themes, with the covenant concept providing a common thread. The themes are the nature of God and the covenant of works, Christ and the covenant of grace, the use of law in the covenant of grace, the terms of the new covenant, the sacraments as seals of the new covenant, and the church and final judgement.[3]

Thomas Grantham, the General Baptist, was another writer who used the organizational principle of six principal subjects. His *St. Paul's Catechism* (1687) began with a series of introductory questions

[1] See, e.g., Sherlock, op. cit.; *The Catechism of the Church of England Briefly Paraphrased and Explained*; Lowth, op. cit.; Edward Boughen, *A Short Exposition of the Catechism of the Church of England* (1668); Thomas Adams, *The Main Principles of Christian Religion* (1675); Towerson, op. cit.; Alexander Nowell, *A Catechisme, or Institution of Christian Religion* (1638 edn.). Boughen (1587–1660?) was rector of Wardchurch, Kent, before his ejection in 1640. *D.N.B.*, s.v.

[2] Perkins, *The Fovndation of Christian Religion* (1677 edn.). For Perkins see *D.N.B.*, s.v.; Keith L. Sprunger, *The Learned Doctor William Ames* (Urbana, Ill., 1972).

[3] Wolfall, *Childrens Bread: Or, A Briefe Forme of Christian Doctrine* [1646]. Wolfall was pastor of a church at Stannington, Northumberland.

and answers before turning to the six major subjects: repentance, faith (incorporating the Nicene Creed), baptism, the laying-on of hands, the resurrection of the dead, and eternal judgement. Brief statements follow, dealing with the duty of prayer (including a very brief exposition of the Lord's Prayer), obedience to superiors, and honour due to the king. Another Baptist, Benjamin Keach, included a thirty-two-page catechism as part of a catch-all child's primer. *The Child's Delight* commences with lessons on the alphabet and vocabulary before coming to the catechism. The latter is divided into two parts; the first covers matters from the existence of God and the covenants to the benefits of Christ for believers; the second includes the offices of Christ (prophet, priest, and king) and his manifestation to man, the nature of faith, the sacraments, and prayer (including the Lord's Prayer). Keach follows the catechism with a two-page confession of faith before including a classic *pot-pourri*, embracing data on days, money, punctuation, letters of admonition, a short dictionary, basic legal documents, a table of interest rates, English and Latin titles, weight-and-measure tables, and mealtime prayers.

The general doctrinal questions covered by Bunyan in his first section are found in most other catechisms. The notable exceptions are soldiers' catechisms and political catechisms,[1] which are really works differing in genre if not form from regular religious catechisms. Confession of sin, faith in Christ, and prayer are also common catechetical topics. Bunyan's treatment of self-denial, however, is unique among the catechisms examined. No other writer devoted either a distinct section or so much attention to this subject. Bunyan included a pointed warning in this section that was clearly applicable to himself:

Q. *Who are likely to miscarry here?*

A. They whose ends in Self-denial are not according to the proposals of the Gospel.

[1] See, e.g., *A Catechisme for Souldiers; to Save Soules and Prevent Blood* (1659), which lays down principles for a just war; *The Souldiers Catechisme: Composed for the Parliaments Army* (1644), a propagandist endeavour to convince the troops they are fighting to rescue Charles I from 'a Popish Malignant Company'; *The Parliaments New and Perfect Catechism* (1647), a satirical blast against Parliament and the army; *The Cavaliers Catechisme, and Confession of His Faith* (1647), a pious Royalist work.

Q. *Who are they?*

A. They that suffer through Strife and Vain-glory; or thus, they who seek in their sufferings, the praise of Men more than the Glory of Christ, and profit of their Neighbour.[1]

As a man deprived once again of the freedom to preach to his congregation, Bunyan was apparently susceptible to the temptations of the martyr. Cockayne, it should be recalled, remarked after his death on his proneness to pride.[2]

The personal and experiential touches in Bunyan's catechism set it apart from most others. Human experience, for example, is used to prove that children are born sinners, for 'the first things that bloom and put forth themselves in Children, shew their Ignorance of God, their disobedience to Parents, and their innate enmity to Holiness of life...'.[3] Experience as well as Scripture is pointed to as proof of 'the desperate wickedness that is in thine heart...'.[4] Some personal experience may lie behind Bunyan's remark that children are 'so rude as to mock the Prophets and Ministers of God . . . but it is a poor Heaven that is not worth enduring worse things than to be mocked...'.[5] More poignant is another passage in the catechism clearly alluding to his personal experiences in 1674 and 1675:

Q. *When else do I sin against the Preaching of the Word?*

A. When you mock, or despise or reproach the Ministers; also when you raise lies and scandals of them, or receive such lies or scandals raised: you then also sin against the preaching of the Word, when you Persecute them that Preach it, or are secretly glad to see them so used . . .[6]

The reference to Bunyan's persecution by the authorities needs no further comment. The references to lies and scandal involve at least in part the Agnes Beaumont scandal of 1674, in which this Edworth girl was carried on horseback behind Bunyan to Gamlingay. Her distraught father's anger may or may not have been a factor in his death, which rumour said was maliciously caused. A trial cleared her, but the scandal was obviously distasteful to

[1] Below, p. 39.
[2] Cockayne's preface to *The Acceptable Sacrifice*, Offor, i. 686.
[3] Below, pp. 12–13. [4] Below, p. 22. [5] Below, p. 19.
[6] Below, p. 16.

Bunyan, who lashed out against the 'ignorant' persons who spread false tales.[1]

The personal and experiential element in Bunyan's catechism contrasts sharply with the manner of most of the others. Benjamin Keach's catechism occasionally strikes a personal note, but this is more pronounced in Dorothy Burch's work.[2] This lady from Stroud, Kent, was one of a number of women who took advantage of the Civil War upheavals to assert her mind on religious issues.[3] The local parson blasted her as one of the 'poore ignorant simple people', but this did not prevent her from writing one of the better catechisms of the century, certainly from the standpoint of clarity. It does not reflect the same personal qualities as does Bunyan's catechism, but it is nevertheless based on her experience. 'It came to my minde to see what God had taught me; I set pen to paper, and asking my selfe questions, and answering of them . . .'.[4]

Bunyan's catechism contains an implicit repudiation of the position on original sin taken by Edward Fowler in their earlier debate on justification.

Q. *But do not some* [including Fowler] *hold that we are sinners only by imitation?*

A. Yes, being themselves deceived. But God's Word saith, we are Children of Wrath by Nature, that is, by Birth and Generation.[5]

The attack against Fowler was, however, primarily carried on by Bunyan in his other 1675 work, *Light for Them That Sit in Darkness*.[6]

Some catechisms were far more polemical in content than Bunyan's. A Quaker catechism by Robert Barclay was published in 1673, in which 'thou shalt easily observe the whole Principles of the People, called *QUAKERS*, plainly couched in Scripture-Words, without Addition or Commentary . . .'.[7] Appended to the catechism and an accompanying confession is a critical examination by Barclay

[1] *The Narrative of the Persecution of Agnes Beaumont in the Year 1674*, ed. G. B. Harrison (1929).

[2] Burch, *A Catechisme of the Severall Heads of Christian Religion* (1646).

[3] Greaves, 'The Ordination Controversy and the Spirit of Reform in Puritan England', *Journal of Ecclesiastical History*, xxi (July 1970), 235–6, and the references there cited; Claire Cross, '"He-Goats before the Flocks": A Note on the Part Played by Women in the Founding of Some Civil War Churches', *Studies in Church History*, viii (1972), 195–202.

[4] Burch, *A Catechisme*, sig. A2v.

[5] Below, p. 12.

[6] Below, pp. 90 ff.

[7] B[arclay], *A Catechism and Confession of Faith* [1673], p. 8.

of the use of Scripture by the Westminster Divines in their confession and catechisms. George Fox's *Catechisme for Children* (1657) is obviously polemical. It commences with the unusual question, '*Is no lie of the Truth?*', to which the answer is, 'No, for the Truth checks and reproves the Lyer, and he is not of Truth'. The point of the catechism is a defence of the Quaker concept of the Inner Light, with its affirmation of the principle that *every* man has '*a light from Gods Covenant*', enabling him to see his sin and 'the Mediator between God and him . . .'.[1]

Thomas Grantham's catechism, less personal and more scholarly (for example, in its use of church fathers and of Greek), includes polemical elements, notably an explicit attack on the Quaker concept of spiritual baptism. Keach also attacks the Friends, asserting that Christ is 'not made known by the works of Creation, nor by the light within; for tho' by these things . . . we may know there is a God, yet hereby we cannot know there is a Saviour . . .'. Keach also repudiates the Catholic doctrines of purgatory, prayer to the saints, and transubstantiation.[2] Sherlock's catechism, explicitly intended to counteract the growth of the sects, includes a penultimate section treating objections against the catechism. The atypical *Cavaliers Catechisme* (1647) is polemical in a political as well as a religious sense, giving due stress to obedience to royalty and a general doctrine of non-resistance. Opposed to such polemical tendencies, Edward Wetenhall took issue with those who would 'make up Catechisms rather of the Systems of the Opinions of some Factions, than of the Principles of the common Christianity . . .'.[3]

Just as catechisms vary with respect to political emphasis, so they also differ with regard to the difficulty of language and technical content of their answers. No catechetical writer rivals Baxter for the sophisticated level of theological terminology. Of his three catechisms the shortest asks only three questions. The first is simple enough:

Q. *What is the Christian Religion?*

A. The Christian Religion is the Baptismal Covenant made and

[1] Fox, op. cit., pp. 1, 24–5.

[2] Keach, *The Child's Delight*, 3rd edn. (1703?), pp. 39–40, 42–3, 48–9 (the quotation is from p. 49).

[3] Wetenhall, *The Catechism*, sig. A3^v.

kept: Wherein GOD the Father, Son and Holy Ghost, doth give Himself to be our reconciled God and Father, our Saviour and our Sanctifier; And we believingly give up our selves accordingly to Him: Renouncing the Flesh, the World, and the Devil. Which Covenant is to be oft renewed, specially in the Sacrament of the Lords Supper.[1]

The covenant theme, it might be noted, is present in a number of catechisms,[2] but not Bunyan's. Once Baxter has proceeded through his three queries and responses, he amplifies on the Christian faith in three further points, the first of which states: 'I believe that there is one GOD; An Infinite Spirit of Life, Understanding and Will; Perfectly powerful wise and good; The Father, the Word, and the Spirit; The Creator, Governor, and End of all things; Our absolute Owner, our most just Ruler, and our most gracious Benefactor, and most amiable Good.'[3] Bunyan covers doctrinal ground with less sophistication than most catechists, more questions, briefer answers, and simpler language. His most complex answer dealing with God's nature is this: 'No Spirit is Eternal but he, no Spirit is Almighty but he, no Spirit is Incomprehensible and Unsearchable but he; He is also most Merciful, most Just, most Holy . . .'[4]

Baxter's second, larger catechism is even more technical, using such theological terms as matter, form, genus, species, accident, formal virtues, volative or willing virtue, penetrability, habitual and actual holiness, and sentential and executive justification.[5] This catechism, it must be remembered, does not appear in a handbook for the professional but in *The Poor Man's Family Book*. It was intended for youth, who were in need of a further explanation of the contents of the first catechism, because children 'learn the words

[1] Baxter, *The Poor Man's Family Book* (1674), p. 60.

[2] See, e.g., Sherlock, op. cit., p. 55; Owen, op. cit., pp. 19, 33–4, 36–7, 53–4; Alleine, op. cit., pp. 19, 25–7; Burch, op. cit., sigs. A7^{v}–A8^{r}; Keach, op. cit., pp. 22–3; Stockton, *A Scriptural Catechism* (1672), pp. 21–3; Wolfall, op. cit., chaps. i–v; John Cotton, *Milk for Babes* (1646), pp. 10–11; W. Cotton, *A New Catechisme Drawn out of the Breasts of the Old and New Testament* (1648), *passim*; Ezekiel Rogers, *The Chief Grounds of Christian Religion* (1648), pp. 3 ff.; John Stalham, *A Catechisme for Children* (1644), p. 8.

[3] Baxter, *The Poor Man's Family Book*, p. 63.

[4] Below, p. 10.

[5] Baxter, *The Poor Man's Family Book*, pp. 65–92.

while they are mindless of the sence . . .'.[1] Even the learned Dr. Owen used a more practical approach in catechizing. His work is erudite but comprehensible.

Q. *What is God in himselfe?*

A. An eternall infinite, incomprehensible spirit, giving beeing to all things, and doing with them whatsoever hee pleaseth.[2]

In content this answer is much closer to Bunyan's catechism than any of Baxter's.

Catechisms often ask, 'What is God?', but Bunyan's does not specifically do this. The question is answered in the quotation cited above, and in his answer to the question, '*How do you distinguish the God of the Christians, from the gods of other people?*' The reply is direct and clear: 'He is a Spirit . . .'[3] The clarity of this answer and that previously quoted is also a characteristic of the catechism of John Stalham, pastor of a Congregational church at Terling, Essex: 'God is an eternall Spirit, who hath his being of himselfe.'[4]

Dorothy Burch gives a similar reply: 'God is a spirit that hath his being of himselfe, without beginning and ending of dayes . . .'[5] The older catechism of William Perkins, reprinted in 1677, lost some of the forcefulness of a simple answer by seeking more theological precision: 'God is a *Spirit*, or spiritual substance, most wise, most holy, eternal, infinite.'[6] Keach's answer is similar: 'God is a Spirit without beginning, and without ending; who is wonderful in his Essence (or Being) and glorious in his Attributes . . .'[7] These examples, when compared to parallel passages in Bunyan, underscore his ability to bring, in the words of John Wilson and Ebenezer Chandler, 'deep things . . . into a familiar Phrase'.[8]

Two topics are given recurring attention by Bunyan in his catechism—ignorance and faith. It is through ignorance and sin that men live alienated from God. This ignorance is manifest in the

[1] Ibid., sig. A2v. Baxter wrote this work in remembrance of Arthur Dent's *The Plaine Mans Path-Way to Heauen*, which so influenced Bunyan. It also praises Lewis Bayly's *Practise of Pietie*, which also had an impact on Bunyan. *G.A.*, §§ 15–16; Nuttall, in *The Beginnings of Nonconformity*, p. 30.

[2] Owen, *The Principles of the Doctrine of Christ*, p. 11.

[3] Below, p. 9.

[4] Stalham, *A Catechisme for Children*, p. 1. For Stalham see *C.R.*, s.v.; *D.N.B.*, s.v.

[5] Burch, *A Catechisme*, sig. A4r.

[6] Perkins, *The Fovndation*, p. 12.

[7] Keach, *The Child's Delight*, pp. 19–20.

[8] *1692 Folio*, sig. A2v.

first things children do. Ignorance cannot, however, be used as an excuse for sinning against the law of God. Yet those who knowingly sin against 'Light, Knowledg, the Preaching of the Word, Godly Acquaintance, timely Cautions, *&c.*' make their sins worse than those 'commited in grossest Ignorance'.[1] Bunyan repudiates the idea that a man ignorant of his sinful state can be happier than one suffering from feelings of guilt. To be ignorant now is to suffer later, in hell. His catechism is therefore intended as 'a Salve to cure that great want of Knowledg which so much reigns both in young and old'.[2]

In the section of the catechism devoted to faith, Bunyan anticipates the theme of his very popular sermon, *Come, & Welcome, to Jesus Christ*, which was published three years later. The catechism deals with the importance of the sinner coming to Christ, aware of his sins and God's wrath, without waiting to '*first mend and be good*'.[3] The problem of fear arises, prompting the catechumen to ask for encouragement to come. The catechist responds:

A. The Prodigal came thus and his Father received him, and fell upon his neck and kissed him. Thus he received the *Colossians* and consequently all that are saved . . .

Q. *Will you give me one more encouragement?*

A. The Promises are so worded, that they that are Scarlet-sinners, Crimson-sinners, Blasphemous Sinners, have incouragement to come to him with hopes of life . . .[4]

One of these promises, John vi. 37, became the text for the sermon which is expounded and expanded in *Come, & Welcome.*

Bunyan's definition of faith, which is such a central element in his catechism, continues to manifest the appealing qualities of directness, clarity, and simplicity.

Q. *What is believing?*

A. It is such an act of a gracious Soul, as layeth hold on Gods Mercy through Christ . . .

Q. *What is believing on Jesus Christ?*

A. It is a receiving of him with what is in him, as the gift of God to thee a sinner . . .[5]

[1] Cf. *G.A.*, § 83. [2] Below, pp. 13, 15, 31. [3] Below, p. 28.
[4] Below, p. 29. [5] Below, p. 27.

To sum up, Bunyan's oft-neglected catechism compares favourably with other seventeenth-century works in this genre. His literary style is plain and effective, whereas the styles of Baxter and Keach, for example, are not. Like most other Congregationalists, Bunyan keeps polemics to a minimum. The personal and experiential qualities that characterize Bunyan's writing at its best (as, for example, in the implicit autobiographical passage in *Saved by Grace* which echoes *Grace Abounding*[1]) are at times found in the catechism. It is, moreover, relatively original, given the conventionality of the genre, especially in the emphasis given to self-denial. For a man who spent so many years in prison because of his beliefs, that emphasis is particularly fitting.

(iv) *Typology*

The other work of Bunyan published in 1675, *Light for Them That Sit in Darkness*, is a polemical work directed against views advocated by the Quakers, and especially by Edward Fowler, vicar of Northill. The early controversy with Edward Burrough had perhaps faded from Bunyan's mind, but Quaker views with which Bunyan did not agree were asserted by William Penn in *The Sandy Foundation Shaken* (1668), a work Bunyan is known to have read and found objectionable.[2] Penn attacked the doctrine of satisfaction as 'inconsistent with the Dignity of God, and very repugnant to the Conditions, Nature, and Tendency of the second Covenant . . .'.[3] He rejected the doctrine of justification by an imputed righteousness (as later advocated by Bunyan in his tracts on justification[4]), arguing that a man was justified by actually keeping God's commandments. Similar views were asserted by Edward Fowler in 1671, and led to an exchange of pamphlets between him and Bunyan.[5] The fact that both men sought adherents from the same Northill area in the 1670s probably helped to keep the controversy in Bunyan's mind. Certainly the attacks on Fowler's views in both

[1] Below, pp. 201–5.

[2] *1692 Folio*, p. 224.

[3] P[enn], *The Sandy Foundation Shaken* (1668), pp. 19–20.

[4] *A Defence of the Doctrine of Iustification, by Faith* (1672) and *Of Justification by an Imputed Righteousness* in the *1692 Folio*.

[5] Greaves, chap. 3.

of Bunyan's 1675 works, culminating in the vituperative closing paragraph of *Light for Them That Sit in Darkness*, would seem to bear this out. The Quakers too continued to compete with Bunyan for converts, making a further attack on their views necessary in Bunyan's judgement.

The polemical aspects of *Light for Them That Sit in Darkness* thus look to past controversies. There is, however, one aspect of this work that Bunyan developed later in his own career, viz. its typology. Although he wrote of types as early as 1659,[1] his fullest development of this subject appears in his commentary on Genesis, which was incomplete at the time of his death in 1688, and may confidently be ascribed to the period after 1675 because of its advanced treatment of types. At least three other posthumous works deal in varying degrees with typology: *Of the House of the Forest of Lebanon*, *The Saint's Priviledge and Profit*, and (very briefly) *Paul's Departure and Crown.*[2]

The principles upon which the Puritan study of typology is based are best set forth in Samuel Mather's *The Figures or Types of the Old Testament, by which Christ and Heavenly Things of the Gospel Were Preached and Shadowed to the People of God* (1683). This treatise appeared too late, of course, for Bunyan to have used it in writing *Light for Them That Sit in Darkness*, though not for his later works. To understand types, Mather believed it was essential to distinguish between 'the thing preached [which] was the Gospel, though the manner of preaching it was legal; the Kernal was Gospel, though the Shell was Law: The Spirit and Substance, and Mystery of that Dispensation was Evangelical, though it was involved in a legal Shell and outside, and overshadowed with the Shades and Figures of the Law'. Types and shadows, according to Mather, comprised one of the seven ways in which God revealed himself in the Old Testament. The others, as given by Mather, were visions, dreams, voices, inner inspiration and impulses of the Holy Spirit, signs and wonders, and 'a special and peculiar kind of Intimacy and Familiarity'.[3]

[1] Oxford Bunyan, ii. 91–4. Cf. *G.A.*, § 71.

[2] *1692 Folio*, pp. 189, 258 ff., and throughout *Of the House of the Forest of Lebanon.*

[3] Mather, op. cit., pp. 10, 17.

Briefly defined, 'A Type is some outward or sensible thing ordained of God under the Old Testament, to represent and hold forth something of Christ in the New'.[1] The study of types requires distinguishing between the outward or sensible thing (the type), the higher thing which it represents (the antitype), and 'the work of the *Type*, which is to *shadow forth* or represent these *future good things*'.[2] Mather lays down a series of principles to follow in pursuing a study of these types. First, God is the author of types. There are, he writes, three ways in which to determine if something is a divinely ordained type. One is an explicit Scriptural statement. Another is a 'permutation of Names between the *Type* and the *Antitype*', as when Christ is called David. A third is 'when by comparing several Scriptures together, there doth appear an evident and manifest analogy and parallel between things under the Law, and things under the Gospel . . .'. The second guide-line is that types are 'not only Signs to represent Gospel Mysteries . . . but also Seals to assure them of the certain and infallible exhibition [of God's promises] . . . in Gods appointed time'. Types are visible promises, as are sacraments in the New Testament. Thirdly, 'the Types relate not only to the Person of Christ; but to his Benefits, and to all Gospel Truths and Mysteries, even to all New-Testament Dispensations'. Finally, just as there is a resemblance between the type and antitype in some things, so there is a disparity in others, hence types must not be pursued too far.[3]

Mather distinguishes between a type, which is divinely instituted and fixed, and a similitude, which is used only occasionally. A type is not a parable; the latter is a sacred similitude, 'but in a Type the Lord doth not only occasionally use such or such a simile; but sets such a thing apart, sets a stamp of Institution upon it, and so makes it an Ordinance to hold forth Christ and his Benefits'. Neither is a type identical to a ceremony, though all ceremonies are types. Types are of the same nature as sacraments, but different in number. Types, furthermore, are signs of the Messiah to come; sacraments are signs of the Christ that has come.[4] In short, these are the key principles set forth by Mather, which reflect the earlier study of types by numerous writers.

[1] Ibid., p. 67. [2] Ibid., p. 66. [3] Ibid., pp. 67–74. [4] Ibid., pp. 75–6.

The probable source of influence for Bunyan's earliest use of types was Thomas Taylor's *Christ Revealed: or the Old Testament Explained*, first published in 1635. His *Highway to Happinesse* (1633) may have influenced Bunyan's imagery in *The Pilgrim's Progress*, for Taylor depicts sin as a burden on man like that of an actual load.[1] The Apology of *The Pilgrim's Progress*, of course, also includes these well-known lines:

But must I needs want solidness, because
By Metaphors I speak; was not Gods Laws,
His Gospel-laws in older time held forth
By Types, Shadows and Metaphors? . . .[2]

If Bunyan had read Taylor, he was likely to have been introduced to his writings by John Owen, who wrote a preface to *A Collection of the Works of T. Taylor* (1653).

Bunyan discusses types in *Light for Them That Sit in Darkness* in connection with the promises of a Messiah in the Old Testament.

> Indeed the Scriptures of the Old-Testament are filled with Promises of the Messias to come, Prophetical Promises, Typical Promises: For all the Types and shadows of the Saviour, are virtually so many Promises.[3]

Bunyan places the Old Testament types used for Christ in three categories: men, animals, and material objects. In explaining these types in his discourse, he used much less detail than the writers of works dealing solely with typology, but his affinity with them is nevertheless apparent.

Adam is, for Bunyan, a type of Christ 'especially as he was the Head and Father of the first World'.[4] Taylor's fuller treatment of Adam as a type of Christ does not differ from Bunyan, though it goes into more detail. Adam is a type of Christ with respect to creation; both are sons of God; both are men; both are sons of one father, viz. of God alone; both are created in the image of God; both are endowed with perfect wisdom and knowledge; both possessed a 'happy and innocent estate'; Adam was created on the sixth day, and Christ 'towards the sixth age of the world . . .'.

[1] Sharrock, p. 96. [2] *P.P.*, p. 4. [3] Below, p. 60.
[4] Below, p. 60.

Adam is also a type of Christ with respect to office and sovereignty: Adam owned paradise and was lord of all creatures, whereas Christ is lord of heaven and earth; Adam was appointed to care for the Garden of Eden, Christ to sanctify the church, 'the Garden and Paradise of God . . .'; Adam was prophet, priest, and king in his family, Christ in his church. Adam was also a type with regard to 'Conjugation': Eve was 'framed' while Adam slept, and the church was 'framed' while Christ died; Eve came from Adam's side, the church from the side of Christ; Eve was given to Adam while pure and innocent, and the church was married to Christ in the same state; Eve bore to Adam both Cain and Abel, just as the visible church has both elect and reprobate. Finally, Adam is a type with respect to 'propagation': both have 'posterity and seed'; Adam conveys sin to his posterity, but Christ conveys righteousness to his; Adam merited death for his posterity, but Christ merited life for his.[1] Mather also discusses Adam as a type of Christ in his treatise on typology.[2]

Bunyan discusses seven other men as types of Christ, viz. Moses (who is also mentioned in *Come, & Welcome*[3]), a type as mediator and builder of the tabernacle; Aaron and Melchizedec, types as high priests; Samson, a type in dying for the deliverance of Israel from the Philistines; Joshua, a type in giving the land of Canaan to Israel; David, a type especially in subduing Israel's enemies and feeding his people; and Solomon, a type in building the temple and ruling a peaceful kingdom.[4] All these except Aaron are discussed by both Taylor and Mather. These writers also include men not discussed by Bunyan, to wit Joseph, Isaac, and Jonah. Mather also discusses Enoch, Noah, Abraham, Jacob, Elijah, Elisha, and Zerubbabel. With regard to Abraham, Mather comments: 'I confess he is omitted by divers that have handled this Subject . . .'[5]

The passover lamb is discussed as a type of Christ by Bunyan, Taylor, Mather, and Benjamin Keach. According to Bunyan the lamb is a type in five ways. First, it was, like Christ, spotless. Secondly, it was roasted, prefiguring the cursed death of Christ.

[1] Taylor, *Christ Revealed: or the Old Testament Explained* (1635), pp. 6–8.
[2] Mather, op. cit., pp. 68, 82–5.
[3] Below, pp. 314, 323–4.
[4] Below, pp. 60–1.
[5] Mather, op. cit., p. 103.

Thirdly, it was to be eaten, as was Christ's body and blood in the communion. Fourthly, its blood was to be sprinkled on the doors of the houses of the faithful for the avenging angels to see, as Christ's blood was to be sprinkled on the elect 'for the Justice of God to look on . . .' Fifthly, 'by eating the Paschal-Lamb, the People went out of *Egypt*: by feeding upon Christ by Faith, we come from under the *Egyptian* Darkness, *Tyranny* of Satan, *&c.*'[1] Taylor depicted the lamb as a type of Christ in three respects: in name; in qualities, such as meekness, innocence, and obedience; and in '*shadows*, being figured in all those lambs slaine, especially in the Paschall Lamb'. Furthermore the lamb must be without blemish, a male, a year old (i.e. a perfect age), and 'out of their own flockes and folds' (i.e. Christ must be an Israelite). The lamb must be severed from the flock, kept alive four days (Christ's four-year ministry), and slain at the appropriate time of day (the evening). It must be roasted whole (as Christ was pierced and crucified, enduring the whole wrath of God), with no bones broken.[2]

Other sacrificial animals are discussed as types, with Bunyan singling out the red cow of Numbers xix. 2 for mention.[3] Keach, curiously, refers to heifers as metaphors (or types) of various things, but not Christ.[4] The other animals named by Bunyan as types are sacrificial bulls, goats, and birds.[5] Birds represent innocence and are not linked to Christ by Mather, with the exception of the turtle dove. The latter had its head wrung off violently by the priest in order to 'shadow forth' the violence suffered by Christ.[6] Keach discusses the turtle dove as denoting the people of Israel or the church. Goats, according to him, 'signifie the *Captains* or Governours of the People . . .' The bull is, for Keach, a metaphor (or type) for 'a violent, cruel, and proud Enemy, that abuses and infests the miserable . . .'[7] There is thus a clear difference in interests between Keach and Bunyan on the subject of typology.

An example of Bunyan's third category of types is manna. Both

[1] Below, p. 61; cf. p. 106.

[2] Taylor, op. cit., pp. 217, 221–3. Cf. Mather, op. cit., pp. 67–8; K[each], *Τροπολογία: A Key to Open Scripture-Metaphors* (1681–2), ii. 186–7.

[3] Below, p. 61.

[4] Keach, op. cit. i. 154–5.

[5] Below, pp. 61, 84, 112.

[6] Mather, op. cit., pp. 259–60.

[7] Keach, op. cit. i. 154, 156, 158.

manna and Christ came from heaven and were intended to be eaten. 'The Mannah was to be gathered daily, so is Christ to be daily eaten.' The only bread Israel had in the wilderness was manna, as Christ is the only spiritual bread which believers have. 'The Mannah came not by *Moses* Law, neither comes Christ by our Merits.'[1] Taylor treats manna as a type of Christ in terms of both its quality and its quantity. With respect to quality, both have a heavenly origin, and each has a sweet taste (Christ tasting sweet to an afflicted sinner). Manna has a round, hence perfect shape, as Christ is perfect, without beginning or end. Manna is white in colour, signifying purity, and is common to all Israelites, whether rich or poor. The supply of manna was continued throughout the wilderness, as Christ continues with his church until the end of the world. With respect to quantity, manna is like Christ, small in size, but of great power and nourishment. Manna is also freely and abundantly given, as is Christ's grace to the church. Manna fell only around the camp, and Christ is to be found only in the church. Finally, manna fell on the eve of the sabbath in double quantity, as men must be doubly diligent to 'get Christ' in this life.[2] Manna is also treated as a type of Christ by Mather and Keach. The latter sums it up nicely: 'CHRIST, and the Graces of Christ, are called *Manna*, the Antitype of that *Manna* that fell in the Wilderness . . .' He goes on to point out no less than twenty-six similarities and only six disparities.[3]

Bunyan includes two other examples in this third category of type. One of these is the rock struck by Moses to provide water for the Hebrews. As it provided drink for the people in the wilderness, so Christ provides drink for those who forsake this world to follow him. The rock was struck to bring forth water; Christ, to bring forth blood. The drinks thus provided were made available to the thirsty. 'The Water of the Rock in the Wilderness ran after the People . . . Christ also is said by that Type to follow us . . .'[4] Taylor depicts the rock as a type of Christ in three respects: appearance (barren and despised, exalted above the earth, firm and stable, a

[1] Below, p. 62.

[2] Taylor, op. cit., pp. 265–9; cf. pp. 269–88.

[3] Keach, op. cit. ii. 139; cf. 139–42; Mather, op. cit., pp. 173–9.

[4] Below, p. 62.

rock of scandal and offence to the wicked, and a danger to those on whom it falls); purpose (to cleanse, comfort, and make the barren fruitful); and attainment. It can be requested by the people but only given by God. It can give water only after being struck. Moses' rod did the smiting, as 'it was the Law given by *Moses* hand, and our transgression against it that breaks the true Rock'. It was not so much the act of striking, as the act of God that brought forth water and divine blessing. Finally, the water subsequently followed the Israelites, as Christ's work and grace suffice for believers throughout their lives.[1] Keach and Mather also treated the rock as a type of Christ.[2]

Bunyan's last example of a material object as a type of Christ is Mount Moriah. 'That Mount stood in *Jerusalem*; Christ also stands in his Church', and 'upon that Rock was built the Temple'.[3] Nothing quite comparable exists in the works of Taylor, Keach, and Mather. The latter does make mention of 'the *transient Holiness* of places . . . where the Lord gave visible appearances of himself', including Mount Sinai and Mount Tabor.[4] Taylor and Mather discuss a number of additional material objects as types of Christ. Mather, for example, writes in this regard of the pillar of cloud and fire, the Red Sea, the brazen serpent, holy things, and circumcision.[5]

The interest in typology which Bunyan manifests is not in any way distinctive or original. It is, nevertheless, an aspect of his writing which becomes increasingly prominent in his later works, and was important enough to warrant specific mention in the Apology to *The Pilgrim's Progress*. Some grasp of the subject is thus necessary for a more thorough understanding of his works.

(v) *Parallels with* Grace Abounding, The Pilgrim's Progress, *and* The Holy War

The four works in this volume contain numerous passages complementary to *Grace Abounding* and *The Pilgrim's Progress*, as well as some passages that foreshadow *The Holy War*.

[1] Taylor, op. cit., pp. 288–95.
[2] Keach, op. cit. i. 129; ii. 170–3; Mather, op. cit., pp. 179–83.
[3] Below, pp. 62–3.
[4] Mather, op. cit., p. 411.
[5] Ibid., pp. 200–15, 243–65, 302–39.

In *Saved by Grace* (§ 8) there is a theological explanation of why the elect are granted long life prior to conversion; this includes preservation from drowning, as happened twice to Bunyan (*G.A.* § 12). *Come, & Welcome* (p. 334) draws attention to reading good books and hearing believers talk of heavenly things[1] as means to bring the elect to Christ, as Bunyan himself experienced (*G.A.*, §§ 20, 77, 89–90, 117–18). 'Being strangly cast under the Ministry of some Godly Man' (p. 334) is another of the means to effect the sinner's conversion, as Bunyan knew (*G.A.*, §§ 15, 37–9). A warning against the temptation to pursue sports rather than God (*G.A.*, §§ 21, 24) is given in *Saved by Grace* (§ 46) and *Instruction for the Ignorant* (p. 18). *Saved by Grace* includes warnings against merely external professions of religion and seeking to find religious peace by keeping the Ten Commandments (§§ 36, 48), both of which Bunyan pursued in his quest for inner tranquillity (*G.A.*, §§ 30, 32). Another danger to be avoided was the advice of wicked friends (*Come, & Welcome*, p. 336), such as Bunyan's youthful companion Harry with his love of cursing and whoring (*G.A.*, § 43).

The experience that 'God never much charged the guilt of the sins of my ignorance upon me' (*G.A.*, § 83) is explained in the catechism (p. 15). Here Bunyan also uses the concept of a limited day of grace, which once struck such fear in him (*G.A.*, §§ 66–7),[2] to persuade catechumens to repent immediately (p. 18). He had also been troubled by the 'sin against the Holy *Ghost*' (*G.A.*, §§ 103, 148, 174, 180), which is discussed in *Come, & Welcome* (pp. 352, 353) as it similarly distressed others. The Quakers, whose 'errors' were a factor in Bunyan's religious experience (*G.A.*, §§ 123–4), are repudiated in *Light in Darkness*. The profound impact of Luther on Bunyan, who 'found my condition in his experience, so largely and profoundly handled, as if his Book [*Commentary on Galatians*] had been written out of my heart' (*G.A.*, § 129), is reflected in *Come, & Welcome* (p. 296), where Luther is quoted to encourage the sinner to come to Christ. Bunyan's moping in a field, troubled with feelings of guilt and despair (*G.A.*, § 140), is also recalled in *Come, & Welcome* (p. 266). This sermon (p. 335) notes the importance of beholding divine judgement on others as a means to convert the

[1] Cf. below, p. 34. [2] Cf. below, p. 367.

sinner; Bunyan may have been thinking of the effect on him of the story of Francis Spira, 'a book that was to my troubled spirit as salt, when rubbed into a fresh wound . . .' (*G.A.*, § 163). In *Saved by Grace* (§ 12), there is a vivid recollection of the doubts that assailed Bunyan when he was 'somewhat inclining to a Consumption . . .' (*G.A.*, §§ 255 ff.).

Apart from these rather specific parallels, there are abundant parallels between the general themes of *Grace Abounding* and the works in this volume. *Saved by Grace* (§§ 45–51, 68) includes a virtual synopsis of the general themes of *Grace Abounding*, though they are not treated autobiographically. Personal experience is also behind Bunyan's remarks in *Light in Darkness* on feelings of guilt in the conscience (pp. 91, 156). The doubts that plague the would-be convert—the doubts Bunyan experienced—are noted several times in *Come, & Welcome* (pp. 352, 356–7, 363, 366–7). Even the catechism (pp. 20–1) cautions us that it is difficult to attain true knowledge of God, and urges the importance of knowing one's loathsome state. These works, then, repeatedly mirror the personal experience of the author—a trait common to the best in the literature of seventeenth-century nonconformity.[1]

The theme and metaphors of *The Pilgrim's Progress* are also frequently reflected in these works. The concept of the believer's pilgrimage is explicitly stated in *Saved by Grace* (§ 25). The dialogue style of the allegory of the soul appears in the catechism (e.g., p. 19) and in *Saved by Grace* (§ 68). Narrative qualities appear in *Light in Darkness* (pp. 100, 126). The personification of *Shall-come*, in *Come, & Welcome* (pp. 278–9, 281) is akin to that of *Help*, *Good-Will*, *Great-grace*, and *Great-heart* in the allegory. Moreover the emphasis on ignorance in the catechism[2] reminds us of the character Ignorance in *The Pilgrim's Progress*. References to lions abound.[3] Above all, the theological foundation of the allegory is developed in *Saved by Grace*, as it was earlier in *The Doctrine of the Law and Grace Unfolded*. What the allegory does, however, is to make the basic Calvinism of these

[1] Nuttall, *The Holy Spirit in Puritan Faith and Experience* (Oxford, 1946), pp. 7, 26–7.

[2] Cf. below, p. 344.

[3] Below, *Light in Darkness*, pp. 127, 156; *Come and Welcome*, pp. 310, 319, 346, 351, 357; *Saved by Grace*, §§ 11, 73. Cf. *P.P.*, pp. 43, 45–6, 218–19, 242, 251.

doctrinal works more palatable.[1] This is also a key to the popularity of *Come, & Welcome*, where the personal qualities of a warm and open invitation to Jesus mask the colder doctrine of predestination.

There are also more specific reflections of the allegory in these works. In *The Pilgrim's Progress* it is Evangelist who comes to the man wandering in the field, but in *Come, & Welcome* (p. 266) the devil comes to torment the wanderer. Nevertheless, later in the sermon (p. 334) reference is made to such a man 'being strangly cast under the Ministry of some Godly Man', who would be the Evangelist of the allegory. The message he gave to the wandering sinner on the parchment roll, '*Fly from the wrath to come*' (*P.P.*, p. 10) is reiterated in *Saved by Grace* (§ 5) and *Come, & Welcome* (pp. 258, 358). The burden carried by Christian is also noted in *Saved by Grace* (§ 5). This should not make him despair (the Slough of Despond), but he must 'look to Jesus Christ Crucified' to lose his burden,[2] as Christian did (*P.P.*, p. 38). The futile attempt of Christian to find help at Mr. Legality's house by Mount Sinai (*P.P.*, p. 20) is paralleled in *Saved by Grace* (§ 48) and *Light in Darkness* (p. 83). The latter vividly describes how 'the threatning of death, and the Curse of the Law lay in the Way between Heaven-Gates and the Souls of the Children, for their Sins . . .' The straight gate through which Christian passed (*P.P.*, p. 25) is also found in the catechism (p. 18). When he got to the Interpreter's house, he was shown a fire which continued to burn despite water being thrown on it (*P.P.*, p. 32). The scene is repeated, with slight variations, in *Saved by Grace* (§ 47). The same discourse (§ 36) condemns the traits that characterize Formalist and Hypocrisie.

Hill Difficulty gave Christian trouble on his pilgrimage (*P.P.* pp. 41–2), hence the warning in the catechism (p. 32) that faith only comes gradually and through difficulty. Christian reaches the Palace Beautiful (*P.P.*, pp. 45 ff.),[3] which is also mentioned in *Come, & Welcome* (p. 289). The sermon (p. 339) warns of the hazardous nature of the pilgrimage, as Christian discovers when he leaves the Palace Beautiful and encounters Apollyon (*P.P.*, pp. 56 ff.). Victory here is followed by entry into the Valley of the Shadow of

[1] For a more precise account of Bunyan's theology see Greaves, chap. 6.

[2] Below, p. 157.

[3] See Greaves, chap. 5.

Death, where Christian's conscience is assaulted with doubts about blasphemy (*P.P.*, pp. 63–4). These doubts are taken up by Bunyan in *Come, & Welcome* (pp. 264 ff.). The Valley was made more dangerous by a deep ditch (*P.P.*, p. 62), worse than the one depicted in *Come, & Welcome* (p. 360), which was a ditch of temptation used by God to aid the coming sinner. The meeting of Christian with Talkative, the Son of Saywell, gave Bunyan an opportunity to decry those who could speak about religion but lacked the spiritual experience (*P.P.*, pp. 75 ff.). He struck out at the same people in *Light in Darkness* (pp. 127–8), warning that 'such Men as have only the notions of it, are of all Men liable to the greatest Sins, because there *wanteth* in their notions, *the Power of Love*, which alone can constrain them to love Jesus Christ'. The pilgrim then passes through a wilderness (*P.P.*, p. 85), depicted more fully in *Come, & Welcome* (pp. 357–8). The trial at Vanity Fair (*P.P.*, pp. 92 ff.) reflects Bunyan's own trial, as does the use of legal terminology in *Light in Darkness* (pp. 87, 91, 102, 132, 153) and *Saved by Grace* (§ 8). Faithful was martyred at Vanity Fair (*P.P.*, pp. 97–8), indicating Bunyan's keen interest in Foxe's *Acts and Monuments*, which is cited at some length in *Come, & Welcome* (pp. 383–4). Christian and Hopeful finally reach the River of Water of Life (*P.P.*, pp. 110–11), which also figures in *Come, & Welcome* (pp. 255–6, 300, 355).

When Christian and Hopeful journey to By-Path-Meadow, they find the way out blocked by flood waters in which 'they had like to have been drowned nine or ten times' (*P.P.*, p. 113). A similar illustration is used in *Come, & Welcome* (p. 363): 'If therefore the wind of Temptations blow, the waves of doubts and fears will presently arise, and this coming sinner will begin to sink, if he has but little faith.' This is precisely what happened to the two pilgrims (and to Peter in the Gospels), who were taken to Doubting-Castle by Giant Despair (*P.P.*, pp. 113 ff.). Escape from the Castle through the use of the key called Promise (*P.P.*, p. 118) is faintly reminiscent of the passage in *Light in Darkness* (p. 63) depicting types as the key to open the promises. The safe arrival of the pilgrims at their destination is never in doubt theologically.[1] When the pilgrims at last complete their journey the bells ring and the voices of the

[1] Below, *Saved by Grace*, § 12.

angels are lifted up in songs (*P.P.*, pp. 161–2). In *Come, & Welcome* too 'the musick was struck up' and songs were sung (p. 301). The songs are also included in *Light in Darkness* (pp. 110, 130, 159).

There are only a few instances in these works which look ahead to *The Holy War*. The concept of spiritual combat appears in *Light in Darkness* (p. 157), as does the metaphor of sin as 'the great Engine of Hell'. In *Saved by Grace* (§ 44) the sinner is portrayed as having 'struck up a Covenant with Death'. Death is personified in *Come, & Welcome* (p. 257), but even more prophetic of what is to come in *The Holy War* is the statement that 'faith, and doubting, may at the same time have their residence in the same soul' (p. 362). Four years later Bunyan developed this metaphor into a classic account of a battle of rival forces for control of the citadel of self.

INSTRUCTION FOR THE IGNORANT

INSTRUCTION FOR THE IGNORANT

Note on the Text

ONE edition of *Instruction for the Ignorant* was published in Bunyan's lifetime. It was printed for Francis Smith in 1675, who at that time had his place of business at the Elephant and Castle, Cornhill, near the Royal Exchange. His associations with Bunyan extend over a period of nearly three decades, commencing with the publication of *Profitable Meditations* in 1661. *Christian Behaviour* followed two years later, and *The Resurrection of the Dead* in 1665. About a year later Smith published a second edition of *A Few Sighs from Hell*, with later editions in 1672, 1674, 1680, and 1686. Smith published two other Bunyan works in 1672, viz. *A Confession of My Faith* and *A Defence of the Doctrine of Iustification*. In 1675 Smith published not only Bunyan's catechism but also his *Light for Them That Sit in Darkness* and *The Strait Gate*. Four years later Smith printed the fourth edition of *Grace Abounding*.

Further information about Smith's activities is provided in a list of books he published for Bunyan, printed at the end of *Light in Darkness*. Of the ten listed, four have not thus far been mentioned, because Smith's name did not appear on their title-pages. One of the four is *I Will Pray with the Spirit*, the first edition of which has been lost. It has already been argued that this work was written in 1661 or 1662.[1] Extant information on Smith's activities in these years makes the likely date of publication no later than August 1661, when he was imprisoned. Bunyan's *One Thing Is Needful* was also published by Smith, perhaps in 1664, about the same time as *A Mapp of Salvation and Damnation*. A year later Smith published *The Holy City*.

Smith's career was highly colourful. In 1659 he published a controversial work by Captain W. Bray entitled *Plea for the People's Good Cause*. His sectarian political and religious views embroiled him in controversy. His windows were broken and his lodgers were

[1] Oxford Bunyan, ii.

scared away in 1659 on account of his opposition to General Monck and the Royalists. He was imprisoned three times and fined £50 in 1660 for publishing *The Lord's Loud Call to England*. In August 1661 he was gaoled for publishing *Mirabilis Annus*. As a result he lost his trade for two years and suffered losses he calculated at £300. There was further trouble in 1666 when his books were seized at a warehouse near Temple Bar. In 1671 he was convicted of violating the Conventicle Act, and again was unable to practise his trade, this time for six months. By his own reckoning persecution extending over two decades cost him at least £1,400. His difficulties with the law extended into the 1680s, when he published several pamphlets defending his cause. He was probably buried at Farnham, Surrey, on 6 July 1688.[1]

Instruction for the Ignorant was included in the *1692 Folio* edition of Bunyan's works.

THE FIRST EDITION, 1675

Title-page: [within rules] INSTRUCTION | FOR THE | IGNORANT: | Being a Salve to cure that great want | of Knowledg which so much reigns | both in young and old. | Prepared, and presented to them in a | plain and easie Dialogue, fitted to | the Capacity of the weakest. | [rule] | By JOHN BUNYAN. | [rule] | Hos. 4. 6. *My People perish for lack of* | *Knowledg*. | [rule]| [row of ornaments] | [rule] | *LONDON*, | Printed for *Francis Smith* at the Elephant and | Castle in *Cornhil*, near the Royal-Ex- | change, 1675.

Collation: 8°: A–D⁸. Pages: 64.

Contents: A1ʳ title-page, A1ᵛ blank, A2ʳ⁻ᵛ epistle to the church at Bedford, A3ʳ–D8ᵛ text. Single row of ornaments at head of A2ʳ and A3ʳ. A2ᵛ is signed 'J.B.' and followed by a tapered rule. The single row of ornaments at the head of A3ʳ is followed by the abbreviated title, '*Instruction for the Ignorant, &c.*' '*The Conclusion.*', which begins on D8ʳ, is preceded by a rule. On D8ᵛ a rule precedes '*THE END.*' Page 64 is numbered 44.

Running Titles: The epistle has none. For the text it is '*Instruction for the Ignorant.*'

Catchwords: (selected) A8ᵛ for C1ʳ Of C8ᵛ Q. *What* D7ᵛ A. Yes;

Copy Collated: Bodleian, Oxford. This is at present the only copy known to exist. The close cropping of this copy has left only the following signatures: A2, B, C, D, D3, D4.

[1] Plomer, pp. 273–4; *An Account of the Injurious Proceedings of Sir G. Jeffreys . . . against F. Smith* . . . (by Smith, 1680).

The text that follows is based on the Bodleian copy of the first edition. Where that copy is deficient at the foot of a page on account of close cropping, the missing text has been provided from the *1692 Folio*. Obvious printer's errors have been corrected. Erroneous Scriptural references have been corrected in the text, and the original references noted in the critical apparatus. When Bunyan lists more verses than he quotes in his text, the extra citations remain. Biblical quotations have been left as Bunyan cited them, whether accurate or not.

To the Church of Christ in and about *Bedford*, walking in the Faith and Fellowship of the Gospel, your affectionate Brother and Companion in the Kingdom and Patience of *JESUS CHRIST*, wisheth all Grace and Mercy by *Jesus Christ*. Amen.

HOly and beloved, Although I have designed this little Treatise for publick and common benefit, yet considering that I am to you a debtor not only in common Charity, but by reason of special Bonds which the Lord hath laid upon me to you-ward, I could do no less (being driven from you in presence, not affection), but first present you with this little Book; not for that you are wanting in the things contained herein, but to put you again in remembrance of first things, and to give you occasion to present something to your carnal relations that may be (if God will) for their awakening and conversion; accept it therefore as a token of my Christian Remembrance of you.

Next, I present it to all those unconverted, old and young, who have been at any time under my Preaching, and yet remain in their sins: And I entreat them also that they receive it as a token of my love to their immortal Souls; yea, I charge them as they will answer it in the day of the terrible judgment, that they read, ponder, and receive this wholsom Medicine prepared for them. Now the God of Blessing bless it to the awakening of many sinners, and the salvation of their souls by faith in Jesus Christ. Amen.

Yours, to serve you by my
Ministry (when I can) to your
Edification and Consolation,
J. B.

Instruction for the Ignorant, &c.

Quest.

H*Ow many Gods are there?*

Answ.

To the Christians there is but one God, the Father, of whom are all things, and we of him, 1 Cor. 8. 6.

Q. *Why? is not the God of the Christians the God of them that are no Christians?*

A. He is their Maker and Preserver; but they have not chosen him to be their God, *Acts* 17. 24. *Psal.* 36. 6. *Judg.* 10. 14.

Q. *Is there then other gods besides the God of the Christians?*

A. There is none other true God but He: but because they want the grace of Christians, therefore they chuse not Him, but such gods as will suit with, and countenance their lusts, *Joh.* 8. 44.

Q. *What gods are they that countenance the lusts of wicked men?*

A. The Devil, who is the god of this World; the Belly, that god of Gluttons, Drunkards, and riotous persons; and idle pleasures and vanities, which are for the most part the gods of the youth, *Joh.* 8. 44. 2 *Cor.* 4. 4. *Phil.* 3. 19. *Exod.* 32. 6. 1 *Cor.* 10. 7. 2 *Tim.* 2. 22. 1 *John* 5. 21.

Q. *Who is a Christian?*

A. One that is born again, a new creature; one that sits at Jesus feet to hear his Word; one that hath his heart purified and sanctified by Faith which is in Christ, *John* 3. 3, 5, 7. *Act.* 11. 26. *Act.* 15. 9. *chap.* 26. 18. 2 *Cor.* 5. 17.

Q. *How do you distinguish the God of the Christians, from the gods of other people?*

A. He is a Spirit, *John* 4. 24.

Q. *Is there no other Spirit but the true God?*

A. Yes, there are many spirits, 1 *John* 4. 1.

Q. *What spirits are they?*

A. The good Angels, are Spirits; the bad Angels are Spirits; and

6 1 *Cor.* 8. 6.] 1 *Cor.* 8. 9.

the Souls of Men are Spirits, *Heb.* 1. 7, 14. 1 *King.* 22. 21, 22. *Rev.* 16. 13, 14. *Act.* 7. 59. *Heb.* 12. 23.

Q. *How then is the true God distinguished from other Spirits?*

A. Thus; No Spirit is Eternal but he, no Spirit is Almighty but he, no Spirit is Incomprehensible and Unsearchable but he; He is also most Merciful, most Just, most Holy, *Deut.* 33. 27. *Gen.* 17. 1. *Psal.* 145. 3. *Mich.* 7. 18. *Job* 34. 17. 1 *Sam.* 2. 2.

Q. *Is this God, being a Spirit, to be known?*

A. Yes, and that by his Works of Creation, by his Providences, by the Judgments that he executeth, and by his Word.

Q. *Do you understand him by the Works of Creation?*

A. The Heavens declare the Glory of God, and the Firmament sheweth his handy-work: so that the invisible things of him from the Creation of the World, are clearly seen, being understood by the things that are made, even his Eternal Power and Godhead, *Psal.* 19. 1, 2. *Rom.* 1. 20.

Q. *Doth his Works of Providence also declare him?*

A. They must needs do it, since through his Providence the whole Creation is kept in such harmony as it is, and that in despite of Sin and Devils: also if you consider that from an Angel to a Sparrow, nothing falls to the ground without the Providence of our Heavenly Father, *Mat.* 10. 29.

Q. *Is he known by his Judgments?*

A. God is known by his Judgments which he executeth; the wicked is snared in the work of his own hands, *Psal.* 9. 16.

Q. *Is he known by his Word?*

A. Yes, most clearly: for by that he revealeth his Attributes, his Decrees, his Promises, his way of Worship, and how he is to be pleased by us.

Q. *Of what did God make the World?*

A. Things that are seen, were not made of things that do appear, *Heb.* 11. 3.

Q. *How long was he in making the World?*

A. In six days the Lord made Heaven and Earth, the Sea, and all that is in them, and on the seventh day God ended all his works which he had made, *Exod.* 20. 11. *Gen.* 2. 2.

Q. *Of what did God make Man?*

A. The Lord God formed Man of the dust of the Ground, and breathed into his nostrils the breath of Life, and Man became a living soul, *Gen.* 2. 7.

Q. *Why doth it say God breathed into him the breath of Life, is Man's Soul of the very nature of the Godhead?*

A. This doth not teach that the Soul is of the nature of the Godhead, but sheweth that it is not of the same matter as his body, which is dust, *Gen.* 18. 27.

Q. *Is not the Soul then of the nature of the Godhead?*

A. No, for God cannot sin, but the Soul doth; God cannot be destroyed in Hell, but the Souls of the Impenitent shall, *Ezek.* 18. 4. *Mat.* 10. 28.

Q. *How did God make man in the day of his first Creation?*

A. God made Man upright. In the Image of God created he him, *Eccl.* 7. 29. *Gen.* 1. 27.

Q. *Did God when he made Man, leave him without a Rule to walk by?*

A. No: He gave him a Law in his nature, and imposed upon him a positive Precept, but he offered violence to them, and brake them both, *Gen.* 3. 3, 6.

Q. *What was the due desert of that Transgression?*

A. Spiritual death in the day he did it, Temporal Death afterwards, and everlasting Death last of all, *Gen.* 2. 17. *chap.* 3. 19. *Mat.* 25. 46.

Q. *What is it to be spiritually dead?*

A. To be alienate from God, and to live without him in the World, through the Ignorance that is in Man, and through the Power of their Sins, *Ephes.* 4. 18, 19.

Q. *Wherein doth this alienation from God appear?*

A. In the love they have to their sins, in their being loth to come to him, in their pleading idle excuses for their sins, and in their ignorance of the excellent mysteries of his blessed Gospel, *Ephes.* 2. 2, 3, 11, 12. *Rom.* 1. 28. *Ephes.* 4. 18, 19.

Q. *What is temporal death?*

A. To have Body and Soul separate asunder, the Body returning to the Dust as it was, and the Spirit to God that gave it, *Gen.* 3. 19. *Eccles.* 12. 7.

Q. *What is Everlasting Death?*

A. For Body and Soul to be separate for ever from God, and to be cast into Hell-fire, *Luk*. 13. 27. *Mar*. 9. 43.

Q. *Do Men go Body and Soul to Hell so soon as they die?*

A. The Body abideth in the Grave till the sound of the last Trump; but the Soul, if the Man dies wicked, goes presently from the face of God into Hell, as into a Prison, there to be kept till the day of Judgment, 1 *Cor*. 15. 52. *Isa*. 24. 22. *Luke* 12. 20.

Q. *Do we come into the World as upright as did our first Parent?*

A. No; He came into the World sinless, being made so of God Almighty; but we came into the World sinners, being made so by his Pollution.

Q. *How doth it appear that we came into the World polluted?*

A. We are the fruit of an unclean thing, are defiled in our very conception, and are by nature the Children of wrath, *Job* 14. 4. *Psal*. 51. 5. *Ephes*. 2. 3.

Q. *Can you make further proof of this?*

A. Yes, It is said that by one Man came Sin, Death, Judgment, and Condemnation upon all Men, *Rom*. 5. 12, 15, 16, 17, 18, 19.

Q. *Do we then come sinners into the World?*

A. Yes, we are Transgressors from the Womb, and go astray as soon as we are born, speaking lies, *Isa*. 48. 8. *Psal*. 58. 3.

Q. *But as* Adam *fell with us in him, so did he not by faith rise with us in him? for he had no seed until he had the Promise.*

A. He fell as a publick person, but believed the Promise as a single person. *Adam*'s faith saved not the World, though *Adam*'s sin overthrew it.

Q. *But do not some hold that we are sinners only by imitation?*

A. Yes, being themselves deceived. But God's Word saith, we are Children of Wrath by Nature, that is, by Birth and Generation.

Q. *Can you bring further proof of this?*

A. Yes; in that day that we were born, we were polluted in our own Blood, and cast out to the loathing of our persons. Again, the Children of old that were dedicated unto the Lord, a Sacrifice was offered for them at a month old, which was before they were sinners by imitation, *Ezek*. 16. 4, 5, 6, 7, 8, 9. *Num*. 18. 14, 15, 16.

Q. *Can you make this appear by experience?*

A. Yes; The first things that bloom and put forth themselves in

Children, shew their Ignorance of God, their disobedience to Parents, and their innate enmity to Holiness of life; their inclinations naturally run to vanity. Besides, little Children die, but that they could not, were they not of God counted sinners; for death is the wages of sin, *Rom.* 6. 23.

Q. *What is sin?*

A. It is a transgression of the Law, 1 *Joh.* 3. 4.

Q. *A transgression of what Law?*

A. Of the Law of our Nature, and of the Law of the Ten Commandments as written in the holy Scriptures, *Rom.* 2. 12, 14, 15. *Exod.* 20.

Q. *When doth one sin against the Law of Nature?*

A. When you do any thing that your Conscience tells you is a transgression against God or Man, *Rom.* 2. 14, 15.

Q. *When do we sin against the Law as written in the ten Commandments?*

A. When you do any thing that they forbid, although you be ignorant of it, *Psal.* 19. 12.

Q. *How many ways are there to sin against this Law?*

A. Three: By sinful thoughts, by sinful words, and also by sinful actions, *Rom.* 7. 7. *Mat.* 5. 28. *chap.* 12. 37. *Rom.* 2. 6.

Q. *What if we sin against but one of the Ten Commandments?*

A. Whosoever shall keep the whole Law, and yet offend in one point, he is guilty of all: for he that said, do not commit adultery, said also, do not kill; now if thou commit no adultery, yet if thou kill, thou art a transgressor of the Law, *Jam.* 2. 10, 11.

Q. *Where will God punish sinners for their sins?*

A. Both in this World and in that which is to come, *Gen.* 3. 24. *chap.* 4. 10, 11, 12. *Job* 21. 30.

Q. *How are Men punished in this World for sin?*

A. Many ways, as with sickness, losses, crosses, disappointments and the like; sometimes also God giveth them up to their own hearts lusts, to blindness of mind also, and hardness of heart; yea, and sometimes to strong delusions that they might believe lies, and be damned, *Lev.* 26. 15, 16. *Amos* 4. 7, 10. *Rom.* 1. 24, 28. *Exod.* 4. 21. *chap.* 9. 12, 13, 14. *Zeph.* 1. 17. *Rom.* 11. 7, 8. 2 *Thes.* 2. 11, 12.

Q. *How are sinners punished in the World to come?*

A. With a Worm that never dies, and with a Fire that never shall be quenched, *Mar.* 9. 44.

Q. *Whither do sinners go to receive this punishment?*

A. The wicked shall be turned into Hell, and all the Nations that forget God, *Psal.* 9. 17.

Q. *What is Hell?*

A. It is a place, and a state most fearful, *Luk.* 16. 28. *Act.* 1. 25. *Luk.* 16. 23.

Q. *Why do you call it a place?*

A. Because in Hell shall all the damned be confined as in a Prison, in their chains of darkness for ever, *Luk.* 12. 5, 58. *chap.* 16. 26. *Jud.* 6.

Q. *What a place is Hell?*

A. It is a dark bottomless burning lake of Fire, large enough to hold all that perish, *Mat.* 22. 13. *Rev.* 20. 1, 15. *Isa.* 30. 33. *Pro.* 27. 20.

Q. *What do you mean when you say it is a fearful state?*

A. I mean, that it is the lot of those that are cast in thither to be tormented in most fearful manner, to wit, with wrath and fiery indignation, *Rom.* 2. 9. *Heb.* 10. 26, 27.

Q. *In what parts shall they be thus fearfully tormented?*

A. In Body and Soul: for Hell-fire shall kindle upon both beyond what now can be thought. *Mat.* 10. 28. *Luk.* 16. 24. *Jam.* 5. 3.

Q. *How long shall they be in this condition?*

A. These shall go away into everlasting punishment, and the smoak of their torment ascendeth up for ever and ever, and they have no rest day nor night; for they shall be punished with everlasting destruction from the presence of the Lord, and from the glory of his Power, *Mat.* 25. 46. *Rev.* 14. 11. 2 *Thes.* 1. 9.

Q. *But why might not the ungodly be punished with this punishment in this world, that we might have seen it and believe?*

A. If the ungodly should with punishment have been rewarded in this World, it would in all probability have overthrown the whole order that God hath settled here among Men. For who could have endured here to have seen the flames of Fire, to have heard the groans, and to have seen the tears perhaps of damned relations, as Parents or Children. Therefore as Tophet of old was without the City, and as the Gallows and Gibbets are builded without the Towns; so Christ hath ordered that they who are to be punished with this

3 *Psal.* 9. 17.] *Psal.* 9. 27. 6 *Luk.* 16. 23.] *Luk.* 16. 21.

kind of Torment, shall be taken away; *Take him away*, saith he (out of this World) *and cast him into utter darkness* (and let him have his punishment there) *there shall be weeping and gnashing of teeth*. Besides, Faith is not to be wrought by looking into Hell, and seeing the damned tormented before our Eyes; but by hearing the Word of God; for he that shall not believe *Moses* and the Prophets, will not be perswaded should one come from the dead; yea should one come to them in flames to perswade them, *Mat.* 22. 13. *Rom.* 10. 17. *Luk.* 16. 27, 28, 29, 30, 31.

Q. *Are there degrees of torment in Hell?*

A. Yes, for God will reward every one according to their works: Wo to the wicked it shall go ill with him, for the reward of his hands shall be given him, *Isa.* 3. 11.

Q. *Who are like to be most punished there, Men or Children?*

A. The punishment in Hell comes not upon sinners, according to age, but sin: so that whether they be Men or Children, the greater sin, the greater punishment; for there is no respect of persons with God, *Rom.* 2. 11.

Q. *How do you distinguish between great sins, and little ones?*

A. By their Nature, and by the Circumstances that attend them.

Q. *What do you mean by their Nature?*

A. I mean when they are very gross in themselves, 2 *Chron.* 33. 2. *Ezek.* 16. 42.

Q. *What kind of sins are the greatest?*

A. Adultery, Fornication, Murder, Theft, Swearing, Lying, Covetousness, Witchcraft, Sedition, Heresies, or any the like, 1 *Cor.* 6. 9, 10. *Ephes.* 5. 3, 4, 5, 6. *Col.* 3. 5, 6. *Gal.* 5. 19, 20, 21. *Rev.* 21. 8.

Q. *What do you mean by Circumstances that attend sin?*

A. I mean Light, Knowledg, the Preaching of the Word, Godly Acquaintance, timely Cautions, *&c.*

Q. *Will these make an alteration in the sin?*

A. These things attending sinners, will make little sins great, yea greater than greater sins that are commited in grossest Ignorance.

Q. *How do you prove that?*

A. *Sodom* and *Gomorrah* wallowed in all, or most of those gross Transgressions above-mentioned: yea, they were said to be sinners exceedingly, they lived in such sins as may not be spoken of without blushing, and yet God swears that *Israel*, his Church, had done worse than they; and the Lord Jesus also seconds it in that Threatning of his, I say unto you, that it shall be more tolerable in that day for *Sodom* than for thee, *Ezek.* 16. 48. *Mat.* 11. 24. *Luk.* 10. 12.

Q. *And was this the reason, namely, because they had such circumstances attending them as* Sodom *had not?*

A. Yes, as will plainly appear, if you read the three Chapters above mentioned.

Q. *When do I sin against Light and Knowledg?*

A. When you sin against convictions of Conscience, when you sin against a known Law of God, when you sin against Counsels and disswasion of Friends, then you sin against Light and Knowledg, *Rom.* 1. 32.

Q. *When do I sin against Preaching of the Word?*

A. When you refuse to hear God's Ministers, or hearing them, refuse to follow their wholsome Doctrine, 2 *Chron.* 36. 16. *Jer.* 25. 4, 7. *chap.* 35. 15.

Q. *When else do I sin against the Preaching of the Word?*

A. When you mock, or despise or reproach the Ministers; also when you raise lies and scandals of them, or receive such lies or scandals raised: you then also sin against the preaching of the Word, when you Persecute them that Preach it, or are secretly glad to see them so used, 2 *Chron.* 30. 1, 10. *Rom.* 3. 8. *Jer.* 20. 10. 1 *Thes.* 2. 15, 16.

Q. *How will godly acquaintance greaten my sin?*

A. When you sin against their Counsels, Warnings, or Perswasions to the contrary; also when their lives and conversations are reproof to you, and yet against all you will sin. Thus sinned *Ishmael*, *Esau*, *Eli's* sons, *Absalom* and *Judas*, they had good Company, good Counsels, and a good life set before them by their godly Acquaintance, but they sinned against all, and their Judgment was the greater. *Ishmael* was cast away, *Esau* hated, *Eli's* sons died suddenly, *Absalom* and *Judas* were both strangely hanged; *Gen.* 21. 10. *Gal.* 4. 30. *Mal.* 1. 2. 1 *Sam.* 2. 25, 34. 2 *Sam.* 18.

Q. *Are sins thus heightned, distinguished from others by any special name?*

34 1 *Sam.* 2. 25, 34.] 1 *Sam.* 2. 20, 25. 2 *Sam.* 18.] 2 *Sam.* 16.

A. Yes; they are called Rebellion, and are compared to the sin of Witchcraft; they are called wilful sin, they are called Briers and Thorns, and they that bring them forth are nigh unto Cursing, whose end is to be burned, 1 *Sam.* 15. 23. *Heb.* 10. 26. *chap.* 6. 7, 8.

Q. *Are there any other things that can make little sins great ones?*

A. Yes; As when you sin against the Judgments of God: As for example, you see the Judgments of God come upon some for their transgressions, and you go on in their iniquities: also when you sin against the Patience, Long-suffering, and Forbearance of God, this will make little sins great ones, *Dan.* 5. 21, 22, 23, 24. *Rom.* 2. 4, 5.

Q. *Did ever God punish little Children for sin against him?*

A. Yes: When the Flood came, he drowned all the little Children that were in the old World; he also burned up all the little Children which were in *Sodom*: and because upon a time the little Children at *Bethel* mocked the Prophet as he was a-going to worship God, God let loose two she-Bears upon them which tore forty and two of them to pieces, 2 *King.* 2. 23, 24.

Q. *Alas! What shall we little Children do?*

A. Either go on in your sins: or remember now your Creator in the days of your Youth, before the evil dayes come, *Eccles.* 12. 1.

Q. *Why do you mock us, to bid us go on in our sins? you had need pray for us that God would save us.*

A. I do not mock you, but as the wise-man doth; and besides I pray for you and wish your Salvation.

Q. *How doth the wise-man mock us?*

A. Thus; Rejoice, O young man, in thy Youth, and let thy heart chear thee in the days of thy Youth, and walk in the ways of thy heart, and in the sight of thine Eyes; but know thou, that for all these things God will bring thee to Judgment, *Eccles.* 11. 9.

Q. *What a kind of mocking is this?*

A. Such an one, as is mixed with the greatest seriousness; as if he should say, I, do, sinners, go on in your sins if you dare; do, live in your vanities, but God will have a time to judg you for them.

Q. *Is not this just as when my Father bids me be naught if I will, but if I be naught, he will beat me for it?*

A. Yes; or like that saying of *Joshua*, If it seem evil to you to

17 2 *King.* 2. 23, 24.] 2 *King.* 2. 22, 23.

serve the Lord, chuse you this day whom you will serve; serve your sins at your peril, *Josh.* 24. 15.

Q. *Is it not best then for me to serve God?*

A. Yes; for they that serve the Devil must be where he is, and they that serve God and Christ, must be where they are, *Joh.* 12. 26. *Mat.* 25. 41.

Q. *But when had I best begin to serve God?*

A. Just now: Remember *now* thy Creator, *now* thou hast the Gospel before thee, *now* thy heart is tender and will be soonest broken.

Q. *But if I follow my play and sports a little longer, may I not come time enough?*

A. I cannot promise thee that, for there be little Graves in the Church-yard; and who can tell but that thy young life is short: or if thou dost live, perhaps thy day of Grace may be as short, as was *Ishmael's* of old: read also, *Prov.* 1. 24, 25, 26.

Q. *But if I stay a little longer before I turn, I may have more wit to serve God than now I have, may I not?*

A. If thou stayest longer, thou wilt have more sin, and perhaps less wit: for the bigger sinner, the bigger fool, *Prov.* 1. 22.

Q. *If I serve God sometimes and my sins sometimes, how then?*

A. No Man can serve two Masters: Thou canst not serve God and thy Sins. God saith, My Son, give me thy heart. Also thy Soul and Body are his; but the double-minded Man is forbidden to think that he shall receive any thing of the Lord, *Mat.* 6. 24. *Prov.* 23. 26. 1 *Cor.* 6. 20. *Jam.* 1. 7, 8.

Q. *Do you find many such little Children as I am, serve God?*

A. Not many; yet some I do, *Samuel* served him being a Child; when *Josias* was young he began to seek after the God of his Father *David*: And how kindly did our Lord Jesus take it, to see the little Children run tripping before him, and crying *Hosannah* to the Son of David! 1 *Sam.* 3. 1. 2 *Chron.* 34. 3. *Mat.* 21. 15, 16.

Q. *Then I am not like to have many Companions, if I thus young begin to serve God, am I?*

A. Strait is the gate, and narrow is the way that leadeth unto life, and few there be that find it. Yet some Companions thou wilt have.

5–6 *Joh.* 12. 26.] *Joh.* 12. 16.

David counted himself a Companion of all them that love God's Testimonies; all the Godly, though Gray-headed, will be thy Companions; yea, and thou shalt have either one or more of the Angels of God in Heaven to attend on, and minister for thee, *Mat.* 7. 13, 14. *Psal.* 119. 63. *Mat.* 18. 10.

Q. *But I am like to be slighted and despised by other little Children if I begin already to serve God, am I not?*

A. If Children be so rude as to mock the Prophets and Ministers of God, no marvel if they also mock thee: but it is a poor Heaven that is not worth enduring worse things than to be mocked for the seeking and obtaining of, 2 *Kings* 2. 23, 24.

Q. *But how should I serve God? I do not know how to worship him.*

A. The true Worshippers, worship God in Spirit and Truth, *Joh.* 4. 24. *Phil.* 3. 3.

Q. *What is meant by worshipping him in the Spirit?*

A. To worship him in God's Spirit and in mine own; that is, to worship him, being wrought over in my very heart by the good Spirit of God, to an hearty Compliance with his will, *Rom.* 1. 9. *Chap.* 6. 17. *Psal.* 101. 3.

Q. *What is it to worship him in truth?*

A. To do all that we do in his Worship according to his Word, for his Word is truth, and to do it without dissimulation. *Heb.* 8. 5. *Joh.* 17. 17. *Psal.* 26. 6. *Psal.* 118. 19, 20.

You may take the whole thus: Then do you worship God a-right, when in heart, and life, you walk according to his word.

Q. *How must I do to worship him with my spirit and heart?*

A. Thou must first get the good knowledg of him. And thou *Solomon* my Son, said *David*, *Know* thou the God of thy Fathers, and serve him with a perfect heart. Mind you, he first bids *know* him, and then *serve* him with a perfect heart, 1 *Chron.* 28. 9.

Q. *Is it easie to get a true knowledg of God?*

A. No; Thou must cry after Knowledge, and lift up thy voice for Understanding. If thou seekest for her as Silver, and searchest for her as for hid treasure, then shalt thou understand the fear of the Lord, and find the knowledg of God, *Pro.* 2. 1, 2, 3, 4, 5.

Q. *How comes it to be so difficult a thing to attain the true Knowledg of God?*

A. By reason of the pride and ignorance that is in us, as also by reason of our wicked ways, *Psal.* 10. 4. *Eph.* 4. 18, 19. *Tit.* 1. 16.

Q. *But do not every one profess they know God?*

A. Yes; But their supposed knowledge of him varieth as much as doth their faces or complexions, some thinking he is this, and some that.

Q. *Will you shew me a little how they vary in their thoughts about him?*

A. Yes; Some count him a kind of an heartless God, that will neither do evil nor good; some count him a kind of an ignorant and blind God, that can neither know nor see through the Clouds; some again count him an inconsiderable God, not worth the injoying, if it must not be but with the loss of this World, and their Lusts. Moreover, some think him to be altogether such an one as themselves, one that hath as little hatred to sin as themselves, and as little love to holiness as themselves, *Zeph.* 1. 12. *Job* 22. 12, 13. *chap.* 21. 9, 10, 11, 12, 13, 14, 15. *Psal.* 50. 21.

Q. *Are there any more false Opinions of God?*

A. Yes; There are three other false opinions of God. 1. Some think he is all Mercy and no Justice, and that therefore they may live as they list. 2. Others think he is all Justice and no Mercy, and that therefore they had as good go on in their sins and be damned, as turn and be never the better. 3. Others think he is both Justice and Mercy, but yet think also, that his Justice is such as they can pacifie with their own good works, and save themselves with their own right hand (*Rom.* 3. 8. *Jer.* 2. 25. *Job* 40. 14), contrary to these Scriptures, *Hab.* 1. 13. *Isa.* 45. 21.

Q. *How then shall I know when I have the true Knowledg of God?*

A. When thy Knowledg of him and the holy Scriptures agree.

Q. *The Scriptures! do not all false Opinions of him, flow from the Scriptures?*

A. No, in no wise; 'tis true, Men father their errors upon the Scriptures, when indeed they flow from the ignorance of their hearts, *Ephes.* 4. 18.

Q. *But how if I do not understand the holy Bible, must I then go without the true knowledg of God?*

A. His Name is manifested by his Word; the Scriptures are they that testifie of him, and they are able to make the Man of God perfect in all things, and wise unto Salvation, through Faith in Jesus Christ, *John* 17. 6, 7, 8. *John* 5. 39. 2 *Tim.* 3. 15, 16.

Q. *But what must one that knoweth not God do, to get the knowledg of God?*

A. Let him apply his heart unto the Scriptures, as unto a light that shineth in a dark place (even this World) until the day dawn, and the day-Star arise in his heart, *Pro.* 22. 17. *chap.* 23. 12. 2 *Pet.* 1. 19, 20.

Q. *But how shall I know when I have found by the Scriptures, the true knowledg of God?*

A. When thou hast also found the true knowledg of thy self, *Isa.* 6. 5. *Job* 42. 5.

Q. *What is it for me to know my self?*

A. Then thou knowest thy self, when thou art in thine own eyes, a lothsome, polluted, wretched, miserable Sinner, and that not any thing done by thee, can pacifie God unto thee, *Job* 42. 5. *Ezek.* 20. 43, 44. *Rom.* 7. 24.

Of Confession of Sin.

Quest. *YOu have shewed me, if I will indeed worship God, I must first know him aright, now then to the question in hand, pray how must I worship him?*

A. In confessing unto him, *Nehem.* 9. 1, 2, 3.

Q. *What must I confess?*

A. Thou must confess thy transgressions unto the Lord, *Psal.* 32. 5.

Q. *Was this the way of the godly of old?*

A. Yes; *Nehemiah* confessed his sins, *David* confessed his sins, *Daniel* confessed his sins, and they that were Baptized by *John* in *Jordan*, confessed their sins, *Nehem.* 1. 6. *Psal.* 32. 5. *Dan.* 9. 4. *Mat.* 3. 6.

Q. *What sins must I confess to God?*

A. All sins whatsoever; for he that covereth his sins shall not prosper, but whoso confesseth and forsaketh them shall find Mercy, *Pro.* 28. 13. 1 *John* 1. 9.

7 *Pro.* 22. 17] *Pro.* 22. 7.

Q. *But how if I do neither know, nor remember all my sins?*

A. Thou must then search and try thy ways by the holy Word of God, *Lam.* 3. 40. *Psal.* 77. 6.

Q. *But how if I do not make this search after my sins?*

A. If thou dost not, God will: if thou dost not search them out and confess them, God will search them out and charge them upon thee, and tear thee in pieces for them, *Psal.* 50. 21, 22.

Q. *Where must I begin to confess my sins?*

A. Where God beginneth to shew thee them: Observe then where God beginneth with conviction for sin, and there begin thou with confession of it. Thus *David* began to confess, thus *Daniel* began to confess, 2 *Sam.* 12. 7, 8, 9, 10, 11, 12, 13. *Dan.* 9. 3, 4, 5, 6, 7, 8.

Q. *What must I do, when God hath shewed me any sin, to make right Confession thereof?*

A. Thou must follow that Conviction, until it shall bring thee to the Original and Fountain of that sin, which is thine own heart, 1 *King.* 8. 38. *Psal.* 51. 5.

Q. *Is my heart, then, the Fountain and Original of sin?*

A. Yes: For from within out of the heart of Man proceedeth evil thoughts, Adulteries, Fornications, Murders, Thefts, Covetousness, Wickedness, Deceit, Lasciviousness, an evil Eye, Blasphemy, Pride, Foolishness. All these evil things come from within, and defile the Man, *Mar.* 7. 21, 22, 23.

Q. *When a Man sees this, what will he think of himself?*

A. Then he will not only think, but conclude, that he is an unclean thing, that his heart hath deceived him, that it is most desperate and wicked, that it may not be trusted by any means, that every imagination and thought of his heart (naturally) is only evil, and that continually, *Isa.* 64. 6. *Prov.* 28. 26. *Isa.* 44. 20. *Gen.* 6. 5.

Q. *You have given me a very bad character of the heart, but how shall I know that it is so bad as you count it?*

A. Both by the Text, and by Experience.

Q. *What do you mean by Experience?*

A. Keep thine eyes upon thy heart, and also upon Gods Word, and thou shalt see, with thine own eyes, the desperate wickedness that is in thine heart, for thou must know Sin by the Law, that bidding thee do one thing, and thy heart inclining to another, *Rom.* 7. 7, 8. 9.

Q. *May I thus, then, know my heart?*

A. Yes; that is, something of it, specially the Carnality of thy mind, because the carnal mind is enmity against God; for it is not subject to the Law of God, neither indeed can be, *Rom.* 8. 7.

Q. *Can you particularize some few things wherein the wickedness of the heart of man shews it self?*

A. Yes; by its secret hankering after sin, although the Word forbids it: by its deferring of Repentance; by its being weary of holy Duties; by its aptness to forget God; by its studying to lessen and hide Sin; by its feigning it self to be better than it is, by being glad when it can sin without being seen of Men; by its hardening it self against the Threatnings and Judgments of God; by its desperate inclinings to Unbelief, Atheism, and the like, *Pro.* 1. 24, 25, 26. *Isa.* 43. 22. *Mal.* 1. 12, 13. *Judg.* 3. 7. *Jer.* 2. 32. *Psal.* 106. 21. *Hos.* 2. 13. *Pro.* 30. 20. *Jer.* 2. 25. *Rom.* 1. 32. *chap.* 2. 5. *Zeph.* 7. 11, 12, 13.

Q. *Is there any thing else to be done in order to a right confession of sin?*

A. Yes; Let this Conviction sink down into thy heart, that God sees much more wickedness in thee than thou canst see in thy self. *If thy heart condemn thee, God is greater than thy heart, and he knows all things*; besides, he hath set thy secret sins in the light of his Countenance, 1 *Joh.* 3. 20. *Psal.* 90. 8.

Q. *Is there any thing else that must go to a right confession of sin?*

A. Yes; In thy confessions thou must greaten and aggravate thy sin by all just circumstances.

Q. *How must I do that?*

A. By considering against how much Light and Mercy thou hast sinned, against how much Patience, and Forbearance, thou hast sinned; also against what Warnings and Judgments thou hast sinned; and against how many of thine own Vows, Promises, and Ingagements, thou hast sinned: these things heighten and aggravate sin, *Ezra* 9. 10, 11, 12, 13, 14, 15.

Q. *But what need I confess my sins to God, seeing he knows them already?*

A. Confession of sin is necessary, for many Reasons.

Q. *Will you shew me some of those Reasons?*

A. Yes; One is, by a sincere and hearty Confession of sin, thou acknowledgest God to be thy Sovereign Lord, and that he hath right to impose his Law upon thee, *Exod.* 20.

Q. *Can you shew me another Reason?*

A. Yes; By confessing thy sin, thou subscribest to his righteous Judgments that are pronounced against it, *Psal.* 51. 3, 4.

Q. *Can you shew me another Reason?*

A. Yes; By confession of sin, thou shewest how little thou deservest the least Mercy from God.

Q. *Have you yet another reason why I should confess my sins?*

A. Yes; By so doing thou shewest whether thy heart loves it, or hates it: He that heartily confesseth his Sin, is like him who having a Thief or a Traitor in his house, brings him out to condign punishment; but he that forbears to confess, is like him who hideth a Thief or Traitor, against the Laws and Peace of our Lord the King.

Q. *Give me one more reason why I should confess my sins to God?*

A. He that confesseth his sin, casteth himself at the feet of Gods Mercy, utterly condemns and casts away his own righteousness, concludeth there is no way to stand Just and acquit before God, but by and through the righteousness of another; whither God is resolved to bring thee, if ever he saves thy Soul; *Psal.* 51. 1, 2, 3. 1 *Joh.* 1. 9. *Phil.* 3. 6, 7, 8.

Q. *What frame of heart should I be in when I confess my sins?*

A. Do it *heartily*, and to the best of thy power, *thoroughly*. For to feign, in this work, is abominable; to do it by the halves, is wickedness; to do it without sence of Sin, cannot be acceptable; and to confess it with the mouth, and to love it with the heart, is a lying unto God, and a provocation of the eyes of his Glory.

Q. *What do you mean by feigning and dissembling in this work?*

A. When men confess it, yet know not what it is; or if they think they know it, do not conclude it so bad as it is; or when men ask pardon of God, but do not see their need of pardon, this man must needs dissemble.

Q. *What do you mean by doing it by the halves?*

A. When men confess some, but not all that they are convinced of; or if they confess all, yet labour in their Confession to lessen it; or when in their Confession they turn not from all Sin to God, but from one Sin to another. They turned, but not to the most high, none of them did exalt him, *Prov.* 28, 13. *Job* 31. 33. *Jam.* 3. 12. *Hos.* 7. 16.

Q. *What is it to confess Sin without sence of Sin?*

A. To do it through Custom, or Tradition, when there is not guilt upon the Conscience, now this cannot be acceptable.

Q. *What is it to confess it with the mouth, and to love it with the heart?*

A. When men condemn it with their mouth, but refuse to let it go; when with their mouth they shew much love, but their heart goeth after their Covertousness, *Job* 20. 12, 13. *Jer.* 8. 5. *Ezek.* 33. 31.

Q. *But I asked you, what frame of heart I should be in, in my Confessions?*

A. I have shewed you how you should not be. Well, I will shew you now what frame of heart becomes you in your Confessions of Sin. Labour by all means for a sence of the evil that is in Sin.

Q. *What evil is there in Sin?*

A. No Man with Tongue can express what may by the Heart be felt of the evil of Sin; but this know, it dishonoureth God, it provoketh him to wrath, it damneth the Soul, *Rom.* 2. 23. *Ephes.* 5. 5, 6. 2 *Thes.* 2. 12.

Q. *What else would you advise me to in this great work?*

A. When we confess sin, tears, shame, and brokenness of heart becomes us, *Jer.* 50. 4. *Isa.* 22. 12. *Psal.* 51. 17. *Jer.* 31. 19.

Q. *What else becomes me in my Confessions of Sin?*

A. Great detestation of sin, with unfeigned Sighs and Groans, that expresseth thou dost it heartily, *Job* 42. 5, 6. *Ezek.* 9. 4. *Jer.* 31. 9.

Q. *Is here all?*

A. No; Tremble at the Word of God; Tremble at every Judgment, lest it overtake thee; Tremble at every promise, lest thou shouldest miss thereof: for, saith God, *To this man will I look even to him that is poor, and of a contrite Spirit, and that trembles at my Word*, Isa. 66. 2. Heb. 4. 1, 2.

Q. *What if I cannot thus confess my Sins?*

A. Bewail the hardness of thy heart, keep close to the best Preachers, remember that thou hangest over Hell, *by the weak thread of an uncertain life*. And know, God counts it a great evil, not to be ashamed of, not to blush at sin, *Isa.* 63. 17. *Jer.* 6. 15. *Chap.* 8. 12.

Q. *Is there no thanks to be rendered to God in Confessions?*

A. O, Yes; Thank him that he hath let thee see thy sins, thank him that he hath given thee time to acknowledg thy sins; thou mightest now have been confessing in Hell: thank him also that he hath so far condescended as to hear the self-bemoaning sinner, and that he hath promised, *Surely to have Mercy upon such*, Jer. 31. 18, 19, 20.

Of Faith in Christ.

Quest. *I Am glad that you have instructed me into this part of the worship of God, pray tell me also how else I should worship him?*

A. Thou must believe his Word.

Q. *Is that worshipping of God?*

A. Yes; after the way which ye call heresy, so worship I the God of my Fathers, believing all things that are written in the Law, and the Prophets, &c. *Acts* 24. 14.

Q. *Why should believing be counted a part of Gods worship?*

A. Because without faith 'tis impossible to please him, *Heb.* 11. 6.

Q. *Why not impossible to please him without believing?*

A. Because in all true Worship, *a man must believe that God is, and that he is a rewarder of them that diligently seek him.* Besides, he that worships God, must also of necessity believe his Word, else he cannot worship with that reverence and fear that becomes him, but will do it in a superstitious prophane manner: for whatsoever is not of Faith is sin, *Rom.* 14. 23.

Q. *But do not all believe as you have said?*

A. That which is born of the flesh is flesh, and that which is born of the Spirit is Spirit. And again, the Children of the flesh, these are not the Children of God, but the Children of the promise are counted for the Seed, *Joh.* 3. 6. *Rom.* 9. 8.

Q. *What do you mean by that?*

A. Thou must be born twice before thou canst truely believe once, *Joh.* 3. 3, 5.

Q. *How do you prove that?*

A. Because believing is a Christian act, and none are true Christians but those that are born again. But I mean by believing, believing unto Salvation.

Q. *Can you prove this?*

A. Yes; They that believe in the Name of Christ, are such, which are born not of blood, nor of the will of the flesh, nor of the will of man, but of God, *Joh.* 1. 12, 13.

Q. *What is believing?*

A. It is such an act of a gracious Soul, as layeth hold on Gods Mercy through Christ, *Act.* 15. 11.

Q. *Why do you call it an act of a gracious Soul?*

A. Because their minds are disposed that way, by the Power of the Holy-Ghost, *Rom.* 15. 13.

Q. *If such a poor sinner as I am would be saved from the wrath to come, how must I believe?*

A. Thy first question should be, *on* whom must I believe? *Joh.* 9. 35, 36.

Q. *On whom then must I believe?*

A. On the Lord Jesus Christ, *Act.* 16. 31, 32.

Q. *Who is Jesus Christ that I might believe on him?*

A. He is the only begotten Son of God, *Joh.* 3. 16.

Q. *Why must I believe in him?*

A. Because he is the Saviour of the World, 2 *Pet.* 1. 1. 1 *John* 4. 14.

Q. *How is he the Saviour of the World?*

A. By the Fathers designation, and sending, for God sent not his Son into the World to condemn the World, but that the World through him might be saved, *John* 3. 17.

Q. *How did he come into the World?*

A. In Mans flesh, in which flesh he fulfilled the Law, died for our sins, conquered the Devil and Death, and obtained Eternal Redemption for us, *Gal.* 4. 4. *Rom.* 10. 3, 4. *chap.* 8. 3. *Heb.* 2. 14, 15. *chap.* 6. 20. *chap.* 9. 12, 24.

Q. *But is there no other way to be saved but by believing in Jesus Christ?*

A. There is no other name given under Heaven among men whereby we must be saved, and therefore he that believeth not, shall be damned, *Act.* 4. 12. *Mar.* 16. 16. *John* 3. 18, 36.

Q. *What is believing on Jesus Christ?*

A. It is a receiving of him with what is in him, as the gift of God to thee a sinner, *Joh.* 1. 12.

Q. *What is in Jesus Christ to encourage me to receive him?*

A. Infinite Righteousness to justifie thee, and the Spirit without

22 *John* 3. 17.] *John* 3. 13.

measure to Sanctifie thee, *Isa.* 45. 24, 25. *Dan.* 9. 24. *Phil.* 3. 7, 8. *Joh.* 3. 34.

Q. *Is this made mine if I receive Christ?*

A. Yes; If thou receive him as God offereth him to thee, *John* 3. 16.

Q. *How doth God offer him to me?*

A. Even as a rich Man freely offereth an Alms to a Begger, and so must thou receive him, *John* 6. 32, 33, 34, 35.

Q. *Hath he indeed made amends for sin? and would he indeed have me accept of what he hath done?*

A. That he hath made amends for sin, 'tis evident, *because God for Christs sake forgiveth thee.* And 'tis as evident that he would have thee accept thereof, because he offereth it to thee, and hath sworn to give thee the utmost benefit, to wit, Eternal life, if thou dost receive it, yea and hath threatned thee with eternal Damnation if after all this thou shalt neglect so great Salvation, *Ephes.* 4. 32. *Rom.* 3. 24. *Mat.* 28. 19. *Act.* 13. 32, 33, 38, 39. *Heb.* 6. 17, 18. *chap.* 2. 3. *Mar.* 16. 16.

Q. *But how must I be qualified before I shall dare to believe in Christ?*

A. Come, sensible of thy sins and of the wrath of God due unto them, for thus thou art bid to come, *Mat.* 11. 28.

Q. *Did ever any come thus to Christ?*

A. David came thus, *Paul* and the *Jailer* came thus, also Christ's Murderers came thus, *Psal.* 51. 1, 2, 3. *Acts* 9. 6. *Acts* 16. 30, 31. *Act.* 2. 37.

Q. *But doth it not seem most reasonable that we should first mend and be good?*

A. The whole have no need of the Physitian, but those that are sick; Christ came not to call the righteous, but sinners to repentance, *Mar.* 2. 17.

Q. *But is it not the best way, if one can to mend first?*

A. This is just as if a sick man should say, is it not best for me to be well before I go to the Physician; or as if a wounded man should say, when I am cured I will lay on the Plaister.

Q. *But when a poor Creature sees its vileness, it is afraid to come to Christ, is it not?*

16 *Ephes.* 4. 32.] *Ephes.* 5. 1.

A. Yes; But without ground, for he hath said, say to them that are of a fearful heart, be strong, fear not; and to this man will I look, even to him that is poor and of a contrite Spirit, and trembles at my word, *Isa.* 35. 4. *Chap.* 66. 2.

Q. *What incouragement can be given us, thus to come?*

A. The Prodigal came thus and his Father received him, and fell upon his neck and kissed him. Thus he received the *Colossians* and consequently all that are saved, *Luke* 15. *Colos.* 2. 13.

Q. *Will you give me one more encouragement?*

A. The Promises are so worded, that they that are Scarlet-sinners, Crimson-sinners, Blasphemous sinners, have incouragement to come to him with hopes of life, *Isa.* 1. 18. *Mar.* 3. 28. *Joh.* 6. 37. *Luk.* 24. 47. *Act.* 13. 26.

Q. *Shall any one that believeth be saved?*

A. If they believe as the Scriptures have said, if the Scriptures be fulfilled in their believing, *Joh.* 7. 38. *Jam.* 2. 23.

Q. *What do you mean by that?*

A. When Faith, which a Man saith he hath, proveth it self to be of the right kind by its Acts and Operations in the mind of a poor sinner, *Jam.* 2. 19, 20, 21, 22.

Q. *Why? is there many kinds of Faith?*

A. Yes; There is a Faith that will stand with a heart as hard as a rock; a short-winded Faith, which dureth for a while; and in time of temptation such fall away, *Luke* 8. 13.

Q. *Is there any other kind of Faith?*

A. Yes; There is a Faith that hath no more life in it than hath the body of a dead man, *Jam.* 2. 26.

Q. *Is there yet another of these unprofitable Faiths?*

A. Yes; there is a Faith that is of our selves, and not of the special Grace of God, *Eph.* 2. 8.

Q. *Tell me if there be yet another?*

A. There is a Faith that standeth in the Wisdom of men, and not in the power of God, 1 *Cor.* 2. 5.

Q. *Is here all?*

A. No; there is a Faith that seems to be holy, but it will not do, because tis not the most holy Faith, 2 *Pet.* 2. 20. *Jude* 20.

12–13 *Joh. 6. 37.*] *Joh. 6. 36.*   13 *Act.* 13. 36.] *Act.* 13. 26.

Q. *Alas! If there be so many kinds of Faith, that will not profit to Salvation, how easie is it for me to be deceived?*

A. It is easie indeed, and therefore the holy Ghost doth in this thing, so often caution us, be not deceived, let no man deceive you, and if a man thinketh himself to be something, when he is nothing, he deceiveth himself, 1 *Cor.* 6. 9. *Eph.* 5. 6. *Gal.* 6. 3.

Q. *But is there no way to distinguish the right Faith from that which is wrong?*

A. Yes; And that by the manner of its Coming, and Operation.

Q. *What do you mean by the manner of its Coming?*

A. Nay; you must make two questions of this one; that is, what is it for Faith to come? and in what manner doth it come?

Q. *Well then, what is it for Faith to come?*

A. This word *Faith comes*, supposeth, thou wert once without it; it also supposeth that thou didst not fetch it whence it was, it also supposeth it hath a way of coming, *Gal.* 3. 23, 25.

Q. *That I was once without it, you intimated before, but must I take it without proof for granted?*

A. I will give you a proof or two: God hath concluded them all in unbelief, and again it is said Faith comes. And again, the Holy Ghost insinuateth our estate to be dreadful before Faith come, *Rom.* 11. 32. *Chap.* 10. 17. *Gal.* 3. 23.

Q. *Why? How is it with men before Faith comes?*

A. Without Faith or before Faith comes it is impossible to please God, for whether their actions be civil or religious, they sin in all they do. The Sacrifice of the wicked is an abomination, and the plowing of the wicked is sin, *Prov.* 21. 4, 27.

Q. *Is not this a very sad condition?*

A. Yes; But this is not all, for their present unbelief bindeth them over to wrath, by shutting them up to the Law; it also draweth them away from God, and will drown them in everlasting damnation if the grace of God prevent not, *Gal.* 3. 23. *Heb.* 3. 17, 18. *John.* 3. 36.

Q. *What if a man saw himself in this condition?*

A. There are many see themselves in this Condition.

Q. *How came they to see it?*

A. By the preaching and hearing the Word of God, *Joh.* 16. 8, 9.

Q. *Is there another Scripture proves it?*

A. Yes; Then she came and worshipped him, saying, Lord help me, *Mat.* 15. 25.

Q. *What is Prayer?*

A. A sincere sensible affectionate pouring out of the Soul to God in the Name of Christ for what God hath promised, *Prov.* 15. 8. *Jer.* 31. 18, 19. *Psal.* 42. 2, 3, 4. *Job* 14. 13, 14. 1 *Joh.* 5. 14.

Q. *Doth not every body pray?*

A. No; the wicked through the pride of his Countenance will not seek after God; God is not in all his thoughts, *Psal.* 10. 4.

Q. *What will become of them that do not pray?*

A. They do not worship God, and he will destroy them; Pour out thy fury (said the Prophet) upon the heathen, and upon the families that call not upon thy name, *Psal.* 79. 6. *Jer.* 10. 25.

Q. *But seeing God knoweth what we want, why doth he not give us what we need without praying?*

A. His Counsel and Wisdom leadeth him otherwise. Thus saith the Lord, I will yet be enquired of by the house of Israel to do it for them, *Ezek.* 36. 37.

Q. *Why will God have us pray?*

A. Because he would be acknowledged by thee, that he is above thee, and therefore would have thee come to him as the Mean come to the Mighty. Thus *Abraham* came unto him, *Gen.* 18. 27, 30.

Q. *Is there another Reason why I should pray?*

A. Yes; For by Prayer thou acknowledgest, that help is not in thine own power, 2 *Chron.* 20. 6, 12.

Q. *What Reason else have you why I should Pray?*

A. By Prayer thou confessest that help is only in him, *Psal.* 62. 1.

Q. *What other Reason have you?*

A. By Prayer, thou confessest thou canst not live without his Grace and Mercy, *Mat.* 14. 30. *Heb.* 4. 16.

Q. *Are all that pray, heard of the Lord?*

A. No; They looked, that is, prayed, but there was none to save them; even unto the Lord, but he answered them not, 2 *Sam.* 22. 42.

Q. *To What doth God compare the Prayers which he refuseth to answer?*

A. He compareth them to the howling of a Dog, *Hos.* 7. 14.

10 *Psal.* 10. 4.] *Psal.* 40. 4.

Q. *Who be they whose Prayers God will not answer?*

A. Theirs, who think to be heard for their much speaking, and vain repetition, *Mat.* 6. 7.

Q. *Is there any others whose Prayers God refuseth?*

A. Yes; There are that ask and have not, because what they ask, they would spend upon their lusts, *Jam.* 4. 3.

Q. *Is there any other whose Prayer God refuseth?*

A. Yes; If I regard iniquity in my heart, the Lord will not hear my Prayer, *Psal.* 66. 18.

Q. *Is the regarding of sin in our heart such a deadly hindrance to Prayer?*

A. Son of Man, saith God, these men have set up their Idols in their heart, and have put the stumbling block of their iniquity before their face: should I be enquired of at all by them? I will set my face against that man, and will make him a Sign and a Proverb. And I will cut him off from the midst of my people, *Ezek.* 14. 3, 8.

Q. *Whose Prayers be they that God will hear?*

A. The Prayers of the Poor and needy, *Psal.* 34. 6. *Isa.* 41. 17.

Q. *What do you mean by the poor?*

A. Such as have poverty in Spirit, *Mat.* 5. 3.

Q. *Who are they that are poor in Spirit?*

A. They that are sensible of the want and necessity of all those things of God, that prepare a Man to the Kingdom of Heaven.

Q. *What things are they?*

A. Faith, Hope, Love, Joy, Peace, a new Heart, the Holy Ghost, Sanctification, see *Jam.* 2. 5. 2 *Thes.* 2. 16. *Ezek.* 36. 26, 27.

Q. *What do you mean by the needy?*

A. Those whose Souls long and cannot be satisfied without the injoyment of these blessed things, *Psal.* 63. 1. *Psal.* 119. 20.

Q. *Will God hear the prayers of such?*

A. Yes; For he satisfieth the longing Soul, and filleth the hungry Soul with good things, *Psal.* 107. 9.

Q. *How shall I know that I am one of those, to whom God will give these things?*

A. If thou seest a beauty in them beyond the beauty of all other things, *Psal.* 110. 3.

Q. *How else shall I know he heareth me?*

A. If thou desirest them for their beauties sake, *Psal*. 90. 14, 17.

Q. *How else should I know I shall have them?*

A. When thy groanings after them are beyond expression, *Rom*. 8. 26.

Q. *How else should I know, and so be incouraged to pray?*

A. When thou followest hard after God in all his Ordinances for the obtaining of them, *Isa*. 40. 31. *chap*. 64. 5.

Q. *How else shall I know?*

A. When thou makest good use of that little thou hast already, *Rev*. 3. 8.

Q. *Is here all the good signs that my Prayers shall be heard?*

A. No; There is one more without which thou shalt never obtain.

Q. *Pray what is that?*

A. Thou must plead with God, the Name and Merits of Jesus Christ, for whose sake only God giveth thee these things. If we ask any thing in his name he heareth us, and whatsoever you ask the Father in my name, saith Christ, I will do it, *Joh*. 14. 13, 14.

Q. *Doth God always answer presently?*

A. Sometimes he doth, and sometime he doth not, *Isa*. 30. 19. *Dan*. 10. 12.

Q. *Is not God's deferring, a sign of his anger?*

A. Sometimes it is not, and sometimes it is.

Q. *When is it no sign of his anger?*

A. When we have not wickedly departed from him by our sins, *Luk*. 18. 7.

Q. *When is it a sign of his anger?*

A. When we have backsliden, when we have not repented some former miscarriages, *Hos*. 5. 14, 15.

Q. *Why doth God defer to hear their Prayers that have not wickedly departed from him?*

A. He loves to hear their voice, to try their Faith, to see their importunity, and to observe how they can wrestle with him for a blessing, *Song*. 2. 14. *Mat*. 15. 22, 23, 24, 25, 26, 27, 28. *Luk*. 11. 5, 6, 7, 8. *Gen*. 32. 25, 26, 27.

Q. *But is not deferring to answer Prayer a great discouragement to Praying?*

7 *Isa*. 40. 31.] *Isa*. 4. 31.

A. Though it is, because of our unbelief, yet it ought not, because God is faithful. Therefore men ought always to Pray, and not to faint, *Luk.* 18. 1, 2, 3, 4, 5, 6, 7, 8.

Of Self-Denial.

Q. *I Am glad you have thus far granted my request: But you told me that there was another part of God's Worship, pray repeat that again.*

A. It is *Self-denial.*

Q. *Now I remember it well, pray how do you prove that Self-denial is called a part of God's Worship?*

A. It is said of *Abraham*, that when he went to offer up his Son *Isaac* upon the Altar for a burnt-offering, which was to him a very great part of Self-denial, that he counted that act of his, *Worshipping God.*

Q. *Will you be pleased to read the Text?*

A. Yes; And *Abraham* said unto his young Men, abide ye here with the Ass, and I and the Lad will go yonder and Worship, *&c.* This now was when he was agoing to slay his *Isaac*, *Gen.* 22. 5.

Q. *What is self-denial?*

A. It is for a man to forsake his *All*, for the sake of Jesus Christ.

Q. *Will you prove this by a Scripture or two?*

A. Yes; Whosoever he be of you that forsaketh not all that he hath, he cannot be my Disciple, *Luke* 14. 33.

Q. *Indeed this is a full place, can you give me one more?*

A. Yes; What things were gain to me, those I count loss for Christ: yea doubtless and I count all things but loss for the excellency of the knowledge of Christ Jesus my Lord, for whom I have suffered the loss of all things, and do count them but dung, that I may win Christ, *&c. Phil.* 3. 7, 8.

Q. *These two are indeed a sufficient Answer to my Questions; but pray will you now give me some particular instances of the self-denial of them that have heretofore been the followers of Christ?*

A. Yes; *Abel* denied himself, to the losing of his Blood; *Abraham* denied himself, to the losing of his Country and his Fathers House; *Moses* denied himself, of a Crown and a Kingdom, and of ease and

3 *Luk.* 18.] *Luk.* 10. 7, 8.] *om.*

tranquillity; *Joseph* denied himself, of fleshly Lusts, *Gen.* 4. 8. *chap.* 12. 1, 2, 3, 4. *Heb.* 11. 24, 25, 26, 27. *Gen.* 39. 7, 8, 9.

Q. *But these Men each of them denied themselves but of some things, did they?*

A. You see *Abel* lost all, his Blood and all; *Abraham* lost his Country to the hazzard of his Life, so did *Moses* in leaving the Crown and Kingdom, and *Joseph* in denying his Mistress, *Gen.* 12. 13. *Heb.* 11. 27. *Gen.* 39. 10, 11, 12, 13, 14.

Q. *Will you discourse a little particularly of Self-denial?*

A. With all my heart.

Q. *First then, pray in what spirit must this Self-denial be performed?*

A. It must be done in the spirit of Faith, of Love, and of a sound mind. Otherwise, if a Man should sell all that he hath and give to the poor, and his Body to be burnt besides, it would profit him nothing, 1 *Cor.* 13. 1, 2, 3.

Q. *Who are like to miscarry here?*

A. They whose ends in Self-denial are not according to the proposals of the Gospel.

Q. *Who are they?*

A. They that suffer through Strife and Vain-glory; or thus, they who seek in their sufferings, the praise of Men more than the Glory of Christ, and profit of their Neighbour.

Q. *Who else are like to miscarry here?*

A. They that have designs like *Ziba* to ingratiate themselves by their pretended Self-denial into the affections of the godly, and to enrich themselves by this means, 2 *Sam.* 16. 1, 2, 3, 4.

Q. *Are there any other like to miscarry here?*

A. Yes; They that by denying themselves think with the Pharisee, to make themselves stand more Righteous in Gods eyes than others, *Luke* 18. 11, 12.

Q. *Who else are in danger of miscarrying here?*

A. They who have fainted in their Works, they whose Self-denial hath at last been overcome by self-Love, *Gal.* 3. 4. *chap.* 6. 9.

Q. *Shall I propound a few more questions?*

A. If you please.

Q. *What then if a Man promiseth to deny himself hereafter and not now, is not this one step to this kind of Worship?*

A. No, by no means; for the reason why this Man refuseth to deny himself *now*, is because his heart at present sticks closer to his Lusts and the World, than to God and Christ.

Q. *Can you give me a Scripture-instance to make this out?*

A. Yes; *Esau* never intended for ever to part with the Blessing, he intended to have it hereafter; but God counted his not chusing of it at present, a despising of it, and a preferring of his Lusts before it, and therefore when he would, God would not, but reject both him and his tears, *Gen.* 25. 30, 31, 32, 33. *Heb.* 12. 14, 15, 16.

Q. *How and if a man shall say thus, I am willing to deny my self in many things, though he cannot deny himself in all, is not this one step in this part of this Worship of God?*

A. No, in no wise; for this man doth just like *Saul*, he will slay a part, and will keep a part alive; the Kingdom must be taken from him also, 1 *Sam.* 15.

Q. *How if a man be willing to lose all but his Life?*

A. He that will save his life shall lose it, but he that will lose his life for my sake, saith Christ, shall save it unto life Eternal, *Mat.* 16. 25. *Joh.* 12. 25.

Q. *How if a man has been willing to lose all that he hath, but is not now, will not God accept of his willingness in time past, though he be otherwise now?*

A. No; for the true Disciple must deny himself daily, take up his Cross daily and go after Jesus Christ. *Luk.* 9. 23.

Q. *But how if a man carrieth it well outwardly, so that he doth not dishonour the Gospel before men, may not this be counted Self-Denial?*

A. No; If he be not right at heart: for though man looketh on the outward appearance, God looketh at the heart; 1 *Sam.* 16. 7.

Q. *But if I be afraid my heart may deceive me in this great work, if hard things come upon me hereafter, is there no way to find out whether it will deceive me then or no?*

A. I will give you a few answers to this question, and will shew you first whose heart is like to deceive him in this work.

Q. *Will you befriend me so much?*

A. Yes; 1. He that makes not daily Conscience of Self-Denial, is very unlike to abide a disciple for times to come, if difficult. *Judas* did not deny himself daily, and therefore fell when the temptation came, *Joh.* 12. 6.

Q. *Will you give me another Sign?*

A. Yes; He that indulgeth any one secret lust under a proffession, is not like to deny himself in all things for Christ.

Q. *Who are they that indulge their lusts?*

A. They that make provision for them, either in apparel, or diet, or other-wise, *Rom.* 13. 12, 13, 14. *Isa.* 3. 16, 17, 18, 19, 20. *Amos* 6. 3, 4, 5, 6.

Q. *Who else do so?*

A. They that excuse their sins, and keep them disguised that they may not be reprehended as *Saul* did, &c. 1 *Sam.* 15. 18, 19, 20, 21.

Q. *Who else are they that indulge their lusts?*

A. They that heap up to themselves such Teachers that will favour their Lusts, 2 *Tim.* 4. 3, 4. *Isa.* 30. 10.

Q. *Who else do indulge their sins?*

A. They that chuse rather to walk by the imperfect lives of professors than by the holy Word of God: or thus, they that make the miscarriages of some good men, an incouragement unto themselves to forbear to be exact in Self-Denial, these eat up the sins of Gods people as men eat bread, *Hos.* 4. 7, 8, 9.

Q. *Will you now shew me who are like to do this part of Gods Worship acceptably?*

A. Yes; He whose heart is set against sin as sin, is like to deny himself acceptably, *Rom.* 7. 13, 24.

Q. *Who else?*

A. He that hath the sence and savour of forgiveness of sins upon his heart, 2 *Cor.* 5. 14.

Q. *Who else is like to deny himself well?*

A. He that hath his affections set upon things above, where Christ sitteth at the right hand of God, *Col.* 3. 1, 2, 3, 4, 5.

Q. *Who else is like to deny himself well for Christ?*

A. He that seeth a greater treasure in Self-Denial, than in self-seeking, 2 *Cor.* 12. 9. 10, 11. *Heb.* 11. 24, 25, 26.

Q. *Is there none other signs of one that is like to do this part of Gods worship acceptably?*

A. Yes; He that takes up his Cross daily and makes Christ's Doctrine his Example. *Luk.* 6. 47, 48. *Joh.* 12. 25, 26.

Q. *But how do you discover a Man to be such a one?*

A. He keepeth his heart with all diligence, he had rather die than sin; Ill carriages of professors break his heart; nothing is to dear to him as the Glory of Christ, *Prov.* 4. 23. *Numb.* 11. 15. *Phil.* 3. 18. *Act.* 20. 24.

Q. *Pray can you give me some motive to Self-Denial?*

A. Yes; The Lord Jesus denied himself for thee; what sayest thou to that?

Q. *Wherein did Christ deny himself for me?*

A. He left his Heaven for thee; he denied for thy sake to have so much of this World, as hath a Fox, or a Bird, and he spilt his most precious Blood for thee. *Joh.* 6. 38. *Luk.* 9. 58. 2 *Cor.* 8. 9. *Rev.* 1. 5.

Q. *Can you give another motive to Self-Denial?*

A. Yes; What shall it profit a man if he shall gain the whole World and lose his own Soul? *Mar.* 8. 36.

Q. *But why doth God require Self-Denial of them that will be saved?*

A. God doth not require Self-Denial as the means to obtain Salvation, but hath laid it down as proof of the truth of a mans affections to God and Christ.

Q. *How is Self-Denial a proof of the truth of a mans affections to God?*

A. In that for the sake of his service, he leaveth all his injoyments in this World. Thus he proved *Abraham's* affections, thus he proved *Peters* affections, and thus he proved their affections that you read of in the Gospel, *Gen.* 22. 12. *Mat.* 4. 18, 19, 20, 21, 22. *Luke* 9. 57, 58, 59, 60, 61, 62.

Q. *What reason else can you produce why God requireth Self-Denial?*

A. Self-Denial is one of the distinguishing Characters by which true Christians are manifested from the feigned ones: for those that are feigned, flatter God with their mouth, but their hearts seek themselves; but the sincere for the love that he hath to Christ, forsaketh all that he hath for his sake, *Psal.* 78. 36, 37. *Ezek.* 33. 31, 32.

Q. *Is there yet another reason why God requireth Self-Denial of them that profess his name?*

A. Yes; because by Self-Denial the power and goodness of the Truths of God are made manifest to the incredulous World. For they cannot see but by the Self-Denial of Gods people, that there is such

15 *Mar.* 8. 36.] *Luk.* 8. 36.

Power, Glory, Goodness and desirableness in Gods Truth as indeed there is, *Dan.* 3. 16, 28. *Phil.* 1. 12, 13.

Q. *Have you another Reason why God requireth Self-Denial?*

A. Yes; because Self-Denial prepareth a man, though not for the pardon of his sin, yet for that *far more exceeding and eternal weight of Glory, that is laid up only for them that deny all that they have for the Lord Jesus his name and cause in this World*, 2 *Cor.* 4. 8, 9, 10, 17. 2 *Thes.* 1. 5, 6.

Q. *Before you conclude, will you give me a few instances of the severity of God's hand upon some Professors, that have not denied themselves when called thereto by him?*

A. Yes, Willingly; *Lot's* Wife for but looking behind her towards *Sodom* when God called her from it, was stricken from Heaven, and turned into a Pillar of Salt, therefore remember *Lots* Wife, *Gen.* 19. 17, 26. *Luk.* 17. 31, 32.

Q. *Can you give me another instance?*

A. Yes; *Esau* for not denying himself of one morsel of Meat was denied a share in the Blessing, and could never obtain it after, though he sought it carefully with Tears, *Gen.* 25. 32, 33, 34. *Heb.* 12. 16, 17.

Q. *Have you at hand another instance?*

A. Yes; *Judas* for not denying himself, lost Christ, his Soul, and Heaven: and is continued the great Object of God's Wrath among all Damned Souls, *John* 12. 5, 6. *Luke* 22. 3, 4, 5, 6. *Mat.* 26. 14, 15, 16. *Act.* 1. 25.

Q. *Will you give me one more instance and so conclude?*

A. Yes; *Ananias* and *Sapphirah* his Wife, did for the want of Self Denial pull upon themselves such Wrath of God, that he slew them, while they stood in the midst before the Apostles, *Act.* 5. 1, 2, 3, 4, 5, 6, 7, 8, 9, 10, 11.

The Conclusion.

BEfore I wind up this discourse, I would lay down these few things for you to consider of, and meditate upon.

I. Consider, That seeing every one by nature are accounted

18–19 *Heb.* 12. 16, 17.] *Heb.* 12. 14, 15.

sinners; 'Tis no matter whether thy actual sins be little or great, few or many, thy sinful nature hath already laid thee under the curse of the Law.

II. Consider, That therefore thou hast already ground for humiliation, sins to repent of, wrath to fly from, or a Soul to be damned.

III. Consider, That time staies not for thee, and also that as time goes, sin increaseth, so that at last the end of thy time, and the compleating of thy sin, are like to come upon thee in one moment.

IV. Bring thy last day often to thy bed-side, and ask thy heart if this morning thou wast to die, if thou be ready to die or no.

V. Know 'tis a sad thing to lie a dying, and to be afraid to die; to lie a dying and not to know whither thou art a going; to lie a dying, and not to know whether good Angels or bad must conduct thee out of this miserable World.

VI. Be often remembring what a blessed thing it is to be saved, to go to Heaven, to be made like Angels, and to dwell with God and Christ to all eternity.

VII. Consider how sweet the thought of Salvation will be to thee when thou seest thy self in Heaven, whilst others are roaring in Hell.

The Lord Jesus Christ be with thy Spirit.

THE END.

LIGHT FOR THEM THAT SIT IN DARKNESS

LIGHT FOR THEM THAT SIT IN DARKNESS

Note on the Text

ONE edition of *Light in Darkness* was published in Bunyan's lifetime. Like *Instruction for the Ignorant*, it was printed for Francis Smith in 1675. It is listed in the Term Catalogue for Trinity Term, 1675, under the date 19 June,[1] when Bunyan is likely to have been either in London or in prison.

THE FIRST EDITION, 1675

Title-page: [within rules] *Light for them that sit in Darkness*: | OR, A | DISCOURSE | OF | JESUS CHRIST; | AND | That he undertook to accomplish by him- | self the Eternal Redemption of Sinners. | ALSO, | How the Lord Jesus addressed himself to | this Work; with undeniable Demon- | strations that he performed the same. | [thin rule] | Objections to the Contrary, Answered: | [tapered rule] | BY | *JOHN BUNYAN.* | [rule] | *Christ hath redeemed us from the Curse of the Law*, | *being made a Curse for us*, Gal. 3. 13. | [rule] | LONDON, | Printed for *Francis Smith*, at the Elephant and Castle | near the Royal Exchange in *Cornhil*. 1675.

Collation: 8^{0}: A^4, B–M^8, N^4. A4, N2, N3, and N4 are not signed. Pages: [viii]+184. Page 12 is numbered 2; p. 100 is numbered 110.

Contents: $A1^r$ title-page, $A1^v$ blank, $A2^r$–$A4^r$ 'The Author to the Reader.', $A4^v$ 'The ERRATA.', $B1^r$–$N3^v$ text, $N4^{r-v}$ '*Books writ by Mr.* Bunyan, *and printed for* Francis Smith, *at the Elephant and Castle near the Royal Exchange, in* Cornhil.' Single row of ornaments at head of $A2^r$, $B1^r$, and $N4^r$. $A4^r$ is signed 'Joh. Bunyan.' and is followed by a rule. On $A4^v$ a rule (a tapering rule in the B.L. copy) precedes 'The ERRATA.', and a rule follows the list of corrections. On $C5^v$ a rule follows the first twenty lines of the text. A rule follows the first five lines of text on $C8^r$, the first ten lines of text on $D6^r$, and the first three lines of text on $D8^v$. A rule precedes the catchword '*That*' on $E1^v$, and the text on $E2^r$. A rule follows the first twenty-one lines of text on $E4^r$, the first seven lines of text on $E8^r$, the first ten lines of text on $F3^r$, and the first nineteen lines of text on $F5^r$. A rule precedes the text on $G1^v$, and the text on $H1^v$, and another follows the first nine lines of text. A rule precedes '*The Second Demonstration.*' on $H4^v$, '*The Third Demonstration.*'

[1] *The Term Catalogues, 1668–1709 A.D.*, ed. Edward Arber (1903), i. 209–10.

on $I2^{v}$, the catchword '*The*' on $I5^{v}$, '*The Fourth Demonstration.*' on $I6^{r}$, 'The *Fifth Demonstration.*' on 17^{v}, '*The Sixth Demonstration.*' on $K6^{r}$, '*The Seventh Demonstration.*' on $K8^{r}$, '*The Eighth Demonstration.*' on $L2^{r}$, and '*The Ninth Demonstration.*' on $L4^{r}$. A rule follows the first four lines of text on $M1^{r}$. The text on $N3^{v}$ is followed by 'THE END.' The list of books on $N4^{v}$ is followed by a rule.

Running Titles: Preface: 'The preface to the Reader.' Text: '*Light for them | that sit in Darkness.*' The period after '*Darkness*' is omitted on pp. 3, 23, 39, and 55. The *L* in '*Light*' is the wrong fount of type on pp. 10, 18, 34, 50, 66, 82, 98, 130, 146, and 162.

Catchwords: (selected) $B8^{v}$ 3. The $C8^{v}$ Scepter $D5^{r}$ 3. eH $D8^{v}$ God, $E8^{v}$ Death. $F8^{v}$ No $G8^{v}$ *we* $H1^{r}$ *severa* $H2^{r}$ Tha $H4^{r}$ *Thou*· $H8^{v}$ for $I8^{v}$ dent $K8^{v}$ self $L2^{r}$ Jesu $L8^{v}$ der $M8^{v}$ yet

Copies Collated: Bodleian, Oxford; British Library; Elstow^{1}; Elstow^{2}; Bunyan Meeting, Bedford; Guildhall, London. The Bodleian and Elstow^{1} copies are complete, but in the B.L. and Elstow^{2} copies A1 and N4 are missing. The Bunyan Meeting copy lacks I1 and N4. The London Guildhall copy lacks N4. A1 l.2 uncorr. OR A Elstow^{1}, Guildhall, Bunyan Meeting; corr. OR, A all other copies. B.L. (A1 supplied in MS. with date '1674' in a second hand.)

The British Library copy, acquired in February 1947, has been charred by fire. Bound with this copy is an engraving from *The Pilgrim's Progress* depicting Bunyan dreaming while Christian climbs the hill behind him. The Elstow^{1} copy was presented by the Revd. F. W. Potto Hicks of Elkstone, Glos., in January 1952. The Elstow^{2} copy was formerly in the Harmsworth collection (Harmsworth Catalogue 2680; Offor Catalogue 1737), and was presented by the B.L. It is badly charred and in 1973 was still unbound.

The text that follows is based on the Bodleian copy of the first edition.

Light for them that ſit in Darkneſs :

OR, A

DISCOURSE

OF

JESUS CHRIST;

AND

That he undertook to accompliſh by himſelf the Eternal Redemption of Sinners.

ALSO,

How the Lord Jeſus addreſſed himſelf to this Work; with undeniable Demonſtrations that he performed the ſame.

Objections to the Contrary, Anſwered :

BY

JOHN BUNYAN.

Chriſt hath redeemed us from the Curſe of the Law, being made a Curſe for us, Gal. 3. 13.

LONDON,

Printed for *Francis Smith*, at the Elephant and Caſtle near the Royal Exchange in *Cornhil*. 1675.

Title-page of the Bodleian copy of *Light for Them That Sit in Darkness* (1675)

The Author to the Reader.

Gentle Reader,

IT was the great care of the Apostle Paul *to deliver his Gospel to the Churches* in its own simplicity, *because,* SO *it is the Power of God unto Salvation to every one that believeth. And if it was* his *care* so *to deliver it to us, it should be* ours *to seek* so *to continue it: And the rather, because of the Unaptness of the Minds even of the Saints themselves to retain it without commixture. For, to say nothing of the Projects of Hell, and of the cunning craftiness of some that lie in wait to deceive, even the Godly themselves, as they are dull of hearing, so much more dull in receiving, and holding fast the simplicity of the Gospel of Jesus Christ: from their Sense, and Reason, and Unbelief, and Darkness, arise many imaginations, and high thoughts which exalt themselves against the Knowledg of God, and the Obedience of Jesus Christ, wherefore they themselves have much ado to stand compleat in all the Will of God. And were they not concerned in electing love, by which they are bound up in the Bundle of Life, and blessed with the Enjoiment of Saving Grace, which enlighteneth their Souls, and maintaineth their Faith and Hope, they would not only be assaulted, and afflicted with their own Corruptions, but as others, overcome thereby.*

Alas! How ordinary a thing is it for Professors to fall from the Knowledg they have had of the Glorious Gospel of the Blessed God, and to be turned unto Fables, Seducing-Spirits, and Doctrines of Devils through the Intoxications of Delusions, and the Witchcrafts of false Preachers.

Now this their swerving from the Gospel, ariseth:

1\. *Either from their not-having, or (having) not-retaining, the true Knowledge of the Person of the Lord Jesus Christ: Or,*

2\. *From their not-believing the true Causes of his Coming into the World, with his Doing, and Suffering there. Upon one, or both these accounts, I say, it is that they everlastingly perish: for if they have not, and do not also retain the Knowledge of his Person, they want the* HE, *on whom if they believe not, they must die in their Sins: And if they know not the Reason of his Coming, Doing, and Suffering, they are in the same condition also.*

Now those Professors that have had some Knowledg of these things, and yet have lost them, it hath come thus to pass with them; because they first lost the Knowledg of themselves, and of their Sins.

They know not themselves to be such, nothing-ones, *as the Scripture reporteth them to be, nor their Sins to be so heinous as the Law hath concluded: Therefore they either turn again with the Dog to his Vomit, or adhere to a few of the Rags of their own Fleshly Righteousness*, and so become pure in their own Eyes, yet are not purged by Blood, from their Filthiness.

For the Person and Doings of Jesus Christ are only precious to them that get and retain the true Knowledg of themselves, and the due Reward of their Sins by the Law: These are desolate, being driven out of all, these embrace the Rock instead of a Shelter; the Sensible Sinner receiveth him joyfully.

And because a miscarriage in this Great Truth, is the most dangerous and damning Miscarriage: *therefore should Professors be the more fearful of swerving aside there-from. The Man that rejecteth the true Knowledg of the Person of the Lord Jesus, and the Causes of his Doing and Suffering in the World, takes the next way to be guilty of that Transgression, that is not to be purged with Sacrifice for ever. That* FEARFUL *Transgression, for which is left* NO *Offering* AT ALL, *nor any thing to be expected by the Person transgressing, but fearful Judgment, and fiery Indignation which shall devour the Adversary.*

Now for their sakes that have not sinned this Sin, for their sakes that are in Danger thereof, but yet not overcome; for their sakes have I written this little Book, wherein is largely, and yet with few words, discovered the Doctrine of the Person, and Doings and Sufferings of Christ with the true Cause thereof, also a removal of those Objections that the crafty Children of darkness have framed against the same.

And I have been the more plain and simple in my writing, because the Sin against the Holy Ghost is in these days, more common than formerly, and the Way unto it more beautified with colour, and pretence of Truth. I may say of the way to this Sin, it is, as was once the Way to Jerusalem, strewed with Boughs and Branches, and by some there is cried a kind of Hosanna *to them that are treading these Steps to Hell. Oh the plausible Pretences, the golden Names, the feigned Holiness, the demure Behaviours mixt with damnable Hypocrisie, that attends the Persons that have forsaken the Lord Jesus, that have despised his Person, trampled upon him, and counted the Blood of the Covenant, wherewith he was Sanctified, an Unholy thing!*

They have crucified him to themselves, and think that they can go to Heaven without him; yea, pretend they love him, when they hate him; pretend they have him, when they have cast him off; pretend they trust in him, when they bid defiance to his Undertakings for the World.

Reader, let me beseech thee to hear me patiently; read, and consider, and iudg. I have presented thee with that which I have received from God, and the Holy Men of God, who spake as they were moved by the Holy Ghost do bear me witness. Thou wilt say, all pretend to this: Well, but give me the hearing, take me to the Bible, and let me find in thy Heart no favour, if thou find me to swerve from the Standard.

I say again, receive my Doctrine, I beseech thee in Christ's stead receive it; I know it to be the Way of Salvation. I have ventured my own Soul thereon with gladness, and if all the Souls in the World were mine as mine own Soul is, I would through God's Grace venture every one of them there. I have not writ at a venture, nor borrowed my Doctrine from Libraries. I depend upon the sayings of no man: I found it in the Scriptures of Truth, among the true sayings of God.

I have done when I have exhorted thee to pray, and give heed to the Words of God as revealed in the Holy Writ. The Lord Jesus Christ himself give thee Light and Life by Faith in him; to whom with the Father and the good Spirit of Grace be Glory and Dominion now and for ever: Amen.

Joh. Bunyan.

LIGHT for them that sit in DARKNESS.

Of this Man's Seed, hath God according to his promise, raised unto Israel *a Saviour, Jesus.* Acts 13. 23.

THese Words are part of a Sermon, which *Paul* preached to the People that lived at *Antioch* in *Pisidia*; where also inhabited many of the Jews. The Preparation to his Discourse he thus begins; *Men of Israel, and ye that fear God give audience*, ver. 16. by which having prepared their minds to attend, he proceeds and gives a particular relation of Gods peculiar dealings with his People *Israel*, from *Egypt* to the time of *David* their King; *of whom* he treateth particularly.

That he was the *Son of Jessey*, that he was *a King*, that *God raised* him up in mercy, that God gave *Testimony of him*, that he was a Man after God's *own heart*, that he should *fulfil* all his Will, *ver.* 22.

And this he did of purpose, both to ingage them the more to attend, and because they well knew that of the fruit of his Loins *God had promised the Messiah should come.*

Having thus therefore gathered up their minds to hearken, he presenteth them with his Errand; to wit, *That the Messiah was come*, and that the promise was indeed fulfilled, *that a Saviour should be born to Israel.*

Of this Man's Seed (saith he) *hath God according to the promise raised unto Israel a Saviour, Jesus.*

In this Assertion he concludeth,

1. That the Promise had kept its due course in presenting a Saviour to Israel; to wit, in *Davids* Loins; *Of this Man's Seed.*

2. That the time of the Promise was come, and the Saviour was revealed; *God hath raised unto Israel a Saviour.*

3. That Jesus of *Nazareth*, the Son of *Joseph* was he: *He hath raised unto Israel a Saviour, Jesus.*

4 Acts 13. 23.] Acts 13. 32.

From these things we may inquire for the explication of the Words.

1. What *this* Jesus is.

2. What it was for *this* Jesus to be of the *Seed of* David.

3. What it was for *Jesus* to be of this Man's Seed *according to the promise.*

4. And what it was for him to *be raised unto Israel.*

These things may give us light into what shall be spoken after.

Quest. 1. First, *What this Jesus is.*

He is God, and had Personal Being from before all Worlds; therefore not such an one as took being when he was formed in the World; *He is God's natural Son.* The Eternal Son of his Begetting, and Love. *God sent forth his Son*; he was, and was his Son, before he was Revealed. *What is his Name, and what is his Sons Name, if thou canst tell?* Prov. 30. 4. Ezek. 21. 10. He hath an Eternal Generation, such as *none can declare*: not Man, not Angel, *Isa.* 53. 8. He was the delight of his Father before he had made either Mountain or Hill. *While as yet he had not made the Earth, or the Fields, or the highest part of the Dust of the World; all things were made by him, & without him was not any thing made that was made; & he is before all things, and by him all things consist.* It is he with whom the Father consulted when he was about to make Man; when he intended to overthrow *Babel*, and when he sent *Isaiah* to harden the Hearts of *Israel*, *Pro.* 8. 26. *Joh.* 1. 3. *Heb.* 1. 1, 2, 3. *Col.* 1. 17. *Gen.* 1. 26. and 11. 7. *Isa.* 6. 8. This is the Person intended in the Text. Hence also he testifies of himself, that he came down from the Father; that he had Glory with him before the World was. And *what and if you shall see the Son of Man ascend up where he was before*, John 16. 28. Chap. 17. 5. Chap. 6. 62.

Quest. Secondly, *What was it for Jesus to be of* Davids *Seed*? To be of *Davids Seed*, is to spring from his Loins, to come of his Race according to the Flesh: and therefore as he is *Davids* God, so likewise is he *Davids* Son; the *Root*, and also the *Off-Spring of* David: And this the Lord himself acknowledgeth; saying, *I am the Root*, or God, *and the Off-Spring*, and Son *of* David, *and the Bright and Morning Star*, Revel. 22. 16. This is indeed the great Mystery, the Mystery of Godliness.

25 *Heb.* 1. 1, 2, 3.] *Heb.* 1. 2, 3.

If David *called him Lord, how is he then his Son?* see Luk. 2. 4. Rom. 1. 3. 2 Tim. 2. 8. Matt. 22. 45.

And hence it is that he is said *to be wonderful*, because he is both God and Man in one Person. *To us a Child is born, to us a Son is given, and the Government shall be upon his Shoulder, and his Name shall be called Wonderful*, Isa. 9. 6. Wonderful indeed! Wonderful God, Wonderful Man, Wonderful God-Man, and so a Wonderful Jesus & Saviour. He also hath wonderful Love, bore wonderful Sorrows for our wonderful Sins, and obtained for *his* a wonderful Salvation.

Quest. 3. Thirdly, *What it was for Jesus to be of this Mans Seed according to the Promise.*

1. This Word [Promise] doth sometimes comprehend all the Promises which God made to our Fathers from the first Promise to the last; and so the Holy Ghost doth call them. The Promise made unto the Fathers, God hath fulfilled the same to us their Children, *Acts* 13. 32, 33.

2. But the word Promise here, doth in special intend that which God made to *David* himself. *Men and Brethren*, said Peter, *let me freely speak unto you of the Patriarch* David, *that he is both dead and buried, and his Sepulcher is with us unto this day: therefore being a Prophet, and knowing that God had sworn with an Oath to him, that of the Fruit of his Loins according to the Flesh, he would raise up Christ to sit on his Throne; he seeing this before, spake of the Resurrection of Christ, &c.* Acts 2. 29, 30, 31.

Quest. Fourthly, *What it was for Jesus to be raised thus up of God to* Israel.

Here we have two things to consider of.

1. Who *Israel* is.

2. What it was for Jesus to be raised up unto them.

1. *Who* Israel *is*. By *Israel* sometimes we should understand the whole Stock of *Jacob*, the Natural Children of his Flesh; for that name they have of him; for he obtained it when he wrestled with the Angel and prevailed (*Gen.* 32.) and it remained with his Seed in their Generations.

2. By *Israel* we are to understand all those that God hath promised to Christ. The Children of *the Promise are counted for the*

24 31] *om.*

Seed, the elect Jews and Gentiles. These are called *the Israel of God*, and the Seed of *Abraham*, whom Jesus in special regarded in his undertaking the work of Mans Redemption, *Rom.* 9. 6. *Gal.* 6. 16. *Heb.* 2. 14, 15, 16.

2. What it was for Jesus to be raised up unto them.

This word, *raised up*, is diversly taken in the Scripture.

1. It is taken for *sending*, as when he saith, he raised them up Judges, Saviours, and Prophets; he means, he sent them such (*Judges* 2. 16, 18. *Chap.* 3. 9, 15. *Amos.* 2. 11), and thus he raised up Jesus; that is, *he sent him. I came not*, saith he, *of myself, but he sent me. But the Father which sent me gave me a commandment*, Jo. 12.

2. To be raised up intimateth one *invested with power and authority.* Thus he raised up *David* to be the King of *Israel*; he anointed him & invested him with Kingly Power, 1 *Sam.* 16. 13. *Acts* 13. 22. And thus was Jesus Christ raised up: Hence he is called, *the Horn of Salvation: He hath raised up for us an Horn of Salvation in the House of his Servant* David, Luk. 1. 69.

3. To be raised up intimateth quickning and strengthening, to oppose and overcome all opposition. Thus was Jesus raised up from under Sin, Death, the rage of the World, and Hell, that day that God raised him out of the Grave.

Thus therefore was Jesus raised up to *Israel*; that is, he was sent, authorized, and strengthned to, and in the work of their Salvation, to the compleating of it.

The words thus opened, do lay before us these two Observations.

First, *That in all Ages God gave his People a Promise, and so ground for a believing remembrance that he would one day send them a Saviour.*

Secondly, *That when Jesus was come into the World, then was that Promise of God fulfilled.*

To begin with the First, *That in all Ages God gave his People a Promise, and so ground for a believing remembrance, that he would one day send them a Saviour.*

This *Zacharias* testifies when he was filled with the Holy Ghost; for speaking of the Messias, or the Saviour, he saith, *That God spake of him by the mouth of all the Prophets which have been since the World began*: To which I will add that of *Peter; Yea, and all the Prophets from*

17 Luk. 1. 69.] Luk. 2. 69.

Samuel, *and these that follow after, as many as have spoken, have likewise foretold of these days*, Luk. 1. 69, 70. Acts 3. 24.

From these Texts it is evident that in every Generation or Age of the World, God did give his People a Promise, and so ground for a believing-remembrance that he would one day send them a Saviour: for indeed the Promise is not only a ground for a remembrance, but for a believing-remembrance: what God saith is sufficient ground for Faith, because he is Truth and cannot lye or repent. But that is not all, his Heart was engaged, yea all his Heart, in the Promise which he spoke, of sending us a Saviour.

From this Observation I shall make inquiry into these three things.

1. *What it is to be a Saviour.*

2. *How it appears that God in all Ages gave his People a Promise that he would one day send them a Saviour.*

3. *That this was ground for a believing remembrance that a Saviour should one day come.*

First, *What it is to be a Saviour.*

This word Saviour is easie to be understood, it being all one with Deliverer, Redeemer, &c. *A Saviour*, *Jesus*; both words are of the same signification, and are doubled, perhaps to teach us, that the Person mentioned in the Text, is not called *Jesus* only to distinguish him from other Men (for names are given to distinguish) but also, and especially to specifie his Office: his Name is Saviour, because it was to be his Work, his Office, his Business in the World. *His Name shall be called Jesus, for he shall save his People from their sins*, Matt. 1. 21.

Secondly, This word *Saviour* is a word so large, that it hath place in all the undertakings of Christ; for whatever he doth in his Mediation, he doth as a Saviour. He interposeth between God and Man as a *Saviour*. He engageth against Sin, the Devil, Death, and Hell, *as a Saviour*, and triumphed over them by himself as a *Saviour*.

Thirdly, The word *Saviour*, as I said, is all one with Redeemer, Deliverer, Reconciler, Peace-maker, or the like; for though there be variation in the terms, yet *Saviour* is the intendment of them all. By *Redeeming* he becomes a *Saviour*, by *Delivering* he becomes *a Saviour*, by *Reconciling* he becomes a *Saviour*, and by *making Peace* he

2 Luk. 1. 69, 70.] Luk. 2. 69, 70.

becometh a *Saviour*: But I pass this now, intending to speak more to the same question afterwards.

Secondly, How it appears that God in all Ages gave his People a Promise that he would one day send them a Saviour.

It appears evidently, for so soon as man had sinned, God came to him with an heart full of Promise, and continued to renew, and renew, till the time of the promised Messias to be revealed was come.

He promised him under the name of the Seed of the Woman, after our first Father had sinned: *I will put enmity between thee and the Woman, and between thy Seed and her Seed, it shall break thy Head, and thou shalt bruise his Heel* (Gen. 3. 15.). This the Apostle hath his eye upon when he saith, *When the fulness of the time was come, God sent forth his Son made of a Woman, made under the Law, to Redeem them that were under the Law*, Gal. 4. 4, 5.

2. God renewed this Promise to *Abraham*, and here tells him Christ should be his Seed; saying, *In thy Seed shall all Families of the Earth be blessed* (Gen. 12. 3.). Now saith *Paul*; *To* Abraham *and his Seed was the Promise made*; *He saith not unto Seeds, as of many, but as of one, and to thy Seed, which is Christ* (Gal. 3. 16.).

3. He was promised in the time of *Moses* under the name of a Prophet; *I will raise them up* (saith God to him) *a Prophet of their Brethren like unto thee*: This *Peter* expounds of Christ, for *Moses* truly said unto the Fathers: *A Prophet shall the Lord your God raise up unto you of your Brethren like unto me, him shall you hear in all things whatsoever he shall say unto you*, Deut. 18. 18. Acts. 3. 22.

4. He promised him to *David* under the Title of a Son; saying, *I will be to him a Father, and he shall be to me a Son*: For this the Apostle expounded of the Saviour; saying, *Thou art my Son, this day have I begotten thee*: and again, *I will be to him a Father, and he shall be to me a Son*, 2 Sam. 7. 14. Heb. 1. 5.

5. He was promised in the days of *Uzziah*, *Jotham*, *Ahaz*, and *Hezekiah*, Kings of *Judah*.

1. By the name of a Branch. *In that day shall the Branch of the Lord be Beautiful and Glorious*, Isa. 4. 2.

2. Under the name of the Son of a Virgin. *Therefore the Lord himself shall give you a Sign; Behold a Virgin shall conceive and bear a Son, &*

41 Gal. 4. 4, 5.] Gal. 4. 4.

thou shalt call his Name Emmanuel. This *Matthew* expounds of Christ, *Isa.* 7. 14. *Matt.* 1. 22, 23.

3. He was promised under the name of a Rod. *There shall come forth a Rod out of the Stem of* Jesse, *and a branch shall grow out of his Roots, and the Spirit of the Lord shall rest upon him.* This answereth the Text, *David* was the Son of *Jesse*, and Christ the Son of *David*, *Isa.* 11. 1, 2.

4. He is promised under the Title of a King. *Behold, a King shall rule in righteousness; and a Man shall be for a hiding-place from the Wind, and a covert from the Tempest, as Rivers of Waters in a dry place, as the shadow of a great Rock in a weary Land*, Isa. 32. 1, 2.

5. He was promised under the name of an Elect Servant. *Behold, my Servant whom I uphold, mine Elect in whom my Soul delighteth; I have put my Spirit upon him, he shall bring forth Judgment to the Gentiles: he shall not cry, nor lift up, nor cause his voice to be heard in the Streets; a bruised Reed shall he not break, and smoking Flax shall he not quench*, Isa. 42. 1, 2, 3. Matt. 12. 18, 19, 20.

6. He was promised to *Jeremiah* under the name of the Lord our Righteousness. *Behold, the days come, saith the Lord, that I will raise unto* David *a Righteous Branch, and a King shall reign and prosper: he shall execute Judgment in the Earth, in his days* Judah *shall be saved, and* Israel *shall dwell safely, and this is the name wherewith he shall be called, The Lord, our Righteousness*, Jer. 23. 5, 6.

7. He was promised by the Prophet *Ezekiel* under the name of *David* a Shepherd. *And I will set one Shepherd over them, and he shall feed them, even my Servant* David, *he shall feed them: and he shall be their Shepherd, and I the Lord will be their God, and my Servant* David *a Prince among them, I the Lord have spoken it.* Ezek. 34. 23, 24. Joh. 10. 1, 2, 3.

8. He was promised by the Prophet *Daniel* under the name of Messias, or Christ, the most Holy. *And after threescore and two weeks shall the Messiah be cut off, but not for himself.* Dan. 9. 26.

9. He was promised by the Prophet *Micha* under the name of the Ruler of *Israel. But thou* Bethlehem Ephratah, *though thou be little among the thousands of* Judah, *yet out of thee shall he come, that is to be Ruler in* Israel, Mic. 5. 2. Matt. 2. 6.

10. He was promised to *Haggai* as the desire of all Nations. *I will*

2 *Matt.* 1. 22, 23.] Matt. 1. 22. 16 Matt. 12. 18, 19, 20.] Matt. 12. 18. 27 Ezek. 34. 23, 24.] Ezek. 34. 24.

shake all Nations, and the desire of all Nations shall come, and I will fill this house with Glory, saith the Lord of Hosts, Hag. 2. 7.

11. He was promised by *Zechariah* under the name of Servant and Branch. *For behold, I will bring forth my Servant the Branch*: and again, *Behold the Man whose name is the Branch, he shall grow up out of his place, and he shall build the Temple of the Lord, and he shall bear the Glory*, Zech. 3. 8; 6. 12, 13.

12. He was promised by *Malachi* under the name of the Lord, and the Messenger of the Covenant. *Behold, I send my Messenger, and he shall prepare the way before thee, and the Lord whom ye seek shall suddenly come to his Temple; even the Messenger of the Covenant whom ye delight in, behold he shall come saith the Lord of Hosts*, Malachi 3. 1.

Indeed the Scriptures of the Old-Testament are filled with Promises of the Messias to come, Prophetical Promises, Typical Promises: For all the Types and shadows of the Saviour, are virtually so many Promises. Having therefore touched upon the Prophetical, I will briefly touch the Typical Promises also; for as God spake at sundry times to the Fathers, so also in divers manners, Prophetically, Providentially, Typically, and all of the Messias, *Heb.* 1. 1.

The Types of the Saviour were various.

1. Sometimes he was typed out by Men.

2. Sometimes by Beasts.

3. Sometimes by Insensible Creatures.

First, *He was typed forth sometimes by Men.*

1. *Adam* was his Type in many things, especially as he was the Head and Father of the first World. *He was the Figure of him that was to come*, Rom. 5. 14.

2. *Moses* was his Type as Mediator, and as Builder of the Tabernacle, *Heb.* 3. 2, 3.

Aaron was his Type as he was High-Priest, and so was *Melchisedec* before him, *Heb.* 5. 4, 5, 6. *Chap.* 7. 1, 21.

4. *Sampson* was his Type in the effects of his death: for as *Sampson* gave his life for the deliverance of *Israel* from the *Philistins*, Christ gave his Life to deliver us from Sin and Devils.

5. *Joshuah* was his Type in giving the Land of *Canaan* to *Israel*, as Jesus will give the Kingdom of Heaven to the Elect, *Heb.* 4. 8.

7 6. 12, 13.] *om.*   12 3. 1.] 3. 12.   31 *Heb.* 5. 4, 5, 6.] *Heb.* 5. 4, 5.

6. *David* was his Type in many things, especially in his subduing of *Israels* Enemies, and feeding them; hence he is sometimes called David *their King*, and David *their Shepherd*, Ezek. 34. 23, 24.

7. *Solomon* was his Type in his building the Temple, and in his Peaceable Kingdom. Hence it is said, he shall build the Temple of the Lord; and again, Of his Government and Peace there shall be no end.

Beasts were his Types. To instance some:

First, The Paschal-Lamb was his Type, *Exod.* 12.

1. *In its Spotlesness.* Christ was a Lamb without blemish and without spot, 1 *Pet.* 1. 18, 19.

2. *In its being Roasted.* It was a Figure of the cursed Death of Christ (for to be Roasted bespake one accursed, *Jer.* 29. 22.), *Gal.* 3. 13.

3. In that it was to be eaten. *He that eateth my Flesh, and drinketh my Blood, saith Christ, hath Eternal Life*, John 6. 54, 56.

4. In that its Blood was to be sprinkled upon the doors of their houses for the destroying Angel to look on: The Blood of Christ is sprinkled upon the Elect for the Justice of God to look on, *Heb.* 9. 1 *Pet.* 1. 1, 2.

5. By eating the Paschal-Lamb, the People went out of *Egypt*: by feeding upon Christ by Faith, we come from under the *Egyptian* Darkness, *Tyranny* of Satan, *&c.*

Secondly, The Red Cow was his Type, *Numb.* 19. 2, &c.

1. In that she was to be without blemish.

2. In that she was to be slain without the Camp. *Jesus also that he might sanctifie the People with his own Blood, suffered without the Gate*, Heb. 13. 12.

3. In that her Flesh was to be burnt, a Type of the grievous Death of Christ.

4. Her Ashes was to be carried into a clean place without the Camp; a Type of the clean Sepulcher where the Body of Jesus was laid, *John* 19. 38, 39, 40, 41, 42.

There was also divers other Sacrifices, as Bulls, Goats and Birds; which were Types of him, which I here omit.

Thirdly, Insensible Creatures were his Types.

16 John 6. 54, 56.] John 6. 57.   33 42.] *om.*

As first, The Mannah in the Wilderness (*Ex.* 16.), and that,

1. As it came down from Heaven; for so did Christ, *I came down from Heaven*, saith he: and again, *I am the Living Bread which came down from Heaven*, John 6. 51.

2. The Mannah was to be eaten, so is Christ by Faith. *If any man eat of this Bread, he shall live for ever, and the Bread that I will give is my Flesh, which I will give for the life of the World*, John 6. 51.

3. The Mannah was to be gathered daily, so is Christ to be daily eaten.

4. The Mannah was all the Bread that *Israel* had in the Wilderness: Christ is all the Bread that Believers have in this Life for their Souls.

5. The Mannah came not by *Moses* Law, neither comes Christ by our Merits. *Moses gave you not that Bread from Heaven, but my Father giveth you the true Bread from Heaven*, John 6. 32.

Again, The Rock that gave them out Water for their Thirst, was a Type of him (*Numb.* 20.). *They did all drink of the same Spiritual Drink, for they drank of that Spiritual Rock that followed them, and that Rock was Christ*, 1 Cor. 10. 4.

This Rock was his Type in four things.

1. It gave Drink to the People in the Wilderness when they were come out of *Egypt*. Christ gives drink to them that forsake the World for him.

2. The Rock yielded Water by being smitten by *Moses's* Rod: Christ giveth drink, *even his Blood*, by being striken by *Moses's* Law, *Numb.* 20. 11. *Isa.* 53.

3. The water out of this Rock was given to the Thirsty. *I will give to him that is a-thirst, saith Christ, of the Fountain of the water of Life freely*, Revel. 21. 6.

4. The Water of the Rock in the Wilderness ran after the People, *They drank of that Rock that followed them, he opened the Rock and the Waters gushed out, they ran in dry places like a River*. Christ also is said by that Type to follow us: They drank of that Rock that followed them, *and that Rock was Christ*, Psal. 105. 41. 1 Cor. 10. 4.

Again, The Mount *Moriah* was his Type.

1. That Mount stood in *Jerusalem*; Christ also stands in his Church.

2. Upon that Rock was built the Temple. *And upon this Rock*, said Christ, *will I build my Church, and the Gates of Hell shall not prevail against it*, 2 Chron. 3. 1. Mat. 16. 18.

Other things might be urged, but these being virtually of the force of the Promise, and also as a Key to open them, therefore I thought good to place them here with the Promises; because, as they are standing with them, so they are written to beget Faith in the same Lord Jesus Christ.

I come now to the third thing, to wit, *That these Promises were ground for a Believing Remembrance that a Saviour should one day come.*

There is a Remembring, and a Believing Remembring, or such a Remembring that begetteth, and maintaineth Faith in the Heart. *Jacob* had a Believing Remembrance, when he said, *I have waited for thy Salvation, O Lord*, Gen. 49. 18. And so had *David* when he cried, *O that the Salvation of* Israel *was come out of* Zion, Psalm 53. 6. These, with *Simeon* and *Anna*, had not a Remembrance only, but a Believing Remembrance, *that God would send them a Saviour*. They had the Promise not in the Book only, but in their Hearts: This Gospel was mixed in them with Faith; therefore they with their Fellows remembred and believed, or made the Promise the Ground of their Believing that God would one day send them a Saviour.

Let me make some use of this Doctrine.

Here we may see how much the Heart of God was set upon the Salvation of Sinners, he studied it, contrived it, set his Heart on it, and promised, and promised, and promised to compleat it by sending one day his Son for a Saviour, *Ephes.* 1. 3, 4. 2 *Sam.* 14. 14. *Tit.* 1. 2.

No marvel therefore, if when he treateth of the New-Covenant, in which the Lord Jesus is wrapped, and presented in a Word of Promise to the World, that he saith; *I will do it assuredly with my whole Heart and with my whole Soul*, Jer. 32. 41.

Now this is of singular comfort to sensible Sinners; yea, what greater ground of consolation to such, than to hear that the God against whom they have sinned, should himself take care to provide us a Saviour.

There are some poor Sinners in the World, that have given such way to discouragement, from the sence of the greatness of their

26 1. 3, 4.] 1. 3.

Sins, that they dare not think upon God, nor the Sins which they have committed: But the reason is, because they are ignorant that God's Heart was wrapt up in this good work of providing and sending *a Saviour*. Let such hearken now to the Call of God; *Return unto me, for I have redeemed thee*, Isa. 44. 22. Ho! turn again, hearken; the Heart of God is much set upon Mercy, from the beginning of the World he resolved and promised, ay, and sware we should have a Saviour.

2. *Doct.* I now proceed to the second Observation.

That when Jesus was come into the World, then was the Promise of God fulfilled; namely, That he would one day send us a Saviour.

Take three Texts for the Confirmation of this Point.

1. *This is of a truth that Prophet that should come into the World.*

These words were spoken of them that were present at that Miracle of Jesus, when he fed Five Thousand with Five Barly Loaves which a Lad had about him in the Company: for these Men, when they had seen the Marvel, being amazed at it, made confession of him to be the Saviour; *Joh.* 6.

2. *Lord, I believe thou art the Christ the Son of God, which should come into the World*, John 11. 27.

3. *This is a faithful saying, and worthy of all acceptation, that Christ Jesus came into the World to save Sinners*, 1 Tim. 1. 15.

For the explaining of this Observation, I will briefly handle three questions.

1. How this Jesus is to be distinguished from *others of that Name.*

2. What it was for *this* Jesus to come into the World.

3. What it was for him to come to be a *Saviour.*

Quest. 1. For the first, The Jesus in the Text, is distinguished from all others of that Name.

1. By the manner of his Birth, he was born of a Virgin, a Virgin espoused to a Man whose Name was *Joseph*; but he knew her not till she had brought forth her First-born Son, *and he called his name Jesus*, Mat. 1. 25.

2. He is distinguished from others of that Name, by the place of his Birth; to wit, *Bethlehem*, the City of *David*, there he must be Born, there he was Born, *Joh.* 7. 42. *Mat.* 2. 4, 5, 6.

20 John 11.] John 9.

3. He is distinguished by his Linage, *He came of the House and Linage of* David, Luk. 2. 4, 5, 6.

4. He is distinguished by the time of his Birth, to wit, *the Time that the Prophets prefixed*, Gal. 4. 4.

5. But his common Distinction is, *Jesus of Nazareth*; by this Name he is distinguished *one and twenty times* in the New-Testament.

1. His Enemies called him *Jesus of Nazareth*, Mat. 26. 71. Mark. 14. 67. Joh. 18. 5.

2. His Disciples called him *Jesus of Nazareth*, Mat. 21. 11. Luk. 24. 19. Joh. 1. 45. Act. 2. 22.

3. The Angels called him *Jesus of Nazareth*, Mar. 16. 6.

4. And he calleth Himself *Jesus of Nazareth*, Acts 22. 8.

5. Yea, and he goeth also by the Name of *Jesus of Nazareth* among the Devils, *Mar.* 1. 24. *Luk.* 4. 34.

He was called *Jesus of Nazareth*, because he dwelt there with his Mother *Mary* and her Husband. *Nazareth* was his City *where he had been brought up*, whither for shelter *Joseph* carried him when he came up out of *Egypt* with him: in *Nazareth* was his common Abode, *until the time that* John *was cast into Prison*, Luk. 4. 16. Mat. 2. 23. Chap. 4. 12, 13. Wherefore he might well say, *I am Jesus of Nazareth*: Yea, though he was now in Heaven; for Heaven shall not make us forget what Country-men we were when we lived in the World. Jesus, you see here, though Glorified in Heaven, yet forgets not what Countrey-Man he was when he dwelt in the World. I am Jesus of *Nazareth*, saith he, I am the Jesus that thou hatest; and that thou mayest know I am he, I tell thee I dwelt once in the City *Nazareth* in *Galilee: Joseph* and my Mother *Mary* brought me up there, and there I dwelt with them many years. I am Jesus of *Nazareth* whom thou persecutest.

Quest. 2. Secondly, *What was it for Jesus to come into the World?*

Ans. 1. Not his coming in, or by his Spirit in his People; for so he was never out of the World.

2. Neither is it his Appearance in his Ordinances.

3. Nor that coming of his by which he destroyeth Antichrist.

4. Nor his Appearing in his dreadful Providences or Judgments.

But by the coming of Jesus, according to the Text, we are to understand *that*, or *such* a Coming, whereby he was manifest to be

God-Man in one Person, God in our Flesh without us, or distinct in his own Person by himself; Such a Coming by which he was manifested to be in all points like as men are, Sin only excepted. Such a Coming, wherein, or by which, the Son of God became also the Son of Man.

For the further clearing of this, you find it expresly said, he was *born into the World*; Mary, *of whom was born Jesus*. Now when Jesus was *born*, it's said, Where is he that is *born* King of the Jews? *Herod* demanded of them where Christ should be *born*, *Mat.* 1. 16. Chap. 2. 1, 2, 4. *Luk.* 1. 35. Chap. 2. 11.

Now that this was fulfilled according to the very word of the Text, without any juggle, evasion, or cunningly-devised Fable, consider:

1. He is called the First-Born of this Woman, *The Male Child that opened her Womb*, Luk. 2. 7, 23.

2. He was not born till nourished in her Womb the full time, according to the time of Life. *And so it was that while they were at* Bethlehem, *the days were accomplished that she should be delivered, and she brought forth her First-born Son, and wrapt him in swaddling Clothes, and laid him in a Manger*, Luk. 2. 4, 5, 6, 7.

3. She also continued in her Separation at the Birth of Jesus, as other women at the Birth of their Children, until the days of her Purification according to the Law of *Moses* were accomplished, *Luk.* 2. 22.

4. Himself also, as other *Hebrew* Children, was brought to *Jerusalem* to present him unto the Lord; *As it is written in the Law of* Moses, *every Male that openeth the Womb shall be called Holy unto the Lord*, Luk. 2. 23, 24.

5. Thus Jesus also, as other *Hebrew*-Children, when the set Day was come, was Circumcised. *And when eight days were accomplished for the Circumcising of the Child, his Name was called* Jesus, *which was so named of the Angel before he was conceived in the Womb*, Luk. 2. 21.

6. After this, he is often called the Young-Child, the Child Jesus; and further it is said of him, that he grew, that he increased in Wisdom and Stature, *Mat.* 2. 20, 21. *Luk.* 2. 40, 52.

Behold, with what diligence, even to a Circumstance, the Holy Ghost sets forth the Birth of the Lord Jesus, and all to convince the incredulous World, of the true Manner of the coming of the Saviour into the World.

Secondly, The Reality of the Manhood of this Lord Jesus, is yet further manifest, and that;

First, By those natural Infirmities that attend Human Flesh.

Secondly, By the Names the Prophets gave him in the Days of the Old-Testament and the New.

First, By those natural Infirmities that attend Human Flesh.

As 1. At his Birth he could not go, but as carried by his Parents.

2. He was sensible of Hunger, *Luk.* 4. 2.

3. He was sensible of Thirst, John 19. 28.

4. He was sensible of Weariness, *Joh.* 4. 6.

5. He was nourished by Sleep, *Mar.* 4. 38.

6. He was subject to Grief, *Mar.* 3. 5.

7. He was subject to Anger, *Mar.* 3. 5.

8. He was subject to Weep, *Joh.* 11. 35. *Luk.* 19. 41.

9. He had Joy as a Man and rejoyced, *Mat.* 11. 25. *Luk.* 10. 21.

These things, I say, Jesus was subject to as a Man, as the Son of the Virgin.

Secondly, The Reality of his Manhood is yet made manifest by the Names the Prophets gave him, both in the Old-Testament and in the New.

As 1. He is called the *Seed.* The *Seed* of the Woman, the *Seed* of *Abraham*, the *Seed* of *David*, by which is meant he was to come of their Children, *Gen.* 3. 15. Chap. 12. Chap. 22. *Gal.* 3. 16, 17. *Rom.* 1. 3.

2. Therefore it is added (where mention is made of the Fathers) *of whom as concerning the Flesh* Christ came. He was made of the Seed of *David according to the Flesh*: And hence again, he calleth himself the *Off-spring* of *David*; therefore, I say, he is said to be of *their Flesh*, *their* Loins, and is called *their* Son, *Rom.* 1. 4. Chap. 9. 5. *Acts* 2. 30. *Revel.* 22. 16.

3. He *therefore* is frequently called *a Man*, and the Son of Man. *Then shall you see the Son of man coming in the Clouds of Heaven. When the Son of man shall come in his Glory, and all the Holy Angels with him. This Man, because he continueth ever, hath an unchangeable Priesthood.* It

13 *Mar.* 4. 38.] *Mar.* 4. 34. 17 11. 25.] 11. 27. 25 *Rom.* 1. 3.] *Rom.* 1. 4.

is therefore necessary that this Man have somewhat also to offer, Mat. 26. 64. *Chap.* 25. 30, 31. Heb. 7. 24. *Chap.* 8. 3. *Chap.* 10. 12.

4. What shall I say, Himself gave undeniable Demonstration of all this, when he said, he *was* dead; when he called to *Thomas* to put his Finger to, and behold his Hands, to reach to him his Hand and *thrust it into his Side*, and bid him he should not be faithless *but believing*. At another time when he stood in the midst of the Eleven, as they were troubled with the thoughts of Unbelief, he said, *Behold my Hands and my Feet, that it is I my self, handle me, and see: for a Spirit hath not Flesh and Bones, as ye see me have*, Joh. 20. 27. Luk. 24. 39.

Thus have I shewed you what it was for Jesus to come into the World; namely, *To be born of a Woman, to take flesh, and to become God-man in one Person.*

I come now to the third Question; but before I speak particularly to that, I will produce further Testimony that we find upon record, concerning the Truth of all this.

Particular Testimonies, that this Coming of Jesus is his Coming to Save us.

1. S*imeon* the Just gives Testimony of him. *And the Holy Ghost was upon him, and it was revealed unto him by the Holy Ghost that he should not see Death before he had seen the Lord's Christ. And he came by the Spirit into the Temple, and when the Parents brought in the Child Jesus to do for him after the Custom of the Law, then took he him up in his Arms, and blessed God, and said, Lord, now lettest thou thy Servant depart in peace, for mine Eyes have seen thy Salvation*, Luk. 2. 25, 26, 27–32.

The Testimony of Anna.

2. *Anna* a Prophetess, one of a great Age, which departed not from the Temple, but served God with fasting and prayer night and day. *And she coming in at the same instant, gave thanks likewise unto the Lord, and spake of him to all them that looked for Redemption in Jerusalem*, Luk. 2. 36, 37, 38.

1–2 Mat. 26. 64.] Mat. 26. 63. 31 Luk. 2. 36, 37, 38.] Luk. 2. 26, 27, 28.

The Testimony of John Baptist.

3. *John Baptist* as he fulfilled his Ministry, he cried concerning this Jesus, *Behold the Lamb of God, that taketh away the Sins of the World. And he*, saith John, *that sent me to baptize with Water, the same said unto me, Upon whom thou shalt see the Spirit descending and abiding, or remaining, the same is he which shall baptize with the Holy Ghost. And I saw, and bear record that this is the Son of God*, Joh. 1. 29, 30, 31, 32, 33, 34.

The Testimony of the Star and Wise-Men.

4. The Star that appeared at his Birth in the East, and that coasted through the Heavens, till it came over the Place where the young Child Jesus was, that Star gave Testimony that he was the Saviour. This Star alarmed many, especially the Wise-Men of the East, who were brought by it from afar to worship him. *And lo, the Star which they saw in the East, went before them till it came and stood over where the young Child was. And when they saw the Star they rejoiced with exceeding joy. And when they were come into the House, they saw the young Child with* Mary *his Mother, and fell down and worshipped him; and when they had opened their Treasures, they presented unto him Gifts, Gold, and Frankincense, and Myrrhe.* Mat. 2. 9, 10, 11.

The Testimony of the Angels.

1. To *Mary* herself.

And in the sixth Month the Angel Gabriel *was sent from God unto a City of* Galilee *named* Nazareth, *to a Virgin espoused to a Man whose Name was* Joseph, *and the Virgin's Name was* Mary*; and the Angel came in unto her, and said, Hail thou that art highly favoured. And the Angel said unto her, Fear not*, Mary, *for thou hast found favour with God. And behold, thou shalt conceive in thy Womb, and bring forth a Son, and shalt call his Name* Jesus. *He shall be great, and shall be called the Son of the Highest. And the Lord God shall give unto him the Throne of his Father* David, *and he shall reign over the House of* Jacob *for ever, and of his Kingdom there shall be no end*, Luk. 1. 26–33.

2. The Angels Testimony to the Shepherds, as they were feeding their Flocks in the Fields by Night.

And lo, the Angel of the Lord came upon them, and the Glory of the

20 Mat. 2. 9, 10, 11.] *om.* 32 Luk. 1. 26–33.] Luk. 2. 26, 35.

Lord shined round about them, and they were sore afraid; and the Angel said unto them, Fear not, for behold, I bring you good tidings of great joy which shall be to all people; for unto you is born this day in the City of David, *a Saviour, which is Christ the Lord*, Luk. 2. 9, 10, 11.

3. How the Angels Solemnized his Birth among themselves.

And suddenly there was with the Angel a multitude of the Heavenly Host, praising God, and saying, Glory to God in the highest, and on Earth Peace, good-will towards Men, Luk. 2. 13, 14.

The Testimony of God the Father.

1. When he was Baptized.

And Jesus when he was Baptized went up straight-way out of the Water; and lo, the Heavens were opened unto him, and he saw the Spirit of God descending like a Dove, and lighting upon him; and lo, a voice from Heaven, saying, This is my beloved Son, in whom I am well pleased, Mat. 3. 16, 17.

2. The Fathers Testimony of him at his Transfiguration.

And he took Peter, *and* James, *and* John, *and went up into a Mountain to pray: and as he prayed, the fashion of his Countenance was altered, and his Raiment was white and glittering, &c. And there appeared* Moses *and* Elias *talking with him, and a Cloud from Heaven overshadowed them*, at which the three Disciples began to be afraid. *Then there came a voice out of the Cloud saying, This is my beloved Son, hear him*, Luk. 9. 28, 29, 30–35.

This is that Testimony of God which *Peter* speaks of, saying, *We have not followed cunningly devised Fables, when we made known unto you the Power and Coming of our Lord Jesus Christ, but were eye-witnesses of his Majesty; for he received from God the Father Honour and Glory when there came such a voice to him from the Excellent Glory, This is my beloved Son, in whom I am well pleased: And this voice which came from Heaven we heard, when we were with him in the Holy Mount*, 2 Pet. 1. 16, 17, 18.

3. God gave Testimony of him by Signs and Wonders.

Believest thou not that I am in the Father, and the Father in me? The words that I speak unto you, I speak not of my self, but the Father that dwelleth in me, he doth the Works. God also bearing them witness (that preached Salvation by Jesus) *both with Signs and Wonders, and with*

4 Luk. 2. 9, 10, 11.] Luk. 2. 8, 9, 10. 22 30–35.] 30, 35. 29 1. 16, 17, 18.] 1. 26, 27, 28.

divers Miracles and Gifts of the Holy Ghost, according to his own Will, Joh. 14. 10. Heb. 2. 4.

Concerning Jesus, how he put himself upon the Test among his Adversaries.

THe Lord Jesus also putteth himself upon the Test among his Adversaries divers ways.

First, he urgeth the time of the appearing of the Messias, to be come.

The time is fulfilled, and the Kingdom of God is at hand; repent ye and believe the Gospel, (Mar. 1. 15.).

For this he had a three-fold proof.

1. The Heathens had invaded and taken the Land, according to that of *Daniel, Dan.* 9. 25, 26.

2. The Scepter was departed from *Judah*, according to that of *Jacob* (Gen. 49. 10.), to which also suited that Prophecy: *Before the Child shall know to refuse the evil and chuse the good, the Land which thou abhorrest, shall be forsaken of both her Kings.* Isa. 7. 16.

3. The *Roman* Emperor had not only subdued the Nation, and put down the Kingly Race of the Jews; but had set up and established his own Power over them. *In the fifteenth year of the Reign of* Tiberius Cesar, Pontius Pilat *was Governor of* Judea, Herod *was Tetrarch of* Galilee, Philip *Tetrarch of* Iturea, *and* Lysanias *Tetrarch of* Abilene, *all Heathens, and of* Tyberius *his making.*

Besides, The Kingly Race of *Judah* was at this time become so low by reason of the *Roman* oppression, that the chief of them were put to get their living by their own hands, even *Joseph*, the supposed Father of Jesus, was then become a Carpenter: Poor man! when Jesus was born, he was fain to thrust into a Stable, for there was in the *Inn* no room for such Guests as they. The Offering also which was brought unto God the time when Jesus was presented unto the Lord, *was two Turtle-Doves, or two young Pigeons*; a Sacrifice allowed only for them that were *Poor* and could provide no bigger.

17 Isa. 7. 16.] *om.*

And if she be not able to bring a Lamb, then she shall bring two Turtle-Doves or two young Pigeons, the one for a Burnt-Offring, the other for a Sin-Offering, Levit. 12. 8. Besides, Jesus himself saith, *Foxes have Holes, and the Birds of the Air have Nests, but the Son of Man hath not whereon to lay his Head.* Mat. 8. 20.

Now, I say, all these things were so apparent to the Jews, that they could not object; they felt the *Romans* were come, they knew the Scepter was gone, they smarted under the *Roman* Tyranny, and knew the Kingly Race of *Judea* was over-thrown: How then could they object, that the time was not come for Christ to be born?

Further, The People was generally convinced, *that the time was come*, and therefore, saith the Text; *They were in expectation. And as all the People were in expectation, and all men mused in their Hearts of* John, *whether he was the Christ or not*, Luk. 3. 15. The unbiassed People observing the face of things, could do no other but look for the Messias. And hence it is, that the Lord Jesus gives the Pharisees, those mortal Enemies of his, such sore rebukes; saying, *O ye Hypocrites, ye can discern the Face of the Skie, but can you not discern the Signs of the Times? The Kingdom is lost*, the Heathens are come, and the Scepter is departed from *Judea. Ye Hypocrites, ye can discern the Face of the Skie, and of the Earth, but how is it that ye do not discern this Time?* Mat. 16. 3. Luk. 12. 56.

Secondly, He yet again puts himself upon the *Test*, by the Miracles which he wrought before them.

Believe me that I am in the Father and the Father in me, or else believe me for the very works sake (John 14. 11.).

For the Works which the Father hath given me to finish, the same works that I do, bear witness of me, that the Father hath sent me, John 5. 36.

This Proof they could not withstand, but granted that he did many Miracles while they did nothing. *Then gathered the Chief-Priests and Pharisees a Counsel, and said, what do we? for this Man doth many Miracles: if we let him alone all men will believe on him, and the* Romans *shall come, and take away both our Place and Nation*, John 11. 47, 48.

Yea so did Jesus confound them, that by their own Records and Laws by which they were to prove persons clean or unclean; they in reading their Lectures, did justifie him and overthrow themselves.

5 Mat. 8. 20.] *om.*

For instance, it was written in their Law; *If he that hath an Issue spit upon him that is clean*, that Spittle should make him unclean (*Levit.* 15. 8.). Now Jesus whom they counted most unclean because he said he was the Son of God (as they thought speaking Blasphemy) he spits upon people and makes them whole; he spat and made clay with the Spittle and with that clay made a Blind Man see, *Joh.* 9. 6. Also he spit on the Eyes of another and made him see, *Mar.* 8. 23, 24, 25. Again he spit, and with his Spittle touched the Tongue of one that was Dumb, and made him speak immediatly, *Mar.* 7. 33, 34, 35. Thus he proved himself clear of their Accusations, and maintained before them, that by their Law he was guiltless, and the Son of God; for the Miracles which he wrought were to prove him so to be.

Again, In their Law it was written, that whoso touched the Altar of Incense should be Holy (*Exod.* 29. 37.). A Woman with a Bloody Issue toucheth him, and is whole of her Plague. Yea, they brought to him many diseased Persons; *and besought him that they might only touch the Hem of his Garment*; *and as many as touched, were made perfectly whole*, Mar. 5. 28, 29. Mat. 14. 35, 36.

Thus was he justified before them out of their own Law, and had his Glory manifest before their Faces, to their everlasting confusion and contempt.

Indeed, the Jews did make one Objection against Jesus Christ, that seemed to them to have weight in it: and that was because he *first began to appear and manifest his Glory in* Canaan *of* Galilee. At this, I say, they stumbled, it was their sore temptation; for still as some affirmed him to be the Christ, others as fast objected, *shall Christ come out of* Galilee? *art thou also of* Galilee? *search and look, for out of* Galilee *ariseth no Prophet*, John 2. 1, 11. Chap. 7. 40, 41, 42, 52.

But this their stumble might arise either;

1. From the cruelty of *Herod*: Or,

2. From their own not observing and keeping in mind the Alarum that God gave them at his Birth.

1. It might arise or be occasioned through the Cruelty of *Herod*; *for Jesus was born in* Bethlehem *the City where* David *dwelt*: But when *Herod* sent out to kill him, and for his sake killed all the young

29 7. 40, 41, 42, 52.] 7. 40, 41, 42.

Children in *Bethlehem*; then was *Joseph* warned by an Angel of God, to take the young Child and his Mother and fly into *Egypt*, and so he did, and was there till the Death of *Herod* (*Mat.* 2. 1, 13, 16, 19, 20.). After this the Angel comes to them in *Egypt*, and bids them take the young Child and return into the Land of *Israel*; wherefore they arose and went: but hearing that *Herod's* Son that Tyrant ruled in the room of his Father, they were afraid to go to *Bethlehem*, but turned aside into the Parts of *Galilee*, where they remained till the time of his shewing to *Israel*.

2. This stumble of theirs might arise from their not observing and keeping in mind the Alarum that God gave them of his Birth.

1. God began to give them the Alarum at the Birth of *John* the *Baptist*, where was asserted that he was to go before the Face of the Lord Jesus, and to prepare his Ways. *And fear came upon all that dwelt round about them; and all these sayings were noised abroad throughout all the hill-Countries of* Judea, Luk. 1. 65.

2. Again, What a continuation of this Alarum was there also at the Birth of Jesus, which was about three months after *John Baptist* was born. Now come the Angels from Heaven, now comes a strange Star over the Countrey to lead the Men of the East to the Stable where Jesus was born; now was *Herod*, the Priests, the Scribes, and also the City *Jerusalem* awakened and sore troubled: for it was noised by the Wise Men, that Christ the King and Saviour was born. Besides, The Shepherds, *Simon*, and *Anna* gave notice of him to the People; they should therefore have retained the Memory of these things, and have followed God in all his dark Providences, until his Son of Righteousness should arise among them with healing under his Wings.

3. I may add another cause of their stumble. They did not understand the Prophecies that went before of him.

1. He was to come to them out of *Egypt*. *Out of* Egypt *have I called my Son*, Mat. 2. 15.

2. He turned aside into *Cana* of *Galilee*, and dwelt in the City of *Nazareth*; *That it might be fulfilled which was spoken by the Prophets, he shall be called a* Nazaren, Mat. 2. 23.

3. That saying also was to be fulfilled. *The Land of* Zebulon, *and the Land of* Nepthaly, *by the way of the Sea beyond Jordan*, Galilee *of*

the Gentiles, *the People that sat in Darkness saw a great Light*, *and to them that sat in the region and shadow of Death*, *Light is sprung up*, Mat. 4. 12, 13, 14, 15, 16, 17.

At these things then they stumbled, and 'twas a great Judgment of God upon them.

Besides, There seemed to be a Contradiction in the Prophecies of the Scriptures concerning his Coming. He was to be *born* in *Bethlehem*, and yet to *come* out of *Egypt*: How should he be *the Christ*, and *yet* come out of *Galilee*, out of *which* ariseth *no* Prophet? Thus they stumbled.

Hence note, That though the Prophecies and Promises be full and plain *as these were*, that he should be born in *Bethlehem*; yet men's Sins may cause them to be fulfilled in such obscurity, that instead of having benefit thereby, they may stumble and split their Souls thereat.

Take heed then, hunt not Christ from plain Promises with *Herod*, hunt him not from *Bethlehem*, lest he appear to your amazement and destruction from *Egypt*, or in the Land of *Zebulon*. But thus much to the Second Question; to wit, *What it was for Jesus to come into the World*.

I come now to the Third Question.

Quest. 3. *What it was for him to come to be a Saviour.*

For the further handling of this Question I must shew:

1. What it is *to be* a Saviour.

2. What it is *to come* to be a Saviour.

3. What it is for *Jesus to come to be a Saviour*.

To these three briefly.

First, What it is to be a Saviour.

1. A Saviour supposeth some in misery, and himself one that is to deliver them.

2. A Saviour, is either such an one Ministerially, or Meritoriously.

Ministerially, is when one person engageth, or is engaged by virtue of respect or command from Superiours, to go and obtain by conquest or the Kings Redemption, the Captives or Persons grieved by the Tyranny of an Enemy. And thus was *Moses* and *Joshuah*, and the Judges and Kings of *Israel*, Saviours.

Thou deliveredst them into the Land of their Enemies who vexed them, and in the time of their trouble when they cried unto thee, thou heardest them from Heaven; and according to thy manifold mercies thou gavest them Saviours, who saved them out of the Hand of their Enemies, Nehem. 9. 27.

Thus was Jesus Christ a Saviour, he was engaged by virtue of respect and command from God, to obtain by conquest and redemption, the Captives or Persons grieved; *God sent his Son to be the Saviour of the World*, John 4. 42.

Meritoriously, is when the Person engaging, shall at his own proper cost and charge give a sufficient value or price for those he redeemeth.

Thus those under the Law were redeemed by the Mony called the Redemption-Mony. *And* Moses *gave the Mony of them that were redeemed unto* Aaron *and to his Sons*, Numb. 3. 46, 47, 48, 49, 50, 51.

And thus was Jesus Christ a Saviour; he paid full price to Divine Justice for Sinners, even his own precious Blood. *Forasmuch as you know that you were not redeemed from your vain Conversation, received by tradition from your Fathers, with corruptible things, as Silver and Gold, but with the precious Blood of Christ*, 1 Pet. 1. 18, 19.

And forasmuch as in mans redemption, the Undertaker must have respect, not only to the paying of a price, but also to the getting of a Victory; for there is not only Justice to satisfy, but Death, Devil, Hell, and the Grave to conquer: therefore hath he also by himself gotten the Victory over these.

1. He hath abolished Death, 2 *Tim.* 1. 10.
2. He hath destroyed the Devil, *Heb.* 2. 14, 15.
3. He hath been the destruction of the Grave, *Hos.* 13. 14.
4. He hath gotten the Keys of Hell, *Revel.* 1. 17, 18, 19.

And this I say, he did by himself at his own proper cost and charge, when he triumphed over them upon his Cross, *Col.* 2. 14, 15.

Quest. 2. Secondly, What it is *to come* to be a Saviour?

1. *To come to be one*, supposeth one, ordained, and fore-prepared for that work. *Then said he lo, I come a Body, hast thou prepared me*, Heb. 10.

2. To come to be a Saviour, supposeth, one commissionated, or authorized to that Work. *The Spirit of the Lord is upon me, because he hath anointed me* (authorized me) *to preach the Gospel to the Poor: He hath*

8 John 4. 42.] John 4. 14. 14 50, 51.] 51, 52. 22 Justice] Jesus

sent me to bind up the broken-hearted, to preach deliverance to the Captives, and recovering of sight to the Blind, and to set at liberty them that are bruised, Luk. 4. 18.

And upon this account it is, that he is so often called CHRIST, or the *Anointed* one; the Anointed Jesus, or Jesus the Anointed Saviour. *Thou art the Christ the Son of God, that should come into the World. This Jesus whom I preach unto you is Christ: He testified to the Jews, that Jesus was Christ, and he confounded the Jews which dwelt at* Damascus, *proving by the Scriptures that this is the very Christ*, Joh. 11. 27. Acts 17. 3. Chap. 18. 5. Chap. 9. 22. The very Anointed of God, or he whom God authorized and qualified to be the Saviour of the World.

3. To come to be a Saviour, supposeth a resolution to do that work before he goeth back. *I will ransom them from the power of the Grave; I will redeem them from death: O Death I will be thy Plague, O Grave I will be thy Destruction, Repentance shall be hid from mine Eyes*, Hos. 13. 14.

And as he resolved, *So he hath done.*

1. He hath purged our Sins, *Heb.* 1. 2, 3.

2. He hath perfected for ever (by one Offering) them that are sanctified, *Heb.* 10. 14.

3. He hath obtained Eternal Redemption for them, *Heb.* 9. 12. See further, 2 *Tim.* 1. 10. *Heb.* 9. 26. *Col.* 2. 15. *Heb.* 6. 18, 19, 20.

Quest. 3. I come now to the Third Question,

What it is for Jesus to come to be a Saviour.

1. *Ans.* It is the greatest discovery of mans misery and inability, to save himself therefrom, that ever was made in the World. Must the Son of God himself come down from Heaven? or can there be no Salvation? can not one Sinner save another? cannot man by any means redeem his Brother, nor give to God a Ransom for him? cannot an Angel do it? cannot all the Angels do it? no; Christ must come and die to do it.

2dly. It is the greatest discovery of the Love of God, that ever the World had. For God SO *to love the World*, as to send his Son! For God SO to commend his love to the World, as to send it to them in the Blood of his Son! Amazing Love! *John* 3. 16. *Rom.* 5. 8.

3dly. It is the greatest discovery of the Condescention of Christ that ever the World had.

1. *That he should not come to be ministred unto, but to minister; and to give his Life a Ransom for many*, Mat. 20. 28.

2. *That he should be manifest for this purpose, that he might destroy the works of the Devil*, 1 John 3. 8.

3. *That he should come that we might have life, and that we might have it more abundantly*, John 10. 10.

4. *That the Son of God should come to seek and to save that which was lost*, Luk. 19. 10.

5. *That he should not come to judg the World, but to save the World*, John 12. 47.

6. *That Christ Jesus should come into the World to save Sinners of whom I am chief*, 1. Tim. 1. 15.

7. *That he should love us and wash us from our Sins in his own Blood*, Revel. 1. 5. What amazing Condescention and Humility is this! *Phil.* 2. 6, 7, 8, 9.

How Jesus Christ addressed himself to the Work of our Redemption.

I Come then in the next place to shew you HOW Jesus Christ addressed himself to the Work of mans Redemption.

The Scripture saith, *he became poor:* That he made himself *of no reputation, and took upon him the form of a Servant, that he humbled himself unto death, even the Death of the Cross*. But particularly:

1. He took upon him our Flesh.
2. He was made under the Law.
3. He took upon him our Sins.
4. He bore the Curse due to our Sins.

First, *He took upon him our Flesh.* I shewed you before that he came in our Flesh, and now I must shew you the *Reason of it*: namely, Because, *That was the way to address himself to the Work of our Redemption.*

Wherefore, when the Apostle treated of the Incarnation of Christ, he addeth withal the reason, to wit, *That he might be capable to work out the Redemption of men.*

9 *World,*[1]] *World, to* 11 *World to*] *World*

There are three things to be considered in this 1st Head.

1. That he took our Flesh; *for this Reason*, That he might be a Saviour.

2. *How he took flesh*, that he might be our Saviour.

3. *That it was necessary* that he should take our Flesh, if indeed he will be our Saviour.

For the First, That he took our Flesh, for *this Reason, That he might be a Saviour: For what the Law could not do in that it was weak through the Flesh, God sending his own Son in the likeness of sinful flesh, and for sin condemned sin in the Flesh*, Rom. 8. 3, 4.

The Sum of the Words is, forasmuch as the Law could do us no good, by reason of the inability that is in our flesh to do it (for the Law can do us no good until it be fulfilled) and because God had a desire that good should come to us, therefore did he send his Son *in our likeness*, clothed with flesh, to destroy by his doing the Law, the tendency of the Sin that dwells in our flesh. He therefore took our flesh, that our Sin, with its effects, might by him be condemned and overcome.

The Reason therefore why he took flesh, is, Because *he would be our Saviour*.

Forasmuch then as the Children are Partakers of Flesh and blood, he also likewise took part of the same, that through death he might destroy him that had the Power of Death, that is the Devil, and deliver them, who through fear of death were all their life-time subject to bondage, Heb. 2. 14, 15.

In these words it is asserted, that he took our flesh for certain Reasons.

1. Because the Children, the Heirs of Heaven, are Partakers of Flesh and Blood. *Forasmuch then as the Children are Partakers of Flesh and Blood, he also himself took part of the same.* Had the Children, the Heirs, been without flesh, he himself had not taken it upon him: had the Children been Angels, he had taken upon him the Nature of Angels; but because the Children were Partakers of Flesh, therefore, leaving Angels, or refusing to take hold of Angels, *he took Flesh and Blood*, the Nature of the Children; that he might put himself into a capacity to save and deliver the Children. Therefore it follows, *That through death he might destroy him that had the Power of Death, that is the Devil.*

This therefore was another Reason, that he might destroy the Devil.

The Devil had bent himself against the Children: he is *their Adversary*, and goeth forth to make war with them. *The Devil your Adversary: And he went to make war with the Remnant of her Seed*, 1 Pet. 5. 8. Revel. 12. Now the Children could not destroy him, because he had already cast them into sin; defiled their Nature, and laid them under the Wrath of God, Therefore Christ *puts himself among the Children*, and into the Nature of the Children; that he might, by means of his Dying in their Flesh, destroy the Devil; that is, take away Sin, his Work, *that he might destroy the Works of the Devil*; for sin is the great Engine of Hell, by which he overthroweth all that perish: Now this did Christ destroy, by taking on him the similitude of Sinful Flesh; of which more anon.

That he might destroy him that had the Power of Death, that is the Devil, and deliver them. This was the thing in chief intended, that he might deliver *the Children*, that he might deliver *them* from death, the Fruit of their Sin; and from Sin, the Sting of that Death. *That he might deliver them, who through the Fear of Death, were all their Life-time subject to bondage.*

He took flesh therefore, because the Children had it; he took it that he might die for the Children, he took it that he might deliver the Children from the Works of the Devil; *that he might deliver them.* No Deliverance had come to the Children if the Son of God had not taken their Flesh and Blood. *Therefore he took our Flesh that he might be our Saviour.*

Again, In a Saviour there must be not only Merit, but Compassion and Sympathy; because the Children are yet to live by Faith, are not yet come to the Inheritance. *It behoved him therefore in all things to be made like unto his Brethren, that he might be a Merciful and Faithful High-Priest in things pertaining to God, to make Reconciliation for the Sins of the People*, Heb. 2. 17, 18.

Two Reasons are rendred in this Text, *why he must take Flesh*; namely, that he might be their Priest, to offer Sacrifice, to wit, *his Body and Blood for them*; and that he might be merciful and faithful, to pitty and preserve them unto the Kingdom appointed for them.

Mark you therefore, how the Apostle, when he asserteth that the Lord Jesus took our Flesh, urgeth the reason why he took our Flesh. THAT he might destroy the Devil and Death, THAT he might deliver them. It behoved him to be made like unto his Brethren, THAT he might be merciful and faithful, THAT he might make Reconciliation for the Sins of the People. The Reason therefore why he took our Flesh is declared, to wit, *That he might be our Saviour*. And hence you find it so often recorded; *He hath abolished in his Flesh the Enmity*; *He hath slain the Enmity by his Flesh*; *and you who were sometimes Aliens and Enemies in your Minds by wicked works: yet, now hath he reconciled, in the Body of his Flesh, through death, to present you holy and unblameable in his Sight*, Ephes. 2. 15, 16. Col. 1. 21, 22.

How he took Flesh.

I Come now to the Second Question, to wit, *How he took our Flesh*. This must be inquired into, for his taking Flesh was not after the common way, never any took man's Flesh upon him as he, since the Foundation of the World.

1. He took not our flesh like *Adam*, who was formed out of the Ground. *Who was made of the Dust of the Ground*, Gen. 2. 7. Chap. 3. 19.

2. He took not our flesh as we do by Carnal Generation. *Joseph* knew not his Wife, neither did *Mary* know any Man, *till she had brought forth her First-born Son*, Luk. 1. 34. Mat. 1. 25.

3. He took flesh then, *by the immediate working and over-shadowing of the Holy Ghost*: and hence it is said expresly; *She was found with Child of the Holy Ghost. Now the Birth of Jesus Christ was on this wise: When-as his Mother* Mary *was espoused to* Joseph (*before they came together*), *she was found with Child of the Holy Ghost*, Mat. 1. 18. And hence again, When *Joseph* doubted of her Honesty (for he perceived she was with Child and knew he had not touched her) the Angel of God, himself comes down to resolve his doubt, and said, Joseph *thou Son of* David, *Fear not, to take unto thee* Mary *thy Wife*, *for that which is conceived in her, is of the Holy Ghost*, Mat. 1. 20.

But again, Though the Holy Ghost was that by which the Child

Jesus was formed in the Womb, so as to be without Carnal Generation; yet was he not formed in her without, but by her Conception. *Behold, thou shalt conceive in thy Womb, and bring forth a Son, and shalt call his Name* Jesus, Luk. 1. 31. Wherefore, he took flesh not only IN, but OF the Virgin. Hence he is called HER Son, the SEED of the Woman. And hence it is also that he is called the *Seed* OF *Abraham*, the *Seed* OF *David*; THEIR *Seed according to the Flesh*, Luk. 2. 7. Gen. 13. 15. Chap. 12. Chap. 22. Gal. 3. 16. Chap. 4. 4. Rom. 1. 3. Luk. 1. 32. Rom. 9. 5.

And this the Work he undertook, required.

1. It required that he should take *our Flesh*.

2. It required that he should take our Flesh *without sin*, which could not be, had he taken it by reason of a Carnal Generation; for so, all Children are conceived *in*, and polluted *with* sin, *Psal.* 51. And the least pollution, either of flesh or spirit, had utterly disabled him for the Work, *which to do*, he came down from Heaven. Therefore, *Such an High-Priest became us, who is holy, harmless, undefiled, separate from Sinners, and made higher than the Heavens*, Heb. 7. 26.

This Mystery of the Incarnation of the Son of God was thus compleated: I say, That he might be in all points like as we are, *yet without sin*; for sin in the Flesh disableth, and maketh incapable to do the Commandment. Therefore was he thus *made*, thus *made of a Woman*: And this the Angel assigneth as the Reason of this his Marvelous Incarnation: *The Holy Ghost*, saith he, *shall come upon thee, and the Power of the Highest shall overshadow thee; therefore also that Holy thing that shall be born of thee, shall be called the Son of God*, Luk. 1. 35.

The Overshadowing of the Holy Ghost, and the Power of the Highest; the Father, and the Holy Ghost, brought this Wonderful thing to pass; for Jesus is *a Wonderful One*, in his Conception and Birth. This Mystery is that, next to the Mystery of three Persons in one God. It is a great Mystery. *Great is the Mystery of Godliness; God was manifested in the Flesh.*

The Conclusion is, That Jesus Christ *took* our Flesh, that he might be our Saviour; and that he might be our Saviour *indeed*, he THUS took our Flesh.

---

26 Luk. 1. 35.] Luk. 2. 35.

That it was necessary that he should take our Flesh, if he will be our Saviour.

I Come now to the Third Thing, namely, That it was necessary that he should take our Flesh if he will be our Saviour.

And that first, from *the Nature of the Work*; his Work was to save, to save man, sinking man: man that was going down to the Pit, *Job* 33. 24. Now he that will save him that is sinking, must take hold on him. And since he was not to save a *Man*, but *Men*; therefore it was necessary that he should take hold, not of one Person, but of the Common Nature, clothing himself with *part of the same*.

He took not hold of Angels, but took on him the Seed of Abraham. For THAT Flesh was the same with the whole Lump of the Children, to whom the Promise was made; and comprehended in it the Body of them that shall be saved, even as in *Adam* was comprehended the whole World at first, *Rom.* 5.

Hence we are said to be *chosen in him*, to be gathered, *being in him*, to be dead *by him*, to be risen *with him* and to be *set with him*, or *in him in Heavenly Places already*, Ephes. 1. 4, 10. Rom. 7. 4. Col. 3. 1, 2, 3. Chap. 2. 12, 13.

This then was the Wisdom of the great God, that the Eternal Son of his Love should take hold of, and so secure the sinking Souls of perishing Sinners by assuming their Flesh.

Secondly, The *Manner of his doing the Work of a Saviour*, did call for his taking of our Flesh.

He must do the Work *by dying: Ought not Christ to have suffered? Christ must needs have suffered*, Luk. 24. 26. Acts 17. 3. or else no glory follows. The Prophets testified beforehand the Sufferings of Christ, *and the Glory that should follow*, 1 Pet. 1. 11. Yea, they did it by the Spirit, even by the Spirit of Christ himself. This Spirit then did bid them tell the World, yea, testify that Christ must suffer, or no man be blest with Glory. For the threatning of death, and the Curse of the Law lay in the Way between Heaven-Gates and the Souls of the Children, for their sins; wherefore he that will save them, *must answer Divine Justice, or God must lye in saving them without inflicting the Punishment threatned.* Christ then must needs have suffered, the

7 *Job* 33. 24.] *Job*. 34. 24.

Manner of the Work, laid a necessity upon him to take our Flesh upon him; *he must die*, he must die *for us*, he must die *for our Sins.* And this was effectually foretold by all the Bloody Sacrifices that were offered under the Law; The Blood of Bulls, the Blood of Lambs, the Blood of Rams, the Blood of Calves, and the Blood of Goats and Birds. These Bloody Sacrifices, what did they signifie, what were they figures of, *but of the bloody Sacrifice of the Body of Jesus Christ*; their Blood being a Shadow of his Blood, and their Flesh being a Shadow of his Flesh?

Therefore when God declared that he took no pleasure in them, because they could not make the Worshippers perfect as pertaining to the Conscience; *then comes Jesus Christ* to offer his Sinless Body and Soul for the Sin of the People: *For it is not possible that the Blood of Bulls and Goats should take away sin: wherefore, when he cometh into the World, he saith, Sacrifices and Offerings thou wouldest not, but a Body hast thou prepared me; in Burnt-Offerings and Sacrifices for sin thou hast had no pleasure. Then said I, lo, I come, in the Volume of thy Book it is written of me to do thy good Will.* Since Burnt-Offerings cannot do thy Will, my Body shall; since the Blood of Bulls and Goats cannot do thy Will, my Blood shall.

Then follows, By the Will of God we are Sanctified *through the offering up of the Body of Jesus Christ once for all*, Heb. 10. 8, 9, 10.

Thirdly, *The End of the Work* required, That Christ, if he will be our Saviour, should take upon him our Flesh.

The End of our Salvation is, That we might enjoy God, and that he by us might be glorified for ever and ever.

1. That we might enjoy God. *I will dwell in them, and they shall be my People, and I will be their God.* This Indwelling of God, and consequently our Enjoyment of him, begins first in its Eminency, by his Possessing our Flesh in the Person of Jesus Christ. Hence his Name is called *Emmanuel, God with us*; and the Word was made Flesh and dwelt amongst us. The Flesh of Christ, is the Tabernacle which the Lord pitched, according to that saying: *The Tabernacle of God is with men, and he will dwell with them, and they shall be his People, and God himself shall be with them, and be their God*, Revel. 21. 3. Here God beginneth to discover his Glory, and to be desirable to the Sons of Men.

God could not communicate himself to us, nor take us into the Enjoyment of himself, but with respect to that Flesh which his Son took of the Virgin, because sin stood betwixt. Now this Flesh, *only*, *was the Holy Lump*; in this Flesh God could dwell, and forasmuch as this Flesh is the same with ours, and was taken up with intent that what was done, in, and by that, should be communicated to all the Children; therefore through that, doth God communicate of himself unto his People. *God was in Christ reconciling the World unto himself.* And, *I am the Way*, saith Christ, *no man cometh to the Father but by me*, 2 Cor. 5. 19. Joh. 14. 6.

That Passage to the *Hebrews* is greatly to our purpose: *We have boldness, Brethren, to enter into the Holiest (the place where God is), by the Blood of Jesus, by a new and living Way which he hath Consecrated for us through the Vail, that is to say, his Flesh*, Heb. 10. 19, 20. Wherefore by the Flesh and Blood of Christ, we enter into the Holiest; through the Vail, saith he, *that is to say, his Flesh.*

2. As the End of our Salvation, is, *That we might enjoy God*: so also it is that *he* by *us* might be Glorified for ever. *That God in all things might be Glorified through Jesus Christ our Lord.*

Here indeed will the Mistery of his Grace, Wisdom, Justice, Power, Holiness, and Glory, *inhabit Eternal praise*, while we that are counted worthy of the Kingdom of God, shall admire at the Mistery and see our selves, without our selves, even by the Flesh and Blood of Christ (through Faith therein) effectually, and Eternally saved. O! This will be the burden of our Eternal Joy; *God loved us, and gave his Son for us, Christ loved us, and gave his Flesh for our Life*, and his Blood for our Eternal Redemption and Salvation.

That Christ was made under the Law.

BUt Secondly, *Christ was made under the Law. When the fulness of the time was come, God sent forth his Son, made of a Woman, made under the Law*, Gal. 4. 4.

Of right, being found in flesh, he must needs be under the Law, for that there is not any Creature, above or without Law to God

10 2. Cor. 5. 19.] 2 Cor. 5.

(but this is not to the point in hand), Christ was not *therefore* under the Law because he was found in flesh, but he took flesh, and *designedly* put himself, or was made under the Law; wherefore 'tis added, he was made under the Law to *Redeem*, to redeem them that were under the Law. Wherefore here is a design, an Heavenly contrivance, and device on foot. Christ is made, that is, by design, subjected under the Law, for the sake, and upon the account of others: *To redeem them that were under the Law.*

Made under the Law; that is, put himself into the Room of Sinners, into the Condition of Sinners; made himself subject to the same pains and penalties we were obnoxious to. We were under the Law, and it had dominion over us, bound us *upon pain of Eternal Damnation* to do compleatly all things written in the Law. This Condition Christ put himself into, *that he might redeem*: for assuredly we had else perished.

The Law had dominion over us, and since we had sinned, of right it pronounced the Curse, and made all men subject to the Wrath of God. Christ therefore did not only come into our Flesh, *but also into our Condition*, into the Valley and Shadow of Death where we were, and where we are as we are Sinners. He that is under the Law, is under the Edge of the Axe. When *David* was to go visit his Brethren, and to save them from the Hand of *Goliah*, he was to look how his Brethren fared, *and to take their Pledg*, 1 Sam. 17. 18. This is true of Jesus Christ, when he came to save us from the Hand of Death and the Law; he looked how his Brethren fared, took to heart their deplorable Condition, and put himself into the same *Plight*, to wit, *under the Law*, *that he might redeem them that were under the Law*.

I told you before, that he came sinless into the World, that he had a miraculous Conception, and wonderful Birth: And here you see a Reason for it, he was to be put, or made under the Law *to redeem*. He that will be made under the Law *to redeem*, had need be sinless, and spotless himself; for the Law findeth fault with the least, and condemneth man for the first beginning of Sin.

Without this then there could not have been Redemption, nor any the Sons of God by Adoption; no Redemption, because the Sentence of Death had already past upon all; no Sons by Adoption, because that's the Effect of Redemption. God sent forth his Son made of a Woman, made under the Law to redeem them that were under the Law, *That we might receive the Adoption of Sons.* Christ then by being made under the Law, hath recovered *his* from under the Law, and obtained for them the Priviledg of the Adoption of Sons.

For as I told you before, Christ stood a Common Person, presenting in himself the whole Lump of the promised *Seed*, or the *Children* of the Promise; wherefore he comes under the Law *for them*, takes upon him to do what the Law required *of them*, takes upon him to do *it for them.*

He began therefore at the first Tittle of the Law, and going in mans Flesh, for man, through the Law, *He becomes the End of the Law for righteousness, for every one that believeth.* The END of the Law, what is the End of the Law, but perfect and sinless Obedience? that is the End of the Law both with respect to its Nature, and the Cause of its being imposed. God gave the Law, that compleat Righteousness should by that be found upon men, but because sin was got into man's Flesh, therefore this Righteousness, by us, could not be compleated: Now comes Christ the Lord into the World, clothes himself with the Children's Flesh, addresseth himself to the Work of their Redemption, is *made under the Law*; and going through every part of the Law without Sin, he becometh *the End of the Law* for Justifying Righteousness to every one that believeth, *Rom.* 10. 4. For he obeyed not the Law for himself, he needed no obedience thereto: 'Twas we that needed obedience, 'twas we that wanted to answer the Law, we wanted it but could not obtain it, because then the Law was weak through the Flesh; therefore God sent his own Son, and he did our duty for us, even to become the End of the Law to every one that believeth: In this therefore Christ laboured for us, he was made under the Law *to redeem.* Therefore, as I said before, It behoved him to be sinless, because the Law binds over to answer for sin at the Bar of the Judgment of God. Therefore did his God-Head assume our humane Flesh, in a clean and spotless way that he might come under *the Law, to redeem them that were under the Law.*

For consisting of two Natures, and the Personality lieing in the God-Head, which gave value and worth to all things done for us by the Man-hood, the Obedience takes denomination from thence, *to be the Obedience of God.* The Sons Righteousness, the Sons Blood; the Righteousness of God, the Blood of God, *Heb.* 5. 8, 9. *Phil.* 3. 7, 8, 9. *Acts* 20. 28. 1 *John* 3. 16.

Thus Jesus Christ came into the World under the Law to redeem; not simply as God, but God-Man, both natures making one Christ. The God-head therefore did influence and give value to the human Flesh of Christ in all its Obedience to the Law; else there would have been wanting that Perfection of Righteousness which only could answer the Demands and Expectation of the Justice of God, to wit, *Perfect Righteousness by Flesh.*

But the Second Person in the God-head, the Son, the Word, coming under the Law for men in their Flesh, and subjecting himself by that Flesh to every tittle, and demand of the Law; all, and every whit of what was acted, and done by Jesus Christ God-man for us, *it was, and is the Righteousness of God*: and since it was not done for himself, *but for us* (as he saith in the Text, *to redeem*). The Righteousness by which we are set free from the Law, is none other but the Righteousness that alone resideth in the Person of the Son of God.

And that it is absolutely necessary thus it should be, is evident, both with respect to God, and also with respect to Man.

1. With respect to God. The Righteousness is demanded by God: therefore he that comes to redeem, must present before God a Righteousness absolutely perfect; this can be done by none but God.

2. With respect to Man. Man was to present this Righteousness to God, therefore must the Undertaker be man. Man for Man, and God for God, God-Man between God and Men. This Days-man can lay his Hand upon us both, and bring God and Man together in peace, *Job.* 9. 33.

Quest. *But some may say, What need of the Righteousness of one that is naturally God? had* Adam *who was but a meer Man stood in his Innocency and done his duty, he had saved himself and all his Posterity.*

Ans. Had *Adam* stood he had so long secured himself (from the Wages of Sin) and Posterity so long as they were in him. But had

3–4 *Phil.* 3. 7, 8, 9.] *Phil.* 3. 7, 8. 33 meer] mean

Adam sinned, yea, although he had not defiled his Nature with filth, he could never after that have redeemed himself from the Curse of the Law; because he was not equal with God: for the Curse of the Law is the Curse of God, but no man can deliver himself from the Curse of God, having first transgressed. This is evident because Angels, for sin, lie bound in Chains, and can never deliver *themselves.*

He therefore that redeemeth man from under the Law, must, not only do all the good that the Law requireth, but bear all the Penalty that is due by the Law for sin.

Should an Angel assume human Flesh, and in that Flesh do the Law, this Righteousness would not redeem a Sinner, it would be but the Righteousness of an Angel, and so, far short of such a Righteousness as can secure a Sinner from the Wrath of God. *But thou shalt love the Lord thy God with all thy Soul, with all thy Heart, with all thy Mind, with all thy Strength.* If there was no more required of us, now to redeem our selves, it would be utterly impossible for us to do it, because in the best there is sin, which will intermix it self with every duty of Man. This being so, *all* the Heart, *all* the Soul, *all* the Strength, and *all* the Mind, to the exact requirement of the Justice of the Law, can never be found in a Natural Man.

Besides, For this Work there is required a perfect Memory, always to keep in mind the whole Duty of Man, the whole of every tittle of all the Law, *lest sin come in by forgetfulness.*

2. A perfect Knowledg and Judgment, *lest sin come in by ignorance.*

3. An everlasting Unweariedness in all, *lest sin and continual Temptations tire the Soul,* & cause it to fail before the whole be done.

For the Accomplishing this last, he must have,

1. *A Perfect Willingness,* without the least thought to the contrary.

2. *Such an hatred of sin,* as is not to be found, but in the Heart of God.

3. *A full delight in every Duty,* and that in the midst of all temptations.

4. A continuing in all things to the well-pleasing of the Justice of God.

I say, should the penalty of the Law be taken off, should God forgive the Penalty and Punishment due to sins that are past, and only demand good works now, according to the Tenour of the Law, no man could be saved: there would not be found that Heart, that Soul, that Mind and that Strength any-where in the World.

This therefore must cease for ever unless the Son of God will put his Shoulder to the Work; but blessed be God he hath done it: *When the fulness of the time was come, God sent forth his Son, made of a Woman, made under the Law, to redeem them that are under the Law.*

Christ took upon him our Sins.

BUt Thirdly, Christ our Saviour takes upon him our Sins. This is another step to the Work of our Redemption. *He hath made him to be sin for us.* Strange Doctrine! a Fool would think it blasphemy, but Truth hath said it. Truth, I say, hath said, not that he *was* made to be sin, but that GOD made him to be sin. *He hath made him to be sin for us*, 2 Cor. 5. 21.

This therefore sheweth us how effectually Christ Jesus undertook the Work of our Redemption. *He was made to be sin for us.* Sin is the great block and bar to our happiness; sin is the Procurer of all miseries to men both here and for ever. Take away sin, and nothing can hurt us; for death Temporal, death Spiritual, and death Eternal is the Wages of sin, *Rom.* 6. 23.

Sin then, and man for Sin, is the Object of the Wrath of God. If the Object of the Wrath of God, then is his Case most dreadful; for who can bear, who can grapple with the Wrath of God! Men cannot, Angels cannot, the whole World cannot. All therefore must sink under sin, but he who is made to be sin for us; he only can bear sins, *he only can bear them away*; and therefore were they laid upon him. *The Lord laid upon him the Iniquities of us all*, Isa. 53. 6.

Mark therefore, and you shall find, that the Reason why God made him to be sin for us, was, *That we might be made the Righteousness of God in him.* He took our Flesh, he was made under the Law, and was made to be sin for us; that the Devil might be destroyed, that the Captives might be redeemed, *and made the Righteousness of God in him.*

14 2 Cor. 5. 21.] 1 Cor. 5. 21. 27 Isa. 53. 6.] Isa. 53.

And forasmuch as he saith, that GOD *hath made him to be sin*, it declareth that the Design of God, and the Mistery of his Will and Grace was in it. *He hath made him to be sin.* God hath done it, that we might be made the Righteousness of God in him: there was no other way, the Wisdom of Heaven could find no other way, we could not by other means stand just before the Justice of God.

Now what remains, but that we who are reconciled to God by Faith in his Blood, are quit, discharged, and set free from the Law of Sin and Death? Yea, what encouragement to trust in him, when we read *That God made him to be sin for us.*

Quest. *But how was Jesus Christ made of God to be sin for us?*

Ans. Even so as if himself had committed all our Sins; that is, they were as really charged upon him, as if himself had been the Actor and Committer of them all. *He hath made him to be sin*; not only as a Sinner, but as Sin itself. He was as the Sin of the World, that Day he stood before God in our steed. Some indeed will not have Jesus Christ our Lord to be made sin for us, their Wicked Reasons think this to be *wrong Judgment in the Lord*: it seems, supposing, that because they cannot imagine how it should be; therefore God, if he does it, *must do it at his Peril*, and must be charged with doing wrong Judgment, and so, things that become not his Heavenly Majesty: But against this Duncish Sophistry, we set *Paul* and *Isaiah*, the one telling us still, *The Lord laid on him the Iniquities of us all*; and the other, *That God made him to be sin for us.*

But these Men, as I suppose, think it enough for Christ to *die under that Notion only*, not knowing nor feeling the Burden of Sin, and the Wrath of God due thereto. These make him as senceless in his Dieing and as much without reason, as a silly Sheep or Goat who also died for Sin, but so as in name, in shew, and shadow only. They felt not the proper Weight, Guilt, and Judgment of God for Sin.

But thou, Sinner, who art so in thine own Eyes, and, who feelest guilt in thine own Conscience; Know then, that Jesus Christ the Son of the Living God in flesh, was made to be sin for thee, or stood sensibly guilty of all thy Sins before God, and bare them in his own Body upon the Cross.

God charged our Sins upon Christ, and that in their guilt and burden; what remaineth, but that the Charge was real or feigned?

if real, then he hath either perished under them, or carried them away from before God: if they were charged but feignedly, then did he but feignedly die for them, then shall we have but feigned benefit by his Death, and but a feigned Salvation at last; not to say how this Cursed Doctrine chargeth God and Christ with Hypocrisy, the one in saying He made Christ to be sin, the other in saying He bare our sin; when indeed, and in truth, our guilt and burden never was really upon him.

Quest. *But might not Christ die for our Sins, but he needs must bear their Guilt or Burden?*

Ans. He that can sever sin, and guilt, sin and the Burden, each from other, laying sin and no guilt, sin and no burden *on the Person that dieth for Sin*, must do it only in his own imaginary Head. No Scripture, nor Reason, nor Sense, saith, understandeth, or feeleth sin when charged, without its guilt and burden.

And here we must distinguish between sin charged, and sin forgiven. Sin forgiven, may be seen without guilt or burden, though I think not *without shame* in this World: But sin charged, and that by the Justice of God, for so it was upon Christ, this cannot be, but guilt and the burthen, as inseparable companions, must unavoidably lye on that Person. Poor Sinner, be advised to take heed of such deluded Preachers, who with their Tongues smoother than Oil, would rob thee of that Excellent Doctrine, *God hath made him to be sin for us*: for such, as I said, do not only present thee with a feigned deliverance and forgiveness, with a feigned Heaven and Happiness, but charge God and the Lord Jesus as meer Impostors, who while they tell us that *Christ was made of God to be sin for us*, affirm, that it was not so REALLY, suggesting this Sophistical Reason, *no wrong Judgment comes from the Lord.* I say again, this Wicked Doctrine is the next way to turn the Gospel in thy thoughts, to no more than a Cunningly-devised Fable, 2 *Pet.* 1. 16. and to make Jesus Christ in his dying for our Sins, as brutish as the Paschal-Lamb in *Moses*'s Law.

Wherefore, distressed Sinner, when thou findest it recorded in the Word of Truth, that Christ *died for our Sins, and that God hath made him to be sin for us*: Then do thou consider of sin as it is a

31 2 *Pet.* 1. 16.] 2 Pet. 1.

Transgression against the Law of God, and that, as such, it procureth the Judgment of God, torments and afflicts the Mind with guilt, and bindeth over the Soul to answer it: sever not sin and guilt asunder, lest thou be an Hypocrite like these wicked Men, and rob Christ of his true Sufferings. Besides, to see sin upon Christ but not its guilt, to see sin upon Christ, but not the Legal Punishment; what is this but to conclude, that either there is no guilt and punishment in sin, or that Christ bare our sin, but we the Punishment? for the Punishment must be born, because the Sentence is gone out from the Mouth of God against sin.

Do thou therefore, as I have said, consider of sin as a Transgression of the Law, 1 *John* 3. 4. and a Provoker of the Justice of God, which done, turn thine Eye to the Cross, and behold those Sins, in the Guilt and Punishment of them, sticking in the Flesh of Christ. *God condemned sin in the Flesh of Christ. He bare our Sins IN his own Body on the Tree*, Rom. 8. 3. 1 Pet. 2. 24.

I would only give thee this Caution, not sin in the Nature of sin; Sin was not so in the Flesh of Christ, but sin in the Natural Punishment of it, to wit, Guilt, and the Chastising Hand of Justice. *He was wounded for our Transgressions, he was bruised for our Iniquities: The Chastisements of our Peace were upon him, and by his Stripes we are healed*, Isa. 53. 5.

Look then upon Christ crucified to be as the sin of the World, as if He only had broken the Law; which done, behold him perfectly innocent in himself, and so conclude, that for the transgressions of God's People he was stricken: That when the Lord made him to be sin, He made him to be sin FOR US.

He was made a Curse for us.

FOurthly, As he was made Flesh under the Law, and also Sin; so he was made a Curse for us. *Christ hath redeemed us from the Curse of the Law, being made a Curse for us; as it is written, Cursed is every one that hangeth on a Tree.* This Sentence is taken out of *Moses* being passed there upon them that for Sin are worthy of death.

12 1 *John* 3. 4.] 1 *John* 3.   22 Isa. 53. 5.] Isa. 53.   31 *Curse*[1]] *Cross*

And if a Man have committed a Sin worthy of death, and thou hang him on a Tree, his Body shall not remain all night upon the Tree, but thou shalt in anywise bury him that Day, for he that is hanged is accursed of God. By this Sentence *Paul* concludeth that Jesus Christ was Justly hanged, because sin worthy of Death was upon him. Sin, not of his own but ours. Since then he took our Sins, he must be cursed of God; for sin is sin where-ever it lies, and justice is justice where-ever it finds it: wherefore since Jesus Christ will bear our Sin, he must be *numbred with the Transgressors*, and counted worthy to die the Death.

He that committeth sin is worthy of death: This, though Christ did not personally do, his Members, his Body, which is his Church, did: and since he would undertake for them with God, and stand in their Sins before the Eyes of his Justice; He must die the Death by the Law.

Sin and the Curse cannot be severed. Sin must be followed with the Curse of God: Sin therefore being removed from us to the Back of Christ, thither goes also the Curse; for if sin be found upon him, he is the Person worthy to die, worthy *by our Sins*. Wherefore *Paul* here setteth forth Christ clothed with our Sins; and so taking from us the Guilt and Punishment. What punishment, but the Wrath and Displeasure of God. *Christ hath redeemed us from the Curse of the Law, being made a Curse for us.*

In this word [Curse] are two things comprized.

1. The Reality of Sin, for there can be no Curse where there is no Sin; either of the Persons own, or made to be his by his own Consent or the Imputation of Divine Justice. And since Sins are made to be Christ's by Imputation, they are his, though not *naturally*, yet *really*, and consequently the Wages due: He hath made him to be sin; he was made a Curse for us.

2. This word Curse comprizeth therefore the Punishment of Sin, that Punishment properly due to sin from the Hand of God's Justice, which punishment standeth in three things.

1. In charging sin upon the Body and Soul of the Person concerned: and hence we read that both the Body and Soul of Christ, *were made an Offering for Sin*, Isa. 53. 10. Heb. 10. 10.

2. The Punishment standeth in Gods inflicting of the Just merits of sin upon him that standeth charged therewith, and that is Death

in its own nature and strength; to wit, Death with the Sting thereof: *The Sting of Death is sin.* This Death did Christ die, because he died for our Sins.

3. The Sorrows and Pains of this Death therefore must be undergone by Jesus Christ. Now there are divers Sorrows in Death.

1. Such Sorrows as Brutes are subject to.

2. Such Sorrows as Persons are subject to, that stand in sin before God.

3. Such Sorrows as those undergo who are swallowed up of the Curse and Wrath of God for ever.

Now so much of all kind of Sorrow as the Imputation of our Sin, could justly bring from the Hand of Divine Justice, so much of it he had.

1. He had Death.

2. He had the Sting of Death, which is Sin.

3. He was forsaken of God, but could not by any means have those Sorrows which they have that are everlastingly swallowed up of them. *It was not possible that he should be holden of it*, Act. 2. 24.

For where Sin is charged and born, there must of necessity follow the Wrath and Curse of God: Now where the Wrath and Curse of God is, there must of necessity follow the Effects, the *Natural Effects.*

I say, the *Natural Effects*: to wit, the Sence, the Sorrowful Sence of the Displeasure of an Infinite Majesty, and his Chastisements for the Sin that hath provoked him.

There are Effects *natural*, and Effects *accidental*; those Accidental, are such as flow from our weakness, whilst we wrestle with the Judgment of God; to wit, hellish fear, despair, rage, blasphemy, and the like: These were not incident to Jesus Christ, he being in his own Person every way perfect. Neither did he alwayes endure the Natural Effects; his Merits relieved, and delivered him. God loosed the Pains of death, *because it was not possible he should be holden of it*, Acts 2. 24.

Christ then was made a Curse for us, for he did bear our sin; the Punishment therefore, from the Revenging Hand of God must needs fall upon him.

Wherefore, *by these four things*, we see how Christ became our Saviour, he took hold of our Nature, was born under the Law, was made to be sin, and the Accursed of God for us. And observe it; all this, as I said before, was the Handy-Work of God. *God made him Flesh, made him under the Law, God made him to be Sin, and also a Curse for us.* The Lord bruised him, the Lord put him to grief, the Lord made his Soul an Offering for Sin, *Isa.* 53. Not for that he hated him, considering him in his own harmless, innocent, and blessed Person; for he was daily his Delight; but by an act of grace to us-ward, were our Iniquities laid upon him, and he in our stead, bruised and chastised for them. God loved us, *and made him a Curse for us.* He was made a Curse for us, *That the Blessing of* Abraham *might come on the Gentiles, through Faith in Jesus Christ*, Gal. 3. 13, 14, 15.

Further Demonstration of this Truth.

BEfore I pass *this Truth*, I will present thee (Courteous Reader) with two or three Demonstrations for its further confirmation.

First, That Christ did bear our Sin and Curse, is clear *because he died*, and that without a Mediator.

1. He died, *Death is the Wages of Sin*, Rom. 6. 23. Now if death be the Wages of sin, and that be true, *that Christ did die and not sin*, either the Course of Justice is perverted, or else he died for our Sins; *there was no cause of death in him*, yet he died, *Act.* 13. 28. He did no Evil, Guile was not found in his Mouth, yet he received the Wages of Sin. Sin therefore, though not of his own, was found upon him, and laid to his Charge, *because he died. Christ died for our Sins, Christ gave himself for our Sins*, 1 Cor. 15. 1, 2, 3. Gal. 1. 4. 1 Pet. 2. 22.

He then that will conclude that Christ did not bear our Sin, chargeth God foolishly, for delivering him up to death: for laying on him the Wages, when in no sence he deserved the same. Yea he overthroweth the whole Gospel, for that hangeth on THIS hinge, *Christ died for our Sins.*

Object. *But all that die, do not bear the Curse of God for Sin.*

Ans. But all that die without a Mediator do: Angels died the Cursed Death, because Christ took not hold of them; and they for whom Christ never prayeth, they die the Cursed Death, for they perish everlastingly in the unutterable Torments of Hell. *Christ too died*, that Death which is the Proper Wages of Sin, for he had none to stand for him. *I looked*, saith he, *and there was none to help, and I wondred that there was none to uphold: therefore mine own Arm brought Salvation unto me. And he saw that there was no man*: *and he wondered that there was no Intercessor*, *therefore his Arm brought Salvation unto him*, *and his Righteousness sustained him*, Isa. 63. 5. Isa. 59. 16.

Christ then died, or endured the Wages of Sin, and that without an Intercessor, without one between God and he: He grappled immediatly with the Eternal Justice of God, who inflicted on him *Death*, the Wages of Sin: there was no man to hold off the Hand of God; Justice had his full blow at him, and made him a Curse for Sin. He died for sin without a Mediator, he died the Cursed Death.

Secondly, A Second thing that Demonstrateth that Christ died the Cursed Death for Sin: *It is the Frame of Spirit that he was in at the time that he was to be taken.*

Never was poor mortal so beset with the apprehensions of approaching death as was this Lord Jesus Christ; *Amazement beyond measure*, *Sorrow that exceeded* seized upon his Soul. *My Soul*, saith he, *is exceeding sorrowful even unto Death. And he began*, saith Mark, *to be sore amazed*, *and to be very heavy*, Mat. 26. 38. Mar. 14. 33.

Add to this, That Jesus Christ was better able to grapple with death, even better able to do it alone, than the whole World joyn'd altogether.

1. He was anointed with the Spirit without Measure, *Joh.* 3. 34.

2. He had all Grace perfect in him, *John* 1. 16.

3. Never none so soaked in the Bosom of his Fathers Love as himself, *Prov.* 8. 23, 30.

4. Never none so harmless, and without sin as he, and consequently never man had so good a Conscience as he, *Heb.* 7. 26.

5. Never none prepared such a stock of good Works to bear him company at the Hour of Death as he.

6. Never none had greater assurance of being with the Father Eternally in the Heavens than he. And yet behold, when HE comes to die, how weak is he, how amazed at death, how heavy, how exceeding sorrowful; and I say, no cause assigned but the Approach of Death.

Alas! How often is it seen, that we Poor Sinners can laugh at destruction when it cometh: yea, *and rejoice exceedingly when we find the Grave*, Job 3. 22. looking upon death as a part of our Portion; yea, as that which will be a means of our present relief and help, 1 *Cor*. 3. 22.

This Jesus Christ could not do, considered as dying for our Sin, but the nearer death, the more heavy, & oppressed with the thoughts of the Revenging Hand of God. Wherefore he falls into an Agony, and Sweats; not after the common rate, as we do when death is severing Body and Soul. *His Sweat was as it were great drops* (Clodders) *of Blood, falling down to the Ground*, Luk. 22. 44.

What, I say, should be the Reason, but that *death assaulted him with his Sting*. If Jesus Christ had been to die for his Vertues only, doubtless he would have born it lightly, and so he did as he died, bearing witness to the Truth, *He endured the Cross, and despised the Shame*, Heb. 12. 1, 2. How have the Martyrs despised death, and as it were, not been careful of that, having peace with God by Jesus Christ, scorning the most Cruel Torments that Hell and Men could devise and invent; but Jesus Christ could not do so, *as he was a Sacrifice for sin*, he died for sin, he was made a Curse for us, O my Brethren, Christ died many deaths at once, he made his Grave with the Wicked, *and with the Rich in his Death*. Look how many thousands shall be saved, so many deaths did Jesus die; yet it was but once he died. He died thy death, and my death, and so many deaths as all our Sins deserved, who shall be saved from the Wrath to come.

Now to feign that these Sorrows, and this Bloody Agony was not real, but in shew only; What greater Condemnation can be passed upon Jesus Christ, who loved to do all things in the most unfeigned Simplicity? It was therefore because of sin; the Sin that was put into the Death he died, and the Curse of God that was due to Sin; That, That made death so bitter to Jesus Christ; *in Christ that died*. The Apostle speaks as if never any died but Christ, nor indeed did there, *so wonderful a Death as he*, Rom. 8. Death considered simply, as it is a deprivation of natural life could not have these Effects in a Person, personally more Righteous than an Angel. Yea, even Carnal Wicked Men not awakened in their Conscience how securely can they die. It must therefore also be concluded, that *the Sorrows, and Agony of*

20 *Death*] *Deaths*. 27 unfeigned] feigned.

Jesus Christ came from a higher cause, even from the Guilt of sin, and from the Curse of God that was now approaching for that Sin.

It cannot be attributed to the Fear of Men, their Terrour could not make him afraid; that was contrary to his Doctrine, and did not become the Dignity of his Person; it was sin, sin, sin, and the Curse due to sin.

Thirdly, It is evident that Christ did bear and die the Cursed Death for sin; *from the Carriage and Dispensation of God towards him.*

First, from the Carriage of God. God now becomes as an Enemy to him.

1. He forsakes him. *My God, my God, why hast thou forsaken me?* Yea, the Sence of the Loss of God's comfortable Presence abode with him even till he gave up the Ghost.

2. He dealeth with him as with one that hath sinned, he chastiseth him, he bruiseth him, he striketh and smiteth him, *Isa.* 53. and was pleased, that is, his Justice was satisfied, in so doing. *It pleased the Lord to bruise him, he hath put him to grief.*

These things could not be, had he only considered him in his own Personal standing (*where was the Righteous forsaken*). Without the Consideration of Sin, he doth not willingly afflict, nor grieve the Children of Men; that is, not out of pleasure, or without sufficient cause.

Jesus Christ then, since he is under this withdrawing, chastising, bruising, and afflicting Displeasure of God, he is all that time under sin, under our sins, and therefore thus accursed of God, his God.

Secondly, Not only the Carriage of God, but his Dispensations, his visible Dispensations, plainly declare that he stood before God in our Sins, *Vengeance suffered him not to live*. Wherefore God delivered him up. *He spared not his own Son, but delivered him up for us all*, Rom. 8. 32.

1. He delivered him into the Hands of Men, *Mar.* 9. 31.

2. He was delivered into the Hands of Sinners, *Luk.* 24. 7.

3. He was delivered unto Death, *Rom.* 4. 25.

4. Yea, so delivered up, as that they both had him to put him to death, and God left him for that purpose in their Hands: yea, was so far off from delivering him, that he gave way to all things that had a tendency to take his Life from the Earth.

Now may men do what they will with him, *he was delivered to their Will.*

1. *Judas* may sell him.
2. *Peter* may deny him.
3. All his Disciples forsake him.
4. The Enemy apprehends him, binds him, they have him away like a Thief to *Caiaphas* the High-Priest, in whose House he is mocked, spit upon, his Beard is twitched from his Cheeks; now they buffet him and scornfully bow the Knee before him: *Yea, his Visage is so marred more than any mans, and his Form more than the Sons of Men,* Isa. 52. 13, 14, 15.

Now he is sent to the Governor, defaced with Blows and Blood; who delivereth him into the Hand of his Souldiers; they Whip him, Crown him with Thorns, and stick the Points of the Thorns fast in his Temples, by a Blow with a Staff in their Hand: Now is he made a Spectacle to the People, and then sent away to *Herod,* who with his Men of War set him at naught, no God appearing for his Help.

In fine, they at last condemn him to Death, *even to the Death of the Cross,* where they hang him up by Wounds made through his Hands and his Feet, between the Earth and the Heavens, where he hanged for the space of Six Hours, to wit, from Nine in the Morning, till Three in the Afternoon. No God yet appears for his help, while he hangs there; some rail at him, others wagg their Heads, others tauntingly say, *He saved others, himself he cannot save*; some divide his Raiment, casting lots for his Garments before his Face, others mockingly bid him come down from the Cross, and when he desireth succour, they give him Vinegar to drink. *No God yet appears for his help.*

Now the Earth quakes, the Rocks are rent, the Sun becomes black, and Jesus still cries out that he was forsaken of God; and presently boweth his Head and dies: read *Mat.* 26. *Chap.* 27. *Mar.* 14. *Chap.* 15 and *Luk.* 22. *Chap.* 23. *John* 18. *Chap.* 19.

And for all this there is no cause assigned from God, *but Sin. He was wounded for our Transgressions, he was bruised for our Iniquities, and the chastisement of our Peace was upon him, and by his Stripes we are healed,* Isa. 53. 5.

36 Isa. 53. 5.] Isa. 53.

The Sum then is, That Jesus Christ the Lord by taking part of our Flesh, became a Publick Person, not doing, nor dying in a private Capacity, but in the room and stead of Sinners, whose Sin deserved Death and the Curse of God: all which Jesus Christ bare in his own Body upon the Tree. I conclude then, that my Sin is already crucified, and accursed in the Death and Curse Christ under-went.

I come now to some Objections.

Objection First.

CHrist never was a Sinner, God never supposed him to be a Sinner, neither did our Sins become really his, God never reputed him so to have been; therefore hate or punish him as a Sinner he could not; for no false judgment can belong to the Lord.

1. *Ans.* That Christ was not a Sinner *Personally*, by acts, or doings of his own, is granted, and in this sense 'tis true, that God did never suppose him to be a Sinner, nor punished him as such a Sinner, nor did he really (if by really you understand naturally) become our Sin, nor did God ever repute him so.

2. But that Christ stood before God in *our* Sins, and that God did not only suppose him so to stand, but set him in them, put them upon him, and count them as his own, is so true, that he cannot at present be a Christian that denies it. *The Lord hath laid upon him the Iniquities of us all*, Isa. 53. 6. 1 Pet. 2. 24.

3. So then, though God did not punish him for sin of his own committing, yet he punished him for sin of our committing. *The Just suffered for the unjust*, 1 Pet. 3. 18.

4. Therefore it is true, That though Christ did never really become sin of his own, he did really become our Sin, did really become our Curse for sin: If this be denyed, it follows that he became our Sin *but feignedly*, that he was made our Curse, or a Curse for us, *but in appearance*, shew, or in dissimulation; but no such action or work can proceed of the Lord. He did then really lay our Sin, and his Curse upon him for our Sin.

23 Isa. 53. 6. 1 Pet. 2. 24.] Isa. 53. 1 Pet. 2. 22.

2. Object. *But if Christ indeed hath suffered for our Sins, and endured for them that Curse, that of justice is due thereto: then hath he also endured for us the proper torments of Hell, for they are the Wages of our Sins.*

Ans. Many things might be said in answer to this Objection. But briefly;

1. What God chargeth upon the Soul for sin, is one thing, and what followeth upon that Charge, is another.

2. A difference in the Person suffering, may make a difference in the Consequences that follow upon the Charge.

Let us then consider of both these things.

1. The Charge is *Sin*, God charged him with our Sins.

2. The Person then stands guilty before the Judgment of God.

The Consequences are:

1. The Person charged sustains, or suffereth the Wrath of God.

2. This Wrath of God is expressed, and inflicted, on Body and Soul.

The Consequences are:

1. God forsaketh the Person charged, and being left, if he cannot stand, he falleth under the Power of guilt and horror of the same.

If the Person utterly fall under this Charge, as not being able to wrestle with, and overcome this Wrath of God, then despair, horror of Hell, rage, blasphemy, darkness, and damnable anguish immediatly swallow him up, and he lieth for ever and ever in the Pains of Hell, a Monument of Eternal Vengeance.

Now that Christ under-went the Wrath of God 'tis evident, because he bare our Curse; That God forsook him, he did with strong crying and tears acknowledg; and therefore that he was under the Soul-afflicting sence of the loss of God's Favor, and under the sence of his Displeasure must needs flow from the Premises.

But now, because Christ Jesus the Lord, was a Person infinitly differing from all others that fall under the Wrath of God: therefore those things that flow from damned Sinners, could not flow from him.

1. *Despair could not rise in his Heart, for his Flesh did rest in hope;* and said even when he suffered, *Thou wilt not leave my Soul in Hell,* Acts 2. 27.

2. The Everlastingness of the Punishment therefore, not the Terrors that accompany such, could not fasten upon him; for he knew at last that God would Justifie him, or approve of his Works that they were Meritorious.

And mark, Everlasting Punishment is not the proper Wages of sin, but under a supposition that the Person suffering be not able to pay the Debt. *Thou shalt not depart thence till thou hast paid the very last Mite.*

The difference then of the Persons suffering may make a difference, though not in the Nature of the Punishment; yet in the Duration, and Consequences of it.

1. Christ under the Sentence, was as to his own Personal Acts only, altogether innocent; the Damned, only altogether Sinners.

2. Christ had in him, even then the utmost Perfection of all graces and vertues; but the Damned, the Perfection of Sin and Vileness.

3. Christ's Humanity had still Union with his God-head, the Damned, Union only with Sin.

4. Now an Innocent Person, perfect in all graces, as really God, as Man, can better wrestle with the Curse for sin, than either sinful Men or Angels.

1. While they despair, Christ hopes.

2. While they blaspheme, Christ submits.

3. While they rage, Christ justifies God.

4. While they sink under the burden of Sin and Wrath, Christ recovereth by vertue of his Worthiness. Thou wilt not leave my Soul in Hell, *neither wilt thou suffer thy Holy one to see corruption.* He was Gods Holy one, and his Holiness prevailed.

So that it follows not, That because Christ did undergo the Curse due to our Sins, he therefore must have those accidental Consequences which are found to accompany damned Souls.

3. Object. *But the Scripture saith, That the Wages of Sin is everlasting punishment.* Depart from me ye cursed into everlasting fire, prepared for the Devil and his Angels, *Mat.* 25. 41.

Ans. This Objection is partly answered already, in the Answer to that fore-going. But further;

34 *Mat.* 25. 41.] *Mat.* 25.

1. Consider, The Wages of Sin is Death, and punishment under the Wrath of God. *Till those that die the Death for Sin, have paid the utmost Farthing*, Mat. 5. 26. Luk. 12. 58, 59.

2. So then the everlastingness of the Punishment, lieth here; If the Person suffering be not able to make amends to justice for the Sins for which he suffereth; else justice neither would, nor could, *because 'tis just*, keep such still under punishment.

3. The Reason then why fallen Angels, and damned Souls have an everlastingness of Punishment allotted them, is because, by what they suffer: *they cannot satisfy the Justice of God.*

4. The Conclusion then is, though the Rebukes of God for Sin by death and punishment after, be the Rebukes of Eternal Vengeance; yet the Eternity of that Punishment, is for want of merit: could the Damned merit their own Deliverance, *Justice would let them go.*

5. It is one thing therefore to suffer for sin, by the stroke of Eternal Justice, and another thing to abide for ever a Sufferer there: Christ did the First, the Damned do the Second.

6. His Rising therefore from the Dead the third Day doth nothing invalid his Sufferings, but rather sheweth the Power of his Merit. And here I would ask a Question, Had Christ Jesus been more the Object of Faith, if weakness and endless infirmity had kept him under the Curse, than by rising again from the Dead, want of merit causing the one, sufficience thereof causing the other?

7. If men will not believe that Christ hath removed the Curse, because he is risen again; they would much more strongly have doubted it, had he been still in the Grave. But O amazing darkness! to make that an Argument, that his Sufferings wanted merit, which to God himself is sufficient proof that he hath purged our Sins for ever. *For this Man after he had offered up one sacrifice for Sins for ever, sat down on the Right Hand of God*, Heb. 10. 12.

4. Object. *But the Scripture saith, Christ is our Example and that in his very death*, 1 Pet. 2. 21.

Ans. Christ in his Sufferings, and Death, is *both Sacrifice and Example.*

1. A Sacrifice. *Christ our Passeover is Sacrificed for us.* And again, *He gave himself for us, an Offering, and a Sacrifice to God for a sweet-smelling*

3 Mat. 5. 26.] Mat. 5. 25.

Savor. And thus he made Reconciliation for Iniquity, and brought in Everlasting Righteousness, 1 *Cor*. 5. 7. *Ephes*. 5. 1, 2. *Dan*. 9. 24.

2dly. He was also in his Sufferings *Exemplary*, and that in several particulars.

1. In his meek Deportment, while he was apprehended, *Isa*. 53. 7.

2. In doing them good that sought his Life, *Luk*. 22. 50, 51.

3. In his Praying for his Enemies, when they were in their Outrage, *Luk*. 23. 34.

4. *When he was reviled, he reviled not again; when he suffered he threatened not, but committed himself to him that judgeth Righteously*, 1. Pet. 2. 23.

In these respects, I say, *he was Exemplary*, and brought honour to his Proffession by his good Behaviour: And O how beautiful would Christianity be in the Eyes of Men, if the Disciples of our Lord would more imitate him therein!

But what? Because Christ is our *Pattern*, is he not our *Passeover*? or, because we should in *these* things follow his Steps, *died* he not for our Sins? Thus to conclude, would not only argue thee very erroneous, but such a Conclusion would overthrow the Gospel; it being none other but a great slight of Satan, to shut out the whole by a Part, and to make us Blasphemers, while we plead for Holiness.

Look then upon the Death of Christ under a double Consideration.

1. As he suffered from the Hand of God.

2. As he suffered from the Hand of Men.

Now as he suffered by God's Hand, so he suffered for sin; but as he suffered from Men, so he suffered for righteousness sake.

Observe then, That as he suffered for sin, so no *MAN* took away his Life; but as he suffered for righteousness, so THEY slew him by wicked hands: What is it then? Christ must needs have suffered, and the Wisdom of God had so ordained. *That those things which God before had shewed by the Mouth of all his Prophets, that Christ should suffer, he hath so fulfilled*, Acts 3. 18.

Thus therefore we ought to distinguish of the Causes, and Ends of the Death of Christ.

2 1 *Cor*. 5. 7.] 1 *Cor*. 5. 8. *Dan*. 9. 24.] *Dan*. 9. 2.

Again, As Christ suffered for sin, so he would neither be taken at mans pleasure, nor die at mans time.

1. *Not at mans pleasure*, and hence it was that they so often sought his Life in vain, *for his Hour was not yet come*; to wit, the Hour in which he was to be made a Sacrifice for our Sin, *John* 13. *Chap.* 17. 1, 2. *Chap.* 18. 1, 2.

2. *Not at their Time*; but contrary to all expectation, when the *due* time was come, he bowed his Head and gave up the Ghost, *John* 19. 30.

And for this last work he had power given him of God, that is, power to die when he would. *I have power*, said he, *to lay down my Life, and I have power to take it again*; This Power never man had before. This made the Centurion wonder, and made *Pontius Pilat* marvel: And indeed well they might, for it was as great a Miracle as any he wrought in his Life. It demonstrated him to be the Son of God, *Mar.* 15. 38, 39. The Centurion knowing that according to nature he might have lived longer, concluded therefore that his dying at that instant was not, but miraculously. And when *he saw that he so cried out, and gave up the Ghost*, he said, *Truly this Man was the Son of God.*

And the Reason why he had power to die, was, That he might offer his Offering willingly, and at the Season.

1. Willingly. *If his Offering be a Burnt-Sacrifice of the Lord, let him offer a Male without blemish, he shall offer it of his own voluntary Will, at the Door of the Tabernacle of the Congregation before the Lord*, Levit. 1. 3.

2. He must offer it at the Season. *Thou shalt keep this Ordinance* (the Passeover) *in his Season*, Exod. 13. 10.

Now both these Offerings having immediate respect to the Offering of the Body of Christ for sin (for he came in the room of all burnt-Sacrifices), the Passeover also was a Type of him, *Heb.* 10. 3, 4, 5, 6. 1 *Cor.* 5. 7, 8. Therefore, he being now the Priest as well as Sacrifice, must have Power and Will to offer his Sacrifice with acceptation; and this the Scripture testifieth he did where it saith, *In due time Christ died for the Ungodly*, Rom. 5. 6. In due time, that is at the time appointed, at the acceptable time.

35 Rom. 5. 6.] Rom. 5. 8, 9.

Thou must therefore, unless thou art willing to be deceived, look upon the Sufferings of Christ, under a double Consideration, and distinguish between his Sufferings *as our Example*, and his Suffering *for our Sins*. And know, that as he suffered *as our Example*, so he suffered *only* for righteousness sake from the Hands of wicked Men; but as he suffered *for our Sins*, so he suffered (as being by God reputed wicked) the Punishment that was due to sin even the dreadful Curse of God: Not that Christ died two deaths one after another, but he died at the same time upon a double account; for his Righteousness sake from Men; for our sins, from the Hand of God. And, as I said before, had he only suffered for righteousness sake, death had not so amazed him, nor had he been so exceeding heavy in the Thoughts of it; that had never put him into an Agony, nor made him Sweat, as it were, great drops of Blood. Besides, When men suffer only for righteousness sake, God doth not use to hide his Face from them, to forsake them, and make them accursed; But *Christ hath delivered us from the Curse of the Law, being made a Curse for us.*

Object. *But if indeed Christ hath paid the full price for us by his Death, in suffering the Punishment that we should have done: wherefore is the Scripture so silent, as not to declare, that by his Death he hath made satisfaction?*

Ans. No Man may teach God Knowledg, he knoweth best how to deliver his Mind in such words and terms as best agree with his Eternal Wisdom, and the Consciences of these that are truly desirous of Salvation, being over-burdened with the guilt of Sin. Perhaps the Word *Satisfaction* will hardly be found in the Bible; and where is it said in so many words, *God is dissatisfied with our Sins*? Yet 'tis sufficiently manifest, that there is nothing that God hateth but sin, and Sinners for the Sake of sin. What meant he by turning *Adam* out of Paradise, by drowning the Old World, by burning up *Sodom* with Fire and Brimstone from Heaven? What meant he by drowning of *Pharaoh*, by causing the Ground to swallow up *Corah* and his Company, and by his destroying *Israel* in the Wilderness, if not to shew that he was dissatisfied with Sin? That God is also satisfied, yea, more than satisfied by Christ's Sufferings for our Sins, *is apparent*: For granting that he died for them, as these Scriptures declare, *Isa.* 53. 1 *Cor.* 15. 1, 2, 3, 4. *Gal.* 1. 4. 1 *Cor.* 5. 8. 2 *Cor.* 5.

21. *Gal.* 3. 13. 1 *Pet.* 2. 24. *Chap.* 3. 18. 1 *Joh.* 2. 2. *Chap.* 3. 16. *Chap.* 4. 14. *Revel.* 1. 5. *Chap.* 5. 9. *Isa.* 49. 4, 5, 6.

1. It is apparent, because it is said; *That God smelled in that Offering of the Body of Christ for our Sins, a Sweet-smelling Savor. He gave himself for us an Offering, and a Sacrifice to God for a sweet-smelling Savor,* Ephes. 5. 2.

2. It is apparent, because it is said expressly, *That God for Christ's Sake* doth now forgive. *Be ye kind one to another, tender-hearted, forgiving one another, even as God for Christ's Sake hath forgiven you,* Ephes. 4. 32.

3. It is apparent that God is satisfied with Christ's Blood for our Sins, because he hath declared, that he can justifie those that believe in, or rely upon that Blood for Life, in a way of Justice and Righteousness. *Being justified freely by his Grace through the Redemption that is in Jesus Christ, whom God hath set forth to be a Propitiation through faith in his Blood, to declare his Righteousness for the Remission of sins, that are past through the forbearance of God. To declare, I say, at this time his Righteousness, that he might be just, and the Justifier of him that believeth in Jesus,* Rom. 3. 24, 25, 26.

Now, I say, to object against such plain Testimonies, what is it, but

1. To deny that Christ died for Sin; or to conclude,
2. That having so done, he is still in the Grave: Or,
3. That there is no such thing as Sin: Or,
4. No such thing as Revenging Justice in God against it: Or,
5. That we must die our selves for our Sins: Or,
6. That sin may be pardoned without a satisfaction: Or,
7. That every man may merit his own Salvation.

But without shedding of Blood there is no Remission, *Heb.* 9. 22.

To avoid therefore these cursed Absurdities, it must be granted that Jesus Christ by his Death did make satisfaction for sin.

But the word *Satisfaction* may not be used by the Holy Ghost, perhaps, for that it is too short and scanty a Word to express the Blessedness that comes to Sinners by the Blood of Christ.

1. To make satisfaction amounts to no more than compleatly to answer a legal Demand for harms and injuries done. Now this when done to the full, leaveth the Offender there where he was before he committed the Injury. Now if Christ had done no more than this,

he had only paid our debt, *but had not obtained eternal redemption for us.*

2. For a full Satisfaction given by this Man for harms done by another, may neither obtain the Love of the Person offended, nor the smallest Gift which the Person *offending* hath not deserved. Suppose I owe to this Man ten thousand Talents, and another should pay him every Farthing, there remaineth over and above, by that compleat Satisfaction, not one single half-Penny for me. Christ hath therefore done more than to make satisfaction for sin by his Blood. *He hath also made us Kings and Priests to God and his Father, and we shall reign with him for ever and ever*, Revel. 1. 5, 6. Chap. 22. 5.

But take a few more Scriptures for the Proof of the Doctrine before asserted.

First, *We have redemption through his Blood*, Col. 1. 14.

1. Redemption from Sin, *Ephes.* 1. 7.

2. Redemption from Death, *Heb.* 2. 14, 15. *Hos.* 13. 14.

3. Redemption from Satan, *Heb.* 2. 15.

4. Redemption from the World, *Gal.* 1. 4.

5. Redemption to God, *Revel.* 5. 9.

6. Eternal Redemption. *Neither by the Blood of Goats and Calves, but by his own Blood, he entered in once into the Holy Place, having obtained Eternal Redemption for us*, Heb. 9. 12.

Secondly, We are said also to be washed in his Blood.

1. Our Persons are washed; *He loved US, and washed US* from our Sins in his own Blood, *Rev.* 1. 5.

2. His Blood washeth also our Performances, *Our Robes are washed, and made white in the Blood of the Lamb*, Revel. 7. 14.

Thirdly, We are said to be purged by his Blood.

1. Purged from Sin before God. *When he had by himself purged our Sins, he sat down on the Right Hand of God*, Heb. 1. 3.

2. Purged from evil Consciences. *How much more shall the Blood of Christ, who through the Eternal Spirit offered himself without spot to God; purge your Conscience from dead works, to serve the Living God?* Heb. 9. 14.

Fourthly, We are said to be made nigh to God by his Blood. *But now in Christ Jesus, ye who sometimes were afar off, are made nigh by the Blood of Christ*, Ephes. 2. 13.

Fifthly, Peace is said to be made by his Blood.

1. Peace with God, *Col.* 1. 20.
2. Peace of Conscience, *Heb.* 10. 19, 20, 21, 22.
3. Peace one with another, *Ephes.* 2. 14.

Sixthly, We are said to be justified by his Blood. *Much more being now justified by his Blood, we shall be saved from wrath through him,* Rom. 5. 9.

Justified, that is, acquitted:

1. Acquitted before God, *Ephes.* 5. 26, 27.
2. Acquitted before Angels, *Mat.* 28. 5.
3. Acquitted by the Law, *Rom.* 3. 21, 22, 23.
4. Acquitted in the Court of Conscience, *Heb.* 9. 14.

Seventhly, We are said to be saved by his Blood, *Rom.* 5. 8, 9.

Eightly, We are said to be reconciled by his Blood, *Col.* 1. 20, 21, 22.

Ninthly, We are said to be sanctified by his Blood, *Heb.* 13. 12.

Tenthly, We are said to be admitted into the Holiest by his Blood, *Heb.* 10. 19.

Eleventhly, We are said to have Eternal Redemption by his Blood, *Heb.* 9. 12.

Yea Lastly, This Blood which was once spilt upon the Cross, will be the burden of our Song in Heaven it self for ever and ever, *Revel.* 5. 9.

Now if we be redeemed, washed, purged, made nigh to God, have peace with God; if we stand just before God, are saved, reconciled, sanctified, admitted into the Holiest; if we have eternal Redemption by his Blood, and if his Blood will be the burden of our Song for ever: then hath Christ paid the full price for us by his Death; then hath he done more than made satisfaction for our Sins.

Several Demonstrations more, proving the former Doctrine.

BUt before I conclude this Answer, I will give you nine or ten more undeniable Demonstrations, to satisfie you, if God will bless them to you, in the Truth of this great Doctrine, to wit, *That*

9 *Ephes.* 5. 26, 27.] *Ephes.* 5. 25, 26.

Jesus Christ by what he hath done hath paid the full Price to God for the Souls of Sinners, and obtained Eternal Redemption for them.

The first Demonstration.

ANd First, I begin with his Resurrection: THAT God that delivered him up unto death, and that made him a Curse for Sin; THAT God raised him up from the dead. *But God raised him from the Dead*, Act. 3. 15. Chap. 13. 30. Now considering, that at his Death he was charged with our Sins, and accursed to death for our Sins: That Justice that delivered him up *for* them, must have amends made to him, before he acquit him *from* them; for there can be *no* change *in Justice*. Had *he* found him in our Sins in the *Grave*, as *he* found him in them upon the *Tree* (for he had them in his Body on the Tree, 1 *Pet*. 2. 24), he had left him there as he left him upon the Tree: yea, he had as surely *rotted* in the Grave, as ever he *died* on the Tree. But when he visited Christ in the Grave, he found him *a Holy, Harmless, Undefiled, and Spotless Christ*, and therefore he raised him up from the Dead. *He raised him up from the dead, having loosed the Pains of Death; because it was not possible that he should be helden of it*, Act. 2. 24.

Quest. *But why not possible* now *to be helden of death?*

Ans. Because, *the Cause was removed*, Sin was the Cause, *he died for our Sins, he gave himself for our Sins*, 1 Cor. 15. 1, 2, 3. Gal. 1. 4. *These Sins brought him to death*: But when God that had made him a Curse for us, looked upon him into the Grave, he found him *there* without sin, and *therefore* loosed the Pains of Death; for Justice saith, *This is not possible*, because not lawful, that he who lieth sinless before God, should be swallowed up of death; therefore he raised him up.

Quest. *But what did he do with our Sins?* for he had them upon his Back.

Ans. 'Tis said he TOOK them away: *Behold the Lamb of God that taketh away the sin of the World*. 'Tis said he PUT them away. *Now once in the End of the World hath he appeared to put away sin by the Sacrifice of himself*, Joh. 1. 29. Heb. 9. 26. That is, by the *Merit* of his undertaking he brought into the World, and set before the Face of God *such* a Righteousness, that out-weigheth, and goeth far beyond that Sin; and so did hide sin from the Sight of God: Hence, he that is justified, is said, to have his Sins HID, and covered. *Blessed is the Man whose Transgressions are forgiven, and whose Sin is covered*, Rom. 4. 7. covered with the Righteousness of Christ. *I spread my skirt over thee, and covered thy Nakedness*, thy Sins, Ezek. 16. 8. Christ Jesus therefore, having by the Infiniteness of his Merit, taken away, put away, or hidden our Sins from the Face of God; therefore he raised him up from the Dead.

You find in that 16th of *Leviticus* mention made of two Goats, one was to be *slain* for a Sin-Offering, the other to be left *alive*: The Goat that was *slain*, was a Type of Christ in his Death, the Goat that was not *slain*, was a Type of Christ in his Merit. Now this living Goat, HE carried away the Sins of the People into the Land of forgetfulness. *And* Aaron *shall lay both his Hands upon the head of the Live-Goat, and confess over him all the Iniquities of the Children of* Israel, *and all their Transgressions, in all their Sins, putting them upon the Head of the Goat, and shall send him away by the Hands of a fit Man into the Wilderness, and the Goat shall bear upon him all their Iniquities unto a Land not inhabited*, Levit. 16. 21, 22. Thus did Jesus Christ bear away by the Merit of his Death, the Sins and Iniquities of them that Believe; wherefore, when God came to him in the Grave, he found him, Holy and Undefiled, and *raised him up from the Dead.*

And observe it, As his Death was for our Sin, so his Rising again was for our Discharge: for both in his Death and Resurrection he immediately respected our Benefits; *he died for us*, he rose from the Dead for us. *He was delivered for our Offences, and was raised again for our Justification*, Rom. 4. 25. By his Death he carried away our Sins, by his Rising, he brought to us Justifying Righteousness.

There are five Circumstances also attending his Resurrection, that shew us how well-pleased God was with his Death.

1. It must be solemnized with the Company, Attendance and Testimony of Angels, *Mat.* 28. 1, 2, 3, 4, 5, 6. *Luk.* 24. 3, 4, 5, 6. *John* 20. 11, 12, 13.

2dly. At, or just upon his Resurrection, the Graves, where many of the Saints, for whom he died, lay asleep, did open, and they followed their Lord in full Triumph over Death. *The Graves were*

19 Levit. 16. 21, 22.] Levit. 16. 33 20. 11, 12, 13.] 20. 11, 12.

opened, and many Bodies of Saints which slept arose, and came out of their Graves after his Resurrection, and went into the Holy City, and appeared unto many, Mat. 27. 52, 53.

These Saints coming out of their Graves after him; what a Testimony is it, that he, for them, had taken away Sin, and destroyed him that had the Power of Death: yea, what a Testimony was it that he had made amends to God the Father, who granted him at his Resurrection, to have presently out of the Grave, *Of the Price of his Blood, even the Body of many of the Saints which slept. He was declared to be the Son of God with Power by the Spirit of Holiness, and the Resurrection from the Dead*, Rom. 1. 4. It saith not, by *his* Resurrection, though that be true; But by *the Resurrection*, meaning the Resurrection of the Bodies of the Saints which slept, because they rose by vertue of his Blood; and by that he was with power declared to be the Son of God. They I say, were part of his Purchase, some of them for whom Christ died: Now for God to raise them, and that upon, and by vertue of his Resurrection; what is it, but an open Declaration from Heaven, that Christ by his Death hath made amends for us, and obtained Eternal Redemption for us?

3rdly. When he was risen from the Dead, God, to confirm his Disciples in the Faith of the Redemption that Christ had obtained by his Blood, *brings him to the Church*, presents him to them alive, shews him *openly*, sometimes to two or three, sometimes to eleven or twelve, and once to above five hundred Brethren at once, *Acts* 1. 3. Chap. 10. 40. *Luk.* 24. 13, 14, 15, 16, 31. *John* 20. 19. Chap. 21. 1, 2, 3, *&c.* 1 *Cor.* 15. 3, 4, 5, 6, 7, 8.

4thly. At his Resurrection, *God gives him the Keys of Hell and of Death*, Revel. 1. 16, 17, 18. Hell and Death are the Effects and Fruits of Sin. *The Wicked shall be turned into Hell*, and the Wages of Sin is Death. But what then are Sinners the better for the Death and Blood of Christ? O! They that dare venture upon him are much the better, for they shall not perish unless the Saviour will damn them; for he hath the Keys of Hell and of Death. *Fear not, saith he, I am the First and the Last, I am he that liveth, and was dead, and behold, I am alive for evermore, and have the Keys of Hell and Death.* These were given him

3 Mat. 27. 52, 53.] Mat. 27. 52. 20 3rdly.] 3thly. 28 Revel. 1. 16, 17, 18.] Revel. 1. 16, 17.

at his Resurrection; as if God had said, My Son thou hast spilt thy Blood for Sinners, I am pleased with it, I am delighted in thy Merits, & in the Redemption which thou hast wrought; in token hereof, I give thee the Keys of Hell and of Death: I give thee all Power in Heaven and Earth, save who thou wilt, deliver who thou wilt, bring to Heaven who thou wilt.

5thly. At Christ's Resurrection, *God bids him ask the Heathen of him, with a Promise to give him the uttermost parts of the Earth for his Possession.* This Sentence is in the second Psalm, and is expounded by *Paul's* Interpretation of the Words before, to be spoken to Christ at his Resurrection. *Thou art my Son, this Day have I begotten thee.* I have begotten thee, that is, saith *Paul*, from the Dead.

He hath raised up Jesus again, as it is also written in the Second Psalm. *Thou art my Son, this day have I begotten thee*, Act. 13. 30, 31, 32, 33, 34. Now mark at his Raising him from the Dead, he bids him *ask*, *ASK* of me, and that the Heathen: As if God had said, *My Son*, thy Blood hath pacified, and appeased my Justice; I can now in justice, for thy sake, forgive poor Mortals their Sin; ASK them of me, ASK them, though they be Heathens, and I will give them to thee, to the utmost Ends of the Earth. This is then the First Demonstration to prove that Jesus Christ by what he hath done, hath paid full price to God for the Souls of Sinners, and obtained Eternal Redemption for them; namely, his being Raised again from the Dead.

The Second Demonstration.

SEcondly. A Second thing that demonstrateth this Truth, is, *That he Ascended, and was received up into Heaven. So after the Lord had spoken to them, he was received up into Heaven*, Mar. 16. 19.

This Demonstration consisteth of two parts.

1. Of his Ascending.
2. Of his being Received.

First, For his Ascending. *He is ascended on High*, Ephes. 4. 8.

This Act of Ascending answereth to the High-Priest under the Law, who, after they had killed the Sacrifice, he was to bring the

Blood into the most Holy Place, to wit, the inner-Temple, the Way to which, was ascending or going up, 2 *Chron.* 9. 4.

Now consider the *Circumstances* that attended his Ascending, when he went to carry his Blood to present it before the Mercy-Seat: and you will find, they all say amends is made to God for us.

1. At this, He is again attended, and accompanied with Angels, *Act.* 1. 10, 11.

2. He ascendeth with a *shout*, & with the sound of a Trumpet, with sing Praises, sing Praises, sing Praises, *Psal.* 47. 5, 6.

3. The Enemies of mans Salvation are now tied to his Chariot-wheels. *When he ascendeth on High, he led captivity captive*, Ephes. 4. 8. that is, he led Death, Devils, and Hell, and the Grave, and the Curse, captive, for these things were our Captivity. And thus did *Deborah* prophecy of him, when she cried, *Arise* Barak *and lead thy Captivity captive, thou Son of* Abinoam. This *David* also fore-saw when he said, *Thou hast ascended on high, thou hast led Captivity captive*, Judges 5. 12. Psal. 68. 18.

4. The Apostles must be the Beholders of his going up, and must see the Cloud receive him out of their Sight, *Act.* 1. 11, 12.

The Consideration of these things strongly inforceth this Conclusion, *That he hath spoiled what would have spoiled us, had he not by his Bloodshed taken them away*: And I say, for God to adorn him with all this Glory in his Ascension; THUS to make him ride Conqueror up into the Clouds; THUS to go up with sound of Trumpet, with shout of Angels, and with Songs of Praises; and let me add, to be accompanied also with those that rose from the Dead after his Resurrection, who were the very Price of his Blood. This doth greatly demonstrate, *That Jesus Christ by what he hath done, hath paid full price to God for the Souls of Sinners, and obtained Eternal Redemption for them*; he had not else rid thus in Triumph to Heaven.

2. I come now to his being Received: *He was received up into Heaven.* The High-Priest under the Law, when he ascended into the Holiest, he was *there to offer the Blood*; which Holiest was the Type of Heaven, *Exod.* 29. 10, 11. *Heb.* 9. 24. But because the Sacrifices under the Law could not make them that did the Service perfect as pertaining

2 2 *Chron.* 9. 4.] 2 *Chron.* 9. 11 Ephes. 4. 8.] Ephes. 4. 34 *Exod.* 29. 10, 11.] *Exod.* 19. 10, 11.

to the Conscience; therefore they were to stand, not sit, to come out again, not tarry there. *For it is not possible that the Blood of Bulls and Goats, should take away sin; wherefore, when he cometh into the World, he saith, Sacrifice and Offerings thou wouldest not, but a Body hast thou prepared me. In Burnt-Offerings and Sacrifices for sin thou hast had no pleasure. Then said he, lo, I come (in the Volume of thy Book it is written of me) to do thy will, O God*, Heb. 10. 4, 5, 6, 7.

Christ therefore in his entering into Heaven, did it, as High-Priest of the Church of God: Therefore neither did he go in without Blood. *Wherefore, when he came to be an High-Priest of good things to come, by a greater and more perfect Tabernacle, not made with hands, that is to say, not of this Building, neither by the Blood of Bulls and Goats, but by his own Blood, he entered in once into the Holy Place, having obtained Eternal Redemption for us*, Heb. 9. 11, 12, 13, 14.

He entered in having obtained, or because he obtained Eternal Redemption for us: but to pass that,

Consider ye now also those Glorious Circumstances that accompany his Approach to the Gates of the Everlasting Habitation.

1. The Everlasting Gates are set, yea, bid stand open. *Be ye open ye Everlasting Doors, and the King of Glory shall come in. This King of Glory*, is Jesus Christ, and the Words are a Prophecy of his Glorious Ascending into the Heavens, when he went up as the High-Priest of the Church, to carry the Price of his Blood into the Holiest of all. *Lift up your Heads, O ye Gates, even lift them up, ye Everlasting Doors, and the King of Glory shall come in*, Psalm 24. 7, 9.

2dly. At his Enterance, he was *received*, and the Price accepted which he paid for our Souls. Hence it is said, He entered in *by his Blood*; that is, by the Merit of it. *To Receive*, is an Act of Complacency and Delight, and includeth Well-pleasedness *in the Person Receiving*, who is God the Father: And considering that this Jesus, *now received*, is to be received upon our account, or as undertaking the Salvation of *Sinners*: (for he entered into the Heavens *for us*) it is apparent that he entered thither by vertue of his Infinite Righteousness, which he accomplished for us upon the Earth.

7 Heb. 10. 4, 5, 6, 7.] Heb. 10. 4, 5, 6. 14 Heb. 9. 11, 12, 13, 14.] Heb. 9. 12, 13, 14.

3dly. At his Reception, *he received Glory*, and that also for *our* Encouragement. *God raised him up, and gave him Glory, that our Faith and Hope might be in him*, 1 Pet. 1. 19, 20, 21.

He gave him Glory, as a Testimony, that his undertaking the Work of our Redemption was accepted of him.

1. He gave Glory; first *to his Person*, in granting him to sit at his own Right Hand, and this he had, I say, for, or upon the account of the Work he accomplished for us in the World; *When he had offered up one Sacrifice for Sins, for ever, he sat down on the Right Hand of God*, Heb. 10. 12, 13. and this by God's appointment. *Sit thou at my Right Hand.* This Glory is the Highest; it is above all Kings, Princes, and Potentates in this World; it is above all Angels, Principalities, and Powers in Heaven. *He is gone into Heaven, and is on the Right Hand of God; Angels, and Authorities, and Powers being made Subject unto him*, 1 Pet. 3. 22.

2. He gave Glory to his Name, to his Name, JESUS; that Name being exalted above every Name. *He hath given him a Name above every Name, that at the Name of Jesus, every Knee should bow, of things in Heaven, and things on Earth, and things under the Earth, and that every Tongue should confess that Jesus Christ is Lord, to the Glory of God the Father*, Phil. 2. 9, 10, 11.

This Name is said (in another place) to be a Name above every Name that is Named, *not only in this World, but in that also which is to come*, Ephes. 1. 21.

But should [JESUS] have been such a Name, since he undertook for Sinners; had this Undertaker failed in his Work, if his Work had not been accepted with God, even the Work of our Redemption by his Blood? No verily, it would have stunk in both the Nostrils of God and Man, it would have been the most abhorred Name: but JESUS is the *Name*; JESUS, he was called, in order to his Work. *His Name shall be called JESUS, for he shall save*; He was so named of the Angels, *before he was conceived in the Womb*; and he goeth by that Name now he is in Heaven: By the Name Jesus, *Jesus of Nazareth*, because he once dwelt there. This Name, I say, is the Highest *Name*, the Everlasting Name; the Name that he is to go by, to be known by, to be worshipped by, and to be glorified by; yea the *Name* by which also most Glory shall redound to God the Father.

20 Phil. 2. 9, 10, 11.] Phil. 2.

Now what is the Signification of this *Name*, but SAVIOUR? This *Name* he hath therefore, *for his Works Sake*; and because God delighted in his Undertaking, and was pleased with the Price he had paid for us; therefore the Divine Majesty hath given him it, hath made it High, and hath commanded all Angels to bow unto it. Yea, it is the *Name* in which he resteth, and by which he hath magnified all his Attributes.

1. *This is the Name* by which Sinners should go to God the Father.

2. *This is the Name* through which they obtain forgiveness of Sins, *and* ANY *thing. If you ask anything in my Name I will do it*, John 14. 14.

3. *This is the Name* through which our spiritual Services and Sacrifices are accepted, and by which an Answer of Peace is returned into our Bosoms, 1 *Pet.* 2. But more of this anon.

3. *At this Name* Devils tremble, at THIS Name Angels bow the Head, at THIS Name God's Heart openeth, at THIS Name the Godly Man's Heart is comforted: THIS Name none but Devils hate it, and none but those that must be damned despise it, *No man speaking by the Holy Ghost calls Jesus accursed*, or accounteth him still dead, and his Blood ineffectual to save the World.

3dly. He hath also given him the Glory of Office.

1. *He is there a Priest for ever*, intercepting betwixt the Divine Presence, and all that hate us, by his Blood; Sin, Satan, Death, Hell, the Law, the Grave, or the like, cannot be heard, if his Blood be presented to God, as the Atonement for us: This is called the Blood of Sprinkling *which speaks better things than the Blood of Abel*, Heb. 12. 24. By this Blood he entered into Heaven, by this Blood he secureth from wrath, *all that come unto God by him*: but should his Blood have had a Voice in Heaven *to save* withal, had it not merited first, even in the Shedding of it, the Ransom, and Redemption of Souls? 'Tis true, a Man whose Blood cannot save, may with *Abels*, cry out for Vengeance and Wrath on the Head of him that shed it, *but* THIS *Blood speaks for better things*, this Blood speaks *for* Souls, for Sinners, for Pardon. *Having obtained Eternal Redemption for us.*

2. He is there a Fore-runner *for us. Whither the Fore-runner is for us entered, even Jesus*, Heb. 6. 20. This Office of Harbinger, is distinct

10–11 John 14. 14.] John 14.

from, though it comes by vertue of, his Priestly Office: therefore they are both mentioned in the Text, *Whither the Fore-runner is for us entered, even Jesus, made an High-Priest for ever, after the Order of* Melchisedec. He is therefore our Fore-runner by vertue of his Priesthood, his Blood giving worth to all he does.

In this Office of Harbinger, or Fore-runner, he prepareth for Believers their dwelling-Places in the Heavens; their dwelling-Places, according to their Place, State, Calling, Service, or Work, in his Body the Church. *In my Fathers House,* saith he, *are many Mansions, if it were not so I would have told you, I go to prepare a Place for you,* Joh. 14. 2.

This is that is mentioned in the 47*th* Psalm. *He shall chuse our Inheritance for us, the Excellency of* Jacob *whom he loved.* But should he have had Power to chuse our Inheritance for us, to prepare for us our dwelling-Places; should he have Power to give even Heaven it self to a Company of Poor Men, had he not in the first Place obtained by his Blood the Deliverance of our Soul from Death.

3. *He is there a Prophet for us,* by which Office of his, he hath received to communicate the whole Will of the Eternal God, so far as is fit for us to know in this World, or in that which is to come. Hence he is called the Prophet of the Church. The Lord shall raise you up a Prophet, *and this is, of a truth, that Prophet that should come into the World*: But this Office he hath also now in Heaven, by vertue of the Blood he shed for us upon Earth. Hence the New-Testament is called, *The New-Testament in his Blood,* and his Blood is said to be *The Blood of the Everlasting Covenant,* or Testament: Yea such vertue doth his Blood give to the New-Testament or Covenant of Grace, as that severed from that it is nothing worth; *for a Testament is of force after men are dead, otherwise it is of no strength at all, while the Testator liveth,* Heb. 9. 16, 17. So that every Word of *God,* which he hath by Christ given to us, for our Everlasting Consolation, is dipt in blood, is founded in blood, and stands good to Sinners purely (I mean with respect to merit) upon the account of Blood, or because his Blood that was shed for us on the Cross, prevailed for us for the Remission of our Sins. Let no man think to receive any benefit by Christs Prophetical Office; by any of the good Words

11 Joh. 14. 2.] Joh. 14.

of Grace, and forgiveness of Sins that are sprinkled up and down in the New-Testament; *That looketh not for that good to come to him for the Sake of that Blood by which this Testament is established*: For neither was the First Testament dedicated without Blood; for when *Moses* had spoken every Precept to all the People according to the Law; *He took the Blood of Calves, and of Goats with Water, and scarlet Wool, and Hissop and sprinkled both the Book and all the People, saying, This is the Blood of the Testament, which God hath injoyned unto you*, Heb. 9. 18, 19, 20.

The Prophetical Office of Christ standeth of two parts: First in Promises of Grace; Secondly, in Directions of Worship; but neither is this last, to wit, the Doctrine of Worship, or our subjection to that Worship, of any value, any further than as sprinkled also with his Blood: For as in the first Testament, the Tabernacle and all the Vessels of the Ministry were sprinkled with Blood (and it was necessary that so it should be), so the Heavenly Things themselves, must be also purified with Sacrifices, but yet *with better Sacrifice than these*; for now, not *Moses*, but *Christ*, doth sprinkle, not with Blood of Calves, but with his own Blood; neither as entered into places made with Hands, *but from Heaven doth Jesus sprinkle* all that Doctrine of Worship, & subjection of his Saints thereto, which is of his own instituting, and commanding, *Heb*. 9. 23, 24, 25, 26.

4. He hath received there the Office of a King, by which he ruleth in the Church, and over all things for her sake. The Government is laid upon his Shoulders; the Lord God hath given him the Throne of his Father *David*. Hence it is that he saith, *All Power is given me in Heaven and Earth*; but now this Kingly Office, he hath it by his Blood, *because he humbled himself to death, therefore God hath highly exalted him, and given him the Highest Name*. And hence again he is called a LAMB upon the Throne. *In the midst of the Throne & of the four Beasts, and in the midst of the Elders stood a Lamb as it had been slain, having seven horns*, a Demonstration of Kingly Power. But mark, he was a Lamb upon the Throne, he had his Horns as a *Lamb*. Now by LAMB, we are to understand, not only his meek and sweet Disposition, but his Sacrifice; for he was as a *Lamb* to be slain, and Sacrificed; and so his having a Throne and seven Horns as a Lamb, giveth us to understand, that he obtained this Dignity of King, by his Blood. *When he had by himself purged our Sins, he sat down on the Right Hand of*

the Majesty in the Heavens. When he had offered up one Sacrifice for Sins for ever, he sat down on the Right Hand of God, Revel. 5. Heb. 1. 3. Chap. 10. 12.

Now put all these together, to wit, his Resurrection from the Dead, his Ascension, and Exaltation to Office, and remember also that the Person thus Exalted, is the same Jesus of *Nazareth* that sometime was made accursed of God for Sin, and also that he obtained this Glory by vertue of the Blood that was shed for us, and it must unavoidably follow, *That Jesus Christ by what he hath done, hath paid full price to God for Sinners, and obtained Eternal Redemption for them.*

The Third Demonstration.

BUt to proceed; A Third Demonstration, That Jesus Christ by what he hath done, hath paid full price to God for Sinners, and obtained Eternal Redemption for them, is, *because he hath received for them the Holy Spirit of God.*

Thus Jesus hath God raised up, whereof, said *Peter*, we are all Witnesses. *Therefore being by the Right Hand of God exalted, and having received of the Father the Promise of the Holy Ghost, he hath shed forth that which ye now see and hear,* Act. 2. 32, 33.

The receiving of the Holy Ghost at the Hand of the Father, who had bruised him before for the Transgressions of his People. The receiving of it, I say, upon his Resurrection, and that to give them for whom (just before) he had spilt his Blood to make an Atonement for their Souls; argueth that the Divine Majesty found rest and content in that Precious Blood, and found it full price for the Sinners for whom he shed it.

And if you consider the necessity of the giving of this good spirit to Men, and the benefit that they receive by his coming upon them, you will see yet more into the Truth now contended for.

First, Then of the Necessity of giving this good Spirit.

2. And then of the Benefit which we receive at his coming.

First, Of the Necessity of its being given.

1. Otherwise Jesus could never have been proved to be the

2–3 Heb. 1. 3. Chap. 10. 12.] Heb. 4. Chap. 10.

Saviour; for the Promise was, that Messias should have the Spirit given him; given him to communicate. *As for me, this is my Covenant with them* (saith the Lord), *my Spirit which is upon thee, and my Words which I have put in thy Mouth* (*meaning the Redeemer*, ver. 20.) *shall not depart out of thy Mouth, nor out of the Mouth of thy Seed, nor out of the Mouth of thy Seeds Seed, from henceforth and for ever*, Isa. 59. 21.

Here is the Promise of the Spirit to be given to Christ, and by him to his Seed for ever. And this was signified long before in the Anointing of *Aaron* and his Sons. *And thou shalt anoint* Aaron *and his Sons and consecrate them*, Exod. 30. 30.

This Spirit Jesus promised to send unto his, at his Exaltation on the Right Hand of God; The Spirit, I say, in the plentiful *Pourings* of it out. True, the Church in all Ages had something of it by vertue of the Suretyship of the Lord Jesus; but *this* in comparison of what was to come into the Church after his Resurrection, is not reckoned a *Pouring* forth, therefore *Pourings* forth thereof are reserved to the time of the Ascension, and Exaltation of this Jesus. *I will pour out my Spirit in* THOSE *Days.*

Hence Jesus reserves it till his going away, and 'tis expresly said; *The Holy Ghost was not yet given, because Jesus was not yet Glorified.* Accordingly did the Apostles wait after his Resurrection for the pouring forth of the Holy Ghost, and at the set time did receive it, by the giving of which, he declared himself to be the son of God and Saviour of the World, *John* 14. 26. *Chap.* 15. 26. *Chap.* 16. 7. *Act.* 1. 4, 5. *Joel* 2. 28. *Acts* 2. 16, 17. *Joh.* 7. 39. *Rom.* 1. 4.

2. Without the giving of the Holy Ghost, there had wanted a Testimony that his Gospel was the Gospel of Messias. *Moses* his Ministration was confirmed by Signs and Wonders and mighty Deeds, both in *Egypt*, in the Wilderness, and at the Red-Sea; wherefore 'twas necessary that the Doctrine of Redemption by Blood, which is the Doctrine of the Gospel of this Jesus, should be also *confirmed with signs following*. Hence both himself, and Apostles did as frequently work Miracles and do mighty Deeds, as his Ministers now do preach: which Signs and Miracles, and Wonders, confirmed their Doctrine, though themselves, both Master and Scholar was (in appearance the most considerable) mean: yea, they by the means

18 *out*] *out of*

of the Holy Ghost, have so ratified, confirmed, and setled the Gospel in the World, that no Philosopher, Tyrant, or Devil hath been able hitherto, to move it out of its place. *He confirmed the Word with Signs following*, Mar. 16. 20. Heb. 2. 4.

3. As the giving of the Holy Ghost was necessary thus; so was it necessary also to strengthen them that were intrusted with his Gospel.

1. To preach it effectually.
2. To stand to it boldly.
3. And to justifie it to be the Doctrine of Messias incontroulably.

1. To preach it effectually; *in demonstration of the Spirit*, 1 Cor. 2. 4. 2 Cor. 6. 4, 5, 6. Joh. 16. 8, 9.

2. To stand to it boldly; Then *Peter* filled with the Holy Ghost, said: *And they saw the Boldness of Peter and John*, Act. 4. 8, 13.

3. To justify the Doctrine incontroulably. *I will give you a Mouth and Wisdom which all your Adversaries shall not be able to resist or gainsay. And they were not able to resist the Wisdom and Spirit by which he spake*, Luk. 21. 15. Act. 6. 10.

Now, I say, that God should give the Holy Ghost to Jesus, to confirm this Gospel, *Redemption from sin by his Blood*; what is it, but that by his Blood he hath paid full price to God for Sinners, and obtained Eternal Redemption for them?

But again, the Benefit which we receive at the Coming of the Holy Ghost, doth more demonstrate this Truth; hath Christ purchased Sinners, and are they the Price of his Blood? Yes. But how doth that appear? Why, because by the Holy Ghost which he hath received to give us, we are fitted for the Inheritance which by his Blood is prepared for us.

1. By the Spirit of God we are quickned, and raised from a state of Sin, but that we could not be, were it not that an Atonement is made for us; first, by the Blood of Christ our Saviour. This is true; for they that are quickned by the Holy Ghost, are quickned by it through the Word of the Gospel which offereth Justification to Sinners through Faith in his Blood: yea, we are said to be quickned together with him, dead and risen with him: yet so as by the Spirit of God.

14 Act. 4. 8, 13.] Act. 8. 13.

2. We are not only quickned by the Holy Ghost, but possessed therewith; it is given to dwell in our Hearts. *Because ye are Sons, God hath sent forth the Spirit of his Son into your Hearts*, Gal. 4, 4, 5, 6. which Spirit is also our earnest for Heaven, until the Redemption of the purchased Possession; that is, until our Body which is the purchased Possession, be redeemed also out of the Grave, by the Power of the same mighty Spirit of God, *Ephes.* 1. 13, 14.

3. By this Holy Spirit we are made to believe, *Rom.* 15. 13.

4. By this Holy Spirit, we are helped to pray and call God Father.

5. By this Holy Spirit we are helped to understand and apply the Promises.

6. By this Holy Spirit the Joy of Heaven, and the Love of God is shed abroad in the Heart of the Saved.

7. By this Holy Spirit we are made to wait for the hope of Righteousness by Faith, that is, to stand fast through our Lord Jesus in the day when he shall judg the World.

And all this is the Fruit of Redemption by Blood; of Redemption by the Blood of Christ.

This is yet further evident:

1. Because the Work of the Spirit is to lead us into the sayings of Christ; which, as to our Redemption from death, are such as these: *I lay down my Life, that you may have Life. I give my Life a Ransom for many; And the Bread which I will give is my Flesh, which I will give for the Life of the World*, Joh. 6. 51.

2. Because, the Spirit in the Wisdom of Heaven, is not counted a sufficient Testimony on Earth, but as joyned with the Blood of Christ. *There are three that bear witness on Earth, the Spirit, the Water, and the Blood.* These are the Witness of God. The Spirit, because it quickneth; the Blood, because it hath merited; and the Water, to wit, the Word, because by that, *we are clean*, as to life and conversation, 1 *John* 5. 8. *Ephes.* 5. 26. *Rom.* 8. 16. *Psal.* 119. 9.

3. Because, as by the Spirit, so we are sanctified by Faith in the Blood of Jesus, *Heb.* 13. 12.

4. Because when most full of the Spirit, & when that doth work most mightly in us, we are then most in the belief, and admiring

25 Joh. 6. 51.] Joh. 6.

apprehensions of our deliverance from death by the Blood of Jesus, *Revel.* 15. *Chap.* 5. 9.

5. The Holy Ghost breatheth, no-where, so as in the Ministry of this Doctrine; this Doctrine is sent WITH the Holy Ghost from Heaven; yea, as I have hinted, one of the Great Works of the Holy Ghost under the Old-Testament, was to testifie *of the Sufferings of Christ, and the Glory that should follow*, 1 Pet. 1. 11, 12.

Put all these things together and see, if Jesus Christ by what he hath done, hath not paid full price to God for Sinners; *if he hath not obtained Eternal Redemption for them.*

The Fourth Demonstration.

THat Jesus Christ *by what he hath done*, hath paid full price to God for Sinners, *and obtained Eternal Redemption for them*, is evident, if you consider how the preaching thereof hath been from that time to this, *a mighty Conquerer over all kind of Sinners.* What Nation, what People, what kind of Sinners have not been subdued by the preaching of a Crucified Christ. He upon the White Horse with his Bow and his Crown hath conquered, doth conquer, *and goeth forth yet conquering and to conquer*, Revel. 6. 2. *And I, saith he, if I be lifted up from the Earth, will draw all men unto me*: but what was it to be lifted up from the Earth? Why, it may be expounded by that saying; *As Moses lifted up the Serpent in the Wilderness, so must the Son of Man be lifted up, that whosoever believeth in him might not perish but have everlasting life*, Joh. 12. 32. Chap. 3. 14, 15.

He was *then* lifted up, when he was hanged upon a Tree between the Heavens and the Earth as the Accursed of God for us. The Revelation of this, it conquers all Nations, Tongues and People. *And they sang a new Song, saying, thou art worthy to take the Book and to open the Seals thereof, for thou wast slain, and hast redeemed us to God by thy Blood, out of every Kindred, and Tongue, and People, and Nation*, Revel. 5. 9. Hence the Apostle *Paul* chose, above all Doctrines, to preach up a Crucified Christ, and resolved so to do: *For I determined*, saith he, *not to know any thing among you, save Jesus Christ and him crucified*, 1 Cor. 2. 2, 3.

1. The Doctrine of Forgiveness of Sin, conquered his very Murderers. They could not withstand the Grace; them bloody ones, that would kill him what-ever it cost them, could stand no longer, but received his Doctrine, fell into his Bosom, and obtained the Salvation which is in Christ Jesus. *They shall look upon him whom they have pierced and mourn for him, as one mourneth for his only Son, & they shall be in bitterness for him, as one is in bitterness for his first-born*, Zech. 12. 10. Now was this Scripture eminently fulfilled, when the Kindness of a Crucified Christ, broke to pieces the Hearts of them that had before been his Betrayers and Murderers. Now was there a *great mourning in Jerusalem*; now was there wailing and lamentation, mixed with joy and rejoycing.

2. Though *Paul* was mad, exceeding mad against Jesus Christ of *Nazareth*, yea, though he was his avowed Enemy, seeking to put out his Name from under Heaven: yet the Voice from Heaven [*I am Jesus, &c.*] *I am the Saviour*; how did it conquer him, make him throw down his Arms, fall down at his Feet, and accept of the forgiveness of Sins freely by grace, through Redemption by Faith in his Blood.

3. They at *Samaria*, though before *Philip* preached to them, worshipped and admired the Devil in *Magus*, yet when they believed *Philip's* preaching of Christ unto them, and forgiveness of sins through Faith in his Name, great joy was amongst them, and they were baptized both Men and Women, *Act.* 8. He preached, saith the Text, *the things concerning the Kingdom of God, and the Name of Jesus Christ*; that is, all the Blessings of Life, through the Name of Jesus Christ; for he is the Mediator, and without his Blood come no spiritual blessings to men.

4. How was the sturdy Jailer overcome by a Promise of forgiveness of sins by Faith in Jesus Christ? It stopt his Hand of self-murder, it eased him of the gnawings of a guilty Conscience, and fears of Hell-Fire, and filled his Soul with rejoicing in God, *Act.* 16. 30, 31, 32, 33.

5. How were those that used curious arts, that were next to, if not, Witches indeed; I say, how were they prevailed upon, and overcome by the Word of God; which is, the Gospel of good Tidings through Faith in the Blood of Christ? *Act.* 19. 17, 18.

6. How were the *Ephesians*, who sometimes were *far* from God; how, I say, were they made *nigh* by the Blood of Christ! *Ephes.* 2. 13.

7. The *Colossians*, though sometimes dead in their Sins, yet how were they quickned by God, through the Forgiveness *of all their Trespasses*, and they had that through his Blood, *Col.* 2. 13. *Chap.* 1. 14.

What shall I say, no man could as yet stand before, and not fall under the Revelation of the Forgiveness of Sins through a Crucified Christ; as hanged, as dying, as accursed for Sinners; he draws all men unto him, men of all sorts, of all degrees.

Shall I add, how have men broken through the Pricks to Jesus, when he hath been discovered to them! neither Lyons nor Fires, nor Sword, nor Famine, nor Nakedness, nor Peril; neither Death, nor Life, nor Angels, nor Principalities, nor Powers, nor things present, nor things to come, nor Height, nor Depth, nor any other Creature, shall be able to separate us from the Love of God, which is in Christ Jesus our Lord, *Rom.* 8. 35, 36, 37, 38, 39.

The Fifth Demonstration.

THat Jesus Christ by what he hath done, hath paid full price to God for Sinners, and obtained Eternal Redemption for them is evident, *by the Peace and Holiness, that by that Doctrine possesseth mens Souls; The Souls of Men awakned, and that continue so.* By awakened men I mean, such as through the Revelation of their Sin and Misery, groan under the want of Jesus to save them, and that continue sensible that they needs must perish if his benefits be not bestowed upon them.

For otherwise the Gospel ministreth neither Peace nor Holiness to any of the Souls of the Sons of Men; that is to say, not Saving Peace and Holiness. ☞ The Gospel of Grace and Salvation, is above all Doctrines, the most dangerous, if in word only it be received by graceless men: if it be not attended with a Revelation of Men's need of a Saviour: if it be not accompanied in the Soul by the Power of the Holy Ghost. For such Men as have only the notions of it, are of all Men liable to the greatest Sins, because there *wanteth* in their notions, *the Power of Love*, which alone can constrain them to love

Jesus Christ. And this is the Reason of these Scriptures. *They turn the Grace of God into wantonness*; *They turn the Grace of our God into lasciviousness*, Jude 4.

For some when they hear of the Riches of Grace, *through Christ*, that hearing, not being attended with the Faith & Love which is in Christ Jesus; those Men receive the notions of this good Doctrine, only to cloak their wickedness, and to harden themselves in their Villanies.

Others when they hear, being leavened before with the Leaven of some other Doctrine, some Doctrine of the Righteousness of the World, or Doctrine of Devils; forthwith make head against, and speak evil of the blessed Doctrine; and because some that profess it, are not cleansed from their filthiness of flesh and spirit, and do not perfect Holiness in the Fear of God: therefore others conclude that all that profess it are such, and that the Doctrine it self, tendeth to encourage, or at least, to tolerate licentiousness, as they imagined and affirmed of *Paul*, that he should say, *Let us do evil that good may come*, Rom. 3. 8, 9.

The ground of that wicked Conclusion of theirs, was, because he by the Allowance of God affirmed, *That as sin had reigned unto death, so grace reigned unto life in a way of Righteousness by Jesus Christ our Lord.* Nay then, says the Adversary, we may be as unholy as we will, and that by the Doctrine you preach: for, if where sin abounds, grace abounds more, the consequence of a wicked life, is but the hightening, advancing and magnifying of Grace. But what saith the Apostle? my conclusions are true, *That grace doth reign above sin*; but to say, *let us therefore sin*, that Man's Damnation is just; because such an one abuseth, and maketh the most devilish use of the Blessedest Doctrine that ever was heard of in the World amongst Men. Besides, 'tis evident that such know not the Power thereof; nor have felt or savored its blessedness, for where this Gospel cometh in truth, *it naturally produceth Peace and Holiness.*

1. *Peace.* He is our Peace, he is the Prince of Peace, he giveth peace in his High Places.

This word *Peace* hath in it a double respect.

1. It respecteth God: *He hath made peace by the Blood of his Cross*; that is, he hath made peace for us with God, having appeased the

rigor of his Law, and satisfied justice for us. Hence it is said: *The Peace of God which passeth all understanding, shall keep your Hearts and Minds through Christ Jesus*, Col. 1. 20. Phil. 4. 7. *The Peace of God, that is*, the Doctrine of Reconciliation by Christ's being made to be sin for us, THAT *shall keep the Heart*, that is, from despair or fainting under apprehensions of weakness and justice: But yet, this Peace of God, cannot be apprehended nor be of any comfort to the Heart, but as the Man looks for it *through Christ Jesus*. Therefore that clause is added, *through Christ Jesus*: for he is Peace-maker, 'tis he that reconcileth us to God *in the Body of his Flesh through death*; for by his doing and suffering he presented God with Everlasting Righteousness, with Everlasting Righteousness for Sinners: Upon this we have Peace with God. Hence Christ is called King of Righteousness FIRST; *first being by interpretation King of Righteousness, and after that also King of Salem, which is King of Peace*, Heb. 7. 1, 2. For he could not make peace with God, 'twixt us and him, but by being first the Lord of Righteousness, the Lord *our* Righteousness: but having first compleated Righteousness, he then came and preached Peace, and commanded his Ambassadors to make Proclamation of it to the World, 2 *Cor*. 5. 19, 20, 21. For 'twas want of Righteousness, that caused want of Peace: now then righteousness being brought in, it followeth that he hath made peace. *For he is our Peace who hath made both one, and hath broken down the middle Wall of Partition between us. Having abolished in his Flesh the Enmity, even the Law of Commandments, contained in Ordinances, for to make in himself of twain one new Man, so making Peace, and that he might reconcile both unto God, in one Body by the Cross, having slain the Enmity thereby, and came and preached Peace to you that were afar off, and to them that were nigh; for through him we both have access, by one spirit unto the Father*, Ephes. 2. 14, 15, 16, 17, 18.

2dly. This word Peace respecteth our inward quietness of heart which we obtain, by beholding this Reconciliation made by Christ, with God, for us. *Being justified by Faith, we have Peace with God through our Lord Jesus Christ. The God of Peace fill you with all joy and peace in believing*, Rom. 5. 1, 2. *Chap*. 15. 13.

This Peace is expressed diversly:

1. Sometimes it is called QUIETNESS; for it calms the Soul from

20 2 *Cor*. 5. 19, 20, 21.] 2 *Cor*. 5. 19, 21.

those troublous Fears of damning, because of sin. *And the work of Righteousness shall be Peace, and the Effect of Righteousness, Quietness and Assurance for ever*, Isa. 32. 17.

2. Sometimes it is called BOLDNESS; for by the Blood of Christ a Man hath encouragement to approach unto God. *Having, brethren, Boldness to enter into the Holiest by the Blood of Jesus, by a new and living way which he hath consecrated for us through the Vail, that is to say, his Flesh*, Heb. 10. 19, 20.

3. It is sometimes called CONFIDENCE; because by Jesus Christ we have not only encouragement to come to God, but confidence; that if we ask any thing according to his Will, he not only heareth, but granteth the Request which we put up to him. *In whom we have boldness and access, with confidence, by the Faith of Jesus*, Ephes. 3. 12. 1 John 5. 14, 15.

4. Sometimes this Peace is expressed by REST, because a Man having found a sufficient Fulness to answer all his Wants, he sitteth down, and looks no further for satisfaction. *Come unto me all ye that labor and are heavy laden, and I will give you rest*, Mat. 11. 28.

5. It is also expressed by SINGING, because the Peace of God when it is received into the Soul by Faith, putteth the Conscience into a Heavenly and Melodious Frame. *And the Ransomed of the Lord shall return, and come to* Zion *with Songs, and Everlasting Joy upon their Heads, they shall obtain joy and gladness, and sorrow and sighing shall fly away*, Isa. 35. 10.

6. Sometimes it is expressed, or discovered by an Heavenly glorying and boasting in Jesus Christ, because this Peace causeth the Soul to set its Face upon its Enemies with Faith of a Victory over them for ever by its Lord Jesus. *Let him that glorieth glory in the Lord*; and, *My Soul shall make her boasts in the Lord, the Humble shall hear thereof, and be glad*, Jer. 9. 23, 24. Psalm 34. 2.

7. Sometimes it is expressed, or discovered by *Joy, Joy unspeakable*; because the Soul having seen it self reconciled to God, hath not only quietness, but such apprehensions do now possess it of the unspeakable Benefits it receiveth by Christ with respect to the World to come, that it is swallowed up with them. *Whom having not seen, ye love, in whom though now ye see him not, yet believing ye rejoice, with joy unspeakable, and full of glory*, 1 Pet. 1. 8.

8. Lastly: It is expressed, or discovered by *the Triumph* that ariseth sometimes in the Hearts of the Believers; for they at times are able to see Death, Sin, the Devil, and Hell, and all Adversity conquered by, and tied as Captives at the Chariot-Wheels of Jesus Christ: Taken captive, I say, and overthrown for ever. *Thanks be to God who causeth us always to triumph in Christ. O clap your Hands, O ye People, sing unto God with the voice of Triumph*, 2 Cor. 2. 14. Psalm 47. 1.

Now that all this should be a *cheat*, is impossible, that is, it is impossible that Believers should thus have Peace with God through the Blood of his Cross; he having not paid full price to God for them; especially if you consider that the Authors of this Peace, are all the three in the Godhead, and that upon a double account.

1. In that they have given us a Gospel *of Peace*, Rom. 10. 15. or a New-Testament which propoundeth Peace with God through the Redemption that is in Christ. Now as this is called the Gospel of Peace; so 1. It is called, *The Gospel of God*, 1 Thes. 2. 9. 2. The Gospel of Christ, 2 Thes. 1. 8. *Rom.* 15. 19. 3. A Gospel indited by the Holy Ghost, 1 *Thes.* 4. 8.

I say therefore, that Redemption and Salvation, being that throw Christ, and the Truth thereof proclaimed by the Father, the Word, and the Holy Ghost, in the Word of the Truth of the Gospel, it must needs be that we who believe, shall be saved, if we hold the confidence and the rejoicing firm unto the End.

2. As the three in the God-head are the Authors of this Peace, by inditing for us the Gospel of Peace, or the good Tidings of Salvation by Jesus Christ: *So they are the Authors of our Peace, by working with that word of the Gospel in our Hearts.* And hence 1. the Father is called the God of Peace; now *the God of Peace be with you all: And the very God of Peace sanctifie you*, Rom. 15. 33. 1 Thes. 5. 23. And because he is the God of Peace, therefore he filleth those that believe in his Christ, *with joy and peace through believing*, Rom. 15. 13.

2. Again, Christ is called the Prince of Peace; therefore the Prayer is, *Grace be with you and Peace from God the Father, and the Lord Jesus Christ*, 2 Thes. 1. 2.

3. The Holy Ghost also is the Author of this Peace, this inward

16–17 2. The Gospel of Christ, 2 Thes. 1. 8.] 2 Thes. 1. 8. 2. The Gospel of Christ,

Peace; *Even righteousness, and peace, and joy in the Holy Ghost*, Rom. 14. 17.

And, I say, as I also have already said, the procuring or meritorious Cause of this Peace, is the doings and sufferings of Christ. *Therefore by his Doings and Sufferings he paid full price to God for Sinners, and obtained Eternal Redemption for them*: else God would never have indited a Proclamation of Peace for them, and the Tenour of that Proclamation to be the Worthiness of the Lord Jesus: yea, he would never have wrought with that Word in the Heart of them that believe, to create in them Peace, Peace.

Secondly, As peace with God is an Evidence (the Blood of Christ being the Cause thereof), that Christ hath by it paid full price to God for Sinners; so Holiness in their Hearts taking its beginning from this Doctrine, makes this fifth Demonstration of double strength.

1. That Holiness, true gospel Holiness, possesseth our hearts by this Doctrine, 'tis evident; *because the ground of Holiness, which is the Spirit of God in us, is ministred to us by this Doctrine*. When the Apostle had insinuated that the *Galatians* were bewitched because they had turned from the Doctrine of Christ Crucified, he demands of them, *Whether they received the Spirit by the Works of the Law, or by the hearing of Faith*, Gal. 3. 1, 2, 3, 4. That is, whether the Spirit took possession of their Souls by their Obedience to the ten Commandments; or by their giving credit to the Doctrine of the forgiveness of their Sins, by Faith in this Crucified Christ: strongly concluding not by the Law, but by the hearing, or preaching of Faith; that is, of the Lord Jesus as Crucified, who is the Object of Faith.

2. As this Doctrine conveyeth the ground, or ground-Work which is the Spirit; so also it worketh in the Heart those three Graces, Faith, Hope, Love; all which as naturally purifie the Heart from wickedness, as Sope, or Niter, cleanseth the Cloath. *He purified their Hearts by Faith*, by Faith in Christ's Blood. *And everyone that hath this Hope in him, purifieth himself even as he is pure*. And also Love, you shall see what that doth, if you look into the Text, *Act*. 15. 9. 1 *Joh*. 3. 3, 4. 1 *Cor*. 13. Now I say, *this Faith* groundeth it self in the Blood of Christ; Hope waiteth for the full enjoyments of the Purchase of it, *in another world*: and love is begot, and worketh, by

the Love that Christ hath expressed by his Death, and by the Kindness he presenteth us with in his Heart-Blood, *Rom.* 3. 24. 1 *Cor.* 15. 19, 20. 2 *Cor.* 5. 14.

Besides, what arguments so prevailing, as such as are purely Gospel? To instance a few:

1. What stronger, *than a free forgiveness of Sins? A certain Man had two Debtors, the one owed him five Hundred Pence, and the other Fifty, and when they had nothing to pay, he frankly forgave them both, tell me therefore which of them will love him most?* Luk. 7. 41, 42, 47.

2. What stronger argument to holiness, than to see, that though forgiveness comes free to us, *yet it cost Christ Jesus Heart-Blood to obtain it for us? Herein is love, not that we loved God, but that he loved us, and sent his Son to be the Propitiation for our Sins.* And this Love of God in giving his Christ and of Christ, in dying for us, there is no argument stronger to prevail with a sensible and awakened Sinner to judg, *he should live to him that died for him, and rose again*, 2 Cor. 5. 15.

3. What stronger argument to holiness than this? *If any man sins, we have an Advocate with the Father, Jesus Christ the Righteous*, 1 Joh. 2. 1, 2. Unsanctified and graceless wretches, know not how to use these Words of God; the Hypocrites also fly in our faces, because we thus urge them; but a Heart that is possessed with Gospel-ingenuity, or to speak more properly, that is possessed with Gospel-Grace, and with Divine Considerations, cries; if it be thus, O let me never sin against God! *for the Love of Christ constrains me*, 2 Cor. 5. 14.

4. What greater argument to holiness, than to see the Holy Scriptures so furnished with promises of Grace and Salvation by Christ, that a Man can hardly cast his Eye into the Bible, but he espieth one, or another of them? who would not live in such an House, or be servant to such a Prince, who, besides his exceeding in good Conditions, hath Gold and Silver as common in his Palace, as stones are by the High-way side? *Having therefore these Promises, dearly beloved, let us cleanse our selves from all filthiness of flesh and spirit, perfecting holiness in the Fear of God*, 2 Cor. 7. 1.

5. What greater argument to holiness, than to have our Performances, though weak and infirm, from us; yet accepted of God in Jesus Christ, 1 *Pet.* 2. 4, 5, 6?

3 1 *Cor.* 15. 19, 20.] 1 *Cor.* 15. 19. 16 2 Cor. 5. 15.] 2 Cor. 5. 14.

6. What greater argument to holiness, than to have our Soul, our Body, our Life hid, and secured with Christ in God? *Mortifie therefore your Members that are upon the Earth, fornication, uncleanness, inordinate affection, evil concupiscence, and covetousness which is idolatry*, Col. 3. 1, 2, 3, 4, 5, 6.

7. What greater argument to holiness, than to be made the Members of the Body, of the Flesh, and of the Bones of Jesus Christ? *Shall I take the Members of Christ, and make them the Members of an harlot, God forbid*, Ephes. 5. 30. 1 Cor. 6. 15.

Now all these, and five times as many more, having their foundation in the Love, Blood and Righteousness of Christ, and operating in the Soul by Faith, are the great Argument unto that Holiness, to which is annexed eternal Life. 'Tis worth our observing, that in *Act.* 26, at the 18. the Inheritance belongs *to them, that are sanctified by Faith in Jesus Christ*: For all other pretences to holiness, they are but a stollen semblance of that which is true and acceptable; though 'tis common for even that which is counterfeit to be called by the deluded, the True; and to be reckoned to be in them that are utter strangers to Faith, and the Holiness that comes by Faith. *But whosoever compoundeth any like it, or whosoever putteth any of it upon a stranger; shall even be cut off from his People*, Exod. 30. 33. God knoweth which is holiness that comes by Faith in forgiveness of Sins, and acceptance with God, through Christ: and God knows which is only such feignedly; and accordingly will he deal with Sinners in that great Day of God Almighty.

The Sixth Demonstration.

THat Jesus Christ by what he hath done, hath paid full price to God for Sinners, and obtained Eternal Redemption for them, is evident; *because Prayers are accepted of God only upon the account and for the sake of the Name of Jesus Christ: Verily, verily I say unto you, whatsoever ye shall ask the Father in my Name, he will give it you*, Joh. 16. 23. In my Name, in the Name of Jesus Christ of *Nazareth*: in the Name of him that came into the World to save Sinners, by dying

6 7.] *om.*

for them a grievous bloody Death; in his Name that hath by himself put away sin, and brought unto God acceptable Righteousness for Sinners; in his Name; why in his Name, if he be not accepted of God? why in his Name, if his undertakings for us are not well-pleasing to God? But, by these Words, *in my Name*, are insinuated that his Person, and performances, as our undertaker, is accepted by the Father of Spirits. We may not go in our own names, because *we* are Sinners; not in the Name of one another, because *all* are Sinners; but why not in the Name of an Angel? Because they are not those that did undertake for us, or had they, they could not have done our work for us. *He putteth no trust in his Saints, yea the Heavens are not clean in his Sight*, Job 4. 18. Chap. 15. 15. It may further be objected:

Since Jesus Christ is God equal with the Father, and so hath naturally the same Power to give as the Father, why should the Father rather than the Son, be the great Giver to the Sinners of the World? and why may we not go to Christ in the Name of the Father, as well as to the Father in the Name of Christ? I say, how can these things be salved, but by considering that sin and justice put a NECESSITY upon it, that thus must our Salvation be obtained. *Sin* and *Justice* could not reconcile, nor could a means be found out to bring the Sinner and an Holy God together, but by the Intercepting of the Son, who must take upon him to answer Justice, and that by taking our Sins from before the Face of God by bloody Sacrifice, not by Blood of others, as the High-Priests under the Law. *For, as every High-Priest is ordained to offer Gifts and Sacrifices, it is of necessity that this Man have somewhat also to offer*, Heb. 8. 3. which Offering and Sacrifice of his being able to perfect for ever them that are sanctified and set apart for Eternal Life: *Therefore the name of the Person that offered* (even Jesus made of God an High-Priest) is acceptable with God; yea therefore is he made for ever, by his doing for us, the Appeaser of the Justice of God, and the Reconciler of Sinners to him. Hence it is, that HIS *Name* is that which it behoveth us to mention when we come before God, for what God hath determined in his Counsels of Grace to bestow upon Sinners; because, for his *Name sake* he forgiveth them. *I write to you little Children, because your Sins are forgiven you for his Name sake. To him give all the Prophets witness, that through his Name, whosoever believeth in him, shall receive Remission of Sins*, 1. Joh. 2. 12. Act. 10. 43.

They therefore that would obtain the forgiveness of Sins, must ask it of God through the Name of Jesus; and he that shall sensibly and unfeignedly do it, he shall receive the forgiveness of them. *Whatsoever you shall ask the Father in my Name, he will give it you.* Hence it is evident that he hath not only paid full price to God for them, but also obtained Eternal Redemption for them.

And it is observable, the Lord Jesus would have his Disciples make a *Proof* of this, and promiseth, that if they do, they shall experimentally find it so. *Hitherto*, saith he, *ye have asked nothing in my* NAME, *ask and ye shall receive, that your joy may be full*, Ioh. 16. 24. As who should say, O my Disciples, you have heard what I have promised to you, even that my Father shall do for you, whatsoever ye shall *ask him in my Name.* Ask now therefore, and prove me, if I shall not make my Words good: Ask, I say, what you need, and see if you do not receive it to the Joying of your Hearts. *At that day ye shall ask in my Name, and I say not unto you, that I will pray the Father for you.* I do not bid you ask in my Name, as if the Father was yet hard to be reconciled, or unwilling to accept you to mercy: my Coming into the World was the Design of my Father, and the Effect of his Love to Sinners; but there is sin in you, and justice in God; therefore that you to him might be reconciled, I am made of my Father Mediator, wherefore *ask* in my Name; for, *there is none other name given under the Heavens among Men whereby they must be saved*, Act. 4. 12. Ask in my Name, love is let out to you through me, it is let out to you by me in a way of Justice, which is the only secure way for you. Ask in my Name, and my Father will love you. *The Father himself loveth you, because you have loved me, and have believed that I came out from God*, Joh. 16. 27. My Fathers Love is set first upon me, for my Name is chief in his Heart, and all that love me are beloved of my Father, and shall have what they need if ye ask in my Name.

But, I say, what cause would there be to ask in *his* Name more than in the Name of *some other*? since justice was provoked by our Sin; if he had not undertook to make up the difference that by Sin was made betwixt justice and us. For though there be in this Jesus

2 1 Joh. 2. 12.] 1 Joh. 2. 14.

infinite worth, infinite righteousness, infinite merit; yet if he make not with these, interest for us, we get no more benefit thereby than if there were no Mediator: But this Worth and Merit, is in him *for us*; for he undertook to reconcile us to God, it is *therefore* that his Name is with God so prevailing for us poor Sinners: and therefore that we ought to go to God in his Name. Hence therefore it is evident that Jesus Christ hath paid full price to God for Sinners, and obtained Eternal Redemption for them.

The Seventh Demonstration.

THat Jesus Christ, by what he hath done, hath paid full price to God for Sinners, *&c.* is evident, because we are commanded also to give God thanks in his Name. By him therefore let us offer the Sacrifice of Praise continually, that is, the Fruit of our Lips, giving thanks in his Name, *Heb.* 13. 15.

By him therefore; wherefore? because he also, that he might *sanctifie us with his own Blood suffered without the Gate*, ver. 12.

He sanctified us with his Blood, but why should the Father have thanks for this? even because the Father gave him for us, that he might die to sanctifie us with his Blood. *Giving thanks to the Father which hath made us meet to be Partakers of the Inheritance of the Saints in Light, who hath delivered us from the Power of Darkness, and hath translated us into the Kingdom of his dear Son, in whom we have redemption through his Blood, even the forgiveness of Sins*, Col. 1. 12, 13, 14. The Father is to be thanked, for the contrivance was also his, but the Blood, the Righteousness, or that worthiness, for the Sake of which we are accepted of God, is the Worthiness of his own dear Son; as it is meet therefore that God should have thanks, so it is necessary that he have it in his Name for whose sake we indeed are accepted of him.

Let us therefore by him offer Praise.

First, For the Gift of his Son, and for that we stand quit through him in his Sight; and that in despite of all inward weakness, and that in despite of all outward enemies.

When the Apostle had taken such a view of himself as to put himself into a maze, with an out-cry also, *who shall deliver me?* he quiets himself with this sweet conclusion, *I thank God through Jesus Christ*, Rom. 7. 25. He found more in the Blood of Christ to save him, than he found in his own Corruptions to damn him; but that could not be, had he not paid full price for him, had he not obtained Eternal Redemption for him. And can an Holy and Just God require that we give thanks to him in his Name, if it was not effectually done for us by him?

Further, when the Apostle looks upon Death, and the Grave, and strengtheneth them by adding to them Sin and the Law, saying, *The Sting of Death is sin, and the Strength of Sin is the Law*: he presently addeth, *but thanks* be to God which giveth us the Victory through Jesus Christ, 1 *Cor*. 15. 56, 57. The Victory over Sin, Death, and the Law, the Victory over these through our Lord Jesus Christ; but God hath given us the Victory: but it is through our Lord Jesus Christ, through his fulfilling the Law, through his destroying Death, and through his bringing in Everlasting Righteousness. *Elisha* said to the King of *Israel*, that *had it not been that he regarded the Person of* Jehoshaphat, *he would not look to him, nor regard him*, 2 Kin. 3. 14. nor would God at all have looked to, or regarded thee, but that he respected the Person of Jesus Christ.

Let the Peace of God therefore rule in your Hearts, to the which also you are called in one body, and be you thankful, Col. 3. 15. The Peace of God, of that we have spoken before; but how should this rule in our Hearts? he by the next words directs you; *Let the Word of Christ dwell in you richly*; that is, the Word that makes revelation of the Death and Blood of Christ, and of the Peace that is made with God for you thereby.

Giving thanks always for all things unto God & the Father in the Name of our Lord Jesus Christ, Ephes. 5. 20. For all things: for all things come to us through this Name Jesus; Redemption, Translation, the Kingdom, Salvation, with all the good things wherewith we are blessed.

These are the Works of God, he gave his Son, and he brings us to him, and puts us into his Kingdom; that is, his true Body, which *Jeremiah* calleth, *a putting among the Children, and a giving us a Godly heritage of the Host of Nations*, Joh. 6. Jer. 3. 19.

2 Rom. 7. 25.] Rom. 7. 24. 12 1 *Cor*. 15. 56, 57.] 1 *Cor*. 15.

4. *Now thanks be to God, which causeth us always to triumph in Christ*, 2 Cor. 2. 13, 14.

See here our cause of triumph is through Christ Jesus, and God causeth us through him to triumph: First and chiefly, because Christ Jesus hath done our work for us, hath pleased God for our Sins, hath spoiled the powers of Darkness. God gave Jesus Christ to undertake our Redemption; Christ did undertake it, did engage our Enemies, and spoiled them. *He spoiled principalities and powers, and made a shew of them openly, triumphing over them upon the Cross*, Col. 2. 14, 15. Therefore, it is evident that he paid full price to God for Sinners with his Blood, because God commands us, to give thanks to him *in his Name*; through his Name. *And whatsoever ye do in word or deed, do all in the Name of the Lord Jesus, giving thanks unto God, and the Father, by him*, Col. 3. 17.

Take this Conclusion from the whole, no thanks are accepted of God, that come not to him in the Name of his Son; his Son must have the Glory of conveying our thanks to God, because he was he that by his Blood conveyeth his Grace to us.

The Eighth Demonstration.

IN the next place; That Jesus Christ by what he hath done, hath paid full price to God for Sinners, and obtained Eternal Redemption for them, is evident; *Because we are exhorted to wait for, and to expect the full and glorious Enjoyment of that Eternal Redemption, at the second Coming of the Lord from Heaven*: *Let your loins be girded about, and your Lights burning, and you your selves like unto men that wait for their Lord, that when he cometh and knocketh, ye may open unto him immediately*, Luk. 12. 35, 36.

Jesus Christ hath obtained by his Blood Eternal Redemption for us, and hath taken it up now in the Heavens, is (as I have shewed) preparing for us there Everlasting Mansions of rest; and then he will come again *for us*. This Coming is intended in this Text, and this Coming we are exhorted to wait for: and that I may more fully shew the Truth of this Demonstration, observe these following Texts.

1. It is said, *he shall* chuse our Inheritance for us. *He shall chuse our*

inheritance for us, the excellency of Jacob *whom he loved*, Selah. *God is gone up with a Shout, &c.* Psal. 47. 4, 5.

These latter words intend the Ascension of Jesus Christ: His Ascension, when he had upon the Cross made reconciliation for iniquity; his Ascension into the Heavens to prepare our Mansions of Glory for us. For, our Inheritance is in the Heavens; our House, our Hope, our Mansion-House, and our incorruptible and undefiled Inheritance is in Heaven, 2 *Cor.* 5. 1, 2. *Col.* 1. 5, 6. *Joh.* 14. 1, 2. 1 *Pet.* 1. 3, 4, 5.

This is called the Eternal Inheritance, of which we that are called, have received the Promise already, *Heb.* 9. 14, 15.

This Inheritance, I say, he is gone to chuse for us in the Heavens, because by his Blood he obtained it for us, *Heb.* 9. 12. and this we are commanded to wait for: but how ridiculous, yea, how great a cheat would this be, had he not by his Blood obtained it for us.

2. *We wait for his Son from Heaven, whom he raised from the dead even Jesus Christ, which delivered us from the Wrath to come*, 1 Thes. 1. 10. He delivered us by his Blood, and obtained the Kingdom of Heaven for us, and hath promised that he would go and prepare our places, and come again and fetch us thither. *And if I go and prepare a Place for you, I will come again and receive you unto myself, that where I am there ye may be also*, Joh. 14. 3. This then is the Cause that we wait for him, we look for the reward of the Inheritance at his Coming, who have served the Lord Christ in this World.

3. *For our conversation is in Heaven, from whence we look for the Saviour, the Lord Jesus Christ*, Phil. 3. 20. We look for him to come, yet as a Saviour; a Saviour he was at his first Coming, and a Saviour he will be at his second Coming. At his first Coming, he bought and paid for us; at his Second Coming, he will fetch us to himself. At his first Coming, he gave us promise of the Kingdom; at his second Coming, he will give us possession of the Kingdom. At his first Coming, he also shewed us how we should be, by his own Transfiguration; at his second Coming, *he will change our vile Body that it may be fashioned like unto his Glorious Body*, Phil. 3. 21.

4. Hence therefore it is, that his Coming is called, our *blessed Hope. Looking for the Blessed Hope, and glorious Appearing of the Great*

8 2 *Cor.* 5. 1, 2.] 2 *Cor.* 1. 2.

God, and our Saviour Jesus Christ, Tit. 2. 13. A Blessed Hope indeed, if he hath bought our Persons with his Blood, and an Eternal Inheritance *for us* in the Heavens: A blessed Hope indeed, if also at his Coming we be certainly carried thither. No marvel then if Saints be bid to wait for it, and if Saints themselves long for it. But what a disappointment would these waiting Believers have, should all their expectations be rewarded with a Fable? and the result of their Blessed Hope can amount to no more, if our Saviour, the Lord Jesus Christ, either denieth to come, or coming, bringeth not with him the HOPE, the blessed HOPE that is laid up for us in Heaven: *Whereof we have certainly been informed by the Word of the Truth of the Gospel*, Col. 1. 5, 6.

5. *For Christ was once offered to bear the Sin of many, and unto them that look for him, shall he appear the second Time, without sin unto Salvation*, Heb. 9. 28. Here we have it promised that he shall come, that he shall appear the second time, but not with sin, as he did before, to wit, with, and in the Sin of his People when he bare them in his own Body; but *now* without sin, for he *before* did *put them away by the Sacrifice of himself*. Now then let the Saints look for him, not to die for the purchasing of their persons by Blood, but to bring to THEM, and to bring them also to that Salvation, that before, when he died, he obtained of God for them by his Death.

These things are to be expected therefore, by them that believe in, and love Jesus Christ, and that from faith and love serve him in this world; they are to be expected by them, being obtained *for* them by Jesus Christ: And he shall give the Crown, saith *Paul*, not only to me, but to them that love his Appearing, 2 *Tim*. 4. 8, 9.

Now forasmuch as this Inheritance in the Heavens is the Price, Purchase, and Reward of his Blood; how evidently doth it appear, that he hath paid full price to God for Sinners? Would God else have given him the Heaven to dispose of to us that believe, and would he else have told us so! Yea, and what comfort could we have to look for his Coming, and Kingdom, and Glory, as the Fruits of his Death; if his Death had not for that purpose been sufficiently efficacious. *O! the Sufferings of Christ, and the Glory that shall follow*, 1 Pet. 1. 11.

The Ninth Demonstration.

THat Jesus Christ by what he hath done, hath paid full price to God for Sinners, and obtained Eternal Redemption for Sinners is evident, *Because of the Threatnings wherewith God hath threatned, and the Punishments wherewith he punished those that shall refuse to be saved by Christ, or seek to make insignificant the Doctrine of Righteousness by Faith in him.*

This Demonstration consisteth of three parts.

1. It suggesteth that some refuse to be justified or saved by Christ, and also seek to make insignificant the Doctrine of Righteousness by Faith in him.

2. That God doth threaten these.

3. That God will punish these.

That some refuse to be saved by Christ is evident, from many Texts. He is the Stone which the Builders have rejected: He is also disallowed of Men: The Jews stumble at him, and to the Greeks he is foolishness; both saying this Man shall not rule over us, or how can this man save us? *Psal.* 118. 22. *Mat.* 25. 42. 1 *Pet.* 2. 4. 1 *Cor.* 1. 23. *Luk.* 19. 14.

The Causes of mens refusing Christ are many.

1. Their Love to sin.
2. Their Ignorance of his Excellency.
3. Their Unbelief.
4. Their Deferring to come to him in the acceptable Time.
5. Their leaning to their own Righteousness.
6. Their entertaining Damnable Doctrines.
7. Their loving the praise of Men.
8. The meanness of his Ways, his People, *&c.*
9. The just Judgment of God upon them.
10. The Kingdom is given to others.

Now these, as they all refuse him, so they seek more or less, some practically, others in practice and judgment also, to make insignificant the Doctrine of Righteousness by Faith in him.

1. One does it by preferring his Sins before him.
2. Another does it by preferring his Righteousness before him.

18 *Mat.* 25. 42.] *Mat.* 24. 42.

3. Another does it by preferring his Delusions before him.

4. Another does it by preferring the World before him.

Now these God threatneth, these God punisheth.

First, God threatneth them. *Whosoever shall not receive that Prophet, shall be cut off from amongst his People*, Acts 3. 23. The Prophet is Jesus Christ; the Doctrine that he preached was that he would lay down his Life for us, that he would give us his Flesh to eat, and his Blood to drink by Faith: and promised, that if we did eat his Flesh, and drink his Blood, *we should have Eternal Life.* He therefore that seeth not, or that is afraid to venture his Soul for Salvation on the Flesh and Blood of Christ by Faith, he refuseth this Prophet, he heareth not this Prophet; and him God hath purposed to cut off. But would God thus have threatned, if Christ by his Blood and the Merits of the same, had not paid full price to God for Sinners, and obtained Eternal Redemption for them.

Secondly. *Sit thou on my Right Hand until I make thine Enemies thy Foot-stool*, Psal. 110. 1. Mat. 22. 44. Heb. 1. 13. The Honour of sitting at God's Right Hand, was given him because he died, and offered his Body once for all. *This Man when he had offered up one Sacrifice for sins for ever, sat down on the Right Hand of God, from henceforth expecting till his Enemies be made his Foot-stool*, Heb. 10. 11, 12, 13. Expecting, since God accepted his Offering, that those that refused him should be trodden under foot, that is, sunk by him into, and under endless & unsupportable vengeance. But would God have given the World such an account of his sufferings, that by one Offering he did perfect for ever them that are sanctified? yea, and would he have threatned to make those foes his Foot stool, that shall refuse to venture themselves upon his Offering (for they are indeed his Foes) had not his Eternal Majesty been well pleased with the Price he paid to God for Sinners; had he not obtained Eternal Redemption for them?

Thirdly. *He shall come from Heaven with his mighty Angels in flaming-fire, taking vengeance on them that know not God, and that obey not the Gospel of our Lord Jesus Christ*, 2 Thes. 1. 7, 8.

Here he expressly telleth us wherefore they shall be punished: Because they know not God, and obey not the Gospel of our Lord Jesus Christ, where also is notably intimated that he that obeyeth not the Gospel of Christ, knoweth not God, neither in his Justice or Mercy. But what is the Gospel of our Lord Jesus Christ, but good tidings of good things; to wit, Forgiveness of Sins by Faith in his Blood, an Inheritance in Heaven by Faith in his Blood, as the whole of all the foregoing discourse hath manifested? Now, I say, can it be imagined that God would threaten to come upon the World with this Flaming-Fiery-Vengeance to punish them for their Non-subjection to his Sons Gospel, if there had not been by himself paid to God full price for the Souls of Sinners; if he had not obtained Eternal Redemption by his Blood for Sinners?

Fourthly. *And* Enoch, *the seventh from* Adam *also prophesied of these, saying, Behold, the Lord cometh with ten thousands of his Saints, to execute judgment upon all, and to convince all that are ungodly among them of all their ungodly Deeds, which they have ungodly committed, and of all their hard Speeches which ungodly Sinners have spoken against him,* Jude 14, 15.

The LORD that is here said to come with ten thousands of his Saints, is *Jesus Christ* himself: and they that come with him are called *his Saints,* because given to him by the Father, for the Sake of the shedding of his Blood. Now in that he is said to come to execute judgment upon all, and especially those that speak hard Speches against him; 'tis evident that the Father tendereth his *Name* which is, Jesus, a Saviour, and his undertaking for our Redemption; and as evident that the hard Speeches, intended by the Text, are such as vilify him, *as Saviour,* counting the Blood of the Covenant, *unholy,* and trampling him, that is Prince of the Covenant under the Feet of their reproachful Language; this is counted a putting of him to open shame, and a despising the riches of his Goodness, *Heb.* 10. *Chap.* 6. *Rom.* 2. Time would fail to give you a view of the revilings, despiteful sayings, and of the Ungodly Speeches which these abominable Children of Hell, let fall in their Pamphlets, Doctrines, and Discourses, against this Lord the King. But the threatning is, He shall execute judgment upon them for all their ungodly Deeds, and for all their hard Speeches that ungodly Sinners have spoken against him.

Fifthly. *Take heed therefore lest that come upon you which is spoken of in the Prophets: Behold, ye Despisers, and wonder, and perish: for I work a*

Work in your days, a Work which you shall in no wise believe, though a Man declare it unto you, Act. 13. 40, 41.

This Work is the same we have been all this while treating of, to wit, Redemption by the Blood of Christ for Sinners, or that Christ hath paid full price to God for Sinners, and obtained Eternal Redemption for them. This is manifest from *ver*. 23 to *ver*. 29 of this Chapter.

Now, observe, there are, and will be Despisers of this Doctrine, and they are threatened with the Wrath of God. *Behold, ye Despisers, and wonder, and perish*: But would God so carefully have cautioned Sinners to take heed of *despising this Blessed Doctrine*, and have backed his Caution with *a threatning that they shall perish*, if they persist, had not himself received by the Blood of Christ full price for the Souls of Sinners?

Secondly. *As God threatneth, so he punisheth those that refuse his Son, or that seek to vilify or make insignificant, the Doctrine of Righteousness by Faith in him.*

1. He punisheth them with the abidings of his Wrath. *He that believeth not the Son, shall not see life, but the Wrath of God abideth on him*, Joh. 3. 36.

The Wrath of God for men; for sin stands already condemned by the Law; & the Judgment is, that *they who refuse the Lord Jesus Christ*, shall have this Wrath of God for ever lie, and abide upon them: For they want a Sacrifice to pacifie wrath for the Sin they have committed, having resisted, and refused the Sacrifice of the Body of Christ. Therefore it cannot be that they should get from under their present condition who have refused to accept of the undertaking of Christ for them.

Besides, God to shew that he taketh it ill at the Hands of Sinners, that they should refuse the Sacrifice of Christ, hath resolved that *there shall be no more Sacrifice for sin. If therefore we sin wilfully after we have received the Knowledg of the Truth*; *there remaineth no more Sacrifice for sin*, Heb. 10. 26. God doth neither appoint another, neither will he accept another who-ever brings it. And here those sayings are of their own natural force; *How shall we escape, if we neglect so great Salvation*! And again, *See that ye refuse not him that speaketh, for if they escaped not who refused him that spake on Earth* (Moses), *How shall we escape if we turn away from him* (Christ) *that speaketh from Heaven!* Heb. 2. 3. Chap. 12. 25.

This therefore is a mighty Demonstration that Christ by what he hath done, hath paid full price to God for the Souls of Sinners, because God so severely threatneth, and also punisheth them that refuse to be justified by his Blood: he threatneth as you have heard, and punisheth by leaving such men in their Sins, under his heavy and unsupportable Vengeance here.

Secondly. *He that believeth not shall be damned*, Mar. 16. 16. damned in Hell-Fire. He that believeth not, but what should he believe? Why!

1. That Jesus is the Saviour. *If*, saith he, *ye believe not that I am he, ye shall die in your Sins.*

2. He that believeth not that he hath undertaken and compleatly perfected Righteousness for us, shall die in his Sins, shall be damned and perish in Hell-fire: For such have no cloak for their Sin, but must stand naked to the shew of their Shame before the Judgment of God, that fearful Judgment. Therefore, after he had said, there remains for such, no more sacrifice for sin; he adds, *But a certain fearful looking for of judgment*; there is for them left nothing *but the Judgment of God*, and his fiery Indignation which shall devour the Adversaries. *He that despised* Moses's *Law died without mercy under two or three Witnesses; of how much sorer punishment suppose ye shall he be thought worthy, who hath trodden under foot the Son of God, and counted the Blood of the Covenant, wherewith he was sanctified, an Unholy thing, and done despite to the Spirit of Grace?* Heb. 10. 27, 28, 29.

See here, if fury comes not up now into the Face of God: now is mention made of his *fearful* Judgment and *fiery* Indignation. Now, I say, is mention made thereof, when it is suggested that some have light thoughts of him, count his Blood unholy, and trample his Sacrificed Body under the Feet of their Reproaches: *Now is he a Consuming fire*, and will burn to the lowest Hell. *For we know him that hath said, Vengeance belongeth unto me, I will recompence, saith the Lord. And again, The Lord shall judg his People*, Heb. 10. 30. These words are urged by the Holy Ghost, on purpose, to beget in the Hearts of the Rebellious, reverend thoughts, and an high esteem of the Sacrifice

26 Heb. 10. 27, 28, 29.] Heb. 10. 25, 26. 34 30.] 28, 29, 30.

which our Lord Jesus offered once for all upon Mount *Calvary* unto God the Father for our Sins; for that is the very argument of the whole Epistle.

It is said to this purpose in one of *Paul*'s Epistles to the *Thessalonians*, That because men receive not the Love of the Truth, that they might be saved; *For this cause God shall send them strong delusions, that they should believe a ly and be damned*, 2 Thes. 2. 10, 11, 12.

The Truth mentioned in the Place, *is Jesus Christ. I am the Truth*, saith he, *Joh.* 14. 6. The Love of the Truth, is none else but the Love and Compassion of Jesus Christ, in shedding his Blood for Mans Redemption. *Greater love than this hath no man, that a Man lay down his Life for his Friends*, Joh. 15. 13. This then is the Love of the Truth (of Jesus) that he hath laid down his Life for us. Now that the rejectors of this Love, should by this their rejecting procure such wrath of God against them, that rather than they shall miss of damnation, himself will chuse their Delusions for them, and also give them up to the effectual Working of these Delusions: what doth this manifest, but that God is displeased with them that accept not of Jesus Christ for Righteousness, and will certainly order that their end shall be everlasting Damnation: therefore Jesus Christ hath paid full price to God for Sinners, and obtained Eternal Redemption for them.

The Use of the Doctrine.

I come now to make some use of, and to apply this Blessed Doctrine of the Undertaking of Jesus Christ; and of his paying full Price to God for Sinners, and of his obtaining Eternal Redemption for them.

The first Use.

BY this Doctrine, *we come to understand many things which otherwise abide obscure and utterly unknown*, because this Doctrine is accompanied with the Holy Ghost, that Revealer of secrets, and Searcher

7 Thes. 2. 10, 11, 12.] 2 Thes. 2.

of the deep things of God, 1 *Pet.* 1. 12. *Ephes.* 1. 17. 1 *Cor.* 2. The Holy Ghost comes down with this Doctrine, as that in which it alone delighteth: therefore is it called *The Spirit of Wisdom and Revelation in the Knowledg of Jesus Christ. He giveth also the Light of the Knowledg of the Glory of God in the Face of Jesus Christ*, 2 Cor. 4. 6. Little of God is known in the World where the Gospel is rejected: the Religious Jew, and the Wise Gentile may see more of God in a Crucified Christ, than in Heaven and Earth besides: For *in him are hid all the Treasures of Wisdom and knowledg*: not only in his Person, as God, but also in his Undertakings as Mediator. Hence *Paul* telleth us, *That he determined not to know any thing among the* Corinthians *but Jesus Christ and him Crucified*, Col. 2. 2, 3. 1 Cor. 2. 2, 3. I say more of God is revealed in this Doctrine to us, than we can see of him in Heaven and Earth without it.

First, *Here* is more of *his* WISDOM seen, than in his making, and upholding all the Creatures. *His Wisdom*, I say, in *devising means* to reconcile Sinners to an Holy and Infinite Majesty, to be a *Just God*, and YET *a Saviour*; to be *just* to his Law, *just* to his Threatning, *just* to himself, and yet save Sinners, can no-way be understood till thou understandest why Jesus Christ did hang on the Tree; for here only is the Riddle unfolded, *Christ died for our Sins*, and therefore can God in justice save us, *Isa.* 45. 21. And hence is Christ called The Wisdom of God, not only because he is so essentially, but because by him is the greatest Revelation of his Wisdom towards man. In Redemption therefore, by the Blood of Christ, God is said *to abound towards us in all wisdom*, Ephes. 1. 7, 8. Here we see the highest Contradictions reconciled, here Justice kisseth the Sinner, here a Man stands just in the Sight of God, while confounded at his own Pollutions; and here he that hath done no good, hath yet a sufficient Righteousness; even the Righteousness of God which is by Faith of Jesus Christ.

Secondly, *The* JUSTICE *of God*, is *here* more seen, than in punishing all the Damned. *He spared not his own Son*, is a Sentence which more revealeth the Nature of the Justice of God, than if it had said *he spared not all the World.* True, he cast Angels from Heaven, and drowned the Old World; he turned *Sodom* and *Gomorrah* into Ashes, with many more of like nature, but what were all these to the

Cursing of his Son? yea, what were ten thousand such manifestations of his Ireful Indignation against Sin, to that of striking, afflicting, chastising, and making the darling of his Bosom the Object of his Wrath and Judgment? Here it is seen he respecteth not persons, but, judgeth sin, and condemneth him on whom it is found; yea although on Jesus Christ his well-Beloved, *Rom.* 8. 32. *Gal.* 3. 13.

Thirdly, *The Mystery of God's* WILL, is *here* more seen, than in hanging the Earth upon nothing; while he condemneth Christ though Righteous, and justifieth us though Sinners: while he maketh him to be sin for us, and us the Righteousness of God in him, 1 *Pet.* 3. 18. 2 *Cor.* 5. 20.

Fourthly, *The* POWER *of God*, is *here* more seen, than in making of Heaven and Earth; for, for one to bear, and get the Victory over Sin, when charged by the Justice of an Infinite Majesty, in so doing, he sheweth the Height of the Highest Power: For where sin by the Law is charged, and that by God immediatly, there an Infinite Majesty opposeth, and that with the whole of his Justice, Holiness, and Power: So then, he that is thus charged, and engaged for the Sin of the World, must not only be equal with God, but shew it, by over-coming that Curse and Judgement that by Infinite Justice is charged upon him for Sin.

When Angels and Men had sinned, how did they fall and crumble before the Anger of God! they had not power to withstand the terrour, nor could there be worth found in their Persons, or Doings, to appease displeased Justice. But behold here stands the Son of God before him in the Sin of the World, his Father finding him there, curseth, and condemns him to death: but he by the Power of his God-head, and the Worthiness of his Person and Doings, vanquisheth sin, satisfieth God's Justice, and so becomes the Saviour of the World. Here then is Power seen: Sin is a Mighty thing, it crusheth all in pieces, save him whose Spirit is Eternal, *Heb.* 9. 14. Set Christ, and his Sufferings aside, and you neither see the Evil of Sin, nor the Displeasure of God against it; you see them not in their utmost. Had'st thou a view of all the Legions that are now in the pains of Hell, yea, couldest thou hear their shreeks, and groans together at once, and feel the whole of all their burden: much of the evil of Sin, and of the Justice of God against it, would be yet unknown by thee; for thou wouldest want power to feel, and bear the utmost! A Giant shews not his Power, by killing of a little Child, nor yet is his might seen by the resistance that such a little one makes, but then he sheweth his power when he dealeth with one like himself: yea, and the Power also of the other is then made manifest in saving himself from being swallowed up with his Wrath. Jesus Christ also made manifest his Eternal Power and God-head, more, by bearing and over-coming our Sins; than in making, or upholding the whole World: Hence Christ Crucified, is called *the Power of God*, 1 Cor. 1. 23, 24.

Fifthly, The LOVE *and* MERCY *of God*, is more seen in, and by this Doctrine, than any other way. Mercy and Love are seen in that God gives us Rain and fruitful Seasons, and in that he filleth our Hearts with food and gladness; from that bounty he bestoweth upon us as men, as his Creatures. Oh! but herein is Love made manifest *in that Christ laid down his Life for us*: And God commended his Love towards us, *in that while we were yet Sinners Christ died for us*; 1 Joh. 3. 16. Chap. 4. 10. Rom. 5. 8.

Never Love like this, nor did God ever give such discovery of his Love from the beginning to this Day. *Herein is Love, not that we loved God, but that he loved us, and sent his Son to be the Propitiation for our Sins.*

Here is Love, that God sent his Son! his Darling! his Son that never offended! his Son, that was always his delight! Herein is Love that he sent him to save Sinners! to save them by bearing their Sins! by bearing their Curse! by dying their Death! and by carrying their Sorrows! Here is Love in that while we were yet Enemies, Christ died for us! yea, here is Love, *in that while we were yet without strength, Christ died for the Ungodly*, Rom. 5. 6.

The Second Use.

But Secondly, as this Doctrine giveth us the best discovery of God; so also it giveth us the best discovery of our selves, and our own things.

29 Rom. 5. 6.] Rom. 5.

First, It giveth us the best discovery of our selves: Wouldest thou know Sinner, what thou art; *look up to the Cross*, and behold a Weeping, Bleeding, Dying Jesus: nothing could do but that, nothing could save thee but his Blood; Angels could not, Saints could not, *God could not*, because he could not ly; because he could not deny himself. What a thing is Sin, that it should sink all that bear its burden, yea it sunk the Son of God himself into death and the Grave, and had also sunk him into Hell-fire for ever, had he not been the Son of God; had he not been able to take it on his Back, *and bear it away*. O! This Lamb of God. Sinners were going to Hell, Christ was the Delight of his Father, and had a whole Heaven to himself; but that did not content him, Heaven could not hold him. *He must come into the World to save Sinners*, 1 Tim. 1. 15. Ay, and had he not come, thy Sins had sunk thee, thy Sins had provoked the Wrath of God against thee; to thy perdition and destruction for ever. There is no Man, but is a Sinner, there is no Sin but would damn an Angel, should God lay it to his charge. Sinner, the Doctrine of Christ crucified crieth, therefore, aloud unto thee, *that sin hath made thy Condition dreadful*: See your selves, your Sin, and consequently, the Condition that your Souls are in, by the Death and Blood of Christ; Christs Death giveth us the most clear discovery of the dreadful Nature of our Sins. I say again, if sin be so dreadful a thing as to break the Heart of the Son of God (for so he saith it did) how shall a Poor, Wretched, Impenitent, damned Sinner, wrestle with the Wrath of God. Awake Sinners, you are lost, you are undone, you perish, you are damned, Hell-fire is your Portion for ever, if you abide in your Sins, and be found without a Saviour in the dreadful Day of Judgment.

Secondly, For your good Deeds cannot help you, the Blood of Christ tells you so: For by this Doctrine, *Christ died for our Sins*, God damneth to death and hell, the Righteousness of the World. Christ must die, or Man be damned: where is now any room for the Righteousness of Men? room, I say, for Man's Righteousness, as to his Acceptance and Justification. Bring then thy Righteousness to the Cross of Jesus Christ, and in his Blood behold the Demands of Justice; behold them, I say, in the Cries, and Tears, in the Blood and Death of Jesus Christ. Look again, and behold the Person dying;

such an one as *never* sinned, nor offended at *any* time, *yet he dies.* Could an Holy Life, an Innocent, Harmless Conversation have saved one from death, *Jesus had not died.* But he must die, Sin was charged, therefore Christ must die.

Men therefore need to go no further to prove the Worth of their own Righteousness, than to the Death of Christ: They need not be to seek in that Matter till they stand before the Judgement-Seat.

Quest. *But how should I prove the Goodness of mine own Righteousness, by the Death and Blood of Christ?*

Ans. Thus: If Christ must die for Sin, then all thy Righteousness cannot save thee. *If Righteousness comes by the Law, then Christ is dead in vain,* Gal. 2. 21. By this Text 'tis manifest, that either Christ died in vain, or thy Righteousness is vain. If thy Righteousness can save thee, then Christ died in vain. If nothing below, or besides the Death of Christ could save thee, then thy Righteousness is in vain; one of the two must be cast away, either Christ's, or thine. Christ Crucified to save the World, discovereth two great evils in Man's own Righteousness: I mean when brought for Justification and Life.

1. It opposeth the Righteousness of Christ.

2. It condemneth God of Foolishness.

1. It opposeth the Righteousness of Christ; in that it seeketh it self to stand, where should the Righteousness of Christ, to wit, in God's affection for the Justification of thy Person, and this is one of the highest affronts to Christ, that poor man is capable to give him: Right worthily therefore, doth the Doctrine of the Gospel damn the Righteousness of Men, and promiseth the Kingdom of God to Publicans and Harlots rather.

2. It condemneth God of Foolishness: For if Works of Righteousness which we can do, can justifie from the Curse of the Law in the Sight of God, then is not all the Treasures of Wisdom found in the Heart of God and Christ: For this Dolt-headed Sinner, hath now found out a Way of his own, unawares to God, to secure his Soul from Wrath and Vengeance. I say, unawares to God; for he never imagined that such a thing could be, for had he, he would never have purposed before the World began, to send his Son to die for

Sinners. Christ is the Wisdom of God, as you have heard, and that as he is our Justifying Righteousness. God was manifest in the Flesh to save us, is the great Mystery of Godliness. But wherein lyeth the depth of this Wisdom of God in our Salvation, *if Man's Right-hand can save him*? Job 40. 10, 11, 12, 13, 14.

Yea, wherefore hath God also given it out, that there is none other Name given to Men, under Heaven whereby we must be saved: I say again, why is it affirmed, without shedding of Blood is no Remission, if Mans good Deeds can save him?

This Doctrine therefore of the Righteousness of Christ, being rightly preached, and truly believed, arraigneth and condemneth Man's Righteousness to Hell: It casteth it out, as *Abraham* cast out *Ismael*.

BLOOD! BLOOD, the sound of *Blood*, abaseth all the Glory of it. When Men have said all, and shewed us what they can, they have no Blood to present God's Justice with; yet 'tis *Blood that maketh an Atonement for the Soul*, and nothing but *Blood* can wash us from our Sins, *Levit*. 17. 11. *Revel*. 1. 5. *Heb*. 9.

Justice calls for *Blood*, Sins call for *Blood*, the Righteous Law calls for *Blood*; yea the Devil himself must be overcome by *Blood*: Sinner where is now thy Righteousness? Bring it before a Consuming Fire [for our God is a Consuming Fire]; Bring it before the Justice of the Law: yea try if ought but the Blood of Christ can save thee from thy Sins, and Devils; try it, I say, by this Doctrine; go not one step further before thou hast tried it.

Thirdly, By this Doctrine we are made to see, *the worth of Souls*: it cannot be but that the Soul is of Wonderful Price, when the Son of God will not stick to spill his Blood for it. O Sinners, you that will venture your Souls for a little pleasure, surely you know not the worth of your Souls. Now if you would know what your Souls are worth, and the Price which God sets them at, read that Price by the Blood of Christ. The Blood of Christ was spilt to save Souls. *For ye are bought with a Price*, and that Price none other than the Blood of Christ; wherefore glorify God in your Bodies and in your Spirits which are Gods, 1 *Cor*. 6. 20. Sinners, you have Souls, can you behold a Crucified Christ and not Bleed, and not Mourn, and not fall in Love with him?

The third Use.

By this Doctrine Sinners, as Sinners, are encouraged to come to God for mercy, for the Curse due to Sin is taken out of the way. I speak now to Sinners that are awake, and see themselves Sinners. There are two things in special when Men begin to be awakened, that kill their thoughts of being saved.

1. A Sense of sin.
2. The Wages due thereto.

These kill the Heart, for who can bear up under the guilt of Sin? *If our Sins be upon us, and we pine away in them, how can we* THEN *live?* Ezek. 33. 10. How indeed! it is impossible. So neither can Man grapple with the Justice of God. *Can thine Heart endure, or can thine Hands be strong?* they cannot. *A wounded Spirit who can bear?* Men cannot, Angels cannot: wherefore if now Christ be hid, and the blessing of Faith in his Blood denied, wo be to them: such go after *Saul* and *Judas*, one to the Sword, and the other to the Halter, *Ezek.* 22. 14. *Prov.* 18. 14. and so miserably end their days; for come to God they dare not, the thoughts of that Eternal Majesty strikes them through.

But now present such Poor dejected Sinners with a Crucified Christ, and perswade them that the Sins under which they shake and tremble, was long ago laid upon the Back of Christ, and the *Noise*, and *Sense*, and *Fear* of damning, begins to cease, depart, and fly away: Dolours, and Terrours fade, and vanish, and that Soul conceiveth hopes of Life. For thus the Soul argueth, is this indeed the Truth of God, that Christ was made to be Sin for me! was made the Curse of God for me! Hath he indeed born all my Sins, and spilt his Blood for my Redemption? O blessed Tidings, O welcome Grace! *Bless the Lord O my Soul, and all that is within me bless his Holy Name.* Now is peace come, now the Face of Heaven is altered: *Behold all things are become new.* Now the Sinner can abide Gods Presence, yea sees unutterable Glory and Beauty in him: For here he sees Justice smite. While *Jacob* was afraid of *Esau*, how heavily did he drive, even towards the Promised Land? but when *killing* thoughts were turned into *kissing*, and the fears of the Swords Point turned into Brotherly Embraces, what says he, *I have seen thy Face, as though it had been the Face of God, and thou wast pleased with me*? Gen. 33. 10.

So, and far better is it, with a poor distressed Sinner at the Revelation of the Grace of God through Jesus Christ. *God was in Christ reconciling the World unto himself not imputing their Trespasses to them:* O! what work will such a word make upon a wounded Conscience, especially when the next words follow. *For he hath made him to be Sin for us, who knew no sin, that we might be made the Righteousness of God in him.*

Now the Soul sees qualifications able to set him *quit* in the Sight of God: Qualifications *prepared already*, Prepared I say *already*, and that by God through Christ; even such as can perfectly answer the Law. What doth the Law require? If Obedience, *here it is*; if Bloody Sacrifice, *here it is*; if infinite Righteousness, *here it is*. Now then the Law condemns him that Believes, *before God*, no more; for all its Demands are answered, all its Curses are swallowed up in the Death and Curse Christ underwent.

Object. *But reason saith, since Personal Sin brought the Death, surely Personal Obedience must bring us Life and Glory.*

Ans. True, Reason saith so, and so doth the Law it self, *Rom.* 10. 5. but God, we know, is above them both, and he in the Covenant of Grace, saith otherwise: to wit, *That if thou shalt confess with thy Mouth the Lord Jesus, and shall believe in thine Heart that God hath raised him from the Dead, thou shalt be saved*, Rom. 10. 6, 7, 8, 9.

Let Reason then hold his tongue, yea let the Law with all his Wisdom subject it self to him that made it; let it look for sin where God hath laid it; let it *approve* the Righteousness which *God approveth*: yea though it be not *that* of the Law, *but that by Faith of Jesus Christ.*

God hath *made* him our Righteousness; God hath made him our Sin; God hath made him our Curse; God hath made him our Blessing. Methinks this word *God hath made it so*, should silence all the World.

The fourth Use.

Fourthly, *By this Doctrine sufficiency of argument is ministred to the tempted, to withstand, thereby, the assaults of the Devil.*

When the Souls begin to seek after the Lord Jesus, then Satan begins to afflict and distress, as the *Canaanites* did the *Gibeonites*, for making Peace with Jehoshuah, *Jos.* 10. 1, 6.

There are three things that do usually afflict the Soul that is earnestly looking after Jesus Christ.

1. Dreadful accusations from Satan.

2. Grievous defiling and infectious thoughts.

3. A strange readiness in our Nature to fall in with both.

By the first of these the Heart is made continually to tremble. Hence his Temptations are compared to the roaring of a Lyon, 1 *Pet.* 5. 8. For as the Lyon by roaring killeth the Heart of his Prey, so doth Satan, kill the Spirit of these that hearken to him: For when he tempteth, especially by way of accusation, he doth to us, as *Rabshakeh* did to the Jews: *He speaks to us in our own Language.* He speaks our Sin at every word, our guilty Conscience knows it, he speaks our Death at every word, our doubting Conscience feels it.

Secondly, Besides this, there doth now arise even in the Heart such defiling, and foul infectious thoughts, that putteth the Tempted to their wits end: for now it seems to the Soul that the very flood-Gates of the Flesh are opened, and that to sin there is no stop at all; now the Air seems to be covered with darkness, and the Man is as if he was changed into the nature of a Devil: Now if ignorance and unbelief prevail, he concludeth that he is reprobate, made to be taken and destroyed.

Thirdly, Now also he feeleth in him a readiness to fall in with every temptation; a readiness, I say, continually present, *Rom.* 7. 21. This throws all down, now despair begins to swallow it up; now it can neither pray, nor read, nor hear, nor meditate on *God*, but Fire and Smoke continually bursteth forth of the Heart against *him*; now sin and great confusion puts forth it self in all: yea, the more the Sinner desireth to do a duty sincerely, the further off it always finds it self: For by how much the Soul struggleth under these distresses, by so much the more doth Satan put forth himself to resist, still infusing more poison, that if possible it might never struggle more (for strugglings are also as poison to Satan). The Fly in the Spider's Webb, is an emblem of the Soul in such a condition; the Fly is entangled in the Webb, at this the Spider shews himself; if the Fly stir again, down comes the Spider to her, and claps a Foot upon her, if yet the Fly makes a noise, then with poisoned Mouth the Spider lays hold upon her; if the Fly struggle still, then he poisons her more and more; what shall the Fly do now? why she dies, if some-body does not quickly release her. *This is the case of the Tempted, they are entangled in the Webb* (their Feet and Wings are entangled), *now Satan shews himself, if the Soul now struggleth, Satan laboureth to hold it down; if it now shall make a noise, then he bites with blasphemous Mouth* (more poisonous than the Gall of a Serpent). *If it struggle again, then he poisoneth more and more:* insomuch that it needs at last must die in the Net, *if the Man, the Lord Jesus, helps not out.*

The afflicted Conscience understands my words.

Further, though the Fly in the Webb, is altogether uncapable of looking for relief, yet this awakened tempted Christian is not; what must he do therefore? how should he contain hopes of life? If he looks to his Heart there is Blasphemy; if he looks to his duties, there is Sin; if he strives to mourn and lament, perhaps he cannot, unbelief and hardness hinder: shall this Man lie down in despair? No: shall he trust to his duties? No: shall he stay from Christ till his Heart is better? No: What then? Let him NOW look to Jesus Christ Crucified, then shall he see his Sins answered for, then shall he see Death a-dying, then shall he see *Guilt* born by another, and there shall he see the Devil overcome. This sight destroys the Power of the first Temptation; purifies the Heart and inclines the Mind to all good things.

And to encourage thee, tempted Creature, to this most Gospel-Duty: Consider, that when Jesus Christ read his Commission upon the entering into his Ministry, he proclaimed: *The Spirit of the Lord is upon me, because he hath anointed me to preach the Gospel to the Poor, he hath sent me to heal the broken-Hearted, to preach deliverance to the Captives, and recovering of sight to the Blind, to set at liberty them that are bruised, to preach the acceptable Year of the Lord*, Luk. 4. 18, 19.

These things therefore should the Tempted believe, but believing is now sweating-work; for Satan will hold as long as possible, and only stedfast Faith can make him fly: But O! the Toyl of a truly gracious Heart in this Combate, if Faith be weak, he can scarce get higher than his Knees; Lord help, Lord save, and then down again, till an Arm from Heaven takes him up; until Jesus Christ be evidently set forth Crucified for him, and Cursed for his Sin: for then (and not till then) the Temptation rightly ceaseth, at leastwise for a Season. Now the Soul can tend to look about it, and thus consider with it self: If Christ hath born my Sin and Curse, then 'tis taken away from me, and seeing thus to take away sin, was the Contrivance of the God of Heaven, I will bless his Name, hope in his Mercy, and look upon Death and Hell with Comfort. *Thine Heart shall meditate terrour, thou shalt see the Land that is very far off*, Isa. 33. 16, 17, 18.

The fifth Use.

Fifthly, This Doctrine *makes Christ precious to the Believers. Unto you therefore which believe he is precious*, 1 Pet. 2. 7. This Head might be greatly enlarged upon, and branched out into a Thousand particulars, & each one full of weight and glory.

1. By considering what Sin is.
2. By considering what Hell is.
3. By considering what Wrath is.
4. By considering what Eternity is.
5. By considering what the loss of a Soul is.
6. What the loss of God is.
7. What the loss of Heaven is.
8. And what it is to be in utter Darkness with Devils and damned Souls for ever and ever.

And after all to conclude, *from all these Miseries the Lord Jesus delivered me.*

Further, This makes Christ precious, if I consider in the next place:

1. How he did deliver me, 'twas with his Life, his Blood; it cost him Tears, Groans, Agony, Separation from God; to do it he endured his Fathers Wrath, bare his Fathers Curse, and died thousands of deaths at once.

2. He did this, while I was his Enemy, without my desires, without my knowledg, without my deserts, he did it unawares to me.

13 1 Pet. 2. 7.] 1 Pet. 2. 5.

3. He did it freely, cheerfully, yea he longed to die for me; yea, Heaven would not hold him for the Love he had to my Salvation, which also he hath effectually accomplished for me at *Jerusalem.* Honourable Jesus! precious Jesus! loving Jesus! *Jonathan's* Kindness captivated *David*, and made him precious in his Eyes for ever. *I am distressed for thee my Brother* Jonathan (said he) *very pleasant hast thou been to me; thy Love to me was wonderful, passing the Love of Women*, 2 Sam. 1. 26. Why, what had *Jonathan* done? O! He had *delivered* David *from the Wrath of* Saul. But how much more should he be precious to me, who hath saved me from Death and Hell! who hath delivered me from the Wrath of God! *The Love of Christ constraineth us.* Nothing will so edge the Spirit of a Christian as, *Thou wast slain, and hast redeemed us to God by thy Blood:* This makes the Heavens themselves ring with joy and shouting. Mark the Words, *Thou wast slain, and hast redeemed us to God with thy Blood, out of every Kindred, and Tongue, and People, and Nation, and hast made us unto our God, Kings, and Priests, and we shall reign on the Earth.* What follows now? *And I beheld, and heard the Voice of many Angels round about the Throne, and the Beasts, and the Elders, and the Number of them was ten thousand times ten thousand, and thousands of thousands, saying with a loud Voice, Worthy is the* Lamb *that was slain, to receive Power, and Riches, and Wisdom, and Strength, and Honour, and Glory, and Blessing; and every Creature which is in Heaven, and on the Earth, and such as are in the Sea, and all that are therein heard I, saying, Blessing, Honour, Glory, and Power, be unto him that sitteth upon the Throne, and to the* LAMB *for ever and ever*, Revel. 5. 9, 10, 11, 12, 13.

Thus also is the Song, that New-Song, that is said to be sung by the Hundred fourty and four thousand which stand with the LAMB upon Mount *Sion*, with his Fathers Name written in their Fore-heads. These are also called Harpers, Harping with their Harps. *And they sang as it were a new Song before the Throne, and before the four Beasts, and the Elders; and none could learn that Song but the Hundred and fourty and four thousand, which were redeemed from the Earth*, Revel. 14. 1, 2, 3.

But why could they not learn that Song? Because they were not redeemed; none can sing of this Song but the Redeemed: they can give Glory to the Lamb, the Lamb that was slain, and that redeemed them to God by his Blood. 'Tis Faith in his Blood on Earth, that will make us sing this Song in Heaven. These Shoutings, and Heavenly Songs must needs come from Love put into a Flame by the Sufferings of Christ.

The last Use.

If all these things be true, what follows but a Demonstration of the Accursed Condition of those among the Religious in these Nations whose notions put them far off from Jesus, and from venturing their Souls upon his Bloody Death. I have observed such a Spirit as this in the World, that careth not for knowing of Jesus; the Possessed therewith do think, that it is not material to Salvation to venture upon a Crucified Christ, neither do they trouble their Heads or Hearts with inquiring whether Christ Jesus be risen, and ascended into Heaven, or whether they see him again or no, but rather are for concluding, that there will be no such thing: These Men speak not by the Holy Ghost, for in the Sum, they call *Jesus Accursed*; but I doubt not to say that many of them are *Anathematised of God, and shall stand so*, till the Coming of the Lord Jesus, to whom be Glory for ever and ever: *Amen.*

THE END.

SAVED BY GRACE

SAVED BY GRACE

Note on the Text

AT least one edition of *Saved by Grace* was published in Bunyan's lifetime, though no copy is known to exist. The Term Catalogue has the following entry for Trinity Term 1676, dated 12 June:

A Discourse of the Grace of God; shewing, 1. What it is to be saved. 2. What it is to be saved by Grace, etc. By John Bunyan. In Twelves. Price, bound, 6d. Both printed for Francis Smith at the Elephant and Castle in *Cornhill*.[1]

The earliest available text is in the *1692 Folio* of Bunyan's works.

1692 FOLIO EDITION

Title-page: Saved by Grace: | OR, A | DISCOURSE | OF THE | GRACE OF GOD. | SHEWING, | I. What it is to be Saved. | II. What it is to be Saved by Grace. | III. Who they are that are Saved by Grace. | IV. How it appears that they are Saved by Grace. | V. What should be the reason that God should choose to save Sinners | by Grace rather than by any other Means.

Collation: Fol. $_{4}$A–$_{4}$C^{4}. Pages: 24 (i.e. 553–76).

Contents: $_{4}$A1^{r} title and beginning of text, $_{4}$A1^{v}–$_{4}$C4^{r} text, $_{4}$C4^{v} conclusion of text and the epistle to the reader. Text printed in double columns separated by vertical rules. Single ornament at head of $_{4}$A1^{r}. Title on $_{4}$A1^{r} is followed by a rule. Postscript on $_{4}$C2^{r} is preceded by a rule. The epistle to the reader on $_{4}$C4^{v} is preceded and followed by rules. The epistle is signed '*J.B.*'

Running Titles: '*Saved by Grace.*' between rules.

Catchwords: (selected) $_{4}$A2^{v} don $_{4}$A4^{v} *Of* $_{4}$B2^{v} 1. BE- $_{4}$B4^{v} grace, $_{4}$C2^{v} 1. THE $_{4}$C4^{r} Object.

Copies Collated: Bedford Public Library; Bodleian, Oxford: British Library; Cambridge University Library; Folger Shakespeare Library; Yale University Library.

The text that follows is based on the Bodleian copy of the *1692 Folio*. The epistle to the reader has been placed at the beginning.

[1] *The Term Catalogues, 1668–1709 A.D.*, ed. Arber, i. 245.

Saved by Grace:

OR, A

DISCOURSE

OF THE

GRACE of GOD.

SHEWING,

I. What it is to be Saved.
II. What it is to be Saved by Grace.
III. Who they are that are Saved by Grace.
IV. How it appears that they are Saved by Grace.
V. What should be the reason that God should choose to save Sinners by Grace rather than by any other Means.

EPHES. 2. 5.
By Grace ye are saved.

1. IN the first Chapter, from the 4*th.* to the 12*th.* verse, the Apostle is treating of the Doctrine of Election, both with respect to the act it self, the end, and means conducing thereto.

1. The act (he tells us) was Gods free choice of some, *ver.* 4, 5, 11.

2. The end was *God's* Glory in their Salvation, *ver.* 6. 14.

3. The means conducing to that end was Jesus Christ himself, *in whom we have redemption through his blood, the forgiveness of sins, according to the riches of his grace,* ver. 9. This done, he treateth of the subjection of the *Ephesians* to the faith (as it was held forth to them in the word of the truth of the Gospel) as also of their being sealed by the holy Spirit of God unto the day of Redemption, *ver.* 12, 13, 14.

Moreover he telleth them how he gave thanks to God for them, making mention of them in his Prayers, even that *he would make them see what is the hope of his calling, and what the riches of the glory of his inheritance, with the Saints, and what was the exceeding greatness of his power to themward who believe, according to the working of his mighty power, which he wrought in Christ when he raised him from the dead,* &c. 15, 16, 17, 18, 19, 20.

And lest the *Ephesians* at the hearing of these their so many Priviledges, should forget how little they deserved them, he tells them, *That in time past, they were dead in trespasses and sins, and that then they walked in them according to the course of this world, according to the prince of the power of the air, the spirit that now worketh in the children of disobedience,* ch. 2. 2, 3.

Having thus called them back to the remem- 2.
brance of themselves, to wit, what they were in their state of Unregeneracy, he proceedeth to shew them, that their first quickning was by the Resurrection of Christ their head (in whom they before were chosen) and that by him they were already set down in heavenly places (*ver.* 5, 6.) inserting by the way, the true cause of all this blessedness, with what else should be by us injoyed in another World: And that is, the Love and Grace of God: *But God who is rich*

1692 Folio Heading of *Saved by Grace* (1676)

To the READER.

Courteous Reader,

IN this little Book thou art presented with a Discourse of the GRACE *of God, and of Salvation, by that Grace; In which Discourse thou shalt find how each Person in the Godhead, doth his part in the Salvation of the Sinner.*

I. *THE* Father *putteth forth his Grace, thus.*

II. *THE* Son *putteth forth his Grace, thus.*

III. *AND the* Spirit *putteth forth his Grace, thus: Which things thou shalt find here particularly handled.*

THOU shalt also find in this small Treatise, the way of God with the Sinner, as to his CONVERSATION, *and the way of the Sinner with God in the same: Where the Grace of* God, *and the wickedness of the Sinner do greatly shew themselves.*

IF thou findest ME *short in things, impute that to my love to brevity.*

IF thou findest me besides the truth in ought, impute that to mine Infirmity.

BUT if thou findest any thing here, that serveth to thy furtherance and joy of Faith, impute that to the Mercy of God, *bestowed on thee and me,*

Thine to serve thee,

With that little I have,

J. B.

14 *that to*] *that*

To the READER.

EPHES. 2. 5.

By Grace ye are saved.

IN the first Chapter, from the *4th.* to the *12th.* verse, the Apostle 1.
is treating of the Doctrine of **Election**, both with respect to the act it self, the end, and means conducing thereto.

1. The act (he tells us) was Gods free choice of some, *ver.* 4, 5, 11.

2. The end was *God's* Glory in their Salvation, *ver.* 6, 14.

3. The means conducing to that end was Jesus Christ himself, *in whom we have redemption through his blood, the forgiveness of sins, according to the riches of his grace*, ver. 7. This done, he treateth of the subjection of the *Ephesians* to the faith (as it was held forth to them in the word of the truth of the Gospel) as also of their being sealed by the holy Spirit of God unto the day of Redemption, *ver.* 12, 13, 14.

Moreover he telleth them how he gave thanks to God for them, making mention of them in his Prayers, even that *he would make them see what is the hope of his calling, and what the riches of the glory of his inheritance, with the Saints, and what was the exceeding greatness of his power to themward who believe, according to the working of his mighty power, which he wrought in Christ when he raised him from the dead*, &c. 15, 16, 17, 18, 19, 20.

And lest the *Ephesians* at the hearing of these their so many Priviledges, should forget how little they deserved them, he tells them, *That in time past, they were dead in trespasses and sins, and that then they walked in them according to the course of this world, according to the prince of the power of the air, the spirit that now worketh in the children of disobedience*, ch. 2. 1, 2.

Having thus called them back to the remembrance of themselves, 2.
to wit, what they were in their state of Unregeneracy, he proceedeth to shew them, that their first **quickning** was by the Resurrection

11 ver. 7.] ver. 9.   28 ch. 2. 1, 2.] ch. 2. 2, 3.

of Christ their head (in whom they before were chosen) and that by him they were already set down in heavenly places (*ver.* 5, 6.) inserting by the way, the true cause of all this blessedness, with what else should be by us injoyed in another World: And that is, the Love and Grace of God: *But God who is rich in mercy, for his great love where with he loved us, even when we were dead in sins, hath quickned us together with Christ: (by* Grace *ye are saved)*. These last words seem to be the Apostles conclusion rightly drawn from the Premises: As who should say, if you *Ephesians* were indeed dead in trespasses and sins; if indeed you were by nature the children of wrath even as others, then you deserve no more than others. Again, if God hath chosen you, if God hath justified and saved you by his Christ, and left others as good as you by nature to perish in their sins, then the true cause of this your blessed condition is, *the free grace of God*; But just thus it is, *therefore by grace ye are saved*; therefore all the good which you enjoy more than others, it is of meer good will.

By Grace ye are Saved.

3. THE method that I shall choose to discourse upon these words, shall be this: I will propound certain Questions upon the words, and direct particular Answers to them; in which Answers I hope I shall answer also (somewhat at least) the expectation of the godly, and consciencious Reader, and so shall draw towards a conclusion.

The Questions are,

1. What is it to be Saved?
2. What is it to be Saved by Grace?
3. Who are they that are Saved by Grace?
4. How it appears that they that are Saved, are saved by Grace?
5. What might be the reasons which prevailed with God to save us by grace, rather than by any other means?

Now the reason why I propound *these* five Questions upon the words, it is, because the words themselves admit them; the first three are grounded upon the several Phrases in the Text, and the two less, are to make way for demonstration of the whole.

The First Question.

What is it to be [Saved]?

THIS Question supposeth, that there is such a thing as Damna- 4.
tion due to Man for sin: For to save supposeth the person to be saved, to be at present in a sad condition; *saving*, to him that is not lost, signifies nothing, neither is it any thing in it self: *To Save, to Redeem, to Deliver* are in the general terms equivalent, and they do all of them suppose us to be in a state of thraldom and misery: Therefore this word *saved*, in the sence that the Apostle here doth use it, is a word of great worth, forasmuch as the miseries from which we are saved, is the misery of all most dreadful.

The miseries from which they that shall be saved, shall by their Salvation be delivered, are dreadful; they are no less than sin, the curse of God, and flames of Hell for ever: What more abominable than sin? What more insupportable than the dreadful wrath of an angry God? And what more fearful than the bottomless Pit of Hell? I say, what more fearful than to be tormented there for ever with the Devil and his Angels? Now to *save* (according to my Text), is to deliver the sinner from these, with all things else that attend them.

And although Sinners may think that it is no hard Matter to answer this Question; yet I must tell you, there is no Man that can feelingly know what it is to be saved, that knoweth not experimentally something of the dread of these three things; as is evident, because all others do even by their practise count it a thing of no great concern, when yet it is of all other, of the highest concern among Men: For *what shall it profit a Man if he shall gain the whole World and lose his own Soul?* Matt. 16. 26.

But I say, if this word *saved* concludeth our deliverance from sin, 5.
how can he tell what it is to be *saved*, that hath not in his conscience groaned under the burden of sin? Yea, it is impossible else that he should ever cry out with all his Heart, *Men and Brethren, what shall we do?* That is, *Do to be saved?* Acts 2. 37. The Man that hath no Sores or Aches, cannot know the vertue of the Salve, I mean, not know it from his own experience, and therefore cannot prize, nor have that esteem of it, as he hath received cure thereby: Clap *a*

Plaster to a well place, and that maketh not its vertue to appear neither can he to whose flesh it is so applied, by that application understand its worth: Sinners, you I mean, that are not wounded with guilt, and oppressed with the burden of sin, you cannot, I will say it again, you cannot know in this senceless condition of yours, what it is to be saved.

Again, this word *saved* (as I said) concludeth deliverance from the wrath of God; how then can he tell what it is to be saved, that hath not felt the burden of the wrath of God? He, he, that is astonished with, and that trembleth at the wrath of God, he knows best what it is to be saved, *Acts* 16. 29.

Further, this word *saved*, it concludeth deliverance from Death and Hell. How then can he tell what it is to be saved, that never was sensible of the sorrows of the one, nor distressed with the pains of the other? The *Psalmist* says, *The sorrows of Death compassed me, and the pains of Hell got hold upon me, and I found trouble and sorrow: Then called I upon the Name of the Lord:* Mark *then*, *Then called I upon the Name of the Lord: O Lord, I beseech thee, deliver my soul, then*, in my distress, when he knew what it was to be saved, *then* he called, because (I say) *then* he knew what it was to be saved, *Psal.* 18. 4, 5. *Psal.* 116. 3, 4.

I say, this is the Man, and this only that knows what it is to be saved: And this is evident, as is manifest by the little regard that the rest have to saving, or the little dread they have of Damnation: Where is he that seeks and groans for Salvation! I say, where is he that hath taken his flight for Salvation! Because of the dread of the wrath to come. *O generation of Vipers, who hath warned you to flee from the wrath to come?* Matt. 3. 7.

Alas! do not the most set light by Salvation? As for sin, how do they love it, embrace it, please themselves with it, hide it still within their Mouth, and keep it close under their Tongue? Besides, for the wrath of God they feel it not, they fly not from it; and for Hell, it is become a doubt to many if there be any, and a mock to those whose doubt is resolved by Atheism.

6. But to come to the Question, *What is it to be saved? To be saved*, may either respect Salvation in the whole of it, or Salvation in the

28 Matt. 3. 7.] Matt. 2. 9.

parts of it, or both: I think this Text respecteth both: to wit, Salvation compleating, and Salvation compleated; for, *to save*, is a work of many steps, or to be as plain as possible, *to* save, is a work that hath its beginning before the World began, and shall not be compleated before it is ended.

First then, we may be said *to be saved, in the purpose of God before the World began*. The Apostle saith, That *he saved us, and called us with an holy calling, not according to our works, but according to his own purpose and grace, which was given us in Christ before the world began*, 2 *Tim.* 1. 9. This is the beginning of Salvation, and according to this beginning, all things concur and fall out in conclusion: *He hath saved us according to his eternal purpose which he purposed in Christ Jesus.* God in *thus* saving, may be said *to save us*, by determining to make those means effectual for the blessed compleating of our Salvation: And hence we are said, *to be chosen in Christ to Salvation*: And again, *That he hath in that choice given us that grace that shall compleat our Salvation:* Yea, the Text is very full, *He hath blessed us with all spiritual blessings in heavenly places in Christ, according as he hath chosen us in him before the foundation of the world*, Ephes. 1. 3, 4.

Secondly, As we may be said *to be saved in the purpose of God, before* 7.
the foundation of the world, so we may be said *to be* saved, *before we are converted, or called to Christ*. And hence *saved*, is put before *called*; *he hath saved us, and called us*; he saith not, he hath called us, and saved us, but he puts saving before calling. So again, we are said to be *preserved in Christ, and called*, he saith not called and preserved: 2 *Tim.* 1. 9. *Jude* 1. And therefore God saith again, *I will pardon them whom I reserve*, that is, as *Paul* expounds it, those whom I have *elected* and *kept*, *Jer.* 50. 20. *Rom.* 11. 4, 5. and this part of Salvation is accomplished through the forbearance of God. God beareth with his own elect, for Christ's sake, all the time of their unregeneracy, until the time comes which he hath appointed for their Conversion. The sins that we stood guilty of before Conversion, had the judgment due to them been executed upon us, we had not now been in the World to partake of *an heavenly calling*. But the judgment due to them hath been by the patience of God prevented, and we saved all the time of our ungodly and unconverted state, from that Death,

19 Ephes. 1. 3, 4.] Ephes. 1. 2. 4.

and those many Hells, that for our sins we deserved at the Hands of God.

8. And here lies the reason, that long Life is granted to the **Elect** before Conversion, and that all the sins they commit, and all the judgments they deserve, cannot drive them out of the World before Conversion. **Manasseh**, you know, was a great sinner, and for the trespass which he committed he was driven from his own Land, and carried to *Babilon*, but kill him they could not, though his sins had deserved death ten thousand times, but what was the reason? Why he was not yet **called**, *God had chosen him in Christ*, and laid up in him a stock of **grace**, which must be given to *Manasseh* before he dies: Therefore *Manasseh* must be Convinced, Converted, and Saved. That **Legion** of Devils that was in the possessed, *Mark* 5. with all the sins which he had committed in the time of his unregeneracy, could not take away his life before his Conversion: How many times was that poor Creature, as we may easily conjecture, assaulted for his life by the Devils that were in him, yet could they not kill him, yea, though his dwelling was near the Sea-side, and the Devils had power to drive him too, yet could they not drive him further than the Mountains that was by the Sea side: Yea, they could help him often to break his Chains, and Fetters, and could also make him as Mad as a *Bedlam*, they could also prevail with him to separate from Men, and cut himself with Stones, but kill him they could not, drown him they could not; he was saved to be called, he was, notwithstanding all this, preserved in Christ, and called. As it is said of the Young Lad in the Gospel, *Mark* 9. 22. he was by the **Devil** cast oft into the Fire, and oft into the Water to destroy him, but it could not be; even so hath he served others, but they must be *saved* to be *called*. How many Deaths have some been delivered from, and saved out of before Conversion! Some have fallen into Rivers, some into Wells, some into the Sea, some into the hands of Men; yea, they have been justly Arraigned, and Condemned, as the Thief upon the Cross, but must not die before they have been Converted. They were preserved in Christ and called.

Called Christian, how many times have thy sins laid thee upon a sick Bed? and to thine, and others thinking, at the very Mouth of the Grave, yet God said concerning thee, *Let him live*, for he is not yet Converted; behold therefore that the Elect are saved before they are called. *God who is rich in mercy, for his great love wherewith he loved us, even when we were dead in our sins*, Ephes. 2. 4, 5. hath preserved us in Christ, and called us.

Now this Saving of us, arises from six Causes. 9.

1. God hath chosen us unto Salvation, and therefore will not frustrate his own Purposes, 1 *Thes.* 5. 9.

2. God hath given us to Christ; and his gift, as well as his calling, is without repentance, *Rom.* 11. 29. *Joh.* 6. 37.

3. Christ hath purchased us with his blood, *Rom.* 5. 8, 9.

4. They are by God counted in Christ before they are Converted, *Ephes.* 1. 3, 4.

5. They are ordained before Conversion to eternal Life; yea, to be called, to be justified, to be glorified, and therefore all this must come upon them, *Rom.* 8. 29, 30.

6. For all this he hath also appointed them their portion and measure of grace, and that before the World began, therefore that they may partake of all these priviledges, they are *saved* and *called*; preserved in Christ, and called.

Thirdly, To *be* saved, *is to be brought to, and helped to lay hold on,* 10.
Jesus Christ by faith: And this is called saving by grace through faith: *For by grace are ye saved, through faith, and that not of your selves, it is the gift of God*, Ephes. 2. 8.

1. They must be brought unto Christ, yea, drawn unto him: *For no Man* (saith Christ) *can come unto me, except the Father which hath sent me, draw him*: Joh. 6. 44. Men, even the Elect, have too many Infirmities, to come to Christ without help from Heaven, inviting will not do. *As they called them, so they went from them*, therefore he drew them with cords, *Hos.* 11. 2. 4.

2. As they must be brought to, so they must be helped to lay hold on Christ by faith, for as coming to Christ, so faith is not in our own power, therefore we are said to be raised up with him, *through the faith of the operation of God*: And again, we are said *to believe according to the working of his mighty power, which he wrought in Christ when he raised him from the dead.* Col. 2. 12. Eph. 1. 18, 19, 20.

11 *Rom.* 5. 8, 9.] *Rom.* 5. 8.

Now we are said to be saved by faith, because, by faith we lay hold of, venture upon, and put on Jesus Christ for life: *For life*, I say, because God having made him the Saviour, hath given him life to communicate to sinners, and the life that he communicates to them, is the merit of his flesh and blood, which who so eateth and drinketh by faith, hath eternal life, because that flesh and blood hath merit in it sufficient to obtain the favour of God: Yea, it hath done so that day it was offered through the eternal spirit a sacrifice of a sweet smelling savor to him; wherefore God imputeth the **righteousness** of Christ to him that believeth in him, by which righteousness he is personally justified, and saved from that just judgment of the Law that was due unto him, *Joh.* 5. 26. *Chap.* 6. 53, 54, 55, 56, 57. *Ephes.* 4. 32. *Chap.* 5. 2. *Rom.* 4. 23, 24, 25.

Saved by Faith: For although Salvation beginneth in God's purpose, and comes to us through Christ's righteousness, yet is not faith exempted from having a hand in saving of us: Not that it meriteth oft, but is given by God to those which he saveth, that thereby they may embrace and put on that Christ, by whose Righteousness they must be saved.

Wherefore this faith is that which here distinguisheth them that shall be saved, from them that shall be damned. Hence it is said, *He that believeth not, shall be damned*; and hence again it is, that the Believers, are called, *the Children, the Heirs, and the blessed with faithful* Abraham: That *the promise by faith in Jesus Christ might be given to them that believe*, Gal. 3. 26. Rom. 4. 13, 14. Gal. 3. 6, 7, 8, 9.

And here let Christians warily distinguish betwixt the meritorious, and the instrumental cause of their justification. Christ with what he hath done and suffered, is the meritorious cause of our justification; therefore he is said to be made to us of God, Wisdom and Righteousness, and we are said to be justified by his *blood*, and saved from wrath through him, 1 *Cor.* 1. 30. *Rom.* 5. 9, 10. for it was his life and blood that was the price of our Redemption. *Redeemed* (says S. *Peter*) *not with corruptible things, as silver and gold* (alluding to the redemption of money under the Law), *but with the precious blood of Christ*: Thou art therefore (as I have said), to make Christ Jesus the object of thy faith for justification: For by his righteousness thy sins must be covered from the sight of the justice of the Law. *Believe on the Lord Jesus Christ, and thou shalt be saved, for he shall save his people from their sins*, Acts 16. 31. *Mat.* 1. 21.

Fourthly, *To be saved*, is to be preserved in the faith to the end. 11.
He that shall endure to the end, the same shall be saved, Matth. 24. 13. not that perseverance is an accident in Christianity, or a thing performed by humane industry: They that are saved, *are kept by the power of God, through faith unto salvation*, 1 Pet. 1. 3, 4, 5.

But perseverance is absolutely necessary to the compleat saving of the soul, because he that falleth short of the state, that they that are saved, are possessed of, as saved, cannot arrive to that saved state: He that goeth to Sea, with a purpose to arrive at Spain, cannot arrive there, if he be drowned by the way: Wherefore *perseverance* is absolutely necessary to the saving of the soul, and therefore it is included in the compleat saving of us, *Israel shall be saved in the Lord, with an everlasting salvation, they shall not be ashamed nor confounded, world without end*, Isa. 45. 17. perseverance is here made absolutely necessary to the compleat saving of the soul.

But (as I said) this part of Salvation dependeth not upon humane power, but upon him that hath begun a good work in us, *Phil.* 1. 6. This part, therefore, of our Salvation, is great, and calleth for no less than the power of God for our help to perform it, as will be easily granted by all those that consider,

1*st*. That all the power, and policy, malice, and rage of the Devils and Hell it self is against us: Any Man that understandeth this, will conclude, that *to be saved*, is no small thing. The Devil is called a God, a Prince, a Lyon, a roaring Lyon; it is said, that he hath death and the power of it, *&c.* but what can a poor Creature whose habitation is in flesh, do against a God, a Prince, a roaring Lyon, and the power of death it self? Our perseverance therefore lieth in the power of God; *the gates of hell shall not prevail against it.*

2*ly*, All the World is against him that shall be saved, but what is one poor Creature to all the World, especially if you consider, that with the World, is Terror, Fear, Power, Majesty, Laws, Gaols, Gibbets, Hangings, Burnings, Drownings, Starvings, Banishments, and a thousand kinds of Deaths, 1 *Joh.* 5. 4, 5. *Joh.* 16. 33.

3*ly*, Add to this that all the Corruptions that dwells in our flesh, is against us, and that not only in their nature and being, but they lust against us, and war against us, to *bring us into Captivity to the Law of Sin and Death*, Gal. 5. 17. 1 Pet. 2. 11. Rom. 7. 23.

4ly. All the Delusions in the world are against them that shall be saved, many of which are so cunningly woven, so plausibly handled, so rarely polished with Scripture and Reason, that 'tis ten thousand wonders, that the Elect are not swallowed up with them; and swallowed up they would be, were they not Elect, and was not God himself engaged, either by power to keep them from falling, or by grace, to pardon if they fall, and to lift them up again, *Mat.* 24. 24. *Eph.* 4. 14. *Rom.* 3. 10.

5ly. Every Fall of the saved, is against the Salvation of his Soul; but a Christian once fallen, riseth not, but as helped by omnipotent power. O *Israel, thou art fallen by thine iniquity, but in me is thy help*, says God, *Hos.* 13. 9. *chap.* 14. 1. *Psal.* 37. 23.

Christians were you awake, here would be matter of wonder to you, to see a man assaulted with all the power of Hell, and yet to come off a Conqueror: Is it not a Wonder, to see a poor Creature who in himself is weaker than the Moth, *Job* 4. 19. to stand against, and overcome all Devils, all the World, all his Lusts and Corruptions! Or if he fall, is it not a wonder to see him, when Devils and Guilt are upon him, to rise again, stand upon his feet again, walk with God again, and persevere after all this in the Faith and Holiness of the Gospel! He that knows himself, wonders; he that knows Temptation, wonders; he that knows what Falls and Guilt means, wonders; indeed Perseverance is a wonderful thing, and is managed by the power of God; for he only is able to keep us from falling, and to present us faultless before the presence of his Glory, with exceeding Joy, *Jude* 24. Those of the Children of *Israel* that went from *Egypt*, and entred the Land of *Canaan*, how came they thither? why the Text says, *That as an Eagle spreadeth abroad her Wings, so the Lord alone did lead them.* And again, *He bore them, and carried them all the days of old*, *Deut.* 32. 11, 12. *Isa.* 63. 9. *David* also tells us, that *Mercy and Goodness should follow him all the days of his Life, and so he should dwell in the house of the Lord for ever*, Psal. 23. 6.

12. Fifthly, *To be saved*, calls for more than all this; he that is saved, must, when this world can hold him no longer, have a safe Conduct to Heaven; for that is the Place where they that are saved, must to

the full enjoy their Salvation. This Heaven is called, *The End of our Faith*, because it is that which Faith looks at; as *Peter* says, *Received the End of your Faith, the Salvation of our Souls*, and again, *But we are not of them that draw back unto perdition, but of them that believe, to the saving of the Soul*, 1 *Pet.* 1. 9. *Heb.* 10. 39. For (as I said) Heaven is the place for the saved to enjoy their Salvation in, with that perfect gladness that is not attainable here; here we are saved by Faith and hope of Glory; but there we that are saved shall enjoy *the End of our Faith and Hope, even the Salvation of our Souls*, There is *Mount Sion, the heavenly Jerusalem, the general Assembly, and Church of the first born*: There is *the innumerable Company of Angels, and the Spirits of just men made perfect*; there is *God the Judge of all, and Jesus the Mediator of the new Covenant*; there shall our Soul have as much of Heaven as it is capable of enjoying, and that without intermission: wherefore, when we come there, we shall be saved indeed!

But now for a poor Creature to be brought hither, this is the Life of the point: But how shall I come hither? There are *Heights* and *Depths* to hinder, *Rom.* 8. 38, 39.

Suppose the poor Christian is now upon a Sick-bed, beset with a thousand fears, and ten thousand at the end of that; sick-bed Fears! and they are sometimes dreadful ones; fears, that are begotten by the review of the Sin (perhaps) of forty years Profession; fears that are begotten by dreadful and fearful Suggestions of the Devil, the sight of Death, and the Grave, and it may be, of Hell it self; fears that are begotten by the withdrawing, and silence of God and Christ, and by (it may be) the appearance of the Devil himself: Some of these made *David* cry, *O spare me a little, that I may recover strength before I go hence, and be no more*, Psal. 39. 13. *The sorrows of death*, said he, *compassed me, the pains of hell got hold upon me, and I found trouble and sorrow;* these things in another place, he calls, *the bands that the godly have in their Death, and the plagues that others are not aware of. They are not in trouble as other men, neither are they plagued like other men*, Psal. 73. 4, 5. But now, out of all these, the Lord will save his people; not one Sin, nor Fear, nor Devil shall hinder; nor the Grave nor Hell disappoint thee, But how must this be? Why thou must have a safe Conduct to Heaven! What Conduct, a Conduct of

33 Psal. 73. 4, 5.] Psal. 37. 45.

Angels: *Are they not all ministring Spirits, sent forth to minister for them that shall be heirs of Salvation?* Heb. 1. 14.

These Angels therefore are not to fail them that are the saved; but must, as commissionated of God, come down from Heaven to do this Office for them; they must come, I say, and take the care and charge of our Soul, to conduct it safely into *Abraham's* bosom: 'tis not our meanness in the world, nor our weakness of Faith that shall hinder this; nor shall the loathsomness of our Diseases make these delicate Spirits shy of taking this charge upon them: *Lazarus* the Beggar found this a Truth; a Beggar so despised of the rich Glutton, that he was not suffered to come within his Gate; a Beggar full of Sores and noisome putrefaction; yet behold, when he dies, the Angels come from Heaven to fetch him thither; *And it came to pass, that the Beggar died, and was carried by the Angels into* Abraham's *Bosome*, Luke 16. 22.

True, Sick Bed Temptations are oft-times the most violent, because then the Devil plays his last Game with us, he is never to assault us more; besides, perhaps God suffereth it thus to be, that the entring into heaven may be the sweeter, and ring of this Salvation the louder: O 'tis a blessed thing for God to be our God, and our Guide, even unto Death, and then for his Angels to conduct us safely to Glory: This is saving indeed. *And he shall save* Israel *out of all his Troubles:* out of sick-bed Troubles as well as others, *Psal.* 25. 22. *Psal.* 34. 6. *Psal.* 48. 14.

13. Sixthly: To be *saved*, to be *perfectly saved*, calls for more than all this: The Godly are not perfectly saved when their Soul is possessed of Heaven. True, their Spirit is made perfect, and hath as much of Heaven as at present it can hold; but Man consisting of Body and Soul, cannot be said to be perfectly saved so long as but part of him is in the Heavens: his Body is the price of the Blood of Christ, as well as his Spirit; his Body is the Temple of God, and a Member of the Body, and of the Flesh, and of the Bones of Christ; he cannot then be compleatly saved until the time of the Resurrection of the Dead, 1 *Cor.* 6. 13, 15, 19. *Eph.* 5. 30. wherefore when Christ shall come the second time, then will he save the Body from all those things that at present make it uncapable of the Heavens: *For our Conversation is in Heaven, from whence we look for the Saviour the Lord Jesus Christ,*

who shall change this our vile Body, that it may be fashioned like unto his glorious Body, Philip. 3. 20, 21. O! what a great deal of good God hath put into this little word *saved.* We shall not see all the good that God hath put into this word *saved*, until the Lord Jesus comes to raise the Dead. *It doth not yet appear what we shall be*, 1 Joh. 3. 2. but till it appears what we shall be, we cannot see the bottom of this word, *saved.* True, we have the earnest of what we shall be, we have the Spirit of God, *which is the earnest of our inheritance, until the redemption of the purchased possession*, Ephes. 1. 14.

The possession is our body, it is called *a purchased possession*, because 'tis the price of blood; now the redemption of this purchased possession is the raising of it out of the Grave, which raising is called the redemption of our body, *Rom.* 8. 23. *and when this vile body is made like unto his glorious body*, and this body and soul together possessed of the Heavens, then shall we be every way saved.

There are three things from which this body must be **saved**. 14.

1. There is that sinful filth, and vileness that yet dwells in it, under which we groan earnestly all our days, 2 *Cor.* 5. 1, 2, 3.

2. There is Mortality, that subjecteth us to Age, Sickness, Aches, Pains, Diseases, and Death.

3. And there is the Grave and Death it self, for Death is the last Enemy that is to be destroyed: *So when this corruptible shall have put on incorruption, and this mortal shall have put immortality, then shall be brought to pass that saying, that is written, death is swallowed up of victory*, 1 *Cor.* 15. 54.

So then, when this comes to pass, then we shall be saved, then will Salvation in all the parts of it meet together in our glory, then we shall be every way saved, saved in God's Decree, saved in Christ's Undertakings, saved by Faith, saved in Perseverance, saved in Soul, and in Body and Soul; together in the Heavens, saved Perfectly, Everlastingly, Gloriously.

Before I conclude my Answer to the first Question, I would dis- 15.
course a little of the state of our Body and Soul in Heaven, when we shall enjoy this blessed state of **salvation**.

First, Of the Soul, it will then be filled in all the faculties of it, with as much Bliss and Glory, as ever it can hold.

5 1 Joh. 3. 2.] Joh. 3. 2.   13 *Rom.* 8. 23.] *Rom.* 8. 31.

1. The understanding shall then be perfect in knowledge; *now we know but in part*, we know God, Christ, Heaven, and Glory, but in part, *but when that which is perfect is come, then that which is in part shall be done away*, 1 Cor. 13. 9, 10. Then shall we have perfect and everlasting Visions of God, and that Blessed one, his Son Jesus Christ; a good thought of whom doth sometimes so fill us, while in this World, that it causeth *joy unspeakable, and full of glory*.

2. Then shall our Will and Affections be ever in a burning flame of love to God and his Son Jesus Christ; our love here hath ups and downs, but there it shall be always perfect with that perfection which is not possible in this World to be enjoyed.

3. Then will our Conscience have that Peace and Joy, that neither Tongue, or Pen, of Men, or Angels, can express.

4. Then will our Memory be so enlarged to retain all things that hapned to us in this world, so that with unspeakable aptness we shall call to mind all God's Providences, all Sathan's Malice, all our own Weaknesses, all the rage of Men, and how God made all Work together, for his Glory and our good, to the everlasting ravishing of our Hearts.

16. Secondly, For our Body, it shall be raised in power, in incorruption, a spiritual Body and glorious, 1 *Cor*. 15. 42, 44.

The glory of which is set forth by several things.

1. It is compared to the brightness of the Firmament, and to the shining of the Stars, for ever and ever, *Dan*. 12. 3. 1 *Cor*. 15. 40, 41.

2. It is compared to the shining of the Sun: *Then shall the righteous shine forth as the sun in the kingdom of their father; who hath ears to hear, let him hear*, Matt. 13. 43.

3. Their state is then to be equally glorious with Angels, but they which shall be counted worthy to obtain that World, and the Resurrection from the Dead, neither Marry, nor are given in Marriage, neither can they die any more, *for they are equal to the Angels*, Luke 20. 35, 36.

4. It is said, that then this *our vile body shall be like the glorious body of Jesus Christ*, Philip. 3. 20, 21. 1 *Joh*. 3. 2, 3.

4 1 Cor. 13. 9, 10.] 1 Cor. 13. 10. 20–1 in incorruption] in corruption
21 1 *Cor*. 15. 42, 44.] 1 *Cor*. 15. 44. 24–5 1 *Cor*. 15. 40, 41.] 1 *Cor*. 15. 41, 42.

5. And now, when body and soul are thus united, who can imagine what glory they both possess? They will now be both in capacity without jarring to serve the Lord with shouting Thanksgivings, and with a Crown of everlasting Joy upon their Head.

In this World there cannot be that harmony and oneness of Body and Soul, as there will be in Heaven. Here the Body sometimes sins against the Soul, and the Soul again vexes and perplexes the Body with dreadful apprehensions of the Wrath and Judgment of God: While we be in this world, the Body oft hangs this way, and the Soul the quite contrary; but there, in Heaven, they shall have that perfect union as never to jarr more: But now the glory of the Body, shall so suit with the glory of the Soul, and both so perfectly suit with the heavenly state, that it passeth Words and Thoughts.

Thirdly, Shall I now speak of the place that this saved Body and 17.
Soul shall dwell in? why,

1. It is a City, *Heb.* 11. 16. *Ephes.* 2. 19.
2. It is called Heaven, *Heb.* 10. 34.
3. It is called God's House, *Joh.* 14. 1, 2, 3.
4. It is called a Kingdom, *Luk.* 12. 32.
5. It is called Glory, *Colos.* 3. 4. *Heb.* 2. 10.
6. It is called Paradice, *Revel.* 2. 7.
7. It is called Everlasting Habitation, *Luke* 16. 9.

Fourthly, Shall I speak of their Company? why, 18.

1. They shall stand and live in the presence of the glorious God the Judge of all, *Heb.* 12. 23.
2. They shall be with the Lamb, the Lord Jesus.
3. They shall be with innumerable Company of Holy Angels, *Heb.* 12. 22.
4. They shall be with *Abraham*, *Isaac*, and *Jacob*, and all the Prophets in the Kingdom of Heaven, *Luke* 13. 28.

Fifthly, Shall I speak of their Heavenly Raiment? 19.

1. It is Salvation, they shall be cloathed with the Garment of Salvation, *Psal.* 132. 16. *Psal.* 149. 4. *Isa.* 61. 10.
2. This Raiment is called white raiment, signifying their clean and innocent state in Heaven. *And they* (says Christ) *shall walk with me in white, for they are worthy*, Isa. 57. 2. Revel. 3. 4. *chap.* 19. 8.

11 glory of] glory   20 *Colos.* 3. 4.] *Colos.* 3. 3.

3. It is called Glory, *when he shall appear, we shall appear with him in glory*, Col. 3. 4.

4. They shall also have Crowns of righteousness, everlasting Joy and Glory, *Isa.* 35. 10. 2 *Tim.* 4. 8. 1 *Pet.* 5. 4.

20. Sixthly, Shall I speak of their **continuance** in this Condition.

1. It is for ever and ever, *and they shall see his face, and his name shall be in their foreheads, and they shall reign for ever and ever*, Revel. 22. 4, 5.

2. It is Everlastingly: *And this is the will of him that sent me, that every one which seeth the son, and believeth on him, may have everlasting life, Joh.* 6. 40, 47.

3. It is Life Eternal, *My sheep hear my voice, and I know them, and they follow me, and I give unto them eternal life*, Joh. 10. 27, 28. *chap.* 7. 3.

4. It is World without end, *But* Israel *shall be saved in the Lord with an everlasting Salvation, they shall not be ashamed nor confounded World without end*, Isa. 45. 17. *Eph.* 3. 20, 21.

O sinner! What saist thou! How doest thou like being saved? Doth not thy Mouth water? Doth not thy Heart twitter at being saved? Why come then, *The Spirit and the Bride says come, and let him that heareth say come, and let him that is athirst come, and whosoever will, let him take of the water of life freely*, Revel. 22. 17.

QUESTION II.

What is it to be saved by [Grace]?

21. NOW I come to the Second Question, to wit, *What it is to be saved by Grace*. For so are the words of the Text, *By Grace ye are saved.*

But First, I must touch a little upon the word (**Grace**) and shew you how diversly it is taken.

1. Sometimes it is taken for the good will and favour of Men, *Esth.* 2. 17. *Ruth* 2. 2. 1 *Sam.* 1. 18. 2 *Sam.* 16. 4.

2. Sometimes it is taken for those sweet Ornaments, that a life, according to the Word of God, putteth about the Neck, *Prov.* 1. 9. *chap.* 3. 22.

3. Sometimes it is taken for the Charity of the Saints, as 2 *Cor.* 9. 6, 7, 8.

2 Col. 3. 4.] Col. 3. 3. 28 1 *Sam.* 1. 18.] 1 *Sam.* 1. 8. 32–3 2 *Cor.* 9. 6, 7, 8.] 2 *Cor.* 9. 6, 7.

4. But *Grace* in the Text, is taken for God's good will, *the good Will of him that dwelt in the Bush*; and is expressed variously.

1. Sometimes it is called, *his good Pleasure.*

2. Sometimes *the good pleasure of his Will*, which is all one with *the riches of his Grace*, Ephes. 1. 7.

3. Sometimes it is expressed by Goodness, Pity, Love, Mercy, Kindness, and the like, *Rom.* 2. 4. *Isa.* 63. 9. *Tit.* 3. 4, 5.

4. Yea, he stiles himself, *The Lord, the Lord God, merciful, gracious, long-suffering, and abundant in goodness and truth, keeping mercy for thousands, forgiving iniquity, transgressions and sin, and that will by no means clear the guilty*, Exod. 34. 6, 7.

Secondly, As the word Grace signifieth all these, so it intimates 22.
to us, that all these are free Acts of God, free-Love, free-Mercy, free-Kindness: Hence we have other hints in the Word, about the nature of Grace, as,

1. It is an act of *God's Will*, which must needs be free, an act of his *own* Will, of the *good pleasure of his Will*; by every of these Expressions, is intimated, that Grace is a free act of God's goodness towards the Sons of Men.

2. Therefore it is expresly said, *being justified freely by his Grace*, Rom. 3. 24.

3. *And when they had nothing to pay, he frankly forgave them both*, Luk. 7. 42.

4. And again, *Not for your sakes do I this, saith the Lord God, be it known unto you*, Ezek. 36. 32. Deut. 9. 5.

5. And therefore *grace* and the deservings of the Creature are set in flat opposition one to another*: And if it be by Grace, then it is no more of Works, otherwise Grace is no more Grace, but if it be of Works, then it is no more of Grace, otherwise Work, is no more work*, Rom. 11. 6.

The word Grace therefore, being understood, doth most properly set forth the true cause of Man's happiness with God, not but that those Expressions, Love, Mercy, Goodness, Pity, Kindness, *&c*, and the like, have their proper place in our happiness also; had not God loved us; Grace had not acted freely in our Salvation, had not God been Merciful, Good, Pitiful, Kind, he would have turned away from us, when he saw us in our Blood, *Ezek.* 16.

So then, when he saith, *By Grace ye are saved*, it is all one as if he had said, by the good Will, free Mercy, and loving Kindness of God, ye are saved; as the words conjoyned with the Text, do also further manifest: *But God* (saith *Paul*) *who is rich in mercy, for his great love wherewith he loved us, even when we were dead in sin, hath quickned us together with Christ, by Grace ye are saved.*

23. The words thus understood, admits us these few Conclusions.

1. That God in saving of the sinner hath no respect to the sinners goodness, hence it is said, he is *frankly* forgiven and *freely* justified, *Luke* 7. 42. *Rom.* 3. 24.

2. That God doth this to whom, and when he pleases, because 'tis an act of his *own* good pleasure, *Gal.* 1. 15, 16.

3. This is the cause why great sinners are saved, for God pardoneth *according to the riches of his grace*, Eph. 1. 7.

4. This is the true cause that some sinners are so amazed, and confounded at the apprehension of their own Salvation, his Grace is unsearchable, and by unsearchable grace, God oft puzzles, and confounds onr reason, *Ezek.* 16. 62, 63. *Acts* 9. 6.

5. This is the cause that sinners are so often recovered from their back-slidings, healed of their wounds, that they get by their falls, and helped again to rejoyce in Gods mercy; why, *he will be gracious to whom he will be gracious, and he will have compassion on whom he will have compassion*, Rom. 9. 15.

But I must not here conclude this point; we are here discoursing of the Grace of God, and that by it we are saved; saved, I say, by the Grace of God.

Now, God is set forth in the word unto us under a double Consideration.

1. He is set forth in his own eternal Power and Godhead, and as thus set forth, we are to conceive of him by his Attributes of Power, Justice, Goodness, Holiness, Everlastingness, *&c.*

2. But then, we have him set forth in the word of Truth, as consisting of Father, Son, and Spirit, and although this second Consideration containeth in it the nature of the Godhead, yet the first doth not demonstrate the Persons in the Godhead: We are saved by the Grace of God, that is, by the Grace of the Father, who is God; by the Grace of the Son, who is God; and by the Grace of the Spirit, who is God.

Now since we are said to be *saved by* Grace, and *that* the Grace of 24. God, and since also we find in the *word*, that in the Godhead there is Father, Son, and Holy Ghost, we must conclude, that it is by the Grace of the Father, Son, and Spirit, that we are saved; wherefore Grace is attributed to the Father, Son, and Holy Ghost distinctly.

1. Grace is attributed to the Father, as these Scriptures testifie, *Rom.* 1. 7. 1 *Cor.* 1. 3. 2 *Cor.* 1. 2. *Gal.* 1. 3. *Ephes.* 1. 2. *Philip.* 1. 2. *Colos.* 1. 2. 1 *Thes.* 1. 1. 1 *Tim.* 1. 2. 2 *Tim.* 1. 2. 2 *Thes.* 1. 2. *Tit.* 1. 4. *Phil.* 3.

2. Grace is also attributed to the Son, and I first manifest it by all those Texts above mentioned, as also by these that follow, 2 *Cor.* 8. 9. *chap.* 13. 14. *Gal.* 6. 18. *Philip.* 4. 23. 1 *Thes.* 5. 28. 2 *Thes.* 3. 18. *Phil.* 3. *Revel.* 22. 21.

3. It is also attributed to the Holy Ghost, *Zech.* 12. 10. *Heb.* 10. 29. Now he is here called the Spirit of Grace, because he is the Author of Grace as the Father, and the Son: So then it remaineth that I shew you.

First, How we are saved by the Grace of the Father.

Secondly, How we are saved by the Grace of the Son.

Thirdly, And how we are saved by the Grace of the Spirit.

Of the Father's Grace.

First, How we are saved by the Grace of the Father: Now this will 25. I open unto you thus.

1. The Father, by his Grace hath bound up them that shall go to Heaven in an eternal Decree of Election, and here indeed, as was shewed at first, is the beginning of our Salvation, 2 *Tim.* 1. 9. and Election is reckoned not the Sons act, but the Fathers, *Blessed be God and the Father of our Lord Jesus Christ, who hath blessed us with all spiritual Blessings in heavenly places in Christ, according as he hath chosen us in him before the foundation of the World*, Eph. 1. 3, 4. Now this Election is counted an act of Grace, *So then, at this present time also, there is a remnant according to the election of Grace*, Rom. 11. 5.

2*ly*, The Father's Grace, ordaineth, and giveth the Son to undertake for us our Redemption: The Father sent the Son to be the

7 *Rom.* 1. 7.] *Rom.* 7. 25. 8 1 *Thes.* 1. 1.] 1 *Thes.* 1. 2. 13–14 *Heb.* 10. 29.] *Heb.* 12. 19. 29 Eph. 1. 3, 4.] Eph. 1. 4.

Saviour of the World, *In whom we have Redemption through his Blood, the forgiveness of sins, according to the riches of his Grace; that in the Ages to come, he might shew the exceeding riches of his Grace in his kindness to usward, through Christ Jesus*, 1 Joh. 4. 14. Ephes. 1. 7. chap. 2. 7. Joh. 3. 16. chap. 6. 32, 33. chap. 12. 47.

3ly, The Father's Grace giveth us to Christ, to be justified by his Righteousness, washed in his Blood, and saved by his Life. This Christ mentioneth, *Joh.* 6. 37. and tells us, it is his Father's Will that they should be safe-coming at the last Day, and that he had kept them all the Days of his life, and they shall never perish, *Joh.* 6. 38, 39. *chap.* 17. 2, 12.

4ly, The Father's Grace giveth the Kingdom of Heaven to those that he hath given to Jesus Christ; *Fear not little flock, it is your Father's good Pleasure to give you the Kingdom*, Luke 12. 32.

5ly, The Father's Grace provideth, and layeth up in Christ for those that he hath chosen a sufficiency of all Spiritual Blessings to be Communicated to them at their need, for their preservation in the Faith, and faithful perseverance through this life; *not according to our Works, but according to his own Purpose and Grace, which was given us in Christ Jesus, before the World began*, 2 *Tim.* 1. 9. *Ephes.* 1. 3, 4.

6ly, The Father's Grace saveth us by the blessed and effectual Call, that he giveth us the Fellowship of his Son Jesus Christ, 1 *Cor.* 1. 9. *Gal.* 1. 15.

7ly, The Father's Grace saveth us by multiplying Pardons to us for Christ's sake, day by day. *In whom we have redemption through his Blood, even the forgiveness of Sins, according to the Riches of his Grace.*

8ly, The Father's Grace saves us, by exercising Patience and Forbearance towards us all the time of our Unregeneracy, *Rom.* 3. 24.

9ly, The Father's Grace saveth us, by holding of us fast in his Hand, and by keeping of us from all the power of the Enemy. *My Father* (said Christ) *that gave them me is greater than all, and no Man can pull them out of my Father's Hand*, Joh. 10. 29.

10ly, What shall I say? The Father's Grace saveth us, by accepting of our Persons and Services, by lifting up the light of his Countenance upon us, by manifesting of his Love unto us, and by sending of his Angels to fetch us to himself when we have finished our Pilgrimage in this World.

Of the Grace of the Son.

I come now to speak of the Grace of the Son, for as the Father 26.
putteth forth his Grace in the saving of the Sinner, so doth the Son put forth his. *For ye know the Grace of our Lord Jesus Christ, that though he was rich, yet for your sakes he became poor, that ye through his poverty might be made rich*, 2. Cor. 8. 9.

Here you see also, that the Grace of our Lord Jesus Christ is brought in as a Partner with the Grace of his Father, in the salvation of our Souls: Now this is the Grace of our Lord Jesus Christ; he was rich, but for our sakes he became poor, that we through his poverty might be made rich.

To enquire then into this Grace, this condescending Grace of Christ, and that by searching out, how rich Jesus Christ was, and then how poor he made himself, that we through his poverty might have the riches of Salvation.

FIRST, How rich was Jesus Christ?

To which I Answer, First, Generally, Secondly, Particularly.

FIRST Generally, he was rich as the Father: *All things that the Father hath* (said he) *are mine*, Jesus Christ *he is the Lord of all*, *God over all blessed for ever: he thought it no robbery to be equal with God*, being naturally and eternally God, as the Father, *Joh.* 16. 15. *Acts* 10. 36. *Phil.* 2. 6. *Rom.* 9. 4, 5. *Joh.* 10. 30. but of his Godhead he could not strip himself.

SECONDLY, Jesus Christ had glory with the Father, yea, a 27.
manifold glory with him, which he stript himself of.

FIRST, He had the glory of Dominion, he was Lord of all the Creatures, they were under him upon a double account.

1. As he was their Creator, *Colos.* 1. 16.

2. As he was made the Heir of God, *Heb.* 1. 2.

SECONDLY, Therefore the glory of Worship, Reverence, and Fear, from all Creatures was due unto him; the Worship, Obedience, Subjection, and Service of Angels was due unto him, the Fear, Honour and Glory of Kings and Princes, and Judges of the Earth, was due unto him; the obedience of the Sun, Moon, Stars, Clouds, and all Vapours was due unto him: All Dragons, Deeps, Fire, Hail,

5 *became*] *become* 22 *Phil.* 2. 6.] *Phil.* 2. 5.

Snow, Mountains, and Hills, Beasts, Cattel, creeping Things, and flying Fouls; the service of them all, and their worship was due unto him, *Psal.* 148.

THIRDLY, The glory of the Heavens themselves was due unto him; in a word, Heaven and Earth was his.

FOURTHLY, But above all, the glory of Communion with his Father was his; I say, the glory of that unspeakable Communion that he had with the Father before his Incarnation, which alone was worth Ten thousand Worlds, that was ever his.

28. BUT again, As Jesus Christ was possessed with this, so besides he was Lord of Life: This glory also was Jesus Christ's; *in him was Life*; therefore he is called, *the Prince of it*: Because it was in him originally as in the Father, *Acts* 3. 15. he gave to all life and breath, and all things; Angels, Men, Beasts, they had all their life from him.

AGAIN, as he was Lord of glory, and Prince of life, so he was also Prince of Peace, *Isa.* 9. 6. and by him was maintained that harmony, and goodly order which was among *things* in Heaven, and *things* on Earth.

Take *things* briefly in these few Particulars.

1. THE Heavens were his, and he made them.
2. ANGELS were his, and he made them.
3. THE Earth was his, and he made it.
4. MAN was his, and he made him.

NOW this Heaven he forsook for our sakes, *He came into the World to save Sinners*, 1 Tim. 1. 15.

He was made lower than the Angels for the suffering of death, *Heb.* 2. 9.

When he was born, he made himself, as he saith, a Worm, or one of no Reputation, he became the Reproach and By-word of the People, he was born in a Stable, laid in a Manger, earned his Bread with his Labour, being by Trade a Carpenter, *Psal.* 22. 6. *Philip.* 2. 7. *Luke* 2. 7. *Mark* 6. 3. When he betook himself to his Ministry, he lived upon the Charity of the People, when other Men went to their own Houses, Jesus went to the *Mount of Olives*. Hark what himself saith for the clearing of this! *Foxes have Holes, and Birds of the air have Nests, but the Son of Man hath not whereon to lay his Head,*

32 *Luke* 2. 7.] *Luke* 27.

Luk. 9. 2, 3. Joh. 7. 35. and 8. 1. Luke 9. 58. He denied himself of this Worlds good.

AGAIN, As he was Prince of Life, so he for our sakes laid down that also; for so stood the matter, that he, or we, must die; but the Grace that was in his heart wrought with him to lay down his Life; *He gave his Life a Ransom for many*; he laid down his Life, that we might have life; he gave his Flesh and Blood for the life of the World, he laid down his Life for his Sheep.

AGAIN, he was Prince of Peace, but he forsook his Peace also. 29.

1. HE laid aside Peace with the World, and chose upon that account, to be a Man of Sorrows, and acquainted with grief; and therefore was Persecuted from his Cradle to his Cross, by Kings, Rulers, *&c.*

He laid aside his Peace with his Father, and made himself the object of his Father's Curse, insomuch that the Lord smote, stroke, and afflicted him; and in conclusion hid his Face from him (as he expressed with great crying) at the hour of his death.

BUT perhaps some may say, What need was there that Jesus 30.
Christ should do all this? Could not the Grace of the Father save us without this Condescention of the Son?

Answ. AS there is Grace, so there is Justice in God: And Man having sinned, God concluded to save him in a way of Righteousness; therefore it was absolutely necessary, that Jesus Christ should put himself into our very Condition, sin only excepted.

NOW by sin we had lost the glory of God; therefore Jesus Christ lays aside the glory that he had with the Father, *Rom.* 3. 23. *Joh.* 17. 5.

2. MAN by sin had shut himself out of an earthly Paradice, and Jesus Christ will leave his heavenly Paradice to save him, *Gen.* 3. 24. 1 *Tim.* 1. 15. *Joh.* 6. 38, 39.

3. MAN by sin had made himself lighter than Vanity, and this Lord God, Jesus Christ, made himself lower than the Angels to redeem him, *Isa.* 40. 17. *Heb.* 2. 7.

4. MAN by sin lost his right to the Creatures, and Jesus Christ will deny himself of a whole World to save him, *Luk.* 9. 58.

5. MAN by sin had made himself subject to Death, but Jesus Christ will lose his Life to save him, *Rom.* 6. 23.

1 Luk. 9. 2, 3.] Luk. 8. 2, 3. 32 *Heb.* 2. 7.] *Heb.* 2.

6. MAN by sin had procured to himself the Curse of God, but Jesus Christ will bear that Curse in his own Body, to save him, *Gal.* 3. 13.

7. MAN by sin had lost Peace with God, but this would Jesus Christ lose also, to the end Man might be saved.

8. MAN should have been mocked of God, therefore Christ was mocked of Men.

9. MAN should have been scourged in Hell, but to hinder that, Jesus was scourged on Earth.

10. MAN should have been Crowned with Ignominy and Shame, but to prevent that, Jesus was Crowned with Thorns.

11. MAN should have been pierced with the spear of God's Wrath, but to prevent that Jesus was pierced both by God and Men.

12. MAN should have been rejected of God and Angels, but to prevent that, Jesus was forsaken of God, and denied, hated, and rejected of Men, *Isa.* 48. 22. *Matt.* 27. 46. *Prov.* 1. 24, 25, 26. *Psal.* 22. 7. *Matt.* 27. 39. *Luk.* 26. 14. *Psal.* 9. 17. *Psal.* 11. 6. *Matt.* 27. 26. *Dan.* 12. 2. *Joh.* 19. 2, 3, 4, 5. *Numb.* 24. 8. *Zech.* 12. 10. *Joh.* 19. 37.

31. I might thus inlarge, and that by Authority from this Text, *He became poor, that we through his poverty might be made rich*; all the riches he stript himself of, it was for our sakes; all the Sorrows he under-went, it was for our sakes; to the least circumstance of the Sufferings of *Christ*, there was necessity that so it should be, all was for our sakes: *For our sakes he became poor, that ye through his poverty might be made rich.*

And you see, the Argument that prevailed with Christ to do this great service for Man, the Grace that was in his heart; as also the Prophet saith, *in his love, and in his pity he redeemed them*: According to this in the *Corinthians, You know the Grace of our Lord Jesus Christ*; both which, agree with the Text, *By Grace ye are saved.*

I say, this was the Grace of the Son, and the exercise thereof: The Father therefore shews his Grace one way, and the Son his another: 'Twas not the Father, but the Son, that left his Heaven for sinners; 'twas not the Father, but the Son that spilt his Blood for sinners. The Father indeed gave the Son, and blessed be the

18 *Luk.* 26. 14.] *Luk.* 6. 14. 25 *became*] *become*

Father for that; and the Son gave his Life and Blood for us, and blessed be the Son for that.

But methinks we should not yet have done with this Grace of the Son: Thou Son of the Blessed, What Grace was manifest in thy Condescention? Grace brought thee down from Heaven, Grace stript thee of thy Glory, Grace made thee Poor and Despicable, Grace made thee bear such burdens of Sin, such burdens of Sorrow, such burdens of God's Curse as is unspeakable: O Son of God! Grace was in all thy Tears, Grace came bubling out of thy side with the Blood, Grace came forth with every word of thy sweet Mouth, *Psal.* 45. 2. *Luk.* 4. 22. Grace came out where the Whip smote thee, where the Thorns prickt thee, where the Nails and Spear pierced thee: O Blessed Son of God! Here is Grace indeed! Unsearchable Riches of Grace! Unthought of Riches of Grace! Grace to make Angels wonder, Grace to make Sinners happy, Grace to astonish Devils: And what will become of them that trample under foot this Son of God.

Of the Grace of the Spirit.

I come now to speak of the **Grace** of the Spirit, *for he also* **saveth** *us* 32.
by his Grace: The Spirit, I told you, is God, as the Father and the Son, and is therefore also the Author of Grace; yea, and it is absolutely necessary that he put forth his Grace also, or else no flesh can be saved. The Spirit of God hath his hand in saving of us many ways; for they that go to Heaven, as they must be beholding to the Father and the Son, so also to the Spirit of God. The Father chooseth us, giveth us to Christ, and Heaven to us, and the like; the Son fulfils the Law for us, takes the Curse of the Law from us, bears in his own body our sorrows, and sets us justified in the sight of *God.* The Father's Grace is shewed in Heaven and Earth; the Son's Grace is shewed on the Earth, and on the Cross; and the Spirits Grace must be shewed in our Souls, and Bodies, before we come to Heaven.

Quest. BUT some may say, Wherein doth the **saving** Grace of the 33.
Spirit appear?

Answ. IN many things.

IN taking possession of us for his own, in his making of us his House and Habitation, 1 *Cor.* 3. 16. *chap.* 6. 19. *Ephes.* 2. 21, 22. so that though the Father and the Son have both gloriously put forth gracious Acts in order to our Salvation, yet the Spirit is the first that makes seisure of us. Christ therefore when he went away, said not, that he would send the Father, but the Spirit, and that he should be in us for ever, *Joh.* 14. *If I depart* (said Christ), *I will send him, the Spirit of Truth, the Comforter*, Joh. 14. 16. *chap.* 16. 7, 13.

34. The holy Spirit coming into us, and dwelling in us, worketh out many Salvations for us now, and each of them in order also to our being saved for ever.

1. HE saveth us from our darkness, by illuminating of us; hence he is called *the Spirit of Revelation*, because he openeth the blind eyes, and so consequently delivereth us from that darkness, which else would drown us in the Deeps of Hell, *Ephes.* 1. 17.

2. HE it is that convinceth us of the evil of our unbelief, and that shews us the necessity of our believing in Christ; without the conviction of this we should perish, *Joh.* 16. 9.

3. THIS is that Finger of God, by which the Devil is made to give place unto Grace, by whose power else we should be carried headlong to Hell, *Luke* 11. 20, 21, 22.

4. THIS is he that worketh faith in our hearts, without which neither the Grace of the Father, nor the Grace of the Son can save us; *For he that believeth not shall be damned*, Rom. 15. 13. Mark 16. 16.

5. This is he by whom we are born again, and he that is not so born, can neither see nor inherit the Kingdom of Heaven, *John* 3. 3, 5, 6, 7.

6. This is he that setteth up his Kingdom in the heart, and by that means keepeth out the Devil after he is cast out, which Kingdom of the Spirit, whoever wanteth, they lie liable to a worse possession of the Devil than ever, *Mat.* 12. 43, 44. *Luke* 11. 24, 25.

7. By this Spirit we come to see the Beauty of Christ, without a sight of which, we should never desire him, but should certainly live in the neglect of him, and perish, *John* 16. 13. 1 *Cor.* 2. 9, 10, 11, 12. *Isa.* 53. 1, 2.

8 Joh. 14. 16.] Joh. 14. 14. 31 *Mat.* 12. 43, 44.] *Mat.* 13. 33. 34 *John* 16. 13.] *John* 16. 14.

8. By this Spirit we are helped to praise God acceptably; but without it, 'tis impossible to be heard unto Salvation, *Rom.* 8. 26. *Eph.* 6. 18. 1 *Cor.* 14. 15.

9. By this blessed Spirit the Love of God is shed abroad in our hearts, and our hearts are directed into the Love of God, *Rom.* 5. 5. 2 *Thes.* 3. 5.

10. By this blessed Spirit we are led from the wayes of the Flesh into the wayes of Life, and by it our mortal Body, as well as our immortal Soul is quickned in the Service of God, *Gal.* 5. 18, 25. *Rom.* 8. 11.

11. By this good Spirit we keep that good Thing, even the Seed of God, that at the first by the Word of God was infused into us and without which we are liable to the worst Damnation, 1 *John* 3. 9. 1 *Pet.* 1. 23. 2 *Tim.* 1. 14.

12. By this good Spirit we have help and light against all the Wisdom and cunning of the World, which putteth forth it self in its most cursed Sophistications, to overthrow the Simplicity that is in Christ, *Mat.* 10. 19, 20. *Mar.* 13. 11. *Luke* 12. 11, 12.

13. By this good Spirit our Graces are maintained in life and vigour; as, Faith, Hope, Love, a Spirit of Prayer, and every Grace, 2 *Cor.* 4. 13. *Rom.* 15. 13. 2 *Tim.* 1. 7. *Eph.* 6. 18. *Tit.* 3. 5.

14. By this good Spirit we are sealed to the Day of Redemption, *Eph.* 1. 14.

15. And by this good Spirit we are made to wait with Patience until the redemption of the purchased Possession comes, *Gal.* 5. 5.

NOW all these Things are so necessary to our Salvation, that I know not which of them can be wanting; neither can any of them be by any means attained but by this blessed Spirit.

AND thus have I in few Words, shewed you the grace of the 35.
Spirit, and how it putteth forth it self toward the saving of the Soul. And verily, Sirs, it is necessary that you know these things distinctly; to wit, the **Grace** of the Father, the Grace of the Son, and the Grace of the Holy Ghost; for it is not the Grace of one, but of all these Three, that **saveth** him that shall be saved indeed.

The Father's Grace saveth no man without the Grace of the Son; neither doth the Father and the Son save any without the

6 2 *Thes.* 3. 5.] 2 *Thes.* 2. 5.

Grace of the Spirit; for as the Father loves, the Son must die, and the Spirit must sanctifie, or no Soul must be saved.

Some think, that the Love of the Father, without the Blood of the Son, will save them; but they are deceived; *for without shedding of Blood is no remission*, Heb. 9. 22.

Some think, that the Love of the Father, and Blood of the Son will do, without the Holiness of the Spirit of God; but they are deceived also; *for if any man have not the Spirit of Christ, he is none of his*; and again, *without holiness no man shall see the Lord*, Rom. 8. 9. Heb. 12. 14.

There is a Third sort, that think the holiness of the Spirit is sufficient of it self; But they (if they had it) are deceived also; for it must be the Grace of the Father, the Grace of the Son, and the Grace of the Spirit joyntly, that must save them.

But yet, as these three do put forth Grace jointly and truly in the Salvation of a Sinner; so they put it forth (as I also have shewed you before) after a diverse manner: The Father designs us for Heaven; the Son redeems from Sin and Death; and the Spirit makes us meet for Heaven; not by electing, that's the Work of the Father; not by dying, that's the work of the Son; but by his revealing Christ, and applying Christ to our Souls, by shedding the Love of God abroad in our hearts, by sanctifying of our Souls, and taking possession of us as an Earnest of our possessing of Heaven.

QUESTION III.

Who are they that are to be Saved *by Grace?*

36. I COME now to the Third Particular; namely, to shew you who they are that are to be saved by Grace.

FIRST, Not the self-righteous, not they that have no need of the Physician. *The whole have no need of the Physician*, said Christ. *I come not to call the righteous, but sinners to repentance*, *Mar.* 2. 17. And again, *He hath filled the hungry with good things, but sends the rich empty away*, *Luke* 1. 53. Now when I say, not the self-righteous, nor the rich, I mean, not that they are utterly excluded; for St. *Paul* was

32 *Luke* 1. 53.] *Luke* 2. 23.

such an one; but he saveth not such, without he first awaken them to see they have need to be saved by Grace.

SECONDLY, The Grace of God saveth not him that hath sinned the unpardonable Sin. *There is nothing left for him but a certain, fearful looking for of Judgment which shall devour the Adversaries*, Heb. 10. 26, 27.

THIRDLY, That Sinner that persevereth in final Impenitency and unbelief, shall be damned, *Luke* 13. 3, 5. *Rom.* 2. 2, 3, 4, 5. *Mark* 16. 15, 16.

FOURTHLY, That Sinner whose Mind the God of this World hath blinded, that the glorious Light of the Gospel of Christ, who is the Image of God, can never shine into him, *is lost*, and must be damned, 2 *Cor.* 4. 3, 4.

FIFTHLY, The Sinner that maketh Religion his Cloak for wickedness, he is an Hypocrite, and continuing so, must certainly be damned, *Psal.* 125. 5. *Isa.* 33. 14. *Matth.* 24. 50, 51.

SIXTHLY, In a word, every Sinner that persevereth in his wickedness, shall not inherit the Kingdom of heaven: *Know you not that the unrighteous shall not inherit the Kingdom of God: Be not deceived, neither Fornicator, nor Idolater, nor Adulterers, nor Effeminate, nor Abusers of themselves with Mankind, nor Thieves, nor Covetous, nor Drunkards, nor Revilers, nor Extortioners, shall inherit the Kingdom of God: Let no man deceive you with vain words; for because of these things cometh the wrath of God upon the Children of Disobedience*, 1 Cor. 6. 9, 10. Ephes. 5. 5, 6.

Quest. BUT what kind of Sinners shall then be saved? 37.

Answ. THOSE of all these kinds that the Spirit of God shall bring the Father by Jesus Christ; these, I say, and none but these can be saved; because else the Sinners might be saved without the Father, or without the Son, or without the Spirit.

NOW, in all that I have said, I have not in the least suggested, that any Sinner is rejected because his sins, in the nature of them, are great; Christ Jesus came into the world to save the chief of Sinners: It is not therefore the greatness *of*, but the continuance *in* sins, that indeed damneth the Sinner: (But I always exclude him that hath sinned against the Holy Ghost); That it is not the greatness of sin that excludeth the Sinner, is evident;

24 1 Cor. 6. 9, 10.] 2 Cor. 6. 9, 12.

1. FROM the Words before the Text; which doth give an account of what kind of Sinners were here saved *by Grace*; as namely, *they that were dead in trespasses and sins, those that walked in these sins, according to the course of this world, even according to the Prince of the Power of the Air, the Spirit that now worketh in the Children of disobedience, among whom also we have all our conversation in times past, in the lusts of the Flesh, fulfilling the desires of the flesh, and of the mind, and were by nature the Children of wrath even as others*, Eph. 2. 1, 2, 3.

2. IT is evident also from the many Sinners that we find to be saved, by the revealed will of God; for in the Word we have mention made of the Salvation of great Sinners, where their Names and their Sins stand recorded, for our encouragement; as,

1. YOU read of **Manasseth**, who was an Idolater, a Witch, a Persecutor; yea, a Rebel against the Word of God, sent unto him by the Prophets; and yet this man was saved, 2 *Chron.* 33. 2, 3, 4, 5, 6, 7, 8, 9. 2 *King.* 21. 16. 2 *Chron.* 33. 10, 11, 12, 13.

2. YOU read of **Mary Magdalene**, in whom was seven Devils; her Condition was dreadful; yet she was saved, *Luke* 8. 2. *John* 20.

3. YOU read of the Man that had a Legion of Devils in him; O how dreadful was his Condition! and yet by Grace he was saved, *Mark* 5. 1–19.

4. YOU read of them that murthered the Lord Jesus, and how they were converted and saved, *Acts* 2. 23–41.

5. YOU read of the Exorcists in *Acts* 19. 13–19. how they closed with Christ, and were saved by grace.

6. YOU read of *Saul* the Persecutor, and how he was saved by grace, *Acts*. 9. 15.

38. *Object*. BUT thou saist, I am a Backslider.

Answ. SO was *Noah*, and yet he found grace in the eyes of the Lord, *Gen*. 9. 21, 22.

2. SO was *Lot*, and yet God saved him by grace, *Gen*. 19. 35, 36. and, 2 *Pet*. 2. 7, 8, 9.

3. SO was *David*, yet by grace he was forgiven his Iniquities, 2 *Sam*. 12. 7, 8, 9, 10, 11, 12, 13.

8 Eph. 2. 1, 2, 3.] Eph. 2. 2, 3. 24 *Acts* 2. 23–41.] *Acts* 2. 23. 25 *Acts* 19. 13–19.] *Acts*. 19. 13. 32 *Gen*. 19. 35, 36.] *Gen*. 20. 36.

4. So was *Solomon*, and a great one too; yet by grace his Soul was saved, *Psal.* 89. 28, 29, 30, 31, 32, 33, 34.

5. SO was *Peter*, and that a dreadful one; yet by grace he was saved, *Mat.* 26. 69, 70, 72, 74. *Mark* 16. 7. *Acts* 15. 7, 8, 9, 10, 11.

6. BESIDES, For further encouragement, read, *Jer.* 3. *chap.* 33. 25, 26. *chap.* 51. 5. *Ezek.* 36. 25. *Hos.* 14. 1, 2, 3, 4. And stay thy self, and wonder at the Riches of the grace of God.

Quest. BUT how should we find out what Sinners shall be saved? 39.
All it seems shall not: Besides, for ought can be gathered by what you have said, there is as bad saved as damned (set him that hath sinned the unpardonable Sin aside).

Answ. TRUE, there are as bad saved as damned; but to this Question:

1. They that are effectually called, are saved.

2. They that believe on the Son of God shall be saved.

3. They that are sanctified and preserved in Christ, shall be saved.

4. They that take up their Cross dayly, and follow Christ, shall be saved.

Take a Catalogue of them thus:

1. *Believe on the Lord Jesus Christ, and thou shalt be saved*, Mark 16. 16. *Acts* 16. 31.

2. *Confess with thy mouth the Lord Jesus and believe in thine heart that God hath raised him from the dead*, and thou shalt be saved, *Rom.* 10. 9.

3. Be justified by the Blood of Christ, and thou shalt be saved, *Rom.* 5. 9.

4. Be reconciled to God by the death of his Son, and thou shalt be saved by his life, *Rom.* 5. 10.

5. *And it shall come to pass, that whosoever shall call upon the Name of the Lord shall be saved*, Acts 2. 21. See some other Scriptures.

1. *He shall save the humble person*, Job 22. 29.

2. *Thou shalt save the afflicted People*, Psal. 18. 27.

3. *He shall save the Children of the needy*, Psal. 72. 4.

4. *He shall save the Souls of the Needy*, Psal. 72. 13.

5. *O thou my God, save thy servant that trusteth in thee*, Psal. 86. 2.

2 31,] *om.* 31 *Acts* 2. 21.] *Rom.* 10. 13.

6. *He will fulfil the desire of them that fear him, he will hear their cry, and will save them*, Psal. 145. 19.

40. But sinner, if thou wouldst indeed be saved, beware of these four things.

1. BEWARE of delaying repentance, delays are dangerous, and damnable; they are dangerous, because they harden the heart, they are damnable because their tendency is to make thee out-stand the time of Grace, *Psal.* 95. 7, 8. *Heb.* 3. 7, 8, 9, 10, 11.

2. BEWARE of resting in the Word of the Kingdom, without the Spirit and Power of the Kingdom of the Gospel, for the Gospel coming in Word only, saves no body, for the Kingdom of God or the Gospel where it comes to Salvation, is not in Word, but in Power, 1 *Thes.* 1. 4, 5, 6. 1 *Cor.* 4. 19.

3. TAKE heed of living in a profession, a Life that is provoking to God: For that is the way to make him cast thee away in his anger.

4. TAKE heed that thy inside and outside be alike, and both conformable to the Word of his Grace; labour to be like the living Creatures which thou mayest read of in the Book of the Prophet *Ezekiel*, whose appearance and themselves were one, *Ezek.* 10. 22.

In all this, I have advertised you not to be content without the power and spirit of God in your hearts, for without him you partake of none of the Grace of the Father or Son, but will certainly miss of the Salvation of the Soul.

QUESTION IV.

41. *How it appears, that they that are saved, are* Saved *by Grace?*

THIS Fourth Question requireth, that some Demonstration be given of the truth of this Doctrine; to wit, that they that are saved, are saved by Grace.

What hath been said before, hath given some Demonstration of the truth, wherefore first repeating in few words, the sum of what hath been said already, I shall come to further proof.

1. THAT this is true, the Scriptures testifie, because God chose them to Salvation before they had done good, *Rom.* 9. 11.

8 *Psal.* 95. 7, 8.] *Psal.* 95. 7.

2. CHRIST was ordained to be their Saviour before the foundation of the World, *Ephes.* 1. 4. 1 *Pet.* 1. 19, 20, 21.

3. ALL things that concur and go to our Salvation, were also in the same laid up in Christ to be communicated in the dispensation of the fulness of times to them that shall be saved, *Ephes.* 1. 3, 4. 2 *Tim.* 1. 9. *Ephes.* 1. 10. *chap.* 3. 8, 9, 10, 11. *Rom.* 8. 30.

AGAIN, As their Salvation was contrived by God, so as was said, this Salvation was undertaken by one of the three, to wit, the Son of the Father, *Joh.* 1. 29. *Isa.* 48. 16.

Had there been a contrivance in Heaven about the Salvation of Sinners on Earth, yet if the result of that contrivance had been, that we should be saved by our own good deeds, it would not have been proper for an Apostle or an Angel to say, *By Grace ye are saved.* But now, when a Councel is held in *eternity* about the Salvation of sinners in *time*, and when the result of that Councel shall be, that the Father, the Son, and the Holy Ghost will themselves accomplish the Work of this Salvation, *this is Grace*, this is naturally Grace, Grace that is rich and free. Yea, this is unthought of Grace; I will say it again, this is unthought-of Grace; for who could have thought that a Saviour had been in the bosom of the Father, or that the Father would have given him to be the Saviour of Men, since he refused to give him to be the Saviour of Angels, *Heb.* 2. 16, 17.

AGAIN, Could it have been thought, that the Father would have 42.
sent his Son to be the **Saviour**, we should in reason have thought also, that he would never have taken the Work wholly upon himself, especially that fearful, dreadful Soul astonishing, and amazing part thereof! Who could once have imagined, that the Lord Jesus would have made himself so poor, as to stand before God in the nauseous rags of our sins, and subject himself to the Curse and Death that was due to our sin; *but thus he did to save us by Grace.*

Blessed be God, and the Father of our Lord Jesus Christ, who hath blessed us with all Spiritual Blessings in heavenly places in Christ, according as he hath chosen us in him before the foundation of the World, that we should be holy, and without blame before him in love. Having predestinated us unto the adoption of Children, by Jesus Christ, to himself, according to the good pleasure of his Will, to the praise of the Glory of his grace, wherein he hath made us accepted in the beloved: In whom we have redemption through his blood, the forgiveness of sins, according to the riches of his Grace, Ephes. 1. 3. to 7.

43. AGAIN, If we consider the terms and condition upon which this salvation is made over to them that are saved, it will further appear, *we are saved by Grace.*

1. THE things that immediately concern our Justification and Salvation, they are offered, yea, given to us freely, and we are commanded to receive them by faith: Sinner hold up thy lap: God so loved the World that he giveth his Son, that he giveth his Righteousness, that he giveth his Spirit, and the Kingdom of Heaven, *Joh.* 3. 16. *Rom.* 5. 17. 2 *Cor.* 1. 21, 22. *Luke* 12. 32.

2. HE also giveth *Repentance*, he giveth *Faith*, and giveth *Everlasting Consolation, and good hope through Grace*, Acts 5. 30, 31. Philip. 1. 29. 2 *Thes.* 2. 16.

3. HE giveth *Pardon*, and giveth *more Grace*, to keep us from sinking into Hell, then *we have sin* to sink us in thither, *Acts* 5. 31. *Prov.* 3. 34. *Jam.* 4. 6. 1 *Pet.* 5. 5.

4. HE hath made all these things over to us in a Covenant of Grace, we call it a Covenant of Grace, *because 'tis set in opposition to the Covenant of Works, and because it is established to us in the doings of Christ*, founded in his Blood, stablished upon the best Promises made to him, and to us by him: *For all the Promises in him are yea, and in him Amen, to the Glory of God by us*, 2 Cor. 1. 20.

44. But to pass these, and to come to some other Demonstrations for the clearing of this.

FIRST, Let us a little consider, what Man is upon whom the Father, the Son, and the Spirit bestows this grace.

By Nature he is an Enemy to God, an Enemy in his Mind: *The carnal Mind is enmity to God; for it is not subject to the Law of God, neither indeed can be*, Colossians 1. 21. Rom. 8. 7.

SO that the state of Man was this, he was not only overperswaded on a sudden to sin against God, but he drank this Sin like water, into his very Nature, mingled it with every Faculty of his Soul, and Member of his Body; by the means of which, he became alienate from God, and an Enemy to him in his very heart; and wilt thou, O Lord, as the Scripture hath it, *And dost thou open*

16 *Acts* 5. 31.] *Acts.* 5. 3.

thine eyes upon such an one? Job 14. 3. Yea, open thy heart, and take this man, not into Judgment, but into Mercy with thee.

FURTHER, Man, by his Sin, had not only given himself to be a Captive-Slave to the Devil; but continuing in his Sin, he made head against his God, struck up a Covenant with Death, and made an agreement with Hell. But for God to open his eyes upon *such an one*, and to take hold of him by riches of Grace, this is amazing, *Isa.* 28. 16, 17, 18.

SEE where God found the *Jew* when he came to look upon him to save him: *As for thy Nativity* says God, *in the day thou wast born, thy Navel was not cut, neither wast thou washed in water to supple thee; thou wast not salted at all, nor swadled at all; none eye pitied thee, to do any of these things to thee, to have compassion on thee; but thou wast cast out into the open Field, to the loathing of thy person, in the day that thou wast born. And when I passed by thee, and saw thee polluted in thy Blood, I said unto thee, when thou wast in thy Blood, live; yea, I said unto thee when thou wast in thy Blood, live; now, when I passed by thee, and looked upon thee, behold thy time was the time of love; and I spread my skirt over thee, and covered thy Nakedness; yea, I swore unto thee, and entred into a covenant with thee, saith the Lord God, and thou becamest mine:* Sinner, see farther into the Chapter, *Ezek.* 16. All this is the grace of God: every Word in this Text smells of grace.

BUT before I pass this, let us a little take notice of the carriage 45.
of God to Man, and again of Man to God in his **Conversion**.

FIRST, Of **God's** carriage to Man; he comes to him while he is in his **Sins**, in his Blood; he comes to him now, not in the heat, and fire of his Jealousie; but in the cool of the Day, in unspeakable gentleness, mercy, pity, and bowels of Love; not in cloathing himself with vengeance; but in a way of entreaty, and meekly beseecheth the Sinner to be reconciled unto him, 2 *Cor.* 5. 19, 20.

IT is expected among Men, that he which giveth the Offence, should be the first in seeking Peace: But Sinner, betwixt God and Man it is not so; not that we loved God, not that we chose God; *but God was in Christ reconciling the world unto himself, not imputing their trespasses to them.* God is the first that seeketh Peace; and, as I said, in a way of Entreaty, he bids his Ministers pray you in Christ's stead; *as if God did beseech you by us, we pray you in Christ's stead, be ye reconciled to God.* O Sinner, wilt thou not open! Behold, God the Father, and his Son Jesus Christ, stand both at the *door of thy heart*, beseeching *there* for favour from thee, that thou wilt be reconciled to them, with promise, if thou wilt comply, to forgive thee all thy Sins. O grace! O amazing grace! To see a Prince entreat a Beggar to receive an Alms, would be a strange sight; to see a King entreat the Traitor to accept of Mercy, would be a stranger sight than that; but to see God entreat a Sinner to hear Christ say, *I stand at the door and knock*, with an heart-ful, and an heaven-full of grace, to bestow upon him that opens; this is such a sight as dazles the eyes of Angels. What saist thou now, Sinner, Is not this *God rich in Mercy*? Hath not this *God great Love for Sinners*? Nay further, that thou maist not have any ground to doubt that all this is but complementing, thou hast also here declared, *That God hath made his Christ to be Sin for us, who knew no Sin; that we might be made the Righteousness of God in him.* If *God* would have stuck at any thing, he would have stuck at the Death of his Son; but he delivered him up for us freely; *how shall he not then with him, freely give us all things? Rom.* 8. 32.

BUT this is not all; God doth not only beseech thee to be reconciled to him; but farther, for thy encouragement, he hath pronounced in thy hearing, exceeding great and precious Promises; *and hath confirmed them by an Oath, that by two immutable things in which it is not possible that God should lie, we might have a strong consolation who have fled for refuge to lay hold on the hope set before us*, Heb. 6. 17, 18. Isa. 1. 18. chap. 55. 6, 7. Jer. 51. 5.

46. SECONDLY, Let us come now to the Carriage of these sinners to God, and that from the first day he beginneth to deal with their souls, even to the time that they are to be taken up into Heaven.

AND first, to begin with God's *ordinary* dealing with sinners, when as first he ministreth Conviction to them by his Word, how strangely do they behave themselves? They love not to have their Consciences touched; they like not to ponder upon what they have been, what they are, or what is like to become of them hereafter: Such Thoughts they count unmanly, hurtful, disadvantageous;

19 *Rom.* 8. 32.] *Rom.* 8. 25 Heb. 6. 17, 18.] Heb. 6. 18, 19.

therefore they refuse to hearken, they pull away their shoulder, they stop their ears that they should not hear, Zech. 7. 11. And now they are for any thing, rather than the Word: An Ale-house, a Whore-house, a Play-house, Sports, Pleasures, Sleep, the World, and what not, so they may stave off the Power of the Word of God.

2ly, IF God now comes up closer to them, and begins to fasten 47.
Conviction upon the Conscience, though such *Conviction* be the first step to Faith and Repentance, yea, and to Life eternal; yet what shifts will they have to forget them, and wear them off! Yea, although they now begin to see that they must either *turn* or *burn*; yet oftentimes, even then, they will study to wave a present Conversion: They object, they are too young to turn yet; seven years hence time enough, when they are old, or come upon a sick-bed: O what an Enemy is Man to his own Salvation! I am perswaded that God hath visited some of you often with his Word, even twice, and thrice; and you have thrown Water as fast, as he hath by the Word cast Fire upon your Conscience. Christian, what had become of thee, if *God* had took thy denial, for an Answer, and said, Then will I carry the Word of Salvation to another, and he will hear it! Sinner turn (says *God*); Lord, I cannot tend it, says the Sinner: Turn or burn (says *God*); I will venture that, says the Sinner: Turn and be saved (says *God*), I cannot leave my Pleasures, says the Sinner: Sweet Sins, sweet Pleasures, sweet Delights, says the Sinner. But what Grace is it in *God*, thus to parley with the Sinner! O the Patience of *God* to a poor Sinner! What if *God* should now say, Then get thee to thy Sins, get thee to thy Delights, get thee to thy Pleasures, take them for thy Portion, they shall be all thy Heaven, all thy Happiness, and all thy Portion?

3*ly*, BUT *God* comes again, and shews the sinner the necessity of 48.
turning *now*; now, or not at all; yea, and giveth the sinner this conviction so strongly, that he cannot put it off. But behold the sinner has one spark of enmity still. If he must needs turn *now*, he will either turn from one sin to another, from great ones to little ones, from many to few, or from all to one and there stop. But perhaps Convictions will not thus leave him: Why then he will turn from Prophaneness to the Law of *Moses*, and will dwell as long as *God* will let him upon his own seeming goodness. And now observe

him, he is a great stickler for legal performance, now he will be a good Neighbour, he will pay every Man his own, will leave off his Swearing, the Alehouse, his Sports, and Carnal Delights: he will read, pray, talk of Scripture, and be a very busie one in Religion (such as it is): Now he will please *God*, and make him amends, for all the wrong he hath done him, and will feed him with Chapters, and Prayers, and Promises, and Vows, and a great many more such dainty Dishes as these: Perswading himself that now he must need be fair for Heaven, and thinks besides, that he serveth *God* as well as any Man in *England* can. But all this while he is as ignorant of Christ, as the stool he sits on, and no nearer Heaven then was the blind *Pharisee*, only he is got in a cleaner way to Hell, than the rest of his Neighbours are. *There is a generation that are pure in their own eyes, and yet are not purged from their filthiness*, Prov. 30. 12.

Might not *God* now cut off this Sinner, and cast him out of his sight; might he not leave him here to his own choice, to be deluded by, and to fall in his own Righteousness, because he *trusteth to it, and commits iniquity*, Ezek. 33. 13? But Grace, preventing Grace preserves him, 'tis true, this turn of the Sinner (as I said), is a turning short of Christ: But,

49. *4ly*, God in this way of the Sinner will mercifully follow him, and shew him the shortness of his performances, the emptiness of his Duties and the uncleanness of his righteousness, *Isa.* 28. 20. *chap.* 64. 6. This I speak of the sinner, the Salvation of whose Soul is graciously intended and contrived of God, for he shall by Gospel-light be wearied out of all; he shall be made to see the vanity of all, and that the personal righteousness of Jesus Christ, and that only, is it which of God is ordained to save the Sinner from the due reward of his sins; but behold, the sinner now, at the sight and sence of his own nothingness, falleth into a kind of despair; for although he hath it in him, to presume of Salvation, through the delusiveness of his own good opinion of himself, yet he hath it not in himself, to have a good opinion of the Grace of God, in the righteousness of Christ: Wherefore he concludeth, That if Salvation be alone of the Grace of God through the Righteousness of Christ, and that all of a Man's own, is utterly rejected, as to the justification of his person with God, then he is cast away. Now the reason of this sinking of

heart, is the sight that God hath given him, a sight of the uncleanness of his best performance, the former sight of his Immoralities, did somewhat distress him, and make him betake himself to his own good deeds to ease his Conscience, wherefore this was his prop, his stay; but behold, now God hath taken this from under him, and now he falls, wherefore his best doth also now forsake him, and flies away like the Morning-dew, or a Bird, or as the Chaff that is driven with the Whirlwind, and the smoak out of a Chimney, *Hos.* 9. 11. *chap.* 13. 3.

Besides, this revelation of the emptiness of his own righteousness, brings also with it a further discovery of the naughtiness of his heart, in its Hypocrisies, Pride, Unbelief, hardness of Heart, Deadness, and backwardness to all Gospel, and New Covenant Obedience, which sight of himself, lies like Millstones upon his Shoulders, and sinks him yet further into doubts and fears of Damnation. For, bid him now receive Christ, he answers, he cannot, he dares not: Ask him why he cannot, he will answer, He has no faith, nor hope in his heart; tell him that grace is offered him freely, he says, But I have no heart to receive it; besides he finds not, as he thinks, any gracious disposition in his Soul, and therefore concludes, he doth not belong to *God's mercy*, nor hath an interest in the Blood of Christ, and therefore dares not presume to believe; wherefore, as I said, he sinks in his heart, he dies in his thoughts, he doubts,
he despairs, and concludes, he shall never be saved. 24

5ly, BUT behold, the *God* of all grace leaveth him not in this 50.
distress, but comes up now to him closer than ever, he sends the spirit of Adoption, the Blessed Comforter to him, to tell him, *God is Love*, and therefore not willing to reject the broken in heart; bids him cry, and pray for an evidence of mercy to his Soul, and says, *Peradventure you may be hid in the day of the Lord's Anger.* At this the Sinner takes some encouragement, yet he can get no more then that which will hang upon a meer probability, which by the next doubt that ariseth in the heart, is blown quite away, and the Soul left again in his first plight, or worse; where he lamentably bewails his miserable state, and is tormented with a thousand fears of perishing, for he hears not a word from Heaven, perhaps for several Weeks together: Wherefore Unbelief begins to get the mastery of him, and

takes off the very edge and spirit of Prayer, and inclinations to hear the word any longer: Yea, the Devil also claps in with these thoughts, saying, that all your Prayers, and hearing, and reading, and godly Company, which you frequent, will rise up in judgment against you at last; therefore better it is, if you must be damned, to chuse as easie a place in Hell as you can. The Soul at this, being quite discouraged, thinks to do as it hath been taught, and with dying Thoughts, it begins to faint when it goeth to Prayer, or to hear the Word; but behold, when all hope seems to be quite gone, and the Soul concludes, *I die*, *I perish*, in comes on a sudden the Spirit of God again with some good Word of God, which the soul never thought of before; which Word of God commands a Calm in the soul, makes Unbelief give place, encourageth to hope and wait upon God again; perhaps it gives some little sight of Christ to the soul, and of his blessed undertaking for sinners. But behold, so soon as the power of things do again begin to wear off the heart, the sinner gives place to Unbelief, questions God's Mercy, and fears damning again; he also entertains hard Thoughts of God and Christ, and thinks former encouragements were Fancies, Delusions, or meer *Thinkso*'s. And why doth not God now cast the Sinner to Hell, for his thus abusing his mercy and grace? O no! *He will have mercy on whom he will have mercy, and he will have compassion on whom he will have compassion*; wherefore goodness and mercy shall follow him all the days of his Life, *that he may dwell in the house of the Lord for ever*, Psal. 23. 6.

51. *6ly*, GOD therefore, after all these Provocations, comes by his Spirit to the soul again, and brings sealing grace and pardon to the Conscience, testifying to it, that its sins are forgiven, and that freely for the sake of the Blood of Christ, and now has the sinner such a sight of the grace of God in Christ, as kindly breaks his heart with joy and comfort. Now the soul knows that it is to eat Promises; it also knows what it is to eat and drink the flesh and blood of Jesus Christ by faith: now it is driven by the power of his grace, to its knees, to thank *God* for forgiveness of sins, and for hopes of an inheritance amongst them that are sanctified by faith, which is in Christ. Now it hath a Calm and Sun-shine; now *he washeth his steps with Butter, and the Rock poures him out Rivers of Oyl.*

52. *7ly*, BUT after this, perhaps the soul grows cold again; it also

forgets this grace received, and waxeth carnal; begins again to itch after the World, loseth the life and savour of heavenly things, grieves the Spirit of God, wofully backslides, casteth off Closet-Duties quite, or else retains only the formality of them, is a reproach to Religion, grieves the hearts of them that are awake, and tender of God's Name, *&c.* But what will God do now? Will he take this advantage to destroy the Sinner? No. Will he let him alone in his Apostasie? No. Will he leave him to recover himself by the strength of his now languishing graces? No. What then? Why he will seek this Man out, till he finds him, and bring him home to himself again. *For thus saith the Lord God, Behold, I, even I, will both search my Sheep, and seek them out, as a Shepherd seeketh out his Flock, in the day that he is among the sheep that are scattered; so will I seek out my sheep, and will deliver them out of all places where they have been scattered. I will seek that which was lost, and bring again that which was driven away; I will bind up that which was broken, and will strengthen that which was sick*, Ezek. 34. 11–16.

THUS he dealt with the Man that went down from *Jerusalem* to **Jericho**, and fell among Thieves; and thus he dealt with the Prodigal you read of also, *Luke* 10. 30, 31, 32, 33, 34, 35. *Luke* 15. 20.

Of Gods ordinary way of fetching the **Backslider** home, I will not now discourse, namely, whether he always breaketh his bones for his sins, as he broke *David*'s: or whether he will all the days of their Life, for this, leave them under guilt and darkness; or whether he will kill them now, that they may not be damned in the Day of Judgment, as he dealt with them at *Corinth*, 1 Cor. 11. 30, 31, 32. He is wise, and can tell how to imbitter backsliding to them he loveth.

HE can break their Bones, and save them; he can lay them in the lowest pit, in darkness, in the deep, and save them: he can slay them as to this Life, and save them. And herein again appears wonderful grace, that *Israel* is *not forsaken, nor* Judah *of his God*, though *their Land be filled with sin against the Holy One of* Israel, *Jer.* 51. 5.

8*ly*, BUT suppose God deals not either of these ways with the 53.
Back-slider, but shines upon him again, and seals up to him the remission of his sins a second time, saying, *I will heal their Back-slidings, and love them freely*: What will the soul do now? Surely it

will walk humbly now, and holily all its days. It will never back-slide again, will it? It may happen it will not, it may happen it will; it is just as his God keeps him; for although his sins are of himself, his standing is of God; I say, his standing, while he stands, and his recovery, if he falls, are both of God. Wherefore, if God leaves him a little, the next gap he finds, away he's gone again: *My People*, says God, *are bent to back-sliding from me.* How many times did *David* backslide? yea, *Jehosaphat* and *Peter*? 2 *Sam.* 11. *chap.* 24. 2 *Chron.* 19. 1, 2, 3. *chap.* 20. 35. *Mat.* 26. 69, 70, 71. *Gal.* 2. 11, 12, 13. As also in the 3*d.* of *Jeremiah*, 'tis said, *But thou hast played the Harlot with many* Lovers, *yet return unto me, saith the Lord*, Jer. 3. 1. Here is Grace! So many times as the soul backslides, so many times God brings him again (I mean, the soul that must be saved by grace), he renews his Pardons, and multiplies them. *Lo all these things worketh God often-times with Man*, Job 33. 29.

54. 9*ly*, BUT see yet more grace; I will speak here of Heart-wandrings, and of daily Miscarriages; I mean, of these common Infirmities that are incident to the best of saints, and that attend them in their best Performances; not that I intend, for I cannot mention them particularly; that would be a Task impossible; but such there are, worldly Thoughts, unclean Thoughts, too low Thoughts of God, of Christ, of the Spirit, Words, Ways and Ordinances of God, by which a Christian transgresses many times; may I not say, sometimes, many hundred times a day; yea, for ought I know, there are some Saints, and them not long-lived neither, that must receive, before they enter into Life, Millions of pardons from God for these; and every Pardon is an Act of grace, through the redemption that is in Christ's Blood. Seventy times seven times a day we sometimes sin against our Brother, but how many times in that day do we sin against God? *Lord, who can understand his errors? Cleanse thou me from my secret sins*, said David: And again, *If thou, Lord, shouldest mark iniquity, O Lord, who should stand? But there is forgiveness with thee that thou maist be feared*, Mat. 18. 21, 22. Psal. 19. 12. Psal. 130. 3, 4.

BUT to mention some of them; sometimes they question the very Being of *God*, or foolishly ask, how he came to be at first? Sometimes they question the truth of his Word, and suspect the

9 *chap.* 20. 35.] *chap.* 20. 5.

Harmony thereof, because their blind hearts and dull heads cannot reconcile it; yea, all fundamental Truths lie open sometimes to the censure of their Unbelief and Atheism; as namely, whether there be such an one as Christ, such a thing as the Day of Judgment, or whether there will be a Heaven or Hell hereafter? and *God* pardons all these by his grace. When they believe these things, even then they sin, by not having such reverent, high and holy thoughts of them as they ought; they sin also by having too good thoughts of themselves, of Sin, and the World; sometimes, let me say, often, they wink too much at known sin; they bewail not, as they should, the Infirmities of the Flesh; the itching inclinations which they find in their hearts after vanity, go too often from them unrepented of: I do not say, but they repent them in the general. But all these things, O how often doth *God* forgive through the riches of his grace?

THEY sin by not walking answerable to Mercies received; yea, they come short in their Thanks to *God* for them, even then when they most heartily acknowledge how unworthy they are of them; also how little of the strength of them is spent to his praise, who freely poureth them into their bosomes; but from all these sins are they saved by grace.

THEY sin in their most exact and spiritual performance of Duties; they pray not, they hear not, they read not, they give not Alms, they come not to the Lord's Table, or other holy Appointments of *God*, but in, and with much coldness, deadness, wandrings of heart, ignorance, mis-apprehensions, *&c.* They forget *God*, while they pray unto him; they forget Christ, while they are at his Table; they forget his Word, even while they are reading of it.

HOW often do they make Promises to *God*, and afterwards break them? Yea, or if they keep Promise in shew, how much doth their heart even grudge the performing of them? how do they shuck at the Cross? and how unwilling are they to lose that little they have for God, though all they have was given them to glorifie him withal? All these things, and a thousand times as many more dwell in the flesh of Man; and they may as soon go away from themselves, as from these Corruptions; yea, they may sooner cut the Flesh from their Bones, than these motions of sin from their Flesh; these will

8 too] too too

be with them in every Duty; I mean, some or other of them: yea, as often as they look, or think, or hear, or speak. These are with them, especially when the Man intends good in so doing: *When I would do good*, says *Paul*, *evil is present with me*. And God himself complains, that *every imagination of the thought of the heart of Man is only evil, and that continually*, *Rom.* 7. 21. *Gen.* 6. 5.

BY these things therefore we continually defile our selves, and every one of our Performances; I mean, in the judgment of the Law, even mixing iniquity with those things which we hallow unto the Lord. *For from within, out of the heart of Man proceed evil thoughts, adulteries, fornications, murthers, thefts, covetousness, wickedness, deceits, lasciviousness, an evil eye, blasphemy, foolishness; all these things come from within, and they defile the Man*, Mark 7. 21, 22, 23. Now what can deliver the Soul from these, but grace? *By grace ye are saved.*

QUESTION V.

55. *What might be the Reason moved God to ordain, and chuse to save those that he saveth, by his Grace, rather than by any other Means?*

I COME now to answer the Fifth Question: namely, to shew why *God* saveth those that he saveth, by grace, rather than by any other Means.

FIRST, God saveth us by **Grace**, because since sin is in the World, he can save us no other way: Sin and Transgression cannot be removed but by the grace of God, through Christ: Sin is the Transgression of the Law of God, who is perfectly just. Infinite Justice cannot be satisfied with the recompence that Man can make; for if it could, Christ Jesus himself needed not to have died; besides, Man having sinned, and defiled himself thereby, all his Acts are the Acts of a defiled Man: Nay farther, the best of his Performances are also defiled by his hands; their Performances therefore cannot be a recompence for Sin. Besides, to affirm, that God saveth defiled Man for the sake of his defiled Duties; for *so, I say is every Work of his hand*, Hag. 2. 14. What is it but to say, God accepteth of one

13 Mark 7. 21, 22, 23.] Mark 7. 21, 22.

sinful Act as a recompence and satisfaction for another? But *God*, even of old hath declared how he abominates imperfect Sacrifices; therefore we can by no means be saved from sin, but by grace, *Rom.* 3. 24.

SECONDLY, To assert, that we may be saved any other way than by the grace of God, what is it, but to object against the Wisdom and Prudence of God, wherein he aboundeth toward them whom he hath saved by grace? *Ephes.* 1. 5, 6, 7, 8. His Wisdom and Prudence found out no other way; therefore he chuseth to save us by grace.

THIRDLY, We must be saved by Grace because else it follows, that *God* is mutable in his Decrees, for so hath he determined before the foundation of the World; therefore he saveth us not, nor chooseth to save us by any other way than by grace, *Ephes.* 1. 3, 4. *chap.* 3. 8, 9, 10, 11. *Rom.* 9. 23.

FOURTHLY, If Man should be saved any other way than by grace, *God* would be disappointed in his Design to cut off boasting from his Creature, but *God*'s design to cut off boasting from his Creature, cannot be frustrated or disappointed; therefore he will save Man by no other means than by grace; he (I say) hath designed, that no flesh should glory in his presence, and therefore he refuseth their Works; *Not of Works, lest any Man should boast: Where is boasting then? It is excluded, by what Law? Of Works, nay, but by the Law of Faith:* Ephes. 2. 8, 9. Rom. 3. 24, 25, 26, 27, 28.

FIFTHLY, *God* hath ordained, that we should be saved by Grace, that he might have the praise and glory of our Salvation, *That we should be to the praise of the glory of his Grace, wherein he hath made us accepted in the Beloved*, Ephes. 1. 5, 6. Now God will not lose his Praise, and his Glory; he will not give to another; therefore God doth choose to save Sinners but by his Grace.

SIXTHLY, God hath ordained, and doth choose to save us by **Grace**, because were there another way apparent, yet this is the 56.
way that is fastest, and best secureth the Soul. *Therefore it is by Faith, that it might be by Grace, to the end the Promise* (the promise of eternal Inheritance, *Hebr.* 9. 14, 15, 16.) *might be sure to all the Seed*: No other way could have been sure: This is evident in *Adam*, the *Jews*, and I will add, the fallen Angels, who being turned over to

18 frustrated] frustrate

another way than Grace, you see in short time what became of them.

To be saved by Grace, supposeth that God hath taken the Salvation of our Souls into his own hand, and to be sure, it is safer in God's hand than ours. Hence it is called the Salvation of the Lord, the Salvation of God, and Salvation, and that of God.

When our Salvation is in *God's* hand, himself is engaged to accomplish it for us.

1. HERE is the Mercy of *God* engaged for us, *Rom.* 9. 15.

2. HERE is the Wisdom of *God* engaged for us, *Ephes.* 1. 7, 8.

3. HERE is the Power of *God* engaged for us, 1 *Pet.* 1. 3, 4, 5.

4. HERE is the Justice of *God* engaged for us, *Rom.* 3. 24, 25, 26.

5. HERE is the Holiness of *God* engaged for us, *Psal.* 89. 30, 31, 32, 33, 34, 35.

6. HERE is the Care of *God* engaged for us, and his watchful Eye is always over us for our good, 1 *Pet.* 5, 7. *Isa.* 27. 1, 2, 3.

57. What shall I say?

1. GRACE can take us into favour with *God*, and that when we are in our Blood, *Ezek.* 16. 7, 8, 9.

2. GRACE can make Children of us, though by nature we have been Enemies to *God*, *Rom.* 9. 25, 26.

3. GRACE can make them *God's* People, which were not *God's* People, 1 *Pet.* 2. 9, 10.

4. GRACE will not trust our own Salvation in our own hands, *He putteth no trust in his Saints*, Job 15. 15.

5. GRACE can pardon our ungodliness, justify us with Christ's Righteousness, it can put the Spirit of Jesus Christ within us, it can help us up when we are down, it can heal us when we are wounded, it can multiply Pardons, as we through Frailty multiply Transgressions: What shall I say?

1. GRACE, and Mercy is everlasting.

2. 'TIS built up for ever.

3. 'TIS the Delight of God.

4. IT rejoyceth against Judgment.

5. AND therefore it is the most safe and secure way of Salvation, and therefore hath God chosen to save us by his Grace and Mercy

12 *Rom.* 3. 24, 25, 26.] *Rom.* 3. 24, 25. 19 *Ezek.* 16. 7, 8, 9.] *Ezek.* 16. 7, 8.

rather than any other way, *Isa.* 43. 25. *Rom.* 3. 24, 25. *Isa.* 44. 2, 3. *Psal.* 37. 23. *Luk.* 10. 33, 34. *Isa.* 55. 7, 8. *Psal.* 136. *Psal.* 89. 2. *Mala.* 3. 18. *Jam.* 2. 13.

SEVENTHLY, We must be saved by the Grace of *God*, or else 58.
God will not have his Will. They that are saved, are *predestinated to the adoption of Children by Jesus Christ to himself, according to the good pleasure of his Will, to the praise of the Glory of his Grace*, Ephes. 1. 5, 6.

1. BUT if it be his Will, that Men should be saved by Grace, then to think of another way, is against the Will of *God*. Hence they that seek to establish their own Righteousness, are such as are accounted to stand out in defiance against, and that do not submit, to the Righteousness of *God*; that is, to the Righteousness that he hath willed to be, that through which alone we are saved by Grace, *Rom.* 10. 3, 4.

2*ly*. IF it be his Will, that Men should be saved through Grace, then it is his Will that Men should be saved by Faith in that Christ, who is the contrivance of Grace: Therefore they that have fought to be justified another way, have come short of; and perished notwithstanding that Salvation that is provided of *God* for Men by Grace, *Rom.* 9. 31, 32, 33.

3*ly*, *GOD* is not willing that Faith should be made void, and the promise of none effect: Therefore they of the Righteousness of the Law are excluded: *For if the Inheritance be of the Law, then it is no more of Promise, but God gave it to* Abraham *by Promise*, Rom. 4. 14. Gal. 3. 18.

4*ly*, *GOD* is not willing that Men should be saved by their own natural Abilities, but all the Works of the Law, which Men do to be saved by, they are the Works of Mens natural Abilities, and are therefore called, the Work of the Flesh, *Rom.* 4. 1. *Gal.* 3. 1, 2, 3. *Philip.* 3. 3. but, *God* is not willing that Men should be saved by these, therefore, no way but by his Grace.

EIGHTHLY, We must be saved by Grace, or else the main pillars, 59.
and foundations of Salvation, are not only shaken but overthrown; to wit, Election, the New Covenant, Christ, and the Glory of *God*, but these must not be overthrown, therefore we must be saved by *Grace*.

1 *Isa.* 44. 2, 3.] *Isa.* 44. 2, 4. 2–3 *Mala.* 3. 18.] *Mala.* 7. 18.

1. ELECTION, which layeth hold of Men by the grace of *God*, *God* hath purposed that that shall stand; *the election of God standeth sure*, Rom. 9. 11. 2 Tim. 2. 19. Therefore Men must be saved by vertue of the election of grace.

2. THE Covenant of Grace, that must stand: *Brethren, I speak after the manner of Men: Though it be but a Man's Covenant, yet if it be confirmed* (as this is by the Death of the Testator, *Heb.* 9. 16, 17.), *no Man disalloweth, or addeth thereunto*; therefore Man must be saved by vertue of a Covenant of Grace.

3. CHRIST, who is the gift of the Grace of *God* to the World, he must stand, because *he is a sure foundation, the same yesterday, to day, and for ever*, Isa. 28. 16, 17. *Heb.* 13. 8. therefore Men must be saved by grace, through the Redemption that is in Christ.

4. *GOD's* Glory, that also must stand, to wit, the glory of his Grace, for that he will not give to another, therefore Men must so be saved from the Wrath to come, that in their Salvation praise may redound to the glory of his Grace.

60. NINTHLY, There can be but one Will, the Master in our Salvation, but that shall never be the Will of Man, but of *God*; therefore Man must be saved by **Grace**, *Joh.* 1. 11, 12, 13. *Rom.* 9. 16.

TENTHLY, There can be but one *righteousness*, that shall save a Sinner, but that shall never be the righteousness of Men, but of Christ, therefore Men must be saved by grace, that imputeth this righteousness to whom he will.

ELEVENTHLY, There can be but one *Covenant*, by which Men must be saved, but that shall never be the Covenant of the Law, for the weakness and unprofitableness thereof: Therefore Men must be saved by the Covenant of Grace, by which *God* will be merciful to our Unrighteousnesses, and our Sins and Iniquities will remember no more, *Heb.* 8. 6. to 13.

---

20 *Joh.* 1. 11, 12, 13.] *Joh.* 1. 11, 12.

POSTSCRIPT.

A FEW words by way of Use, and so I shall conclude. 61.

The First USE.

FIRST, *Is the Salvation of the sinner by the Grace of God?* Then here you see the reason, Why God hath not respect to the personal vertues of Men in the bringing of them to Glory: Did I say, *personal vertues*, how can they have any to God-ward, that are enemies to him in their minds, by wicked Works? Indeed, Men one to another seem to be, some better, some worse, by nature, but to God they are all alike, *dead in Trespasses and Sins.*

We will therefore state it again; Are Men saved by Grace? Then here you may see the reason, why Conversion runs at that rate among the Sons of Men, that none are **converted** for their good deeds, nor rejected for their bad, but even so many of both, and only so many, are brought home to God, as Grace is pleased to bring home to him.

1. NONE are received for their good deeds, for then they would not be saved by Grace, but by Works. Works and Grace, as I have shewed are in this matter opposite each to other; if he be saved by Works, then not by Grace; if by Grace, then not by Works, *Rom.* 11. 6.

That none are received of God for their good deeds, is evident, not only because he declares his abhorrence of the supposition of such a thing, but hath also rejected the Persons that have at any time attempted to present themselves to God in their own good deeds for justification. This I have shewed you before.

2. MEN are not rejected for their bad deeds. This is evident by *Manasseth*, by the Murderers of our Lord Jesus Christ, by the Men that you read of in the Nineteenth of the *Acts*, with many others, whose sins were of as deep a dye as the sins of the worst of Men, 2 *Chron.* 33. 2–13. *Acts* 2. 23, 41. *ch.* 19. 19.

Grace respecteth, in the Salvation of a sinner, chiefly the purpose of God, wherefore those that it findeth under that purpose, those it justifies freely through the redemption that is in Jesus Christ.

20 *Rom.* 11. 6.] *Rom.* 11.

At Saul's Conversion, *Ananias* of *Damascus*, brought in a most dreadful Charge against him to the Lord Jesus Christ, saying, *Lord, I have heard by many, of this Man, how much evil he hath done to thy Saints at* Jerusalem, *and here he hath authority from the Chief Priests to bind all that call upon thy Name*: But what said the Lord unto him? *Go thy ways for he is a chosen Vessel unto me*, Acts 9. 13, 14, 15. This Man's Cruelty, and Outrage must not hinder his Conversion, because he was a chosen Vessel: Mens good deeds are no argument with God to convert them; Mens bad deeds are no argument with him to reject them. I mean, them that come to Christ by the drawings of the Father; besides Christ also saith, *I will in no wise cast such out*, John 6. 37, 44.

62. SECONDLY, Is the Salvation of the Sinner, by the Grace of God? *Then here you see the reason, why some* Sinners, *that were wonderfully averse to Conversion by nature, are yet made to stoop to the God of their Salvation*: Grace takes them to do, because Grace hath designed them to this very thing: Hence some of the Gentiles were taken from among the rest; God granted them repentance unto life, because he had taken them from among the rest, both by election and calling, for his Name, *Acts* 11. 18. *chap.* 15. 14. These Men, that were not a People, are thus become the People of God; these Men that were not beloved for their Works, were yet beloved by the Grace of God. *I will call them my people, which were not my people, and her beloved, which was not beloved*: But their minds are averse; but are they the People, on whom God doth magnifie the Riches of his Grace? Why then they shall be in the day of his Power made willing, and be able to believe through Grace, *Psal.* 110. 3. *Acts* 18. 27. But doth the guilt, and burden of sin so keep them down, that they can by no means lift up themselves? Why God will by the exceeding greatness of that power, by which he raised Christ from the dead, work in their Souls also by the Spirit of Grace, to cause them to believe and to walk in his ways, *Ephes.* 1. 18, 19, 20.

St. Paul tells us in that Epistle of his to the *Corinthians*, that it was by Grace he was what he was. *By the Grace of God I am what I am*, says he, *and his Grace which was bestowed upon me was not in vain*, 1 Cor. 15. 10. This Man kept always in his mind a warm remembrance, of what he was formerly by nature, and also how he had added to his vileness by practice; yea, moreover, he truly concluded in his own Soul, that had not God by unspeakable grace put a stop to his wicked proceedings, he had perished in his wickedness: Hence he lays his Call and Conversion at the door of the grace of God. *When it pleased God*, says he, *who separated me from my Mothers womb, and called me by his grace, to reveal his Son in me*, Gal. 1. 15, 16. And hence it is again, that he saith, *He obtained Grace and Apostleship*: Grace, to convert his Soul, and the gifts and Authority of an Apostle, to preach the Gospel of the grace of God.

THIS blessed Man ascribes all to the grace of God.

1. *HIS Call*, he ascribes to the grace of God.

2. *HIS Apostleship*, he ascribes to the grace of God.

3. *AND all his Labour in that Charge*, he also ascribes to the grace of God.

THIS Grace of God, it was that which saved from the beginning.

1. *NOAH* found grace in the eyes of the Lord, and was therefore converted, and preserved from the Flood, *Gen.* 6. 7, 8.

2. Abraham found grace in the sight of the Lord; and therefore he was called out of his Countrey, *Gen.* 12. 1, 2.

3. Moses found grace in the eyes of the Lord; and therefore he must not be blotted out of God's Book, *Exod.* 33. 12, 17.

NEITHER may it be imagined, that these Men, were, before grace laid hold on them, better than other Men; for then they would not have been saved by grace: Grace should not have had the dominion and glory of their salvation. But as St. *Paul* says of himself, and of those that were saved by grace in his day, *What, are we better than they? No, in no wise; for we have proved before that both* Jews *and* Gentiles *are all under sin*, Rom. 3. 9. So it may be said of these blessed ones; for indeed this Conclusion is general, and reacheth all the Children of Men, Christ Jesus alone only excepted; But,

THIRDLY, Is the Salvation of the Sinner by the grace of God? 63.
Then here you may see the reason why one Backslider *is recovered, and another left to perish in his* Backsliding.

There was Grace for *Lot*, but none for his Wife: therefore she was left in her transgression; but *Lot* was saved notwithstanding. There was grace for *Jacob*, but none for *Esau*; therefore *Esau* was left in

6 Gal. 1. 15, 16.] Gal. 1. 14, 15.

his Back-sliding, but *Jacob* found Mercy notwithstanding. There was grace for *David*, but none for *Saul*; therefore *David* obtained Mercy, and *Saul* perished in his Backsliding. There was grace for *Peter*, but none for *Judas*; therefore *Judas* is left to perish in his Back-sliding, and *Peter* is saved from his sin. That Text stands good to none but those that are elect by grace, *Sin shall not have dominion over you; for you are not under the Law, but under Grace*, Rom. 6. 14.

IT will be said, Repentance was found in one, but not in the other. Well, but who granted and gave the one Repentance? The Lord turned, and looked upon *Peter*; he did not turn and look upon *Judas*; yea, the Lord told *Peter* before he fell, that he should follow him to the Kingdom of Heaven; but told him, that he should deny him first; but withal, told him also, he should not let his heart be troubled, that is, utterly dejected; for he would go and prepare a place for him, and come again and receive him to himself, *John* 13. 36, 37, 38. *Chap.* 14. 1, 2, 3. That is a blessed Word of God. *The steps of a good man are ordered by the Lord, and he delighteth in his way; though he fall, he shall not be utterly cast down; for the Lord upholdeth him with his hand*, Psal. 37. 23, 24.

The Second USE.

64. MY Second USE shall be to them that are **dejected** in their Souls at the sight and sense of their Sins.

FIRST, Are they that are saved, saved by grace? *Then they that would have their guilty Consciences quieted, they must study the Doctrine of* **Grace**.

IT is Satan's great Design, either to keep the Sinner senseless of his Sins; or if God makes him sensible of them, then to hide and keep from his thoughts the sweet Doctrine of the grace of God, by which alone the Conscience getteth Health and Cure: *For everlasting Consolation, and good Hope is given through grace*, 2 Thes. 2. 16. How then shall the Conscience of the burthened Sinner be rightly quieted, if he perceiveth not the grace of God?

STUDY therefore this Doctrine of the grace of God, Suppose thou hast a Disease upon thee, which is not to be cured by such or such Medicine, the first step to thy Cure, is to know the Medicines: I am sure this is true, as to the Case in hand; the first step to the Cure of a wounded Conscience, is for thee to know the grace of *God*, especially the grace of *God* as to Justification, from the Curse, in his sight.

A Man under a wounded Conscience, naturally leaneth to the works of the Law, and thinks *God* must be pacified by something that he should do, whereas the Word says, *I will have Mercy, and not Sacrifice; for I am not come to call the righteous, but sinners to repentance,* Mat. 9. 13.

Wherefore thou must study the grace of *God. 'Tis a good thing* (saith the Apostle), *that the heart be established with grace.* Thereby insinuating, that there is no establishment in the Soul, that is right, but by the knowledge of the grace of *God*, Heb. 13. 9.

I said, That when a man is wounded in his Conscience, he naturally leaneth to the works of the Law: wherefore thou must therefore be so much the more heedful to study the grace of God; yea, so to study it as rightly, not only in notion, but in thy practices, to distinguish it from the Law. *The Law was given by* Moses, *but Grace and Truth came by Jesus Christ,* John 1. 17. Study it, I say, so as to distinguish it, and that, not only from the Law, but from all those things that Men blasphemously call this grace of God.

There are many things which Men call the **Grace** of God, that is not.

1. THE Light and Knowledge that is in every Man. 65.

2. THAT natural willingness that is in Man to be saved.

3. THAT Power that is in Man by nature, to do something, as he thinketh, towards his own Salvation.

I name these Three: There are also many other which some will have entituled the **Grace** of God: But do thou remember, that the grace of God is his good-will and great love to Sinners in his Son Jesus Christ; *by the which good will they are sanctified through the offering up of the Body of Jesus Christ, once for all,* Heb. 10. 10.

AGAIN, When thou hast smelt out this grace of God, and canst distinguish it from that which is not, then labour to strengthen thy Soul with the blessed knowledge of it. *Thou therefore, my Son,* said *Paul, be strong in the grace that is in Christ Jesus,* 2 Tim. 2. 1. Fortifie thy Judgment and Understanding; but especially labour to get down all into thy Conscience, that that may be *purged from dead works, to serve the living God.*

66. And to enforce this Use upon thee yet farther, consider, a Man gets yet more advantage by the knowledge of, and by growing strong in this **Grace** of God.

1. IT ministreth to him matter of Joy; for he that knows this grace aright, he knows *God* is at peace with him, because he believeth in Jesus Christ, *who by grace tasted death for every man*; *by whom also we have access by faith into this grace wherein we stand, and rejoyce in hope at the glory of God*, Rom. 5. 1, 2, 3. And indeed, what joy, or what rejoycing is like rejoycing here? To rejoyce in hope of the glory of God, it is to rejoyce in hope to enjoy him for ever, with that eternal glory that is in him.

2*ly*, AS it manifesteth matter of joy and rejoycing; so it causeth much fruitfulness in all holiness and godliness. *For the grace of God that bringeth Salvation, hath appeared to all men, teaching us, that denying ungodliness, and worldly lusts, we should live soberly, righteously, and godly in this present World*, Tit. 2. 11, 12. Yea, it so naturally tendeth this way, that it can no sooner appear to the soul, but it causeth this blessed fruit in the heart and life: *We our selves were sometimes foolish, disobedient, deceived, serving divers lusts and pleasures; living in malice and envy, hateful and hating one another; but after the love and kindness of God our Saviour appeared.* What then? Why then, *he that believeth, being justified by his grace*, and expecting *to be an heir according to the hope of eternal life, is careful to maintain good works*, Tit. 3. 3, 4, 5, 6, 7, 8.

See also that in St. *Paul*'s Epistle to the *Colossians*, *We give thanks*, says he, *to God and the Father of our Lord Jesus Christ, praying always for you since he heard of your Faith in Christ Jesus, and of the love which ye have to all the Saints; for the hope which is laid up for you in heaven; whereof ye heard before in the word of the Truth of the Gospel, which is come unto you, as it is also in all the world, and bringeth forth fruit, as it doth also in you, since the day you heard it, and knew the grace of God in truth*, Col. 1. 3, 4, 5, 6.

67. 3*ly*, THE knowledge of, and strength that comes by the **grace** of God, is a sovereign Antidote against all, and all manner of Delusions that are, or may come into the world. Wherefore S. *Peter*

33 Col. 1. 3, 4, 5, 6.] Col. 1. 3, 4.

exhorting the Believers to take heed that they were not carried away with the Errors of the wicked, and so fall from their own stedfastness, adds, as their only help, this exhortation; *But grow in grace, and in the knowledge of our Lord and Saviour Jesus Christ*, 2 Pet. 3. 18.

1. SUPPOSE it should be urged, That Man's own Righteousness saveth the Sinner; why then we have this at hand, *God hath saved us, and called us, not according to our works, but according to his own purpose and grace, which was given us in Christ*, &c. 2 *Tim.* 1. 9.

2. SUPPOSE it should be urged, That by the Doctrine of free grace, we must not understand, God's extending free forgiveness as far as we have, or do sin. The Answer is, *But where Sin abounded, Grace hath much more abounded; that as Sin hath reigned unto Death, so grace might reign through Righteousness* (through the Justice of God, being satisfied by his Son), *unto eternal Life*, Rom. 5. 20, 21.

3. SUPPOSE it should be urged, That this is a Doctrine tending to loosness and lasciviousness; the Answer is ready: *What shall we say then? shall we continue in sin that Grace may abound? God forbid: How shall we that are dead to sin, live any longer therein?* for the Doctrine of free grace believed, is the most Sin-killing Doctrine in the world, *Rom.* 6. 1, 2.

4. SUPPOSE Men should attempt to burthen the Church of God with unnecessary Ceremonies, and impose them, even as the false Apostles urged Circumcision of old, saying, unless you do these things, ye cannot be saved. Why, the Answer is ready: *Why tempt ye God to put a yoak upon the necks of the Disciples, which neither our Fathers, nor we were able to bear; but we believe that through the grace of our Lord Jesus Christ, we shall be saved, even as they*, Acts 15. 1, 10, 11. But not to enlarge;

5ly, THIS Doctrine, *By* Grace *ye are saved*, it is the only remedy 68.
against despairing thoughts, at the apprehension of our own unworthiness: as;

1. THOU criest out, O cursed Man that I am, my sins will sink me into Hell.

Answer. Hold Man, there is a God in Heaven that is *the God of all grace*, 1 Pet. 5. 10. Yet thou art not the Man of all sin; if God be the God of all grace, then if all the sins in the world were thine, yet the

God of all Grace can pardon, or else it should seem, that sin is stronger in a Man penitent, to damn, than the grace of God can be to save.

2. BUT my sins are of the worst sort; Blasphemy, Adultery, Covetousness, Murther, *&c.*

Answer, *All manner of Sins and Blasphemy shall be forgiven unto Men, wherewith soever they shall blaspheme: Let the wicked forsake his way, and the unrighteous man his thoughts, and let him return unto the Lord, and he will have mercy upon him, and to our God for he will abundantly pardon,* Matt. 12. 31. Mark 3. 28. Isa. 55. 7, 8.

3. BUT I have a stout and rebellious heart, a heart that is far from good.

Answ. *Hearken to me* (saith God), *ye stout-hearted, that are far from righteousness, I bring near my righteousness*: that is the righteousness of Christ, by which stout-hearted sinners are justifyed, though ungodly, *Isa.* 46. 12, 13. *Philip.* 3. 7, 8. *Rom.* 4. 5.

4. BUT I have an heart as hard as any stone.

Answer. *A new heart also will I give you* (says God) *and a new spirit will I put within you, and I will take away the stony heart out of your flesh, and I will give you an heart of flesh,* Ezek. 36. 26.

5. BUT I am as blind as a Beetle, I cannot understand any thing of the Gospel.

Answer. *I will bring the blind a way that they know not, I will lead them in paths that they have not known; I will make darkness light before them, and crooked things straight; these things will I do unto them, and not forsake them,* Isa. 42. 16.

6. BUT my heart will not be affected with the Sufferings and Blood of Christ.

Answer. *I will pour upon the house of* David, *and the inhabitants of* Jerusalem, *the spirit of grace and supplication, and they shall look upon me whom they have pierced, and they shall mourn for him as one mourneth for his only Son, and shall be in bitterness for him, as one that is in bitterness for his first-born,* Zech. 12. 10.

7. BUT though I see what is like to become of me If I find not Christ, yet my Spirit, while I am thus, will be, running after Vanity, Foolishness, Uncleanness, Wickedness.

26 Isa. 42. 16.] Isa. 41. 16.

Answer. *Then will I sprinkle clean water upon you, and you shall be clean, from all filthiness, and from all your Idols will I cleanse you*, Ezek. 36. 25.

8. BUT I cannot believe in Christ.

Answer. BUT God hath promised to make thee believe. *I will also leave in the midst of thee an afflicted and poor People, and they shall trust in the Name of the Lord*: And again, *There shall be a Root of* Jesse, *and he shall rise to reign over the Gentiles, and in him shall the Gentiles trust*, Zeph. 3. 12. *Rom.* 15. 12.

9. BUT I cannot pray to God for Mercy.

Answer. BUT God hath graciously promised a Spirit of Prayer, yea, *Many People and strong Nations, shall come to seek the Lord of Hoasts in* Jerusalem, *and to pray before the Lord*: *They shall call on my Name, and I will hear them, I will say, it is my People, and they shall say, the Lord is my God*; Zech. 8. 22. chap. 13. 9. chap. 12. 10.

10. But I cannot repent.

Answer. *The God of our Fathers raised up Jesus whom ye slew, and hanged on a Tree: Him hath God exalted with his right hand to be a Prince and a Saviour, to give repentance to* Israel, *and the forgiveness of sins*, Acts 5. 30, 31.

Thus might I inlarge, for the Holy *Bible* is full of this exceeding Grace of God. O these words, *I will*, and *you shall*, they are the Language of a Gracious God: They are Promises by which our God has engaged himself to do that for poor Sinners, which would else be left undone for ever.

The Third USE.

THIRDLY, Are they that are saved, saved by Grace? Then let 69. Christians labour to advance God's **Grace**.

1. IN Heart.

2. IN Life.

FIRST in Heart, and that in this manner.

1. BELIEVE in God's Mercy, through Jesus Christ, and so advance the Grace of God; I mean, venture heartily, venture confidently, for there is a sufficiency in the Grace of *God*. *Abraham* magnified the Grace of *God*, *when he considered not his own body now*

dead, neither yet the barrenness of Sarah's *Womb: When he staggered not at the promise of God through unbelief, but was strong in faith, giving Glory to God*, Rom. 4. 19, 20.

2. ADVANCE it by heightning of it in thy thoughts: Have always good and great thoughts of the Grace of *God*, narrow and slender thoughts of it are a great disparagement to it.

And to help thee in this matter, consider.

70. 1. THIS Grace is compared to a Sea, *and thou wilt cast all our sins into the depth of the Sea*, Mich. 7. 19. now a Sea can never be filled up by casting into it.

2. THIS Grace is compared to a Fountain, to an open Fountain: *In that day there shall be a Fountain opened to the House of* David, *and to the Inhabitants of* Jerusalem *for sin and for uncleanness*: Now a Fountain can never be drawn dry, *Zech.* 13. 1.

3. THE Psalmist crys out concerning the Grace and Mercy of God, *it endureth for ever*, he says so twenty six times in one Psalm: surely he saw a great deal in it, surely he was taken a great deal with it, *Psal.* 136.

4. St. *PAUL* says, the God of all Grace, *can do more then we ask, or think*, Ephes. 3. 20.

5. THEREFORE as God's Word says, so thou shouldest conclude of the Grace of *God.*

3. COME boldly to the Throne of Grace by hearty Prayer, for this is the way also to magnifie the Grace of *God*: This is the Apostles Exhortation, *Let us therefore come boldly to the Throne of Grace, that we may obtain mercy, and find grace to help in time of need*, Heb. 4. 16.

See here a little, and wonder.

WE have been all this while discoursing of the *Grace of God*; and now we are come to his *Throne*; as *Job* says, *even to his Seat*; and behold, *that is a Throne of Grace.* O, when a God of Grace is upon a Throne of Grace, and a poor Sinner stands by, and begs for Grace, and that in the name of a gracious Christ, in and by the help of the Spirit of Grace, can it be otherwise, but such a sinner must obtain mercy and grace, to help in time of need? But not to forget the Exhortation, *Come boldly.* Indeed we are apt to forget this Exhortation; we think, being we are such abominable sinners, we should

23 3.] 3*ly*, 26 Heb. 4. 16.] Heb. 4. 15.

not presume to come boldly to the Throne of Grace: But yet so we are bidden to do; and to break a Commandment here, is as bad as to break it in another place.

YOU may ask me, What is it to come boldly? 71.

Answer 1. It is to come confidently, *Let us draw near with a true heart, in full assurance of faith, having our hearts sprinkled from an evil conscience, and our bodies washed with pure water*, Heb. 10. 21, 22.

2. TO come boldly, it is to come frequently, at Morning, at Noon, and at Night will I pray: We use to count them bold Beggers that come often to our Door.

3. TO come boldly, it is to ask for great things when we come: That's the bold Beggar, that will not only ask, but also choose the thing that he asketh.

4. To come boldly, it is to ask for others as well as our selves; to beg Mercy and Grace for all the Saints of *God* under Heaven, as well as for our selves: *Praying with all Prayer and Supplication in the Spirit for all Saints*, Ephesians 6. 18.

5. TO come boldly, it is to come and take no nay; thus *Jacob* came to the Throne of grace. *I will not let thee go except thou bless me*. Gen. 32. 26.

6. To come boldly, it is to plead God's Promises with him, both in a way of Justice and Mercy, and to take it for granted, God will give us (because he hath said it), whatever we ask in the Name of his Son.

4ly, LABOUR to advance God's Grace in thy heart, by often admiring, praising and blessing God in secret for it, God expects it: *He that offereth praise glorifies me*, says he: *By Jesus Christ therefore let us offer the sacrifice of praise to God continually*; that is, *the fruit of our lips, giving thanks in his Name*, Psal. 50. 23. Hebr. 13. 15.

BUT again Secondly, As we should advance this Grace in our 72.
hearts, so we should do it in our life: We should in our Conversation adorn the Doctrine of God our Saviour in all things. 'Tis a great word of the Apostle; *Only let your Conversation be as becomes the Gospel of Christ*, which is the Gospel of the Grace of *God*, *Philip*. 1. 27. God expecteth that there should in our whole life be a blessed tang of the Gospel; or that in our life among Men there should be preached to them the Grace of the Gospel of God.

The Gospel shews us, That God did wonderfully stoop and condescend for our good, and to do accordingly it is to stoop and condescend to others.

The Gospel shews us, That there was abundance of pity, love, bowels, and compassion in God towards us, and accordingly we should be full of bowels, pity, love, and compassion to others.

The Gospel shews us, That in God there is a great deal of willingness to do good to others.

The Gospel shews us, That God acteth towards us, according to his truth and faithfulness, and so should we be in all our actions one to another.

By the Gospel *God* declares, that he forgiveth us ten thousand Talents, and we ought likewise to forgive our Brother the hundred Pence.

73. And now before I conclude this Use let me give you a few heart indearing Considerations, to this so good and so happy a Work.

FIRST, Consider, God hath *saved* thee, by his Grace: Christian, God hath *saved* thee, thou hast escaped the Lyon's Mouth, thou art delivered from Wrath to come, advance the grace that saves thee, in thy heart and life.

SECONDLY, Consider, God left Millions in their sins that day he saved thee by his grace: He left Millions out, and pitched upon thee: It may be Hundreds also, yea Thousands, were in the day of thy Conversion, lying before him under the preaching of the Word as thou wert, yet he took thee: Considerations of this nature affected *David* much, and God would have it affect thee to the advancing of his Grace in thy Life and Conversation, *Psal.* 78. 67, 68, 69, 70, 71. *Deut.* 7. 7.

THIRDLY, Consider, perhaps the most part of those that God refused, that day that he called thee by his Grace, were as to Conversation far better than ever thou wert. *I was a Blasphemer, I was a Persecutor, I was an injurious Person, but I obtained mercy!* O this should affect thy heart, this should engage thy heart to study to advance this Grace of *God*, 1 *Tim.* 1. 14, 15.

FOURTHLY, Perhaps in the day of thy Conversion thou wast more unruly than many: Like a Bullock unaccustomed to the Yoak, hardly tamed, thou wast brought home by strong hands; thou wouldest not drive, the Lord Jesus must take thee up, lay thee upon his Shoulder, and carry thee home to his Father's House, this should engage thy heart to study to advance the Grace of God, *Luke* 15. 1, 2, 3, 4, 5.

FIFTHLY, It may be, many did take even offence at God in his converting and saving of thee by his Grace, even as the elder Son was offended with his Father for killing the fatted Calf for his Brother, and yet that did not hinder the Grace of *God*, nor make God abate his love to thy Soul: This should make thee study to advance the Grace of *God* in thy heart and life, *Luke* 15. 25, 26, 27, 28, 29, 30, 31, 32.

SIXTHLY, Consider again, that God hath allowed thee but a little time for this good work, even the few days that thou hast now to live, I mean for this good work among sinful Men, and then thou shalt go to receive that wages that Grace also will give thee for thy work to thy eternal joy.

SEVENTHLY, Let this also have some place upon thy heart, every Man shews subjection to the God that he serveth: Yea, though that *God* be none other but the Devil and his Lusts, and wilt not thou, *O Man! saved of the Lord!* Be much more subject to the Father of Spirits and Live: Alas! They are pursuing their own Damnation, yet they sport it, and Dance all the way they go. They serve that God with chearfulness and delight, who at last will plunge them into the everlasting gulf of Death, and torment them in the fiery flames of Hell: But thy God is the God of Salvation, and to God thy Lord belongs the issues from death: wilt not thou serve him with joyfulness in the enjoyment of all good things? Even him by whom thou art to be made blessed for ever.

Object. *This is that which kills me,* **Honour** *God I cannot; my heart* 74.
is so wretched, so spiritless, and desperately wicked I cannot.

Answer. What dost thou mean by *cannot*?

1. IF thou meanest, thou hast no strength to do it, thou hast said an untruth, for *stronger is he that is in us, than he that is in the World*, 1. Joh. 4. 4.

2. IF thou meanest thou hast no will, then thou art out also, for every Christian (in his right mind) is a willing Man, and the day of God's Power hath made him so, *Psal.* 110. 3.

20 Live] Love 33 1. Joh. 4. 4.] Joh. 4. 4.

3. IF thou meanest, that thou wantest Wisdom, that's thine own fault: *If any Man lacks wisdom, let him ask it of God, who giveth to all Men liberally, and upbraideth not*. Jam. 1. 5.

75. Object. *I cannot* do *things as I would.*

Answer. No more could the best of the Saints of old, *to will is present with me*, said *Paul*, *but how to perform that which is good I find not*: And again, *the flesh lusteth against the spirit, and the spirit against the flesh, and these are contrary the one to the other, so that ye cannot do the things that ye would*: Rom. 7. 18. *Gal*. 5. 17.

And here indeed lies a great discovery of this truth, *ye are saved by Grace*, for the Children of God, whilst here, notwithstanding their Conversion to God, and Salvation by Christ through Grace, are so infirm and weak, by reason of a body of death that yet remaineth in them, that should even the sin that is in the best of their performances be laid to their charge, according to the tenour of a Covenant of Works, they would find it impossible ever to get into glory. But why do I talk thus? 'Tis impossible that those that are saved by grace should have their Infirmities laid to their charge as afore, *for they are not under the Law*, they are included by the Grace of *God*, in the Death and Blood of the Son of *God*, who ever liveth to make intercession for them at the right hand of God. Whose intercession is so prevalent with the Father, as to take away the iniquity of our holy things from his sight, and to present us holy and unreprovable, and unblameable in his sight: To him, by Christ Jesus, through the help of the blessed Spirit of Grace, be given, Praise, and Thanks, and Glory, and Dominion, by all his Saints, now and for ever, *Amen*.

FINIS.

16 to get into] into get in

COME, & WELCOME, TO JESUS CHRIST

COME, & WELCOME, TO JESUS CHRIST

Note on the Text

SIX editions of *Come, & Welcome* were published in Bunyan's lifetime. These included three different 'third' editions, published in 1685 and 1686. The first edition was published by Benjamin Harris in 1678, and the second edition, also by Harris, in 1684. The original third edition was printed for Benjamin Harris in 1685, and was to be sold by John Harris. This was also the arrangement for the fourth and fifth (called 'third') editions, published in 1686. The sixth edition was printed in 1688 by J. A. for John Harris.

Benjamin Harris first appears as a bookseller in the Term Catalogue for Michaelmas 1673, when he issued Benjamin Keach's *War with the Devil*. He was an ardent Protestant. During the furor caused by the Popish Plot, he published a large number of broadsides, ballads, news-sheets, and tracts, attacking the papacy and the Jesuits. The year after publishing the first edition of *Come, & Welcome*, Harris published *An Appeal from the Country to the City, for the Preservation of His Majesty's Person and the Protestant Religion.* The government prosecuted him for this, ordering him to find security for his good behaviour for three years. In 1681 he again ran foul of the authorities by issuing *A Protestant Petition.* He was tried, fined £500, and put in the pillory. Three years later came the second edition of *Come, & Welcome*, with the original third edition the following year. His legal difficulties apparently prompted him to leave London for Boston, Mass., where he set up a book, coffee, tea, and chocolate shop in 1686. He must have had nothing directly to do with the publication of the fourth and fifth editions of *Come, & Welcome.* In 1690 he issued the first newspaper in America (*Public Occurrences*), which was suppressed because he lacked permission. Harris returned to England late in 1695, and died *c.* 1708.[1]

[1] Plomer, pp. 144–6.

THE FIRST EDITION, 1678

Title-page: [within double rules] Come, & Welcome | TO | JESUS CHRIST. | OR, | A plain and profitable Discourse | upon the Sixth of *John*, 37 *Vers.* | Shewing the *Cause*, *Truth*, and | *Manner* of the Coming of a Sin- | ner to *Jesus Christ*; with his | Happy Reception, and Blessed | Entertainment. | [rule] | Written by *J. Bunyan.* | [rule] | *And they shall come which were ready* | *to Perish*, Isa. 27. 13. | [rule] | *LONDON*, | Printed for *B. Harris* at the *Stationers* | *Arms* in *Swithings Rents* in *Cornhil* by | the *Royal Exchange*, 1678.

Collation: 8°: A–T^{8}. Pages: 304. ($4 signed: *1–2* [3]4–109 '101' 111–60 157–65 *166* 167–85 '189' 187–297 *298*).

Contents: A1^{r} title-page, A1^{v} blank, A2^{r}–T7^{r} text, L5^{v} blank, T7^{v} '*ERRATA.*', T8^{r-v} blank. Large ornament at head of A2^{r}, followed by a short title, 'Come, & Welcome, | TO | JESUS CHRIST. | [rule] | '. A rule precedes the text on L6^{r} and Q1^{v}, and a rule follows the text on Q3^{v} and Q6^{v}. A rule follows the first twelve lines of text on R1^{r}, and a rule follows the first sixteen lines of text on S8^{r}. The conclusion of the text on T7^{r} is followed by '*FINIS.*' The errata on T7^{v} is preceded and followed by rules.

Running Titles: 'Come, & Welcome, | to Jesus Christ.' Misprints in the running titles: 'Come, & welcome,' instead of 'to Jesus Christ.' on C7^{r}. C8^{v} reads 'to Jesus Christ.' instead of 'Come, & welcome,'. L5^{v} omits the running title. (Misprints in punctuation are not noted here.)

Catchwords: (selected) A2^{r} Now, [for 'Note,'] A8^{v} True, B8^{v} First, C8^{v} *Objecti-* D8^{v} A E8^{v} gave F8^{v} *to* G8^{v} though H8^{v} with I8^{v} *Lord* K8^{v} *fend*, L1^{v} *Ninethly*, [*for* '*Ninthly*,'] L8^{v} 23, 24. M7^{r} *Seventh*, for '*Seventhly*,' M8^{v} And N8^{v} to O8^{v} he P8^{v} *Ninethly*, Q8^{v} *Ninethly*, R2^{r} 1. He [for '2. He'] R8^{v} *Tenthly*, S8^{v} was T6^{v} upon

Copies Collated: Bodleian, Oxford; British Library; Huntington Library; Pierpont Morgan Library; the William Andrews Clark Library, Los Angeles.

The lower lines of the title-page of the Huntington copy are slightly damaged. On p. 237, l. 29, the Bodleian copy has apparently been hand-corrected to read '*out.*' instead of '*out*,' as in the other copies.

THE SECOND EDITION, 1684

Title-page: [within rules] Come, and Welcome, | TO | Jesus Christ. | Or, a plain and profitable | DISCOURSE | On *John 6. Vers.* 37. | Shewing the Cause, Truth, and | Manner of the Coming of a | Sinner to Jesus Christ; with | his Happy Reception, and | Blessed Entertainment. | [rule] | Written by *JOHN BUNYAN*, | Author of the *Pilgrims Progress.* | [rule] | *And they shall come which were ready to* | *Perish*, Isa. 27. 13. | [rule] | The Second Edition with

Additions. | rule | *London*, Printed for *Benj. Harris*, at the | *Stationers-Armes* and *Anchor* under the | *Piazza* of the *Royal-Exchange*, 1684.

Collation: 12°: illustration, Title-page (*A* 1, 2 but plate seems to be disjunct), B–F^{12}, $_2F^{12}$, G–L^{12}. ($ 5 signed—E5, F2, I5,). Pages: *1–4* 1–158 '155' 160–243 '442' 245–258 '265' 260–264.

Contents: illustration, A1^r title-page, A1^v blank, B1^r–L12^v text. The only illustration is that which precedes the title-page. In the centre of the illustration Jesus is depicted placing his left hand on the head of a kneeling leper, while his disciples look on behind him. At the bottom of the illustration is the text from Matt. viii. 2–3, '*Lord, if thou wilt, thou canst make me clean, And he put forth* | *his hand, and touched him, Saying, I will be thou clean—*'. Single row of ornaments at the head of B1^r, followed by the abbreviated title, 'Come, and Welcome, | TO | JESUS CHRIST. | [rule] |'. A rule follows the first nine lines of text on I11^v and on L6^v. The conclusion of the text on L12^v is followed by '*FINIS.*' On p. 213 only, there is a change to smaller type after the first five lines. This change in type is apparently to be explained by an omission on the part of the printer, which he corrected before press by resetting this page in smaller type. There is no addition of consequence by Bunyan to account for the change in type.

Running Titles: 'Come, and Welcome, | to Jesus Christ.' On pp. 38, 64, 72, 110, 118, 206, and 214 the *W* in 'Welcome' is in the wrong fount of type. In all other instances the printer has used one of two standard *W*s. There are numerous variations in punctuation. Pages 225, 231, 235, and 237 have 'Iesus'; p. 230 has 2£0; p. 241 has 'Chist'; p. 244 has 'Welcom'; p. 247 has 'Chrest'.

Catchwords: (selected) B12^v them C12^v *Answ.* D12^v then E12^v Lump $_1$F12^v And [should be '*Secondly,*'] $_2$F7^v feel [for 'feels,'] $_2$F12^v *shall* G12^v being [for 'hearing'] H7^r *the* [for '*them,*'] I12^v these K12^v *Seven-* L2^v there, [for 'ther,'] L4^v *metns* [for '*ments*'] L12^r sails

Copies Collated: British Library; Elstow[1]; Elstow[2]; Yale University Library.

The Yale copy and the Elstow[1] copy have an uncorrected state of sheet L. On both the inner and outer formes the running titles have been improperly reversed. Consequently, e.g., the running title for L1^r appears on L12^v, and that for L4^r appears on L9^v.[1] When this was corrected, the spelling errors in the running titles were not altered. As a result, the first state has 'Chrest' on p. 258 (L9^v), the corrected state has 'Chrest' on p. 247 (L4^r). The first state also has 'Chist' on p. 264 (L12^v), the corrected state has 'Chist' on p. 241 (L1^r). The first state has the page number correctly

[1] For the layout of a sheet of common duodecimo see Philip Gaskell, *A New Introduction to Bibliography* (Oxford, 1972), fig. 55.

placed for p. 255 (L8r), the second state places the number in the upper left corner.

In the Yale copy, pp. 161–4 (G9 and G10) have been damaged. The Elstow[1] copy was formerly in the Harmsworth collection (2768), and was presented by the B.L. to the Moot Hall (17) in 1960. It has been charred and is incomplete. The illustration, title-page, and pp. 169–70 are missing. Elstow[2] (34. 1) was formerly in the Offor and Harmsworth collections. It is charred, coverless, and (in 1973) unbound, and p. 263 is badly damaged. The B.L. copy has been rebound.

THE THIRD EDITION, 1685

Title-page: [within double rules] Come and Welcome | TO | **Jesus Christ**: | Or, a plain and profitable | DISCOURSE | On *John* 6. Verse 37. | SHEWING | The Cause, Truth and Manner of | the Coming of a *Sinner* to **Jesus** | **Christ**; with his Happy Reception, | and Blessed Entertainment. | [rule] | Written by *JOHN BUNIAN*, | Author of the *Pilgrims Progress*. | [rule] | *And they shall come which were ready* | *to Perish*, Isai. 27. 13. | [rule] | *The Third Edition, with Additions.* | [rule] | *London*: Printed for *Benj. Harris*, and are to be | sold by Jo. Harris, at the *Harrow*, over a- | gainst the Church in the *Poultry*. 1685.

Collation: 12°: A–K[12], L[6]. Pages: 1–252. F3, F5, L4, L5, and L6 are not signed.

Contents: A1r blank, A1v illustration, A2r title-page, A2v blank, A3r–L6v text. The illustration precedes the title-page. The text at the bottom of the illustration reads, '*Lord, if thou wilt, thou canst make me clean, And he put forth* | *his hand, and touched him, Saying, I will be thou clean—*'. A row of ornaments at the top of A3r precedes the abbreviated title, '*Come, and Welcome* | TO | JESUS CHRIST. | [rule] |'. A rule precedes the text on I6r. Another rule follows the first eleven lines of text on K12v. The conclusion of the text on L6v is followed by '*FINIS*.'

Running Titles: '*Come, and Welcome* | *to* Jesus Christ.' There are numerous errors in punctuation. The fount of type used for the *C* in '*Come*' varies. Page 232 has '*Welcom*'. Page 252 reads '*Come, and Welcome*, &c.'

Catchwords: (selected) A12v Work B7v *come* [for '*Come*'] B10r obtained [omitted at the top of B10v] B11v Cry, [top of B12r has 'Cry'] B12v business; C11r with, [top of C11v has 'with'] C12v I told D9v But, [top of D10r has 'But'] D12v in E12v *will* F12v *mise*, G12v 'Tis H12v it I12v 5. he K12v truth L3v [no catchword] L5v *Fourthly*,

Copy Collated: Yale University Library.

The copy has been cropped, and some of the pages are damaged.

THE FOURTH EDITION, 1686[1] ('THIRD')

Title-page: [within double rules] Come and Welcome | TO | **Jesus Christ**: | Or, A Plain and Profitable | DISCOURSE | On *John* 6. Verse 37. | SHEWING | The Cause, Truth and manner of the | coming of a *Sinner* to **Jesus Christ**; | with his happy Reception, and blessed | Entertainment. | [rule] | Written by *JOHN BUNYAN*, | Author of the *Pilgrims Progress.* | [broken rule] | *And they shall come which were ready* | *to Perish, Isaiah* 27. 13. | [rule] | *The third Edition, with Additions.* | [rule] | *LONDON*: Printed for *B.H.* and are to be | Sold by *J. Harris*, at the *Harrow*, over a- | gainst the Church in the *Poultrey*. 1686.

Collation: 12°: illustration, A–H^{12}, I^{9}, ⟨I^{12}⟩. Pages: illustration+1–210+[1–6]. B4 is misprinted B5.

Contents: illustration, A1^{r} title-page, A1^{v} blank, A2^{r}–I9^{r} text, I9^{v}–⟨I11$^{v?}$⟩ a catalogue of books printed for and sold by John Harris, ⟨I12^{r-v} blank?⟩. The only illustration is that which precedes the title-page. It is superficially like the illustration in the second edition, but there are obvious differences, e.g. in the clouds, the birds, the loin-cloth of the leper, the tree stump in the lower right foreground, the trees in the background, the buildings of the town, etc. The text at the bottom of the illustration now reads, '*Lord if thou wilt, thou canst make me clean, And he put* | *forth his hand and touched him, saying, I will be thou clean*'. A double rule at the top of A2^{r} precedes the abbreviated title, '*Come, and Welcome* | TO | JESUS CHRIST. | [rule] |'. A rule follows the first twenty-five lines of text on H4^{v}. On I1^{r} the signature and catchword '*The*' are between rules. On I4^{v} a rule is placed between the end of the text and the catchword '*The*'. On I9^{r} '*FINIS.*' is placed between two rules, following the completion of the text. In the pagination the numbers 69–78 are absent. Pages 131–219 are in smaller type than the preceding pages. The catalogue of books at the end reverts to the original, larger type.

Running Titles: '**Come, and Welcome** | **to** Jesus Christ.' Misprints: pp. 32, 68, '**Com**'; pp. 134, 146, 148, 180, 204, 210, comma omitted after '**Come**'; pp. 178, 186, full stop after '**Welcome**'; *J* in 'Jesus' is wrong fount of type on pp. 41, 67, 103, 133, 219; *I* is substituted for *J* in 'Jesus' on pp. 153, 167, 203, 211.

Catchwords: (selected) A12^{v} *be* B12^{v} Salvation; C12^{v} *which* D12^{v} thereof E12^{v} ing F12^{v} company G12^{v} *tween* H12^{v} possedssed [for 'possessed'] I8^{r} Coming-

Copy Collated: British Library (C. 111. 9.).

This copy has charred edges, and was rebound in 1957. It was once part of the Offor collection.

THE FIFTH EDITION, 1686² ('THIRD')

Title-page: [within double rules] *Come, and Welcome*, | TO | **Jesus Christ**: | Or, A Plain and Profitable | DISCOURSE | On *John* vi. Verse xxxvii. | SHEWING | The Cause, Truth, and Manner of the | Coming of a *Sinner* to **Jesus Christ**; | With his Happy Reception, and | Blessed Entertainment. | [rule] | Written by *JOHN BUNYAN*, | Author of the **Pilgrims Progress**. | [rule] | *And they shall come which were ready to* | *Perish*, Isaiah 27. 13. | [rule] | *The Third Edition, with Additions*. | [rule] | *LONDON*: Printed for B.H. and are to be | sold by *J. Harris*, at the *Harrow*, over against | the Church in the *Poultrey*. 1686.

Collation: 12°: illustration, A–I^{12}. Pages: 1–2 1–216.

Contents: illustration, A1^{r} title-page, A1^{v} blank, A2^{r}–I9^{r} text, I9^{v}–I11^{v} a catalogue of books printed for and sold by John Harris, I12^{r-v} blank. The only illustration is that which precedes the title-page, and appears to be from the setting of that used in the earlier B.L. fourth edition ('Third') of 1686. A double rule at the top of A2^{r} precedes the abbreviated title, '*Come and Welcome*, | TO | JESUS CHRIST. | [rule] |'. A rule follows the first twenty-five lines of text on H4^{v}. On I1^{r} the signature and catchword '*The*' are between rules. On I4^{v} a rule is placed between the end of the text and the catchword '*The*'. On I9^{r} '*FINIS.*' is placed between two rules, following the completion of the text. In the pagination the numbers 73–82 are absent. Pages 131–219 are in smaller type than the preceding pages. The catalogue of books at the end reverts to the original, larger type.

Running Titles: '**Come and Welcome**, | **to** Jesus Christ.' Running title of the catalogue, '*A Catalogue of Books*, &c.'

Catchwords: (selected) A12^{v} *he* B12^{v} Salvation; C4^{r} mise. [for 'mise,'] C12^{v} *which* D12^{v} thereof E12^{v} ing F12^{v} Company [for 'company'] G12^{v} *tween* H12^{v} possessed I8^{r} Coming

Copies Collated: British Library (C. 71. a. 4.); Bunyan Meeting, Bedford.

THE SIXTH EDITION, 1688 ('FOURTH')

Title-page: [within double rules] *Come, and Welcome*, | TO | **Jesus Christ**: | Or, A Plain and Profitable | DISCOURSE | On *John* VI. Verse xxxvii. | SHEWING | The Cause, Truth, and Manner of the | Coming of a *Sinner* to **Jesus Christ**; | with his Happy Reception, and | Blessed Entertainment. | [rule] | Written by *JOHN BUNYAN*, | Author of the **Pilgrims Progress**. | [rule] | *And they shall come which were ready to* | *Perish*, Isaiah 27. 13. | [rule] | *The Fourth Edition.* | Licensed and entred according to Order. | [rule] | *LONDON*: Printed by *J.A.* for *John Harris*, | at the *Harrow*, over against the Church in | the *Poultrey*. 1688.

Collation: 12°: illustration, A–H^{12}. Pages: 1–2 1–192.

Contents: illustration, A1^r title-page, A1^v blank, A2^r–H10^r text, H10^v–H12^v a catalogue of books printed for and sold by John Harris. The illustration precedes the title-page, and appears to be identical to that used in the third edition. A single row of ornaments at the top of A2^r precedes the abbreviated title, '*Come and Welcome* | TO | JESUS CHRIST. | [tapered rule] |'. A rule precedes the text on G4^r. A rule precedes the text on G5^v. A rule follows the first fourteen lines of text on G7^r, the first four lines of text on G8^v, the first fourteen lines of text on H2^r, and the first seventeen lines of text on H5^v. The conclusion of the text on H10^r is followed by '*FINIS.*' between two rules. The end of the catalogue of books on H12^v is followed by a rule.

Running Titles: '**Come and Welcome,** | **to** Jesus Christ.' Running title of the Catalogue, '*Books sold by* John Harris.'

Catchwords: (selected) A12^v *Acts* B12^v now C12^v Sounds D12^v 1. In E12^v know F2^r *Second* [for '*The Second*'] F7^r thlness, [for 'thiness',] F12^v lief, G12^v of H3^r at [not repeated in the text on H3^v] H9^v Body,

Copies Collated: British Library (C. 111. e. 10.); British Library (C. 111. e. 13.); Yale University Library; Folger Shakespeare Library.

Numerous subsequent editions of *Come, & Welcome* were published. Part of its appeal was the manner in which the essentially Calvinist doctrines were set forth with an evangelical warmth and simplicity. Virtually any interested reader could find encouragement in the sermon to regard himself as one of the elect who were coming to Christ. A seventh ('fifth') edition was printed by G. L. for John Harris in 1690. Harris brought out an eighth edition the following year, a ninth in 1694, and a tenth in 1697. Another 'eighth' was printed by T. Mead for Elizabeth Harris in 1700. The same year the twelfth edition was published by Benjamin Harris. The latter also published a 'tenth' edition in 1702, and a different 'tenth' edition in 1707. Harris brought out an 'eleventh' edition in 1715, with further issues the same year to be sold by himself and T. Norris, and by himself and A. Bettesworth. Harris also published another 'eleventh' edition in 1715 to be sold by himself and E. Tracy. A 'twelfth' edition was printed in 1719 by Vavasour Harris and sold by H. Tracy. The place of publication for all of the above was London. American editions were published at Boston by Nicholas Boone in 1728, at Exeter, New Hampshire, by H. Ranlet in 1801, at New York and Boston by James Eastburn, and Bradford and

Read in 1812, and at Philadelphia by George W. Mentz in 1815 and 1818.[1]

The text that follows is based on the Bodleian copy of the first edition. Authorial additions to later editions are included in the text and indicated in the apparatus. Variant readings in subsequent editions are also included in the apparatus. Changes in spelling, capitalization, italicization, and punctuation in subsequent editions are not noted.

The history of the text is that of a vertical descent, with each successive edition in Bunyan's lifetime providing copy for the next. Mistakes, however, are often corrected from one edition to the next, usually by the printer having recourse to an earlier edition.

Each edition is indicated in the apparatus by the year of its publication. The three 'third' editions are indicated *1685*, *1686*^{1}, and *1686*^{2} respectively.

An authorial addition or revision is noted in the apparatus for the edition in which it *first* appears. Its retention through subsequent editions is indicated by a hyphen, e.g. *1684–1688*. An indication such as *1686*^{1}–*1686*^{2} indicates that the variant appeared only in these two editions, and that the next edition (in this case *1688*) reverts to the original reading.

[1] David E. Smith, 'Publication of John Bunyan's Works in America', *Bulletin of the New York Public Library*, lxvi (Dec. 1962), 645.

Come, & Welcome,

TO

JESUS CHRIST.

OR,

A plain and profitable Discourse upon the Sixth of *John*, 37 *Vers.* Shewing the *Cause*, *Truth*, and *Manner* of the Coming of a Sinner to *Jesus Christ*; with his Happy Reception, and Blessed Entertainment.

Written by *J. Bunyan.*

And they shall come which were ready to Perish, Isa. 27. 13.

LONDON,

Printed for *B. Harris* at the *Stationers Arms* in *Swithings Rents* in *Cornhil* by the *Royal Exchange*, 1678.

Title-page of the first edition of the Bodleian copy of *Come, & Welcome, to Jesus Christ* (1678)

Come, & Welcome,

TO

JESUS CHRIST.

John 6. 37.

All that the Father giveth me, shall come to me; and him that cometh to me, I will in no wise cast out.

A Little before in this Chapter you may read, That the Lord JESUS walked on the Sea to go to *Capernaum*, having sent his Disciples before in a Ship: But the Winds was contrary, by which means the Ship was hindred in her Passage: Now about the fourth watch of the night, Jesus came Walking upon the Sea, and overtook them; at the sight of whom they were afraid.

Note, *When Providences are black and terrible to Gods People, the Lord Jesus shews himself to them in wonderful manner, the which, somtimes they can as little bear, as they can the things that before were terrible to them. They were afraid* of the Wind, and the Water; they were also afraid of their Lord and Saviour, when He appeared to them in that State.

But He said, *be not afraid, it is I. Note, That the* **End** *of the appearing of the Lord Jesus unto his people (though the manner of his appearing be never so terrible), is to alay their fears and perplexities.*

Then they received him into the Ship, and immediately the Ship was at the Land whither it went.

Note, *When Christ is absent from his people, they go on but slowly, and with great difficulty; but when he joyneth himself unto them, Oh! how fast they stear their course, how soon are they at their Journies end!*

9 Winds] Wind *1685–1688*   16 *before were*] *were before 1685–1688*   17 the Water] Water *1688*   22 *is*] *as 1688*   24 the Land whither *1685*] the Land whether *1678–1684*] Land whither *1686*[1]*–1688*

The people now among whom he last preached, when they saw that both Jesus was gon, and his Disciples, they also took shipping and came to *Capernaum* seeking for Jesus. And when they had found him, they wonderingly asked him, *Rabbi, when camest thou hither?* But the Lord Jesus, slighting their complement, answered, *Verily, Verily, ye seek me, not because ye saw the Miracles, but because ye did eat of the Loaves and were filled.*

Note, *A People may follow Christ far, for base ends, as these went after him beyond-Sea for Loaves; a mans belly will carry him a great way in Religion: yea, a mans belly will make him venture far for Christ.*

Note again, *They are not feigning complements, but gracious intentions that crowns the work in the eye of Christ*: Or thus, *It is not the toyl, and business of professors, but their love to him, that makes him approve of them.*

Note again, *When men shall look for friendly entertainment at Christ's Hand (if their hearts be rotten) even then will they meet with a check and rebuke:* Ye seek me not because ye saw the Miracles, but because ye did eat of the Loaves, and were Filled.

Yet observe again, *He doth not refuse to give, even to these, good counsel; he bids them Labor for the meat that endureth to eternal Life.* O how willingly would Jesus Christ have even those Professors that come to him with pretences only, come to him sincerely, that they may be saved.

The Text, you will find, is after much more discourse with, and about this people; and it is uttered by the Lord Jesus as the conclusion of the whole, and intimateth, that since they were Professors in pretence only; and therefore such as his soul could not delight in as such, that he would content himself with a Remnant that his Father had bestowed upon him. As who should say, *I am not like to be Honoured in your Salvation; but the Father hath bestowed upon me a people, and they shall come to me in Truth; and in them will I be satisfied.* The Text therefore may be called *Christ's repose*; in the fulfilling whereof, he resteth himself content, after much Labor, and many Sermons spent, as it were, in vain. As he saith by the Prophet: *I have Labored in vain, I have spent my strength for nought, and in vain,* Isa. 49. 4.

12 *crowns*] *Crown 1685–1688* 34 Sermons *1684–1688*] Sermon *1678*

But as there he saith, *my Judgment is with the Lord, and my work with my God*: So in the Text, he saith, *All the Father giveth me, shall come to me; and them that cometh to me, I will in no wise cast out.* By these words therefore, the Lord Jesus comforteth himself under the consideration of the dissimulation of some of his followers.

He also thus betook himself to *rest* under the consideration of the *little effect* that his Ministry had even in *Capernaum*, *Corazin* and *Bethsaida. I thank thee O Father*, said he, *Lord of Heaven and Earth, because thou hast hid these things from the wise and prudent, and hast revealed them to babes: even so Father, for so it seemed good in thy sight*, Matt. 11. 25. Luke 10. 21.

The Text, in the general standeth of two parts, and hath special respect to the Father, and the Son: As also to their joynt management of the Salvation of their People. *All that the Father giveth me, shall come to me; and him that cometh to me, I will in no wise cast out.*

The first part of the Text, as is evident, respecteth the Father and his gift; the other part, the Son and his reception of that gift.

First, For the gift of the Father, there is this to be considered about it; to wit,

The gift it self, and that is a gift of certain *persons* to the Son. The Father giveth, and that gift shall come; *And* **Him** *that cometh.* The gift then is of Persons; the Father giveth Persons to Jesus Christ.

Secondly, Next, you have the Sons *reception* of this gift, and that sheweth it self in these particulars.

1. In his hearty acknowledgment of it, *to be a gift*: *The Father giveth me.*

2. In his taking notice, after a solemn manner, of **All**, and *every* part of the gift: *All that the Father giveth me.*

3. In his resolution to bring them to himself. *All the Father giveth me, shall come to me.*

4. And in his determining, that not any thing shall make him dislike them in their coming. *And him that cometh to me, I will in no wise cast out.*

3 *them*] *him 1684–1688* 7 even] *om. 1684–1688* 14 their] the *1684–1688*
20 about it] *om. 1684–1688*

These things might be spoken to at large, as they are in *this* method presented to view; but I shall chuse to speak to the words,

1. By way of Explication.
2. By way of Observation.

First, By way of Explication. [All] *that the Father giveth me*. This word, All, is often used in Scripture; and is to be taken more largely, or more strictly, even as the Truth, or argument for the sake of which it is made use of, will bare: wherefore, that we may the better understand the mind of Christ, in the use of it here, we must consider, that it is Limited, and Restrained, only to those that shall be Saved; to wit, to those that *shall come to Christ*; even to those that he will, *in no wise cast out*. Thus also the word All *Israel*, is sometimes to be taken (though sometimes it is taken for the whole Family of *Jacob*). *And so* All Israel *shall be saved*, Rom. 11. By All *Israel*, here he intendeth, not All of *Israel* in the largest sence: *For they are not* All Israel *which are of* Israel; *neither because they are of the Seed of* Abraham *are they* All *Children, but in* Isaac *shall thy seed be called: That is, they which are the Children of the flesh; these are not the Children of God, but the Children of the promise are counted for the seed*, Rom. 9. 6, 7, 8.

This Word, All, must therefore be limited, and enlarged, as the truth, and argument, for the sake of which it is used, will bare; else we shall abuse Scriptures and Readers, & our selves, & All. *And I, if I be lifted up from the earth, said Christ, will draw* All *men after me*, Joh. 12. 32. Can any man imagine, that by All, in this place, he should mean All, and every individual man in the World; and not rather, That All, that is consonant to the scope of the place? And if by being lift up from the earth, he means, as he should seem, his being taken up into Heaven; and if by drawing All men after him, he meant a drawing of them into that place of Glory: then must he mean, by All *Men*, Those, and only Those, that shall in truth be eternally Saved from the Wrath to Come. *For God hath concluded them* All *in unbelief, that he might have mercy upon* All, Rom. 11. 32. Here again you have All and All, two Alls, but yet a great disparity between the all made mention of in the first place, and that all

11 that[2]] whom *1685–1688* 16 *of the 1684–1688*] *the 1678* 18 *which*] *who 1685–1688* 20 must therefore] therefore must *1686[1]–1688* 29 of[1]] *om. 1686[1]–1688* 32–p. 243, l. 1 Here again . . . second.] *add 1684–1688*

made mention of in the second. Those intended in this Text, are the *Jews*, even All of them, by the first [All], that you find in the words. The second All doth also intend the same People; but yet only so many of them as God will have Mercy upon. *He hath concluded them* All *in unbelief, that he might have Mercy upon* All. The All also in the Text, is also to be limited, and restrained to the Saved, and to them only. But again:

The word [Giveth] *or hath given*, must be restrained after the same manner, to the same limited number. *All that the Father giveth me.* Not all that are *given*, if you take the *gift* of the Father to the Son, in the largest sence. For in that sence, there are *Many* given to him that shall never come unto him. Yea, many are *given* to him, *that he will cast out.* I shall therefore first, shew you the truth of this, and then, in what sence the gift, in the Text, must be taken.

First, That All that are given to Christ, if you take the *Gift* of the Father to him, in the largest sence, cannot be intended in the Text; is evident:

1. Because, then all the men, yea all the things in the World must be Saved. *All things, saith he, are delivered unto Me of my Father*, Mat. 11. v. 27. This I think, no rational man in the world, will conclude. Therefore, the Gift intended in the Text, must be restrained to some, to a *Gift* that is *given* by way of *speciality* by the Father to the Son.

2. It must not be taken for All, that in any sence are given by the Father to him; because, the Father hath given some, yea, many to him to be dashed in pieces by him. *Ask of me, said the Father to him, and I will give thee the Heathen for thine inheritance, and the uttermost parts of the earth for thy possession*; But what must be done with them? Must he Save them All? No, *Thou shalt brake them with a rod of iron, thou shalt dash them in pieces like a potters vessel*, Psal. 2. This method he useth not with them that he saveth by his Grace, but with those, that Himself and Saints shall rule over in Justice and Severity (*Rev.* 2. 26, 27.) Yet, as you see, *they are given to him.* Therefore the gift intended in the Text, must be restrained to *some*; to a *gift* that is given, by way of *speciality*, by the Father to the Son.

6 is also] is likewise *1684–1688* 12 *given* to] *given* unto *1685–1688* 19 *of my*] *by the 1685–1688* 20 v.] ver. *1684*] *om. 1685–1688* 22 that is] thats *1686*[1]] that's *1686*[2]*–1688*

In *Psalm* 18. he saith plainly, That some are given to him, that he might destroy them. *Thou hast given me the necks of mine enemies, that I might destroy them that hate me*, ver. 40. These therefore cannot be of the number of those that are said to be given in the Text; for those, even All of them shall come to him, *and he will in no wise cast them out.*

3. Some are given to Christ, that he by them might bring about some of his high and deep designes in the world. Thus *Judas* was given to Christ, to wit, that by him, even as was determined before, he might bring about *His* death, and so the Salvation of his Elect by his Blood. Yea, and *Judas* must so manage this business, as that he must lose himself for ever in the bringing of it to pass. Therefore the Lord Jesus, even in his losing of *Judas*, applies himself to the Judgment of his Father, if he had not in that thing, done the thing that was right, even in suffering of *Judas* so to bring about his Masters death, as that he might by so doing bring about his own eternal Damnation also.

Those, saith he, that thou gavest me, have I kept, and none of them is lost, but the Son of perdition, that the Scripture might be fulfilled, Joh. 17. 12. Let us then, grant that *Judas* was given to Christ, but not as others are given to him, to wit, not as those made mention of in the Text; for then he should not have failed to have been so received by Christ, & kept to Eternal life. Indeed he was given to Christ, but he was given to him to lose him, in the way that I have mentioned before; that is, he was given to Christ, that he by him might bring about his own death, as was before determined; and that, in the overthrow of him that did it. Yea, he must bring about his Dying for us in the loss of the instrument that betrayed him, that he might even fulfill the Scripture in his destruction, as well as in the Salvation of the rest. *And none of them is lost, but the Son of perdition, that the Scripture might be fulfilled.*

The gift therefore in the Text, must not be taken in the Largest sence, but even as the Words will bare; to wit, for such a gift as he

3 ver.] vers. *1685*] verse *1686*[1]–*1688* 6 3. *1684–1688*] 3ly. *1678* 8 as was] as he was *1688* 11 the bringing of] bringing *1685–1688* 13–14 the thing that] what that *1684*] that which *1685–1688* 15 that] *add 1684–1688* by so doing] *add 1684–1688* 16 also] *add 1684–1688* 17 *saith*] said *1688* 20 to wit] *om. 1684–1688* 21 not] *om. 1685–1688* so] *add. 1684–1688* 24 that is] *om. 1684–1688*

accepteth, and promiseth to be an Effectual means of their Eternal Salvation. *All that the Father giveth me, shall come to me; and him that cometh to me, I will in no wise cast out.* Mark, They shall come, *that are in special given* to me, and they shall by no means be rejected. For this is the Substance of the Text.

Those therefore intended, as the gift, in the Text, they are those that are given by Covenant to the Son; those that in other places are called the **Elect**, the **Chosen**, the **Sheep**, and the **Children** of the promise, *&c.*

These be they that the Father hath given to Christ to keep them; those, that Christ hath promised Eternal Life unto, those to whom he hath given his Word, and that he will have with him in his Kingdom to behold his Glory, as these Scriptures declare. *This is the will of the Father that sent me, that of all that he hath given me, I should lose nothing, but should raise it up at the last day. And I give unto them Eternal Life, and they shall never perish; neither shall any man pluck them out of my Hand, my Father that gave them me is Greater than All; and no man is able to pluck them out of my Fathers Hand. As thou hast given him Power over all Flesh, that he should give Eternal Life to as many as thou hast given him. Thine they were, and thou gavest them me, and they have kept thy word. I pray for them, I pray not for the world, but for those that thou hast given me; for they are thine. And all mine are thine, and thine are mine; and I am glorified in them.*

Keep through thine own Name, those whom thou hast given me, that they may be one, as we are. Father, I will that those whom thou hast given me, may be with me where I am, that they may behold my Glory which thou hast given me; for thou lovedst me before the Foundation of the World, John 6. 39. Chap. 10. 28. Chap. 17. 2, 6, 9, 10, 24.

All these sentences are of the same import with the Text; and the **Alls**, and **Manies**; those, they, *&c.* in these several sayings of Christ, are the same with **All** the given in the Text. **All** *That the Father giveth.*

So that (as I said before), the word **All**, as also other words, must **not** be taken in such sort as our foolish fancies, or groundless opinions

1 their] *om. 1684–1688* 2 Salvation] Salvation to *1684–1686*[1]] Salvation too *1686*[2]] Salvation to *1688* 6 they] *om. 1684–1688* 13 as these Scriptures declare] *om. 1684–1688* 15 *should*[1]] *shall 1685–1688* *at*] *om. 1686*[1]*–1688*

will prompt us to, but do admit of an enlargment or a restriction, according to the true meaning and intendment in the Text. We must therefore diligently consult the meaning of the Text by compareing it with other the Sayings of God; so shall we be better able to find out the mind of the Lord, in the Word which he has given us to know it by.

All *that the* [*Father*] *giveth.*

By this word [*Father*] Christ describeth the person giving, by which we may learn several useful things. 1. That the Lord God, and Father of our Lord Jesus Christ, is equally concerned with the Son in the Salvation of his People. True, his acts, as to our Salvation, are divers from those of the Son, he was not capable of doing *that*, or *those* things for us as did the Son; he Died not, he Spilt not Blood for our *Redemption* as the Son; but yet he hath a hand, a great hand in our Salvation too. As Christ saith, *The Father himself loveth you*, and his love is manifest in chusing of us, in giving of us to his Son, yea, and in giving his Son also to be a ransom for us. Hence he is called, *The Father of Mercies, and the God of all comfort*. For here even the Father, hath himself found out, and made way for his grace to come to us through the sides, and the heart Blood of his well beloved Son, *Col.* 1. 12. The father therefore is to be remembred and adored as one having a chief hand in the Salvation of sinners. *We ought to give thanks to the Father, who hath made us meet to be partakers of the inheritance of the Saints in light: for the Father sent the Son to be the Saviour of the World*, 1 *Joh.* 4. 14. *Col.* 1. 12. As also we see in the Text, the *Father giveth* the sinner to Christ to save him.

Secondly, Christ Jesus the Lord by this word *Father*, would *familiarize* this giver to us. Naturally the Name of God is dreadful to us, specially when he is discovered to us by those names that declare his Justice, Holiness, Power, and Glory: but now this word *Father*, is a familiar word, it frighteth not the sinner, but rather inclineth his heart to love, and be pleased with the remembrance of him. Hence Christ also when he would have us pray with Godly boldness, puts this word *Father* into our mouths; Saying, when ye

2 intendment in] intent of *1684–1688* 10 equally] *om. 1684–1688* 12 divers] diverse *1685–1688* 29 specially] especially *1685–1688* 33 pray] to pray *1685–1688*

pray, say *Our Father which art in Heaven*: concluding thereby, that by the *familiarity* that by such a word is intimated, the Children of God may take more boldness to pray for, and ask great things. I my self have often found, that when I can say but this word *Father*, it doth me more good, than when I call him by any other Scripture Name; and 'tis worth your Noting, that to call God by this relative Title, was rare among the Saints in Old-Testament times; seldom do you find him called by this name, no, sometimes not in three or four whole books: but now, in New-Testament times, he is called by no name so often as this, both by the Lord Jesus himself, and by the Apostles afterwards. Indeed the Lord Jesus was he that first made this name common among the Saints, and that taught them, both in their Discourses, their Prayers, and in their Writings, so much to use it; it being more pleasing to, and discovering more plainly our interest in God, than any other Expression; for by this one name we are made to understand that all our Mercies are the off-spring of God, and that we also that are called, are his children by adoption.

All that the Father [*giveth*].

This word [*giveth*] is out of Christs ordinary Dialect, and seemeth to intimate, at the first sound, as if the Fathers gift to the Son, was not an act that is past, but one that is present and continuing; when indeed this gift was bestowed upon Christ when the Covenant, the Eternal Covenant was made between them before all worlds. Wherefore in those other places when this gift is mentioned, it is still spoken of, as of an act that is past. As, *All that He* hath *given* me; to as many as thou hast *given* me; Thou gavest them me; and those which thou hast given me. Therefore of necessity this must be the first and chief sence of the Text. I mean of this word [giveth]: otherwise the Doctrine of Election, and of the Eternal *Covenant which* was made between the Father and the Son (in which Covenant, this gift of the Father is most certainly comprized) will be shaken, or at leastwise questionable by erronious and wicked men. For they may say that the Father gave not all those to Christ that shall be saved, before the World was made, for that this Act of giving is an Act of continuation.

6 and] *om. 1684–1688* 9 whole] *om. 1685–1688* 27 those] *these 1688*
33–5 For they . . . continuation.] *add 1684–1688*

But again this word [*giveth*] is not to be rejected, for it hath its proper use, and may signifie to us;

First, That though the act of giving, among men doth admit of the time past, or the time to come, and is to be only spoken of with reference to the time: yet with God it is not so. Things past, or things to come, are alwayes present with God, and with his Son Jesus Christ: *He calleth things that are not* (that is, to us) *as though they were*; and again, *known unto God are all his works from the foundation of the world.* All things to God are present, and so the gift of the Father to the Son, although to us as is manifest by the Word, it is an act that is past, *Rom.* 4. 17. *Acts* 15. 18.

Secondly, Christ may Express himself thus, to shew, that the Father hath not only given him this portion in the Lump, before the world was; but that those that he hath so given, he will give him again: that is, will bring them to him at the time of their conversion; *for the Father bringeth them to Christ* (Joh. 6. 44.).

As it is said, *She shall be brought unto the King, in raiment of needle work.* That is, in the righteousness of Christ, for it is God that imputeth that to these that are saved, *Psal.* 45. 14. 1 *Cor.* 1.

A man giveth his daughter to such a man, first in order to marriage, and this respects the time past; and he giveth her again at the day appointed, in marriage. And in this last sense, perhaps, the Text may have a meaning: that is, that all that the Father hath before the world was, given to Jesus Christ, he giveth them again to him, in the day of their espousals. Or,

Thirdly, In that Christ saith [*giveth*] instead of *hath given*, he may do it to shew, that this gift of the Father, to him, is now as new, as sweet, as pleasant and desirable, as if it had never bin given before.

Things that are given among men, are oft-times best at first, to wit, when they are new; and the reason is, because, all earthly things wax old; but with Christ it is not so: this gift of the Father is not old, and deformed, and unpleasant in his eyes; and therefore to him 'tis always new. When the Lord spake of giving the Land

4 only] *om. 1684–1688* 5 the] such *1684–1688* 10 as is manifest by the Word,] *add, 1684*] as is manifest by the World, *1686*[1]*–1686*[2]] as is manifest by the Word, *1688* 10–11 it is an act that is past] *om. 1685* 11 18.] 10. *1678–1688* 14 hath] had *1685–1688* 19 these] those *1688* 25 Or,] *om. 1686*[1]*–1688* 26–8 Thirdly . . . before.] *om. 1686*[1]*–1688* 31 wax *1684–1688*] war *1678*

of *Canaan* to the *Israelites*, he saith not, that he *had* given, or *would* give it to them; but thus, *The Lord thy God giveth thee this good Land*, Deut. 9. 6. not but that he had given it to them, while they were in the Loyns of their Fathers, Hundreds of Years before. Yet he saith *now*, he giveth it to them, as if they were now also in the very act of taking possession, when as yet, they were on the other side *Jordane*. What then should be the meaning? Why, I take it to be this: That the Land should be to them alway *as new*; *as new*, as if they were taking possession thereof but now. And so is the gift of the Father, mentioned in the Text, to the Son; it is always new, as if it were alwayes giving.

All that the Father giveth [*Me.*]

In these words, you find mention made of two persons, the *Father* and the *Son*; the Father giving, and the Son receiving, or accepting of his Gift. This then in the first place, clearly demonstrateth, that the Father and the Son, though they, with the Holy Ghost, are one and the same Eternal God; yet as to their personality are distinct. The Father is one, the Son is one, the Holy Spirit is one. But because there is in this Text, mention made but of two of the three, therefore a word about those two. The *Giver* and *Receiver* cannot be the same person, in a proper sence, in the same act of giving and receiving. He that giveth, giveth not to himself but to an other; the Father giveth not to the Father, to wit, to *Himself*, but to the *Son*; the Son receiveth not of the Son, to wit, of *Himself*, but of the Father: so when the Father giveth Commandment, he giveth it not to himself but to another; as Christ saith, He hath given **Me** a Commandment, *Joh.* 12. 49. So again, *I am one that beareth witness of my self, and the Father that sent me beareth witness of me*, *Jo.* 8. 18.

Further, here is something implyed that is not expressed, to wit, that the Father hath not given all Men to Christ; that is, in that sence as is intended in this Text: though in a larger, as was said before, he hath given him every one of them. For then all should be saved: He hath therefore disposed of some another way. He gives some up to Idolatry, He gives some up to uncleanness, to vile

4 the Loyns of] *add 1684–1688* 11 giving] new *1685–1688* 15 his] this *1685–1688* 20 those] these *1686*[2]*–1688* 28 8.] 10. *1678–1688* 31 this] the *1686*[2]*–1688* 31–2 though in . . . them.] *add 1684–1688*

affections, and to a reprobate mind. Now these he disposeth of in his Anger, for their destruction (*Acts* 7. 42, *Rom.* 1. 24, 26, 28.) that they may reap the fruit of their doings, and be filled with the reward of their own ways. But neither hath He thus disposed of all men; he hath even of Mercy reserved some *from* these Judgments, and those are they that he will Pardon, as he saith, *for I will pardon them whom I reserve*, Jer. 50. 20. Now these he hath given to Jesus Christ by Will, as a Legacy and Portion. Hence the Lord Jesus sayes, *This is the Fathers Will which hath sent me*, *that of all which he hath given me I should lose nothing*, *but should raise it up again at the last day*, Joh. 6. 29.

The Father therefore in *giving* of them to Him to save them, must needs by so doing declare unto us these following things.

1. That he is Able, to answer this designe of God, to wit, to save them to the uttermost Sin, the uttermost temptation, *&c.* Heb. 7. 25. Hence he is said, *To lay help upon one that is Mighty*, *Mighty to save*: And hence it is again, that God did even of old promise to send *his* people a Saviour; a great one, *Psal.* 89. 19. *Isa.* 63. 1. To save, is a great work, and calls for Almightyness in the Undertaker: hence he is called the Mighty God, the Wonderful Counseller, *&c.* Sin is strong, Satan is also strong, Death and the Grave are strong, and so is the Curse of the Law; therefore it follows, that this Jesus must needs be by God the Father, accounted Almighty, in that he hath given his Elect to him, to save them, and to deliver them from these, and that in despite of all their Force, and Power.

Yea, he gave us Testimony of this his Might, when he was imployed in that part of our deliverance, that called for a Declaration of it. He abolished Death: He destroyed him that had the power of Death; he was the Destruction of the Grave; he hath finished Sin, and made an end of it, as to its Damning effect upon the Persons that the Father hath given him. He hath vanquished the curse of the Law, Nailed it to his *Cross*, Triumphed over them upon his *Cross*, and made a shew of these things openly, 2 *Tim.* 1. 10. *Heb.* 2. 14, 15. *Hos.* 13. 14. *Dan.* 9. 24. *Gal.* 3. 13. *Col.* 2. 14, 15.

8 and Portion] *add 1684–1688* 11 6.] 36. *1678–1688* 12 in *giving* of *1687–1688*] *giving 1678* 13 by so doing] *om. 1684–1688* 16 *upon one*] *on one 1685–1688* 24 hath *1685–1688*] have *1678–1684* to deliver] deliver *1686*[1]*–1688* 26 Yea,] And *1684–1688* 30 effect] effects *1684–1688*

Yea, and even now, as a sign of his Triumph and Conquest, he is alive from the Dead, and hath the Keys of Hell and Death in his own keeping, *Revel.* 1. 18.

2ly. The Fathers giving of them to him to save them, declares unto us that he *is*, and *will* be faithful in his Office of Mediator, and that therefore they shall be secured from the fruit, or wages of their Sins, which is Eternal Damnation, by his Faithful Execution of it. And indeed it is said, even by the Holy Ghost himself, *That he is faithful to him that appointed him*; that is, to this work of saving those that the Father hath given him, *for that purpose*; *as* Moses *was faithful in all his House*: Yea, and more faithful too, for *Moses* was faithful in Gods house, but as a Servant. *But Christ as a Son*, *over his own house*, Heb. 3.

And therefore this Man is counted worthy of more glory than *Moses*, even upon this account, because more Faithful than he; as well as because of the dignity of his person. Therefore in him, and in his truth and faithfulness, God rested wel-pleased, and hath put all the government of this People upon his shoulders. Knowing, that nothing shall be wanting in him, that may any way perfect this design. And of this, He, to wit the Son, hath already given a proof; for when the time was come, that his Blood was by Divine Justice required for their Redemption, Washing, and cleansing: he as freely poured it out of his Heart, as if it had been Water out of a vessel; not sticking to part with his own Life, that the life which was laid up for them in Heaven, might not fail to be bestowed upon them. And upon this account (as well as upon any other) it is, that God calleth him his *righteous servant*, Isa. 53. For his righteousness could never have been compleat, if he had not been to the uttermost faithful to the work which he undertook; It is also, because he is faithful, and true, that in Righteousness he doth Judge and make Work for his peoples deliverance. He will faithfully perform this trust reposed in him: The Father knows this, and hath therefore given his Elect unto him.

Thirdly, The Fathers giving of them to Him to save them,

4 2ly.] 2. *1685–1688* 5 of Mediator] *add 1684–1688* 6 or] and *1685–1688* 7 by his Faithful Execution of it] *add 1684–1688* 18 this] his *1688* 25 them] his People *1684–1688* 29 which] *om. 1685–1688*

declares unto us that he is, and will be gentle and patient towards them under all their provocations and miscarriages. It is not to be imagined, the tryals and provocations that the Son of God hath all along had with these people that have been given to him to save them: indeed he is said to be a *tryed stone*, for he has been tryed, not only by the devil, guilt of sin, death, and the curse of the Law, but also by his peoples ignorance, unruliness, falls into sin, and declining to errors, in life, and Doctrine. Were we but capable of seeing how this Lord Jesus has been tryed, even by this people, ever since there was one of them in the world, we should be amazed at his Patience and gentle Carriages to them. It is said indeed, the *Lord is very pitiful*, *slow to anger*, *and of great mercy*: and indeed, if he had not so been, he could never have indured their manners, as he has done from *Adam* hitherto. Therefore is his pitty and bowels towards his Church, preferred above the pitty and bowels of a mother towards her Child. *Can a woman forget her sucking Child*, *that she should not have Compassion on the Son of her Womb? yea they may forget*, *yet will I not forget thee*, *saith the Lord*, Isa. 49. 15.

God did once give *Moses*, as Christs Servant, an handful of this people to carry them in his bosom, but no further than from *Egypt* to *Canaan*; and this *Moses*, as is said of him by the Holy Ghost, was the Meekest man that was then to be found in the Earth: yea, and he loved the people at a very great rate, yet neither would his meekness nor love hold out in this work; he failed, and grew pationate even to the provoking of his God to Anger under this work that God had laid upon him. *And Moses said unto the Lord*, *wherefore hast thou afflicted thy Servant?* But what was the affliction? Why the Lord had said unto him, *carry this people in thy bosom as a nursing father beareth the sucking child*, *unto the Land that he sware unto their fathers. And how then?* Not I, sayes *Moses*, *I am not able to bear all this people*, *because it is too heavy for me: if thou deal thus with me*, *kill me I pray thee out of hand*, *and let me not see my Wretchedness*, Numb. 11. 11, 12, 13, 14. God gave them to *Moses* that he might carry them in his

1 unto us] *om. 1684–1688* 4 to save] that save *1684*] that saves *1685–1688* 8 and Doctrine *1684–1688*] in Doctrine *1678* 9 this[2]] his *1685–1688* 13 so been] been so *1685–1688* 18 *will I*] *I will 1685–1688* 19 this] his *1685–1688* 25 of] *om. 1686[1]–1688* 26 that God had laid upon him] *om. 1684–1688* 30 *And how then?*] add *1684–1688*

bosom; that is, that he might shew gentleness and patience towards them, under all the provocations wherewith they would provoke him from that time, till he had brought them to their Land, but he failed in the work, he could not exercise it, because he had not that sufficiency of patience towards them: But now, it is said of the person speaking in the Text, *That he shall gather his Lambs with his arm, shall carry them in his bosom, and shall gently lead them that are with young*, Isa. 40. 10, 11. Intimating, that this was one of the qualifications that God looked for, and knew was in him, when he gave his Elect to him to save them.

Fourthly, The fathers giving of them to him to save them, declare to us that he hath a Sufficiency of wisdom to wage with all those difficulties that would attend him in his bringing of his Sons and Daughters unto glory; 1 *Cor.* 1. 30. He hath made him *to us* to be Wisdom, yea he is called Wisdom it self; and God saith moreover, that he shall deal prudently, *Isa.* 52. 13. And indeed, he that shall take upon him to be the Saviour of the people, had need be Wise, because their adversaries are subtile above any. Here they have to incounter with the Serpent, who for his Subtilty out-witted our Father and Mother when their wisdome was at highest (*Gen.* 3.). But if we talk of Wisdom, our Jesus is wise, wiser than *Solomon*, wiser than all men, wiser than all the Angels; he is even the Wisdom of God. *Christ the Wisdom of God* (1 *Cor.* 1. 24.). And hence it is, that he turneth sin, temptation, persecutions, falls, and all things, for good unto this people (*Rom.* 8.).

Now these things thus concluded on, do shew us also the great, and wonderful love of the Father, in that he should chuse out one every way so well prepared for the work of mans Salvation. Herein indeed perceive we the love of God. *Huram* gathered, *that God loved Israel*, because he had given them such a King as *Solomon* (2 *Chro.* 2. 11.). But how much more may we behold the love that God hath

1 that is,] *om. 1684–1688* 2–3 under all . . . Land,] *add 1684–1688* 4 it] *add 1688* 11 of them to him to save] of them to save *1684–1685*] of him to save them *1686*[1]*–1688* 12 to us] *om. 1684–1688* 14 1 *Cor.* 1. 30.] *add 1684–1688* 16 *Isa.* 52. 13.] *add 1684–1688* 18 have] are *1685–1688* 22 the[1]] *om. 1685–1688* 23 1 *Cor.* 1. 24.] 1 Col. 1. *1678–1684*] Col. 1. 1. *1685–1688* 24 temptation] Temptations *1686*[1]*–1688* 25 this] his *1685–1688*

bestowed upon us, in that he hath given us to his Son, and also given his Son for us?

All that the Father giveth me [*shall come.*]

In these last words, there is closely inserted an answer unto the Fathers end in giving of his Elect to Jesus Christ. The Fathers end was, that they might *come* to him, and be *Saved* by him; and *that*, sayes the Son, shall be done, neither Sin nor Satan, neither Flesh nor World, neither Wisdom nor Folly, shall hinder their coming to me. *They* **shall** *come to me, and him that cometh to me, I will in no wise cast out.*

Here therefore the Lord Jesus positively determineth to put forth such a sufficiency of all Grace that shall Effectually perform this promise. *They shall come.* That is, he will *cause* them to come, by infusing of an effectual blessing into all the means that shall be used to that end. As was said to the evil Spirit, that was sent to perswade *Ahab*, to go and fall at *Ramah Gilead. Go, Thou shalt perswade him, and prevail also; go forth and do so*, 1 King. 22. 22. So will Jesus Christ say to the *means* that shall be used for the bringing of those to him that the Father hath given him. I say, he will bless it effectually, to this very end; it shall perswade them, and shall prevail also. Else, as I said, the Fathers end would be frustrate. For the Fathers will is, that *of all that he hath given him he should lose nothing, but should raise it up at the last day*, in order next unto himself, Christ the first-fruits, afterwards those that are his at his Coming (1 *Cor.* 15). But this cannot be done, if there should fail to be a work of grace effectually wrought, though but in any one of them. But this shall not fail to be wrought in them, even in all that the Father hath given him to save. *All that the Father hath given me, shall come to me*, &c. But to speak more distinctly to the words; *They shall come.* Two things I would shew you from these words.

First, *What it is to come to Christ.*

Secondly, *What force there is in* **this** *promise, to make them come to him.*

First, I would shew you first what it is to come to Christ: This word *come*, must be understood spiritually, not carnally; for many came to him carnally, or bodily, that had no saving advantage by

7–8 neither Sin . . . to me.] *add 1684–1688* 11 such] *add 1684–1688* that] as *1684–1688* 26 that] *om. 1684–1688* 33 first[2]] *om. 1685–1688*

him; multitudes did thus come unto him in the days of his flesh, yea innumerable companies. There is also at this day a Formal, customary Coming to his Ordinances, and ways of Worship, which availeth not any thing: but with them I shall not now medle with these, for they are not intended in the Text. The Coming then, intended in the Text, is to be understood of the *Coming of the* **minde** *unto him, even the moving of the heart towards him. I say, the moving of the heart towards him, from a sound Sense of the absolute want that a man hath of him for his Justification and Salvation.*

This Description of Coming to Christ, divideth it self into two heads.

First, *That coming to Christ, is a moving of the mind towards him.*

Secondly, *That it is a moving of the mind towards him from a Sound Sense of the absolute want that a man hath of him for his Justification and Salvation.*

To speak to the first, That it is a moving of the mind towards him. This is evident, because coming hither or thither, if it be voluntary, is by an act of the Mind or will; so coming to Christ, is through the inclining of the will. *Thy people shall be willing*, Psal. 110. 3. This willingness of heart, is it, which sets the mind a moving after, or towards him. The Church expresseth this moving of her mind towards Christ, by the moving of her bowels: *My beloved put in his hand by the hole of the door, and my Bowels were moved for him*, Song. 5. 4. My bowels; the passions of my mind and affections; which passions of the affections, are expressed by the yerning, and sounding of the bowels. The yerning or passionate working of them, the Sounding of them, or their making an Noise for him, *Gen.* 43. 30. 1 *King* 3. 26. *Isa.* 16. 11.

This then is the coming to Christ, even a moving towards him with the minde. *And it shall come to pass, that every thing that liveth, which moveth whithersoever the water shall come, shall live.* Ezek. 47. 9.

The water, in this Text, is the Grace of God, in the Doctrine of it: the living things, are the Children of men to whom this Grace of God, by the Gospel is preached: now saith he, *Every living thing*

4 but with them] *add 1684–1688* 4–5 with these] *om. 1684–1688* 7 *unto*] *to 1686[1]–1688* 18 Mind or] *add 1684–1688* 23 *for*] *from 1684–1688* 27 an] a *1684–1688* 33 this] the *1685–1688*

which moveth whithersoever the waters shall come, shall live. Now see how this word moveth is Expounded by Christ himself in the Book of the Revelations: *The Spirit and the Bride say, come. And let him that heareth, say, come. And let him that is athirst, come. And whosoever will, that is willing, let him take the water of life freely,* Revel. 22. 17.

So that, to move in thy mind and will after Christ, is to be coming to him. There are many poor souls that are coming to Christ, that yet cannot tell how to believe it; because they think, that coming to him, is some strange and wonderfull thing: and indeed so it is; but I mean, they overlook the inclination of their will; the moving of their mind, and the sounding of their bowels after him: and count these none of this strange and wonderful thing: when indeed it is a work of greatest wonder in this world, to see a man who was sometimes dead in sin, possessed of the devil, an enemy to Christ, and to all things spiritually good. I say, to see this man moving with his minde after the Lord Jesus Christ, is one of the highest wonders in the world.

Secondly, *It is a moving of the minde towards him, from a Sound Sense of the absolute want that a man hath of him for his Justification and Salvation.* Indeed, without this Sense of a lost condition, without him there will be no moving of the mind towards him: a moving of their mouth there may be, *with their mouth they shew much love,* Ezek. 33. 31. Such a people as this will come, as the true people cometh; that is in shew, and outward appearance: and they will sit before Gods Ministers, as *his people Sit before them; and they will hear his words too, but they will not do them*: that is, will not come inwardly with their mindes; *for with their mouth they shew much love, but their heart* (or minde) *goeth after their Covetousness.* Now all this is, because they want an effectual sense of the misery of their state by nature; for not till they have that, will they in their minde move after him. *Therefore, thus it is said Concerning the true Commers. At that day the great Trumpet shall be blown, and* **They** *shall come which were ready to perish in the Land of* Assyria, *and the outcasts of the land of* Egypt, *and shall worship the Lord in his Holy Mountaine at* Jerusalem (Isa. 27. 13.). They are then you see, the out-casts, and those that are ready to perish, that indeed

1 Now] And *1684–1688* 22 33. 31. *1684–1688*] 32. *1678* 35 you see,] (as you see) *1684–1688*

have their mindes Effectually moved to come to Jesus Christ. *This sense of things*, was that which made the three thousand come, that made *Saul* come, that made the Jaylor come, and that indeed makes all others come, that come Effectually. *Acts* 2. Chap. 8 and 16.

Of the true coming to Christ, the three Leapers were a famous Semblance, of whom you read in 2 *King*. 7. 3, *&c.* The famine in those days was sore in the Land, there was no bread for the people; and as for that Sustinence that was, which was *Asses* Flesh, and *Doves* Dung that was only in *Samaria*; & of these the Leapers had no share, for they were thrust without the City. Well, now they sat in the Gate of the City; and hunger was, as I may say, making his last Meal of them; and being therefore half dead already, what do they think of doing? why, first they display the dismal colours of death before each others faces, and then resolve what to do, saying, *If we say we will go into the City, then the famine is in the City, and we shall die there; if we sit still here, we die also; now therefore* **Come**, *and let us fall into the Host of the Syrians; if they save us alive, we shall live; if they kill us, we shall but die.* Here now was necessity at work, and this necessity drove them to go thither for life, whither else they would never have gon for it. Thus it is with them that in truth come to Jesus Christ: Death is before them, they see it and feel it; he is feeding upon them, and will eat them quite up, if they come not to Jesus Christ; and therefore they come even of necessity, being forced thereto by that Sense they have of their being utterly and everlastingly undone, if they find not safety in him.

These then are they that will come: indeed these are they that are invited to come. *Come unto me all ye that Labor, and are Heavy Laden, and I will give you rest*, Matt. 11. 28.

Take two or three things to make this more plain, to wit, that coming to Christ, floweth from a sound sense of the absolute need that a Man hath of him, as afore.

1. *They shall come with Weeping, & with Supplication will I lead them; I will cause them to walk by the Rivers of Waters in a plain way, wherein they shall not stumble*, Jer. 31. 9. Mind it, they come with Weeping

4 *Acts* 2. Chap. 8 and 16.] *Acts* 2. 8, 16. *1684–1688* 6 in[1]] *om. 1685–1688* 16 *and*] *om. 1685–1688* 19 whither *1685–1688*] whether *1678–1684* 26 then] *om. 1684–1688* 28 11. 28.] 11. 21. *1684–1688* 33 *the*] *om. 1684–1688*

and Supplication; they come with Prayers, and Tears. Now Prayers, and Tears, are the effects of a right Sense of the need of Mercy. Thus a senseless Sinner cannot Come, he cannot Pray, he cannot Cry, he cannot come sensible of what he sees not, nor feels. *In those Days, and at that time, the Children of* Israel *shall come; they and the Children of* Judah *together, going & weeping: they shall seek the Lord their God: they shall ask the way to* Zion *with their Faces thitherward, saying, come and let us joyn our selves to the Lord in a perpetual Covenant that shall not be forgotten*, Jer. 50, 4, 5.

Secondly, This coming to Christ, it is called a running to him, as flying to him; a flying to him from Wrath to come. By all which Termes, is set forth the sense of the man that comes, to wit, That he is affected with the sense of his sin, and the Death due thereto; that he is sensible, that the avenger of Blood pursues him, and that therefore he is cut off, if he makes not speed to the Son of God for Life; *Mat.* 3. 7. *Psal.* 143. 9. Flying is the last work of a man in danger, all that are in danger do not Fly; No, not all that see themselves in danger: flying is the last work of a man in danger; all that hear of danger will not fly. Men will consider if there be no other way of escape, before they Fly. Therefore, as I said, flying is the last thing. When all Refuge fails, and a man is made to see that there is nothing left him but Sin, Death and Damnation, unless he flyes to Christ for Life: then he flies, and not till then.

Thirdly, That the true coming is, from a sense of an absolute need of Jesus Christ to save, *&c.* is evident by the *Out-cry* that is made by them that come, even as they are coming to him; Mat. 14. 30. Acts 2. 37. Act. 16. 30. *Lord save me or I perish*; *Men and Brethren what shall we do*; *Sirs what must I do to be saved*, and the like. This Language doth sufficiently discover that the truly coming Souls, are Souls sensible of their need of Salvation by Jesus Christ; and moreover, that there is nothing else that can help them but Christ.

Fourthly, It is yet further evident, by these few things that follow, it is said that such are *pricked in their Hearts*, that is, with the sentence of Death by the Law, and the least prick in the Heart kills a Man, *Acts* 2. 37. such are said, as I said before, to *Weep*, to *Tremble*, and

11 to him] *add 1684–1688* 26 that] to *1684–1688* 26–7 Mat. 14. 30. Acts 2. 37. Act. 16. 30.] *add 1684–1688* 27 *me*] *add 1684–1688*

to be *astonished* in themselves at the evident and unavoidable danger that attends them, unless they fly to Jesus Christ, *Acts* 9. *chap.* 16.

Fifthly, Coming to Christ is attended with an honest, and sincere forsaking of all for him. *If any Man come to me, and hate not his Father, and Mother, and Wife, and Children, and Brethren, and Sisters, yea, and his own Life also, he cannot be my Disciple; And whosoever doth not bear his Cross, and come after me, cannot be my Disciple*, Luk. 14. 26, 27.

By *these*, and *the like* expressions elsewhere, Christ describeth the true Commer, or the man that indeed is coming to him; he is one that casteth all behind his Back; he leaveth all, he forsaketh all, he hateth all things that would stand in his way to hinder his coming to Jesus Christ. There are a great many pretended Commers to Jesus Christ in the World. And they are much like to the man that you read of in (*Matt.* 21. 30.) that said at his Fathers bidding, *I go Sir, and went not*. I say, there are a great many such Commers to Jesus Christ; they say, when Christ calls by his Gospel, *I come Sir*, but still they abide by their Pleasures, and carnal Delights. They come not at all, only they give him a Courtly Complement; but he takes notice of it, and will not let it pass for any more than a Lie. He said, *I go Sir, and went not*, he dissembled and lied. Take heed of this, you that flatter your selves with your own deceivings, words will not do with Jesus Christ: coming is coming, and nothing else will go for coming with him.

Before I speak to the other Head, I shall answer some Objections that usually lie in the way of those that in Truth are coming to Jesus Christ.

Objection 1.

Though I cannot deny, but my mind runs after Christ, and that too as being moved thereto from a sight, and consideration of my lost Condition (For I see without him I perish): yet I fear my ends are not right in coming to him.

Quest. Why? what is thine end, in coming to Jesus Christ?

Answer, My end is, that I might have Life, and be saved by Jesus Christ.

2 *chap.*] *om. 1685–1688*   4 of] *om. 1688*   *to*] *unto 1684–1688*   *hate*] *hateth 1688*   14 at] to *1684–1688*   24 speak *1684–1688*] spake *1678*   33 *Answer*] *Ans. 1686*[1]] *Answ. 1686*[2]*–1688*

This is thy Objection; well, let me tell thee, that to come to Christ *for Life, and to be saved*: though at present thou hast no other end, is a lawful, and good coming to Jesus Christ. This is evident, because Christ propoundeth *Life*, as the only Argument to prevail with sinners to come to him, and so also blameth them because they come not to him for *Life. And ye will not Come to me that ye might have Life*, Joh. 5. 40. Besides, there are many other Scriptures whereby he allureth Sinners to come to him, in which he propoundeth nothing to them but their safety. As, *He that believeth in him, shall not perish; he that believeth, is passed from Death to Life. He that believeth, shall be Saved. He that believeth on him is not condemned.* And believing, & coming, are all one. So that you see, to Come to Christ for Life, is a lawful coming, and good.

And let me add over and above, that for a man to come to Christ *for Life*, though he comes to him for nothing else but *Life*: he gives much honour to him.

First, He Honoureth the Word of Christ, and consenteth to the Truth of it, and that in these two general Heads.

1. He Consenteth to the Truth of all those sayings, that Testifieth that Sin is most abominable in it Self, dishonourable to God, and damnable to the Soul of Man, for thus saies the Man that cometh to Jesus Christ, *Jer.* 44. 4. *Rom.* 2. 23. Chap. 6. 23. 2 *Thes.* 2. 12.

2. In that he believeth, as the Word hath said, that there is in the Worlds best things, Righteousness and all, Nothing but Death and Damnation, for so also saies the Man that comes to Jesus Christ for Life, *Rom.* 7. 24, 25. Chap. 8. 2, 3. 2 *Cor.* 3. 6, 7, 8.

Secondly, He Honoureth Christs Person, in that he believeth, that there is Life in Him, and that he is able to Save him from Death, Hell, the Devil, and Damnation, for unless a Man believes this, he will not come to Christ for Life, *Heb.* 7. 24, 25.

1 thy] the *1684–1688* 5 so] *add 1684–1688* 7 5. 40.] 5. *1678*] 5. 3. *1684–1688* 14 1. In that he believeth, that he alone hath made Attonement for Sin, *Rom.* 5.] transposed here, *1686*[1]*–1688*, from p. 261, l. 5 to l. 6, in the earlier editions 15 he gives] it is to give *1684–1688* 20 Testifieth] testifie *1685–1688* 21–2 for thus . . . Christ,] *add 1684–1688* 21 saies *1684–1686*[2]] saith *1688* 26–7 for so . . . for Life,] *add 1684–1688* 27 7. 24, 25.] 7. 24, 35. *1684–1688* 30–1 for unless . . . for Life,] *add 1684–1688*

Thirdly, He Honoreth him, in that he believeth that he is Authorized of the Father to give Life to those that come to him for it (*Joh.* 5. 11, 12. Chap. 17. 1, 2, 3.).

Fourthly, He Honoureth the Priest-Hood of Jesus Christ.

1. In that he believeth, that he alone hath made Attonement for Sin, *Rom.* 5.

2. In that he believeth, that Christ hath more Power to Save from Sin by the Sacrifice that he hath Offered for it, than hath all Law, Devils, Death, or Sin to Condemn. He that believes not this, will not come to Jesus Christ for Life, *Acts* 13. 38. *Heb.* 2. 14, 15. *Revel.* 1. 17, 18.

Thirdly, In that he believeth that Christ, according to his office, will be most faithfull, and mercifull in the discharge of his office. This must be included in the Faith of him that comes for Life to Jesus Christ, 1 *Joh.* 2. 1, 2, 3. *Heb.* 2. 17, 18.

Fourthly, Further, he that cometh to Jesus Christ for life, taketh part with him against Sin, and against all the ragged and imperfect righteousness of the world; yea, and against false Christs, and damnable errors that set themselves against the worthiness of his merits and sufficiency. This is evident, for that such a Soul singleth Christ out from them all as the only one that can save.

Fifthly, Therefore, as *Noah*, at Gods command, thou preparest this Ark, for the saving of thy self, by the which also thou condemnest the world, and art become Heir of the righteousness which is by faith (*Heb.* 11. 7.). Wherefore coming sinner, be content; he that cometh to Jesus Christ, believeth too that he is willing to shew mercy to, and to have Compassion upon him (though unworthy) that comes to him for life. And therefore thy Soul lieth not only under a special Invitation to come, but under a Promise too of being accepted and forgiven, *Mat.* 11. 28.

All these particular parts, and qualities of faith, are in that Soul that comes to Jesus Christ for Life, as is evident to any indifferent Judgment.

p. 261, l. 5 to l. 6 1. In that . . . *Rom.* 5.] transposed in the later editions, *1686*[1]–*1688*, to p. 260, as noted above 6 *Rom.* 5.] *Rom.* 2. *1685* 9–10 He that . . . for Life,] *add 1684–1688* 14–15 This must . . . Christ,] *add 1684–1688* 17 all] *om. 1684–1688* 20–1 This is . . . can save.] *add 1684–1688* 21 one *1684*] *om. 1685–1688* 27 to[2]] *om. 1685–1688*

For, will he that Believeth not the Testimony of Christ concerning the baseness of Sin, & the insufficiency of the Righteousness of the World, come to Christ for Life? No.

He that believeth not this Testimony of the word, *comes not*: He that believeth that there is Life any where else, *comes not*: He that questions whether the Father hath given Christ power to forgive, *comes not*: He that thinketh that there is more in Sin, in the Law, in Death, and the Devil, to Destroy, than there is in Christ to Save, *comes not*: He also that questions his faithful Management of his Office of Priesthood for the salvation of sinners, *comes not.*

Thou then that art indeed the *comeing* Sinner, believest all this. True, perhaps thou dost not believe with that full Assurance: nor hast thou leisure to take Notice of thy Faith as to these Distinct acts of it: But yet all this Faith is in him that cometh to Christ for Life. And the Faith that thus Worketh, is the Faith of the best and purest kind; because this Man comes alone as a Sinner, and as seeing that Life is, and is to be had, only in Jesus Christ.

Before I conclude my Answer to this Objection, take into thy consideration these two things.

First, That the Cities of Refuge, were Erected for their sakes that were dead in Law, and that yet would live by grace; even for those that were to fly thither for life from the avenger of blood that pursued after them. And it is worth your Noting, that those that were upon their flight thither, are in a peculiar manner called the people of God. *Cast ye up, Cast ye up, saith God, prepare ye the way, take up the stumbling block out of the Way of* **My** *people*, Isa. 57. 14. This is meant of preparing the way to the City of refuge, that the Flying slayers might escape thither, and live; which slayers are here by way of speciality called the people of God: even those of them that escaped thither for life.

Secondly, Consider that of *Ahab*, when *Benhadad* sent to him for life, saying, *Thus saith thy Son Benhadad, I pray thee let me live*. Though *Benhadad* had sought the Crown, Kingdom, yea and also the life of *Ahab*; yet how effectually doth *Benhadad* prevaile with him. Is

10 Office of] *om. 1684–1688* 14 that cometh] coming *1686[1]–1688* 20 their sakes] those *1685–1688* 22–3 pursued] pursueth *1686[1]–1688* 26 *block 1686[1]–1688*] *blocks 1678–1685* 27 Flying] *add 1684–1688* 28 and live] *om. 1684–1688* 29 speciality] specialty *1688*

Benhadad yet alive? said *Ahab*, he is my brother; yea, go ye, bring him to me: so he made him ride in his Chariot, 1 *King*. 20 chap.

Coming Sinner what thinkest thou? if Jesus Christ, had as little Goodness in him as *Ahab*, he might grant an humble *Benhadad* life; thou neither beggest of him his Crown or Dignity: Life, eternal life will serve thy turn: how much more then shalt thou have it, since thou hast to deal with him who is goodness and mercy it self; yea since thou art also called upon, yea greatly encouraged by a promise of life, to come to him for Life. Read also these Scriptures, *Numb*. 35. 11, 14, 15. *Josh*. 20. 1, 2, 3, 4, 5. *Heb*. 6. 16, 17, 18, 19, 20.

Objection 2.

When, I say, I only seek my self, I mean, I do not find that I do design Gods Glory in mine own Salvation by Christ, and that makes me fear, I do not come aright.

Answer, Where doth Christ Jesus require such a Qualification, of those that are coming to him for Life? come thou for Life, and trouble not thy head with such Objections against thy Self, and let God and Christ alone to Glorify themselves in the Salvation of such a worm as thou art. The Father saith to the Son, *Thou art my Servant*, O Israel, *in whom I will be Gloryfied*. God, propoundeth Life to Sinners, as the argument to prevail with them to come to him for Life; and Christ sayes plainly, *I am come, that ye might have Life*, John 10. 10. He hath no need of thy designes, though thou hast need of his. Eternal Life, pardon of Sin, and Deliverance from Wrath to come, Christ propounds to thee, and these be the things that thou hast need of; besides, God will be gracious, and merciful to worthless, undeserving wretches; come then as such an one. Therefore lay no stumbling blocks in thy way to him, but come to him for life, & live, *Joh*. 5. 34. *Chap*. 10. 10. *Chap*. 3. 36. *Mat*. 1. 21. *Prov*. 8. 35, 36. 1 *Thes*. 1. 10. *Joh*. 11. 25, 26.

The Jayler was only for knowing at first, what he should do to

2 1 *King*. 20 chap.] 1 *Kings* 20. Chapter. *1684*] 1 Kings 20. *1685–1688* 5 or] and *1685–1688* 9 to²] unto *1685–1688* 11 *Objection*] Obj. *1685–1686*[1] 15 *Answer*] Answ. *1686*[2]*–1688* 22 10. 10.] 12. 10. *1686*[1]*–1688* 27 one. Therefore lay] one: and lay *1684–1688* 28 thy] the *1685–1688* 29 8. 35, 36.] 8. 36, 37. *1678–1688* 31 to p. 264, l. 1 The Jayler . . .: But] When the Jayler said, Sirs, what must I do to be Saved? *1684–1688*

be Saved: But *Paul* did not so much as once ask him, what is your *End*, in this Question; do you design the Glory of God in the Salvation of your Soul? He had more wit; he knew that such Questions as these would have bin but Fools bables about, instead of a sufficient salve, to so weighty a Question, as this was. Wherefore since this poor wretch lacked Salvation by Jesus Christ; I mean, to be saved from Hell and Death, which he knew (now) was due to him for the sins that he had committed: *Paul* bids him, like a poor condemned sinner as he was, to proceed still in this his way of self-seeking: saying, *Believe on the Lord Jesus Christ and thou shalt be saved.* Acts 16. 30, 31, 32.

I know, that afterwards, thou wilt desire to glorifie Christ, by walking in the way of his precepts; but at present thou wantest life; the avenger of blood is behind thee, and the devil like a Lyon is roaring against thee: well, come now, and obtain life from these; and when thou hast obtained some comfortable perswasion that thou art made partaker of life by Christ, then, and not till then, thou wilt say, *Bless the Lord O my Soul, and all that is within me bless his holy name. Bless the Lord O my Soul, and forget not all his benefits. Who forgiveth all thine iniquities, and healeth all thy diseases; who redeemeth thy life from distruction, and Crowneth thee with loving kindness, and tender mercies.* Psal. 103. 1, 2, 3, 4, 5.

Objection 3.

But I cannot believe that I come to Christ aright, because, sometimes, I am apt to question his very Being, and Office to save.

Thus to do is horrible: but may'st thou not Judge amiss in this matter?

How can I Judge amiss, when I Judge as I feel? Poor Soul! thou maist Judge amiss for all that. Why, saith the sinner, I think that these questionings come from my Heart.

Answ. Let me answer. That which comes from thy heart, comes from thy *will* and *affections*, from thy *understanding*, *Judgement* and

5 was] *om. 1685–1688* 6 lacked] lacken *1686*[2] Jesus] *add 1685–1688* 14–15 Lyon is roaring against] *roaring Lion is behind 1685–1688* 17 till *1686*[1]–*1688*] tell *1678–1685* 29 saith the sinner,] *add 1684–1688*

Conscience. For these must acquiess in thy questioning, if thy questioning be with thy heart. And how say'st thou (for to name no more), dost thou with thy Affection and Conscience thus question?

Answ. *No, my Conscience trembles when such thoughts come in to my mind, and my affections are otherwise inclined.*

Then I conclude, that these things are either suddenly injected by the devil, or else are the fruits of that body of sin and death that yet dwels in thee, or perhaps from both together.

If they come wholly from the devil, as they seem, because thy Conscience and affections are against them; or if they come from that body of death, that is in thee (and be not thou curious in enquiring from whether of them they come, the safest way is to lay enough at thy own door) nothing of this should hinder thy coming, nor make thee conclude thou comest not aright.

And before I leave thee, let me a little query with thee farther about this matter.

First, Doest thou like these wicked blasphemies?

Answ. No, no: their presence and working kills me.

Secondly, Doest thou mourn for them, pray against them, and hate thy self because of them?

Answ. Yes, yes: but that which afflicts me, is, I do not prevail against them.

Thirdly, Dost thou sincerely chuse (mightest thou have thy choice), that thy heart might be affected and taken with the things that are best, most heavenly, and holy?

Answ. With all my heart, and death the next hour (if it were Gods will), rather than thus to sin against him.

Well then, thy not liking of them, thy mourning for them, thy praying against them, and thy loathing of thy self because of them, with thy sincere chusing of those thoughts for thy delectation that are heavenly, and holy: clearly declares that these things are not countenanced either with thy Will, Affections, Understanding, Judgement or Conscience; and so, that thy heart is not in them, but that rather they come immediatly from the devil or arise from the body of death that is in thy flesh: of which thou oughtest thus to

8 in] within *1685–1688* 15 farther] *om. 1686[1]–1688* 29 of] *om. 1686[1]–1688*

Say, *Now then, it is no more I that doth it, but sin that dwells in me.* Rom. 7. 16, 17.

I will give thee a pertinent instance. In *Deut.* 22. Thou mayest read of a betrothed damsel, one betrothed to her beloved; one that hath given him her heart and mouth, as thou hast given thy self to Christ; yet she was met with as she walked in the field, by one that forced her, because he was stronger than she. Well, what judgment now doth God the righteous judge pass upon the damsel for this? *The man only, that lay with her, saith God, shall die; but unto the damsel thou shalt do nothing; there is in the damsel no sin worthy of death. For as when a man riseth against his Neighbor, and slayeth him, even so is this matter: he found her in the field, and the betrothed damsel cryed, and there was none to save her.* Deut. 22. 25, 26, 27.

Thou art this damsel, the man that forceth thee with these blasphemous thoughts, is the devil; and he lighteth upon thee in a fit place, even in the field, as thou art wandering after Jesus Christ; but thou cryest out, and by thy cry, did'st shew that thou abhorrest such wicked leudness. Well, the Judge of all the earth will do right, he will not lay the Sin at thy door, but at his that offered the violence: and for thy comfort, take this into consideration also, *That he came to heal them that are oppressed with the devil,* Acts 10. 38.

Objection 4.

But saith another, I am so heartless, so slow, and, as I think, so indifferent in my coming, that, to speak truth, I know not whether my kind of coming, ought to be called a coming to Christ.

Answ. You know that I told you at first, that coming to Christ, is a moving of the heart, and affections towards him.

But, *saith the Soul, my dulness, and indifferency in all holy Duties, demonstrate my heartlessness in coming: and to* **come**, *and* **not** *with the heart, signifies nothing at all.*

Answ. The moving of the heart after Christ, is not to be discerned (at all times) by thy sensible, affectionate performing of duties; but rather by those secret groanings, and complaints which thy soul makes to God against that sloth that attends thee in Duties.

1 *it is*] *it 1685*] *it's 1686*[1]*–1688* 10 *sin*] Sin that is *1684* 14 forceth] forced *1685–1688* 20 also] *om. 1685–1688* 31 *Answ.*] *Answer. 1684–1688*

Secondly, But grant it to be even as thou say'st it is, that thou *comest so slowly*, &c. yet since Christ bids them come, that comes not at all; surely they may be accepted that come, though attended with those infirmities, which thou at present groanest under. He saith, *And him that cometh:* he saith not, if they come sensibly so fast: But, *And him that cometh to me I will in no wise cast out*. He saith also in the Ninth of the *Proverbs*, *As for him that wanteth* **understanding**; that is, an heart, for oft-times the understanding is taken for the heart. **Come**, *eat of my bread, and drink of the wine that I have Mingled.*

Thirdly, Thou may'st be vehement in thy spirit in coming to Jesus Christ, and yet be plagued with sensible sloth. So was the Church, when she cryed, *Draw me, we will run after thee*. And *Paul*, when he said, *When I would do good, evil is present with me* (Song 1. 4. Rom. 7. Gal. 5. 19.). The works, strugglings and oppositions of the Flesh, *are more manifest*, than are the works of the Spirit in our hearts, and so are sooner felt, than they. What then, let us not be discouraged at the sight and feeling of our own infirmities, but run the faster to Jesus Christ for Salvation.

Fourthly, Get thy heart warmed with the sweet promise of Christs acceptance, of the coming sinner, and that will make thee make more hast unto him. Discouraging thoughts, they are like unto cold weather, they benumb the senses, and make us go ungainly about our business; but the sweet and warm gleads of the promise, are like the comfortable beams of the Sun, which liven and refresh. You see how little the *Bee* and *Flye* do play in the Air in Winter; why, the cold hinders them from doing of it; but when the Wind and Sun is warm, who so busie as they?

Fifthly, But again, he that comes to Christ, flyes for his life: now there is no man that Flyes for his life, that thinks he speeds fast enough on his Journey; no, could he, he would willingly take a mile at a step. Oh I come not fast enough, say'st thou: Oh my sloth and heartlesness, say'st thou. *O that I had wings like a dove, for then*

2 comes] come *1685–1688* 5 sensibly] sensible *1684–1688* 7 Ninth] Eighth *1678–1688* of the] of *1685–1688* 8 oft-times] oftentimes *1684–1688* 14 *me*] *men 1688* 1. 4.] 14. *1685–1688* 15 Gal. 5. 19.] *add 1684–1688* 24 of the] of *1684–1688* 27 of] *om. 1685–1688* 32 Oh I . . . thou:] *om. 1685–1688*

would I fly away, and be at rest—I would hasten mine escape from the windy storme and tempest, Psal. 55. 6, 8.

Poor coming Soul, thou art like the man that would ride full gallop, whose horse will hardly trot: now the desire of his minde, is not to be judged of, by the slow pace of the dull jade he rides on; but by the hitching and kicking and Spurring, as he sits on his back. Thy flesh is like this *dull* **Jade**, it will not Gallop, after Christ. It will be backward, though thy soul and heaven lies at stake; but be of good comfort, Christ judgeth not according to the fierceness of outward motion (*Mark* 10. 17.) but according to the sincerity of the heart, and inward parts. *Joh.* 1. 47. *Psal.* 51. 6. *Mat.* 26. 41.

Sixthly, *Ziba* in appearance came to *David* much faster than did *Mephibosheth*: but yet his heart was not so upright in him to *David* as was his. Tis true, *Mephibosheth* had a Check from David, for said he, *Why wentest thou not with me Mephibosheth?* said he; but when *David* came to Remember that Mephibosheth was *Lame* (for that was his plea) *Thy Servant is Lame*, 2 Sam. 19. he was content, and concluded he would have come after him faster than he did: And *Mephibosheth* appealed to *David*, who was in those days as an Angel of God to know all things that are done in the earth, if he did not believe that the reason of his backwardness lay in his *Lameness*, and not in his mind. Why poor coming sinner, thou canst not come to Christ with that outward fierceness of *Carrear*, as many others do; but doth the reason of thy backwardness lie in thy mind, and will, or in the sluggishness of the flesh? canst thou say sincerely, *The Spirit truly is willing, but the flesh is weak*? Mat. 26. 41. Yea, canst thou appeal to the Lord Jesus, who knoweth perfectly the very inmost thought of thy heart; that this is true, then take this for thy comfort, he hath said, *I will assemble her that halteth, I will make her that halteth a remnant, and I will save her that halteth* (Mich. 4. 6, 7. Zeph. 3. 19.); what canst thou have more from the sweet lips of the Son of God? But,

Seventhly, I read of some that are to follow Christ in Chains; I say,

1 *fly 1685–1688*] *flee 1678–1684* mine] *my 1685–1688* 8 lies] lie *1688* 14–15 for said he] *add 1684–1688* 15 *thou not*] *not thou 1685–1688* said he] *om. 1684–1688* 16 came *1684–1688*] come *1678* 21 and] *add 1684–1688* 22 in] add *1686[2]–1688* 23 fierceness of *Carrear*] swiftness of *Carier 1685*] swiftness of *Curier 1686[1]–1686[2]*] swiftness of *Career 1688*

to come after him in *Chaines*, *Thus saith the Lord*, *the labor of* Egypt, *and the Merchandize of* Ethiopia, *and the* Sabeans, *men of stature*, *shall come over unto thee*, *and they shall be thine: They shall come after thee; in Chaines shall they come over*, *and they shall fall down unto thee*, *they shall make Supplication unto thee; saying*, *surely there is none else to save*. Isa. 45. 14. Surely they that come after Christ in Chaines, come to him in great difficulty, because their steps, by their chaines, are straightened.

And what Chaines so heavy, as those that discourage thee? thy Chain which is made up of guilt and filth is heavy; it is a wretched bond about thy neck, by which thy strength doth fail (*Lam.* 1. 14. chap. 3. 17.). But come, though thou comest in chaines, 'tis glory to Christ that a sinner come after him in Chaines. The chinking of thy *Chaines* though troublesome to thee, are not, nor can be obstruction to thy Salvation, 'tis Christs work and Glory to save thee from thy *Chains*, to enlarge thy steps, and set thee at Liberty. The blind man, though called, surely could not come apace to Jesus Christ, but Christ could stand still, and stay for him. True, he rideth upon the Wings of the Wind: But yet he is long Suffering, and his long Suffering is Salvation to him that cometh to him. *Mark* 10. 49. 2 *Pet*. 3. 9.

Eighthly, Hadest thou seen those that came to the Lord Jesus in the days of his flesh, how slowly, how hobblingly they come to him by reason of their infirmities; and also how friendly, and kindly, and graciously he received them, and gave them the desire of their hearts, thou wouldest not, as thou dost, make such Objections against thy self, in thy coming to Jesus Christ.

Objection 5.

But (sayes another) *I fear I come too late*, *I doubt I have stayed too long*, *I am afraid the Door is Shut*.

Answ. Thou canst never come too late to Jesus Christ, *if Thou dost come*. This is manifest, by two instances.

First, By the Man that came to him at the Eleventh Hour. This Man was Idle all the day long: He had a whole Gospel day to come

7 by their] by the *1686[1]–1688* 12 come] comes *1685–1688* 12–15 The chinking . . . Liberty.] *add 1684–1688* 19 *Mark* 10. 49.] *Mark*. 19. 49. *1684–1686[1]*] *Mat*. 19. 49. *1686[2]–1688* 22 come] came *1684–1688*

in, and he play'd it all away, save only the last hour thereof. But at last, at the Eleventh Hour he came, and goes into the Vineyard to Work with the rest of the Labourers, that had born the Burden, and heat of the day. Well, but how was he received of the Lord of the Vineyard? Why, when pay-day came, he had even as much as the rest, yea had his mony first. True, the others Murmured at him, but what did the Lord Jesus Answer them? *Is thine Eye Evil because mine is Good? I will give to this last even as unto thee*, Mat. 20.

Secondly, The other instance is, *The Thief upon the Cross*: He came late also, even as at an Hour before his Death; yea, he stayed from Jesus Christ, as long as he had liberty to be a Theif, and longer too; for could he have deluded the Judge, and by lying words, have escaped his Just Condemnation; for ought I know, he had not come as yet, to his Saviour: but being Convicted, and Condemned to Die; yea, fastned to the Cross, that he might Die like a Rogue, as he was in his Life; behold the Lord Jesus, when this wicked one, *even now*, desireth Mercy at his Hands, tells him, and that without the least reflexion upon him, for his former Mis-spent Life, *To Day thou shalt be with me in Paradice*, Luke 23. 43.

Let no Man turn this Grace of God into Wantonness; my design is now to encourage the coming Soul.

Object. But is not the Door of Mercy Shut against some before they Die?

Answ. Yes. And God forbids that Prayers should be made to him for them, *Jer.* 7. 16. *Jud.* 22.

Quest. *Then, why may not I doubt that I may be one of these?*

Answ. By no means, if thou art coming to Jesus Christ; because when God Shuts the Door upon Men, he gives them no heart, to come to Jesus Christ. *None comes, but those to whom it is given of the Father:* But thou comest, therefore it is given to thee of the Father.

Be sure therefore, if the Father hath given thee an Heart to come to Jesus Christ, the Gate of Mercy yet stands Open to thee: For it stands not with the Wisdom of God, *To give strength to come to the Birth, and yet to Shut up the Womb*, Isa. 66. 9. to give grace to thee to come to Jesus Christ, and yet Shut up the Door of his Mercy

4 received of] received by *1685–1688* 8 *give to*] *give unto 1685–1688*
27 *Answ.*] *Answer. 1684* 34 to thee] *om. 1684–1688*

upon thee. *Encline your Ear, saith he, come unto me, hear, and your Souls shall Live; And I will make an Everlasting covenant with you, even the sure Mercies of David*, Isa. 55. 3.

Object. *But it is said that some knocked when the Door was Shut.*

Answ. Yes, But the Texts in which these Knockers are Mentioned, are to be referred unto the day of Judgment, and not to the coming of the Sinner to Christ in this Life. (See the Texts, *Mat.* 25. 11. *Luke* 13. 24, 25.)

These therefore concern thee nothing at all; that art coming to Jesus Christ, thou art coming **Now**! *Now is the acceptable time, behold now is the day of Salvation*, 2 Cor. 6. 2. now God is upon the Mercy-Seat, now Christ Jesus Sits by continually pleading the Virtue of his Blood for Sinners: and now, even as long as this World lasts, this word of the Text shall still be free, and fully fulfilled. *And him that cometh to Me, I will in no wise cast out.*

Sinner! the greater Sinner thou art, the greater need of Mercy thou hast, and the more will Christ be gloryfied thereby: come then, come and try, come tast, and see how good the Lord is to an Undeserving Worthless Sinner.

Objection 6.

But (sayes another) *I am fallen since I began to come to Christ, therefore I fear I did not come aright, and so consequently that Christ will not receive me.*

Answ. Falls are dangerous, for they dishonour Christ, wound the conscience, and cause the Enemies of God to speak reproachfully. But it is no good argument, *I am fallen, therefore I was not coming aright to Jesus Christ.* If *David*, and *Solomon*, and *Peter* had thus objected against themselves, they had added to their griefs, and yet they had at least, as much cause to do it, as thou. A Man whose steps are ordered by the Lord, and whose goings the Lord delights in, may yet be over-taken with a Temptation, that may cause him to fall, *Psal.* 37. 23, 24. Did not *Aaron* fall, yea, and *Moses* himself? what shall we say of *Hezekiah*, and *Jehosaphat*? There are therefore *falls*,

1 *your*] *thine 1686[1]–1688* 9 art] are *1686[2]* 12 Virtue] Victory *1684–1688* 19 Worthless] *om. 1684–1688* 24 *Answ.*] *Answer*, *1684* 28–9 they had] *om. 1684–1688* 29 to do it] *om. 1685–1688* 32 , and] *add 1685–1688*

and *falls*; falls pardonable, and falls unpardonable; falls unpardonable are falls against Light, from the Faith to the despising of, and trampling upon Jesus Christ, and his blessed undertakings (*Heb.* 6. 2, 3, 4, 5. Chap. 10. 28, 29.). Now as for such, there remaines no more Sacrifice for sin: Indeed, they have no heart, no mind, no desire to come to Jesus Christ for life, therefore they must perish; nay, sayes the Holy Ghost, 'tis impossible that they should be renewed again unto repentance. Therefore, *these* God hath no Compassion for, neither ought we; but for other falls, though they be dreadfull (and God will Chastise his people for them) they do not prove thee a graceless man, one not Coming to Jesus Christ for life.

It is said of the Child in the Gospel, *That while he was yet a-coming, the Devil threw him down, and tore him*, Luk. 9. 42.

Dejected Sinner, is it a wonder that thou hast caught a fall in thy Coming to Jesus Christ? Is it not rather to be wondred at, that thou hast not caught before this, a thousand times a thousand falls! Considering,

First, What fools we are by nature.

Secondly, What weaknesses are in us.

Thirdly, What mighty powers, the fallen Angels, our implacable Enemies, are.

Fourthly, Considering also how often the Coming-man is benighted in his Journey, and also what stumbling-blocks do lie in his way.

Fifthly, Also his familiers (that were so before) now watch for his haulting, and seek by what means they may, to cause him to fall by the hand of their strong ones.

What then? must we, because of these Temptations, incline to fall? No. Must we not fear falls? yes. *Let him that thinketh he standeth, take heed lest he fall.* 1 Cor. 10. 12. Yet let him not be utterly cast down. *The Lord upholdeth all that fall, and raiseth up all those that are bowed down.* Make not light of falls: yet hast thou fallen? *ye have*, said Samuel, *done all this wickedness, yet turn not aside from following the*

14 is it *1678–1684*] it is *1685–1688* a[1]] no *1685–1688* thy] *om. 1684–1688* 18 *First,*] 1. *1685–1688* 19 *Secondly,*] 2. *1685–1688* 20 *Thirdly,*] 3. *1685–1688* 22 *Fourthly,*] 4. *1685–1688* 25 *Fifthly,*] 5. *1685–1688* 30 1. Cor. 10. 12.] *add 1684–1688* be utterly] utterly be *1684–1688* 31 *all*[2]] *om. 1684–1688* *those*] *om. 1684*

Lord, but serve him with a perfect heart, and turn not aside, for the Lord will not forsake his people (and he counteth the coming sinner one of them) *because it hath pleased the Lord to make you his people*, 1 Sam. 12. 20, 21, 22.

Shall come to me.

Now we come to shew, what force there is in this Promise to make them come to him. *All that the father giveth me shall come to me.*

I will Speak to this promise,

First. In general.

Secondly. In particular.

In general. This word [*shall*] is confined to **these** [**all**] that are given to Christ. **All** *that the father giveth me*, **shall** *come to me*. Hence I conclude,

First, That coming to Jesus Christ aright, is an effect of their being (of God) given to *Christ* before. Mark, *they* shall come! Who? *those* that are given; they *come* then, because they *were given. Thine they were*, *and thou gavest them me*. Now this is indeed a Singular comfort to them that are coming in truth to Christ, to think that the reason why they come, is because they were given of the Father before to him. Thus then may the coming Soul reason with himself as he comes. Am I coming indeed to Jesus Christ? this coming of mine is not to be attributed to me, or my goodness, but to the grace and gift of God to Christ: God gave first my Person to him, and therefore hath now given me a heart to come to him.

Secondly, This word, *shall come*, maketh thy coming, not only the fruit of the gift of the Father, but also of the purpose of the Son; for these words are a divine purpose, they shew us the Heavenly determination of the Son. The Father hath given them to me, and they shall, yea, they shall come to me. Christ is as full in his resolution to save those given to him, as is the Father in the giving of them. Christ prizeth the gift of his Father, he will lose nothing of it: he is resolved to save it every whit by his Blood, and to raise it up again at the last day: and thus he fulfills his Fathers will, and accomplisheth his own desires. *Joh*. 6. 39.

18–20 to think . . . to him.] *add 1684–1688*   24 to come to him] to come to come *1685*] *to come 1686*[1]*–1688*   25 coming] cometh *1685*   30 in the] in *1686*[1]*–1688*   31–4 Christ prizeth . . . *Joh*. 6. 39.] *add 1684–1688*

Thirdly, These words, *shall come*, make thy coming to be also the effect of an absolute Promise. Coming sinner, thou art concluded in a Promise; thy coming is the fruit of the faithfulness of the Promise, of the faithfulness of an absolute Promise. 'Twas this promise, by the vertue of which thou at first received'st strength to come: And this is the Promise, by the vertue of which thou shalt be effectually brought to him. It was said to Abraham, *At this time, will I come, and* Sarah *shall have a Son*: this Son was *Isaac*. Mark, Sarah *shall have a Son*; There is the promise: and *Sarah* had a Son, there was the fullfilling of the promise. And therefore was *Isaac* called the child of the promise, *Gen.* 17. 19. Chap. 18. 10. *Rom.* 9. 9. *Sarah* shall have a Son, but how if *Sarah* be past age? why still the promise continues, to say, *Sarah shall have a Son*, but how if *Sarah* be Barren? why still the Promise says, Sarah *shall have a Son*. But *Abrahams* body is now dead; why, the promise is still the same; Sarah *shall have a Son*. Thus you see what vertue there is in an absolute promise. It carrieth enough in its own bowels to accomplish the thing promised, whether there be means or no in us to effect it: wherefore this promise, in the Text, being an absolute promise; by vertue of it, not by vertue of our selves, or by our own enducements, do we come to Jesus Christ: for so are the words of the Text. *All that the Father giveth me* shall *come to me*.

Therefore is every sincere commer to Jesus Christ, called also a Child of the promise. *Now we brethren, as* Isaac *was, are the Children of the promise*, Gal. 4. 28. That is, we are the Children that God hath promised to Jesus Christ, and given to him; yea, the Children that Jesus Christ hath promised shall come to him. *All that the Father giveth me, shall come*.

Fourthly, This word [*shall-come*] engageth Christ to Communicate all manner of Grace to those thus given him, to make them effectually to come to him. *They shall come*; that is, not if they will, but if grace, all grace, if power, wisdom, a new heart and the holy spirit, and all Joyning together, can make them come. I say, this word [*shall-come*] being absolute, hath no dependance upon our own will,

3–4 of the Promise, of the faithfulness] *om. 1684–1688* 13–14 but how . . . *a Son.*] *add 1684–1688* 20 by[3]] *add 1684–1688* by our] by your *1686[1]–1688* 29 *Fourthly*] *Fourth 1686[1]–1688* 34 own] *add 1684–1688* or power, or goodness; but it ingageth for us even God himself, Christ himself, the Spirit himself. When God had made that Absolute promise to *Abraham*, that *Sarah should have a Son*, Abraham did not at all look at any qualification in himself, because the promise looked at none, but as God had by the promise absolutely promised him a Son; so he considered now not his own body now dead, nor yet the barrenness of *Sarah's* Womb. *He staggered not at the promise of God through unbelief, but was strong in faith, giving glory to God, being fully perswaded that what* **He** *had promised,* **He** *was able to perform*, Rom. 4. He had promised, and had promised absolutely, *Sarah shall have a Son*. Therefore *Abraham* looks that **He**, to wit, God must fulfil the condition of it. Neither is this Expectation of *Abraham*, disapproved by the Holy Ghost, but accounted good and laudable, it being that by which he gave Glory to God. The Father also hath given to Christ, a certain number of Souls for him to save, and he himself hath said, *They shall come to him*. Let the Church of God then live in a Joyful Expectation of the utmost accomplishment of this promise, for assuredly it shall be fulfilled, and not one thousandth part of a Tittle thereof shall fail. *They shall come to me.*

And now, before I go any further, I will more particularly enquire into the nature of an *Absolute Promise*.

First, We call that an Absolute promise, that is made without any condition; or more fully thus, That is an absolute promise of God, or of Christ, which maketh over to this or that man, any Saving Spiritual blessing, without a condition to be done on our part for the obtaining thereof. And this we have in hand is such a one: Let the best Master of Arts on Earth, shew me if he can any condition in this Text, depending upon any qualification in us, which is not by the same promise concluded, shall be by the Lord Jesus effected in us.

Secondly, An Absolute promise therefore is, as we say, without **if**, or **and**; that is, it requireth nothing of us, that it self might be accomplisht. It saith not, They shall *if they will*; but *they shall*: not they shall, if they use the means; but *they shall*. You may say, that

2 had] hath *1686[1]–1688* 6 now[1]] *add 1684–1688* 19 *They shall come to me.*] *add 1684–1688* 26–30 And this . . . in us.] *add 1684–1688* 26 a one *1684*] an one *1685–1688*

a will, and the use of the means, is supposed, though not expressed. But I answer; No, by no means; that is, as a condition of this promise: If they be at all included in the promise, they are included there as the fruit of the Absolute promise, not as if it expected the qualification to arise from us. *Thy people shall be willing in the day of thy power*, Psal. 110. 3. That is another absolute promise: But doth that Promise suppose a willingness in us, as a condition of Gods making of us willing? they shall be willing, if they *are* willing; or they shall be willing, if they *will* be willing. This is ridiculous, there is nothing of this supposed. The promise is absolute, as to us; all that it ingageth for its own accomplishment, is the mighty power of Christ: and his Faithfulness to accomplish.

The difference therefore betwixt the absolute, and the conditional promise, is this.

First, They differ in their *terms*. The absolute promises say, *I will*, and you shall: the other, *I will*, *if you will*; or do this, and thou shalt live; *Jer*. 31. 31, 32, 33. *Ezek*. 36. 24, 25, 26, 27, 28, 29, 30, 31, 32, 33. *Heb*. 8. 7, 8, 9, 10, 11, 12. *Jer*. 4. 1. *Ezek*. 18. 30, 31, 32. *Mat*. 19. 21.

Secondly, They differ in their way of Communicating of good things to men; the absolute ones Communicate things freely, only of Grace; the other, if there be that qualification in us, that the promise calls for, not else.

Thirdly, The absolute promises therefore ingage God, the other ingage us: I mean God only, us only.

Fourthly, Absolute promises must be fulfilled; Conditional may, or may not be fulfilled. The absolute ones must be fulfilled, because of the faithfulness of God; the other may not, because of the unfaithfulness of men.

Fifthly, Absolute promises have therefore a sufficiency in themselves to bring about their own fulfilling; the Conditional have not so. The absolute promise, is therefore a big-bellied promise, because it hath in it self a fulness of all desired things for us; and will, when the time of that promise is come, yeild to us mortals, that which will veryly save us: yea, and make us capable of answering of the demands, of the promise that is conditional. Wherefore,

6 *thy*] *the 1684* 8 of] *om. 1685–1688* 11 own *1685–1688*] one *1678–1684* 12 : and his . . . accomplish] *add 1684–1688* 13 and the] and *1685–1688*

though there be a real, yea an eternal difference in these things (with others) betwixt the conditional and absolute promise: yet again in other respects there is a blessed Harmony betwixt them, as may be seen in these particulars.

First, The Conditional promise calls for Repentance, and the absolute promise gives it, *Acts* 5. 30, 31.

Secondly, The Conditional promise *calls* for *faith*, the absolute promise *gives it*, Zeph. 3. 12. Rom. 15. 12.

Thirdly, The Conditional promise *calls* for a *new heart*, the absolute promise *gives it*, Ezek. 36.

Fourthly, The Conditional promise *calleth* for *Holy Obedience*, the absolute promise giveth it, or causeth it, *Ezek.* 36. 27.

And as they Harmoniously agree in this; so again the Conditional promise blesseth the man, who by the absolute promise is endued with its fruit: As for instance,

First, The absolute promise maketh men upright, and then the Conditional follows saying, *Blessed are the undefiled in the way, who walk in the Law of the Lord*, Psal. 119. 1.

Secondly, The absolute promise giveth to this man, the fear of the Lord; and then the Conditional followeth saying, Blessed is every *one that feareth the Lord*, Psal. 128. 1.

Thirdly, The absolute promise giveth faith, and then this Conditional follows saying, *Blessed is she that believeth*, Zeph. 3. 12. Luk. 1. 45.

Fourthly, The Absolute promise brings free forgiveness of Sins; and then says the Conditional, *Blessed are they, whose Transgressions are forgiven, and whose sin is covered*, Rom. 4. 7, 8.

Fifthly, The Absolute promise says, that Gods elect shall hold out to the end; then the Conditional follows with his blessing, *He that shall endure to the end, the same shall be saved*, 1 Pet. 1. 4, 5, 6. Mat. 24.

Thus do the promises gloriously serve one another, *and us*, in this their harmonious agreement.

Now the promise under consideration, is an absolute promise; *All that the Father giveth me*, **shall** *come to me.*

5 and] *om. 1685–1688* 6 promise] *om. 1685–1688* 12 giveth it *1684–1688*] giveth *1678* 18 *Law*] *way 1684–1688* 23 *she*] *he 1686*[1]*–1688*

This promise therefore is, as I said, a big-bellied promise, and hath in it self all those things to bestow upon us, that the conditional calleth for at our hands. *They shall come!* Shall they come? yes, *They shall come.* But how if they want those things, those Graces, Power and Heart, without which they cannot come? Why, Shall *come* answereth all this, and all things else that may in this manner be objected. And here I will take the liberty a little to amplifie things.

Object. 1. *But they are dead, dead in Trespasses and Sins, how shall they then come?* Answ. Why? *Shall-come, can raise them from this Death. The hour is coming, and now is, That the dead shall hear the Voice of the Son of God, and they that hear, shall Live.* Thus therefore is this impediment, by *shall-come*, swallowed up, or quite removed out of the way. They shall Heal, they shall Live.

Object. 2. *But they are Satans Captives, he takes them Captive at his Will, and he is stronger than they; How then can they come?*

Answ. Why? *Shall-come*, hath also provided an help for this. Satan had bound that Daughter of *Abraham* so, that she could by no means lift up her self; but yet, *shall-come*, set her free in Body and Soul both. Christ will have them turned from the Power of Satan to God. But what! Must it be, if they turn themselves, or do something to Merit of him to turn them! No, he will do it freely of his own good Will. Alas! Man whose Soul is possessed by the Devil, is turned whither soever That Governor listeth; is taken Captive by him, notwithstanding his natural Powers, at his Will; but what will he do? will he hold him, when *shall-come* puts forth itself (will he then let him) for comeing to Jesus Christ? No: that cannot be, his Power is but the Power of a fallen Angel; but *shall-come*, is the Word of God: therefore *shall-come* must be fulfilled, *And the Gates* of Hell Shall not prevail against it.

There was Seven Devils in *Mary Magdalen*, too many for her to get from under the Power of; but when the time was come, that *shall-come* was to be fulfilled upon her, they give place, fly from her, and she comes [indeed] to Jesus Christ, according as it is written, *All that the Father giveth me shall come to me.*

1 as I said,] *add 1684–1688* 7 a little] *om. 1686*[1]*–1688* 8 1.] *add 1688* 12 swallowed up, or quite] *om. 1685–1688* 12–13 They shall . . . Live.] add *1684–1688* 18 in Body and Soul both] both in Body and Soul *1684–1688* 24 his[1]] its *1684–1688* 30 was] were *1685–1688* 33 according as it is written,] *add 1684–1688*

The Man that was possessed with a *Legion* (Mark 5.) was too much, by them, captivated, for him by humane force to come; yea, had he had (to boot) all the men under Heaven to help him, had he that said, he *shall-come*, with-held his mighty power: but when this promise was to be fulfilled upon him, then he comes, nor could all their power hinder his coming. It was also this *shall-come*, that preserved him from death, when by these evil spirits he was hurled hither and thither; and 'twas by the vertue of *shall-come*, that at last he was set at liberty from them, and inabled indeed to *come* to Christ. *All that the father giveth me shall come to me.*

Object. 3. *They shall (you say) but how if they will not! man cannot come without his will: but if he will not, he will not; and if so, then what can* **shallcome**, *do?*

Answ. True, there are some men say, *we are Lords, we will come no more unto thee*, Jer. 2. 31. But as God says in another case (if they are Concerned in shall-come to me) *They shall know whose word shall stand, mine or theirs*, Jer. 44. 28. Here then is the case, we must now see who will be the liar, he that saith, *I will not*, or he that saith, *he shall come to me.* You *shall come*, sayes God. *I will not come* sayes the sinner. Now as sure as he is concerned in this *shall-come*, God will make that man eat his own words: for *I will not*, is but the unadvised Conclusion of a Crazy-headed sinner: but *shall-come*, was spoken by him that is of power to perform his word, *Son, go work to day in my vineyard*, said the Father: but he answered and said, *I will not*. What now? Will he be able to stand to his refusal, will he pursue his desperate denial! No: He *afterwards repented, and went*. But how came he by that repentance? Why it was wrapped up, for him, in the *absolute* promise; and therefore not withstanding he said, *I will not*, he afterwards repented and went. By this parable, Jesus Christ sets forth the obstinacy of the sinners of the world, as touching their coming to him; they will not *come*, though threatned, yea though life be offered them upon condition of coming.

But now when, *shall-come*, the absolute promise of God, *comes* to be fulfilled upon them, then they come; because by *that* promise

8 'twas by] it was *1685–1686*[2]] was by *1688*   11–12 *man cannot . . . if he will not, he will not;*] *om. 1686*[1]*–1688*   15 *unto*] *under 1686*[1]*–1688*   19 sayes[2]] saith *1685–1688*   21 but] *om. 1684–1688*

a cure is provided against the rebellion of their will; *Thy people shall be willing in the day of thy power*, Psal. 110. 3. Thy People, what People, why the People that thy Father hath given thee. The Obstinacy and Plague that is in the will of that People, shall be taken away, and they shall be made willing, *shall come*, will make them willing to come to thee.

He that had seen *Paul* in the midst of his out-rage against Christ, his Gospel, and people: would hardly have thought that he would ever have been a follower of Jesus Christ, specially since he went not against his Conscience in his persecuting of them. He thought verily that he ought to do what he did. But we may see, what *shall-come* can do, when it comes to be fulfilled upon the Soul of a rebellious sinner: he was a Chosen vessel, given by the Father to the Son; and now the time being come, that *shall-come*, was to take him in hand, behold he is over-mastered, astonished, and with trembling, and reverence, in a Moment becomes *willing* to be obedient to the Heavenly call, *Acts* 9.

And were not they far gone (that you read of in *Acts* the Second) who had their hands and hearts in the Murder of the Son of God; and to shew their resolvedness never to repent of that horrid fact, said, *His Blood be on us and our Children*? But must their obstinacy rule, must they be bound to their own ruin by the rebellion of their Stubborn wills? No: not *those* of *these* that the Father gave to Christ, wherefore at the times appointed, *shall-come* Brakes in among-them; the absolute promise takes them in hand, and then they *come* indeed, crying out to *Peter*, and the rest of the *Apostles*, *Men and brethren, what shall we do?* No Stubborness of mans will can stand, when God hath absolutely said the contrary, *shall-come*, can make them come as doves to their windows, that had afore resolved never to come to him.

The Lord spake unto *Manasseth*, and to his people (by the Prophets) but he would not hear, no, he *would not*: but shall *Manasseth* come off thus? no, he *shall not*. Therefore, he being also one of those

1 a cure] *add 1684–1688* 2–6 Thy People . . . to thee.] *add 1684–1688* 7 outrage] Outrages *1686*[1]*–1688* 9 specially] especially *1684–1688* 18 of in *Acts* the Second] of, *Acts* 2. *1685–1688* 23 that] *om. 1685–1688* 29–30 that had . . . to him] *add 1684–1688* 32 he would not hear] he would hear *1685–1686*[2]] *would he hear? 1688*

whom the Father had given to the Son, and so falling within the bounds and reach of **shall-come**: At last *Shall-come* takes him in hand, and then he comes indeed. He comes Bowing, and Bending; He humbled himself greatly, and made Supplication to the Lord, and prayed unto him, and he was intreated of him, and had mercy upon him, 2 *Chro.* 33.

The Thief upon the Cross, at first, did rail, with his fellow, upon Jesus Christ; but he was one that the Father had given to him, and therefore *shall-come*, must handle him, and his rebellious will. And behold, so soon as he is dealt with all, by vertue of that absolute promise, how soon he buckleth, leaves his railing, falls to Supplicating of the Son of God for mercy; *Lord*, saith he, *remember me, when thou comest into thy Kingdome*, Mat. 27. 44. Luk. 23. 40, 41, 42.

Object 4. *They shall come*, say you, *but how if they be blind, and see not the way; for some are kept off from Christ, not only by the obstinacy of their will, but by the blindness of their minde: now if they be blind, how shall they come?*

Answ. The question is not, Are they blind? but, are they with in the reach, and power of *shall come*; if so, *That* Christ, that said they *shall-come*, will find them eyes, or a guide, or both, to bring them to himself. *Must is for the King*. If they *shall-come*, they *shall-come*: no impediment shall hinder.

The *Thessalonians* darkness did not hinder them from being the Children of Light: *I am come*, said Christ *that they that see not, might see*. And if he saith, *See ye blind, that have eyes*, who shall hinder it? *Ephes*. 5. 8. Joh. 9. 39. Isa. 29. 18. Chap. 43. 8.

This promise therefore, is, as I said, a big-bellied promise, having in the bowels of it, all things that shall accur to the compleat fulfilling of it self. They *shall-come*. But 'tis objected that they are blind: well, *shall-come*, is still the same, and continueth to say, they *shall-come to me*. Therefore he saith again, *I will bring the blind by a way that they know not, I will lead them in paths that they have not known. I will make darkness light before them, and Crooked things straight, these things will I do unto them, and not forsake them*, Isa. 42. 16.

2–3 *Shall-come . . .* then] *add 1684–1688* 4 humbled] humbles *1686*[1]*–1688*
6 2 *Chro*. 33.] 2 *Chron*. 3. 33. *1684–1688* 15 *some 1684–1688*] *same 1678*
21 *Must is for the King*.] *add 1684–1688* 32 *have not known*] *know not 1686*[1]*–1688*

Mark, I will bring them though they be blind, I will bring them by a way they know not; I will, I will, and therefore *they shall-come to me*.

Object. 5. *But how if they have exceeded many in sin, and so made themselves far more abominable? They are the Ring-leading Sinners in the Country, the Town or Family.*

Answ. What then? Shall that hinder the execution of *shall-come*? It is not Transgressions, nor Sins, nor all their Transgressions, in all their sins (if they by the Father are given to Christ to save them) that shall hinder this promise, that it should not be fulfilled upon them. *In those days, and at that time, saith the Lord, the iniquities of* Israel *shall be sought for, and there shall be none, and the sins of* Judah, *and they* shall *not be found*, Jer. 50. 20. Not that they *had* none (for they abounded in Transgression, 2 *Chron.* 33. 9. *Ezek.* 16. 48), but God would pardon, cover, hide, and put them away, by vertue of his absolute promise, by which they are given to Christ to save them. *And I will cleanse them from all their iniquity, whereby they have sinned against me; and I will pardon all their iniquity, whereby they have Transgressed against me. And it* shall *be to me for a name of joy, a praise, and an honour before all the Nations of the Earth, which shall hear of all the good that I do unto them; and they shall fear and tremble for all the goodness, and all the prosperity that I procure to it*, Jer. 33. 8, 9.

Object. 6. *But how if they have not Faith and Repentance? how shall they come then?*

Answ. Why? he that saith they *shall-come*, shall he not make it good? If they *shall-come*, they *shall-come*; and he that hath said, they *shall-come*, if faith and repentance be the *way* to come, as indeed they are, then faith and repentance shall be given to them: for *shall-come*, must be fulfilled on them.

First, Faith *shall* be given them; *I will also leave in the midst of thee an afflicted, and poor people, and they* shall *trust in the name of the Lord. There* shall *be a Root of* Jesse, *and he* shall *rise to raign over the Gentiles; and in him* shall *the Gentiles trust*, Zeph. 3. 12. Rom. 15. 12.

Secondly, They *shall* have repentance: He is exalted to give repentance; *They* shall *come weeping and seeking the Lord their God. And*

4 5.] *om. 1685–1686*[2]   13 50. 20.] 32. 30.   21 *that*] *om. 1684–1688*

again, with Weeping and Supplication will I lead them, Acts 5. 30, 31. Jer. 31. 9. Chap. 50. 4.

I told you before, that an absolute promise, hath all *conditional* ones in the belly of it, and also provision to answer all those qualifications that *they* propound to him that seeketh for *their* benefit: And it must be so, for if *shall-come* be an absolute promise, as indeed it is, then it must be fulfilled upon every of those, concerned therein I. say, it **must** be fulfilled, if God can by Grace, & his absolute Will, fulfil it. Besides, since Coming, and Believing is all one (according to *Joh.* 6. 35.) *He that cometh to me shall never hunger, and he that believeth in me shall never thirst.*

Then, when he saith, they *shall come*, 'tis as much as to say, they *shall believe*, and consequently repent to the saving of the Soul. So then the present want of faith and repentance, cannot make this promise of God of none effect; because that this promise hath in it to give, what others call for and expect. I will give them an heart, I will give them my spirit, I will give them repentance, I will give them faith. Mark these words, *If any man be in Christ, he is a new Creature.* But how came he to be a new Creature, since none can Create but God? why, God indeed doth make them new Creatures. *Behold*, saith *he*, *I make all things new.* And hence it follows, even after he had said, they are new Creatures; *And all things are of God*: that is, all this new Creation standeth in the several operations, and special workings of the Spirit of grace, who is God, 2 *Cor.* 5. 17, 18.

Object. 7. *But how shall they escape all those dangerous, and damnable opinions, that like rocks, and quick-sands, are in the way in which they are going?*

Answ. Indeed this age, is an age of errors, if ever there was an age of errors in the world; but yet the gift of the Father, laid claim to by the Son in the Text, must needs escape them, and in conclusion come to him. There are a company of *shall-comes* in the Bible, that doth secure them. Not but that they may be assaulted by them; yea, and also for the time, intangled and detained by them from the Bishop of their Souls: but these *Shall-comes*, will break those Chains and Fetters, that those given to Christ are intangled in, and they *hall-come*, because he hath said they shall-come to him.

2 Chap. 50. 4.] Chap. 50. 5. *1678*] *om. 1684–1688*

Indeed, errors are like that whore, of whom you read in the *Proverbs*, that sitteth on her seat on the High-places of the City, *To call Passingers who go right on their way* (Pro. 9. 13, 14, 15, 16.). But the persons, as I said, that by the Father are given to the Son to save them, are at one time or other, secured by, *Shall come to me.*

And therefore, of such it is said; God will guide them with his eye, with his Counsel, by his spirit, and that in the way of peace; by the springs of water, and into all truth, *Psal.* 32. 8. *Psal.* 73. 24. *Joh.* 16. 13. *Luk.* 1. 79. *Isa.* 47. 10. So then, he that hath *such* a guide (and all that the Father giveth to Christ, shall have it) he shall escape those dangers, he shall nor Err in the way; yea, though he be a fool, he shall not Err therein (*Isa.* 35.) for of every such an one it is said, *Thine ears shall hear a word behind thee, saying; This is the way, walk in it, when ye turn to the right hand, and when ye turn to the left*, Isa. 30. 21.

There were Thieves and Robbers before Christs coming, as there are also now: But, saith he, *The sheep did not hear them.*

And why did they not hear them, but because they were under the power of *shall come*? that absolute promise, that had that grace in it self to bestow upon them, as could make them able rightly to distinguish of voices. *My sheep hear my voice.* But how came they to hear it? why, to them it is given to know and to hear, and that distinguishingly, *Joh.* 10. 8, 16. *Chap.* 5. 25. *Eph.* 5. 14.

Further, the very plain Sentence of the Text makes provision against all these things; for, saith it, *All that the Father giveth me, shall come to* me; that is, shall not be stopped, or be allured to take up any where short of Me; nor shall they turn aside, to abide, with any besides Me.

Shall Come [*to me*].

To me!] By these words there is further insinuated (though not expressed) a double cause of their coming to him.

First, There is in Christ, a fulness of Al-sufficiency of *that*, even of all *that* which is needfull to make us happy.

Secondly, Those that indeed come to him, do therefore come to him that they may receive it at his hand.

2 on *1678–1684*] in *1685–1688*   3 *call*] *all 1685–1688*   7 Counsel *1688*] *counsels 1678–1686*[2]

For the first of these, *There is in Christ a fulness of all Sufficiency of all that, even of all that which is needfull to make us happy*. Hence it is said, *For it pleased the Father, that in him should all fulness dwell*. And again, *Of his fullness, all we have received, and grace for grace*, Colos. 1. 19. Joh. 1. 16. It is also said of him, that his riches is unsearchable, *The unsearchable riches of Christ*, Ephes. 3. 8. Hear what he saith of himself, *Riches and honour are with* Me, *even durable riches and righteousness; my fruit is better than Gold, yea than fine Gold; and* My *revenue than Choice silver: I lead in the way of Righteousness, in the midst of the paths of Judgement, that I may cause them that love* Me *to inherit Substance. And I will fill their treasures*, Prov. 8. 18, 19, 20, 21.

This in general, but more particularly.

First, There is that *Light* in Christ, that is Sufficient to lead them out of, and from all that darkness, in the midst of which all others, but them that come to him, stumble, and fall, and perish: *I am the light of the world*, saith he; *he that followeth* me *shall not abide in darkness, but shall have the Light of Life*, Joh. 8. 12. Man by nature is in darkness, and walketh in darkness, and knows not whither he goes, for darkness hath blinded his eyes; neither can any thing but Jesus Christ, lead men out of this darkness; Natural Conscience cannot do it; the Ten Commandments, though in the heart of man, cannot do it: this prerogative belongs only to Jesus Christ.

Secondly, There is that life in Christ, that is to be found no where else, *Joh*. 5. 40. Life as a principle in the Soul, by which it shall be acted and enabled to do that which through him is pleasing to God. *He that believeth* in, or cometh, *to* me, saith he, as the Scriptures have said, *out of his belly shall flow Rivers of Living Water*, Joh. 7. 38. Without this life a man is dead, whether he be bad, or whether he be good, that is good in his own, and other mens esteem. There is no true and Eternal life, but what is in the Me that speaketh in the Text.

There is also life for those, that come to him, to be had by faith in his flesh, and blood. *He that eateth Me, even he shall live by Me*, Joh. 6. 57.

And this is a life against that Death, that comes by the guilt of sin, and the curse of the Law, under which all men are, and forever

11 8.] *om. 1685–1688* 23 that[1]] *om. 1688*

must be, unlesse they eat the Me, that speaks in the Text. *Whoso findeth* Me, saith he, *findeth life*; deliverance from that everlasting death, and destruction, that without Me he shall be devoured by, *Prov.* 8.

Nothing is more desirable than life, to him that hath in himself the Sentence of Condemnation; and here only is life to be found. *This life*, to wit, Eternal life, *this life is in his Son.* That is, in him that saith in the Text, *All that the Father hath given* Me *shall come to* Me, 1 Joh. 5. 11.

Thirdly, The person speaking in the Text, is he alone by whom poor sinners have Admittance with, and Acceptance to the Father, because of the Glory of his righteousness, by and in which he presenteth them amiable, and spotless in his sight; neither is there any way besides him, so to come to the Father; *I am the way*, sayes he, *the truth, and the life; no man cometh to the Father but by* Me, Joh. 14. 6. All other ways to God, are dead and damnable, the destroying Cherubins, stand with flaming swords turning every way to keep all others from his presence (*Gen.* 3. 24.), I say, all others but them that come by him.

I am the door, by Me, saith he, *if any man enter in, he shall be saved*, Joh. 10. 1, 2, 9.

The person speaking in the Text, is He, and only He, that can give stable, and everlasting peace; therefore, saith he, My *peace I give unto you.* My peace, which is a peace with God, peace of Conscience, and that of an everlasting duration. My peace, peace that cannot be Matched, *not as the world giveth give I unto you*; for the worlds peace is but Carnal, and Transitory; but mine is Divine and Eternal, Hence it is called, the peace of God, and *That* passeth all understanding.

Fourthly, The person speaking in the Text, hath enough of all things truly Spiritually good, to satisfie the desires of every longing Soul. *And Jesus stood, and Cried, saying, If any man thirst, let him come unto me, and drink.* And to him that is athirst, I will give of the fountain of the water of life freely, *Joh.* 7. 37. *Rev.* 21. 6.

9 5. 11.] 5. 10. *1678–1688*   11 with] to *1684–1688*   to] with *1684–1688*   21 9.] *om. 1678–1688*   26 *giveth 1685–1688*] *gived 1678–1684*   31 desires] desire *1688*

Fifthly, With the person speaking in the Text, is power to perfect and defend, and deliver those that come to him for safegard. *All power*, saith he, *in heaven, and earth, is given unto* **Me**, *Mat.* 28. 18.

Thus might I multiply instances of this nature in abundance. But

Secondly, they that in truth, do come to him, do therefore come to him, that they may receive it at his hand. They come for light, they come for life, they come for reconciliation with God; they also come for peace, they come that their Soul may be satisfied with Spiritual good, and that they may be protected by him against all Spiritual, and Eternal damnation; and he alone is able to give them all this, to the filling of their joy to the full, as they also find, when come to him.

This is evident,

First, From the plain declaration of those that already are come to him. *Being Justified by faith, we have peace with God through our Lord Jesus Christ, by whom also we have access with boldness into this grace, wherein we stand, and rejoyce in hope of the glory of God*, Rom. 5. 1, 2.

Secondly, 'Tis evident also, in that while they keep their eyes upon him, they never desire to change him for another, or to add to themselves, some other thing, together with him to make up their Spiritual Joy. *God forbid*, said *Paul*, *that I should Glory, save in the Cross of our Lord Jesus Christ.* Yea and I count all things but loss for the excellency of the knowledge of Christ Jesus my Lord, for whom I have suffered the loss of all things; and do count them but dung, that I may win Christ, and be found in him; not having mine own Righteousness, which is of the Law, but that which is thorough the faith of Christ, the righteousness which is of God by faith, *Philipians* 3. 7, 8, 9.

Thirdly, 'Tis evident also by their earnest desires, that others might be made partakers of their blessedness. Brethren, said *Paul*, my hearts desire and prayer to God for *Israel* is, that they might be saved, that is, that way that he expected to be saved himself, as he saith also to the *Galatians*. *Brethren*, saith he, *I beseech you, be as I am, for I am as ye are*. That is, I am a sinner as you are; now I beseech you seek for life, as I am seeking of it: as who should say, For there is a sufficiency in the Lord Jesus both for me and you.

22 count] account *1685–1688* 28 *Philipians*] *Phil. 1684–1688*

Fourthly, 'Tis evident also, by the Triumph that such men make over all their enemies, both Bodily, and Ghostly: *Now, thanks be to God*, said *Paul, who causeth us always to triumph in Jesus* Christ. And who shall separate us from the Love of Christ our Lord? And again, *O death where is thy sting! O Grave, where is thy victory! The sting of death is Sin, and the strength of sin, is the Law; but thanks be to God, who giveth us the victory thorow our Lord Jesus Christ.* 2 Cor. 2. 14. Rom. 8. 35. 1 Cor. 15. 55, 56, 57.

Fifthly, 'Tis evident also, for that they are made, by the Glory of that which they have found in him, to suffer, and endure what the Devil and Hell it self hath or could invent, as a means to separate them from him. Again, *Who shall separate us from the Love of Christ? Shall tribulation, or distress, or persecution, or famine, or nakedness, or peril, or Sword (as it is written, for thy sake we are killed all the day long, we are accounted as sheep for the slaughter)? Nay, in all these things we are more than Conquerors, through him that loved us. For I am perswaded, that neither death, nor life, nor Angels, nor principalities, nor powers, nor things present, nor things to come, nor height, nor depth, nor any other Creature shall be able to separate us from the Love of God, which is in Christ Jesus*, Rom. 8. 35–39.

Shall come [to Me]. O the heart attracting glory that is in Jesus Christ (when he is discovered), to draw those to him that are given to him of the Father. Therefore, those that came of old rendered this, as the cause of their coming to him. *And we beheld his glory, as of the only begotten of the Father*, Joh. 1. 14. And the reason why others come not, but perish in their sins, is for want of a sight of his glory. *If our Gospel be hid, it is hid to them that are lost, in whom the God of this world hath blinded the minds of them that believe not, lest the Glorious Light of the Gospel of Christ, who is the image of God, should shine unto them*, 2 Cor. 4. 3, 4.

There is therefore heart-pulling glory in Jesus Christ, which, when discovered, draws the man to him; wherefore, by, *shall-come to* **Me**, Christ may mean; when his glory is discovered, then they **must** come, then they *shall-come to* **Me**. Therefore, as the True Comers come with Weeping and Relenting, as being sensible of their own

8 57.] *om. 1678–1688* 20 35–39.] *om. 1678–1688* 23 came *1685–1688*] come *1678–1684* 28 *lest*] *least 1686*[1] 30 4. 3, 4.] 4. *1684–1688*

Vileness; so again it is said, *That the Ransomed of the Lord shall return, and come to* Zion, *with Singing and Everlasting Joy upon their Heads; they shall obtain Joy and Gladness, and Sorrow and Sighing shall flye away:* That is, at the Sight of the Glory of that Grace, that shews it self to them *now*, in the Face of our Lord Jesus Christ, and in the Hopes that they *now* have of being with Him in the Heavenly Tabernacles. Therefore, it saith again; *With Gladness and Rejoycing shall they be brought; they shall enter into the King's Palace*, Isa. 35. 10. *Chap.* 51. 11. Psal. 45. 15.

There is therefore Heart-attracting Glory in the Lord Jesus Christ; which, when discovered, subjects the Heart to the Word, and **Makes** us Come to him.

'Tis said of *Abraham, That when he dwelt in* Mesopotamia, *the God of Glory appeared unto him* (Act. 7. 2, 3.), *saying, Get thee out of thy Country.* And what then? why, away he went from his House and Friends, and all the World could not stay him. **Now**, as the Psalmist sayes, *Who is the King of Glory?* He answers, The Lord mighty in Battle: And who was that, but He that spoiled Principalities and Powers, when he did Hang upon the Tree, Tryumphing over them thereon? And who was that, but Jesus Christ, even the Person speaking in the Text? Therefore, he said of *Abraham, He saw his Day*; Yea, saith he to the *Jews, Your Father* Abraham *rejoiced to see my Day; and he saw it, and was Glad*, Psal. 24. 8. Col. 2. 14, 15. Jam. 2. 23. Joh. 8. 56.

Indeed, the Carnal Man sayes (at least) in his Heart, Isa. 53. 1, 2, 3. There is no Form or Comliness in Christ; and when he shall see him, there is no Beauty that he should desire him; *But he lies:* This he speaks, as having never seen him. But they that stand in his House, and look upon him through the Glass of his Word, by the Help of his Holy Spirit, they will tell you other things. *But we*, say they, *all with open Face beholding, as in a Glass, the Glory of the Lord, are changed into the same Image, from Glory to Glory*, 2 Cor. 3. 17, 18. They see Glory in his Person, Glory in his Undertakings, Glory in the Merit of his Blood, and Glory in the Perfection of his Righteousness; yea, Heart-affecting, Heart-sweetening, and Heart-changing Glory!

14 3.] *om. 1678–1688* 23 Jam. 2. 23.] Jam. 1. 1. *1678–1688* 24–5 Isa. 53. 1, 2, 3.] *add 1684–1688* 26 he should] *we should 1688* 28 look *1685–1688*] looks *1678–1684* 34 Heart-sweetening, and] *add 1684–1688*

Indeed, his Glory is veiled, and cannot be seen, but as discovered by the Father (*Matth.* 11. 27.). It is veiled with Flesh, with Meanness of Descent from the Flesh, and with that Ignominy and Shame that attended him in the Flesh; but they that can, in God's Light, see through these things, they shall see Glory in him; yea, such Glory, as will draw, and pull their Hearts unto him.

Moses was the Adopted Son of *Pharoah's* Daughter; and, for ought I know, had bin King at last, had he now conformed to the present Vanities that was there at Court; but he could not, he would not do it: Why? what was the matter? Why? he saw more in the worst of Christ (bear with the Expression), than he saw in the best of all the Treasures of the Land of *Egypt. He refused to be called the Son of* Pharaoh's *Daughter; choosing rather to suffer Affliction with the People of God, than to enjoy the Pleasures of Sin for a Season: Esteeming the Reproach of Christ greater Riches, than the Treasures in* Egypt; *for he had respect to the Recompence of Reward. He forsook* Egypt, *not fearing the Wrath of the King: But what emboldened him thus to do?* Why? he endured; for he had a Sight of the Person speaking in the Text: *He endured, as seeing Him who is Invisible.* But, I say, would a Sight of Jesus have thus taken away *Moses's* Heart from a Crown, and a Kingdom, *&c.* had he not by that Sight seen more in Him, than was to be seen in them? *Heb.* 11. 24, 25, 26, 27.

Therefore, when he saith, *Shall come to Me*, he means, They shall have a Discovery of the Glory of the Grace that is in Him; and the Beauty and Glory of *that* is of such Vertue, that it constraineth, and forceth, with a Blessed Violency, the Hearts of those that are given to Him.

Moses, of whom we spake before, was *no Child*, when he was thus taken with the Beauteous Glory of this Lord: He was *Forty Years old*, and so consequently was able, being a Man of that Wisdom and Opportunity as he was, to make the best Judgement of the Things, and of the Goodness of them that was before him in the Land of *Egypt*. But he, even he it was, that set that low Esteem upon the Glory of *Egypt*, as to count it not worth the medling with, when he had a Sight of this Lord Jesus Christ. This wicked World thinks, that the Fancies of a Heaven, and a Happiness hereafter,

3 Ignominy *1685–1688*] Ignomy *1678–1684* 22 27.] *om. 1678–1688*

may serve well enough to take the Heart of such, as either have not the Worlds good Things to delight in; or that are Fools, and know not how to delight themselves therein: But let them know again, that we have had Men of all Ranks and Qualities, that have been taken with the Glory of our Lord Jesus, and have left All to follow Him: As *Abel*, *Seth*, *Enoch*, *Noah*, *Abraham*, *Isaac*, *Jacob*, *Moses*, *Samuel*, *David*, *Solomon*; and who not, that had either Wit or Grace to savour Heavenly things? Indeed, none can stand off from Him, nor any longer out against Him, to whom he Reveals the Glory of his Grace.

And him that cometh to Me, I will in no wise cast out.]

By these Words, our Lord *Jesus* doth set forth (yet more amply) the great Goodness of his Nature towards the Coming Sinner. Before he said, They *Shall come*; and here he declareth, *That with Heart and Affections he will receive them.* But by the way, let me speak one Word or two, to the seeming Conditionality of this Promise, with which now I have to do. *And him that cometh to Me, I will not cast out:* Where it is evident (may some say), That *Christ's* Receiving us to Mercy, depends upon our Coming; and so our Salvation by *Christ* is Conditional: If we Come, we shall be Received; if not, we shall not: for that is fully intimated by the Words. The Promise of Reception is only to him that Cometh: *And him that cometh.* I Answer; that the Coming in these Words mentioned, as a Condition of being Received to Life, is that which is promised, yea, concluded to be effected in us by the Promise going before. In those latter Words, Coming to *Christ* is implicitly required of us; and in the Words before, that Grace that can make us come is positively promised to us. It is, as if he should say; All that the Father giveth Me, shall come, to *me*; and him that cometh to *me*, I will in no wise cast out thence. We come to *Christ*, because it is said, We *Shall come*; because it is given to us *to Come*: So that, the Condition which is expressed by *Christ* in these latter Words, is absolutely promised in

14 here] *om. 1688* 16 seeming] *add 1684–1688* 27 that can make us come] *add 1684–1688* 28 It is, as if he should say;] *om. 1684–1688* 29 *me*[1] *1684–1688*] Heaven *1678* *me*[2] *1684–1688*] Heaven *1678* 32 latter *1684–1688*] later *1678*

the Words before. And indeed, the Coming here intended, is nothing else but the Effect of, *Shall come to Me. They Shall come, and I will not cast them out.*

And him that cometh.]

He saith not, and him that *is come*, but, him that cometh.

To speak to these Words,

1. In general.
2. More particularly.

In general: They suggest unto us these four Things:

First, That *Jesus Christ* doth build upon it; that since the Father *gave* his People to him, they shall be enabled to *Come* unto him. *And him that cometh:* As who should say; I know, that since they are *Given* to Me, they shall be enabled to *Come* unto Me. He saith not, **If** *they come*, or **I Suppose** they will Come; but, *And him that cometh.* By these Words therefore he shews us, that he addresseth himself to the Receiving of them whom the Father gave to him, to save them: I say, he addresseth himself, or prepareth himself to Receive them: By which, as I said, he concludeth or buildeth upon it, that they shall indeed Come to Him. He looketh that the Father should bring them into his Bosom, and so stands ready to embrace them.

Secondly, *Christ* also suggesteth by these Words, That he very well knoweth who are given to him; not by their Coming to him, but by their being Given to him. *All that the Father giveth Me, shall come to Me: And him that cometh*, &c. This *Him* he knoweth to be one of them, that the Father hath Given him; and therefore, he Receiveth him, even because the Father hath Given him to Him, *Joh.* 10. *I know my Sheep*, saith he: Not only those, that already have Knowledge of him; but those too, that yet are ignorant of him. *Other Sheep have I* (said he) *which are not of this Fold:* Not of the *Jewish-Church*; but those that lie in their Sins, even the Rude and Barbarous *Gentiles*. Therefore, when *Paul* was afraid to stay at *Corinth*, from a Supposition, that some Mischief might befal him there: *Be not*

2–3 *They Shall . . . out.*] *add 1684–1688* 5 He saith . . . that cometh.] *add 1684–1688* 17–18 I say . . . Receive them:] *add 1684–1688* 19–20 He looketh . . . embrace them.] *add 1684–1688* 25 Receiveth] Received *1684–1686*[2] 26 *Joh.* 10.] *add 1684–1688*

afraid (said the Lord *Jesus* to him) *but speak; and hold not thy peace, for I have much People in this City*, Joh. 10. 16. Act. 18. 9, 10. The People that the Lord here speaks of, were not at this time accounted His, by reason of a Work of Conversion that already had passed upon them; but by Vertue of the Gift of the Father, for he had given them unto him: Therefore, was *Paul* to stay here, to speak the Word of the Lord to them; that by his Speaking, the Holy-Ghost might effectually work over their Souls, to the causing them to Come to him; who was also ready with Heart and Soul, to receive them.

Thirdly, *Christ* by these Words also suggesteth, That no more come unto Him, than indeed are given him of the Father: For the *Him* in this place, is one of the *All*, that by *Christ*, was mentioned before. All *that the Father giveth Me, shall come to Me;* and *every* Him, of that All, I will in no wise cast out. This the Apostle insinuateth, where he saith; *He gave some Apostles, and some Prophets, and some Evangelists, and some Pastors and Teachers, for the perfecting of the Saints, for the work of the Ministry, for the edifying of the Body of* Christ*: Till we* All *come in the Unity of the Faith, and of the Knowledge of the Son of God, unto a Perfect Man, unto the Measure of the Stature of the Fulness of* Christ, *Ephes.* 4. 11, 12, 13.

Mark, As in the Text, so here, he speaketh of *All*; *Untill we* All *come. We All!* All who? Doubtless, *All* that the Father giveth to *Christ*. This is further insinuated, because he calleth *this* All, The *Body* of Christ, the Measure of the Stature of the Fulness of *Christ*: By which he means, the Universal Number given, to wit, The true Elect Church; which is said to be his Body and Fulness, *Ephes.* 1. 22, 23.

Fourthly, And *Christ Jesus* by these Words further suggesteth, That he is well content with this Gift of the Father to him. All *that the Father giveth Me, shall come to Me; and him that cometh to Me, I will in no wise cast out*. I will heartily, willingly, and with great Content of Mind receive him. They shew us also, that *Christ's* Love in Receiving, is as large as his Father's Love in Giving, and no larger.

8 over *1684–1688*] out *1678* 9 to him] *add 1684–1688* 12 come *1684–1688*] came *1678* are *1684–1688*] was *1678* 19 *the Faith*] *Faith 1688* 29 And] *om. 1684–1688*

Hence he thanks him for his Gift; and also thanks him for hiding of Him, and his Things, from the rest of the Wicked, *Mat.* 11. 25. *Luk.* 10. 21.

But, *Secondly*, and more particularly. *And [him] that cometh. And [him]!* This word *Him*; By it, *Christ* looketh back to the Gift of the Father; not only in the Lump, and whole of the Gift, but to every *Him* of that Lump. As who should say; I do not only accept of the Gift of my Father in the General, but have a special Regard to every of them in Particular; and will secure not only some, or the greatest part; but *Every Him*, every Dust: Not an Hooff of all shall be lost, or left behind. And indeed, in this he consenteth to his Father's Will; which is, That of All that he hath given him, he should lose Nothing, *Joh.* 6. 39.

And him.] *Christ Jesus* also, by his thus dividing the Gift of his Father into *Hims*, and by his speaking of them in the *Singular Number*, shews, what a particular Work shall be wrought in each one, at the time appointed of the Father. *And it shall come to pass in that Day*, saith the Prophet, *that the Lord shall beat off from the Channel of the River, to the Stream of* Egypt*; and ye shall be gathered one by one, O ye Children of Israel.* Here are the *Hims* one by one to be gathered to him by the Father, *Isa.* 27. 12. He shews also hereby, That no Lineage, Kindred, or Relation, can at all be profited by any Outward or Carnal Union, with the Person that the Father hath given to *Christ*. 'Tis only *Him*, the Given *Him*, the Coming *Him*, that he intends absolutely to secure. Men make a great ado with the Children of Believers, and Oh the Children of Believers: But if the Child of the Believer is not the *Him* concerned in this absolute Promise, it is not these Mens great cry nor yet what the Parent or Child can do, that can interest him in this Promise of the Lord Christ, this absolute Promise.

And him.] There are divers sorts of Persons, that the Father hath given to *Jesus Christ*: They are not all of one Rank, of one Quality. Some are High, some Low; some are Wise, some Fools; some are more Civil, and Complying with the Law; some more Profane, and averse to Him, and his Gospel. Now, since those that are given to

6 to] to the *1688* 20–1 Here are . . . Father,] *add 1684–1688* 25–30 Men make . . . absolute Promise.] *add 1684–1688*

him, are in some sense so divers; and again, since he yet saith, *And* Him *that cometh*, &c. He by that doth give us to understand, that he is not, as Men, for picking and choosing, to take a Best, and leave a Worst; but he is for *Him*, that the Father hath given him; and that cometh to him. *He will not alter nor change it; a Good for a Bad, or a Bad for a Good*, Levit. 27. 9, 10. But will take him as he is, and will save his Soul.

There is many a sad Wretch given by the Father to *Jesus Christ*; but not one of them all is despised, or slighted by him.

It is said of those that the Father hath given to *Christ*, That they have done worse than the Heathen; That they were Murderers, Thieves, Drunkards, Unclean Persons, and what not? But he has Received them, Washed them, and Saved them. A fit Emblem of this Sort, is that wretched Instance mentioned in the Sixteenth of *Ezekiel*, that was cast out in a Stincking Condition, to the loathing of its Person in the day that it was Born: A Creature in such a wretched Condition, that no Eye pittied, to do any of the Things there mentioned unto it, or to have Compassion upon it: No Eye, but his that speaketh in the Text.

And Him.] Let him be as red as Blood, let him be as red as Crimson: Some men are blood-Red sinners, Crimson sinners, Sinners of a double die; dipt, and dipt again before they come to Jesus Christ. Art thou that readest these Lines, such an one? speak out man, Art thou such an one? and art thou now coming to Jesus Christ for the Mercy of Justification, that thou mightest be made white in his Blood, and be covered with his Righteousness? Fear not; for as much as this thy coming betokeneth, that thou art of the number of them, that the Father hath given to Christ; for he will in no wise cast thee out. *Come now*, saith Christ, *and let us reason together; though your sins be as scarlet, they shall be as white as snow; though they be as Red as Crimson, they shall be as wooll.* Isa. 1. 18.

And him] There was many a strange *him* came to Jesus Christ, in the days of his flesh; but he received them all, without turning any away. *Speaking unto them of the Kingdom of God, and Healing such as had need of healing*, Luk. 9. 11. Chap. 4. 40. These words *And him*, are therefore words to be wondered at: That not one of them, who by

6–7 But will . . . Soul.] *add 1684–1688*

vertue of the Fathers gift, and drawing, are coming to Jesus Christ; I say, that not one of them, what ever they have been, what ever they have done, should be rejected, or set by, But admitted to a share in his saving grace. 'Tis said in *Luke*, that the people *wondred at the gracious words that proceeded out of his mouth*, Luk. 4. 22. Now, this is one of his gracious words; these words are like drops of honey, as it is said; *Prov.* 16. 24. *Pleasant words are as an honey-Comb, sweet to the Soul, and health to the bones.* These are gracious words indeed, even as full as a faithful, and a merciful High Priest could speak them. *Luther* saith, *When Christ speaketh, he hath a mouth as wide as Heaven and Earth:* That is, to speak fully to the incouragement of every sinfull *him*, that is coming to Jesus Christ. And that his word is certain, hear how himself confirms it: *Heaven and Earth*, saith he, *shall pass away*; *but my word shall not pass away*, Isa. 63. 1. Mat. 24. 35.

It is also confirmed by the testimony of the Four Evangelists, who gave faithful relation of his loving reception of all Sorts of coming sinners, whether they were publicans, harlots, thieves possessed of Devils, Bedlams, and what not? *Luk.* 19. 1, 2, 3, 4, 5, 6, 7, 8. *Mat.* 21. 31. *Luk.* 15. Chap. *and* Chap. 23. 41, 42. *Mark* 16. 9. Chap. 5. 1, 2, 3, to 9.

This then shews us,

First, *The greatness of the merits of Christ.*

Secondly, *The willingness of his heart to impute them for Life to the great, if coming, sinners.*

First, This shews us the greatness of the Merits of Christ; for it must not be supposed, that his words are bigger than his worthyness. He is Strong to execute his word; he can *Do*, as well as *Speak*. *He can do exceeding abundantly more than we ask or think*, even to the uttermost, and out side of his word (*Ephes.* 3. 20.).

Now then, since he concludeth Any Coming Him: it must be concluded, that he can save to the uttermost Sin, Any coming-Him.

Do you think, I say, that the Lord Jesus did not think before he

7 *Prov.* 16. 24.] *add 1684–1688* 13 his] this *1688* confirms *1684–1688*] confines *1678* 20 21. 31.] 21. 21. *1678–1688* Chap. *and* Chap.] and *chap. 1685–1688* 16. 9.] 19. 9. *1678–1688* 34–p. 297, l. 2. Do you . . . *Isa.* 63. 1.] *add 1684–1688*

spake? He spake all in Righteousness, and therefore by his word we are to Judge how Mighty he is to Save, *Isa.* 63. 1.

He speaketh in Righteousness, in very faithfulness, when he began to build this blessed Gospel Fabrick, the Text: It was for that, he had first sat down, and counted the cost; and for that he knew he was able to finish it. What Lord, **Any** *him*! **Any** *him*, that *cometh* to thee! This is a Christ *worth* looking after, this is a Christ *worth* coming to.

This then, should learn us diligently to consider the Natural force of every word of God: and to judge of Christ's ability to save; not by our sins, or by our shallow apprehensions of his Grace; but by his word, which is the true measure of Grace.

And if we do not judge thus, we shall dishonor his Grace, lose the benefit of his word, and needlesly fright our selves into many Discouragements, though coming to Jesus Christ. *Him*, *any* him that cometh, hath sufficient from this word of Christ, to feed himself with hopes of Salvation. As thou art therefore coming, O thou coming sinner, Judge thou, whether Christ can save thee, by the true Sense of his words? Judge, coming sinner, of the Efficacy of his Blood, of the perfection of his Righteousness, and of the prevailancy of his intercession, by his word. *And him*, saith he, *that cometh to me, I will in no wise cast out*. In *no wise*, that is, for no Sin: Judge therefore by his word, how able he is to save thee? It is said of Gods Sayings to the Children of *Israel*; *There failed not ought of any good thing, which the Lord had spoken to the house of* Israel*; all came to pass.* And again; *Not one thing hath failed of all the good things which the Lord your God spoke concerning you, all are come to pass unto you; and not one thing hath failed thereof*, Josh. 21. 45. Chap. 23. 14.

Coming sinner, what promise thou findest in the word of Christ, strain it whither thou canst, so thou dost not corrupt it, and his Blood and Merits will answer all, what the word saith, or any true Consequence that is drawn there-from, that we may boldly venture upon; As here in the Text, he saith; *And* **Him** *that cometh*; indefinitely; without the least intimation of the rejection of any, though

1 spake] spakes *1684*] speakes *1685–1688* 16 sufficient] *add 1684–1688* 30 whither *1685–1688*] whether *1678–1684* 33–4 indefinitely *1685–1688*] indefinitively *1678–1684*

never so great, if he be a coming-sinner. Take it then for granted, that thou, whoever thou art, if coming, art intended in these words: neither shall it injure Christ at all, if, as *Benhadad's* Servants *served Ahab*, thou shalt catch him at his word. *Now*, saith the Text, *The Men did diligently observe whether any thing would come from him*; to wit, any word of grace; *and did hastily catch it*: And it happened, that *Ahab* had called *Benhadad*, his *brother*. The men replyed therefore, *Thy brother Benhadad?* catching him at his word, 1 *King*. 20. 33. Sinner, coming sinner, serve Jesus Christ thus, and he will take it kindly at thy hands. When he in his argument called the *Canaanitish* woman, **Dog**, she catcht him at it, and said; *Truth Lord, yet the Dogs eat of the Crumbs that fall from their Masters Table*. I say, she catcht him thus in his words, and he took it kindly; saying, *O woman, great is thy faith! be it unto thee even as thou wilt*, Mat. 15. 26, 27, 28. Catch him, coming sinner, catch him. In his words surely he will take it kindly, and will not be offended at thee.

Secondly, The other thing that I told you, is shewed us from these words, is this; *The willingness of Christ's heart, to impute his merits for Life to the great, if coming, sinner. And him that cometh to me, I will in no wise cast out.*

The awakned coming sinner, doth not so easily question the power of Christ, as his willingness to save him. *Lord, if thou wilt, thou canst*, said one, *Mar*. 1. 40. He did not put the **If** upon his power, but upon his will: he concluded, he *could*; but he was not as fully of perswasion, that he *would*. But we have the same ground to believe, he *will*, as we have to believe he *can*; and indeed, ground for both, is the Word of God. If he was not willing, why did he promise? why did he say, he would receive the coming sinner? Coming Sinner, take notice of this we use to plead practices with Men, and why not with God likewise? I am sure we have no more ground for one then the other, for we have to plead the promise of a Faithful God. *Jacob* took him there; *Thou saidst*, says he, *I will surely do thee Good*, Gen. 32. 12. For, from this promise he concluded, that it followed in reason, *He must be willing*.

7 had] *add 1684–1688* 14 27, 28.] *om. 1678–1688* 15–16 In his . . . at thee.] *add 1684–1688* 17 us] *om. 1685–1688* 29–32 Coming Sinner . . . God.] *add 1684–1688* 31 one then *1684*] one than *1685*] the one than *1686[1]–1688*

The Text also gives some ground for us, to draw the same conclusion. *And him that cometh to me, I* **will** *in no wise cast out.* Here is his willingness asserted, as well as his power suggested. It is worth your observation, that *Abraham's* Faith considered rather Gods power, than his willingness; that is, he drew this Conclusion, *I shall have a Child*, from the Power that was in God to fulfill the Promise to him: for he concluded, he was willing to give him one, else he would not have promised one. *He staggered not at the promise of God through unbelief, but was strong in faith, giving glory to God; being fully perswaded, that what he had promised, he was* **able** *to perform*, Rom. 4. 20, 21. But was not his faith *exercised*, or tryed, about his willingness too? No, there was no shew of reason for that, because he had promised it; indeed, had he not promised it, he might Lawfully have doubted it; but since he had promised it, there was left no ground at all for doubting; because his willingness to give a Son, was demonstrated in his promising him a Son. These words therefore, are sufficient ground to incourage any coming sinner, that Christ is willing to his power, to receive him; and since he hath *power* also to do what he *will*, there is no ground at all left to the coming sinner, any more to doubt; but to come in full hope of acceptance, and of being received unto grace and mercy. *And him that* [*cometh*]. He saith not, And him that is **Come**; but, and him that **Cometh**; that is, and him, whose heart *begins* to move after me, who is *leaving* all for my sake; *him*, who is looking out, who is on his Journey to me. We must therefore distinguish betwixt *coming*, and being *come* to Jesus Christ. He that is *come* to him, has attained of him more sensibly, what he felt before he wanted; than he has, that but yet is *coming* to him.

A Man that is *come* to Christ, hath the advantage of him that is but *coming* to him; and that in seven things.

First, He that is *come* to Christ, is nearer to him, than he that is but *coming* to him; for he that is *but* coming to him, is yet, in some sense, at a distance from him; as it is said of the coming prodigal; *And while he was yet a great way off, Luk.* 15. 20. Now, he that is nearer to him, hath the best sight of him; and so, is able to make the best Judgement of his wonderful grace & beauty, as God saith; *Let them come near, then let them speak.* And as the Apostle *John* saith;

4 Gods *1684–1688*] his *1678*   5 this] his *1686*[1]   33 20.] *om. 1678–1688*

And we have seen, and do testifie, that God sent his Son to be the Saviour of the world, Isa. 41. 1. 1 Joh. 4. 14. He that is not yet come, though he is *a-coming*, is not fit, not being indeed capable, to make that Judgement of the worth and glory of the Grace of Christ, as he is that is come to him, and hath seen and beheld it. Therefore Sinner suspend thy Judgment till thou art come nearer.

Secondly, He that is *come* to Christ, has the advantage of him that is but *coming*, in that he is eased of his burden; for he that is but coming, is not eased of his burden, *Mat.* 11. 28. He that is *come*, has cast his burden upon the Lord; by Faith he hath seen himself released thereof: but he that is but *coming*, hath it yet, as to sense, and feeling, upon his own shoulders. *Come unto me, all ye that Labor, and are heavy Laden*, implies, that their burden, though they are coming, is yet upon them; and so will be, till indeed they are *come* to him.

Thirdly, He that is *come* to Christ, has the advantage of him that is but *coming*: in this also, namely; He hath drank of the Sweet, and Soul-refreshing Water of Life; but he that is but *coming*, hath not: *If any man thirst, let him* Come *unto me and drink.*

Mark, he must Come to him, before he drinks; according to that of the Prophet: *Ho every one that thirsteth,* Come *ye to the Waters.* He drinketh not as he cometh, but when he is *come* to the Waters, *Joh.* 7. 37. *Isa.* 55. 1.

Fourthly, He that is *come* to Christ, hath the advantage of him, that as yet is but coming: in this also, to wit, He is not so terrified with the noise, and, as I may call it, *Hue and Cry*; which the Avenger of blood makes at the heels of him, that yet, is but coming to him. When the Slayer was upon his flight to the City of his refuge, he had the noise or fear of the Avenger of blood at his heels; but when he was come to the City, and was entred there-into, that noise ceased: Even so it is with him, that is but coming to Jesus Christ; he heareth many a dreadful Sound in his ears; sounds of death and damnation; which he that is *come*, is at present freed from. Therefore he saith; Come, *and I will give you rest:* And so he saith again; *We* that have believed, do enter into rest, as he said, *&c.* Heb. 4.

3 *a-coming*] *coming 1685–1688* 5 come] to come *1684–1688* 5–6 Therefore . . . nearer.] *add 1684–1688* 9 eased of his burden] *add. 1684–1688* 22 55. 1.] 45. 1. *1678–1688* 31 ears] Ear *1685–1688* 34 Heb. 4.] *add 1684–1688*

Now the believing there intended, is a believing on Christ; as *come* unto him for rest, is only found in him, by them that are **Come** to him.

Fifthly, He therefore that is *come* to Christ, is not so subject to those dejections, and castings down, by reason of the rage and assaults of the evil one; as is the man, that is but coming to Jesus Christ (tho he has Temptations too). [*And while he was yet a-coming, the Devil threw him down, and* **Tore** *him*, Luk. 9. 42.] For he has, though Satan still Roareth upon him, those experimental comforts, and refreshments (to wit) in his treasury, to present himself with, in times of Temptation and Conflict; which he that is but *coming*, has not.

Sixthly, He that is *come* to Christ, has the advantage of him that is but coming to him: in this also, to wit, He hath upon him the Wedding Garment, *&c.* But he that is *coming*, has not. The *Prodigal*, when coming home to his Father, was cloathed with nothing but Rags, and was tormented with an empty belly: but when he was *come*, the best Robe is brought out; also, the Gold Ring, and the shooes; yea, they are put upon him, to his great rejoycing. The fatted Calf was killed for him; the musick was struck up, to make him merry: and thus also the Father himself Sang of him; *This my Son was dead, and is alive again; was lost, and is found*, Luk. 15. 18, 19, 20, 21, 22, 23, 24.

Seventhly, In a word, he that is *come* to Christ, his groans, and tears, his doubts, and fears, are turned into Songs and Praises; for that he hath now received the atonement, and the earnest of his inheritance: But he that is but yet a *coming*, hath not those Praises, nor Songs of deliverance with him, nor has he as yet, received the atonement, and earnest of his Inheritance, which is, the Sealing testimony of the Holy Ghost, through the sprinkling of the Blood of Christ upon his Conscience; for he is not come: *Rom.* 5. 11. *Ephes.* 1. 13. *Heb.* 12. 22, 23, 24.

And him that [*Cometh*].

There is further to be gathered from this word [*Cometh*], these following particulars.

1–3 Now the . . . to him.] *om. 1684–1688* 23 22, 23, 24] &c. *1685–1688*

First, That *Jesus Christ* hath his Eye upon, and takes notice of the First Moving of the Heart of a Sinner after himself: Coming-Sinner, thou canst not move with Desires after *Christ*, but he sees the Working of those Desires in thy Heart. *All my Desires*, said *David*, *are before thee*, *and my Groanings are not hid from thee*, Psal. 38. 9. This he spake, as he was coming (after he had back sliden) to the Lord *Jesus Christ*. 'Tis said of the Prodigal, *That while he was yet a great way off*, *his Father saw him*, had his Eye upon him, and upon the going out of his Heart after him, *Luk*. 15. 20.

When *Nathaniel* was *come* to *Jesus Christ*, the Lord said unto them that stood before him; *Behold*, *an* Israelite *indeed*, *in whom there is no Guile*. But *Nathaniel* answered him, *Whence knowest thou me? Jesus* answered, *Before that* Philip *called thee*, *when thou wast under the Fig-Tree*, *I saw thee*. There, I suppose, *Nathaniel* was pouring out of his Soul to God for Mercy, or that he would give him good Understanding about the *Messias* to come: And *Jesus* saw all the Workings of his honest Heart at that time, *Joh*. 1. 47, 48.

Zacheus also had some secret Movings of Heart, such as they was, towards *Jesus Christ*; when he ran before, and climbed up the Tree to see him; and the Lord *Jesus Christ* had his Eye upon him: Therefore, when he was come to the Place, he looked up to him, bids him *come* down; *For to Day* (said he) *I must abide at thy House*: To wit, in order to the further Compleating the Work of Grace in his Soul, *Luk*. 19. 1, 2, 3, 4, 5, 6, 7, 8. Remember this, Coming-Sinner!

Secondly, As *Jesus Christ* has his Eye upon; so he hath his Heart open, to receive the Coming Sinner. This is verified by the Text: *And him that cometh to Me*, *I will in no wise cast out*. This is also discovered by his preparing of the Way, in his making of it Easie (as may be) to the Coming-Sinner; which Preparation is manifest by them Blessed Words, *I will in no wise cast out*: Of which, more when we come to the Place. And while he was yet a great way off, his Father saw him, *and had Compassion on him; and ran*, *and fell on his Neck*, *and kissed him* (Luk. 15. 20). All these Expressions do strongly prove, that the Heart of Christ is open to receive the Comming-Sinner.

2 himself] him *1686*[2]*–1688* 10 unto] to *1685–1688* 18 was] were *1685–1688*

Thirdly, As Jesus Christ has his Eye upon, and his Heart open to receive; so he hath resolved already, that nothing shall alienate his Heart from receiving the Coming-Sinner. No Sins of the Coming-Sinner, nor the Length of the Time that he hath abode in them, shall by any Means prevail with Jesus Christ to reject him. Coming-Sinner, thou art coming to a loving Lord Jesus!

Fourthly, These Words therefore are dropt from his Blessed Mouth, on purpose, that the Coming Sinner might take Encouragement to continue on his Journey, until he be come indeed to Jesus Christ. It was doubtless, a great Encouragement to Blind *Bartlimeus*, that Jesus Christ stood still, and called him, when he was crying; *Jesus, thou Son of* David, *have Mercy on me:* Therefore, 'tis said, He cast away his Garment, *Rose up, and* **Came** *to Jesus*, Mark 10. 46, *&c.* Now, if a Call to *come* hath such Encouragement in it, what is a Promise of Receiving such, but an Encouragement much more? And observe it, though he had a Call to *come*, yet not having a Promise, his Faith was forced to work upon a meer Consequence: Saying, He calls me; and surely, since he calls me, he will grant me my Desire. Ah! but Coming-Sinner, thou hast no need to go so far about, as to draw (in this Matter) Consequences; because thou hast plain Promises: *And him that cometh to me, I will in no wise cast out.* Here is full, plain; yea, what Encouragement one can desire: For, suppose thou was admitted to make a Promise thy self, and Christ should attest, that he would fulfil it upon the Sinner, that cometh to him; Couldest thou make a better Promise? Couldest thou invent a more full, free, or larger Promise? A Promise, that looks at the first Moving of the Heart after Jesus Christ! A Promise, that declares, yea, that ingageth Christ Jesus to open his Heart, to receive the Coming-Sinner: Yea, further; A Promise, that Demonstrateth that the Lord Jesus is resolved freely to receive, & will in no wise cast out, nor means to reject the Soul of the Coming sinner. For all this lieth fully in this Promise, and doth naturally flow therefrom. Here thou needest not make use of far-fetcht Consequences, nor strain thy Wits, to force encouraging Arguments from the Text. Comming-Sinner, the Words are plain; *And him that cometh to Me, I will in no wise cast out.*

7 dropt] drop *1685*] drop'd *1686*[1]–*1688* 23 was] wast *1685–1688*

And **Him** *that* [*Cometh*].

There are two Sorts of sinners that are coming to Jesus Christ.

First, *Him that hath never, while of late, at all, began to come.*

Secondly, *Him that came formerly, and after that went back; but hath since bethought himself, and is now coming again.*

Both these sorts of sinners are intended by the **Him** in the Text, as is evident; because, **Both** are now the coming Sinners.

And **Him** *that cometh*, &c.

For the first of these; the sinner that hath never, while of late, began to come, his way is more easie: I do not say, more plain, and open, to come to Christ, than is the other (those last not having the Clog of a guilty Conscience, for the sin of Back-sliding hanging at their Heels). But all the incouragement of the Gospel (with what invitations are therein contained), to coming sinners, are as *free*, and as *open* to the one as to the other; so that they may with the *same* freedom and liberty, as from the word, both alike claim interest in the promise. *All things are ready*: All things, for the coming back-sliders, as well as for the others: *Come to the Wedding*: *And let him that is a thirst, come*, Mat. 22. 1, 2, 3, 4. Revel. 22. 17.

But having spoken to the first of these already, I shall here pass it by; and shall speak a word or two to him that is coming, after back-sliding, to Jesus Christ for life.

Thy way, O thou sinner of a double dye, thy way is *open* to come to Jesus Christ: I mean, *thee* whose heart, after long back-sliding, doth think of turning to him again. Thy way, I say, is open to him, as is the way of the other sorts of Comers; as appears by what follows.

First, *Because the Text makes no Exception against thee*; it doth not say, And *any* him; **But**, a back-slider; *any him*, **But** *him*: The Text doth not thus object, but indefinitely openeth wide its *Golden Arms*, to every coming soul, without the least Exception. Therefore thou

30 indefinitely *1685–1688*] indifinitively *1678–1684*

maist come. And take heed that thou shut not that door against thy Soul by unbelief, which God has opened by his Grace.

Secondly, Nay, the Text is so far from excepting against thy coming, that it strongly suggesteth, that thou art one of the souls intended, O thou coming back-slider: Else, what need that Clause have been so inserted, *I will in no wise cast out*: No, as who should say, though those that come now, are such as have formerly back-sliden, I will in **No** wise cast away the Fornicator, the Covetous, the Railer, the Drunkard, or other common Sinners; nor yet the Back-slider neither.

Thirdly, That the Back-slider is intended, is evident,

First, For that he is sent to *By* **Name**: *Go, tell his Disciples, and* **Peter**, Mark 16. 7. But *Peter* was a Godly Man: True; but he was also a Back-slider: yea, a desperate Back-slider. He had Denyed his Master once, twice, thrice; Cursing and Swearing, that he knew him not. If this was not Back-sliding; if this was not an High and Eminent Back-sliding; yea, a higher Back-sliding than thou art capable of, I have thought amiss.

Again, When *David* had back-sliden, and had committed Adultery and Murder in his Back-sliding, he must be sent to by **Name**. *And*, saith the Text, *the Lord sent* Nathan *to* **David**. And he sent him to tell him, after he had brought him to unfeigned Acknowledgment of his Fact; *The Lord hath also put away, or forgiven* **Thy** *Sin*, 2 Sam. 12. 1, 13.

This Man also was far gone; He took a Man's Wife, and Kill'd her Husband; and endeavoured to cover all with wicked dissimulation; he did this, I say, after God had exalted him, and shewed him great favor, wherefore his Transgression was greatned also by the Prophet with mighty aggravations: yet, he was accepted, and that with gladness, at the first step he took in this returning to Christ; for the first step of the back-sliders return, is to say sensibly, and unfeignedly, *I have sinned*: But he had no sooner said this, but a pardon was produced, yea thrust into his bosom. *And Nathan said unto* **David**, *the Lord hath also put away* **Thy** *sin.*

1–2 And take . . . his Grace.] *add 1684–1688* 6 No,] *om. 1684–1688* 23 of his Fact] *om. 1684–1688* 24 13.] *om. 1678–1688* 32 this] thus *1686*[1]–*1688*

Secondly, As the person of the back-slider is mentioned by **Name**, so also is his **Sin**, that if possible thy Objections against thy returning to Christ, may be taken out of thy way. I say it is mentioned by Name, and mixed as mentioned with words of grace and favor. *I will heal their backsliding*, and love them freely, (*Hos.* 14. 4.) What sayest thou now back-slider!

Thirdly, Nay further, thou art not only mentioned by *name*, and thy *sin* by the *nature* of it, but thou thy self who art a *returning back-slider*, *put*

First, Among Gods **Israel**. *Return O back-sliding* Israel, *saith the Lord, and I will not cause mine anger to fall upon you:* **For** *I am mercifull, saith the Lord, and will not keep anger for ever*, Jer. 3. 12.

Secondly, Thou art put among his **Children**, among his Children to whom he is *married*. Turn O back-sliding Children, for I am married unto you, *vers.* 14.

Thirdly, Yea after all this, as if his heart was so full of Grace for them, that he was pressed untill he had uttered it before them, he adds, *Return ye back-sliding Children, and I will heal your back-slidings.*

Fourthly, Nay further, the Lord hath considered, that the *shame* of thy *sin* hath stopped thy mouth, and made thee almost a prayer-less man; and therefore he saith unto thee, *Take with you words, and turn unto the Lord, and say unto him, take away all iniquity and receive us graciously*: See his grace! that himself should put words of incouragement into the heart of a back-slider: As he saith in another place, *I taught* Ephraim *to go, taking him by the Arms. This* is teaching him to go indeed, to put words into his mouth, to hold him up by the Arms, by the Chin, as we say, *Hos.* 14. 1, 2, 3, 4. *Chap.* 11. 3.

From what hath been said I conclude, even as I said before, that the **Him** in the Text, *And him that cometh*, includeth both these sorts of Sinners, and therefore both should freely come.

Question, *But where doth Jesus Christ, in all the words of the New-Testament, Expresly speak to a returning back-slider with words of Grace and Peace? For what you have urged as yet, from the New Testament, is nothing but Consequences drawn from this* Text. *Indeed it is a full* Text *for*

3 it is] thy sin also *1684–1688* 3–4 by Name] *add 1684–1688* 10 Among] Amongst *1685–1688* 18 *back-slidings*] *back-sliding 1686[1]–1688* 26 to put words into his mouth] *om. 1686[1]–1688* 31 Question] Quest. *1685–1688* *words*] *word 1685–1686[1]*

carnal ignorant sinners that come, but to me who am a back-slider it yeeldeth but little relief.

Answ. First, How! but little incouragement from the Text, when it saith, *I will in no wise cast out*? What more could have been said? what is here omitted that might have been inserted, to make the promise more full and free? Nay, take all the promises in the Bible, all the freest promises, with all the variety of expressions of what nature or extent soever, and they can but amount to the expressions of this very promise; *I will in* **no wise** *cast out*: I will for nothing, by no means, upon no account, however they have sinned, however they have back-sliden, however they have provoked, cast out the coming sinner. But,

Secondly, *Thou sayst, where doth Jesus Christ in all the words of the New Testament, speak to a returning back-slider with words of Grace and Peace?* that is, under the name of a back-slider.

Answ. Where there is such plenty of examples in receiving back-sliders, there is the less need of Express words to that intent; one promise, as the Text is, with those Examples that are annexed, are instead of many promises. And besides, I reckon that the Act of receiving, is of as much, if not of more incouragement, than is a bare promise to receive; for receiving is as the promise, and the fulfilling of it too: So that in the *Old* Testament thou hast the promise, and in the *New*, the fulfilling of it: and that in divers examples.

1. In *Peter. Peter* denyed his Master, once, twice, thrice, and that with open oath; yet Christ receives him again without any the least hesitation or stick. Yea he slips, stumbles, falls again, in down right Dissimulation, and that to the hurt and fall of many others; but neither of this doth Christ make a bar to his Salvation, but receives him again at his return, as if he knew nothing of the fault, *John* 21.

Secondly, The rest of the disciples, even all of them, backslide and leave the Lord Jesus in his greatest straights: *Then all the Disciples forsook him and fled, they returned* (as he had fore-told), *every one to his own, and left him alone*; but this also, he passes over as a very light matter; not that it was so indeed, in it self, but the abundance of

4 saith] is said *1686*[1]*–1688* 21 as the *1684–1688*] as *1678* 24 1.] *First, 1688* 30 *John* 21.] *Gal.* 2. *1678–1688*

grace that was in him did lightly *role* it away; for after his Resurrection, when at first he appeared unto them, he gives them not the least check for their perfidious dealing with him, but salutes them with words of Grace, saying; *All hail*, *be not afraid*, *Peace be to you; All Power in Heaven and Earth is given unto me*. True, he rebuked them for their unbelief, for the which thou also deservest the same; for, 'tis unbelief that alone puts Christ and his benefits from us, *Mat*. 26. 56. *Joh*. 16. 32. *Mat*. 28. 9, 10, 18. *Luk*. 24. 36. *Mar*. 16. 14.

Thirdly, The man that after a large profession, lay with his Fathers Wife, committed a high Transgression, even such an one, that at that day was not heard of, no, not among the Gentiles. Wherefore this was a desperate back-sliding; yet at his return, he was received, and accepted again to Mercy, 1 *Cor*. 5. 1, 2. 2 *Cor*. 2. 6, 7, 8.

Fourthly, The Thief that stole, was bid to steal no more; not at all doubting but that Christ was ready to forgive him this Act of backsliding, *Ephes*. 4. 28.

Now all these are Examples, particular instances of Christs readiness to receive the Backsliders to Mercy; and observe it, examples and proofs that he *hath* done so, are to our unbelieving hearts, stronger incouragements, than bare Promises, that so he *will* do. But again, the Lord Jesus hath added to these for the incouragement of returning Backsliders, to come to him,

First, *A Call to come*, and he will receive them, *Revel*. 2. 1, 2, 3, 4, 5, 14, 15, 16, 20, 21, 22. *Chap*. 3. 1, 2, 3, 15, 16, 17, 18, 19, 20, 21, 22. Wherefore, New Testament Backsliders have incouragement to come.

Secondly, A Declaration of readiness to receive them that Come, as here in the Text, and in many other places is plain: Therefore, *Set thee up these Marks*, *make thee these high heaps* (of the golden Grace of the Gospel), *set thine heart towards the high-way*, *even the way that thou wentest* (when thou didst backslide) *turn again*, *O Virgin of Israel; turn again to these thy Cities*, Jer. 31. 21.

And him that [*Cometh*]. He saith not, And *him* that talketh, that professeth, that maketh a shew, a noise, or the like, but *him that*

3 with him *1684–1688*] with them *1678* 6 thou also] also thou *1686*[1]*–1688* 'tis] it is *1685–1688* 8 16. 32.] 16. 52. *1688* 10 an] a *1684–1688* 21 these *1684–1688*] those *1678*

Cometh. Christ will take leave to judge, who, among the many that make a Noise, they be that indeed are *coming to him.* It is not him that saith he *comes*, nor him of whom others affirm that he *comes*; but him that Christ himself shall say *doth Come*; that is concern'd in this Text. When the Woman that had the bloody Issue came to him for Cure, there were others as well as she, that made a great bussle about him, that touched, yea thronged him; Ah, but Christ could distinguish this woman from them all. *And he looked round about upon them all, to see* **her** *that had done this thing*, Mar. 5. 25, 26, 27, 28, 29, 30, 31, 32. He was not concerned with the thronging, or touchings of the rest; for theirs were but accidental, or, at best, void of that which made her touch acceptable. Wherefore Christ must be Judg who they be that in Truth are coming to him; *Every mans way is right in his own Eyes, but the Lord weigheth the Spirits:* It standeth therefore every one in hand to be certain of their coming to Jesus Christ; for as thy coming is, so shall thy Salvation be: If thou comest indeed, thy Salvation shall be indeed; but if thou comest but in outward appearance, so shall thy Salvation be: But of coming see before, as also afterwards in the Use and Application.

And him that cometh [*to me*].

These words [*to me*], are also well to be heeded; for by them, as he secureth those that come to him, so also he shews himself unconcerned with those that in their coming rest short, or turn aside to others; For you must know, that every one that comes, comes not to Jesus Christ; some that come, come to *Moses*, and to his Law, and then take up for Life; with these Christ is not concerned; with these this Promise hath not to do. *Christ is become of none* effect *unto you, whosoever of you are justified by the Law, ye are falen from grace*, Gal. 5. 3, 4. Again, some that came, come no farther than to Gospel Ordinances, and there stay, they come not through them to Christ; with these neither is he concerned; nor will their *Lord, Lord*, avail them any thing in the great and dismal day. A man may come too,

9 5.] *om. 1678–1688* 21 well to be] to be well *1688* 23 or] to *1685–1688* 25 come, come *1685–1688*] come, came *1678–1684* 29 came, come] came, came *1686*[1]*–1688* farther] further *1684–1688* 30 come] came *1685–1688*

and also go from the place and Ordinances of Worship, and yet not be remembred by Christ. *So I saw the wicked buried*, said Solomon, *who had come and gone from the place of the Holy, and they were forgotten in the City; when they had so done, this is also Vanity*, Eccles. 8. 10.

[*To me.*] These words therefore, are by Jesus Christ very warily put in, and serve for *caution*, and *incouragement*: for *caution*, lest we take up, in our coming, any where short of Christ; and for *incouragement* to those that shall in their coming, come past all, till they come to Jesus Christ; *And him that cometh to me, I will in no wise cast out.*

Reader, If thou lovest thy Soul, take this *Caution* kindly at the hands of Jesus Christ. Thou seest thy Sickness, thy Wound, thy necessity of Salvation; well, go not to King *Jareb*, for he cannot Heal thee, nor Cure thee of thy Wound (*Hos.* 5. 13.). Take the *Caution*, I say, lest Christ, insteed of being a Saviour to thee, becomes a Lion, a young Lion to tare thee, and go away, *vers.* 14.

There is a coming, but not to the most High; there is a coming, but not with the whole Heart, but as it were feignedly; therefore take the *Caution* kindly, *Jer.* 3. 10. *Hos.* 7. 16.

And him that cometh [*To me*]. Christ, as a Saviour, will stand alone, because his own Arm alone hath brought Salvation unto him; He will not be joyned with *Moses*, nor suffer *John* Baptist to be tabernacled by him: I say, thay must vanish, for Christ will stand alone (*Luk.* 9. 28, 36.), yea, God the Father will have it so; therefore, they must be parted from him, and a Voice from Heaven must come to bid the Disciples hear, **only** *the beloved Son.* Christ will not suffer any Law, Ordinance, Statute, or Judgement, to be partners with him in the salvation of the Sinner. Nay, he saith not, And him that cometh to my **word**; but, And him that cometh to **me**. The words of Christ, even his most blessed and free Promises, such as this in the Text, are not the Saviour of the World; for **that** is Christ himself; Christ himself **only**. The Promises therefore, are but to incourage the coming sinner to come to Jesus Christ, and not to rest in them short of Salvation by him.

And him that cometh [*To me*]. The man therefore that comes aright, casts all things behind his back; and looketh at, nor hath

6 lest] least *1686*[1]   14 lest] least *1686*[1]   26 Statute] Stature *1686*[1]
30 is] in *1686*[1]–*1686*[2]

his expectation from ought but the Son of God alone, as *David* said, *My Soul, wait thou* **only** *upon God, for my expectation is from him: He only is my Rock, and my Salvation; he is my Defence, I shall not be moved*, Psal. 62. 5, 6. His Eye is to Christ, his Heart is to Christ, and his expectation is from him, from him **only**.

Therefore, the man that comes to Christ, is one that hath had deep Considerations of his own sins, slighting thoughts of his own Righteousness, and high thoughts of the Blood and Righteousness of Jesus Christ; yea he sees, as I have said, more vertue in the Blood of Christ to save him, than there is in all his sins to damn him. He therefore setteth Christ before his Eyes, there is nothing in Heaven or Earth, he knows, that can save his Soul, and secure him from the Wrath of God, but Christ; that is, nothing but his personal Righteousness, and Blood.

And him that cometh to me, I will [in no wise] cast out. In no wise: By these words there is somthing expressed, and somthing implyed. That which is expressed, is Christ Jesus his unchangable Resolution to Save the Coming sinner; *I will in no wise* reject him, or deny him the benefit of my Death and Righteousness. This word therefore is like that which he speaks of the everlasting damnation of the sinner in Hell-fire, *He shall by no means depart thence; that is, never*, never, never come out again; no, not to all Eternity, *Mat.* 5. 26. *chap.* 25. 46. So that, as he that is condemned into Hell-fire, hath no ground of hope for his deliverance thence; so him that cometh to Christ, hath no ground to fear he shall ever be cast in thither.

Thus saith the Lord, If Heaven above can be measured, or the Foundation of the Earth searched out beneath, I will also cast away all the seed of Israel, *for all that they have done, saith the Lord*, Jer. 31. 37.

Thus saith the Lord, if my Covenant be not with Day and Night, and if I have not appointed the Ordinances of Heaven, and Earth, then will I cast away the Seed of Jacob. But Heaven can not be measured, nor the Foundations of the Earth searched out beneath; his Covenant is also with day and night, and he hath appointed the Ordinances of Heaven; therefore he will not cast away the Seed of *Jacob*, who are the coming ones; but will certainly save them from the dreadful

4 6.] *om. 1678–1688*   22 5. 26.] 5. 25. *1678–1688*   31 nor the *1684–1688*] not the *1678*   32 his] this *1686*[1]*–1688*

Wrath to come, *Jer.* 33. 25, 26. *chap.* 50. 4, 5. By this therefore it is manifest, that it is not the greatness of sin, nor thy long continuance in it, no, nor yet thy back-sliding, nor the pollution of thy Nature, that can put a bar in against, or be an hinderance of the Salvation of the coming sinner. For, if indeed this could be, then would this solemn and absolute Determination of the Lord Jesus, of its self fall to the ground, and be made of none effect: *But his Counsel shall stand, and he will do all his pleasure.* That is, his pleasure in this; for this promise, this irreversible conclusion, ariseth of his Pleasure; and he will stand to it, and will fulfil it, because it is his pleasure.

Suppose that one man had the sins, or as many sins as an hundred, and another should have an hundred times as many as he; yet if they come, this word, *I will in no wise cast out*, secures them both alike.

Suppose a man hath a desire to be saved, and for that purpose is coming in truth to Jesus Christ, but he by his debauched Life, has damned many in hell: why, the dore of hope is by these words set as open for him, as it is for him that hath not the thousandth part of his Transgressions. *And him that cometh to me, I will in no wise cast out.*

Suppose a man is coming to Christ to be Saved, and hath nothing but sin, and an ill-spent life to bring with him; Why, let him come, and welcome to Jesus Christ, *And he will in no wise cast him out*, Luk. 7. 43. Is not this Love that passeth knowledg? is not this Love the wonderment of Angels? and is not this Love worthy of all acceptation at the hands and hearts of all coming sinners?

Secondly, That which is *implyed* in the words, is

First, The coming Souls hath those that continually lie at Jesus Christ, to cast them off.

Secondly, *The coming Souls are afraid, that these will prevail with Christ to cast them off.*

For these words are spoken to satisfie us, and to stay up our Spirits against these two dangers: *I will in no wise cast out.*

2 is] was *1684–1688* thy] the *1684–1688* 3 thy[1]] the *1684–1688* 7 its] it *1685–1688* 9 this promise] his promise *1684–1688* 10 and he] he *1684–1688* 24 7. 43.] 7. 41. *1678–1688* 26 all] *add 1685–1688* 28 *hath those*] *have those 1684*] *have these 1685–1686*[2]] *have those 1688* 29 *off.*] *om. 1678–1688* 30 *these*] *those 1688*

First, For the First, *Coming Souls have those that continually lye at Jesus Christ to cast them off.*

And there are three things, that thus bend themselves against the coming sinner.

First, There is the **Devil**, that Accuser of the brethren, that accuses them before God, day and night, *Revel.* 12. 10. This Prince of Darkness is unwearied in this work; he doth it, as you see day and night, that is, without ceasing: He continually puts in his Caveats against thee, if so be he may prevail. How did he ply it against that good man *Job*, if possible he might have obtained his destruction in Hell fire? He objected against him, that he served not God for nought, and tempted God to put forth his Hand against him; urging, that if he did it, he would Curse him to his face; and all this, as God witnesseth, *He did without a Cause*, Job 1. 9, 10, 11. *chap.* 2. 4, 5. How did he ply it with Christ against *Joshua* the high Priest? *And he shewed me* Joshua, said the Prophet, *the high Priest, standing before the Angel of the Lord, and Satan standing at his right hand to resist him*, Zech. 3. 1. *To resist him*; that is, to prevail with the Lord Jesus Christ to resist him: Objecting, the uncleanness and unlawful Marriage of his Sons with the Gentiles; for that was the Crime that Satan laid against them, *Ezra* 10. 18. Yea, and for ought I know, *Joshua* was also guilty of the fact; but if not of that, of Crimes no whit inferior; for he was *Cloathed with filthy Garments, as he stood before the Angel*: neither had he one word to say in vindication of himself, against all that this wicked one had to lay against him: But notwithstanding that, he came off well; but he might for it, thank a good Lord Jesus, because he did not resist him, but contrariwise took up his cause, pleaded against the Devil, excused his infirmity, and put justifying Robes upon him before his Adversaries Face.

And the Lord said unto Satan, The Lord Rebuke thee, O Satan, even the Lord that hath chosen Jerusalem *Rebuke thee. Is not this a Brand pluckt out of the Fire? And he answered and spake to those that stood before him, saying, Take away the filthy Garments from him; and to him he said, Behold, I have caused thine iniquities to pass from thee, and will Cloath thee with chang of Raiment.*

18 1.] *om. 1678–1688* 25 lay] say *1684–1688* 28 excused] excusing *1685–1688* 33 *Garments*] *Garment 1684–1688*

Again, how did Satan ply it against *Peter*, when he desired to have him that he might sift him as Wheat; that is, if possible, sever all Grace from his heart, and leave him nothing but flesh and filth, to the end he might make the Lord Jesus loath and abhor him; *Simon, Simon, said Christ, Satan hath desired to have you, that he might sift you as Wheat*. But did he prevail against him? No, *But I have prayed for thee, that thy Faith fail not*. As who should say, *Simon*, Satan hath desired me that I would give thee up to him, and not only thee, but all the rest of thy Brethren (for that the word you, imports); but *I* will not leave thee in his hand, *I* have prayed for thee, thy faith shall not fail: *I* will secure thee to the Heavenly Inheritance, *Luk*. 22. 30, 31, 32.

Secondly, As Satan, *so every sin*, of the coming-sinner, comes in with a Voice against him, if perhaps they may prevail with Christ to cast off the Soul. When *Israel* was coming out of *Egypt* to *Canaan*, how many times had their sins thrown them out of the mercy of God, had not *Moses* as a Type of Christ, stood in the breach to turn away his Wrath from them, *Psal*. 106. 23. Our Iniquities testify against us, and would certainly prevail against us, to our utter rejection and Damnation, had we not an Advocate with the Father Jesus Christ the Righteous, 1 *Joh*. 2. 1, 2.

The sins of the old World cryed them down to Hell, the sins of *Sodom* fetched upon them Fire from Heaven, which devoured them; the sins of the *Egyptians* cryed them down to Hell, because they came not to Jesus Christ for Life. Coming-sinner, thy sins are no whit less than any; Nay, perhaps, they are as big as all theirs: Why is it then that thou livest when they are dead, and that thou hast a promise of Pardon when they had not? *Why thou art coming to Jesus Christ*, and therefore sin shall not be thy ruin.

Thirdly, As *Satan*, and *Sin*; so the *Law* of *Moses*, as it is a Perfect Holy Law, hath a Voice against thee before the Face of God: *There is one that accuseth you, even* Moses's *Law*, Jo. 5. 45. Yea, it accuseth all Men of Transgression, that have sinned against it; for as long as Sin is Sin, there will be a Law to accuse for Sin: But this Accusation shall not prevail against the Coming-Sinner; because 'tis Christ

31 thee] you *1685–1688* 32 45.] *om. 1678–1688* 33 have] hath *1686*^{2}

that dyed, and that ever lives, to make Intercession for them that *Come to God by him*, Rom. 8. Heb. 7. 25.

These things, I say, do accuse us before Christ *Jesus*; yea, and also to our own Faces, if perhaps they might prevail against us. But these words, *I will in no wise cast out*, secureth the Coming-Sinner from them all.

The Coming-Sinner is not saved because there is none that comes in against him; but because the Lord Jesus will not hear their Accusations; will not cast out the Coming-Sinner.

When *Shimei* came down to meet King *David*, and to ask for Pardon for his Rebellion; up starts *Abishai*, and puts in his Caveat, saying; *Shall not* Shimei *dye for this?* This is the Case of him that comes to Christ; He hath this *Abishai*, and that *Abishai*, that presently steps in against him, saying; Shall not this Rebel's Sins destroy him in Hell? Read further; *But* David *answered; What have I to do with you, ye Sons of* Zeruiah, *that you should this day be Adversaries to me? Shall there any Man be put to Death this Day in* Israel*? for do not I know, that I am King this Day over* Israel? 2 *Sam.* 19. 16, 17, 18, 19, 20, 21, 22.

This is Christ's Answer by the Text, to all that accuse the Coming-*Shimeis*; What have I to do with you, that accuse the Coming-Sinners to me? I count you Adversaries, that are against my shewing Mercy to them. Do not I know, that I am Exalted this Day to be King of Righteousness, and King of Peace. *I will in no wise cast them out.*

Secondly, But again; These Words do closely imply, that the Coming-Souls are afraid, that these Accusers will prevail against them; as is evident, because the Text is spoken for their Relief and Succour: For that need not be, if they that are coming, were not subject to fear, and despond upon this account. Alas! there is Guilt, and the Curse lies upon the Conscience of the Coming-Sinner!

Besides, He is Conscious to himself, what a Villain, what a Wretch he hath been against God, and Christ. Also, he now knows, by woful Experience, how he hath been at *Satan*'s Beck, and at the Motion of every Lust. He hath now also, new Thoughts of the

2 *God*] *him 1684–1688*   7 that] *add 1685–1688*

Holyness, and Justice of God: Also, he feels, that he cannot forbear sinning against him; *For the Motions of Sin, which are by the Law, do still work in his Members, to bring forth Fruit unto Death* (Rom. 7. 5.). But none of this needs be, since we have so Good, so Tender-hearted, and so Faithful a *Jesus* to come to; who will rather overthrow Heaven and Earth, than suffer a tittle of this Text to fail: *And him that comes unto me, I will in no wise cast out.*

Now, We have yet to enquire into, two things that lie in the Words, to which there hath yet been nothing said: As,

1. *What it is to cast out.*

2. *How it appears, that Christ hath Power to Save, or to Cast out.*

For the First of these, *What it is to Cast out*; to this I will speak,

1. Generally.

2. More Particularly.

More Generally;

First, *To cast out*, Is to Slight, and Despise, and Contemn; as it is said of *Saul's* Shield, *It was vilely cast away*; that is, Slighted and Contemned. Thus it is with the Sinners, that come not to Jesus Christ; He Slights, Despises, and Contemns them; that is, *Casts them away*, 2 Sam. 1. 21.

Secondly, Things cast away, are reputed as Menstruous Cloaths, and as the Dirt of the Street, *Isa.* 3. 24. *Psal.* 18. 42. *Matth.* 5. 13. Chap. 15. 17. And thus it shall be with the Men, that come not to Jesus Christ; they shall be counted as Menstruous, and as the Dirt in the Streets.

Thirdly, To be cast out, or off; it is, To be abhorred, not to be pityed; but to be put to perpetual Shame, *Psal.* 44. 9. *Psal.* 89. 38. *Amos* 1. 11.

But more particularly, To come to the Text: The Casting-out here mentioned, is not limited to this, or the other Evil: Therefore, it must be extended to the most extream and utmost Misery; Or thus:

He that cometh to Christ, shall not want any thing, that may make him Gospelly Happy in this World, or that which is to come:

3 *still*] *add 1684–1688* 5.] *om. 1678–1688* 6 tittle *1688*] little *1678–1686*^{2} 7 *comes unto*] *cometh to 1685–1688* 9 yet] *om. 1686*^{2}*–1688* 11 *to Cast*] *cast 1686*^{1}*–1688* 20 1. 21.] 1. 2. *1678–1688* 22 24.] 22. *1678–1688*

Nor shall he want any thing, that cometh not, that may make him Spiritually and Eternally Miserable!

But further: As it is to be Generally taken, so it respecteth Things that are now; and also, Things that shall be hereafter.

For the Things that are now; they are either,

1. More General;

2. Or more Particular.

First, More General, thus:

It is *To be cast out* of the Presence and Favour of God.

Thus was *Cain cast out: Thou hast driven* (or cast) *me out this Day from thy Presence; and from thy Face* (that is, from thy Favour) *shall I be hid.* A dreadful Complaint! but the Effect of a more dreadful Judgement! *Gen.* 4. 13, 14. *Jer.* 23. 39. 1 *Chron.* 28. 9.

Secondly, *To be cast out*, is to be cast out of God's Sight: God will look after them no more, care for them no more; nor will he watch over them any more for Good (2 *King.* 17. 20. *Jer.* 7. 15.). Now, they that are so, are left like Blind Men, to wander, and fall into the Pit of Hell: This therefore, is also a sad Judgement! Therefore, here is the Mercy of him that *Cometh* to Christ; He shall not be left to wander at Uncertainties: The Lord Jesus Christ will keep him, as a Shepheard doth his Sheep, *Psal.* 23. *Him that cometh to me*, *I will in no wise cast out.*

Thirdly, *To be cast out*, Is to be denyed a Place in God's House; and to be left as Fugitives and Vagabonds, to pass a little time away in this Miserable Life; and after that, to go down to the Dead, *Gal.* 4. 30. *Gen.* 4. 13, 14. Chap. 21. 10. Therefore, here is the Benefit of him that *Cometh* to Christ; He shall not be denyed a Place in God's House: They shall not be left, like Vagabonds in the World. *Him that cometh to me*, *I will in no wise cast out*; See *Prov.* 14. 26. *Isa.* 56. 3, 4, 5. *Ephes.* 2. 19, 20, 21, 22. 1 *Cor.* 3. 21, 22, 23.

Fourthly, In a word; *To be cast out*, Is to be Rejected, as are the Fallen Angels: For, their Eternal Damnation began at their being cast down from Heaven to Hell. So then, *Not to be cast out*, Is to have a Place, a House, and Habitation there; and to have a Share in the Priviledges of Elect Angels.

4 are now . . . Things that] *om. 1684–1688* 11 *Presence; and from thy*] *om. 1684–1688*

These Words therefore, *I will not cast out*, will prove great Words one Day, to them that come to Jesus Christ, 2 *Pet.* 2. 4. *Joh.* 12. 31. *Revel.* 12. *Luk.* 20. 35.

Secondly, and more Particularly.

First, Christ hath Everlasting Life for him that cometh to him, and he shall never Perish; *For he will in no wise cast him out*: But for the rest, they are Rejected, *Cast out*; and must be Damned, *Joh.* 10. 27, 28.

Secondly, Christ hath Everlasting Righteousness, to cloath them with, that come to him; and they shall be covered with it, as with a Garment: But the rest shall be found in the Filthy Rags of their own stinking Polutions, and shall be wrapt up in them, as in a Winding-sheet; and so bear their Shame before the Lord, and also, before the Angels, *Dan.* 9. 24. *Isa.* 57. 2. *Revel.* 3. 4–18. Chap. 15, 16.

Thirdly, Christ hath pretious Blood, that like an open Fountain, stands free for him to wash in, that comes to him for Life; *And he will in no wise cast him out*: But they that come not to him, are Rejected from a Share therein, and are left to ireful Vengeance for their Sins, *Zech.* 13. 1. 1 *Pet.* 1. 18, 19. *Joh.* 13. 8. Chap. 3. 36.

Fourthly, Christ hath precious Promises; and they shall have a Share in them, that come to him for Life: *For he will in no wise cast them out.* But they that come not, can have no Share in them; because they are *True* only in him: For in Him, and only in Him, all the Promises are *Yea*, and *Amen.* Wherefore, they that come not to him, are no whit the better for them, *Psal.* 50. 16. 2 *Cor.* 1. 20, 21.

Fifthly, Christ hath all Fulness of Grace in himself, for them that come to him for Life; *And he will in no wise cast them out*: But those that come not to him, are left in their Graceless State; and as Christ leaves them, Death, Hell, and Judgement finds them. *He that findeth me* (saith Christ) *findeth Life, and shall obtain Favour of the Lord; but he that sins against me, wrongeth his own Soul: All that hate Me, love Death*, Prov. 8. 33, 34, 35, 36.

Sixthly, Christ is an Intercessor; and ever liveth to make Intercession for them, that come to God by him: *But their Sorrows shall be*

2 12. 31.] 21. 31. *1686*[2]*–1688* 3 *Revel.* 12.] *om.* *1685–1688* 25 for] from *1684* 26 all] also *1685–1688* 28 to] unto *1685–1688*

multiplyed, that hasten after another (or other) *Gods* (their Sins and Lusts); *Their Drink-Offerings will he not offer, nor take up their Names into his Lips*, Psal. 16. 4. Heb. 7. 25.

Seventhly, Christ hath wonderful Love, Bowels, and Compassions, for those that come to him! For, *He will in no wise cast them out*. But the rest will find him a Lyon Rampant; he will, one Day, tear them all to peices. Now, *Consider this* (saith he) *ye that forget God; lest I tare you in peices, and there be none to deliver you*, Psal. 50. 22.

Eighthly, Christ is He, by, and for whose sake, those that come to him, have their Persons and Performances accepted of the Father; *And he will in no wise cast them out:* But the rest must flye to the Rocks and Mountains, for Shelter, but all in vain, to hide them from his Face, and Wrath, *Revel.* 6. 15, 16, 17.

But again; These Words [*Cast out*] have a special Look to what will be hereafter; even at the Day of Judgement: For then, and not till then, will be the great *Anathema*, and *Casting out*, made manifest, even manifest by Execution. Therefore, here to speak to this, and that under these two Heads; As,

1. *Of the Casting out it self.*

2. *Of the Place into which they shall be cast, that shall then be cast out.*

First, The Casting out it self, standeth in two Things;

1. In a Preparitory Work.

2. In the manner of Executing the Act.

The Preparitory Work standeth in these three Things:

First, It standeth in *their* Separation, that have not come to him, from them that have, at that Day: Or thus; At the Day of the great *Casting out*, those that have not (*now*) come to him, shall be separated from them that *have*; for *them* that have, *He will not cast out. When the Son of Man shall come in his Glory, and all the Holy Angels with him, then he shall sit upon the Throne of his Glory; and before him shall be gathered all Nations; and he shall separate them one from another, as a Shepheard divideth the Sheep from the Goats*, Matth. 25. 31, 32.

This dreadful Separation, therefore, shall then be made, betwixt them that (*now*) come to Christ, and them that come not: And good Reason; for since they would not with us come to him, *now* they have time; Why should they stand with us, when Judgement is come?

8 *you*[1]] *ye 1686*[1]–*1686*[2]   9 He] none *1685–1686*[2]] known *1688*

Secondly, They shall be placed before him according to their condition; they that have come to him, in great Dignity, even at his right hand, *For he will in no wise cast them out:* but the rest shall be set at his left hand, the place of disgrace and shame; for they did not come to him for Life.

Distinguished also shall they be, by fit terms: Those that came to him, he calleth *Sheep*, but the rest are **Frowish** *Goats. And he shall separate them one from another, as the Shepherd divideth the Sheep from the Goats*; and the *Sheep will be set on the right hand* (next Heaven-Gate, for they came to him); *but the Goats on his left*, to go from him into Hell, because they are not of his Sheep.

Thirdly, Then will Christ proceed to conviction of those that came *not* unto him, and will say, *I was a stranger, and ye took me not in*, or did not come unto me. Their excuse of themselves, he will slight as dirt, and proceed to their final Judgment. Now when these wretched rejectors of Christ shall thus be set before him in their sins, and convicted, this is the preparitory work upon which follows the manner of Executing the Act which will be done.

First, In the presence of all the Holy Angels.

Second. In the presence of all them that in their life-time came to him, by saying unto them. *Depart from me ye Cursed into everlasting Fire prepared for the Devil and his Angels*; with this Reason annexed to it; For you were cruel to me and mine, particularly discovered in these words; *For I was an hungred, and ye gave me no meat; thirsty, and ye gave me no drink; I was a Stranger, and ye took me not in; Naked, and ye Clothed me not; Sick, and in Prison, and ye visited me not*, Mat. 25. 41, 42, 43.

Lastly, Now it remains, that we speak of the place into which these shall be cast, which in the general you have heard already, to wit, the Fire prepared for the Devil and his Angels: but in particular, it is thus described.

First, It is called **Tophet**: *For* Tophet *is ordained of Old, yea, for the King* (the Lucifer). *It is prepared, he hath made it deep and large, the*

6 came] come *1685–1688* 9 *he*] *be 1685–1686*[2] 19 all] *add 1684–1688*
20 *Second.*] Secondly *1684–1688* 22 this] the *1686*[1]*–1688*

pile thereof is Fire and much Wood, and the Breath of the Lord like a stream of Brimstone doth kindle it, Isa. 30. 33.

Secondly, It is called **Hell**, *It is better for thee to enter into Life halt, or lame, than having two feet to be cast into Hell*, Mar. 9. 45.

Thirdly, It is called the *Wine press of the Wrath of God. And the Angel thrust in his Sickle into the Earth, and gathered the Vine of the Earth* (that is them that did not come to Christ) *and cast them into the great Wine press of the Wrath of God*, Rev. 14. 19.

Fourthly, It is called a *Lake of Fire. And whosoever was not found written in the Book of Life, was cast into the Lake of Fire*, Rev. 20. 15.

Fifthly, It is called a **Pitt**. *Thou hast said in thy Heart, I will Ascend into Heaven, I will Exalt my Throne above the Stars of God, I will sit also upon the Mount of the Congregation, in the sides of the North—Yet thou shalt be broutght down to Hell, to the sides of the* **Pitt**, *Isa.* 14. 13, 14, 15.

Sixthly, It is called a *bottomless Pit, out* of which the smoak and the Locusts came, and *into* which the great Dragon was cast; and it is called **Bottomless**, to shew the endlesness of the fall that they will have into it, that come not, in the acceptable time to Jesus Christ, *Rev.* 9. 1, 2. *chap.* 20. 3.

Seventhly, It is called *Outer Darkness: Bind him hand and foot, and cast him into outer Darkness; and cast ye the unprofitable Servant into outer Darkness, there shall be Weeping, and Nashing of Teeth*, Mat. 22. 13. *chap.* 25. 30.

Eighthly, It is called a *Furnace of Fire. As therefore the Tares are gathered and burned in the Fire, so shall it be in the end of this World: the Son of Man shall send forth his Angels, and they shall gather out of his Kingdom, all things that Offend, and them that do Iniquity; and shall cast them into a Furnace of Fire, there shall be Wailing and Gnashing of Teeth: And again, So shall it be in the end of the World, the Angels shall come forth, and sever the wicked from among the just, and shall cast them into a Furnace of Fire; there shall be wailing and gnashing of Teeth*, Matt. 13. 40, 41, 42, 43, 48, 49, 50.

Lastly, It may not be amiss, if in the conclusion of this, *I* shew in few words, to what the things that torment them in this state, are

1 *and the Breath*] *the Breath 1686*[1]*–1688* 2 30. 33.] 30. 32. *1678–1688* 16 Locusts *1688*] Locust *1678–1686*[2] 23 25. 30.] 25. 13. *1684–1688* 26 *they*] *he 1688* 32 40,] *om. 1678–1688*

compared. Indeed some of them have bin occasionally mentioned already; as that they are compared,

1. To wood that burneth.

2. To Fire.

3. To Fire and Brimstone: But

4. It is compared to a Worm, a gnawing Worm, a never dying gnawing Worm: *They are cast into Hell, where their Worm dieth not*, Mar. 9. 44.

Fifthly, It is called unquenchable Fire, *He will gather his Wheat into his Garner: but will burn up the Chaff with unquenchable Fire*, Matt. 3. 12. Luk. 3. 17.

Sixthly, It is called everlasting destruction. *The Lord Jesus shall descend from Heaven with his mighty Angels in flaming Fire, taking Vengance on them that know not God, and that obey not the Gospel of our Lord Jesus Christ; Who shall be punished with Everlasting Destruction from the presence of the Lord, and from the Glory of his Power*, 2 Thes. 1. 7, 8, 9.

Seventhly, It is called *Wrath without mixture*, and is given them in the Cup of his Indignation. *If any man Worship the Beast, and his Image, and receive his mark in his forehead, or in his hand, the same shall drink of the Wine of the Wrath of God, which is powred out without mixture, in the Cup of his Indignation, and he shall be tormented with Fire and Brimstone in the presence of the Holy Angels, and in the presence of the Lamb*, Rev. 14. 9, 10.

Eighthly, It is called the second Death, *And death and hell were cast into the Lake of Fire, this is the second Death. Blessed and holy is he that hath part in the first Resurrection, on such the second Death hath no Power*, Rev. 20. 14. *chap.* 20. *v.* 6.

Ninthly, It is called Eternal Damnation, *But He that shall blaspheme against the Holy Ghost, hath never forgiveness, but is in danger of Eternal Damnation.*

Oh These three Words!
Everlasting Punishment!
Eternal Damnation!
And for Ever and Ever!

How will they gnaw, and eat up all the expectation of the end of

21 *of the Wine*] *om.* *1684–1688* 28 20. *v.* 6.] 2. *v.* 6. *1678–1688*

the misery of the Cast-away sinners. *And the smoke of their Torment, ascended up for Ever, and Ever, and they have no rest Day nor Night*, &c. Rev. 14. 11.

Their behaviour in Hell, is set forth but by four things as *I* know of.

1. By calling for Help and Relief in Vain.
2. By Weeping.
3. By Wailing.
4. By gnashing of Teeth.

And now we come to the second thing that is to be enquired into Namely,

How it appears that Christ hath Power to save, or to Cast out: For by these words, *I will in no wise cast out*, he declareth that he hath power to do both.

Now this enquiry admits us to search into two things.

1 *How it appears that he hath power to save.*

2 *How it appears that he hath power to cast out.*

That he hath power to save, appears by that which follows.

First, To speak only of him as he is Mediator: He was Authorized to this blessed work by his Father before the World began. Hence the Apostle saith, He hath chosen us in him, before the Foundation of the World; that is, chosen us in him to be Saved by him, as *Ephesians* the first makes manifest. Hence it is again, that we are said to be Blessed in him before the Foundation of the World, with all those things that effectually will produce our Salvation. Read the same Chapter, with 2 *Tim*. 1. 9.

Secondly, He was promised to our first Parents, that he should in the fulness of time, bruise the Serpents Head; and as *Paul* expounds it, redeem them that were under the law: hence since that time, he hath bin reckoned as slain for our Sins, by which means all the Fathers under the first Testament were secured from the wrath to come; hence he is called, *The Lamb slain from the Foundation of the World*. Rev. 13. 8. Gen. 3. 15. Gal. 4. 4, 5.

Thirdly, *Moses* gave Testimony of him by the Types and Shadows, and Bloody Sacrifices, that he commanded from the Mouth of God, to be in use for the support of his peoples Faith, until the

22–4 that is . . . the World] *om*. *1686*[1]*–1688* 36 for] to *1688*

time of Reformation; which was the time of this Jesus his Death. *Heb.* 9. and 10th. Chapters.

Fourth, At the time of his Birth, it was Testified of him by the Angel, *That he should Save his People from their Sins.* Mat. 1. 20, 21.

Fifth, It is Testified of him in the days of his Flesh, that he had Power on Earth to forgive Sins. *Mark* 2. 5, 6, 7, 8, 9, 10.

Sixth, It is Testified also of him by the Apostle *Peter; that God hath exalted him with his own Right Hand to be a Prince, and a Saviour, to give Repentance to* Israel, *and forgiveness of Sins.* Acts 5. 30, 31.

Seventh, In a word, This is every where Testified of him, both in the Old Testament and in the New.

And good reason, that he should be acknowledged and trusted in, as a Saviour.

1. He came down from Heaven to be a Saviour, *Joh.* 6. 38, 39, 40.

2. He was Anointed, when on Earth to be a Saviour, *Luk.* 3. 22.

3. He did the Works of a Saviour. As

First, He Fulfilled the Law, and became the End of it for Righteousness, for them that believe in him, *Rom.* 10. 3, 4.

Secondly, He laid down his Life as a Saviour, He gave his Life as a Ransom for many, *Mat.* 20. 28. *Mar.* 10. 45. 1 *Tim.* 2. 6.

Thirdly, He hath Abolished Death, Destroyed the Devil, put away Sin, got the Keys of Hell and Death, is Ascended into Heaven; is there accepted of God, exalted of God, and bid Sit at his Right Hand as Saviour, and that because his Sacrifice for our Sins pleased God, 2 *Tim.* 1. 10. *Heb.* 2. 14, 15. *Ephes.* 4. 7, 8. *Joh.* 16. 10, 11. *Acts* 5. 30, 31. *Heb.* 10. 12, 13.

Fourthly, God hath sent out, and proclaimed him as Saviour, and tells the World that we have redemption through his Blood, that he will Justifie us if we believe in his Blood, and that he can Faithfully, and Justly do it. Yea, God doth beseech us to be reconciled to him by his Son; which could not be, if he were not Anointed by him to this very End, and also if his Works and undertakings were

3 *Fourth*] *Fourthly 1684–1688* it was] 'twas *1685–1688* 5 *Fifth*] *Fifthly 1684–1688* 7 *Sixth*] *Sixthly 1684–1688* 8 *hath*] *had 1684–1688* 9 *Sins*] *Sin 1685–1686*[2] 10 *Seventh*] *Seventhly 1684–1688* 11 in] *om. 1686*[1]*–1688* 24 accepted] excepted *1686*[1] exalted of God] *om. 1684–1688* his] the *1686*[1]*–1688* 25 as] as a *1684–1688* our] *om. 1686*[1]*–1688* 28 as] as a *1684–1688*

not accepted of him as considered a Saviour, *Rom.* 3. 24, 25. 2 *Cor.* 5. 18, 19, 20, 21.

Fifthly, God hath received already Millions of Souls into his Paradice, because they have received this Jesus for a Saviour, and is resolved to cut him off, and to cast him out of his presence, that will not take him for a Saviour, *Heb.* 12. 22, 23, 24, 25, 26.

I intend brevity here; therefore a word to the Second, and so conclude.

How it appears that he hath Power to cast out.

This appears also by what follows.

First, The Father (for the service that he hath done him as Saviour) hath made him Lord of all, even Lord of Quick and Dead. *For to this End Christ both Died, and Rose, and Revived, that he might be Lord both of the Dead and Living*, Rom. 14. 9.

Secondly, The Father hath left it with him, to quicken whom he will, to wit, with saving Grace, and to cast out whom he will, for their Rebellion against Him, *Joh.* 5. 21.

Thirdly, The Father hath made him Judge of Quick and Dead, hath committed all Judgment unto the Son, that all Men should honour the Son, even as they honour the Father, *Joh.* 5. 22.

Fourthly, God will Judge the World by this Man; the day is Appointed for Judgment, and he is Appointed for Judge. *He hath Appointed a day in the which he will Judge the World in Righteousness by that Man*, Acts 17. 31, 32.

Therefore we must all appear before the Judgment-Seat of Christ, that every one may receive for the things done in the Body, according to what they have done. If they have closed with Him, Heaven and Salvation; if they have not, Hell and Damnation.

And for these Reasons he must be Judge.

First, Because of his Humiliation, because of his Fathers Word he humbled himself, and he became Obedient unto Death; even the Death of the Cross: *Therefore God hath highly Exalted him, and given him a Name above every Name; that at the Name of Jesus, every Knee should bow; both of things in Heaven, and things on Earth, and things under*

3 received already] already received *1688* 5 him[1]] them *1685–1688* him[2]] them *1685–1688* that] that he *1684–1686*[2] 19–20 that all Men should honour the Son,] *om. 1684–1686*[2]] and appointed that all should honour the Son *add 1688* 20 5. 22.] 22. 5. *1688* 34 *should*] *shall 1686*[2]

the Earth; and that every Tongue should confess that Jesus Christ is Lord, to the Glory of God the Father.

This hath respect to his being Judge, and his Sitting in Judgment upon Angels and Men, *Phil.* 2. 7, 8, 9, 10, 11. *Rom.* 14. 10, 11.

Secondly, That all Men might honour the Son, even as they honour the Father. *For the Father Judgeth no Man, but hath Committed all Judgment unto the Son; that all Men should honour the Son, even as they honour the Father*, Joh. 5. 22, 23.

Thirdly, Because of his Righteous Judgment, this work is fit for no Creature; it is only fit for the Son of God. For he will reward every Man according to his Ways, *Rev.* 22.

Fourthly, Because he is the Son of Man. He hath given him authority to execute Judgment also, because he is the Son of Man, *Joh.* 5. 27.

Thus have I in brief passed through this Text by way of explication; my next Work is, to speak to it by way of Observation: but I shall be also as brief in that, as the Nature of the thing will admit.

All that the Father giveth me shall come to me, and him that cometh to me I will in no wise cast out, Joh. 6. 37.

AND now to come to some Observations, and a little briefly to speak to them, and then conclude the whole.

The words thus Explained, affords us many, some of which are these:

First, *That God the Father, and Christ his Son, are two Distinct Persons in the God-head.*

Secondly, *That by them* (not Excluding the Holy Ghost) *is contrived, and determined, the Salvation of some of fallen Man-kind.*

Thirdly, *That this contrivance, resolved it self into a Covenant between these Persons in the God-head, which standeth in giving, on the Fathers part; and Receiving, on the Sons.* All that the Father *giveth me*, &c.

Fourthly, *That every one that the Father hath given to Christ (according to the mind of God in the Text) shall certainly come to him.*

11 22.] 2. 2. *1685–1688*   15–16 explication] Explications *1685–1686*[2]   20 to come] come *1684–1688*   22 affords] afford *1685–1688*   27 *of some*] *om. 1684–1688*

Fifthly, *That coming to Jesus Christ, is therefore not by the will, wisdom, or power of man: but by the gift, promise, and drawing of the Father.* [*All that the Father giveth me,* **shall** *come.*]

Sixthly, *That Jesus Christ will be careful to receive, and will not in any wise reject, those that come, or are coming to him.* [*And him that cometh to me, I will in no wise cast out.*]

There are besides these, some other Truths, *implyed*, in the Words: As

Seventhly, *They that are coming to Jesus Christ, are oft-times heartily afraid that he will not receive them.*

Eighthly, *Jesus Christ would not have them, that in Truth are Coming to him, once think, that he will cast them out.*

These Observations, lie, all of them in the Words, and are plentifully confirmed by the Scriptures of Truth; but I shall not at this time speak to them all, but shall pass by the first, second, third, fourth, and sixth; partly because, I design brevity, and partly because they are touched upon, in the Explicatory part of the Text. I shall therefore begin with the *Fifth* Observation, and so make that the *first* in order, in the following discourse.

First, Then, *Coming to Christ, is not by the will, wisdom, or power of Man, but by the gift, promise, and drawing of the Father.* This Observation standeth of two parts.

First, that coming to Christ, is not by the Will, Wisdom, or Power of Man.

Secondly, But by the Gift, Promise, and Drawing of the Father. That the Text carrieth this Truth in its bosom, you will find, if you look into the Explication of the first part thereof, before; I shall therefore here follow the Method propounded, *viz.* shew

First, *That coming to Christ is not by the will, wisdom, or power of man: this is true,* because the Word doth flatly deny it.

First, It denyeth it to be by the **Will** of man. *Not of blood, nor of the* **Will** *of the flesh, nor of the* **Will** *of man.* And again, *It is not of him that* **Willeth**, *nor of him that* **Runneth**. Joh. 1. 13. Rom. 9. 16.

Secondly, It denyeth it to be of the **Wisdome** of man, as is manifest from these considerations.

25 of] *om. 1686*[1] 28 *viz.* shew] *add 1688* 30 flatly deny it] positively say it is not *1684–1688* 31 be] be holy *1686*[1]*–1688*

First, *In the Wisdome of God it pleased him, that the World by Wisdome should not know him:* Now if by *their* Wisdom they cannot *know* him, it follows, by *that* Wisdome, they cannot come unto him; for coming to him, is not before, but after some knowledge of him, 1 *Cor.* 1. 21. *Acts* 13. 27. *Psal.* 9. 10.

Secondly, The Wisdome of Man, in Gods Account, as to the Knowledge of Christ, is reckoned foolishness. *Hath not God made* **Foolish** *the Wisdome of this World? and again, the Wisdome of this World is* **Foolishness** *with God.* If God has made *Foolish*, the Wisdome of this World; and again, if the Wisdom of this World is *Foolishness* with Him: then verily it is not likely, that by that, a Sinner should become so Prudent, as to come to Jesus Christ: especially if you Consider,

Thirdly, That the Doctrine of a Crucified Christ, and so of Salvation by him, is the very thing, that is counted foolishness, to the Wisdom of this World; Now, if the very Doctrine of a Crucified Christ, be counted foolishness by the Wisdom of this World, it cannot be, that by that Wisdom, a man should be drawn out, in his Soul, to come to him, 1 *Cor.* 1. 20. Chap. 2. 14. Chap. 3. 19. Chap. 1. 18, 23.

Fourthly, God counteth the Wisdom of this World, one of his greatest Enemies, therefore by that Wisdom no man can come to Jesus Christ. For it is not likely that one of Gods greatest Enemies, should draw a man to that which best of all pleaseth God, as coming to Christ doth. Now, that God counteth the Wisdom of this World, one of his greatest Enemies, is evident.

First, For that it casteth the greatest contempt upon his Sons undertakings, as afore is proved, in that it counts his Crucifixion foolishness; Though **That** be one of the Highest Demonstrations of Divine Wisdom, *Ephes.* 1. 7, 8.

Secondly, Because God hath threatned to destroy it, and bring it to naught, and cause it to perish; Which surely he *would not do*, was it not an Enemy; would it direct men to, and cause them to close with Jesus Christ. See *Isa.* 29. 14. 1 *Cor.* 1. 19.

Thirdly, He hath rejected it from helping in the Ministry of his

9 has] hath *1685–1688* 16 this] the *1686*[1]*–1688* 21 counteth] counted *1684–1688* 28 it] he *1685–1688*

Word, as a fruitless business, and a thing that comes to naught. 1 *Cor.* 2. 4, 6, 12, 13.

Fourthly, Because it causeth to perish, those that seek it, and pursue it, 1 *Cor.* 1. 18, 19.

Fifthly, And God has proclaimed, *That if any man will be wise in this World*, he must be a fool in the Wisdom of this World; and that's the way to be wise in the Wisdom of God. *If any man will be wise in this World, let him become a fool, that he may be wise. For the Wisdom of this World is foolishness with God*, 1 Cor. 3. 18, 19, 20.

Thirdly, *Coming to Christ, is not by the power of man.* This is evident, partly,

First, From that which goeth before: For mans power, in the puttings forth of it, in this matter, is either stirred up by Love, or sense of Necessity: but the Wisdom of this World, neither gives man love to, or sense of a need of Jesus Christ; therefore his power lieth still, *as from that.*

Secondly, What power has he, *that is dead*, as every natural man, spiritually, is; Even dead in Trespasses and sinnes. Dead, even as dead to Gods New-Testament things; as he that is in his Grave, is Dead to the things of this World. What power hath he then, whereby to come to Jesus Christ. *Joh.* 5. 25. *Ephes.* 2. 1. *Col.* 2. 13.

Thirdly, God forbids the mighty man's glorying in his strength, and sayes positively, *By strength shall no man prevaile:* and again, *Not by might, nor by power, but by my Spirit, saith the Lord*, Jer. 9. 23, 24. 1 Sam. 2. 9. Zech. 4. 6. 1 Cor. 1. 27, 28, 29, 30, 31.

Fourthly, *Paul* acknowledgeth that man, nay, converted man of himself, hath not a Sufficiency of power in himself *to think a good thought*; if not to do that which is least, *for to think, is less than to come*; then no man by his own power can come to Jesus Christ, 2 *Cor.* 3. 5.

Fifthly, Hence we are said to be made willing to come, by the power of God; to be raised from a state of sin to a state of Grace, by the power of God; and to *believe*, that is, to *come*, through the exceeding working of his mighty power, *Psal.* 110. 3. *Col.* 2. 12. *Ephes.* 1. 18–20. See also *Job* 40. 6–14.

22 glorying] glory *1686^{2}–1688* 25 1.] *om. 1686^{2}–1688* 35 40. 6–14.] 40. 6. 14. *1685*] 46. 14. *1686^{1}–1688*

But this needed not, if either man had power, or will, to come; or so much, as graciously to think of being, willing to come (of themselves) to Jesus Christ.

I Should now come to the proof of the Second part of the Observation, but that is occasionally done already, in the Explicatory part of the Text; To which I referr the Reader: For I shall here only, give thee a Text or two more to the same purpose, and so come to the use and application.

First, It is Expresly said, *No man can come to me*, *Except the Father which hath sent me*, *draw him*. By this Text, there is not only insinuated, that in man is want of *power*, but also of *will*, to come to Jesus Christ, they must be *drawn*; they come not, if they be not *drawn*: and observe, it is not man, no nor all the Angels in Heaven, that *can* draw one sinner to Jesus Christ. *No man cometh to me*, *except the* Father *which hath sent me*, *draw him*. Joh. 6. 44.

Secondly, Again, *No man can come to me*, *except it were given him of my Father*. Joh. 6. 65. It is an heavenly gift that maketh man come to Jesus Christ.

Thirdly, Again, *It is written in the Prophets*, *they shall be all Taught of God; every one therefore that hath heard and learned of the Father*, *cometh to me*. Joh. 6. 45.

I Shall not enlarge; but shall make some use and application, and so come to the next Observation.

First, Is it so? Is coming to Jesus Christ, *Not by the will*, *wisdom*, *or Power of man; but by the gift*, *promise*, *and drawing of the Father?* Then they are to blame, that cry up the will, wisdom, and power of man, as things Sufficient to bring men to Christ.

There are some men, who think they may not be Contradicted, when they plead for the will, wisdom, and power of man, in reference to the things that are of the Kingdom of Christ: But I will say to such a man, he never yet came to understand, that himself is, what the Scripture teacheth Concerning him: Neither did he ever know, what coming to Christ is, by the teaching, gift, and drawing of the Father. He is such an one that hath set up Gods Enemy in opposition to him, and that continueth in such acts of defiance; and

2 being] *add 1684–1688*   15 *sent 1684–1688*] *sent to 1678*   31 came] come *1684–1686*[1]   34 an] a *1686*[1]*–1688*

what his end, without a new birth, will be, the Scripture teacheth also: But we will pass this.

Secondly, Is it so? Is coming to Christ, by the gift, promise, and drawing of the Father? then let Saints here learn, to ascribe their coming to Christ; to the gift, promise, and drawing of the Father. Christian man, bless God, who hath given thee to Jesus Christ, by promise; and again, bless God for that he hath drawn thee to him. And why is it thee! Why not another! O that the glory of Electing love, should rest upon thy head; and that the glory of the Exceeding grace of God, should take hold of thy heart, and bring thee to Jesus Christ.

Thirdly, Is it so? that coming to Christ is by the Father, as aforesaid; then this should teach us to set an high esteem *upon them that indeed are coming to Jesus Christ*: I say, an high esteem on **Them**, for the sake of him, by vertue of whose grace, they are made to come to Jesus Christ.

We see, that when men, by the help of humane abilities, do arrive to the Knowledge of, and bring to pass, that which, when done, is a wonder to the World: how he that did it, is esteem'd and commended. Yea, how are his wits, parts, industry, and unweariedness in all, admired; and yet the man, as to this, is but of the World, and his work, the effect of natural ability: The things also attained by him, end in vanity, and vexation of Spirit. Further, perhaps in the pursute of this his Acheivement, he sins against God, wasts his time vainly, and at long run loses his Soul, by neglecting of better things: Yet he is admired! But, I say, if this mans parts, labor, diligence, and the like, will bring him to such applause, and esteem in the World; what esteem should we have, of such an one that is by the Gift, promise, and power, of God, coming to Jesus Christ.

First, This is a man, with whom God is, in whom God works and walks; a man whose motion is Governed & Steared by the mighty hand of God, and the effectual working of his power. *Hear's a Man!*

Secondly, This man by the power of Gods might, which worketh in him, is able to cast a whole World behind him, with all the lusts, and pleasures of it; and to Charge through all the difficulties that Men and Devils can set against him. *Hear's a Man!*

13 an] a *1686*[1]*–1688* 24 Acheivement] Achievements *1684–1688*

Thirdly, This man is Travelling to Mount *Zion*, the Heavenly Jerusalem: The City of the living God; And to an innumerable company of Angels; And the Spirits of Just men made Perfect; to God the Judge of all, and to Jesus. *Hear's a Man!*

Fourthly, This man can look upon death with comfort, can laugh at destruction, when it cometh; and longs to hear the Sound of the last Trump; And to see his Judge coming in the Clouds of Heaven. *Hear's a Man indeed!*

Let Christians then esteem each other as such: I know you do it; but do it more, and more. And that you may, consider these two or three things:

First, These are the Objects of Christs esteem. *Mat.* 12. 48. *chap.* 15. 22, 23, 24, 25, 26, 27, 28. *Luk.* 7. 9.

Secondly, These are the Objects, of the esteem of Angels. *Dan.* 9. 22. chap. 10. 11. chap. 12. 1. *Heb.* 1. 14.

Thirdly, These have been the Objects of the esteem of Heathens, when but convinced about them. *Dan.* 5. 11. *Acts* 5. 13. 1 *Cor.* 14. 24, 25.

Let each of you, then, esteem other better than themselves, Philip. 2. 3.

Fourthly, Again, Is it so? that no man comes to Jesus Christ, by the will, wisdom, and power of man; But by the Gift, Promise, and Drawing of the Father. *Then this shews us how horribly ignorant of this such are, who make the man that is coming to Christ, the Object of their contempt and rage.* These are also unreasonable, and wicked men, *men in whom is no faith*, 1 Thes. 3. 2.

Sinners, did you but know what a blessed thing it is, to come to Jesus Christ, and that by the help, and drawing of the Father, they do indeed come to him; You would Hang and Burn in Hell, a Thousand years, before you would turn your spirit, as you do, against him that God is drawing to Jesus Christ, and also against the God that draws him.

But faithless Sinners, let us a little Expostulate the matter. What hath this man done against thee, that is coming to Jesus Christ? why dost thou make him the Object of thy scorn; doth his coming to Jesus Christ offend thee? Doth his pursuing of his own Salvation

15 12. 1.] 12. 4. *1678–1688* 17 5. 11.] 5. 10. *1678–1688* 19 2. 3.] 3. 2. *1678–1688* 22 *horribly*] *horrible 1685–1688*

offend thee? Doth his forsaking of his sins, and pleasures offend thee?

Poor Coming man! *Thou Sacrificest the abomination of the Egyptians before their eyes; and will they not stone thee?* Exod. 8. 26.

But I say, why offended at this? is he ever the worse, for coming to Jesus Christ, or for his loving, and serving of Jesus Christ? Or is he ever the more a fool, for flying from that which will dround thee in Hell fire, and for seeking Eternal life? Besides, pray Sirs, consider it, this he doth, not of himself, but by the drawing of the Father. Come, let me tell thee in thine ear, thou that will not, come to him thy self, and him that would, thou hindrest.

First, Thou shalt be judged for one, that hath hated, maligned, and reproached *Jesus Christ*, to whom this poor sinner is coming.

Secondly, Thou shalt be judged too, for one that hath hated the *Father*, by whose powerful drawing, this sinner doth come.

Thirdly, Thou shalt be taken, and judged for one that has done despite to the Spirit of Grace, in him, that is by its help, coming to Jesus Christ. What sayst thou now? Wilt thou stand by thy doings, wilt thou continue to contemn, and reproach the living God? Thinkest thou, that thou shalt weather it out well enough, at the day of Judgement? *Can thy heart indure, or can thine hands be strong in the days, that I shall deal with thee, saith the Lord?* Joh. 15. 18, 19, 20, 21, 22, 23, 24, 25, 26. Jude 14, 15. 1 Thes. 4. 8. Ezek. 22. 14.

Fifthly, Is it so? *That no man comes to Jesus Christ by the will, Wisdome and power of man, but by the gift, promise, and drawing of the Father:* Then this sheweth us, how it comes to pass, that weak means is so powerful as to bring men out of their sins, to a hearty pursute after Jesus Christ: When God bid *Moses* speak to the people, he said, *I will speak with thee*, Exod. 19. 9. When God speaks, when God works, Who can let it? None, none. Then the work goes on. *Elias threw his Mantle upon the Shoulders of* Elisha: and what a wonderful work followed. When Jesus fell in with the crowing of a Cock, what work was there! O when God is in the Means, then shall that Means (be it never so weak, and contemptible in it self), work wonders,

3 *abomination*] *abominations 1685–1688* 10 *will*] *wilt* 1686^2*–1688* 21 *thy*] *thine* 1686^1*–1688* 22 *days 1688*] *day* *1678–*1686^2 23 14, 15.] 14. 14, 15. *1678–1685*] 14. 15. *1685–1688* 22. 14.] 22. 13. *1684–*1686^2 29 9.] *om. 1678–1688*

1 *Kings* 19. 19. *Matt.* 26. 74, 75. *Mar.* 14. 71, 72. *Luk.* 22. 60, 61, 62.

The World understand not, nor believe that the walls of *Jerico* shall fall at the Sound of Rams Horns; but when God will Work, the means must be effectual. A word weakly spoken, spoken with difficulty, in Temptation, and in the midst of great contempt and scorn, works Wonders; *If the Lord thy God will say so too.*

Sixthly, Is it so? *doth no Man come to Jesus Christ, by the Will, Wisdom, or Power of Man; but by the Gift, Promise, and Drawing of the Father:* Then here is room for Christians to stand and admire, to stand and wonder, at the effectual working of Gods Providences, that he hath made use of, as means to bring them to Jesus Christ.

For although Men are drawn to Christ by the Power of the Father: yet that Power putteth forth it self in the use of means; and that means, is Divers; somtimes this, somtimes that: for God is at liberty to work, by which, and when, and how he will; but let the means be what it will, and as Contemptible as may be; yet God that Commanded the Light to Shine out of Darkness, and that out of Weakness, can make Strong; can, nay, doth oft-times make use of very unlikely means, to bring about the Conversion and Salvation of his People. Therefore, you that are come to Christ (and that by unlikely means), stay your selves, and wonder; and wondering, magnifie all mighty Power, by the working of which, the Means hath bin made effectual to bring you to Jesus Christ.

What was the providence, that God made use of, as a Means either more remote, or more near, to bring thee to Jesus Christ? Was it the Removing of thy Habitation, the change of thy Condition, the Loss of Relations, Estate, or the like? was it thy casting of thine Eye upon some good Book, thy hearing of thy Neighbours talk of Heavenly Things, the beholding of Gods Judgments, as executed upon others, or thine own Deliverance from them; or thy being strangly cast under the Ministry of some Godly Man? O take notice of such providence, or providences! They were sent and managed by mighty Power, to do thee good. God himself, I say,

9 *or*] *and 1686*[1]*–1688* 10 to stand and admire] *om. 1684–1688* 24 working] work *1684–1688*

hath Joyned himself unto this Chariot: Yea, and so blessed it, that it failed not to accomplish the thing for which he sent it.

God blesseth not to every one his Providences in this manner How many Thousands are there in this world, that pass every day under the same Providences? but God is not in them, to do that work by them, as he hath done for thy poor Soul, by his effectual working with them. O! That Jesus Christ should meet thee in this Providence, that Dispensation, or the other Ordinance! This is Grace indeed! At this, therefore, it will be thy Wisdom to admire, and for this to bless God.

Give me leave, to give you a tast of some of those Providences, that have been effectual, through the Management of God, to bring Salvation to the Souls of his People.

First, The first shall be, That of the *Woman* of *Samaria*. It must happen, that she must needs go out of the City to draw Water (not before, nor after, but) just when Jesus Christ her Saviour was come from far, and set to rest him (being weary) upon the Well: What a blessed Providence was this? Even a Providence Managed by the Almighty Wisdom, and Almighty Power, to the Conversion and Salvation of this poor Creature. For by this Providence, was this Poor Creature, and her Saviour, brought together; that that blessed Work might be fulfilled upon the Woman, according to the purpose afore determined by the Father, *Joh.* 4.

Secondly, What a Providence was it, that there should be a *Tree* in the way, for *Zachus* to climb, thereby to give Jesus an opportunity to call that, Chief of the *Publicans*, home to himself, even before he came down there-from? *Luk.* 19.

Thirdly, was it not also wonderfull, that the *Thief*, which you read of in the Gospel, should by the providence of God be cast into prison, to be condemned, even at that Sessions that Christ himself was to die; Nay, and that it should happen too, that they must be hanged together, that the Thief might be in hearing and observing of Jesus in his last words, that he might be converted by him before his death? *Luk.* 23.

Fourthly, What a strang providence was it, and as strangly

3 blesseth] blessed *1685–1686*[2] 19 the[1]] *add 1686*[1]*–1688* 25 an] *om. 1686*[1]*–1688*

managed by God, that *Onesimus*, when he was run away from his Master, should be taken, and, as I think, cast into that very prison, where *Paul* lay bound for the word of the Gospel; that he might there be by him converted, and then sent home again to his Master, Philem. *Behold, all things work together for Good; to them that love God; to them*, who are the called according to his purpose, *Rom.* 8. 28.

Nay, I have, my self, known some that have been made to go to hear the Word preached, against their wills: others have gone, not to hear; but to see, and to be seen; nay, to jear and flout others; again, to catch and carp at things. Some also to feed their adulterous eyes, with the sight of beautifull Objects, and yet God hath made use, even of these things, even of the wicked, and sinfull proposals of sinners, to bring them under *that* grace, that might save their souls.

Seventhly, Doth no man come to Jesus Christ, *but by the drawing*, &c. *of the Father*? then let me here caution those poor sinners, that are spectators of the change, that God hath wrought in them that are coming to Jesus Christ, not to attribute *this* work and change, to other things and causes.

There are some poor sinners in the World, that plainly see a change, a mighty change in their Neighbors, and Relations, that are coming to Jesus Christ: But as I said, they being ignorant, and not knowing whence it comes, and whither it goes (*For so is every one that is Born of the Spirit*, John 3. 8.)

Therefore, they Attribute this Change to other Causes; as,

1. To Melancholy.
2. To sitting alone.
3. To overmuch Reading.
4. To their going to too many Sermons.
5. To too much studying, and musing on what they hear.

Also, they conclude on the other side;

First, That it is for want of merry company.

Secondly, For want of Physick, and therefore they advise them to leave off Reading, going to Sermons, the company of sober People,

6 28.] *om.* *1678–1688* 9 be] to be *1684–1688* 10 again,] as also *1684–1688* 12 even of[1]] of even *1686[2]–1688* even[2]] and even *1686[1]–1688* 13 *that* grace] the Grace *1686[1]–1688*

and to be merry, to go a Gossipping, to busie themselves in the things of this World, not to sit musing alone, *&c.*

But come poor ignorant sinner, let me deal with thee, it seemes thou art turned *Counsellor for Satan*: I tell thee, thou knowest not what thou dost. Take heed of spending thy judgment after this manner; thou judgest foolishly, *And saist in this, to every one that passeth by, that thou art a Fool.*

What! count Convictions for sin, mournings for sin, and Repentance for sin, Melancholy! This is like those that on the other side, said, *These men are Drunk with new Wine*, &c. or as he that said, *Paul* was Mad, *Acts* 2. 13. *chap.* 26. 24.

Poor ignorant sinner, canst thou judge no better? What! Is sitting alone, pensive under Gods Hand; Reading the Scriptures, and hearing of Sermons, *&c.* the way to be undone! The Lord open thine Eyes, and make thee to see thine Error: Thou hast set thy self against God, thou hast despised the Operation of his Hands, thou attemptest to Murther Souls. What! canst thou give no better Counsel touching those whom God hath Wounded, than to send them to the Ordinances of Hell for help; thou biddest them be merry and lightsome: but dost thou not know that *The heart of Fools is in the House of Laughter*, Eccles. 7. 4. Thou bidest them shun the hearing of Thundring Preachers; *But is it not better to hear the Rebuke of the wise, than for a man to hear the Song of Fools?* verse 5. Thou bidst them busy themselves in the things of this World: but dost thou not know that the Lord bids, *First seek the Kingdom of God, and the Righteousness thereof*? Matt. 6. 33.

Poor ignorant sinner, hear the Counsel of God to such, and learn, thy self, to be wiser. *If any be afflicted, let him Pray, is any merry, let him sing Psalms. Blessed is he that heareth me, and hear for time to come: Save your selves from this untoward Generation; search the Scripture, give attendance to Reading. It is better to go to the House of Mourning, than to the House of Feasting*, Jam. 5. 13. Prov. 8. 32, 33, 34. *Acts* 2. 40. *Joh.* 5. 39. 1 *Tim.* 4. 13. *Eccles.* 7. 1, 2, 3.

And wilt thou judg him that doth thus, art thou almost like

8 mournings] Mourning *1688*   10 or] *add 1684–1688*   11 2. 13.] 2. 23. *1685–1688*   26 33.] 36. *1678–1688*   31–2 *than to the House of Feasting*] *om. 1686*[1]*–1688*   32 34.] *om. 1678–1688*

Elemas the Sorcerer, that sought to turn the Deputy from the Faith, thou seekest to pervert the right ways of the Lord; take heed, lest some heavy judgment overtake thee, *Acts* 13. 8, 9, 10, 11, 12, 13.

What! Teach men to quench convictions; take men off from a serious consideration of the evil of sin, of the Terrors of the world to come, and of how they shall escape the same! What! Teach men to put God and his Word out of their minds by running to merry Company, by running to the World, by Gossipping, *&c.* This is as much as to bid them say to God, *Depart from us, for we desire not the knowledge of thy ways; Or, what's the Almighty that we should serve Him! Or, what profit have we, if we keep his Ways?* Here's a Devil in Grain! What: bid men walk according to the course of this world, according to the *Prince of the Power of the Air, the Spirit that now worketh in the Children of Disobedience*, Ephes. 2. 2.

Object. *But we do not know, that such are comming to Jesus Christ, truly we wonder at them, and think they are Fools.*

Answ. *First*, Do you not know that they are coming to Jesus Christ? then they may be coming to him for ought you know, and why will you be worse than the Brute, *to speak evil of the things ye know not*? What! are ye made to be taken and destroyed, must ye utterly Perish in your own Corruptions? 2 *Pet.* 2. 12.

Secondly, Do you not know them? let them alone then. If you cannot speak good of them, speak not bad. *Refrain from these Men, and let them alone; for if this Council, or this Work, be of men, it will come to nought; but if it be of God, ye cannot overthrow it, lest haply ye be found, even to fight against God.* Acts 5. 38, 39.

Thirdly, But why do you wonder at a work of Conviction, and Conversion; know you not, that this is the Judgment of God upon you, ye despisers? *To behold, and wonder, and perish.* Acts. 13. 40, 41.

Fourthly, But why wonder, and think they are Fools? Is the way of the just an abomination to you, see that passage and be ashamed, *He that is upright in the way is an Abomination to the wicked*, Pro. 29. 27.

Fifthly, Your wondring at them, argues, that you are strangers to your selves, to conviction for sin, and to hearty desires to be saved: as also to coming to Jesus Christ.

15 2. 2.] 2. *1678–1688*   20 *ye*] *you 1684–1688*

But how shall we know, that such men are coming to Jesus Christ?

Ans. Who can make them see that Christ has made blind! (*Joh.* 9. 39.) Nevertheless, because I endeavor thy Conviction, Conversion, and Salvation, Consider,

1. Do they cry out of Sin, being burdened with it, as of an exceeding bitter thing?

2. Do they fly from it, as from the Face of a deadly Serpent?

3. Do they Cry out of the insufficiency of their own Righteousness, as to justification in the sight of God?

4. Do they Cry out after the Lord Jesus, to save them?

5. Do they see more Worth, and Merit, in one drop of Christs Blood to save them, than in all the sins of the World to Damn them?

6. Are they tender of sinning against Jesus Christ?

7. Is his Name, Person, and Undertakings, more precious to them, than is the Glory of all the World?

8. Is his Word most Dear unto them?

9. Is Faith in Christ (of which they are convinced by Gods Spirit, of the want of; and that without it, they can never close with Christ) Precious to them?

10. Do they savor Christ in his Word, and do they leave all the World for his Sake; and are they willing (God helping them) to run all hazzards, for his Name, for the love they bear to him?

11. Are his Saints precious to them?

If these things be so, whether thou seest them or no, these men are coming to Jesus Christ, *Rom.* 7. 9, 10, 11, 12, 13, 14. *Psal.* 38. 3, 4, 5, 6, 7, 8. *Heb.* 6. 18, 19, 20. *Isa.* 64. 6. *Phil.* 3. 7, 8. *Psal.* 54. 1. *Psal.* 109. 26. *Acts* 16. 30. *Psal.* 51. 7, 8. 1 *Pet.* 1. 18, 19. *Rom.* 7. 24. 2 *Cor.* 5. 2. *Acts* 5. 41. *Jam.* 2. 7. *Phil.* 3. 7, 8. *Song.* 5. 10, 11, 12, 13, 14, 15. *Psal.* 119. *Joh.* 13. 35. 1 *Joh.* 4. 7. *chap.* 3. 14. *Joh.* 16. 9. *Rom.* 14. 23. *Heb.* 11. 6. *Psal.* 19. 10, 11. *Jer.* 15. 16. *Heb.* 11. 24, 25, 26, 27. *Acts* 20. 22, 23, 24. *chap.* 21. 13. *Tit.* 3. 15. 2 *Joh.* 1. *Ephes.* 4. 16. *Phil.* 7. 1 *Cor.* 16. 24.

3 9. 39.] 2. 3. 9. *1686[1]–1688* 5 burdened] burned *1686[1]–1686[2]* 16 all] *om. 1686[1]–1688* 17 his] this *1684–1688* most] more *1684–1688* 23 all] *om. 1685–1688*

The Second Observation.

I come now to the Second Observation propounded to be spoken to; to witt,

That they that are coming to Jesus Christ are oft-times heartily afraid, that Jesus Christ will not receive them.

I told you, that this Observation is implyed in the Text, and I gather it from the largeness, and openness of the Promise [*I will in no wise cast out*]. For had there not been a proneness in us *to fear Casting out*, Christ needed not to have, as it were, waylaid our fear, as he doth, by this great and strange Expression, *In no wise* [*And him that Cometh to me, I will in no wise cast out*]. There needed not, as I may say, such a Promise, be invented by the Wisdom of Heaven, Worded at such a Rate, as it were, on purpose to dash in peeces at one blow, all the Objections of Coming Sinners; if they were not prone to admit of such Objections, to the discouraging of their own Souls. For this Word, *in no wise*; cutteth the Throat of all Objections; and it was dropt by the Lord Jesus, for that very end; and to help the Faith that is mixed with Unbelief.

And it is as it were, the sum of all Promises: neither can any Objection be made, upon the unworthyness that thou findest in thee, that this Promise will not asoile.

But I am a great sinner, sayst thou.

I will in no wise cast out, sayes Christ.

But I am an old sinner, sayst thou.

I will in no wise cast out, sayes Christ.

But I am a hard hearted sinner, sayst thou.

I will in no wise cast out, sayes Christ.

But I am a back-sliding sinner, sayst thou.

I will in no wise cast out, sayes Christ.

But I have served Satan all my dayes, sayst thou.

I will in no wise cast out, sayes Christ.

But I have sinned against Light, sayst thou.

I will in no wise cast out, sayes Christ.

But I have sinned against mercy, sayst thou.

I will in no wise cast out, sayes Christ.

2–3 spoken to] spoken *1686*[2] 33 sayes] say *1684*

But I have no good thing to bring with me, say'st thou:
I will in no wise cast out, sayes Christ.

Thus I might go on, to the end of things, and shew you, that still this promise was provided to answer all Objections; And doth answer them: But I say, what need it be, if they that are coming to Jesus Christ, are not sometimes, yea oft-times, heartily afraid, *that Jesus Christ, will cast them out*?

I will give you, now, two instances, that seem to imply the truth of this observation.

In the Nineth of *Matthew*, at the Second *Verse*, you read of a man, that was sick of the Palsie; and he was coming to Jesus Christ, being born upon a bed by his Friends: He also was coming himself, and that upon another account than any of his friends was aware of; even for the pardon of sins, and the Salvation of his Soul. Now so soon as ever he was come into the presence of Christ, Christ bids him *be of good chear*; it seems then, his heart was fainting, but what was the cause of this fainting, not his bodily Infirmity, for the cure of which his Friends did bring him to Christ, but the guilt, and burden of his sins; for the pardon of which himself did come to him, therefore he proceeds, *Be of good chear*, *thy sins are forgiven thee.*

I say, Christ saw him sinking in his mind, about how it would go with his most Noble part; and therefore, first, he applies himself to him, upon that account. For though his friends, had Faith enough as to the cure of the Body, yet he himself had little enough as to the Cure of his Soul: Therefore, Christ takes him up as a man falling down, saying, *Son*, *be of good Cheer*, *thy Sins are forgiven thee.*

That about the Prodigal, seemes pertinent also to this matter; *When he was come to himself*, *he said*, *how many hired Servants of my Father have Bred enough*, *and to spare*, *and I perish for Hunger*. *I will arise now and go to my Father*. Heartily spoken. But how did he perform his Promise? I think, not so well as he promised to do: And my ground for my Thoughts is, because his Father, so soon as he was come at him, fell upon his Neck and Kist him: Implying methinks, as if the Prodegal by this time was dejected in his mind; and

4 all] *add 1684–1688* 6 oft-times] often times *1685–1688* 13 was] were *1686*^{2}*–1688* 17–18 not his . . . to Christ,] *add 1684–1688* 19 for the pardon . . . come to him,] *add 1684–1688* 29 *have*] *hath 1686*^{2}*–1688* 33 at] to *1684–1688*

therefore, his Father gives him the most sudden and familiar token of Reconciliation.

And Kisses were of old time often used to remove Doubts and Fears. Thus *Laban*, and *Esau*, *Kiss Jacob*. Thus *Joseph*, *Kissed his Brethren*, and thus also *David*, *Kissed Absolom*, *Gen.* 31. 55. *chap.* 33. 1, 2, 3, 4, 5, 6. *chap.* 48. 9, 10. 2 *Sam.* 14. 33.

'Tis true, as I said, at first setting out, he spake heartily, as sometimes Sinners also do in their beginning to come to Jesus Christ: But might not he, yea, in all probability he had (between the first step he took, and the last, by which he accomplished that journey), many a thought, both this way, and that; as whether his Father would receive him, or no? As thus; I said, I *would go to my Father*: but how, if when I come at him, he should ask me, *Where I have all this while bin*; What must I say then? Also, if he asks me, *What is become of the portion of Goods that he gave me*; What shall I say then? If he asks me, *Who have bin my Companions*; What shall I say then? If he also shall ask me, *What hath bin my Preferment in all the time of mine absence from him*; What shall I say then? Yea, and if he ask me, *Why I came home no sooner*; What shall I say then? Thus, I say, might he reason with himself; And being Conscious to himself, that he could give but a bad Answer to any of these Interogatories; no marvel, if he stood in need first of all, *of a Kiss* from his Fathers Lips. For, had he answered the first, in Truth he must say, *I have bin a haunter of Taverns, and Alehouses*; and as for my Portion, *I spent it in Riotous Living*; my Companions, *were Whores, and Drabs*: As for my preferment, the highest was, *that I became a Hoggard*: and as for my not coming home till now, *Could I have made shift to have staid abroad any longer, I had not lain at thy Feet for Mercy now.*

I say, these things considered, and considering again, how prone poor man is, to give way, when truly awakned, to despondings, and heart-misgiveings; no marvel if he did sink in his mind, between the time of his first setting out, and that of his coming to his Father.

3. But *Thirdly*, methinks I have for the confirmation of this Truth, the consent of all the Saints that are under Heaven, to witt, *That*

14 asks] ask *1686*^{2}*–1688* 17 shall] should *1688* 24 *haunter*] *hunter 1685–1686*^{2} 26 *Hoggard*] *Hogherd 1684–1688* 27 *have staid*] *staid 1688* 31 did] *om. 1684–1688*

they that are Coming to Jesus Christ, are oft-times heartily afraid that he will not receive them.

Quest. *But what should be the Reason?*

I will Answer to this Question thus.

First, It is not for want of the revealed Will of God, that manifesteth grounds for the Contrary, for that there is a sufficiency of; yea, the Text it self, hath laid a sufficient Foundation, for incouragement, for them that are Coming to Jesus Christ.

And him that Cometh to me, I will in no wise cast out.

Secondly, It is not for want of an Invitation to Come, for that is full, and plain, *Come unto me, all ye that Labor, and are heavy Laden, and I will give you Rest*, Mat. 11. 28.

Thirdly, Neither is it, for want of a manifestation of Christs willingness to receive, as those Texts above named, with that which follows, declareth. *If any man Thirst, let him come unto me and drink*, Joh. 7. 37.

Fourthly, It is not for want of exceeding great and precious Promises, to receive them that Come. *Wherefore, come out from among them, and be ye separate, saith the Lord, and touch not the unclean thing, and I will receive you, and I will be a Father unto you, and ye shall be my Sons and Daughters, saith the Lord Almighty.* 2 *Cor.* 6. 17, 18.

Fifthly, It is not for want of Solemn Oath, and Ingagement, to save them that come: *For, because he could swear by no Greater, he swore by Himself;—That by Two Immutable Things, in which it was impossible that God should Lie, we might have a strong Consolation, who have fled for Refuge, to lay hold on the Hope set before us*, Heb. 6. 15, 16, 17, 18.

Sixthly, Neither is it for want of great Examples of God's Mercy, that have come to Jesus Christ, of which we Read most plentifully in the Word.

Therefore, it must be concluded, It is for want of that which follows:

First, It is for want of the Knowledge of Christ: Thou knowest but little of the Grace and Kindness that is in the Heart of Christ: Thou knowest but little of the Vertue and Merit of his Blood: Thou

6 that there is a sufficiency of] of that there is a sufficiency *1684–1688* 10 an] any *1685–1688* 15 *man*] *om. 1684–1688* 16 7. 37.] 7. 3. *1684–1688* 25 *a*] *om. 1688*

knowest but little of the Willingness, that is in his Heart to save thee; And this is the reason of the Fear that ariseth in thy Heart, and that causeth thee to doubt, that Christ will not receive thee. Unbelief is the Daughter of Ignorance: Therefore, Christ saith; *O Fools, and slow of Heart to Believe*, Luk. 24. 25.

Slowness of Heart to believe, flows from thy Foolishness in the Things of Christ: This is evident to all that are acquainted with themselves, and that are seeking after Jesus Christ: The more Ignorance, the more Unbelief; the more Knowledge of Christ, the more Faith. *They that know thy Name, will put their Trust in thee*, Psal. 9. 10. He therefore, that began to come to Christ but the other day, and hath yet but little Knowledge of him, he fears that Christ will not receive him: But he that hath been longer acquainted with him, he is *Strong, and hath over-come the Wicked One*, 1 Joh. 2.

When *Joseph's* Brethren came into *Egypt* to buy Corn, it is said; Joseph *knew his Brethren, but his Brethren knew not him.* What follows? Why, great Mistrust of Heart about their speeding well; specially, if *Joseph* did but answer them Roughly; calling them *Spies*, and questioning their *Truth*, and the like. And observe it; So long as their Ignorance about their Brother remained with them, whatsoever *Joseph* did, still they put the worst Sense upon it: For instance; *Joseph* upon a time, bids the Steward of his House bring them Home, to Dine with him, to Dine even in *Joseph*'s House: And how is this resented by them? Why, they were afraid: *And the men were afraid, because they were brought into* (their Brother) Joseph's *House.* And they said, *He seeketh occasion against us, and will fall upon us, and take us for Bond-men, and our Asses*, Gen. 42. Chap. 43. What! Afraid to go to *Joseph*'s House? He was their *Brother*; He intended to Feast *them*; to *Feast* them, and to Feast with them. Ah! but they were ignorant, *That he was their Brother*: And so long as their Ignorance lasted, so long their Fear terrifyed them. Just thus it is with the Sinner, that but of late is coming to Jesus Christ: He is ignorant of the Love and Pity that is in Christ to Coming-Sinners: Therefore he doubts, therefore he fears, therefore his Heart mis-gives him.

Coming-Sinner, Christ inviteth thee to Dine and Sup with him:

1 his] the *1684–1686*[2]   8 *that*] *om. 1686*[1]*–1688*   24 were[1]] are *1685–1688*
25 *into*] *unto 1684–1688*   29 and to *1686*[1]*–1688*] and *1678–1684*

He inviteth thee to a Banquet of Wine; yea, to come into his Wine-Cellar, and his Banner over thee shall be Love, *Revel.* 3. 20. *Song* 2. *Chap.* 5. But I doubt it, sayes the Sinner: But 'tis answer'd; He calls thee, invites thee to his Banquet, to his Flaggons, Apples; to his Wine, and to the Juyce of his Pomgranate. O I fear, I doubt, I mistrust! I tremble in Expectation of the contrary! *Come out of the Man, thou Dastardly Ignorance!* Be not afraid Sinner, only Believe: *He that cometh to Christ, he will in no wise cast out.*

Let the Coming-Sinner therefore seek after more of the good Knowledge of Jesus Christ: Press after it; Seek it as Silver; and dig for it, as for hid Knowledge. This will embolden thee: This will make thee wax Stronger and Stronger. *I know whom I have Believed; I know him*, said *Paul:* And what follows? Why, *And I am perswaded, that he is able to keep that which I have committed to him, against that Day*, 2 Tim. 1. 13.

What had *Paul* committed to Jesus Christ? The Answer is, He had committed to him *his Soul*. But why did he Commit his Soul to him? Why, because he *knew* him: He *knew* him to be Faithful, to be Kind: He *knew*, he would not fail him, nor forsake him; And therefore, he laid his Soul down at his Feet; and committed it to him, to keep against that Day, But,

Secondly, Thy Fears, that Christ will not receive thee, may be also a *Consequent* of thy earnest, and strong Desires after thy Salvation by him. For this I observe; That strong *Desires* to *have*, are attended with strong *Fears* of *missing*. What a Man most sets his Heart upon, and what his Desires are most after, he (oft-times) most fears, he shall not obtain. So the Man, the Ruler of the Synagogue, had a great desire, that his Daughter should live; and that Desire was attended with Fear, that she should not: Wherefore, Christ saith unto him, *Be not afraid*, Mark 5. 36.

Suppose a Young Man should have his Heart much set upon a Virgin, to have her to Wife: If ever he Fears he shall not Obtain, it is when he begins to love; now, thinks he, some body will step in betwixt my Love, and the Object of it; either they will find Fault with my Person, my Estate, my Conditions, or somthing.

4 to his Flaggons] Flaggons *1685–1688* 11 Knowledge] Treasure *1684–1688*
25 a] *om. 1685–1688* 27 the Ruler] Ruler *1684–1688*

Now thoughts begin to work, she doth not like me, or something. And thus it is with the Soul at first Coming to Jesus Christ; thou lovest him, and thy love produceth Jealousy, and that Jealousy, oft-times, beget Fears.

Now thou fearest the Sins of thy Youth, the Sins of thine old Age, the Sins of thy Calling, the Sins of thy Christian Duties, the Sins of thy Heart, or somthing: thou thinkest somthing or other will alienate the Heart and Affections of Jesus Christ from thee; thou thinkest he sees somthing in thee, for the sake of which he will refuse thy Soul.

But be content, a little more Knowledge of him, will make thee take better heart, thy earnest desires shall not be attended with such burning Fears: Thou shalt hearafter say, *This is my Infirmity* (Psal. 77. 10.).

Thou art *Sick of Love*; a very sweet Disease, and yet every Disease has some weakness attending of it; yet I with this Distemper (if it be lawful to call it so) was more Epidemical. Dye of this Disease, I would gladly do; 'tis better than Life it self, though it be attended with Fears. But thou cryest, *I cannot obtain*: Well, be not too hasty in making Conclusions: If Jesus Christ had not put his Finger in at the Hole of the Lock, thy Bowels would not have been troubled for him (*Song* 5.). Mark how the Prophet hath it: *They shall walk after the Lord; he shall Roar like a Lyon: When he shall Roar, the Children shall Tremble from the* East*: They shall Tremble like a Bird out of* Egypt, *and as a Dove out of the Land of* Assyria, Hos. 11. 10, 11.

When God *Roars* (as oft-times the Coming Soul hears him Roar), what Man, that is coming, can do otherwise than Tremble? (*Amos* 3. 8.) But Trembling he comes: *He sprang in, and came Trembling, and fell down before* Paul *and* Silas, Act. 16. 29.

Should you ask him that we mentioned but now; How long is it, since you began to fear you should miss of this Damosel you Love so? The Answer would be; Ever since I began to Love her: But did you not fear it before? No; nor should I fear it now, but that I vehemently Love her. Come Sinner, let us apply it: How long is

5 fearest] feareth *1685–1688* 13 *my*] *mine 1678* 14 10.] *om. 1678–1688*
30 29.] *om. 1678–1688* 33 would] will *1684–1688*

it since thou begannest to Fear, that Jesus Christ will not Receive thee? Thy Answer is; Ever since I began to desire, that he would save my Soul. I began to Fear, when I began to Come: And the more my Heart burns in Desires after him, the more I feel my Heart fear, I shall not be Saved by him.

See now; Did not I tell thee, That thy Fears were but the Consequence of strong Desires? Well, fear not, Coming-Sinner; Thousands of Coming-Souls are in thy Condition, and yet they will also get safe into Christ's Bosom. *Say* (sayes Christ) *to them that are of a fearful Heart, Be strong, fear not;—Your God will come and Save you*, Isa. 35. 4. Chap. 63, 1.

Thirdly, Thy Fear that Christ will not Receive thee, *May arise from a Sense of thine own Unworthyness.* Thou seest what a poor, sorry, wretched, worthless Creature thou art; And seeing this, thou fearest Christ will not Receive thee. *Alas*, say'st thou, *I am the Vilest of all Men; a Town-Sinner, a Ring-leading-Sinner! I am not only a Sinner my self, but have made others two-fold worse the Children of Hell also. Besides, Now I am under some Awakenings, and Stirrings of Mind after Salvation; even now I find my heart Rebellious, Carnal, Hard, Treacherous, Desperate, prone to Unbelief, to Despair: It forgetteth the Word; it wandreth, it runneth to the Ends of the Earth. There is not (I am perswaded) one in all the World, that hath such a desperate wicked Heart, as mine is: My Soul is careless to do Good; but none more earnest to do that which is Evil.*

Can such an one as I am, Live in Glory? Can an Holy, a Just, and Righteous God, once think (with Honour to his Name) of Saving such a Vile Creature as I am? I fear it. Will he shew Wonders to such a dead Dog as I am? I doubt it.

I am cast out, to the loathing of my Person; yea, I loath my self: I stink in mine own Nostrils. How can I then be accepted by an Holy and Sin-abhorring God? (Psal. 38. 5, 6, 7. Ezek. 16. Chap. 20. 42, 43, 44.) *Saved I would be; and, Who is there, that would not, were they in my Condition? Indeed, I wonder at the Madness and Folly of others, when I see them so Merry in their Chains; while I see them Leap and Skip so carelessly about the Mouth of*

1 begannest] begunnest *1684–1688* 8 also] *om. 1684–1688* 13 *Unworthyness*] *Unweariedness 1684–1688* 30 *an*] *a 1686[1]–1688* 31 16.] 10. *1684–1688* 33–4 *so Merry . . . see them*] *om. 1685–1688* 34 *carelessly*] *carless 1684–1688*

Hell. Bold Sinner, How darest thou tempt God, by Laughing at the Breach of his Holy Law? But Alas! They are not so bad one way, but I am worse another: I wish, my Self were any Body but my Self: And yet here again, I know not what to wish. When I see such, as I believe, are coming to Jesus Christ; O I bless them! But am confounded in my self, to see how unlike (as I think) I am to every good Man in the World. They can Hear, Read, Pray, Remember, Repent; be Humble, and Do every thing better than so Vile a Wretch as I.

I, Vile Wretch, am good for nothing, but to burn in Hell-fire; and when I think of that, I am confounded too.

Thus the Sense of Unworthyness, creates and heightens Fears in the Hearts of them that are coming to Jesus Christ; But indeed, it should not: For, who needs the Physitian, but the Sick? Or, who did Christ come into the World to Save, but the Chief of Sinners? (*Mar*. 2. 17. 1 *Tim*. 1. 15.) Wherefore, the more thou seest thy Sins, the faster fly thou to Jesus Christ. And let the Sense of thy own Unworthyness, prevail with thee yet to go faster. As it is with the Man that carrieth his broken Arm in a Sling to the Bone-setter; still as he thinks of his broken Arm, and as he feels the Pain and Anguish, he hastens his Pace to the Man: And if Satan meets thee, and asketh, Whither goest thou? Tell him, Thou art Maimed, and art going to the Lord Jesus. If he objects thine own Unworthiness, Tell him; That even as the Sick seeketh the Physitian, and as he that hath broken Bones, seeks him that can Set them: So thou art going to Jesus Christ for Cure and Healing, for thy Sin-sick-Soul.

But it oft times happeneth to the Coming-Soul, as it happeneth to him that flies for his Life; He despairs of Escaping, and therefore delivers up himself into the Hand of the Pursuer. But, up, up, Sinner; be of good chear, Christ came to Save the Unworthy Ones: Be not Faithless, but Believe. Come away Man; the Lord Jesus calls thee, saying; *And him that cometh to me, I will in no wise cast out*.

Fourthly, Thy Fear that Christ will not Receive thee, may arise

6 *every*] *a very 1685–1688* *Man*] *many 1688* 15 2. 17.] 1. 17. *1678–1688*
21 Whither *1685–1688*] Whether *1678–1684* 23 and] *om. 1685–1688*
27–8 the Coming-Soul . . . happeneth to] *om. 1685–1688*

from a Sense of the exceeding Mercy of being Saved. Sometime Salvation is in the Eyes of him that desires it, so great, so huge, so wonderful a thing, that the very Thoughts of the Excellency of it, ingenders Unbelief about obtaining it, in the Heart of those that unfeignedly desire it. *Seemeth it to you* (said *David*) *a Light thing, to be a King*'s *Son-in-Law*, 1 Sam. 18. 23. So the Thoughts of the Greatness and Glory of the Thing propounded; as Heaven, Eternal Life, Eternal Glory, to be with God, and Christ, and Angels: These are great Things; Things too Good (saith the Soul, that is little in his own Eyes), Things too Rich (saith the Soul, that is truly poor in Spirit), for me.

Besides, the Holy Ghost hath a way to greaten Heavenly things, to the understanding of the coming sinner; yea, and at the same time to greaten too the sin, and unworthiness of that sinner. Now the Soul staggeringly wonders, saying; What! to be made like Angels, like Christ! To live in Eternal bliss, joy and felicity! This is for Angels, and for them that can walk like Angels.

If a *Prince*, *a Duke*, or *Earl*, should send (by the Hand of his Servant) to some poor, sorry, beggarly scrub, to take her for his Master, to wife; and the Servant should come and say, My Lord and Master, such an one, hath sent me to thee, to take thee to him to wife: he is rich, beautiful; and of excellent qualities; he is Loving, Meek, Humble, Well-spoken, *&c.* What now would this poor, sorry, beggarly Creature think? what would she say, or how would she frame an answer? When *King David* sent to *Abigail* upon this account, and though she was a rich woman, yet she said, *Behold, Let thine hand maid be a Servant to wash the feet of the Servants of my Lord* (1 Sam. 25. 40, 41.). She was confounded, she could not well tell what to say, the offer was so great, beyond what could in reason be expected.

But suppose this great person should Second his Sute, and send to this Sorry Creature again; What would she say now? Would she not say, *you Mock me*? But what if he affirms that he is in good earnest, and that his Lord *must* have her to wife, yea, suppose he should prevail upon her to Credit his Message, and to address

2 it,] *om. 1684–1688* 5 said] saith *1686*[1]*–1688* 18 or] a *1685–1688*
19 to[1]] for *1685–1688*

her self for her Journey: Yet behold, every thought of her pedigree confounds her; also her sense of want of beauty, makes her ashamed: and if she doth but think of being imbraced, the unbelief that is mixed with that thought, whirls her into tremblings: And now she calls her self fool for believing the Messenger, and thinks not to go: If she thinks of being bold, she Blushes, and the least thought that she shall be rejected, when she comes at him, makes her look as if she would give up the Ghost.

And is it a wonder then, to see a Soul that is drowned with the sense of glory, and a sense of its own nothingness, to be confounded in it self, and to fear that the glory apprehended, is too great, too good, and too rich for such an one?

That thing, Heaven and Eternal Glory, is so great; and I that would have it, so small, so sorry a Creature, that the thoughts of obtaining, confounds me.

Thus, I say, doth the greatness of the things desired, quite dash and overthrow the mind of the desirer: O it is too bigg, it is too big! It is too great a mercy.

But coming sinner, let me reason with thee, Thou say'st it is too bigg, too great. Well, will things that are less, satisfie thy Soul? will a less thing than Heaven, than Glory, and Eternal life, answer thy desires? No, nothing less: yet I fear they are too big, and too good for me, ever to obtain. Well, as big, and as good as they are, God giveth them to such as thou; They are not too big for God to give. No, not too big to give freely: be content, let God give like Himself; he is that Eternal God, and he giveth like himself. When *Kings* give, they do not use to give as poor men do. Hence it is said, that *Nabal* made a feast in his house, *Like the feast of a King*: And again, *All these things did* Araunah, *as a King*, *give unto David*, 1 Sam. 25. 2 Sam. 24. Now God is a great King, let him give like a King; Nay let him give like himself, and do thou receive like thy self: He hath all, and thou hast nothing. God told his people of old, that he would save them in truth, and in righteousness; and that they should return to, and injoy the Land, which before, for their sins, had spued them out: and then adds, under a supposition of their coun-

9 with] in *1686[1]–1688* 23 ever] even *1686[1]–1688* 26 he[2]] *om. 1684–1688*

ting the mercy too good, or too big: *If it be marvellous in the eyes of the remnant of this people in these days, should it also be Marvellous in mine eyes, saith the Lord of hosts*, Zech. 8. 6.

As who should say, they are now in Captivity, and little in their own eyes; therefore they think the mercy of returning to *Canaan*, is a mercy too marvellously big for them to injoy; but if it be so in their eyes, it is not so in mine: I will do for them, *like God*, if they will but receive my bounty, *like sinners*.

Coming sinner, God can give his heavenly *Canaan*, and the glory of it unto thee; yea none ever had them, but as a *gift*, a *free* gift: He hath given us his **Son**, *how shall he not then with him also freely give us all things?* Rom. 8. 32.

It was not the worthiness of *Abraham*, or *Moses*, or *David*, or *Peter*, or *Paul*: But the mercy of God that made them inheritors of Heaven. If God thinks thee worthy, judge not thy self unworthy; but take it, and be thankfull. And it is a good signe, he intends to give thee, if he hath drawn out thy heart to ask. *O Lord, thou hast heard the desire of the humble, thou wilt prepare their heart, thou wilt encline thine ear* (Psal. 10. 17.).

When God is said to encline his ear, it implies an intention to bestow the mercy desired: Take it therefore, thy Wisdom will be to receive, not *sticking* at thine own unworthiness. It is said, *He raiseth up the poor out of the dust, and lifteth up the beggar from the dunghill, to set them among Princes, and to make them inherit the thrown of glory*. Again, *He raiseth up the poor out of the dust, and lifteth some needy* **Out** *of the dunghill, that he may set him with Princes, even with the Princes of his people*. 1 Sam. 2. 8. Psal. 113. 7, 8.

You see also, when God made a Wedding for his Son, he called not the great, nor the rich, nor the mighty, *but the poor, the maimed, the halt, and the blind* (Mat. 22. Luk. 14.).

Fifthly, Thy fears that Christ will not receive thee, may arise from the hideous Roarings of the Devil, who pursues thee. He that hears him Roar, must be a mighty Christian, if he can, at that time, deliver himself from fear. He is called a Roaring Lyon, and then, to alude to that in Isaiah, *if one look into them, they have darkness*

12 Rom. 8.] *om.* *1686*^{2}*–1688* 32.] *om.* *1678–1688* 18 *heart*] *Hearts* *1686*^{1}*–1688*
22 thine] thy *1684–1688* 32 Roarings] Roaring *1686*^{1}*–1688*

and sorrow, and the Light is darkned in their very Heaven, 1 Pet. 5. 8. Isa. 5. 30.

There are two things, among many, that Satan useth to Roar **Out**, after them, that are coming to Jesus Christ.

1. *That they are not Elected.* Or,

2. *That they have sinned the sin against the Holy Ghost.*

To both these I answer briefly.

First, Touching election, out of which thou fearest thou art excluded: Why coming sinner, even the Text it self affordeth thee help against this doubt, and that by a double argument.

First, That coming to Christ, is by vertue of the gift, promise, and drawing of the Father; but thou art a coming, therefore God hath given thee, promised thee, and is drawing thee to Jesus Christ. Coming sinner, hold to this: and when Satan beginneth to Roar again, Answer: but I feel my heart moving after Jesus Christ; but that would not be, if I were not given by promise, and drawing, to Christ by the power of the Father.

Secondly, Jesus Christ hath promised, that *him that cometh to Him, he will in no wise cast out*: And if he hath said it, will he not make it good; I mean, even thy Salvation? for, as I have said already; *Not to cast out*, is to receive, and admit to the benefit of Salvation: if then the Father hath given thee, as is manifest by thy coming; and if Christ will receive thee, thou coming Soul; as 'tis plain he will, because he hath said, *he will in no wise cast thee out*: Then be confident, and let those conclusions, that as naturally flow from the Text, as light from the Sun, or water from the fountain, stay thee.

If Satan therefore objecteth, *but thou art not elected*; Answer. But I am coming, Satan, I am coming; and that I could not be, but that the Father draws me; and I am coming to such a Lord Jesus, as *will in no wise cast me out*. Further, Satan, were I not elect, the Father would not draw me, nor would the Son so graciously open his bosom to me. I am perswaded, that not one of the non-elect, shall ever be able to say (no, not in the day of judgement) I did sincerely come to Jesus Christ. Come they may feignedly, as *Judas* and *Magus*

1 *darkned*] *darkness* *1685–1688* 3 useth] used *1685–1686*[2] 16 I] it *1686*[1]–*1688* 24 hath] had *1685* 28 *elected*] *Ejected* *1686*[1]–*1686*[2]

did; But that is not our question: Therefore, O thou honest-hearted coming sinner, be not afraid, but come!

As to the Second part of the Objection, about sinning the sin against the Holy Ghost: The same argument overthrows that also. But I will argue thus.

First, Coming to Christ, is by vertue of a special gift of the Father; but the Father giveth no such gift to them that have sinned that sin; therefore thou that art coming, hast not committed that sin. That the Father giveth no such gift to them that has sinned this sin; Is evident,

1. Because such have sinned themselves out of God's Favour, *They shall never have Forgiveness*, Matth. 12. 32. But it is a special Favour of God to give unto a Man, to come to Jesus Christ; because thereby he obtaineth Forgiveness: Therefore, he that cometh, hath not sinned that Sin.

2. They that have sinned the Sin against the Holy-Ghost, have sinned themselves out of an Interest in the Sacrifice of Christ's Body and Blood; *There remains for such, no more Sacrifice for Sin*: But God giveth not Grace to any of them to come to Christ, that have no share in the Sacrifice of his Body and Blood: Therefore, thou that art coming to him, hast not sinned that Sin; *Heb.* 10. 26.

Secondly, Coming to Christ, is by the Special Drawing of the Father: *No Man cometh to me, except the Father which hath sent me, draw him:* But the Father draweth not him to Christ, for whom he hath not alotted Forgiveness by his Blood. Therefore, they that are coming to Jesus Christ, have not sinned that Sin; because he hath alotted them Forgiveness by his Blood, *Joh.* 6. 44.

That the Father cannot draw them to Jesus Christ, for whom he hath not alotted Forgiveness of Sins, is manifest to Sense: For that would be a plain Mockery, a Flam; neither becoming his Wisdom, Justice, Holyness, nor Goodness.

Thirdly, Coming to Jesus Christ, lays a Man under the Promise of Forgiveness, and Salvation: But it is impossible, that he that hath sinned that Sin, should ever be put under a Promise of these. Therefore, he that hath sinned that Sin, can never have Heart to come to Jesus Christ.

Fourthly, Coming to Jesus Christ, lays a Man under his Intercession; *For he ever Liveth to make Intercession for them that come,*

Heb. 7. 25. Therefore, he that is coming to Jesus Christ, cannot have sinned that Sin.

Christ has forbidden his People, to pray for them that have sinned that Sin; and therefore, will not pray for them himself: But he prays for them that come.

Fifthly, He that hath sinned that Sin, Christ is to him of no more Worth, than is a Man that is Dead; *For he hath Crucified to himself, the Son of God:* Yea, and hath also counted his Precious Blood, as the Blood of an Unholy Thing; *Heb.* 6. *chap.* 10. Now, he that hath this low Esteem of Christ, will never come to him for Life: But the Coming-Man has an high Esteem of his Person, Blood, and Merits. Therefore, he that is coming, has not Committed that Sin.

Sixthly, If he that hath sinned this Sin, might yet come to Jesus Christ; then must the Truth of God be overthrown: which saith in one Place; *He hath never Forgiveness:* and in another, *I will in no wise cast him out:* Therefore, that he may never have Forgiveness, he shall never have Heart to come to Jesus Christ. *It is impossible, that such an one should be Renewed, either to, or by Repentance*, Heb. 6. Wherefore, never trouble thy Head, nor Heart, about this Matter: He that cometh to Jesus Christ, cannot have sinned against the Holy Ghost.

Sixthly, Thy Fears that Christ will not Receive thee, *may arise from thine own Folly, in Inventing; yea, in thy Chalking out to God a way to bring thee Home to Jesus Christ.* Some Souls that are coming to Jesus Christ, are great Tormentors of themselves upon this account: They conclude, that if their Coming to Jesus Christ is right, they must needs be brought Home thus and thus: As to instance;

1. Sayes one, If God be bringing of me to Jesus Christ, then will he load me with the Guilt of Sin, till he makes me Roar again.

2. If God be indeed a bringing of me home to Jesus Christ, then must I be assaulted with dreadful Temptations of the Devil.

3. If God be indeed a bringing of me to Jesus Christ; then even when I come at him, I shall have wonderful Revelations of him.

This is the way that some Sinners appoint for God: But, perhaps, he will not walk therein; yet will he bring them to Jesus Christ: But now, because they come not the Way of their own Chalking

9 *chap.*] *om. 1684–1688* 29 of] *om. 1685–1688* 31 bringing] bringer *1685–1688*

out, therefore they are at a loss. They look for Heavy Load and Burden; but, perhaps, God gives them a Sight of their lost Condition, and addeth not that heavy Weight and Burden. They look for fearful Temptations of Satan; but God sees, that yet they are not fit for them: Nor is the Time come, that he should be Honoured by them in such a Condition. They look for great and glorious Revelations, of Christ, Grace and Mercy: But perhaps, God only takes the Yoke from off their Jaws, and lays Meat before them. And now again, they are at a loss, yet a-coming to Jesus Christ: *I drew them* (saith God) *with the Cords of a Man, with the Bands of Love: I took the Yoke from off their Jaws, and laid Meat unto them*, Hos. 11. 4.

Now, I say, if God brings thee to Christ, and not by the Way that thou hast appointed, then thou art at a loss; and for thy being at a loss, *Thou mayst thank thy self*. God hath more ways than thou knowst of, to bring a Sinner to Jesus Christ: But he will not give thee before-hand an Account, by which of them he will bring thee to Christ; *Isa*. 40. 13. *Job* 33. 13.

Sometimes, he hath his Way *in the Whirlwind*; but sometimes *the Lord is not there*, Nah. 1. 3. 1 King. 19. 11.

If God will deal more gently with thee, than with others of his Children, grudge not at it: Refuse not the Waters that go softly, lest he bring upon thee the Waters of the Rivers, strong and many; even these two smoaking Fire-brands, the *Devil*, and *Guilt* of Sin; *Isa*. 8. 6, 7. He said to *Peter*, *Follow me*: And what Thunder did *Zacheus* hear or see? Zacheus, *come down*, said Christ; *and he came down* (sayes *Luke*) *and Received him Joyfully*.

But had *Peter*, or *Zacheus*, made the Objection that thou hast made; and *Directed the Spirit of the Lord, as thou hast done*; they might have looked long enough, before they had found themselves coming to Jesus Christ.

Besides, I will tell thee; That the greatness of Sense of Sin, the hideous Roarings of the Devil, yea, and abundance of Revelations, will not prove that God is bringing the Soul to Jesus Christ: As *Balaam*, *Cain*, *Judas*, and others can witness.

9 Jesus] *om.* *1686²–1688* 11 11. 4.] 11. 14. *1685–1688* 22 upon] up *1685–1686²*] up to *1688* 24 said] saith *1686¹–1688* 32 Roarings] Roaring *1686¹–1688*

Further; Consider, that what thou hast not of these things *now*, thou mayst have *another* time, and that to thy Distraction: Wherefore, instead of being discontent, because thou art not in the Fire, because thou hearest not the Sound of the Trumpet, and Alarum of War; *Pray, that thou enter not into Temptation:* Yea, come boldly to the Throne of Grace, and obtain Mercy, and find Grace to help in that time of need; *Psal.* 88. 15. *Matth.* 26. 40, 41. *Heb.* 4. 16.

Poor Creature! Thou criest, If I were Tempted, I could come faster, and with more Confidence to Jesus Christ: Thou sayest thou knowst not what. What sayes *Job*? *With-draw thy Hand from me, and let not thy Dread make me afraid: Then call thou, and I will answer; or let me speak, and answer thou me*, Job 13. 22. It is not the overheavy Load of Sin, but the Discovery of Mercy; not the Roaring of the Devil, but the Drawing of the Father, that makes a Man come to Jesus Christ: *I my self know all these Things.*

True, sometimes, yea, most an end, they that come to Jesus Christ, come the Way that thou desirest; the Loaden, Tempted Way: But the Lord also leads some by the Waters of Comfort. If I was to chuse, when to go a long Journey; to wit, Whether I would go it in the Dead of Winter, or in the Pleasant Spring (though if it was a very profitable Journey, as that of coming to Christ is, I would chuse to go it through Fire and Water, before I would lose the Benefit). But I say, if I might chuse the time, I would chuse to go it in the Pleasant Spring; because the Way would be more Delightsome, the Dayes longer and Warmer, the Nights shorter, and not so Cold. And it is observable, that that very Argument that thou usest to weaken thy Strength in the Way, that very Argument Christ Jesus useth to incourage his Beloved to come to him: *Arise* (saith he) *my Love, my Fair One, and come away;* (Why?) *For lo, the Winter is past, the Rain is over and gone, the Flowers appear in the Earth, the time of the Singing of Birds is come, and the Voyce of the Turtle is heard in our Land. The Fig-Tree putteth forth her Green Figs, and the Vine, with her tender Grapes, give a good Smell: Arise my Love, my Fair One, and come away*, Song 2. 10, 11, 12, 13.

2 *now*] here *1686*[1]–*1688* 13 22.] 2. *1678–1688* 18 Loaden] Loading *1684–1688* 24 But I say . . . the time,] *add 1684–1688*

Trouble not thy self therefore, Coming-Sinner. If thou seest thy lost Condition by Original and Actual Sin; if thou seest thy Need of the spotless Righteousness of Jesus Christ; if thou art willing to be found in him, and to take up thy Cross and follow him: Then pray for a fair Wind, and good Weather, and come away. Stick no longer in a Muse and Doubt about Things, but come away to Jesus Christ: Do it, I say, lest thou tempt God to lay the Sorrows of a Travelling Woman upon thee. Thy Folly in this thing, may make him do it. Mind what follows: *The Sorrows of a Travelling Woman shall come upon him: Why? He is an unwise Son; so he should not stay long in the Place of the breaking forth of the Children*, Hos. 13. 13.

Seventhly, Thy Fears that Christ will not Receive thee, may arise from those Decayes that thou findest in thy Soul, even while thou art coming to him: Some, even as they are coming to Jesus Christ, do find themselves grow worse and worse; And this is, indeed, a sore Tryal to the poor Coming-Sinner.

To explain my self: There is such an one a coming to Jesus Christ; who, when at first, he began to look out after him, was Sensible, Affectionate, and broken in Spirit: but now is grown Dark, Sensless, Hard-hearted, and inclining to neglect Spiritual Duries, *&c.* Besides, he now finds in himself, Inclinations to Unbelief, Atheisme, Blasphemy, and the like: Now he finds, he cannot Tremble at God's Word, his Judgements, nor at the Apprehensions of Hell-fire: Neither can he, as he thinketh, be sorry for these Things. Now, this is a sad Dispensation: The Man under the Sixth Head, complained for want of Temptations; but thou hast enough of them: Art thou glad of them, Tempted, Coming-Sinner? They that never were Exercised with them, may think it a fine thing to be within the Range; but he that is there, is ready to sweat Blood for Sorrow of Heart, and to howl for Vexation of Spirit.

This man is in the Wilderness, among the wild Beasts: *here* he sees a Bear, *there* a Lyon, *Yonder* a Leopard, a Wolf, a Dragon: Devils of all sorts, doubts of all sorts: Fears of all sorts Haunt and Molest his Soul. Here he sees smoak, yea, feels fire and brimstone,

1 therefore] *om. 1684–1688* 11 *the Children 1686*[1]*–1686*[2]] *Children 1678–1685, 1688* 12 arise] rise *1684–1688* 23 Judgements] Judgment *1685–1686*[2] 25–6 complained] complaineth *1685–1688* 31 the[2]] *om. 1686*[1]*–1688* 33 Fears] Fear *1684* Haunt] Haunts *1684*

scattered upon his secret places; he hears the sound of an Horrible Tempest.

O! My friends, even the Lord Jesus that knew all things, even He, saw no pleasure in Temptations, nor did He desire to be in them: Wherefore one Text saith, *he was led*, and an other, *he was driven* of the Spirit into the wilderness, to be tempted of the Devil. *Mat.* 4. 1. *Mar.* 1. 12.

But to return, Thus it happeneth sometimes to them that are coming to Jesus Christ. A sad hap indeed; one would think, that he that is flying from Wrath to come, has little need of such Clogges as these; And yet so it is, and wofull experience proves it: The Church of old Complained, *that her enemies over-took her, between the straights.* Just between hope and fear, Heaven and Hell, *Lam.* 1. 3.

This man feeleth the infirmity of his flesh; he findeth a *proneness* in himself to be desperate: now he chides with God, Flings and Tumbles like a Wild Bull in a net, and still the guilt of all returns upon himself, to the Crushing of him to peices; Yet he feeleth his heart so hard, that he can find, as he thinks, no kind falling under any of his Miscarriages. Now he is a lump of confusion in his own eyes, whose Spirit, and Actions are without order.

Temptations serve the Christian, as the Shepheards dogs serveth the silly sheep, that is coming behind the flock; he runs upon it, pulls it down, Worries it, Wounds it, and grievously bedabbleth it with dirt and wet in the lowest places of the Furrows of the field: And not leaving it, untill it is half dead; nor then neither, except God rebuke.

Here is *now* room for fears of being cast away. *Now* I see I am lost, sayes the sinner; *This* is not coming to Jesus Christ, sayes the sinner; such a desperate hard, and wretched heart as mine is, cannot be a gracious one, saith the sinner: And bid such an one be Better; he sayes, I cannot, no I cannot.

Quest. *But what will you say to a Soul in this condition?*

Answ. *I will say, that Temptations have attended the best of Gods people; I will say, that Temptations come to do us good; and I will say also,*

14 3.] *om. 1678–1688* 24 Worries *1685–1688*] worry *1678–1684* Wounds *1685–1688*] wound *1678–1684*

that there is a difference betwixt growing worse and worse, and thy seeing more clearly how bad thou art.

There is a man of an ill-favoured countenance, who hath too high a conceit of his beauty; and wanting the benefit of a glass, he still stands in his own conceit; at last a Limner is sent unto him, who draweth his ill-favoured face to the life: now looking thereon, he begins to be convinc't that he is not half so handsome, as he thought he was. Coming sinner, thy Temptations are these painters, they have drawn out thy ill-favoured heart to the life, and have set it before thine eyes, and now thou seest how ill favoured thou art.

Hezekiah was a good man, yet when he lay sick (for ought I know) he had some what too good an opinion of his heart; and for ought I know also, the Lord might, upon his recovery, leave him to a Temptation, that he might better know All that was in his heart. Compare, *Isa.* 38. 1, 2, 3. with 2 *Chron.* 32. 31.

Alas! we are sinfull out of measure, but see it not to the full, untill an hour of Temptation comes: But when it comes, it doth as the Painter doth, it draweth out our heart to the life: Yet the sight of what we are, should not keep us from coming to Jesus Christ.

There are two ways, by which God lets a man into a sight of the Naughtyness of his heart: One is, by the light of the Word, and spirit of God; and the other is, by the Temptations of the Devil. But by the first, we see our naughtiness one way, and by the second, another. By the Light of the Word, and Spirit of God, thou hast a sight of thy naughtyness, as by the light of the Sun, thou hast a sight of the spots, and defilements that are in thy house or raiment. Which light gives thee to see a necessity of cleansing, but maketh not the blemishes to spread more abominably. But when Satan comes, when he tempts, he puts life and rage into our sins, and turnes them, as it were, into so many devils within us. Now like prisoners they attempt to brake through the prison of our body; they will attempt to get out at our eyes, mouths, ears, any ways; To the Scandal of the Gospel, and Reproach of Religion, to the darkning of our evidences, and damning of our souls.

22 Word] World *1686*[2] 25 Word] World *1686*[2] 26 as] and *1684–1688*
33 mouths] Mouth *1686*[1]*–1688*

But I shall say, as I said before, this hath oft times been the Lot of Gods people. And, *No Temptation hath over-taken thee, but such as is common to man; and God is faithfull, who will not suffer thee to be tempted above what thou art able*, 1 Cor. 10. 13. See the Book of *Job*, the Book of *Psalms*, and that of the *Lamentations*. And remember further, that Christ himself was tempted to blaspheme, to worship the devil, and to Murder himself (*Mat.* 4. *Luk.* 4.). Temptations, worse then which, thou canst hardly be over-taken with. But he was sinless. That is true. And he is thy Saviour, and that is as true: Yea, it is as true also, that by his being tempted, he became the Conqueror of the tempter, and a succourer of those that are tempted, *Col.* 2. 14, 15. *Heb.* 2. 17. chap. 4. 15, 16.

Quest. *But what should be the reason, that some that are coming to Christ, should be so Lamentably cast down, and buffeted with Temptations?*

Answ. It may be for several causes.

First, Some that are coming to Christ, cannot be perswaded, untill the Temptation comes, that they are so vile as the Scripture saith they are: True, they see so much of their wretchedness, as to drive them to Christ; but there is an *over*, and *above*, of wickedness, which they see not. *Peter* little thought that he had had Cursing, and Swearing, and Lying, and an inclination in his heart to deny his Master, before the Temptation came: But when that indeed, came upon him, then he found it there to his sorrow. *Joh.* 13. 36, 37, 38. *Mark* 14. 36, 37, 38, 39, 40, 68, 69, 70, 71, 72.

Secondly, Some that are coming to Jesus Christ, are too much affected with their own graces, and too little taken with Christs person; wherefore God, to take them off from doteing upon their own Jewels, and that they might look more to the person, undertaking, and merits of his Son, plunges them into the ditch by Temptations. And this I take to be the meaning of *Job*. *If I wash me*, said he, *with snow-water, and make my self never so clean, yet wilt thou plung me in the ditch, and mine own clothes shall abhor me*, Job 9. 30, 31. *Job* had been before a little too much Tampering with his own graces, and setting his excellencies a little too high (as these Texts make manifest, *Job* 33. 8, 9, 10, 11, 12. chap. 34. 5, 6, 7, 8, 9. chap.

12 *Heb.* 2. 17.] *Heb.* 2. 15. *1686[1]–1688* 33 31] *om.* *1685–1688* before] *om.* *1684–1688*

35. 2, 3. chap. 38. 1, 2. chap. 40. 1, 2, 3, 4. chap. 42. 3, 4, 5, 6.). But by that the Temptation was ended you find him better taught.

Yea, God doth oft-times, even for this thing as it were, take our graces from us, and so leave us almost quite to our selves, and to the tempter, that we may learn not to love the *Picture*, more than the *person* of his Son. See how he dealt with them in the *Sixteenth* of *Ezek.* and the *Second* of *Hosea.*

Thirdly, Perhaps thou hast been given too much, to Judge thy brother, to condemn thy brother, because a poor tempted man: And God, to bring down the pride of thy heart, letteth the tempter loose upon thee, that thou also mayest feel thy self weak. *For pride goeth before destruction, and an haughty spirit before a fall.* Pro. 16. 18.

Fourthly, It may be thou hast dealt a little too roughly with those that God hath this way wounded; not considering thy self, lest thou also be tempted: and therefore God hath suffered it to come unto thee, *Gal.* 6. 1.

Fifthly, It may be thou wast given to slumber, and sleep, and therefore these Temptations were sent to awaken thee. You know that *Peters* Temptation came upon him, after his sleeping; then, instead of watching and praying; then he denyed, and denyed, and denyed his Master, *Mat.* 26.

Sixthly, It may be thou hast presumed too far, and stood too much in thine own strength, and therefore is a time of Temptation come upon thee. This was also one cause, why it came upon *Peter. Though all men forsake thee, yet will not I.* Ah! that's the way to be tempted indeed, *Joh.* 13. 36, 37, 38.

Seventhly, It may be, God intends to make thee wise, to speak a word in season, to others that are afflicted; and therefore he suffereth thee to be Tempted. *Christ was tempted, that he might be able to succour them that are tempted.* Heb. 2. 18.

Eighthly, It may be *Satan* hath dared God, to suffer him to tempt thee; promising himself, that if he will but let him do it, *thou wilt curse him to his face.* Thus he obtained leave against *Job*; wherefore take heed, tempted soul, lest thou provest the devils sayings true. *Job* 1. chap. 2.

2 Temptation was] Temptations was *1685–1686*[2]] Temptations were *1688*
7 *Ezek.*] *Ezekiel 1684–1688* 14 lest] least *1686*[2] 32 himself] *add 1684–1688*

Ninethly, It may be thy graces must be tryed in the fire, that that rust that cleaveth to them, may be taken away, and themselves proved, both before Angels and Devils, to be far better than of Gold that perisheth; it may be also, that thy graces are to receive special Praises and Honour, and Glory, at the coming of the Lord Jesus (to Judgement) for all the exploits that thou hast Acted by them against Hell, and its infernal crue, in the day of thy Temptation, 1 *Pet.* 1. 6, 7.

Tenthly, It may be, God would have others learn by thy sighs, groans and complaints under Temptation, to beware of those sins; for the sake of which, thou art at present delivered to the Tormentors.

But to conclude this, put the worst to the worst (and then things will be bad enough), suppose that thou art to this day without the grace of God, yet thou art but a miserable Creature, a sinner, that has need of a blessed Saviour; and the Text presents thee with one as good, and kind, as heart can wish: who also for thy incouragement saith, *And him that cometh to me, I will in no wise cast out.*

To come therefore to a word of Application.

IS it so? *That they that are coming to Jesus Christ, are oft-times heartily afraid, that Jesus Christ will not receive them.* Then this teacheth us these things:

First, That faith, and doubting, may at the same time have their residence in the same soul. *O Thou of little faith, wherefore didst thou doubt?* Mat. 14. 31. He saith not, O! Thou of **No** faith; but O! Thou of **Little** faith. Because he had a little faith in the midest of his many doubts. The same is true, even of many that are coming to Jesus Christ: They come, and fear they come not, and doubt they come not. When they look upon the promise, or, a word of incouragement by faith, then they *come*; but when they look upon themselves, or the difficulties that lie before them, then they *doubt*. Bid me **Come**, said *Peter*: **Come**, said Christ. So he went down out of the Ship to go

2 rust] rest *1686*[2] 3 to be] *add 1684–1688* 28 not] *add 1684–1688*
28–9 they come not] *add 1684–1688*

to Jesus, but his hap was to go to him upon the water; There was the Tryal. So it is with the poor desiring Soul. Bid me **Come**, sayes the sinner: **Come**, sayes Christ, and *I will in no wise cast thee out*. So he **Comes**, but his hap is to come upon the water, upon drowning difficulties; if therefore the wind of Temptations blow, the waves of doubts and fears will presently arise, and this coming sinner will begin to sink, if he has but little faith.

But you shall find here, in *Peters* little faith, a twofold act; to wit, *Coming*, and *Crying*; Little faith *cannot* come *all* the way without crying: So long as its holy boldness lasts, so long it can come with peace; but when it's *So*, it can come no farther, It will go the rest of the way with crying. *Peter* went as far as his little faith would carry him; he also cryed as loud as his little faith would help, *Lord save me, I perish*: And so with coming and crying, he was kept from sinking, though he had but a little faith. *Jesus stretched forth his hand, and caught him, and said unto him; O! Thou of little faith, wherefore didst thou doubt?*

Secondly, Is it so? *That they that are coming to Jesus Christ, are ofttimes heartily afraid, that Jesus Christ will not receive them:* Then this shews us a reason of that Dejection, and those castings down, that very often we perceive to be in them, that are coming to Jesus Christ: Why, it is because they are afraid that Jesus Christ will not receive them. The poor World, they Mock us, because, we are a dejected people; I mean, because we are sometimes so: But they do not know the cause of our Dejections. Could we be perswaded, even then, when we are Dejected, that Jesus Christ, would indeed receive us: It would make us Fly over their Heads, and would put more gladness into our hearts, than in the time in which their Corn, and Wine, and Oyl increases, *Psal.* 4. 6, 7. But,

Thirdly, Is it so? *That they that are coming to Jesus Christ, are ofttimes heartily afraid that he will not receive them.* Then this shews, that they that are coming to Jesus Christ, are an awakned, sensible, considering people. For, fear cometh from sense, and consideration of things. They are sensible of sin, sensible of the Curse due thereto;

5 of] of the *1684–1686*[2] 11 it's *So*, it *1688*] it, *So 1678–1686*[2] 13 loud] far *1685–1688* 18 Is it] It is *1685–1686*[1] *that are*] *are 1684* 27 would . . . Heads, and] *add 1684–1688* 29 and[1]] *om. 1684–1688* 30 Is it] It is *1685–1686*[1] 33 and] *om. 1685–1688*

They are also sensible of the Glorious Majesty of God, and of what a blessed, blessed thing it is, to be received of Jesus Christ: The glory of Heaven, and evil of sin, these things they consider, and are sensible of. *When I remember, I am afraid; when I consider, I am afraid,* Job 21. 6. chap. 23. 15.

These things dash their spirits, being awake, and sensible; Were they dead like other men, they would not be afflicted with *fear*, as they are; For dead men, Fear not, Feel not, Care not; but the living, and sensible man, he it is, that is oft-times heartily afraid, that Jesus Christ will not receive him. I say, the dead, and senseless, are not distressed. *They* presume, *they* are groundlessly confident. *Who so bold as blind Bayard.* These indeed *should* fear, and be *afraid*, because they are not coming to Jesus Christ. O! The Hell, the Fire, the Pit, the Wrath of God, and Torments of Hell, that are prepared for poor neglecting sinners: *How shall we escape, if we neglect so great Salvation!* (Heb. 2. 3.) But they want sense of things, and so cannot fear.

Fourthly, Is it so? *That they that are coming to Jesus Christ, are oft-times heartily afraid, that he will not Receive them;* Then this should teach *Old* Christians to pity and pray for *Young* Comers: *You know the Heart of a Stranger, for you your selves were Strangers in the Land of* Egypt. You know the Fears, and Doubts, and Terrors, that take hold of them; for that they sometimes took hold of you. Wherefore, pity them, pray for them, encourage them; they need all this: Guilt hath over-taken them, Fears of the Wrath of God hath over-taken them: Perhaps, they are within the Sight of Hell-fire; and the Fear of going thither, is burning-hot within their Hearts. You may know, how strangely Satan is suggesting his Devilish Doubts unto them, if possible, he may sinck, and drown them with the Multitude, and weight of them. Old Christians, mend up the Paths for them, take the Stumbling-blocks out of the way; lest that which is Feeble and Weak be turned aside, but let it rather be Healed, *Heb.* 12.

---

5 23.] 36. *1678–1688* 15 *great*] *great a 1685* 29 drown *1685–1688*] drown'd *1678–1684* 30 Paths] Path *1684–1688*

I come now to the next Observation, *and shall speak a little to that; to wit,*

THat Jesus Christ would **Not** *have them, that in truth are coming to him,* **Once** *think, That he will cast them out.*

The Text is full for this: For, he saith; *And him that cometh to me, I will in no wise cast out.* Now, if he saith, *I will not*, he would not have us think, *He will.*

This is yet further manifest by these Considerations:

First, Christ Jesus did forbid even them, that *as yet*, were not coming to him, **Once** to think him such an one: *Do not think* (said he) *that I will accuse you to the Father*, Joh. 5. 45.

These (as I said) were such, that as yet, were not coming to him: For he saith of them a little before; *And ye will not come to me*: For the Respect they had to the Honour of Men, kept them back. Yet, I say, Jesus Christ gives them to understand, that though he might Justly reject them, yet he would not; but bids them not **Once** *to think, that he would accuse them to the Father.* Now, not to Accuse (with Christ), is to Plead for: For Christ in these things, stands not Neuter between the Father and Sinners. So then, If Jesus Christ would not have them think, that **Yet** will not come to him, that he will Accuse them; then he would not that they should think so, that in truth are coming to him. *And him that cometh to me, I will in no wise cast out.*

Secondly, When the Woman taken in Adultery (even in the very Act), was brought before Jesus Christ: So he carryed it, both by Words and Actions, that he evidently enough made it manifest, that Condemning, and Casting-out, were such Things; for the Doing of which, he came not into the World.

Wherefore, when they had set her before him, and had laid to her charge her Heinous Fact, he stooped down, and with his Finger wrote upon the Ground, as though he heard them not. Now, What did he do by this his Carriage, but testify plainly, That he was not for Receiving Accusations against poor Sinners, who-ever accused by? And observe; Though they continued asking, thinking at last

5 for] of *1685–1688*   34 continued] continue *1686*[1]*–1688*

to force him to Condemn her; yet then he so answered, as that he drove all Condemning Persons from her. And then he adds, for her Encouragement to come to him; *Neither do I Condemn thee; go, and Sin no more*, Joh. 8. 1, 2, 3, 4, 5, 6, 7, 8, 9, 10, 11, 12.

Not but that he indeed abhorred the Fact; but he would not Condemn the Woman for the Sin, because that was not his Office: *He was not sent into the World, to condemn the World, but that the World through Him might be saved*, Joh. 3. 17. Now, if Christ, though urged to it, would not Condemn the Guilty Woman, though she was far at present from coming to him; he would not that they should **Once** think, that he will cast them out, that in truth are coming to him: *And him that cometh to me, I will in no wise cast out.*

Thirdly, Christ plainly bids the Turning Sinner, **Come**; and forbids him to Entertain any such Thought, as that *He will cast him out. Let the Wicked forsake his Way, and the Unrighteous Man his Thoughts; and let him Turn unto the Lord, and he will have Mercy upon him; and to our God, for he will abundantly Pardon*, Isa. 55. 7.

The Lord, by bidding the Unrighteous forsake his Thoughts; doth in special forbid, as I have said (to wit), those Thoughts, that hinder the Coming-Man in his Progress to Jesus Christ; *His Unbelieving Thoughts.*

Therefore, he bids him, not only forsake his Ways, but his Thoughts: *Let the Wicked forsake his Ways, and the Unrighteous Man his Thoughts.* 'Tis not enough to forsake *one*, if thou wilt come to Jesus Christ; because the *other* will keep thee from him. Suppose a Man forsakes his wicked Wayes, his debauched and filthy Life; yet if these Thoughts, *That Jesus Christ will not Receive him*, be entertained and nourished in his heart; them Thoughts will keep him from coming to Jesus Christ.

Sinner, Coming-Sinner; Art thou for coming to Jesus Christ? *Yes*, sayes the Sinner. Forsake thy wicked Wayes then. *So I do*, sayes the Sinner. Why comest thou then so slowly? *Because I am hindred.* What hinders? Has God forbidden thee? *No.* Art thou not willing to come faster? *Yes: Yet I cannot.* Well, prethee be plain with me, and tell me the Reason and Ground of thy Discouragement: *Why?* (saith the Sinner) *though God forbids me not, and though I am willing to come*

15 *Way 1685–1688*] *Ways 1678–1684*

faster; yet there naturally ariseth this, and that, and the other Thought in my Heart, that hinders my Speed to Jesus Christ. Sometimes, I think, I am not Chosen; sometimes, I think, I am not Called; sometimes, I think, I am come too late; and sometimes, I think, I know not what it is to Come. Also, One while I think, I have no Grace; and then again, that I cannot Pray; and then again, I think, that I am a very Hypocrite: And these Things keep me from coming to Jesus Christ.

Look ye now! Did not I tell you so? There are Thoughts yet remaining in the Heart, even of those that have forsaken their wicked Wayes; and with those Thoughts they are more plagued, than with any thing else; because they hinder their Coming to Jesus Christ: For the Sin of *Unbelief* (which is the Original of all these Thoughts), is that which besets a Coming-Sinner *more* easily, than doth his Wayes; *Heb.* 12. 1, 2, 3, 4.

But now, since Jesus Christ commands thee to forsake these Thoughts; forsake them, Coming-sinner: And if thou forsake them not, thou Transgressest the Commands of Christ, and abidest thine own Tormentor, and keepest thy self from Establishment in Grace: *If ye will not Believe, ye shall not be Established*, Isa. 7. 9.

Thus you see, how Jesus Christ setteth himself against such Thoughts, that any way discourage the Coming-Sinner; and thereby, truly vindicates the Doctrine we have in hand; To wit, *That Jesus Christ would not have them, that in truth are coming to him,* **Once** *think, that he will cast them out.* And him that cometh to me, I will in **No wise** cast out.

I come now to the Reasons *of the* Observation.

1. IF Jesus Christ should allow thee *Once* to think, that he will Cast thee out; he must allow thee to think, that he will falsify his Word: For he hath said, *I will in no wise cast out*. But Christ would not that thou shouldst count him as One, that will falsify his Word: For he saith of himself, *I am the Truth*; Therefore, he would not, that any that in Truth are coming to him, should **Once** think, that he will cast them out.

3 *am come 1685–1688*] *come 1678–1684* 9 that] who *1686*[1]*–1688*

Secondly, If Jesus Christ should allow the Sinner, that in Truth is coming to him, Once to think, that he will cast him out: Then he must allow, and so countenance the first Appearance of Unbelief; the which, he counteth his greatest Enemy; and against which, he has bent even his Holy Gospel. Therefore, Jesus Christ would not, that they that in Truth are coming to him, should Once think, that he will cast them out: See *Mat.* 14. 31. *chap.* 21. 21. *Mark* 11. 23. *Luk.* 24. 25.

Thirdly, If Jesus Christ should allow the Coming-Sinner, Once to think, that he will cast him out; then he must allow him to make a Question, Whether he is willing to Receive his Father's Gift? For the Coming-Sinner is his Father's Gift; as also sayes the Text: But he testifieth, *All that the Father giveth him, shall come to him; and him that cometh, he will in no wise cast out.* Therefore, Jesus Christ would not have him, that in Truth is coming to him, Once to think, that he will cast him out.

Fourthly, If Jesus Christ should allow them Once to think (that indeed are coming to him) that he will cast them out; he must allow them to think, that he will despise and reject the Drawing of his Father: For No Man can come to him, but whom the Father draweth: But it would be high Blasphemy, and damnable Wickedness, Once to imagine thus. Therefore, Jesus Christ would not have him that cometh, Once think, that he will cast him out.

Fifthly, If Jesus Christ should allow those, that indeed are coming to him, Once to think, that he will cast them out; He must allow them to think, that he will be Unfaithful to the Trust, and Charge, that his Father hath committed to him; which is to Save, and not to Lose, any thing of that which he hath given unto him to Save; *Joh.* 6. 39. But the Father hath given him a Charge, to save the Coming-Sinner: Therefore, it cannot be, that he should allow, that such an one should Once think, that he will cast them out.

Sixthly, If Jesus Christ should allow, that they should Once think, that are coming to him, that he will cast them out: Then he must allow them to think, that he will be unfaithful to his Office of Priest-hood: For, as by the first part of it, he paid Price for, and

18 cast them *1688*] cast him *1678–1686*[2] 28 unto] *add 1685–1688* 29 39. *1686*[1]] 36. *1678–1685, 1686*[2]*–1688* 31 them *1686*[1]*–1686*[2]] *him 1678–1685, 1688*

Ransomed Souls; so by the Second Part thereof, he continually maketh Intercession to God for them that come, *Heb.* 7. 25. But he cannot allow us to question his Faithful Execution of his Priest-hood: Therefore, he cannot allow us **Once** to think, that the Coming-Sinner shall be cast out.

Seventhly, If Jesus Christ should allow us **Once** to think, that the Coming-Sinner shall be cast out: Then he must allow us to question, his Will, or Power, or Merit to Save. But he cannot allow us **Once** to question any of these: Therefore, not **Once** to think, that the Coming-Sinner shall be cast out.

1. He cannot allow them to question his **Will**: For he saith in the Text, *I will in no wise cast out*.

2. He cannot allow us to question his **Power**: For the Holy Ghost saith, He is **Able** to save to the uttermost, them that come.

3. He cannot allow them to question the *Efficacy of his Merit*: For the Blood of Christ cleanseth the Commer from all Sin, 1 *Joh.* 1. Therefore, he cannot allow, that he that is coming to him, should **Once** think, that he will cast him out.

Eighthly, If Jesus Christ should allow the coming sinner, **Once** to think, that he will cast him out; he must allow him to give the lie, to the manifest testimony of the Father, Son, and Spirit: yea to the whole Gospel contained in *Moses*, the *Prophets*, the book of *Psalms*, and that commonly called the New-Testament: But he cannot allow of this, therefore, not that the coming sinner should **Once** think that he will cast him out.

Ninethly, Lastly. If Jesus Christ should allow him that is coming to him, **Once** to think that he will cast him out: He must allow him to question his Fathers Oath; Which he in truth, and Righteousness, hath taken; that they might have a strong Consolation, who have fled for refuge to Jesus Christ: But he cannot allow this, therefore he cannot allow that the coming sinner should once think that he will cast him out, *Heb.* 6.

---

11 them] us *1688*   14 uttermost] utmost *1685–1688*   16 them] us *1688*

I come now to make some General Use *and* Application *of the whole*, *and so to draw towards a* Conclusion.

THe First Use, a *Use of Information.* And it Informeth us, That Men by Nature are far off from Christ.

Let me a little improve *this Use*, by speaking to these Three Questions.

1. *Where is he, that is not coming to Jesus Christ?*
2. *What is he, that is not coming to Jesus Christ?*
3. *Whither is he to go, that cometh not to Jesus Christ?*

First, *Where is he?*

1. *Answ.* He is far from God, he is without him; even alienate from him, both in his Understanding, Will, Affections, Judgment, and Conscience; *Ephes.* 2. 12. *chap.* 4. 18.

2. He is far from Jesus Christ, who is the only Deliverer of Men from Hell-Fire; *Psal.* 73. 27.

3. He is far from the Work of the Holy Ghost, the Work of Regeneration, and a Second Creation; without which, no Man shall see the Kingdom of Heaven; *Joh.* 3. 3.

4. He is far from Righteousness, from that Righteousness that should make him Acceptable in God's Sight; *Isa.* 46. 12, 13.

5. He is under the Power and Dominion of Sin; Sin reigneth in and over him; it dwelleth in every Faculty of his Soul, and Member of his Body: So that, from Head to Foot, there is no place clean; *Isa.* 1. 6. *Rom.* 3. 9, 10, 11, 12, 13, 14, 15, 16, 17, 18.

6. He is in the Pest-house, with *Uzziah*; and excluded the Camp of *Israel*, with the Leapers; 2 *Chron.* 26. 21. *Numb.* 5. 2.

7. His Life is among the Unclean; *He is in the Gall of Bitterness, and in the Bond of Iniquity*, Job 36. 14. Act. 8. 23.

8. He is in Sin, in the Flesh, in Death, in the Snare of the Devil, and is taken Captive by him at his Will; 1 Cor. 15. 17. *Rom.* 8. 8. 1 *Joh.* 3. 14. 2 *Tim.* 2. 26.

7 *not*] *om. 1686[1]–1688* 8 *not*] *om. 1688* 9 *Whither 1684–1686[1], 1688*] *Whether 1678, 1686[2]* 13 4. 18.] 4. 8. *1685, 1686[2]–1688* 19 from Righteousness] more Righteous *1685–1686[2]*] from being Righteous *1688* 20 12, 13.] 14. *1678–1688*

9. He is under the Curse of the Law; and the Devil dwells in him, and hath the Mastery of him; *Gal.* 3. 13. Eph. 2. 2, 3. Acts 26. 18.

10. He is in Darkness, and walketh in Darkness, and knows not whither he goes; for Darkness has blinded his Eyes.

11. He is in the Broad-way, that leadeth to Destruction; and holding on, he will assuredly go in at the Broad-gate, and so down the Stairs to Hell.

Secondly, *What is he, that cometh not to Jesus Christ?*

1. He is counted one of God's Enemies; *Luk.* 19. 14. *Rom.* 8. 7.

2. He is a Child of the Devil, and of Hell; for the Devil begat him, as to his sinful Nature; and Hell must swallow him at last, because he cometh not to Jesus Christ; *Joh.* 8. 44. 1 *Joh.* 3. 8. *Mat.* 23. 15. *Psal.* 9. 17.

3. He is a Child of Wrath, an Heir of it; 'tis his Portion, and God will repay it him to his Face; *Ephes.* 2. 1, 2, 3. *Job* 21. 29, 30, 31.

4. He is a Self-Murderer; he wrongeth his own Soul, and is one that loveth Death; *Prov.* 1. 18. *Chap.* 8. 35, 36.

5. He is a Companion for Devils, and Damned Men; *Prov.* 21. 16. *Mat.* 25. 41.

Thirdly, *Whither is he like to go, that cometh not to Jesus Christ?*

1. He that cometh not To him, is like to go *Further* from him; for every Sin, is a Step further from Jesus Christ; *Hos.* 11.

2. As he is in Darkness, so he is like to go on in it: For Christ is the Light of the World; and he that comes not to him, walketh in Darkness, *Joh.* 8. 12.

3. He is like to be removed at last, as far from God, and Christ, and Heaven, and all Felicity, as an Infinite God can remove him; *Mat.* 13. 41.

But, *Secondly*, This Doctrine of coming to Christ, informeth us, *Where poor destitute Sinners may find Life for their Souls*; and that is in Christ: This Life is in his Son; he that hath the Son, hath Life: And again; *Whoso findeth me, findeth Life, and shall obtain Favor of the Lord*, Prov. 8. 35.

10 for] so *1685–1688* 16 Murderer *1684–1688*] Murder *1678* 22 for] so *1685–1688* 28 13.] 12. *1678–1688* 33 35.] *om. 1678–1688*

Now, for further Enlargement, I will also here propound three more Questions:

1. *What Life is in Christ?*

2. *Who may have it?*

3. *Upon what Terms?*

First, *What Life is in Jesus Christ?*

1. There is Justifying Life in Christ. Man, by Sin, is Dead in Law; and Christ only can deliver him by his Righteousness, and Blood, from his Death, into a State of Life: *For God sent his Son into the World, That we might Live through him*, 1 Joh. 4. 9. That is, through the Righteousness which he should accomplish, and the Death that he should dye.

2. There is Eternal Life in Christ: Life that's endless; Life for ever, and ever. *He hath given us Eternal Life; and this Life is in his Son*, 1 Joh. 5. 11.

Now, Justification, and Eternal Salvation, being both in Christ, and no where else to be had for Men, Who would not come to Jesus Christ?

Secondly, *Who may have this Life?*

I answer; Poor, Helpless, miserable Sinners: Particularly,

1. Such as are willing to have it; *Whosoever will*, Let *him take the Water of Life*, Revel. 22. 17.

2. He that Thirsteth for it: *I will give to him that is a Thirst*, *of the Fountain of the Water of Life*, Revel. 21. 6.

3. He that is weary of his Sins. *This is the Rest*, *whereby ye may cause the Weary to rest; and this is the Refreshing*, Isa. 28. 12.

4. He that is Poor and Needy. *He shall spare the Poor and Needy, and shall save the Souls of the Needy.*

5. He that followeth after him, crying for Life. *He that follows me, shall not walk in Darkness, but shall have the Light of Life*, Joh. 8. 12.

Thirdly, *Upon what Terms may he have this Life?*

Answ. **Freely**: Sinner, Dost thou hear? Thou may'st have it **Freely**. Let him take the Water of Life **Freely**: I will give him of the Foun-

5 3.] *om.* 1686[2]   15 11.] *om. 1678–1688*   22 *Water*] *Waters 1688*   25 *ye*] *you 1684–1688*   29 crying] cryeth *1685–1688*

tain of the Water of Life **Freely**. *And when they had nothing to pay, he* **Frankly** *forgave them both*, Luk. 7. 42.

Freely, without Money, or without Price. *Ho! Every one that Thirsteth, come ye to the Waters; and he that hath no Money, Come ye, Buy and Eat: Yea, come, buy Wine and Milk, without Mony, and without Price*, Isa. 55. 1.

Sinner, Art thou Thirsty? art thou Weary? are thou Willing? Come then, and regard not your Stuff; for all the Good that is in Christ, is offered to the Coming-Sinner, without Mony, and without Price. He has Life to give away, to such as want it, and that have not a Penny to purchase it; and he will give it Freely: Oh, What a blessed Condition is the Coming-Sinner in!

But, *Thirdly*, This Doctrine of Coming to Jesus Christ for Life; *Informeth us, That* **It** *is to be had no where else:* Might it be had **Any** where else, the Text, and Him that spoke it, would be but little set-by: For, What great Matter is there in, *I will in no wise cast out*, if another stood by that could Receive them? But here appears the Glory of Christ, that none but He can Save! And, here appears his Love, that though none can Save but He, yet he is not Coy in Saving! *But him that comes to me* (saith he) *I will in no wise cast out.*

That none can Save but Jesus Christ, is evident from *Acts* 4. 12. *Neither is there Salvation in any other; and he hath given us Eternal Life, and this Life is in his Son.* If Life could have been had any where else, it should have been in the Law; but it is not in the Law: For, by the Deeds of the Law, no Man living shall be Justifyed; and if not Justifyed, then no **Life**. Therefore, **Life** is no where to be had, but in Jesus Christ; *Gal.* 3.

Quest. *But why would God so order it, that* **Life** *should be had no where else, but in Jesus Christ?*

Answ. There is Reason for it; and that both with Respect to God, and to Us.

First, *With Respect to God.*

First, That it might be in a way of *Justice*, as well as *Mercy*: And

2 42.] *om. 1678–1688* 4 *ye*[2]] *om. 1684–1688* 16 great] greater *1684–1688*
17 Receive *1684–1688*] *Received 1678* 31 and to] and *1686*[1]*–1688*

in a way of Justice it could not have been, if it had not been by Christ; because He, and He only, was able to answer the Demand of the Law; and give for Sin, what the Justice thereof required. All Angels had been Crushed down to Hell for ever, had that Curse been laid upon them for our Sins, which was laid upon Jesus Christ: But 'twas laid upon Him, and He bare it, and answered the Penalty, and Redeemed his People from under it, with that Satisfaction to Divine Justice, that God himself doth now proclaim; That he is Faithful and Just to forgive us, if by Faith we shall venture on Jesus, and trust to what he has done for Life; *Rom.* 3. 24, 25, 26. 1 *Joh.* 1. 9.

Secondly, Life must be by Jesus Christ, that God might be Adored, and Magnifyed, for finding out this Way. This is the Lord's Doings, that in all Things he might be Glorifyed, through Jesus Christ our Lord.

Thirdly, It must be by Jesus Christ, that Life might be at God's dispose; who hath great Pity for the Poor, the lowly, the Meek, the Broken in heart; and for them that others care not for, *Psal.* 34. 6. *Psal.* 138. 6. *Psal.* 25. *Psal.* 51. 17. *Psal.* 147. 3.

Fourthly, Life must be in Christ, to cut off boasting from the lips of men. This also is the Apostles reason, in *Rom.* 3. 26, 27. And *Ephes.* 2. 8, 9, 10.

Secondly, Life must be in Jesus Christ, with *respect to us.*

First, That we might have it upon the easiest Termes, to wit, *Freely*, as a gift, not as wages; was it in *Moses* hand, we should come hardly at it. Was it in the *Popes* hand, we should pay soundly for it: but thanks be to God, it is in Christ, laid up in him, and by him, to be communicated to sinners upon easie Termes, even for receiving, accepting and imbraceing with Thanksgiving. As the Scriptures plainly declare, *Joh.* 1. 11, 12. 2 *Cor.* 11. 4. *Heb.* 11. 13. *Col.* 3. 13, 14, 15.

Secondly, Life is in Christ *for us*, that it might not be upon so brittle a foundation, as indeed it would, had it been any where else. The Law it self is weak because of us, as to this: But Christ is a

9 on] to *1686*[1]*–1688* 10–11 1 *Joh.*] *Iohn 1684–1688* 21 3. 26, 27.] 3. 20, 27. *1685–1688*

tryed stone, a sure foundation, one that will not fail to bear thy burden, and to receive thy Soul, coming sinner.

Thirdly, Life is in Christ, that it might be sure to all the seed. Alas! the best of us, was life left in our hands, to be sure, we should forfeit it, over, and over, and over: or was it in any other hand, we should by our often back-slidings, so offend him, that at last he would shut up his bowels in everlasting displeasure against us. But now it is in Christ, it is with one that can pity, pray for, pardon, yea multiply pardons: It is with one that can have Compassion upon us, when we are out of the way; with one that hath an heart to fetch us again, when we are gone astray; with one that can pardon without upbraiding. Blessed be God, that life is in Christ! For **Now** 'tis sure, to all the seed.

But Fourthly. This Doctrine of coming to Jesus Christ for life, informs us of the evil of Unbelief; that wicked thing, that is the only, or chief hindrance to the coming sinner. Doth the Text say, **Come**? Doth it say, *And him that cometh to me, I will in no wise cast out?* Then what an evil is that, that keepeth sinners from coming to Jesus Christ? And that evil is unbelief. For by faith we come, by Unbelief we keep away. Therefore **It** is said to be that, by which a Soul is said to depart from God; because it was that, which at first caused the world to go off from him; and that also that keeps them from him to this day. And it doth it the more easily, because it doth it with a wile. This sin may be called, *The White Devil*; for it often-times in its Mischievous doings in the Soul, shews as if it was an Angel of Light. Yea, it Acteth like a Counsellor of Heaven: Therefore a little to discourse of this evil disease.

First, It is that sin, *above all others*, that hath some shew of *reason* in its attempts. For it keeps the Soul from Christ, by pretending its present unfitness, and unpreparedness; as want of more sense of sin, want of more repentance, want of more humility, want of a more broken heart.

Secondly, It is the sin, that most Suiteth with the *Conscience*: the Conscience of the coming sinner, tells him that he hath nothing good, that he stands inditable for Ten Thousand Tallents; that he is a very ignorant, blind, and hard-hearted sinner, unworthy to be

5 in] *om. 1684* 17 *to me 1688*] *om. 1678–1686*[2]

once taken notice of by Jesus Christ: And will you (says Unbelief) in such a case as you now are, presume to come to Jesus Christ?

Thirdly, It is the sin that most Suiteth with our *Sense of feeling*. The coming sinner, feels the workings of sin, of all manner of sin, and wretchedness, in his flesh: He also feels the Wrath, and Judgement of God due to sin, and oft-times staggers under it: Now, sayes unbelief, you may see you have no grace, for that which works in you, *is corruption*; You may also perceive, that God doth not love you, because the Sense of his Wrath abides upon you: Therefore how can you bear the face to come to Jesus Christ?

Fourthly, It is the sin, above all others, that most Suiteth with the *Wisdom* of our flesh: the Wisdom of our flesh, thinks it prudence to question a while, to stand back a while, to hearken to both sides a while, and not to be rash, sudden or unadvised, in too bold a presuming upon Jesus Christ: And this Wisdom Unbelief falls in with.

Fifthly, It is that sin above all other, that continually is whispering the Soul in the ear, with mistrusts of the faithfulness of God, in keeping promise to them that come to Jesus Christ for life. It also suggesteth mistrust, about Christs willingness to receive it, and save it. And no sin can do this so artificially as Unbelief.

Sixthly, It is also that sin, which is always at hand, to enter an Objection against this or that Promise, that by the Spirit of God is brought to our heart, to comfort us; and if the poor coming sinner, is not aware of it, it will by some evasion, slite, trick or cavil, quickly wrest from him the Promise again, and he shall have but little benefit of it.

Seventhly, It is that above all other sins, that weakens our Prayers, our faith, our love, our diligence, our hope and expectations: It even taketh the heart away from God in duty.

Eighthly, Lastly. This sin, as I have said even now, it appeareth in the Soul with so many sweet pretences to safety, and security; that it is, as if it were, Counsel sent from Heaven. Biding the Soul be wise, wary, considerate, well advised, and to take heed of too rash

11 with] *om. 1688* 20 suggesteth] suggests *1686[1]–1688* 21 artificially *1684–1688*] Artificiently *1678* 25 slite] Sight *1685–1686[1]* 31 *Eighthly*] *Eightly 1678–1688* 33 if] *om. 1686[1]–1688*

a venture upon Believing. Be sure first, that God loves you; take hold of no promise untill you are forced by God unto it; neither be you sure of your Salvation, doubt it still, though the testimony of the Lord has been often confirmed in you: live not by faith, but by sense: and when you can neither see nor feel, then fear and mistrust, then doubt, and question all. This is the Devilish counsel of Unbelief, which is so covered over with specious pretences, that the wisest Christian can hardly shake off these reasonings.

But to be brief: Let me here give thee, Christian Reader, a more particular description of the qualities of Unbelief, by opposing Faith unto it, in these Twenty five particulars.

First. Faith, believeth the word of God, but Unbelief questioneth the certainty of the same, *Psal.* 106. 24.

Secondly. Faith, believeth the word, *because it is true*; but Unbelief doubteth thereof, *because it is true*, 1 Tim. 4. 3. Joh. 8. 45.

Thirdly. Faith, sees more in a promise of God to help, than in all other things to hinder: But Unbelief, notwithstanding Gods promise, saith, How can these things be? *Rom.* 4. 19, 20, 21. 2 *King.* 7. 2. *Joh.* 3. 4, 12.

Fourthly, Faith will make thee see love in the heart of Christ, when with his mouth he giveth reproofs: But Unbelief will imagine wrath in his heart, when with his mouth, and word, he saith he loves us, *Mat.* 15. 22, 23, 24, 25, 26, 27, 28. *Numb.* 13. 2 *Chron.* 14. 3.

Fifthly, Faith will help the Soul to wait, though God deferres to give: but Unbelief will take snuff, and throw up all, if God make any tarrying, *Psal.* 25. 5. *Isa.* 8. 17. 2 *King.* 6. 33. *Psal.* 106. 13, 14.

Sixthly, Faith will give comfort in the midst of fears; but Unbelief causeth fears in the midst of comfort, 2 *Chro.* 20. 20, 21. *Mat.* 8. 26. *Luk.* 24. 36, 37.

Seventhly, Faith will suck sweetness out of Gods rod; but Unbelief can find no comfort in his greatest mercies, *Psal.* 23. 4. *Numb.* 21. 5.

Eighthly, Faith maketh great burdens light; but Unbelief maketh light ones intollerably heavy, 2 *Cor.* 4. 13, 14, 15, 16, 17, 18. *Mal.* 1. 2, 13.

7 specious] spacious *1684* 23 *Chron. 1685–1688*] chap. *1678–1684* 26 106.] 100. *1685, 1686[2]–1688* 31 5.] *om. 1684–1688* 33 intollerably] intolerable *1684–1686[2]* 13] 1 *1685–1688*

Ninethly, Faith helpeth us up when we are down; but Unbelief throws us down, when we are up, *Mich.* 7. 8, 9, 10. *Heb.* 4. 11.

Tenthly, Faith bringeth us near to God, when we are far from him; but Unbelief puts us far from God, when we are near to him: *Heb.* 10. 22. *Chap.* 3. 12, 13.

Eleventhly, Where Faith reigns, it declareth Men to be the Friends of God; but where Unbelief reigns, it declareth them to be his Enemies: *Jam.* 2. 23. *Heb.* 3. 18. *Rev.* 21. 8.

Twelfthly, Faith putteth a Man under Grace; but Unbelief holdeth him under Wrath: *Rom.* 3. 24, 25, 26. *Chap.* 4. 16. *Ephes.* 2. 8. *Joh.* 3. 36. 1 *Joh.* 5. 10. *Heb.* 3. 17. *Mark* 16. 16.

Thirteenthly, Faith purifieth the Heart; but Unbelief keepeth it polluted and impure: *Acts* 15. 9. *Tit.* 1. 15, 16.

Fourteenthly, By Faith, the Righteousness of Christ is imputed to us; but by Unbelief, we are shut up under the Law to Perish: *Rom.* 4. 23, 24. *Chap.* 11. 32. *Gal.* 3. 23.

Fifteenthly, Faith maketh our Work acceptable to God through Christ; but whatsoever is of Unbelief, is Sin: For without Faith, it is impossible to please him; *Heb.* 11. 4. *Rom.* 14. 23. *Heb.* 11. 6.

Sixteenthly, Faith giveth us Peace and Comfort in our Souls; but Unbelief worketh Trouble and Tossings, like the restless Waves of the Sea: *Rom.* 5. 1. *Jam.* 1. 6.

Seventeenthly, Faith makes us see Preciousness in Christ; but Unbelief sees no Form, Beauty, or Comlyness in him: 1 *Pet.* 2. 7. *Isa.* 53. 1, 2, 3.

Eighteenthly, By Faith we have our Life in Christ's Fulness; but by Unbelief, we starve and pine away: *Gal.* 2. 20.

Nineteenthly, Faith giveth us the Victory over the Law, Sin, Death, the Devil, and all Evils; but Unbelief layeth us Obnoxious to them all: 1 *Joh.* 5. 4, 5. *Luk.* 12. 46.

Twentyeth, Faith will shew us more Excellency in Things not seen, than in them that are; but Unbelief sees more in Things that are here, than in Things that will be here-after: 2 *Cor.* 4. 18. *Heb.* 11. 24, 25, 26, 27. 1 *Cor.* 15. 32.

1 up] *om. 1685–1688* 8 2.] 5. *1678–1688* 10 4. 16.] 14. 16. *1685–1688* 22 1. 6.] 6. 1. *1684–1688* 32–3 that are here, than in Things] *om. 1686[1]–1688*

Twenty-First, Faith maketh the Ways of God pleasant, and amiable: but Unbelief maketh them heavy, and hard: *Gal.* 5. 6. 2 *Cor.* 12. 10, 11. *Joh.* 6. 60. *Psal.* 2. 3.

Twenty-Second, By Faith, *Abraham*, *Isaac*, and *Jacob*, possessed the Land of Promise; But because of Unbelief, neither *Aaron*, nor *Moses*, nor *Miriam*, could get thither: *Heb.* 11. 9. *Heb.* 3. 19.

Twenty-Third, By Faith, the Children of *Israel* passed through the *Red Sea*; but by Unbelief, the Generality of them perished in the *Wilderness*: *Heb.* 11. 29. *Jude* 5.

Twenty-Fourth, By Faith, *Gidion* did more with Three-hundred men, and a few empty Pitchers, than all the *Twelve Tribes* could do; because they believed not God: *Judg.* 7. 16, 17, 18, 19, 20, 21, 22. *Numb.* 14. 11, 14.

Twenty-Fifth, By Faith, *Peter* walked on the Water; but by Unbelief, he began to sink: *Mat.* 14. 21, 22, 23, 24, 25, 26, 27, 28, 29, 30, 31.

Thus might many more be added, which, for brevity sake, I omit: Beseeching every one, that thinketh he hath a Soul to Save, or be Damned, to take heed of Unbelief. Lest, seeing there is a Promise left us of Entering into his Rest, any of us, by Unbelief, should indeed come short of it.

The Second Use; a Use of Examination.

WE come now to a *Use of Examination.* Sinner, Thou hast heard of the Necessity of Coming to Christ; also, Of the Willingness of Christ, to Receive the Coming-Soul: Together, with the Benefit, that *They* by him shall have, *that* indeed come to Him. Put thy self now upon this Serious Enquiry; *Am I, indeed, come to Jesus Christ?*

Motives, plenty, I might here urge, to prevail with thee to a Conscientious Performance of this Duty; As,

1 maketh] makes *1684–1688* Ways] way *1686[1]–1688* amiable] admirable *1686[1]–1688* 6 *Heb.* 3.] Chap. 3. *1685–1688* 13 14. 11, 14. *1688*] 14. 11, 44. *1678–1686[1]*] 14. 11. 44. *1686[2]* 15–16 25, 26, 27, 28, 29, 30, 31.] *om. 1678–1688* 19 Lest] Least *1686[1]–1688* 20 his Rest] his, or *1686[1]–1686[2]*

1. Thou art in Sin, in the Flesh, in Death, in the Snare of the Devil, and under the Curse of the Law; if thou art not coming to Jesus Christ.

2. There is no way to be delivered from these, but by coming to Jesus Christ.

3. If thou comest, Jesus Christ will Receive thee, and will *in no wise cast thee out.*

4. Thou wilt *not* Repent it in the Day of *Judgement*, if *now* thou comest to Jesus Christ.

5. But thou wilt surely Mourn at last, if now thou shalt refuse to come: And,

6. Lastly, Now thou hast been invited to come; now will thy Judgment be greater, and thy Damnation more fearful, if thou shalt yet Refuse, than if thou hadst never heard of Coming to Christ.

Object. *But we hope, we are come to Jesus Christ.*

Answ. 'Tis well, if it proves so. But lest thou should speak without Ground, and so fall unawares into Hell Fire; Let us Examine a little.

First, Art thou, indeed, come to Jesus Christ? What has thou left behind thee? What didst thou come away from, in thy Coming to Jesus Christ?

When *Lot* came out of *Sodom*, he left the *Sodomites* behind him; *Gen.* 19.

When *Abraham* came out of *Chaldea*, he left his Country and Kindred behind him; *Gen.* 12. *Acts* 7.

When *Ruth* came to put her Trust under the Wings of the Lord God of *Israel*; she left her Father, and Mother; her Gods, and the Land of her Nativity behind her; *Ruth* 1. 15, 16, 17. *Chap.* 2. 11, 12.

When *Peter* came to Christ, he left his Nets behind him; *Mat.* 4. 18, 19, 20.

When *Zacheus* came to Christ, he left the Receipt of Custom behind him; *Luk.* 19.

When *Paul* came to Christ, he left his own Righteousness behind him; *Philip.* 3. 7, 8.

When those that used Curious Arts came to Jesus Christ, they

2 thou] you *1684–1688* art] are *1684–1688* 16 lest] least *1686[1]–1688* should] shouldst *1685–1688* 18 come] coming *1686[2]* 19 Coming] come *1686[2]* 29 19, 20.] *om. 1678–1688* 31 19.] 18. *1685–1688*

took their Curious Books, and burned them; though in another Man's Eye, they were counted worth Fifty-Thousand Peices of Silver: *Acts* 19. 18, 19, 20.

What say'st thou, Man? Hast thou left thy Darling Sins, thy *Sodomitish* Pleasures, thy Acquaintance, and vain Companions; thy unlawful Gain, thy Idol Gods, and Righteousness, and thy unlawful Curious Arts, behind thee? If any of these be with thee, and thou with them, in thy Heart and Life, thou art not yet come to Jesus Christ.

Secondly, Art thou come to Jesus Christ? Prethee tell me, What *moved* thee to come to Jesus Christ? Men do not usually come, or go, to this or that Place, before they have a *Moving* Cause; or rather, a Cause moving them thereto: No more do they come to Jesus Christ (I do not say), before they *have* a Cause; but before *that* Cause *moveth* them to come: What say'st thou? Hast thou a Cause *moving* thee to come? To be at present, in a State of Condemnation, is *Cause* sufficient for Men to come to Jesus Christ for Life: But that will not do, except that Cause move them; the which, it will never do, until their Eyes be opened, to see themselves in that Condition. For it is not a Man's being under Wrath, but his seeing it, that moveth him to come to Jesus Christ. Alas! *All* Men by Sin, are under Wrath; yet but few of that *All*, come to Jesus Christ: And the Reason is, because they do not see their Condition. *Who hath warned you, to flee from the Wrath to come*, Mat. 3. 7. Until Men are warned, and also, receive the Warning, they will not come to Jesus Christ.

Take three or four instances for this:

1. *Adam* and *Eve* came not to Jesus Christ, until they Received the Alarum; the Conviction of their Undone State by Sin: *Gen.* 3.

2. The Children of *Israel* cryed not out for a Mediator, before they saw themselves in danger of Death by the Law; *Exod.* 20. 18, 19.

3. Before the *Publican* came, he saw himself lost and undone; *Luk.* 18. 13.

6 and Righteousness] thy Righteousness *1684–1688* 11 to come *1685–1688*] come *1678–1684* 18 that] the *1686*[1]*–1688* 22 come *1684–1688*] came *1678*

4. The *Prodigal* came not, until he saw Death at the Door, ready to devour him: *Luk.* 15. 17, 18.

5. The Three-Thousand came not, until they knew not what to do, to be Saved; *Acts* 2. 37, 38, 39.

6. *Paul* came not, until he saw himself lost and undone; *Acts* 9. 3, 4, 5, 6, 7, 8, 11.

7. Lastly, Before the Jayler came, he saw himself undone; *Acts* 16. 29, 30, 31. And I tell thee, It is an easier thing to perswade a Well-Man to go to the Physitian for Cure, or a Man without Hurt, to seek out for a Playster to Cure him; than it is to perswade a Man, that sees not his Soul-Disease, to come to Jesus Christ. *The Whole have* **No** *need of the Physitian:* Then, Why should they go to him? The full Pitcher can hold no more; then, Why should it go to the Fountain? And, if thou comest full, thou comest not aright; and be sure, Christ will send thee Empty away: *But he healeth the Broken in Heart, and bindeth up their Wounds*, Mar. 2. 17. *Psal.* 147. 3. *Luk.* 1. 53.

Thirdly, Art thou *Coming* to Jesus Christ? Prethee tell me, What seest thou in him, to allure thee to forsake all the World, to come to him? I say, What hast thou seen in him? Men must see something in Jesus Christ, else, they will not come to him.

1. What Comlyness hast thou seen in his Person? Thou comest not, if thou seest no Form, nor Comlyness in him; *Isa.* 53. 1, 2, 3.

2. Until those mentioned in the *Song*, were convinced, that there was more Beauty, Comlyness, and Desirableness in Christ, than in Ten-Thousand; they did not so much as ask, Where he was, nor incline to turn aside after him; *Song* 5. *Chap.* 6.

There be many Things on this side Heaven, that **Can** and **Do**, carry away the Heart; and so will do, so long as thou Livest, if thou shalt be kept blind, and not be admitted to see the beauty of the Lord Jesus.

Fourthly, Art thou *come* to the Lord Jesus; what hast thou found in him, since thou camest to him?

Peter found with him the words of eternal life, *Joh.* 6. 68.

8 easier] easie *1686*[1]–*1686*[2] 10 out] *om. 1684–1688* 12 *the*] *a 1688*
34 words] word *1684–1688*

They that *Peter* makes mention of, found him a Living stone, even such a living stone as Communicated life to them, 1 *Pet.* 2.

He saith himself, they that come to him, *&c.* Shall find rest unto their Souls; hast thou found rest in him, for thy Soul? *Mat.* 11.

Let us go back to the times of the Old Testament.

First, *Abraham* found that in him, that made him Leave his Countrey for him, and become for his sake a Pilgrim, and stranger in the earth, *Gen.* 12. *Heb.* 11.

Secondly, *Moses* found that in him, that made him forsake a Crown, and a Kingdome for him too.

Thirdly, *David* found so much in him, that he counted, to be in his house one day, was better than a Thousand; yea, to be a door keeper there-in, was better, in his esteem, than to dwell in the Tents of wickedness, *Psal.* 84. 10.

Fourthly, What did *Daniel*, and the three Children find in him, to make them run the hazzard of the Fiery Furnace, and the Den of Lyons, for his sake? *Dan.* 3. chap. 6.

Let's come down to Martyrs.

First, *Stephen* found that in him, that made him Joyfully and quietly, yeild up his life for his name, *Acts* 7.

Secondly, *Ignatius* found that in him, that made him, *Chuse to go through the Torments of the Devil, and Hell it self; rather than not to have him*, *Acts* and *Mon.* vol. 1. *pag.* 25.

Thirdly, What saw *Romanus* in Christ, when he said to the rageing Emperor, who threatned him with fearful Torments; *Thy Sentence O Emperor, I Joyfully imbrace, and refuse not to be Sacrificed, by as Cruel Torments as thou canst invent*? pag. 116.

Fourthly, What saw *Menas* the Egyptian in Christ, when he said under most Cruel Torments; *There is nothing in my mind, that can be compared to the Kingdome of Heaven; neither is all the World, if it was weighed in the ballance, to be preferred with the price of one Soul; who is able to separate us from the Love of Jesus Christ our Lord; and I have Learned of my Lord, and King not to fear them, that kill the body*, &c.? pag. 117.

Fifthly, What did *Eulalia* see in Christ, when she said, as they

10 and] *om. 1688* 16 hazzard] hazards *1688* 20 7.] 17. *1686*[1]*–1688* 22 *than not*] *then 1684*] than not *1685*] then not *1686*[1]*–1688* 23 vol. 1.] *Vol.* 4. *1686*[1]*–1688* 24 *Romanus*] *Romans 1684* 31 *weighed*] *weighted 1684* *the*[1]] *a 1684–1688* *preferred 1685–1688*] *conferred 1678–1684*

was pulling her one Joynt from another; *Behold O Lord, I will not forget thee: what a pleasure is it for them O Christ! that remember thy Tryumphant Victories*? pag. 121.

Sixthly, What, think you, did *Agnes* see in Christ, when rejoyce-ingly she went to meet the Souldier, that was appointed to be her Executioner? *I will willingly* (said she) *receive into my Paps, the length of his Sword, and into my Breasts will draw the force thereof even to the hilts; that thus I, being married to Christ my Spouse, may surmount and escape all the darkness of this World*, pag. 122.

Seventhly, What do you think did *Julitta*, see in Christ, when, at the Emperors telling of her; that, except she would worship the Gods, she should neither have Protection, Laws, Judgements, nor life: She replied, *Fare-well life, Welcome Death: Fare-well Riches, Welcome poverty. All that I have, if it were a Thousand times more, would I rather lose, than to speak one wicked and blasphemous word against my Creator*? pag. 123.

Eighthly, What did *Marcus Arethusius*, see in Christ, when after his enemies had cut his flesh, anointed it with honey, and hanged him up in a basket, for flies and bees to feed on, *he would not* (*give to up-hold Idolatry*) *one half penny to save his life*? pag. 129.

Ninethly, What did *Constantine*, see in Christ, when he used *to kiss the wounds of them that suffered for him*? pag. 135.

Tenthly, But what need I give, thus, particular instances of words, and smaller actions, when by their lives their blood, their induring hunger, sword, fire, pulling a sunder, and all Torments that the Devil, and Hell could devise, for the love they bare to Christ, after they were come to him?

What hast thou found in him sinner?

What! come to Christ, and find nothing in him (when all things that are worth looking after, are in him; or if any thing, yet not enough to wean thee from thy sinfull delights, and fleshly lusts: Away, away: thou art not come to Jesus Christ.

He that is come to Jesus Christ, hath found in him, that, as I said, that is not to be found any where else. As,

1 was] were *1688* 3 *Victories*] *Victorious 1684*] *Victorie 1685–1688* 7 *his*] *this 1688* *Breasts*] *Breast 1686[2]–1688* 12 neither] never *1684–1688* 17 *Eighthly*] *Eightly 1678–1688* 30 after] for *1688*

First, He that is come to Christ, hath found God in him reconciling the world unto himself, not imputing their trespasses to them: And so God is not to be found in Heaven and earth besides, 2 *Cor.* 5. 19, 20.

Secondly, He that is come to Jesus Christ, hath found in him a fountain of grace, sufficient, not only to pardon sin, but to Sanctifie the Soul, and to preserve it from falling in this evil World.

Thirdly, He that is come to Jesus Christ, hath found vertue in him: **That** vertue, that if he does but touch thee with his Word; or thou, him by Faith: Life is forthwith conveyed into thy Soul: It makes thee wake as one that is waked out of his sleep: it awakes all the powers of thy Soul. *Psal.* 30. 11, 12. *Song.* 6. 12.

Fourthly, Art thou come to Jesus Christ? thou hast found glory in him, glory that Surmounts, and goes beyond: *Thou art more glorious than the mountaines of prey*, Psal. 67. 4.

Fifthly, What shall I say? thou hast found Righteousness in him; Thou hast found rest, peace, delight, Heaven, glory and eternal life. Sinner, be advised, Ask thy heart again, saying; Am I come to Jesus Christ? For, upon this one question, *Am I* **Come**, or, *am I* **Not**, Hangs Heaven and Hell, as to thee. If thou canst say, *I am come*; and God shall approve that saying; Happy, Happy, Happy man art thou! but if thou art *not come*, what can make thee happy: Yea what can make *that* man Happy, that for his not coming to Jesus Christ for life, must be damned in Hell?

The Third Use; a Use of Encouragement.

COming Sinner, I have now a word for thee; be of good comfort, *He will in no wise cast out.* Of all men, thou art the blessed of the Lord; the Father hath prepared his Son to be a Sacrifice for thee; and Jesus Christ thy Lord is gone to prepare a place for thee, *Joh.* 1. 29. *Heb.* 10. *Joh.* 14.

What shall I say to thee? thou comest to a full Christ, thou canst not want any thing, for Soul or body, for this World, or that to come, but it is to be had, in, or by Jesus Christ.

11 thy] the *1684–1688* 14 *prey 1685–1688*] *pray 1678–1684* 29 *Joh.* 14.] *om. 1684–1688*

As it is said of the Land, that the *Dannits* went to possess, So, and with much more truth, it may be said of Christ: He is such *an one, with whom there is no want of any good thing that is in Heaven or earth.*

A Full Christ, is thy Christ.

First, He is full of **Grace**. Grace is sometimes taken for *love*, and take it so here. He is full of *love*; never any *loved* like Jesus Christ. *Jonathans* love went *beyond* the love of *Women*; but the love of Christ *passes knowledge*. It is beyond the love of all the Earth, of all Creatures, even of Men and Angels. His love prevailed with him to lay aside his Glory, to leave the Heavenly place, to cloth himself with flesh, to be born in a Stable, to be laid in a Manger, to live a poor life in the World, to take upon him our sicknesses, infirmities, sins, curse, Death, and the Wrath that was due to man. And all this he did, for a base, undeserving, unthankfull people: yea, for a people that was at Enmity with him. *For when we were yet without strength, in due time Christ died for the ungodly. For scarcely for a righteous man will one die, yet peradventure for a good man, some would even dare to die. But God commended his love towards us, in that while we were yet sinners Christ dyed for us. Much more then being now justified by his blood, we shall be saved by his life. For if when we were Enemies, we were reconciled to God by the Death of his Son: much more, being reconciled, we shall be saved by his life*, Rom. 5. 6, 7, 8, 9, 10.

Secondly, He is full of **Truth**. Full of grace, and truth. **Truth**, that is, faithfulness in keeping promise, even this of the Text (with all other), *I will in no wise cast out.* Hence it is said, that his words be true, and that he is the faithfull God that keepeth covenant. And hence it is also that his promise is called Truth, *Thou wilt fulfill thy truth unto* Jacob, *and thy mercy to* Abraham, *which thou hast sworn unto our Fathers, from the days of old.* Therefore it is said again, that both himself, and words are Truth. I am the Truth, the Scriptures of Truth, thy Word is Truth, thy Law is the Truth, and my mouth, saith he, shall speak truth, *Joh.* 14. 6. *Dan.* 10. 21. *Joh.* 17. 17. 2 *Sam.* 7. 28. *Pro.* 8. 7. *Psal.* 119. 142. *Eccles.* 12. 10. *Isa.* 25. 1. *Mal.* 2. 6. *Acts* 26. 25. 2 *Tim.* 2. 12, 13.

5–6 and take it . . . full of *love*;] *om. 1684–1688* 9 Men] Man *1684–1685* 13 that] to that *1684–1686*[1] 19 *by his blood*] *add 1684–1688* 20 *his*] *om. 1686*[1]*–1688* 28 *to*] *unto 1685–1688* 31 the] *om. 1686*[1]*–1688* 32 speak] spake *1684*

Now I say, his word is truth, and he is full of truth, to fulfill his truth even to a Thousand Generations. Coming sinner, he will not deceive thee, come boldly to Jesus Christ.

Thirdly, *He is full of* **Wisdome**, *He is made unto us of God Wisdome, Wisdome* to manage the affairs of his Church in general, and the affairs of every coming sinner, in particular. And upon this account he is said to be *head over all things*, 1 *Cor*. 1. *Ephes*. 1. Because he manages all things that are in the world by his *Wisdom*, for the good of his Church; all mens Actions, all Satans Temptations, all Gods Providences, all Crosses, Disappointments; all things what ever, are under the hand of Christ (Who is the *Wisdom* of God), and he ordereth them all for good to his Church; And can Christ help it (and be sure he can), nothing shall happen, or fall out in the world, but it shall, in despite of all opposition, have a good tendency to his Church and people.

Fourthly, *He is full of the* **Spirit**, to communicate it to the coming Sinner; he hath therefore received it without measure, that he may communicate it to every member of his body, according as every mans measure thereof is allotted him by the Father. Wherefore he saith, that he that comes to him, *Out of his belly shall flow rivers of Living water*, Joh. 3. 34. Tit. 3. 5, 6. Acts 1. Joh. 7. 31, 32, 34, 35, 36, 37, 38.

Fifthly, *He is indeed a store-house*, full of all the graces of the Spirit. *Of his fulness have all we received, and grace for grace*. Here is *more* Faith, *more* Love, *more* Sincerity, *more* Humility, *more* of every Grace; and of this, even more of this he giveth to every Lowly, Humble, Penitent coming Sinner: wherefore coming Soul, thou comest not to a barren wilderness, when thou comest to Jesus Christ, *John* 1. 16.

Sixthly, *He is full of Bowels and Compassion*; And they shall feel, and find it so, that come to him for Life. He can *bear* with thy Weaknesses, he can *pity* thy Ignorance, he can be *touched* with the Feeling of thine Infirmities, he can *affectionately* forgive thy Transgressions, he can *heal* thy Back-slidings, and *Love thee Freely*. His Compassions fail not: *And he will not break a bruised Reed, nor quench the smoaking Flax: He can pity them, that no Eye pities, and be afflicted in*

4 *God*] *Gods 1686*[2] 31 Weaknesses] Weakness *1688* 32 thine] thy *1684–1688*

all thy Afflictions; Mat. 26. 41. Heb. 5. 2. Chap. 2. 17, 18. Mat. 9. 2. Hos. 14. 4. Ezek. 16. 5, 6. Isa. 63. 9. Psal. 78. 38. Psal. 86. 15. Psal. 111. 4. Psal. 112. 4. Lam. 3. 22. Isa. 42. 3.

Seventhly, *Coming Soul*, *the* Jesus *that thou art coming to*, *is full of* **Might**, *and Terribleness*, *for thy Advantage*; He can suppress all thine Enemies: He is the Prince of the Kings of the Earth; He can bow all Men's Designes for thy Help: He can break all Snares laid for thee in the Way: He can lift thee out of all Difficulties, where-with thou may'st be surrounded. *He is Wise in Heart*, *and Mighty in Power.* Every Life under Heaven is in his Hand; yea, the Faln Angels tremble before him: And he will save thy Life, Coming-Sinner; 1 *Cor.* 1. 24. *Rom.* 8. 28. *Mat.* 28. 18. *Rev.* 15. *Psal.* 19. 3. *Psal.* 27. 4, 5, 6. *Job* 9. 4. *Joh.* 17. 2. *Mat.* 8. 29. *Luk.* 8. 28. *Jam.* 2. 19.

Eighthly, *Coming-Sinner*, *The Jesus to whom thou art coming*, *is* **Lowly** *in Heart*; He despiseth not any: 'Tis not thy outward Meanness, nor thy inward Weakness; 'tis not because thou art Poor, or Base, or Deformed, or a Fool, that he will despise thee. *He hath chosen the Foolish*, *the Base*, *and despised Things of this World*, *to confound the Wise*, *and Mighty.* He will bow his Ear to thy Stammering Prayers; he will pick out the Meaning of thy inexpressible Groans; he will respect thy weakest Offering, if there be in it but thy Heart: *Mat.* 11. 29. *Luk.* 14. 21. *Prov.* 9. 4, 5, 6. *Isa.* 38. 14, 15. *Song.* 5. 16. *Joh.* 4. 27. *Mark* 12. 33, 34. *Jam.* 5. 11.

Now, Is not this a Blessed Christ, Coming-Sinner? Art thou not like to fair well, when thou hast Embraced him, Coming-Sinner! But,

Secondly, Thou hast yet another Advantage by Jesus Christ, that art coming to him: For he is not only **Full**, but **Free**. He is not sparing of what he has; he is open-hearted, and open-handed. Let me in a few Particulars shew thee this:

First, *This is evident*, *because he calls thee*; He calls upon thee, to come unto him; the which he would not do, was he not **Free** to give: Yea, he bids thee, when come; *Ask*, *Seek*, *Knock*: And for thy Encouragement, adds to every Command, a Promise; **Seek**, and ye shall find; **Ask**, and ye shall have; **Knock**, and it shall be opened unto you. If the Rich Man should say thus to the Poor, would not

28 art] are *1684–1685, 1686*[2]

he be reckoned a Free-hearted Man? I say, Should he say to the Poor, *Come* to my Door, *Ask* at my Door, *Knock* at my Door, and you shall Find and Have; Would he not be counted Liberal? Why? thus doth Jesus Christ: Mind it, Coming-Sinner; *Isa.* 55. 3. *Psal.* 50. 15. *Mat.* 7. 7, 8, 9.

Secondly, *He doth not only bid thee Come, but tells thee, He will heartily do thee Good*; Yea, he will do it with Rejoycing: *I will rejoyce over them to do them Good, with my whole Heart, and with my whole Soul*, Jer. 32. 41.

Thirdly, *It appeareth that he is* Free, *because he giveth without Twitting*: He gives to all Men Liberally, and upbraideth not; *Jam.* 1. 5. There are some, that will not deny to do the Poor a Pleasure, but they will mix their Mercies with so many *Twitts*, that the Persons on whom they bestow their Charity, shall find but little Sweetness in it. But Christ doth not do so, Coming-Sinner; He casteth all thine Iniquities behind his Back; Thy Sins and Iniquities he will remember no more: *Isa.* 38. 17. *Heb.* 8. 12.

Fourthly, That Christ is Free, is manifest by the Complaints that he makes against them, that will not come to him for Mercy: I say, he complains, saying; *O Jerusalem, Jerusalem! How often would I have gathered thy Children together, as a Hen gathereth her Chickens under her Wings, and ye would not?* Matth. 23. 37. I say, he speaks it by way of Complaint. He saith also in another place; *But thou hast not called upon me, O* Jacob*; but thou hast been weary of me, O* Israel; Isa. 43. 22. Coming-Sinner, See here the Willingness of Christ to Save; See here, how Free he is to communicate Life, and all good Things, to such as thou art? He complains, if thou comest not; he is displeased, if thou callest not upon him.

Hark, Coming-Sinner, once again; When *Jerusalem* would not come to him for Safe-guard, *He beheld the City, and wept over it, saying; If thou hadst known, even thou, at least in this thy day, the Things that belong to thy Peace; but now they are hid from thine Eyes*, Luk. 19. 42.

Fifthly, Lastly, *He is open and* Free Hearted to do thee Good, as is seen by the Joy and Rejoycing, that he manifesteth at the coming home of poor *Prodigals:* He receives the lost Sheep with Rejoycing; the lost Groat with Rejoycing: Yea, when the Prodigal came home,

10 Liberally] Liberty *1686[1]–1686[2]* 23 *but thou hast . . . of me*] *om. 1686[1]–1688* 26 comest *1688*] comes *1678–1686[2]* 31 42.] 41. *1678–1688*

what Joy and Mirth, what Musick and Dancing, was in his Father's House? *Luk.* 15.

Thirdly, Coming-Sinner, I will add another Encouragement for thy Help.

First, God hath prepared a *Mercy-Seat*, a Throne of Grace *to Sit on*; that thou may'st come *thither* to him, and that he may *from thence* Hear thee, and Receive thee: *I will Commune with thee* (saith he) *from above the Mercy-Seat*, Exod. 25. 22.

As who should say; Sinner, When thou comest to me, thou shalt find me upon the *Mercy Seat*; where also I am alwayes found of the Undone, Coming, Sinner: Thither I bring my Pardons; there I Hear, and Receive their Petitions, and Accept them to my Favour.

Secondly, God hath also prepared a *Golden Altar* for thee, to offer thy Prayers, and Tears upon: A *Golden* Altar! It is called a *Golden* Altar, to shew what Worth it is of in God's Account: For this Golden Altar, is Jesus Christ; This Altar sanctifies thy Gift, and makes thy Sacrifices acceptable. This Altar, then, makes thy Groans, *Golden* Groans; thy Tears, *Golden* Tears; and thy Prayers, *Golden* Prayers, in the Eye of that God thou comest to, Coming Sinner: *Rev.* 8. *Mat.* 23. 19. *Heb.* 10. 10, 15. 1 *Pet.* 2. 5.

Thirdly, God hath *Strowed all the way* (from the Gate of *Hell*, where thou wast, to the Gate of *Heaven*, whither thou art going), *with Flowers out of his own Garden*: Behold! How the promises, Invitations, Calls, and Encouragements, like Lillies, lye round about thee; (Take heed, that thou doest not tread them under foot, Sinner!). With Promises, did I say? Yea, he hath mixed all those with his *Own* Name, his *Sons* Name; also, with the Name of Mercy, Goodness, Compassion, Love, Pity, Grace, Forgiveness, Pardon, and what not, that may encourage the coming Sinner.

Fourthly, He hath also, for thy Encouragement, laid up the Names, and set forth the Sins, of those that have been Saved: In his Book they are fairly written, that thou through Patience, and Comfort of the Scriptures, mightst have Hope.

1. In this Book is Recorded *Noah*'s Name, and Sin; and how God had Mercy upon him.

9 should] shall *1686*[1]–*1688* shalt] shall *1684* 11 Pardons] Pardon *1688*
22 whither] whether *1684*

2. In this Record is fairly written the Name of *Lot*, and the Nature of his Sin; and how the Lord had Mercy upon him.

3. In this Record, thou hast also fairly written, the Names of *Moses*, *Aaron*, *Gidion*, *Sampson*, *David*, *Solomon*, *Peter*, *Paul*; with the Nature of their Sins, and how God had Mercy upon them: And all to Encourage thee, Coming-Sinner.

Fourthly, I will add yet another Encouragement, for the Man that is coming to Jesus Christ. Art thou coming? Art thou coming, indeed? Why?

1. Then this thy Coming, *Is by Vertue of God's Call.* Thou art **Called**; *Calling* goes before *Coming*: Coming is not of Works, but of him that *Calleth. He went up into a Mountain, and called to him whom he would, and* **They** *came to him*, Mark. 3. 13.

Secondly, Art thou coming? *This is also by the Vertue of Illumination.* God has made thee see; and therefore, thou art coming. So long as thou wast Darkness, thou lovedst Darkness; and couldst not abide to come, because thy Deeds were Evil: But, being now Illuminated, and made to see, what, and where thou art; and also, what, and where thy Saviour is: Now thou art coming to Jesus Christ. *Blessed art thou* Simon Bar-Jona! *for Flesh and Blood hath not Revealed it unto thee* (said Christ) *but my Father which is in Heaven*; Matth. 16. 15, 16, 17.

Thirdly, Art thou coming, *this is because God has* **Inclined** thine heart to come; God hath called thee, illuminated thee, and *inclined* thy heart to come, and therefore thou comest to Jesus Christ. It is God that worketh in thee to **Will**, and to come to Jesus Christ. Coming sinner, bless God, for that he hath given thee a **Will**, to come to Jesus Christ. It is a Sign that thou belongest to Jesus Christ, because God has made thee *willing* to come to him (*Psal.* 110. 3.). Bless God for *slaying* the enmity of thy mind; had *he* not done it, thou wouldest, *as yet*, have hated thine own Salvation.

Fourthly, Art thou coming to Jesus Christ, *it is God that giveth thee* **Power**; *power* to pursue thy *Will* in the matters of thy Salvation, is the gift of God. 'Tis God that worketh in you both to *Will* and to **Do**, *Phil.* 2. 13. not that God worketh *Will* to come, where he

12 *into*] *in* 1686^{1}–1686^{2} 14 *by the* 1686^{2}–*1688*] *by* *1678*–1686^{1} 22 17.] *om.* *1678–1688* 30 enmity] Enemy 1686^{1}–*1688* 35 to^{1}] *om. 1684–1688*

gives no *power*; but thou shouldest take notice, that *power* is an aditional Mercy. The Church saw that *will* and *power* were two things, when She cried, *Draw me, we will run after thee* (Song. 1. 4.): and so did *David* too, when he said, *I will run the ways of thy Commandments, when thou shalt enlarge my Heart. Will* to come, and *power* to pursue thy will, is a double Mercy, coming Sinner.

Fifthly, All thy strange, passionate, sudden rushings forward after Jesus Christ (coming Sinners know what I mean), they also are thy helps from God. Perhaps thou feelest at sometimes, more than at others, strong stirrings up of heart, to fly to Jesus Christ; now thou hast at this time a sweet, and stiff gale of the Spirit of God filling thy sails with the fresh gales of his good Spirit; and thou ridest at those times, as upon the wings of the wind, being carried out beyond thy self, beyond the most of thy prayers, and also above all thy fears and temptations.

Sixthly, coming Sinner, hast thou not, now and then, a kiss of the sweet lips of Jesus Christ? I mean, some blessed word droping like an Honey-Comb upon thy Soul to revive thee, when thou art in the midst of thy dumps.

Seventhly, Does not Jesus Christ sometimes give thee a glimps of himself, though perhaps, thou seest him not so long a time as while one may tell twenty?

Eighthly, Hast thou not sometimes as it were the very warmth of his wings over-shadowing the face of thy Soul, that gives thee as it were a gload upon thy Spirit, as the bright beams of the Sun do upon thy body, when it suddenly breaks out in the midst of a cloud, though presently all is gone again?

Well, all these things are the good hand of thy God upon thee, and they are upon thee to constrain to provoke and to make thee willing, and able to come (coming Sinner) that thou mightest in the end be Saved.

FINIS.

3 *we*] *and we 1688*   6 a] *om. 1686*^{1}*–1688*   15 fears] fear *1684–1686*^{2} 18 an] a *1686*^{1}*–1688*   revive] receive *1686*^{1}*–1686*^{2} 26 in the midst] *om. 1684–1688*

NOTES TO
INSTRUCTION FOR THE IGNORANT

p. 12, l. 24. *a publick person.* Cf. Oxford Bunyan, ii. 28, l. 23, and note.

p. 14, l. 34. *Tophet of old.* Cf. Isa. xxx. 33; *Come, & Welcome*, above, p. 320, l. 32.

p. 15, ll. 31–3. Cf. *G.A.*, § 83.

p. 18, ll. 11–12. *Q. But if I follow my play and sports a little longer, may I not come time enough?* Cf. *G.A.*, §§ 21, 24.

p. 18, l. 35. *Strait is the gate.* This quotation from Matt. vii. 14 is the theme of Bunyan's 1676 discourse, *The Strait Gate*. Cf. *P.P.*, p. 25.

p. 24, ll. 10–11. *to condign punishment.* A legal phrase, meaning appropriate punishment. Cf. the 1642 Declaration of the House of Commons in *Historical Collections of Private Passages of State*, ed. John Rushworth (1721–2), v. 25: 'That the Authors . . . shall be . . . brought to this House to receive condign Punishment'. *O.E.D.*

p. 25, ll. 1–3. The condemnation of confession of sin merely as custom and not from a sense of guilt recalls the attack on external religious forms in *I Will Pray with the Spirit*, Oxford Bunyan, ii. 249–50, 252, 264.

p. 25, ll. 31–4. This warning was a basic theme in *A Few Sighs from Hell*, Oxford Bunyan, i. It is repeated in a different context later in the catechism (above, p. 31, ll. 15–19).

p. 32, ll. 2–4. The reference here to John vi. 37 foreshadows the theme of Bunyan's popular sermon, *Come, & Welcome*, on that verse published three years later.

p. 34, l. 14. *their Conversation is in Heaven.* Cf. *G.A.*, §§ 37–9.

p. 44, ll. 6 ff. The remarks on death that conclude the catechism are more fully developed in the closing three chapters of *The Life and Death of Mr. Badman*, Offor, iii. 655–65.

NOTES TO
LIGHT FOR THEM THAT SIT IN DARKNESS

p. 50, l. 5. 2 Pet. ii. 22.

p. 50, ll. 5–6. Isa. lxiv. 6.

p. 50, ll. 7–8. Cf. Ezek. xxiv. 13.

p. 51, l. 12. *I have ventured my own Soul.* Cf. *G.A.*, § 337. Bunyan may have been influenced in this regard by Walter Cradock, the Welsh Independent. See Geoffrey F. Nuttall, *The Welsh Saints, 1640–1660* (Cardiff, 1957), p. 34.

p. 51, l. 15. *nor borrowed my Doctrine from Libraries.* Cf. the similar statement in *Solomon's Temple Spiritualized*: 'I have not for these things fished in other men's waters . . . ' Offor, iii. 464. For an account of doctrinal influence on Bunyan see Oxford Bunyan, ii. xvi–xxi.

p. 54, l. 14. Rom. viii. 3.

p. 58, ll. 9–11. Geneva Version.

p. 61, l. 4. *Solomon was his Type in his building the Temple.* Cf. the thesis of *Solomon's Temple Spiritualized*: 'There lies, as wrapt up in a mantle, much of the glory of our gospel matters in this temple which Solomon builded . . .' At the beginning of this work Bunyan declared again that Solomon was a type of Christ 'as the builder of his church'. Offor, iii. 464, 465.

p. 61, l. 24. Geneva Version.

p. 63, ll. 27–9. *the New-Covenant . . . in a Word of Promise.* For Bunyan's development of the promissory nature of the covenant of grace, see Greaves, 'John Bunyan and Covenant Thought in the Seventeenth Century', *Church History*, xxxvi (June 1967), 156–63.

p. 63, l. 35–p. 64, l. 2. Cf. *G.A.*, § 173.

p. 69, ll. 14–20. Matt. ii. 9–11.

p. 80, ll. 11–12. *sin is the great Engine of Hell.* Cf. the development of this metaphor in *The Holy War*. Offor, iii. 276.

p. 84, ll. 13–18. Heb. x. 4–7.

p. 84, ll. 30–1. Matt. i. 23.

p. 84, ll. 31–2. John i. 14.

p. 85, ll. 18–19. 1 Pet. iv. 11.

p. 86, ll. 9 ff. In this section Bunyan is repudiating the view of Edward Fowler or his curate. 'The benefit we get by his perfect obedience [to the law] is this, that it qualified him to be a satisfactory Sacrifice for our sins, which without it he could not be; but Christ never obeyed the law *for us* so as that, *his* obedience should be looked on as *ours*; for then what necessity can there be of our own *personal* obedience.' *Dirt Wip't Off* (1672), p. 52. Cf. also William Penn's argument that Christ fulfilled the law as an example for believers, but not on their behalf. 'Unless we become doers of that Law, which Christ came not to destroy, but as our Example, to fulfil, we can never be justified before God . . .' *The Sandy Foundation Shaken* (1668), p. 26.

p. 86, l. 19. *into the Valley and Shadow of Death*. Cf. Ps. xxiii. 4; *P.P.*, pp. 61–5, 74, 241–6, 252.

p. 87, l. 3. Gal. iv. 5.

p. 87, ll. 34–5. Gal. iv. 5.

p. 89, ll. 13–15. Deut. vi. 5; Matt. xxii. 37.

p. 90, ll. 6–7. Gal. iv. 4–5.

p. 90, ll. 29–30. 2 Cor. v. 21.

p. 91, ll. 16–30. The position Bunyan is attacking here was advocated by a number of writers. The debate ultimately hinged on the interpretation of 2 Cor. v. 21. According to Richard Baxter the import of this verse is that Christ 'was made a Sacrifice for sin: But never was a Sinner indeed, or in Gods esteem . . . Christ never undertook to be reputed of God one that was truly and formally wicked or a sinner . . .' *Catholick Theologie* (1675), Bk. I, pt. 2, chap. xlv. The views of the Arminian Independent John Goodwin were akin to Baxter's (and Fowler's); *Imputatio Fidei* (1642), pt. 1, pp. 171–2; pt. 2, p. 26. Penn, of course, rejected the whole doctrine of satisfaction to which this debate related. *The Sandy Foundation Shaken*, pp. 16, 19. For a sound exposition of Penn's thought, see Melvin Endy, *William Penn and Early Quakerism* (Princeton, 1973).

p. 91, l. 22. *Duncish Sophistry*: specious reasoning, with which the name of Duns Scotus had come to be commonly and erroneously associated.

p. 91, ll. 32–5. Cf. Owen: 'Christ so took and bare our sins, and had them so laid upon him, as that he underwent the punishment due unto them, and that in our stead: therefore, he made satisfaction to the justice of God for them.' *The Works of John Owen*, ed. W. H. Goold (1850–5), x. 280; cf. 269.

p. 91, l. 36–p. 92, l. 8. Cf. John Goodwin: 'It hath no foundation, either in the Scriptures or Reasons to say, that Christ by any imputation of sinne, was made formally a sinner: nor that sinne in any other sense should be said to be imputed to him, then as the punishment due unto it was inflicted on him.' *Imputatio Fidei*, pt. 2, p. 26.

p. 92, ll. 21–33. This is an attack against Fowler or his curate. 'God doth not, nay he *cannot* pass a false judgment . . .' *Dirt Wip't Off*, p. 45.

p. 93, ll. 9–10. Cf. Owen, 'This is eminently seen in this business of satisfaction,—that God, as a creditor, doth exactly require the payment of the debt by the way of punishment.' *Works*, x. 272; cf. 260–70.

p. 93, ll. 30–2. Gal. iii. 13.

p. 94, ll. 1–3. Deut. xxi. 22–3.

p. 94, ll. 6–14. The Arminians rejected this. Cf. John Goodwin: 'The sentence or curse of the *Law*, was not properly executed upon *Christ* in his death, but this death of *Christ* was a ground or consideration unto *God*, whereupon to dispence with his *Law*, and to let fall or suspend the execution of the penalty or curse therein threatned.' *Imputatio Fidei*, pt. 2, p. 33.

p. 94, l. 9. Isa. liii. 12.

p. 94, l. 10. Cf. Deut. xxi. 22.

p. 94, ll. 21–2. Gal. iii. 13.

p. 94, ll. 24 ff. Bunyan develops this thesis at length in *A Defence of the Doctrine of Justification, by Faith*. In the reply by Fowler or his curate it was argued that Christ did not suffer the *same* punishment due to sinners, but one as acceptable to God, answering the demands of divine government just as if all men had perished for their sins. *Dirt Wip't Off*, p. 51.

p. 95, l. 2. 1 Cor. xv. 56.

p. 98, l. 14. *How have the Martyrs despised death*. Bunyan is reflecting on his reading of Foxe's *Acts and Monuments*. Cf. the extensive references in *Come, & Welcome*, above, pp. 383–4.

p. 98, ll. 19–20. Isa. liii. 9.

p. 98, ll. 34–5. Cf. *The Life and Death of Mr. Badman*, chaps. xviii–xix.

p. 99, l. 11. Matt. xxvii. 46.

p. 99, ll. 16–17. Isa. liii. 10.

p. 99, l. 19. Cf. Ps. xxxvii. 25.

p. 100, ll. 1–2. Cf. Luke xxiii. 25.

p. 100, ll. 18–19. Phil. ii. 8.

p. 100, l. 24. Matt. xxvii. 42.

p. 101, ll. 27–33. Cf. Fowler's or his curate's contrary view: 'It is blasphemy to say, that Christ was accursed of God in any other sense than this, *that* he suffered such a kind of death as was by the law of *Moses* pronounced accursed . . . Christ was alwayes Gods beloved Son, nor was he ever more a darling of heaven than when he hung upon the Cross. And that the Reader may be truly informed in the Doctrine of Christ's Satisfaction (false notions whereof make this *I.B.* talk most gross things), I entreat him to get and carefully peruse the Learned Dr. *Stillingfleets* Treatise upon that Subject; there you will find that Christ did not suffer the very *same* punishment that is due to sinners, but that what he suffered for sinners sakes was as Satisfactory, and answered the ends of Government as much, as if all mankind had perished . . .' *Dirt Wip't Off*, pp. 50–1.

p. 103, ll. 7–8. Luke xii. 59.

p. 103, ll. 26–7. Acts ii. 27.

p. 103, ll. 33–4. Cf. Rom. vi. 22.

p. 104, ll. 18–23. Cf. Thomas Goodwin: 'God is resolved not to stoop one whit unto man, no nor to Christ his surety. Justice will not only be satisfied, and have a sufficient ransom collected and paid, as at Christ's death, but he must come and bring his bags up to heaven . . .' *The Works of Thomas Goodwin*, ed. J. C. Miller (1861), iv. 62.

p. 106, ll. 11–12. John x. 18.

p. 107, l. 17. Gal. iii. 13.

p. 107, ll. 34–6. Cf. Lewis Bayly, '*Gods Iustice* could not be *satisfied* but by such a *Sacrifice*' as Christ made. *The Practise of Pietie*, 3rd edn. (1614), p. 751. Thomas Goodwin similarly wrote that God's justice had the honour to be satisfied by a price paid upon it, that so the severity of it might appear and be held forth in our salvation'. *Works*, iv. 62.

p. 108, l. 26. The position Bunyan is attacking here was expressly asserted by Penn, who argued that remission was 'by believing his [Christ's] Testimony, and obeying his Precepts, and not by a pretended satisfaction'. *The Sandy Foundation Shaken*, p. 18.

p. 108, ll. 31 ff. For Bunyan's concept of satisfaction see Greaves, pp. 36–41.

p. 110, l. 28. *Christ paid the full price for us by his Death*. Cf. *The Holy War*: 'Mansoul is mine by right of purchase. I have bought it, O Diabolus, I have bought it to myself.' Offor, iii. 288.

p. 110, l. 33–p. 111, l. 2. Cf. 1 Cor. vi. 20; Heb. ix. 12.

p. 111, ll. 7–11. Cf. Bayly: 'Christ tooke by *imputation* al their sinnes and guiltinesse vpon him to satisfie *Gods iustice* for them . . .' *The Practise of Pietie*, pp. 692–3.

p. 112, l. 22. Rom. vi. 4.

p. 113, ll. 8–9. Matt. xxvii. 6, 52.

p. 113, l. 29. Ps. ix. 17.

p. 114, ll. 7–9. Ps. ii. 8.

p. 114, l. 14. Acts xiii. 33.

p. 115, ll. 28–30. Cf. 1 Cor. vi. 20; Heb. ix. 12.

p. 117, l. 10. Acts ii. 34.

p. 117, l. 30. Matt. i. 21.

p. 117, ll. 30–1. Cf. Matt. i. 23.

p. 118, ll. 18–19. 1 Cor. xii. 3.

p. 118, l. 22. Ps. cx. 4; Heb. v. 6.

p. 118, l. 34. Heb. ix. 12.

p. 119, ll. 12–13. Ps. xlvii. 4.

p. 119, ll. 22–3. Deut. xviii. 18.

p. 119, l. 25. 1 Cor. xi. 25.

p. 119, l. 26. Heb. xiii. 20.

p. 120, ll. 2–3. Cf. Heb. ix. 20.

p. 120, ll. 25–6. Matt. xxviii. 18.

p. 120, ll. 27–8. Phil. ii. 8–9.

p. 121, ll. 9–10. Cf. 1 Cor. vi. 20; Heb. ix. 12.

p. 122, ll. 18–19. Joel ii. 28.

p. 122, l. 20. John vii. 39.

p. 123, l. 20. Cf. Eph. i. 7; Col. i. 14.

p. 124, l. 23. Cf. John x. 15, 17–18; xx. 31.

p. 124, ll. 23–4. Cf. Matt. xx. 28; Mark x. 45.

p. 126, l. 11. Zech. xii. 11.

p. 126, ll. 15–16. Acts ix. 5.

p. 126, ll. 25–6. Acts viii. 12.

p. 128, ll. 20–2. Rom. v. 21.

p. 128, ll. 26–7. Cf. Rom. vi. 1.

p. 129, l. 10. Col. i. 22.

p. 132, ll. 4–6. Cf. 1 Cor. vi. 20; Heb. ix. 12.

p. 133, ll. 4 ff. There is an implicit repudiation of Fowler in the ensuing pages, where Bunyan discusses incitements to holiness. Fowler's *Design of Christianity* (1672) was based on the thesis that '*the Promoting of* Holiness *was the Design of* our Saviour's whole Life and Conversation among Men . . .' The intent of the gospel, according to Fowler, was to make men partakers of an inward and real righteousness; only in a secondary sense were they to be '*accepted* and rewarded' as if they were '*completely* righteous'. Fowler accepted the concept of the imputation of Christ's righteousness, but only to the extent that it 'consists in dealing with *sincerely* righteous Persons, as if they were *perfectly* so, for the sake of Christ's Righteousness'. The purpose of such imputation was to 'excite Men in their Endeavours after a Righteousness as this is', viz. 'to make men holy'. There was, nevertheless, some requirement of holiness on man's part prior to such imputation. 'Were it possible that *Christ's Righteousness* could be *imputed* to an *unrighteous* Man, I dare boldly affirm, that it would signify as little to his Happiness, while he continues so, as would a gorgeous and splendid Garment to one that is almost starved with Hunger . . .' op. cit. (1760 edn.), pp. 31, 100–1, 190–1. Bunyan makes clear in this section that the major incentive to live a holy life, as he sees it, is the recognition of the atoning work of Christ, with the free benefits thereof for sinners.

p. 133, ll. 12–13. 1 John iv. 10.

p. 133, ll. 25–8. This was not always the case for Bunyan. See *G.A.*, § 197. For the kind of experience he is depicting in the text, see, e.g., *G.A.*, § 245.

p. 136, l. 6. John xvi. 23.

p. 136, ll. 17–19. John xvi. 26.

p. 138, ll. 24–5. Col. iii. 16.

p. 141, ll. 18–19. Heb. ix. 26.

p. 143, ll. 7–9. Cf. 1 Cor. xi.

p. 144, ll. 29–32. The reference here is especially to Fowler and Penn.

p. 145, ll. 9–10. Acts xiii. 41.

p. 146, ll. 12–13. John viii. 24.

p. 148, ll. 3–4. Eph. i. 17.

p. 149, l. 35–p. 150, l. 2. Cf. Bunyan's fuller description of hell in *A Few Sighs from Hell*, Offor, iii. 681 ff.

p. 150, ll. 20–1. 1 John iv. 10.

p. 151, l. 2. *look up to the Cross*. Cf. *P.P.*, p. 38.

p. 151, ll. 18–19. *sin hath made thy Condition dreadful*. Cf. *G.A.*, § 67.

p. 153, ll. 6–8. Acts iv. 12.

p. 153, ll. 8–9. Heb. ix. 22.

p. 153, l. 22. Deut. iv. 24.

p. 154, ll. 29–30. Ps. ciii. 1.

p. 154, l. 31. 2 Cor. v. 17.

p. 155, ll. 4–6. 2 Cor. v. 19.

p. 155, ll. 7–9. 2 Cor. v. 21. Cf. *G.A.*, § 113.

p. 155, l. 11. Cf. Rom. ix. 23.

p. 156, l. 5. *Dreadful accusations from Satan.* Cf. *G.A.*, §§ 51, 60, 70, 97, 103, 107–8, 110, 132–3, 181, etc.

p. 156, l. 6. *Grievous defiling and infectious thoughts.* Cf. *G.A.*, §§ 70, 81, 96, 101, 136–7, 139, etc.

p. 156, l. 7. *A strange readiness in our Nature to fall in with both.* Cf. *G.A.*, §§ 52, 60–1, 98–100, 111, 134, 138, etc.

p. 156, ll. 12–13. Isa. xxxvi. Cf. Acts ii. 6. Also cf. Fowler: 'Here's a *Rabshak Dirt Wip't Off*, p. 7.

p. 156, l. 22. *he concludeth that he is reprobate.* Cf. *G.A.*, §§ 59 ff., 142, 145, 150 165.

p. 156, ll. 28–9. *Fire and Smoke continually bursteth forth of the Heart against him.* Cf. *P.P.*, p. 20.

p. 156, ll. 31–4. *the Soul struggleth . . . (for strugglings are also as poison to Satan).* Charles Doe entitled his proposal to publish Bunyan's works *The Struggler.* In it Doe described Bunyan's own religious experience in these words: 'he did not take up religion upon trust, but grace in him continually struggling with himself and others, took all advantages he lit on to ripen his understanding in religion . . .' Offor, iii. 765.

p. 156, l. 24–p. 157, l. 4. The emblem of the sinner and the spider is used in *A Book for Boys and Girls*, Offor, iii. 752–4.

p. 157, ll. 20–5. Cf. *P.P.*, p. 38.

p. 157, l. 36. *this Combate.* This imagery is fully developed in *The Holy War.*

p. 158, ll. 3–4. *the Temptation rightly ceaseth, at leastwise for a Season.* There are repeated references to temporary lapses of temptation in *G.A.* Cf. *P.P.*, pp. 38, 41–6.

p. 159, l. 11. 2 Cor. v. 14.

NOTES TO *SAVED BY GRACE*

p. 168, ll. 5–7. Eph. ii. 4–5.

p. 169, ll. 12–16. Cf. Thomas Goodwin, whose concept of God's nature reflects, as does Bunyan's, the influence of Martin Luther: 'I shall but further superadd that noticed saying of Luther (which, out of deep experience of the wrath of God in his soul, at his first humiliation and conversion he had learned), The wrath of God is hell, the hell of devils and all damned spirits.' Moreover, 'the Scriptures do set out this . . . wrath of God under the similitude, resemblance, and representation of fire, and sometimes, when hell-fire is spoken of, the wrath of God is intended thereby'. *Works*, x. 501; cf. 504. See Greaves, pp. 31–2.

p. 169, ll. 30–3. Cf. *G.A.*, §§ 76–8.

p. 170, ll. 7–9. Cf. *P.P.*, p. 17.

p. 170, ll. 12–15. Cf. *G.A.*, §§ 6, 86, 260.

p. 170, ll. 25–6. *Where is he that hath taken his flight for Salvation!* Cf. *P.P.*, p. 10: 'Whither must I fly?' Also cf. Luther: 'Whither shall I flie from the wrath of Christ, that angry Iudge . . .?' *A Commentarie of Master Doctor Martin Luther upon the Epistle of S. Paul to the Galathians* (1635 edn.), p. 202ᵛ.

p. 171, ll. 11–12. Eph. iii. 11.

p. 172, l. 22. *Mad as a Bedlam*: a lunatic. Cf. *P.P.*, p. 91: 'But they that were appointed to examine them, did not believe them to be any other than Bedlams and Mad . . .' The Hospital of St. Mary of Bethlehem, an asylum for the mentally ill, was rebuilt near the London Wall in the same year *Saved by Grace* was published.

p. 172, l. 31. *fallen into Rivers*. Cf. *G.A.*, § 12.

p. 173, ll. 9–10. This is one of the themes developed throughout Bunyan's sermon, *Come, & Welcome*, published two years later, in 1678.

p. 174, ll. 1–2. *by faith we . . . venture upon . . . Jesus Christ*. Cf. *Light in Darkness*, above, p. 51, l. 12; *G.A.*, § 37.

p. 174, ll. 14 ff. For Bunyan's concept of faith, see Greaves, pp. 69–75.

p. 174, l. 18. *put on that Christ*. Cf. Christian's new coat in *P.P.*, pp. 38, 41.

p. 174, ll. 21–2. Mark xvi. 16.

p. 174, ll. 26–7. *distinguish betwixt the meritorious, and the instrumental cause of their justification*. Cf. Baxter: 'Christ's righteousness is nevertheless the *meritorious cause of our righteousness* or justification, though he justify us by the instrumentality of his *donative Covenant*, as giving us right to our *Union, and Justification and Life*; and though our Faith and Repentance be the condition of our Title.' *Catholick Theologie* (1675), Bk. I, pt. 2, p. [26c].

p. 174, ll. 33–5. 1 Pet. i. 18–19.

p. 175, ll. 25–6. *The Devil is called . . . a Lyon, a roaring Lyon.* Cf. *P.P.*, p. 242.

p. 175, l. 30. Matt. xvi. 18.

p. 175, l. 34. *Gibbets.* Cf. *Instruction for the Ignorant*, above, p. 14, l. 35.

p. 176, ll. 36–7. *a safe Conduct to Heaven.* Cf. *P.P.*, pp. 306–11.

p. 177, ll. 8–9. 1 Pet. i. 9.

p. 177, ll. 9–13. Heb. xii. 22–4.

p. 177, ll. 28–30. Ps. cxvi. 3.

p. 178, ll. 20–1. *Angels . . . conduct us safely to Glory.* Cf. *P.P.*, p. 157: '*Angels help us not comfortably through death.*'

p. 179, l. 11. *'tis the price of blood.* Cf. Thomas Goodwin: 'The death of Jesus Christ is so far from derogating from grace, or that God hath received a price, that because it is his own price, and he himself set the price, and he would be at the cost, and he would have his Son die in obedience to him, that here comes the ὑπερβάλλων, the exceeding riches of it.' *Works*, ii. 292.

p. 179, ll. 13–14. Phil. iii. 21.

p. 180, ll. 6–7. Cf. *G.A.*, §§ 38, 252; and the similar experience of Baxter, *Reliquae Baxterianae*, ed. M. Sylvester (1696), i, pt. 1, § 3 (p. 3).

p. 181, l. 3. *jarring*: quarrelling, disputing, wrangling. Cf. Oliver Cromwell to William Lenthall, Speaker of Parliament, 25 Nov. 1649: 'If the Father . . . be so kind, why should there be such jarrings and heart-burnings amongst the children?' *The Writings and Speeches of Oliver Cromwell*, ed. W. C. Abbott (Cambridge, Mass., 1937, 1939), ii. 173.

p. 183, l. 1. *Grace . . . is taken for God's good will.* Cf. *P.P.*, pp. 25–8. Cf. also *Water of Life*, Offor, iii. 545: 'The original of grace to sinners is the good will of God . . .' This understanding of grace is frequently stated in the writings of Thomas Goodwin. Grace is God's 'everlasting purpose and good-will . . .' *Works*, ii. 227; cf. ix. 238, 252.

p. 183, ll. 1–2. Deut. xxxiii. 16.

p. 183, l. 3. Eph. i. 9.

p. 183, l. 4. Eph. i. 5.

p. 183, ll. 6–7. Cf. Owen: mercy and grace are the 'Goodness, Kindness, and Benignity of God in Christ'. *An Exposition on the Third, Fourth, and Fifth Chapters of . . . Hebrews* (1674), p. 323.

p. 183, ll. 12–14. Cf. *The Saints' Privilege*, Offor, i. 644. This emphasis on the freeness of divine grace is discussed at some length by Thomas Goodwin. 'Grace . . . always imports such a freedom as is moved with nothing, but it is merely out of the good pleasure of one's own goodness; that is properly grace.' It 'superadds to his love and mercy a freeness, as being extended to us upon no motives of incentives in us, but *ex proprio suo motu*'. *Works*, ii. 290; vi. 92; cf. i. 124; ii. 222, 318; vi. 89, 196; viii. 91; ix. 129, 162, 236. Also cf. Lewis Bayly: '*Goodnesse*, whereby God *willingly communicateth* his good with his creatures: and because hee communicates it *freely*, it is termed *Grace*.' *Practise of Pietie*, pp. 53–4.

p. 184, ll. 29–30. *his Attributes of Power, Justice, Goodness, Holiness, Everlastingness, &c.* Cf. *An Exposition . . . of Genesis*, Offor, ii. 414: 'In his attributes of wisdom, power, justice, holiness, mercy, &c., he is also inconceivably perfect and infinite . . .'

p. 186, ll. 6–11. Again Bunyan is foreshadowing his sermon, *Come, & Welcome*.

p. 186, ll. 21–2. *effectual Call*. Cf. above, p. 197, l. 15. A distinction must be made between a soteriological calling (as in this case) and a vocational calling. This is not done, e.g., by Charles H. George, 'A Social Interpretation of English Puritanism', *Journal of Modern History*, xxv (December 1953), 332, 340.

p. 186, ll. 25–6. Eph. i. 7.

p. 186, ll. 35–7. Cf. *P.P.*, pp. 157–63.

p. 188, ll. 11–12. John i. 4.

p. 189, l. 6. Matt. xx. 28.

p. 189, l. 11. Isa. liii. 3.

p. 189, l. 12. *from his Cradle to his Cross*. Cf. *G.A.*, §§ 119–20.

p. 189, l. 21. *As there is Grace, so there is Justice in God*. Cf. *Ebal and Gerizim*, Offor, iii. 744: . . . God, as he is love So he is justice . . .

p. 190, l. 21. 2 Cor. viii. 9.

p. 190, ll. 25–6. 2 Cor. viii. 9.

p. 190, l. 29. Isa. lxiii. 9.

p. 190, l. 30. 2 Cor. viii. 9.

p. 193, ll. 15–18. *the Wisdom and cunning of the World . . . putteth forth it self in its most cursed Sophistications, to overthrow the Simplicity that is in Christ*. Cf. *The Holy City*: 'Words easy to be understood do often hit the mark, when high and learned ones do only pierce the air.' Offor, iii. 398.

p. 195, ll. 32–4. This is the theme of Bunyan's last sermon, *Good News for the Vilest of Men* (1688).

p. 196, ll. 13–15. Cf. *G.A.*, § 171.

p. 199, ll. 10–11. *a contrivance in Heaven about the Salvation of Sinners*. This is an aspect of the covenant of grace. See Greaves, pp. 103–4.

p. 200, l. 8. *hold up thy lap*: hold up the front part of your skirt to catch something. Cf. Thomas Heywood: 'Hold up your lapps; tho' them you cannot see That bring this gold.' *Love's Mistress*, II. i, *The Dramatic Works of Thomas Heywood* (1874), v. 109. *O.E.D.*

p. 200, ll. 18–22. This is developed at length in *Law and Grace*, Oxford Bunyan, ii. 83 ff.

p. 201, ll. 5–6. *a Covenant with Death, and . . . an agreement with Hell*. In *The Holy War* Diabolus bound Mansoul to a 'covenant with death, and agreement with hell'. The Biblical basis for this concept is Isa. xxviii. 15. Offor, iii. 267.

p. 202, ll. 8–9. Rev. iii. 20.

p. 202, ll. 14–16. 2 Cor. v. 21. Cf. *G.A.*, § 113.

p. 202, ll. 31–6. Cf. *G.A.*, §§ 10, 21.

p. 203, l. 4. *Sports, Pleasures*. Cf. *G.A.*, §§ 22–4.

p. 203, ll. 10, 21. *turn or burn*. The phraseology is evocative of Foxe's *Acts and Monuments*.

p. 203, ll. 16–17. Cf. *P.P.*, pp. 32–3.

p. 203, l. 23. *sweet Pleasures, sweet Delights*. Cf. *G.A.*, §§ 24, 35, 70.

p. 203, ll. 35–6. *turn from Prophaneness to the Law of Moses*. Cf. *G.A.*, § 30.

p. 204, ll. 1–2. *a good Neighbour*. Cf. *G.A.*, §§ 31–2.

p. 204, l. 37–p. 205, l. 1. *this sinking of heart, etc*. Cf. *G.A.*, §§ 39, 48, 59, 62, 78.

p. 205, ll. 17–24. Cf. *G.A.*, §§ 48, 67, 81, 84.

p. 205, ll. 27–8. 1 John iv. 8.

p. 205, l. 30. Zeph. ii. 3.

p. 205, ll. 36–7. *several Weeks together*. Cf. *G.A.*, § 75.

p. 206, ll. 2–5. Cf. *G.A.*, § 176.

p. 206, l. 2. *claps in*: enters with alacrity and briskness. Cf.: 'Truly, sir, I would desire you to clap into your prayers . . .' Shakespeare, *Measure for Measure*, IV. iii.

p. 206, ll. 6–15. Cf., e.g., *G.A.*, §§ 113–14, 191, 202, 215, 218.

p. 206, ll. 21–2. Rom. ix. 15.

p. 206, ll. 35–6. Job xxix. 6.

p. 207, ll. 36–7. Jer. iii. 22.

p. 209, l. 31. *shuck*: shirk, draw back from. Cf. *Seasonable Counsel*: 'those bitter pills, at which we so . . . shuck . . .' Offor, ii. 693. Also cf. *The Saint's Knowledge*: 'sickness, losses, crosses, persecution and affliction . . . make us shuck . . .' Offor, ii. 11.

p. 211, ll. 33–5. Rom. iv. 16.

p. 214, ll. 5–8. Gal. iii. 15.

p. 214, ll. 26–31. Cf. *G.A.*, § 186; Greaves, pp. 97–111.

p. 215, l. 10. Eph. ii. 1.

p. 216, ll. 6–10. Again, this theme is developed in *Come, & Welcome.*

p. 216, ll. 23–5. Rom. ix. 25.

p. 217, l. 7. Rom. i. 5.

p. 217, l. 34–p. 218, l. 7. These lines reflect the strict Calvinist doctrine of a limited atonement. Bunyan is not, however, consistent in his statements on this subject. See Greaves, pp. 41–4.

p. 219, l. 24. For Bunyan's earlier controversy with the Quakers on this subject see *Some Gospel-Truths Opened* and *A Vindication of Some Gospel-Truths*, Oxford Bunyan, i.

p. 220, ll. 1–2. Heb. ix. 14.

p. 221, ll. 16–17. This charge was commonly hurled against Antinomians and many other sectaries. Fowler or his curate made such an accusation against Bunyan in *Dirt Wip't Off.* Baxter attacked Bunyan's *Law and Grace* as an Antinomian work which 'ignorantly subverted the Gospel of Christ . . .' *The Scripture Gospel Defended* (1690), sig. A2^{r}.

p. 221, ll. 33–4. Cf. *G.A.*, §§ 78, 84, 88.

p. 222, l. 21. *as blind as a Beetle*. Cf. Nicholas Udall's translation of Erasmus' paraphrase of Mark i. 5: 'Jerusalem . . . albeit she were in very dede as blynde as a betell.' *The First Tome or Volume of the Paraphrase of Erasmus upon the Newe Testamente* (1548). Cf. 'as pureblinde as a bettle'. Sir Thomas Chaloner, *The Praise of Folie* (1549), sig. N3^{v}, cited in William George Smith, *The Oxford Dictionary of English Proverbs*, 2nd edn. (Oxford, 1948), p. 50.

p. 224, l. 29. Job xxiii. 3.

p. 227, ll. 19–20. Heb. xii. 9.

p. 228, l. 19. Gal. v. 18.

NOTES TO
COME, & WELCOME, TO JESUS CHRIST

p. 239, l. 20. John vi. 20.

p. 240, l. 4. John vi. 25.

p. 240, ll. 5–7. John vi. 26.

p. 242, l. 14. Rom. xi. 26.

p. 243, ll. 25–7. Ps. ii. 8.

p. 243, ll. 28–9. Ps. ii. 9.

p. 245, l. 7. *given by Covenant to the Son.* See Oxford Bunyan, ii. 88 ff.; *Saved by Grace*, above, p. 199; Greaves, pp. 103–4.

p. 245, ll. 15–18. John x. 28–9.

p. 245, ll. 24–5. John xvii. 11.

p. 246, ll. 15–16. John xvi. 27.

p. 246, l. 18. 1 Cor. i. 3.

p. 247, l. 1. Matt. vi. 9.

p. 247, ll. 19–32. See above, pp. 244–5.

p. 252, l. 5. Isa. xxviii. 6.

p. 252, ll. 11–12. James v. 11; Neh. ix. 17.

p. 254, ll. 21–2. John vi. 39.

p. 255, ll. 17–19. *coming hither or thither, if it be voluntary, is by an act of the Mind or will; so coming to Christ, is through the inclining of the will.* Bunyan may have been influenced here by the voluntarist ideas of William Ames. See Nuttall, *Visible Saints: The Congregational Way, 1640–1660* (Oxford, 1957), p. 106. Bunyan, of course, would stress that it is divine grace that so inclines man's will.

p. 255, ll. 32–3. For the development of the theme of grace as the water of life, see Bunyan's 1688 discourse, *The Water of Life.*

p. 257, ll. 13–14. *they display the dismal colours of death.* There is a faint hint here of the more obvious use of colours in *The Holy War*; cf. Offor, iii. 341–2.

p. 257, l. 21. *Death is before them, they see it.* This imagery is vividly depicted in *The Holy War*, particularly in the standard of Diabolus, with its 'flaming flame, fearful to behold, and the picture of Mansoul burning in it'. Offor, iii. 343.

p. 257, l. 21. *and feel it.* There is a marked tendency among sectaries to write and preach in terms of sensual perception. Here the perception of spiritual death is physically depicted, but the spiritual perception of the Holy Spirit is similarly described. See Nuttall, *The Holy Spirit*, pp. 38–40; *G.A.*, § 78.

p. 258, l. 11. *a flying to him from Wrath to come.* Cf. *P.P.*, p. 10, where this is the message on the '*Parchment Roll*' given to the Man by the Evangelist. Cf. *Saved by Grace*, above, p. 170, ll. 25–6, and note.

p. 260, l. 9. John iii. 15.

p. 260, ll. 9–10. John v. 24.

p. 260, ll. 10–11. Mark xxvi. 16.

p. 260, l. 11. John iii. 18.

p. 263, ll. 19–20. Isa. xlix. 3.

p. 265, ll. 4–14. Cf. *P.P.*, pp. 63–4; *G.A.*, §§ 99–102.

p. 266, ll. 14–16. Cf. *P.P.*, p. 9.

p. 267, ll. 7–8. Prov. ix. 4.

p. 267, ll. 9–10. Prov. ix. 5.

p. 267, l. 24. *gleads*: embers, or, in this case, rays. Cf. 'Those few weak gleeds of grace, that are in me, might soon go out, if they were not thus refreshed.' Again, 'yet, when I stir up these embers to the bottom, there are found some living gleeds, which do both contain fire, and are apt to propagate it'. Joseph Hall, *Occasional Meditations* (1656 edn.), §§ 22, 37.

p. 267, ll. 26–8. There is no use of this 'bee and fly' motif in *A Book for Boys and Girls*. The bee is the subject of one emblem, but it represents sin. Offor, iii. 751.

p. 267, ll. 29–31. Cf. above, p. 258, l. 11; *P.P.*, p. 10.

p. 268, ll. 3–7. Cf. the emblem of the horse and rider, *A Book for Boys and Girls*, Offor, iii. 758–9.

p. 268, l. 23. *fierceness of Carrear (1678–1684)*. Originally Bunyan appears to have intended this to mean a fierce encounter, or a fierce, persistent action. Cf. Milton: 'Mortal combat or carreer with Lance.' *Paradise Lost* (1667), i. 766; and Thomas Traherne: 'Quickly stopt in his careir of vertue.' *Christian Ethicks* (1675), xxv. 389. *O.E.D.*

p. 269, ll. 8 ff. Cf. *G.A.*, §§ 230, 277.

p. 269, ll. 28–9. Cf. *G.A.*, §§ 66–7; Oxford Bunyan, ii. 211, l. 35.

p. 270, ll. 29–30. Cf. Jer. vi. 39, 44.

p. 271, ll. 14–15. John vi. 37.

p. 272, ll. 31–2. Ps. cxlv. 14.

p. 273, ll. 16–17. John xvii. 6.

p. 276, ll. 6–9. Bunyan's insistence on the absolute nature of the divine promise places him in the tradition of strict rather than moderate Calvinism. See Greaves, pp. 104–7. In *The Pilgrim's Progress* (p. 25), Christian must ask *Good-Will* (divine grace) 'if you are *willing* to let me in'. Yet previously (above, p. 255, ll. 17–19) Bunyan stated that coming is an act of the will, though the will *must* be so inclined by Christ. Baxter, a moderate Calvinist, says essentially the same thing: 'to his Elect God freely giveth, as leave, so a will to enter sincerely into Covenant with him, and faithfully to keep Covenant, and so the continuance of the Priviledges of the Covenant'. *Plain Scripture Proof of Infants Church-Membership and Baptism* (1651), p. 227.

p. 277, l. 30. Matt. xxiv. 13.

p. 278, ll. 5 ff. The characterization of *Shall-come* is evocative of the allegorized characters of *The Pilgrim's Progress*, notably *Good-Will*, *Help*, *Great-grace*, and *Great-heart*.

p. 278, ll. 9–11. John v. 25.

p. 278, ll. 22–9. These lines encompass the outline of *The Holy War*, though the idea of captivity and rescue is used in the account of *Doubting-Castle*. *P.P.*, pp. 113–18.

p. 278, ll. 29–30. Matt. xvi. 18.

p. 279, ll. 23–4. Matt. xxi. 28.

p. 279, l. 26. Matt. xxi. 29.

p. 280, l. 21. Matt. xxvii. 25.

p. 280, l. 26. Acts ii. 37.

p. 283, ll. 25–31. Bunyan is likely here to be thinking particularly of his own recent controversies with Edward Fowler, Henry Danvers, Thomas Paul, John Denne, William Kiffin, and perhaps William Penn and (earlier) Edward Burrough.

p. 285, ll. 13–22. Bunyan here returns to the theme of his polemical work, *Light for Them That Sit in Darkness*.

p. 286, ll. 23–4, 26. John xiv. 27.

p. 287, ll. 20–1. Gal. vi. 14.

p. 287, ll. 33–4. Gal. iv. 12.

p. 289, ll. 27–8. *they that stand in his House, and look upon him through the Glass of his Word.* Cf. the Interpreter's House in *The Pilgrim's Progress*, pp. 28–37, and the emblem of the looking-glass in *A Book for Boys and Girls*, Offor, iii. 759–60.

p. 291, ll. 15–28. Cf. above, p. 276, ll. 6–9. Also cf. Owen: 'The nature of the covenant overthrows this proposal, that they that are covenanted withal shall have such and such good things if they fulfil the condition, as though that all depended on this obedience, when the obedience itself, and the whole condition of it, is a promise of the covenant, Jer. xxxi. 33 . . .' 'The condition of the covenant is not said to be required, but it is absolutely promised . . .' *Works*, x. 207, 236.

p. 292, l. 27. John x. 14.

p. 294, ll. 25–30. The section added to the second edition is directed against Paedobaptists, who, if strict Calvinists, had difficulty reconciling infant baptism as a seal of the covenant of grace with the empirical fact that not all of those baptized subsequently lived as visible saints. See Greaves, *Church History*, xxxvi. 161–2; *Law and Grace*, Oxford Bunyan, ii. 182.

p. 295, ll. 13–19. There is no direct use of this 'fit Emblem' in *A Book for Boys and Girls*, though the emblem of the beggar bears a slight similarity. Offor, iii. 758.

p. 295, ll. 21–2. *Sinners of a double die.* Cf. Sir Thomas Herbert: 'A Treason of an ugly dye.' *Some Yeares Travels*, 4th edn. (1677), 244. *O.E.D.*

p. 296, ll. 10–11. I have not been able to locate this quotation (assuming it is accurate) in Luther. The theme is clearly present in the one work of Luther's Bunyan is known to have read, viz. *A Commentarie . . . upon . . . Galathians* (1635 edn.), p. 236[r]. Cf. similar phraseology in *G.A.*, § 249.

p. 300, ll. 16–17. Cf. above, p. 255, ll. 32–3.

p. 301, l. 20. *the musick was struck up.* Cf. *P.P.*, pp. 160–1.

p. 304, l. 24. *sinner of a double dye.* Cf. above, p. 295, l. 21, and note.

p. 306, l. 18. Jer. iii. 22.

p. 309, ll. 13–14. Prov. xvi. 2.

p. 312, ll. 1–5. The greatness of sin, long continuance in a sinful life, backsliding, and natural corruption are all problems dealt with by Bunyan in *Grace Abounding*; cf. §§ 84, 115, 175, 252.

p. 312, ll. 7–8. Isa. xlvi. 10.

p. 313, ll. 23–4. Zech. iii. 3.

p. 313, ll. 30–5. Zech. iii. 2–4.

p. 314, l. 17. *Moses as a Type of Christ.* Cf. above, p. xlvii; *Light in Darkness*, above, p. 60.

p. 320, ll. 7–10. Matt. xxv. 32–3.

p. 320, ll. 13–14. Matt. xxv. 43.

p. 320, l. 32. *Tophet.* Cf. *P.P.*, p. 10; *Instruction for the Ignorant*, above, p. 14, l. 34, and note.

p. 322, ll. 29–31. Mark iii. 29.

p. 323, ll. 34–6. Cf. above, p. xlvii; *Light in Darkness*, above, p. 60.

p. 326, ll. 28–30. The nature of the covenant between Father and Son is discussed in *Law and Grace*, Oxford Bunyan, ii. 88 ff. See Greaves, pp. 103–4; and *Saved by Grace*, above, p. 199, ll. 10–11.

p. 334, ll. 29–30. *thy casting of thine Eye upon some good Book.* Cf. *G.A.*, §§ 15–16, 40–1.

p. 334, ll. 30–1. *thy hearing of thy Neighbours talk of Heavenly Things.* Cf. *G.A.*, §§ 37–41.

p. 334, ll. 31–2. *the beholding of Gods Judgments, as executed upon others.* Cf. *G.A.*, §§ 13, 164; *P.P.*, pp. 34–7, and the note to p. 34, l. 8 (p. 318).

p. 334, l. 32. *thine own Deliverance from them.* Cf. *G.A.*, §§ 12–13.

p. 334, l. 33. *strangly cast under the Ministry of some Godly Man.* Cf. *G.A.*, §§ 77, 117; *P.P.*, pp. 9–10.

p. 334, l. 34. *such providence.* Cf. *G.A.*, §§ 37, 157.

p. 337, ll. 6–7. Eccles. x. 3.

p. 338, ll. 10–12. Job xxi. 14–15.

p. 338, ll. 12–13. *Here's a Devil in Grain!* I have been unable to locate another citation of this proverb.

p. 338, ll. 16–36. This passage may reflect internal dissension in the Bedford congregation.

p. 339, ll. 22–3. *run all hazzards.* Cf. *P.P.*, pp. 175, 182–3, and *The Heavenly Footman.*

p. 341, ll. 28–30. Luke xv. 17–18.

p. 342, l. 12. Luke xv. 18.

p. 342, l. 26. *Hoggard*: hogherd. Cf. Du Parc: 'Our Regent (who had in him no more humanity than a Hoggard)'. *Francion* (trans. 1655), iv. 3. *O.E.D.*

p. 347, l. 16. *a Town-Sinner*. Cf. *G.A.*, §§ 26, 43.

p. 348, ll. 4–10. Cf. *G.A.*, §§ 38–40, 48, 53–7.

p. 351, l. 32. *hideous Roarings of the Devil*. Cf. *P.P.*, p. 242.

p. 352, l. 5. *That they are not Elected*. Cf. *G.A.*, §§ 57, 59, 75; *Law and Grace*, Oxford Bunyan, ii. 214, ll. 34–5.

p. 352, l. 6. *That they have sinned the sin against the Holy Ghost*. Cf. *G.A.*, §§ 132–252; *Law and Grace*, Oxford Bunyan, ii. 201, ll. 19–22.

p. 352, ll. 28 ff. These simple directions to determine election, coupled with the frequent allusions to Bunyan's personal experience, are major factors in explaining the popularity of this work.

p. 353, l. 29. *a Flam*. Cf. Thomas Fuller: 'His Flamens and Arch-Flamens, seeme . . . Flamms and Arch-Flamms, even notorious Falshoods.' *The Church-History of Britain* (1655), I. ii. § 9. 12. *O.E.D.*

p. 354, l. 15. Mark iii. 29.

p. 354, l. 22. *Chalking out to God*. Cf. *P.P.*, p. 6: '*This Book it chaulketh out before thine eyes, The man that seeks the everlasting Prize . . .*'

p. 354, l. 35–p. 355, l. 1. *their own Chalking out*. See above, p. 354, l. 22.

p. 355, ll. 25–6. Luke xix. 5–6.

p. 356, l. 16. *I my self know all these things*. Here is the explicit acknowledgment of the abundant personal allusions that abound in this work. Cf. *Law and Grace*, Oxford Bunyan, ii. 159, ll. 14–15.

p. 356, ll. 18–19. *the Loaden, Tempted Way*. Cf. *G.A.*, § 20: 'I was for the present greatly loaden therewith, and so went home when the Sermon was ended, with a great burden upon my spirit.' Cf. Hugh Binning: 'This we preach unto you, that until you be wearied and loaden, you will not cast your burden on Jesus.' *Sermons* (1845 edn.; first published, 1653), p. 427. *O.E.D.* The 'Loaden, Tempted Way' is that followed by Christian in the first part of *The Pilgrim's Progress*.

p. 356, l. 19. *some by the Waters of Comfort*. Essentially this is true of Christiana in the second part of *The Pilgrim's Progress*.

p. 357, l. 31. *This man is in the Wilderness*. Cf. *P.P.*, pp. 1–3, 61–5, 241–6.

p. 358, l. 10. *flying from Wrath to come*. Cf. above, p. 258, l. 11, and note.

p. 358, ll. 10–11. *such Clogges as these*. In the spiritual sense clogs are impediments, such as doubts and temptations. The analogy is with the clogs on a falcon to control its flight.

p. 360, ll. 27–8. *doteing upon their own Jewels*. Cf. *P.P.*, p. 288, where Christiana and her daughters are bedecked by the shepherds with spiritual jewels, following Mercy's request for the looking-glass. See James F. Forrest, 'Mercy with Her Mirror', *Philological Quarterly*, xlii (January 1963), 121–6.

p. 360, ll. 29–30. *plunges them into the ditch by Temptations.* Cf. *P.P.*, pp. 62, 64.

p. 362, ll. 23–4. *faith, and doubting, may at the same time have their residence in the same soul.* This theme figures prominently in *The Holy War*.

p. 362, ll. 26 ff. Cf. the treatment of *Little-faith* in the following passages with that in *P.P.*, pp. 125–9, 132.

p. 362, ll. 31–2. Matt. xiv. 28–9.

p. 363, ll. 13–14. Matt. xiv. 30.

p. 363, ll. 15–17. Matt. xiv. 31.

p. 364, ll. 11–12. *Who so bold as blind Bayard.* Bunyan may have borrowed this line from Fowler (or his curate): '*But who so bold as blind Bayard.*' *Dirt Wip't Off*, p. 28. Cf. 'As . . . boldly as blind bayard rusheth into the battle'. *The Works of T. Jackson*, iii. 33. *O.E.D.*

p. 364, ll. 20–1. Exod. xxiii. 9.

p. 365, l. 13. John v. 40.

p. 367, l. 31. John xiv. 6.

p. 369, ll. 14–15. Heb. vii. 25.

p. 372, ll. 27–8. Ps. lxxii. 13.

p. 373, ll. 22–3. 1 John v. 11.

p. 374, ll. 7–8. *Satisfaction to Divine Justice.* See *Light in Darkness*, above, p. 108, ll. 32 ff.; Greaves, pp. 36–41.

pp. 383–4. George Offor has determined that Bunyan used the 1632 edition of Foxe's *Actes and Monuments*, which was published in three volumes. Note also the influence of Foxe in *I Will Pray with the Spirit*, Oxford Bunyan, ii. 239; *Saved by Grace*, above, p. 203, ll. 10, 21; and *Light in Darkness*, above, p. 98, l. 14.

p. 386, ll. 2–3. Ps. xxxiv. 10.

p. 386, l. 5. *Grace is sometimes taken for love.* For a discussion of Bunyan's concept of grace see Greaves, pp. 27–35. Cf. *Saved by Grace*, above, p. 183, l. 1, and the corresponding note.

p. 386, ll. 7–8. Eph. iii. 19.

p. 386, ll. 27–9. Mic. vii. 20.

p. 388, ll. 17–19. 1 Cor. i. 27.

p. 390, l. 21. *Strowed*: strewn, scattered. Cf. 'Thick as Autumnal Leaves that strow the Brooks In Vallombrosa.' Milton, *Paradise Lost*, i. 302. Cf. Dryden's translation of Virgil's *Pastorals*, vii. 76 (1697): 'And lavish Nature laughs, and strows her Stores around.'

p. 391, l. 11. *Calling goes before Coming*. Cf. *Saved by Grace*, above, p. 186, ll. 20–1, and the corresponding note.

p. 392, ll. 4–5. Psalm cxix. 32.

p. 392, l. 25. *gload*: warming sensation, warming glance. The form usually encountered is that of the verb (cf. Spenser, *The Faerie Queene*, IV. iv. 23: 'Like sparke of fire that from the anvile glode') but Bunyan uses the substantive form.